THE MODERN LIBRARY
OF THE WORLD'S BEST BOOKS

THE PERSONAL HISTORY

OF HENRY THE EIGHTH

THE

Personal History

OF

HENRY THE EIGHTH

Francis Hackett

THE MODERN LIBRARY · NEW YORK

TO SIGNE TOKSVIG

CONTENTS

CONTENTS

THE PERSONAL HISTORY

OF HENRY THE EIGHTH

BOOK ONE

Henry's Boyhood

They sawe already in the East a faire morning like unto the color of roses, and all starres voyded, saving only Venus, the sweete Governesse of heaven.

BALDASSARE CASTIGLIONE

I

IN THE hot month of August, 1501, a solemn little Spanish girl took ship at Corunna, to be married into an English family.

The circumstances were peculiar. The girl was not yet sixteen years of age, she did not know a word of French or English, and the only personal impression she had of the boy she was to marry was gained from a small and woodenish portrait. It was true that from the age of twelve he had written her love letters. That is to say, his tutor had written them for him. Composed in Latin, they were full of sonorous words and round appropriate sentiments. The girl had spelled them out for herself, since she had been brought up to study Latin. She had responded in the same high strain, and now she was being shipped by her father and her mother to marry the youth across the sea. Peasant girls have still sometimes this fate in the twentieth century.

But Catalina did not pity herself. A princess-royal by birth, she was of the superb lineage that makes its own laws, and of the stern Spanish mettle that knows its duty. For fourteen years her father and her mother had been considering whether she was to go to this strange land and this unknown bridegroom, and it could never have crossed her mind to question their decision. White-faced, with chin set, swathed in veils, no one who went on board with her could have known what she hoped or what she feared, as a person, except perhaps her Italian confessor, Geraldino, and even to him this girl could never have conveyed what it meant to be taken from her people and from her habit and custom—what it meant to decide, though she could not know it, that she was never to set eyes on her own country again.

She was no romantic Spanish type. Of the cluster of excited girls who looked back on the glorious bay of Corunna when they had set sail, this bride-to-be, the most excited and the least willing to reveal it, was also the least beautiful. The English king, Henry VII, had requested that the rest of them should be selected for their physical beauty, and he seemed to have been obeyed. Veiled from observation, they scintillated with that mischief and fire which invest high-spirited youth setting out on a great adventure, and more than one of them had that astonishing allure of the Spaniard of race, that sweeping black glance which unites such dignity with such gorgeous suppressed passion. But, loyal and devoted to their mistress, they naturally subdued themselves as they came near her. Catalina was not awkward, no more so than any sober convent girl of her age, and her standing had always been that of a royal princess; but she had much less the air of a princess than certain of her dazzling maids of honor. With her high round alabaster brow, her eyes like blue rosary beads, her hidden auburn hair, her heavy chin, there was that look of a lay nun about her, even at slender fifteen and a half. Her maids were the poetry of a royal presence; she was the stiff prose.

This sobriety was due partly to her temperament and partly to the obligation of being a Spanish princess at the opening of the sixteenth century.

Had she been the child of a muleteer, Catalina would have taken herself seriously, stood on her rights and stood by her duties. Being the daughter of Ferdinand and Isabella, she did not take herself any the less seriously. She was the youngest of the family. She had been born in the thick of a great campaign. The Holy War against the Moors had shot her earliest landscapes with a valiant blood-red, and the banishment of the Jews during the years that succeeded had intensified her sense of race and of rank, of family and of true religion. She had the immense seriousness of a plain young girl, who is profoundly good by nature, who feels called on to devote her life to a national purpose, and who has been brought up in a period of crisis by two extremely strong-willed and active parents. For a rather slow and conscientious girl, with dignity and stamina, this was calculated to make her staid beyond her years. Her gravity had been increased by solicitude for her remarkable mother, who was soon to succumb to dropsy, and since in addition she herself had had malaria in May, when she left her ailing mother at Granada, and since her journey across Spain had inflicted on her one hardship after another, it was no wonder that she was going North with anxiety as well as the quiver of young anticipation.

II

Unfortunately for Catalina, her departure was being financed in the mood of parents who, having laid themselves out with lavishness on a recent great occasion, pick on the next occasion for retrenchment and for the practice of the most acid little economies.

Four years before, a magnificent double marriage had been

staged by Ferdinand and Isabella. To send out their daughter
Juana to Antwerp for Philip the Handsome, and to fetch back
Margaret of Austria for their boy Juan was a symmetrical linking of fortunes that appealed to Spanish grandiosity. An imposing fleet, consisting of a hundred and fifty vessels, had been
chartered without regard to expense, and everything had been
arranged except the weather. The royal display, the royal un-
foreseeingness about the weather, the toppling pride, the
wreckage, had all resulted in a tightening of heart strings and
purse strings, and Catalina was being held down to a half dozen
boats. If Juan had lived, perhaps this new marriage might have
been undertaken with more gusto. But Prince Juan, the only
male child that had been reared by Ferdinand and Isabella, had
survived his glorious nuptials only by a few months. And this
cruel disappointment had daunted the parents.

England, besides, was not the Holy Roman Empire. A match
with England at this moment was a match with a minor power.
During the fourteen years that the marriage had been debated,
with Bishop Fox coming to argue and assure, Ferdinand and
Isabella had both watched with dubiousness the clambering
Tudor dynasty. Henry VII had indeed landed on the throne,
but to each of his legs had clung one aspirant after another; and
while he had managed to kick them off, with unfailing nimble-
ness, it was not yet certain that his was a stable monarchy.
English history had been decidedly skittish for many years,
and only its previous stability, and its long history of useful
antagonism to the French, inclined Ferdinand and Isabella to
consider the marriage at all. Under the circumstances, half a
dozen vessels seemed a liberal allowance.

Catalina, however, was emigrating in royal style. In its
modest proportion, the right thing was being done by her, as
befitting a dynastic marriage. Her bastard half-brother, who
had been an archbishop since he was six years old, was not of

the party, but Archbishop Fonseca was accompanying her. One of the bravest of the grandees who had served all through the Granada campaign had gone on board, clanking in gilded armor. On account of the dowry, which was no less an important item than Catalina herself, several sallow gentlemen of the utmost punctilio were included, with many necessary clerical and diplomatic small fry. There were enough of the customary officials to support the façade of pride, the master of ceremonies and the ladies of the bedchamber, people in whose hands is the stage management of royal etiquette, who help royalty to play their part, who prompt them about what to wear and what to spend, what to say and what to do—the priesthood of the royal ritual, the custodians of the high tradition. It was, in its way, such a complicated host as goes with any person whose prestige must be kept up, and for a Spaniard like Catalina the intention was grandiose even if the means had been skimped. But motherly judgment was exhibited in certain of the details. Because of Catalina's knowing no English, and having no ultimate confidence in the English art of housekeeping, she was bringing with her all the people who would enable her to set up house in England just as she would at home, including a comptroller, a marshal, a cup-bearer, a cook, a washerwoman, a scullion and a chimney-sweep. These, with her confessor, girded her for the brave plunge into the unknown.

III

But her plunge into the unknown, her voyage to Southampton that was to land her at Plymouth, her voyage to Arthur that was to land her with Henry, her voyage with Henry that was to send her adrift on such mountainous gray seas, could never be measured solely by the circumstance of her being a princess. She was also a Spaniard.

In these faces still around her, on her little ship, there was nothing indefinite or vague. When the eyes were bright, they sparkled with the opulence of Southern stars. When they were dull, they were dull as mud. Their very cheeks were significant; they either curved like a goat's skin full of wine or were flat like the goat's skin emptied, little existing for their positive natures between strong sensuality and strong asceticism. A sculptor in wood might have carved the brown visages of Catalina's sailors: the trials of their seafaring life were no more to them than hard weather to the lean hills from which they came. The soldiers who had ridden with her across the Spain which the sun smites with iron hand seemed to have in their veins something of his midday fierceness and his disturbing intensity. The beggars who had turned their seamed and pitted faces toward the royal cavalcade demanded charity with the thirst of arid river-beds excoriated by torrents. In all this life of Spain that imbued the girl with the convictions of early reality which color a lifetime, the note of the temperate zone to which she was voyaging was permanently distrained by the Orient and darkened by the claims of Africa.

In the moral drama of such a Spaniard there was always a trace of ancestral fierceness, a certain elemental directness and simplicity. Appetites so vigorous and senses so vivid do not lend themselves to temperance, to tolerance, to modulation. They spring out of assertive instincts, the proud gush of a fountain. In religious rapture they seek for a ravishing, mystic ecstasy. By lust they understand a fire that eats out a man's marrow. By impotence of any sort they mean something extravagantly grotesque and ludicrous. Poverty with them is not a lack of money, but a sort of economic leprosy, an incapacity for money. They tame themselves with difficulty to the lessons of experience, since in experience they press so eagerly to savor the purity, the heroism, that matches their prompt imaginings. The middle class, that was doing its practical best to come into existence in Spain, could not build itself out of a nobility that aimed at unquestioned privileges and around these privileges flung the cloak of its honor. Neither could the middle class build itself out of serfs who needed a noble as a clapper needs a bell. Where the Italians with their great pagan heritage, their vast and roomy mythology, their spacious humanism, could rise through their practiced intellect into a sense of happy reality, or into the cool repose of compromise, and even outside the ether of faith could breathe the zero of disillusion and still live by the assurance of beauty, the Spaniards, burdened with the epic temperament, could achieve order in their lives only by riveting themselves to an implacable faith. In the possession of this faith and this righteousness, their minds could move independently of the hampering world: and if the Jew or the Moor clashed with their prepossession, the answer was not to share the present world with them, but to hate them, to pursue and to uproot them.

Such a temperament is anarchic. No righteousness is so proud or so narrow as the Spanish, because no sincerity is so primitive. Without an object, it defeats itself by its sheer unbendingness, but given an object, raised to militancy by some religious or national fever, it becomes capable of sustained exaltation.

No one would have suspected Catalina of being exalted to look at her, and in the abounding practicality and good sense of her mother there was a corrective to the national temperament. But even Isabella was not beyond the reach of those somber and tragic provocations that came from one unofficial member of her family, the spiritual father Thomas Torquemada.

Torquemada is one of those salient Spaniards who intensify one's beliefs in the boundless possibilities of human nature. He was the nephew of a famous cardinal, a man of proud lineage, and naturally fitted to be the adviser of that "handful of dust," the Queen of Castile. He was the man who made Isabella promise that should she ever come to the throne she would devote herself to the extirpation of heresy, for the glory of God and the exaltation of the Catholic faith. Through Torquemada, it may be said, she became Isabella the Catholic. Though she drove in the Jews and Moors as well as drove them out, she was precisely the kind of woman who took to a bristling religiousness, and got strength from it, and added to her power by her humility. She was born for a crusade or a holy war, and in the intervals of war-fever she embroidered with her own pious hands the veil that her monks were to drape over the Holy Sepulchre.

The Prince of Peace was not Torquemada's savior. Lean, ascetic, ominous, with black fires in his hollow eyes, Torquemada reminds one of certain Spanish landscapes that look like suburbs of hell. Nature in these landscapes has never smiled: she is either sallow or livid, with a sinister glare as of the end of the world, and a cheerless cadaverous concentration, as if one were bending over the pale lips and waxen grin of death. The Spaniard who has taken into his soul the aspect of these desolate mountains, these bitter valleys, these sardonic forests, and who has felt in his bones the sweltering and sullen heat of these macabre heights and blistering voids, is all ready to believe in a God of fire and blood and sacrifice, not so far removed from the deity of ancient Mexico, where the brain reels before the comprehension of his tropical extravagance and becomes a mere mob of hysterical delusions. Torquemada was born with that Spanish contempt for pain which soon becomes a contempt for pity. He held himself in check on the edge of delusions, but they darted out from under his iron control like a fringe of flame. He was not a bad man so much as a very dangerous man. And the thing that made him dangerous was the willingness of Isabella to see as a corona of light this burning edge of fanaticism. To make him her counselor was like installing a very reckless and masterful alchemist in a children's kitchen. Those who admire power above everything, and think of moderation as feebleness, forget these cowled magicians. The young Catalina had been reared, no less than the fanatical young Isabel and the hysterical Juan and the melancholic Juana, in the zone of Torquemada's influence. Her personality had been steeped in brimstone at an early age, and when she came to transmit her own beliefs as a mother she was still in some measure this kind of child.

She was no less a Spaniard, at any rate, because she was to leave the hot suns of Spain and the voluptuous winds of Africa to cease to be Catalina and to become Catherine of Aragon. Positive and durable in character, of a race that can be disagreeable as asafœtida and as strongly delicious as Malaga, she kept in her marrow that definiteness of trait which makes a Spaniard either hopelessly chaotic or graphically extreme. That Catherine was a Spaniard cannot be forgotten. Alongside the Frenchman, who has blended North and South with exquisite intelligence, the Spaniard is like a clang of brasses or the unlatching vibration of a guitar among the intense precisions of the violin. With his heroic conception of absolute personal honor, of absolute chastity (even though he could provide for bastards by the ten thousand) his capacity for endurance under a siege like Perpignan, that could enable him to go from eating cats and dogs to eating the corpses of his enemy and the corpses of his late companions, his bold and firm policies, that disregard the slight but important difference between stone walls and his skull, his joyous cruelty, his lust, his abasement, his humility, his devouring introspection —the Spaniard is a passionate and emotional creature who must heed the laughter of Cervantes to become a civilized being.

From the very heart of this race sprang Catherine of Aragon,

the square-cut Catalina, who embarked at Corunna to go
North to be married, and who was never, except through the
tears of her imagination, to gaze on Spain again.

IV

Catherine did not arrive serenely. Her vessels met with contrary winds, driving her south of Corunna, and then they had
to battle against a smashing hurricane in the Bay of Biscay,
until the voyage dragged out so long that the King of England
sent to find her. It was a wretched, sea-green company of Spaniards that crawled from their little coops in October and gazed
at last on the commodious calm of Plymouth.

Plymouth rose to greet them. It was not so many years since
the French had burned this town itself; a union with Spain
would mean a solid front against France, and safer trade with
Flanders. But it was the sight of the young princess that kin-
dled the people. She was the daughter of a great kingdom, she
was coming to marry the first English prince in whose veins ran
the Red Rose and the White, she was fresh and young and
a bride. From the russet country around trotted knights of the
shire, abbots, squires in harness, and a show of fine curious
ladies bundled against the rain. A joyous and hilarious rabble,
fascinated by every detail of the Spanish gear, streamed with
Catherine to the church where, with tremulous fervor, she and
her escorts gave thanks to God for having protected their lives.
It was a moment generous and appealing, when a gleam of
sympathy seemed to warm every one's heart, and this popularity that Catherine won on her arrival she was never to lose
in England. She accepted herself as royal, and gave herself to
the people. "She could not have been received with greater re-
joicings," reported a vaunting Spaniard, "if she had been the
Savior of the world."

Word having reached London that the bride had at last
landed, a royal reception was prepared for her at Lambeth.

The progress was slow. Early in November King Henry VII set out with his boy Arthur, his council and several hundred guards. Catherine was nearing Hampshire. How should she be received? At Winchfield, Ayala, the former ambassador, came to greet Henry and to affirm that the bride could not be seen by any one till the wedding morning. This astounding rigidity of custom huffed the king. He consulted his council, and, as usual, decided for himself. Disregarding the thunderheads of Spanish disapproval, he rode ahead to the house of the Bishop of Bath. There, without changing, wet and splashed, he made his entry. This was not Spanish etiquette, but Henry was master. "I'll see and speak with her," he announced, "even if she were gone to bed." The wholly surprised and embarrassed Catherine was summoned. Henry meant no ill. He beamed where he could not speak, and he rubbed his hands when his blond youngster, who had stopped to change after the wet gallop, came coughing into the presence of his future wife.

Arthur, Prince of Wales, was barely fifteen years old. Flushed and glistening after his toilet, he must for the moment have seemed well, but it was not an easy encounter. He could say nothing to Catherine. Catherine could say nothing to him. But they could kiss ceremoniously, gaze, smile, while courtiers exchanged compliments, and at last boyish inquiries—about dogs and birds—could be addressed to the girl from a far country, Arthur's question being put into Latin by a bishop, turned into Castilian by a priest, and the answer—"Yes, they are white birds"—going back from Castilian into Latin and so on the return journey to the terminus. This round-table colloquy, which was not likely to lead either to grave misunderstanding or to grave intimacy, at last gave way to stately dances. Catherine showed her steps to the admiring son and father; and the meeting, with all its hidden emotions and forced inexpressiveness, came to a close.

The father, whose drawn face with bluish gills and hollow

temples spoke of ill health, looked with bright eyes vigilant and
alert, his smile as thin as his fine hands. No peasant had ever
made a match for his boy more keenly, no Hindu had ever
bargained more tenaciously for a valuable girl-bride. This wedding had been plotted for fourteen years. It was England's
safe reëntry into Europe, a strong link with a great rising
power, an offset against France and a princely dowry. To clear
the Tudor title for Catherine's sake, Henry had sent to the
block the witless Warwick, cutting him down as if he had been
a weakly sapling that marred the view. The goal was reached,
the goal for which he had panted. The actual cash that Catherine was bringing voluptuously interested him. He enveloped
her with approbation, the dowry-in-the-flesh.

Of this cupidity Catherine knew nothing. She had set herself to carry out the will of her parents and the will of Spain,
and this path she pursued, murmuring her lesson to herself like
a child sent on a message.

But if she were a princess to the courtiers, she seemed a
fellow-being to Henry VII's wife. The good Elizabeth saw in
this girl a dynastic bride, such as she had been herself. Remembering how in her own time with her son Henry she had
suffered much, in spite of the scroll with the Magnificat written
upon it that was wrapped around her, she bethought herself
that she should find for this future mother the thing that would
most ease her. In England at this time Our Lady's girdle was
shown in not less than eleven places, and Our Lady's milk, in a
condensed form, in eight places. One of these girdles the good
Queen procured for Catherine to present to her when the time
should come. Though the older woman and the girl could not
speak directly together, Catherine's eyes could read sympathy
in Elizabeth, and she felt gratitude.

Another comfort to her was the boyish chivalry of Arthur's
younger brother, Henry, who took on himself so bravely the
part of her squire.

Henry was ten, but big for his years. He was a handsome boy, round as an Italian Cupid, with odd expectant eyebrows and regarding eyes. To call him beautiful would not have been impossible, but the fair child with his golden hair and his cream complexion owed not a little to the perfect harmony of white satin. His face, in truth, was round as a porringer, and his strong little features were islanded with a gravity that might be sulky and lowering and yet, so happy was his mien, made him cherubic and infantile. What made him even more infantile was his air of grand responsibility. He was to accompany Catherine as she perambulated on her mule. This gave him his cue, since he was already a superb horseman and sat erect in his saddle with the innate confidence of the uncurbed.

The young prince was not shy. If he were silent and non-committal in his gravity, he could break out into the sudden assertive urgency of the willful. A prettiness like his, that had sunned itself in outpoured admiration, could scarcely help a recipience at once imperious and innocent. Frankly a child, with petulance in his tilted lip, his clustering curls, his brimming curiosity, he had garnered the love of his acute grandmother, Margaret Beaufort, and had won the best efforts of Skelton his tutor, that sharp, tart, exasperated man. A tender nature, in one sense, he had been ensconced in the perfect favor of his environment. While Arthur had been holding court at Ludlow, on the border of unquiet Wales, doing the "dirty work" that is traditionally the eldest son's, Henry had been nestling among the younger brood, Margaret and Mary and Edmund, and there flowed from him that radiance of the princely, as if he had forever been glowing in his downy tenderness and ripening on a southern wall.

But Henry was not merely the radiant boy. Under the guidance of his strong-willed, narrow grandmother, he had undoubtedly been given the "conventional maxims, stock passions, and theological sanctions" that went by the name of education: yet his mind had been vigorously cultivated. When More and Erasmus had been brought to see him two years before, he had himself the aplomb to ask in writing for a tribute from Erasmus's pen. Already, with a diligence that enchanted the scholarly Margaret, he had made headway in Latin; and as French was his father's language, he was at home in English and French. But his hidden eagerness, one may surmise, was to be the parfit knight. His mind was still pearled with the roseate ideals of the middle ages; he knew Hercules, Hector, Troilus, Bevis of Hampton, Robin Hood, Amadis and Lanzilote, "a thousand histories and fables of love and wantonness and ribaldry." It was as Catherine's knight that he must have escorted her through London. With her wide-brimmed hat cocked on her head, her cardinal's coif, and her Spanish colors, she was a novel figure in London; out into the rough cobbled streets tumbled the cheery populace to see their future Queen, and the boy by her side, proud as a peacock, drank in the incense and the cheers.

v

The ceremony was everything that man could desire. It began at St. Paul's and ended in the bed. It swam in wine. The London that had been charmed at Catherine in her Spanish style, and with the lad Henry always at her side as cavalier, was even more excited by the vision of the bride, with her auburn hair streaming down her shoulders and vested in white satin. The wedding party floated from the banquet hall at Westminster Hall to the bedchamber in the Bishop of London's. It was usual for hilarious youths to pull off the bride's garters, which were loosened in advance, but this was no roistering wedding. In the bedchamber, glowing with the red flames of many candles, packed with nobility and clergy, humming with Latin, the youthful bride and still more youthful bridegroom were secreted behind the bed-curtains, and there stripped to the skin before they knelt according to pious custom. Given their final cup of warm sweet wine after the bed had been blessed, the horde withdrew, and Arthur and Catherine were locked in for the night, not to consummate their marriage, which was never the acceptable behavior, but to spend the first night under God's holy blessing.

And in the anteroom, within calling distance, hovered the whispering attendants of the Prince and Princess of Wales.

In the celebrations that followed on the wedding, Catherine rejoiced her courtiers by the dignity with which she and her flashing maids of honor went through those dances that brought before the English court all the brocaded ceremony of the Alhambra. The King and Queen were suitably impressed, and in return they watched their own Arthur's performance with his aunt; but what enchanted every one was the boyish impetuosity with which Henry, his sister's partner, "suddenly threw off his robe, and danced in his jacket with the said Lady Margaret in so goodly and pleasant a manner that it was to King Henry and Queen Elizabeth great and singular pleasure." Henry and Elizabeth were still young enough to enjoy the verve of their offspring, and the court still simple enough to idolize a boy.

VI

When the feasts were over, King Henry had leisure to stroke his chin. He and Puebla, the Spanish ambassador, had made a capital plan by which he would not have to buy Arthur any plate or any jewels. Catherine was to come provided with them and they were to be credited as part of the dowry; but when they had been used by the young couple they were to be refused as second-hand. So Henry and Puebla had put their heads together, and so they had connived.

"Señor," said Puebla, "if the Princess uses all this now, and you afterwards refuse to accept it, my sovereign lords will be ashamed to take from her what she has already used as her own on her person as well as in her household. They must then leave it to her, and fulfill their obligations toward you!"

So Puebla plotted to give Arthur the benefit of Spanish pearls, jewels, gold plate, silver plate and tapestry, that would otherwise cost Henry the equivalent of half a million dollars. Henry chuckled and assented. To outwit his brother Ferdinand seemed to him sweet.

But, having persuaded Henry to leave these goods with Catherine, until they were used, Puebla turned the tables on his confederate. On rereading his instructions, he said, he was forced to conclude that Henry must hand over a receipt for the full value of the goods in Catherine's hands.

Henry was caught in his own trap. A miser to the core, he could not bear to be exposed in his malady. Seizing his cap, he came to Catherine's lodgings like any commoner, and before her chamberlain and her duenna he bitterly explained the whole situation.

"I see now that there is a crafty design," he declared, "and I shall not consent that it be attributed to me. I should not like to be held for a person who asks what is due to me before the time. God be praised, I am not in want, and, if it were necessary, I could for love of their highnesses and you, my señora daughter, spend a million of gold without contracting a debt."

When he mentioned their highnesses, Henry removed his cap, as was his custom. As he still could not force himself to provide "so much as a pin," however, he had to decide on the course which would combine honor with frugality. The Spaniards, seeing that Arthur's chest was weak, and remembering Juan, felt that Ferdinand and Isabella "would be rather pleased than dissatisfied if they for sometime did not live together." But Henry induced Catherine's confessor to say differently. He went among his councilors, eyes half-closed, probing. And within a few days he made it known that, having sympathy with those who are young and in love, he could not separate the bridal couple. He ordered that they go to their court at Ludlow, live together and take their meals together, "so that Arthur must use the things of the Princess."

"Though the opinions of many were adverse to this course," he himself wrote tenderly to Spain, "yet were we unwilling to allow the Prince and Princess to be separated at any distance from each other. Thus much we wished to show unto you by this letter, that you may understand our excessive love which we bear toward the most illustrious Lady Catherine, our common daughter, even to the danger of our own son."

So the matrimonial skiff was launched, and King Henry turned his mind to other cares. His own wife, now thirty-six, was going to have her seventh child, and the marriage portion for little Margaret, who was to marry the King of Scotland, had to be drained from parliament. A beardless boy, Thomas More by name, had had the insolence to oppose this grant. To turn the screws on More's father, to throw him in prison and fine him, while the young man headed for Flanders, was the natural rebuke for such opposition.

VII

At Ludlow the toy court was installed. There are few things on this earth so socially symbolic as a castle—pride surrounded by stagnant water. Catherine and Arthur became the center of a set group of the most staid and the most loyal standard-bearers, English and Spanish, and the boy began jousting and practicing the chivalrous technique. It was a community of extreme conservatism, high piety and formal courtesy, where those steeped in tradition took the Prince and Princess in leading strings. And Arthur ate off Catherine's plate.

For five months the regal life was mimicked, when a sudden alarm shook the little court. Arthur had collapsed. Was it consumption, or was it some mysterious malady? The courtiers, anxious and baffled, hovered round the boy, while the official medicine men consulted their folios. Arthur's wife, who could only speak to him through an interpreter, was alienated by something beyond her powers. The youth was mortally ill. For a few days there was a tense, frightened waiting. Then the heir to the throne died.

VIII

Had Catherine of Aragon been a commoner, her widowhood at seventeen would have been a merely personal affair, and her fate would now have been left to chance and love. She might have married again, and her cheeks bloomed with new roses, or she might have remained a dowered aunt, who passed white-faced and a little red-nosed on a round of family visits, a center of critical interest or fond affection. But this career, purely personal, was not open to her. She was a dynast. She was a pawn in the new game of Europe, and her fate was caught up in it. She found herself in the center of a revolving ring of kings and king-makers, who circled round her as she stood there, bewildered and alone. The nature of this game, to which she had been born and to which she had been fitting herself with the ardor of her flesh and the vigor of her blood, was at the same time wholly beyond her own powers of scrutiny. She was an actor in it, anxious to play her part and yet unaware of its intentions, bumping into its sharp corners like a blindfolded child. Even if she had eyes to see, or the valor of a saint, it could not have been certain that Catherine could have found her way. As it was, she wore her bandage tight, and obeyed the rôle to which she was consigned.

With Arthur's death her fortune went into eclipse. As the Spaniards mourned by Arthur's coffin, and attended the pale widow, the future hung gray and heavy. To return to Spain, when a huge dowry had been half paid, when a voyage so painful had been safely undertaken to England, when England was still just as necessary to the Spanish empire as before, was too bitter a reversal. The tragedy of Ludlow made the Spaniards infinitely thoughtful rather than crushed. There was still young Henry, who shortly would become Prince of Wales. He was six years younger than Catherine, but Henry was not a sickly body like Arthur. Henry was the picture of health, so big, so robust, so beautiful. The late Prince of Wales paled out like the last star of a short night, and over the horizon glowed this unseen sun.

There was, however, a predicament. There were ten months to wait. Had Catherine actually been married to Arthur? A great deal of rustling and whispering went on between the Spanish lady in waiting, the Spanish chamberlain, the Spanish confessor, followed by long confabulations behind doors, all in a privacy thick with significance.

The cause of this agitation was Leviticus. All the girl's future, and the future of the King and Queen of England, narrowed down to one crucial point on which the Spaniards had to take a blunt position. If Catherine and the poor boy who was dead had actually lived together as male and female, then all the stars in their courses could more easily be reversed than the fact of this embrace be obliterated. Was Catherine a virgin? So the deft Italian Geraldino asked gravely of Juan de Cuero. So Juan de Cuero inquired excitedly of Donna Elvira Manuel. If she were no longer a virgin, only the shrugs, the gesticulations, the cocked eyebrows of the Spaniards could convey the misfortune of it. Had she, or had she not, created a mystical barrier between herself and Henry? On both sides of this mystical barrier the Spanish contingent ran up and down, tearing their hair. It is written in the Bible: "Thou shalt not uncover the nakedness of thy brother's wife; it is thy brother's nakedness." And again, "And if a man shall take his brother's wife, it is impurity; he hath uncovered his brother's nakedness; they shall be childless." Those maledictions smote on the heart of the Spaniards. No more awful doom could be spoken to a dynast than "they shall be childless." It was true that Manuel of Portugal had married Catherine's two sisters, and the second union was not childless, far from it, but the words of the Bible were directed at brothers, not sisters. Catherine had already trembled on the verge of her marriage to Arthur because King Henry, who had imprisoned the Earl of Warwick until he became half-witted, had decided before the wedding to cut his head off, in order to clear Arthur's title to the throne. Catherine had quailed at this ugly emergency. She feared God's vengeance. And now who should raise in her young mind this question of Leviticus, this blasting curse, if she were untruthful?

One can imagine that this question created a terrifying fear in Catherine's soul, and that she confronted her conscience in anguish. When a Spaniard is afraid, he is afraid: one sees her kneeling on bare stone, her face the color of gray paper. Her whole body trembles, so that she can feel her legs tremble, and her arms tremble, and her teeth chatter as if she had the ague. Her soul curdles in her body and causes her mortal elements to shrink away from her immortal, as if she were possessed. She leans on her prie-Dieu, powerless, and strives to pray. But words do not come to her. She thinks of her mother, who is brave. She clings to her mother with the intensity that has in it something as primitive as the earliest caves. At last, with her frantic appeal to her mother, the blood that has been drawn up by her heart as by a sponge, and that has deserted the rest of her poor body, begins once more to creep into the members, which, ashamed of their feebleness, take on a little life. Her face loses its round-eyed terror. Her teeth cease to chatter. She stands on her feet, breathes deeply and closes her eyes. "Come," she calls to Donna Elvira. "I am ready."

A triumphant lady in waiting leaves Catherine to sweep to

and wrong, with her positive religion and social discipline, she combined an exacting sense of what a princess owed her people. Catherine looked up to her mother with love and awe. Her widowhood was for her a mere interval until her fresh betrothal, and that betrothal was argued and dictated and enforced by Isabella with the insistence peculiar to her nature. Since the English held that the marriage had been consummated, Isabella and Ferdinand, though saying "It is well known in England that the Princess is still a virgin," asked the Pope to issue a dispensation on the score that it had been consummated. No obstacle could daunt Isabella, or no subterfuge repel her. And by 1503 her diplomacy was crowned. A day or two before Henry reached the age of twelve, he was brought to a bishop's palace in Fleet Street and there betrothed to Catherine in person. He accepted it, as she accepted it, with a grand docility. Such a betrothal meant more, however, to a girl of eighteen than to an open-eyed, twelve-year-old boy.

Once Isabella was dead, in 1504, there commenced a drama in which all Europe took part, and which Catherine's fate rolled back and forth, in the trough of waves too high for her vision and too strong for her oars.

Though the favors and gestures of chivalry still flourished, Henry VII, seeking bribes from accused nobles, was more in tune with his time than Isabella, proudly punishing a nobleman who offered one. The game of dynasty was the game of all monopoly of power—finite in its outlook yet infinite in its appetite. And, in this game, England had to be a sharper. She had been driven from France humiliatingly after the breathtaking advance of Joan of Arc. Civil war had later weakened her, and though wealth dazzled the visitor from every goldsmith's window in Cheapside, the Yorkist was still lurking on the Continent, and the Tudor dynasty was young. Henry VII had himself become a widower with Henry as his sole remaining boy, now aged thirteen. Into the close fabric of his mind the one idea that rooted firmly was his family's fortune. England he dragged after him, like a hand-cart. The reward was Tudor supremacy, and if Ferdinand was frugal and frigid in Spain, and if Louis the Eleventh had been a miser in France, this contemporary of theirs was of the same breed, snuffing his candle with his own fingers to pinch a halfpenny from the moon.

Human meanness was a small price to pay for dynastic magnificence, and in his boy he beheld the future king. Young Henry, who was now taller than his father, bright in color, red and gold, with a sweet voice that was beginning to break, had been led to leave his book-learning, for which he was apt, to be taught his paces as a prince. He was not of his father's meager figure. He took after his grandfather, Edward IV, and he had it in him to be as careless, gay and popular as that tall and masterful prince. Those who remembered young Henry's grandfather before he grew very fat recalled how handsome he had been, how he had taken his ease and pleasures more than any prince living, with thought for nothing but the ladies, and that beyond measure, and for hunting and the merry life. They said that this young prince was the very image of his grandfather, who was of very fine stature and towered above every one, wearing those costly garments and new monkish cloaks of his that were lined inside with the most sumptuous furs.

But the canny Henry VII wanted something more than soft comfort for his gifted offspring. The older Tudor bent his brows over the younger Tudor's deer hunting and bride hunting, archery and policy, theology, tennis and the lute. To give the boy the means that would command an impregnable place in Europe was the ambition of the father, while at the same time he could not afford to risk his immediate marriage, since sons had been known to oust their fathers. The renaissance shimmered in the distance, its light gilding a few fine spires on English soil, but King Henry had no eye for the renaissance. He cupped Europe in his hands and hunched over it, to pick the best joint bargain for himself and his son. It was a study in chicane and price-cutting, consolidation and monopoly. It was the tutorship by an expert, jealous for and jealous of his own sweet flesh and blood.

The boy might have been solemnly betrothed to Catherine in 1503, but with the death of Isabella Catherine was no longer a bargain. She was no longer the daughter of the monarchs of Spain. Her father had lost his consort and had become merely Ferdinand, King of Aragon. Castile had passed to Mad Juana, who was married to the handsome Hapsburg, and who, even if she was so jealous as to pull the hair of Philip's beloved in open court, was only too glad to bring her fair Philip to power in Castile. The Hapsburg stock went up, and with it followed the craving eyes of Henry VII.

A practical man can usually find a precedent. Margaret of Austria had been sent to Paris for the Dauphin, as an impressionable child. She had been trained for him. But when a chance had come for Charles to marry the heiress of Brittany, Margaret had been bundled home, *sans compliments*. Catherine in England had no better claim. King Henry knew that after Pope Alexander's death Pope Julius had granted the dispensation for marriage, expressly stating that Arthur and Catherine had been man and wife. But why must this Spanish match be persisted in? Might not a better bride be found for young Henry? The King's closest councilor was Bishop Fox, the man who had given his word of honor not to harm Tyrrell at Calais, and who, Tyrrell once on board, had handed him to his death. "To serve the King's will, he will not stick to agree to his father's death." Since Archbishop Warham was always in the wings to say that this papal dispensation was not valid, Bishop Fox could at any time he brought forward to say that it was valid. Canon law was obedient. It stood on a revolving stage; with one turn Catherine was owned and with two twirls she

could be disowned. Hence Henry spread Europe before him,
asking for the most adroit, the most strategic, the most profitable marriage.

XI

In consequence he caused much pain. Catherine's position at
the court was intolerable. Every time she saw the king he said,
"Why does not his Highness keep his word and pay the
dowry? It is only our goodwill that makes us give you food to
eat. You have no claim on us." Those stinging reproaches
could not be answered, because the girl was in a false position.
She was marriageable and not married, a resident and yet not
invited, betrothed and not paid for. She went trembling-lipped
to old Puebla, and every word she said to that rascal was carried
back to Henry. She complained to her chamberlain, who dryly
pointed out that she was not paying her servants. For four
months, though she was living at Clapham in the same house
as young Henry, she was not allowed to say a word to him. Her
only hope of relief was her father, but her father was in the
same situation as Henry VII. He too was a man of middle age
who had just found his bearings as a widower, and his daughter's troubles were an annoyance to him. He needed to
strengthen himself in Naples and consequently he was interested in Germaine de Foix, the gay Navarrese whom he later
married, shortening his days by his efforts to have an heir.

Catherine sent letters to her father saying in every other
line, "I supplicate your Highness," "I supplicate your Highness." "For the love of our Lord," she begged, "consider how I
am your daughter." Not a maravedi had she been given by her
father since she left Spain, her servants had stuck by her
though in rags, and she had not a penny for alms. "I have
nothing for chemises; wherefore, by your Highness's life, I
have now sold some bracelets to get a dress of black velvet, for
I was all but naked: since I departed from Spain I have noth-

ing except two new dresses, for till now those I brought from there have lasted me; although now I have nothing but the brocade dresses. On this account I supplicate your Highness to command to remedy this; for certainly I shall not be able to live in this manner."

Catherine might as well have tried to impress flint. The money troubles of his daughter, thirty days distant by fast courier, filled Ferdinand with annoyed indifference. She signed herself, "The humble servant of your Highness, who kisses your hands, The Princess of Wales." But the Prince of Wales, to whom she was betrothed, was held apart from her. Catherine heard rumors that he was to marry Marguerite, sister to Francis. She heard rumors that her own father did not believe she was to marry the Prince in the end. Knowing her plainness, being six years older than Henry, her dowry unpaid, her agent a rogue, and her servants restive, Catherine began to lose control. "I am in the greatest trouble and anguish in the world," she burst out. Pale-faced and shaking, she ran to King Henry and his council, and, breaking into tears, she begged for a little assistance. These men, Henry, Fox, Warham, frowned on her and told her to respect her honor and dignity. She sought elsewhere some human aid in her misery, but she was still isolated. Her scoundrel of an agent, Puebla, the dean of ambassadors, so feeble that he had to be carried about in a litter, though he still resided in a house of ill fame, could write to Ferdinand in all rectitude, "She imagines she need not observe such order and seclusion as she does at court, but that she ought to enjoy greater freedom!"

And at this moment, in the midst of this discouragement, her "husband" Henry, the day he was fourteen years old, was taken secretly before Bishop Fox, to sign a protest against his betrothal with Catherine. The dispensation was on record. The betrothal was on record. This protest was also on record. Whichever way the cat jumped, the Tudor was ready to jump

with it. No longer a child, Henry could scarcely close his eyes
to the system into which he was being initiated by his father
and by the clerical councilors on whom his father leaned.

XII

Catherine, a princess-royal, and prospective Queen of England, thought she would die. Her malaria had kept its grip on
her for seven years, but worse than her malaria was her humiliation. She was twenty years old, isolated, desperate, biting her
fingernails in fury and anxiety, without the faintest touch of
coquetry or of artifice to relieve the grim façade of her destiny.
Yet a change came, such a change as Wyatt's cat bringing him
his pigeon when he was starving in prison. Catherine's hunger
was for some human being who would value her and on whom
she could rely. She found a young confessor. A Spanish grandee
described him in a few words: "May God destroy me if I see
in the friar anything for which she should have so much affection, for he has neither learning, nor appearance, nor manners,
nor competency, nor credit." These things might have been
just as true of Fray Diego Fernandez as they were of his Grace
Henry VII, but "young, and light, and haughty, and scandalous
in an extreme manner," this friar was what the woman needed,
a fierce partisan. He was seized with wrath at the state of
Catherine's affairs. The first Spaniard whom she had found to
act on her behalf, he sharpened his wits and took her cause in
hand.

The situation was, in fact, far from hopeless. Death, which
had cut Catherine's value, raised it again. In 1505 Philip and
Mad Juana had started for Spain. In the storm that forced them
to land in England, Juana's one care had been to don her best
dress, so that her corpse would be properly respected as royal,
but instead of a shipwreck she and Philip had a royal reception, and, under the thumb of King Henry's hospitality,
Philip promised gilded terms for the English merchants in

Flanders, promised to yield up the Yorkist Pole, and promised his own sister Margaret of Austria as a bride for the veteran Henry VII. These arrangements, setting Catherine dismally in the background, were hardly formed before Philip, overheated at a game of ball, died of a congestion at Burgos. Once more Castile dazzled King Henry. He wanted it, even if he had to marry Mad Juana.

In this the bold-eyed friar saw Catherine's chance. Henry's marriage to Juana was the bait she could use for her own purposes, and so he counseled her.

Catherine, who had tactlessly relieved her feelings about the King to Puebla, now, with that heavy fidelity of hers, changed her tone deliberately. "They fancy I have no more in me than appears outwardly," she said scornfully, "and that I shall not be able to see through his designs, but that I shall be satisfied with his promises as if I had not had experience of them. But I dissimulate with him and praise all he does." So she had learnt her diplomatic lesson, and so she wrote her father.

It was now Henry VII's turn to want something through Catherine, namely the hand of her crazy sister. Henry was bald, toothless and wheezing. He was one of those elderly potentates who bring with them a whiff of the backstairs. The prospect of his remarriage he had been canvassing for some years with avidity. Once Arthur was dead, he had promptly weaved after Catherine herself. When Isabella had died, he had taken in view that doughty lady, Louise of Savoy, after his addresses had been rejected by Juana of Naples. Then he had considered Louise's daughter Marguerite. Now, with Philip's light quenched, he stood on the Castile doorstep with his little smile, asking for Mad Juana. This was the best prospect of all.

Puebla urged his case for him. "There is no king in the world," Puebla wrote to Juana's father, "who would make so good a husband to the Queen of Castile as the King of England, whether she be sane or insane." She would soon recover her

reason when wedded to such a husband as Henry, and King
Ferdinand would, in any event, be sure to retain the regency
of Castile. If the Queen's madness should prove incurable,
Puebla added, it would perhaps not be inconvenient that she
should live in England, for the English seem little to mind her
insanity, especially "since they have been assured that her de-
rangement of mind would not prevent her bearing children."

Catherine joined the chorus, under her friar's direction.

XIII

Ferdinand, by the successes of the Great Captain in Italy, was
now anything but a mere King of Aragon. With an irony more
adept than Henry's own, he took pains to give his assent to
Henry's marriage to his insane daughter, at the same time
dwelling on the mental state of the lady that Henry burned to
marry.

"I shall never consent that she wed with any one else than
the King of England, my brother, and shall employ with
the greatest love and goodwill all my industry and energy to promote that. But you must know that the said Queen, my daughter, still carries about with her the corpse of King Philip, her
late husband. Before I arrived they could never persuade her
to bury him, and since my arrival she has declared that she
does not wish the said corpse to be buried. . . . I touched on
this matter, in order to know whether she was inclined to
marry, without, however, mentioning any person. She answered
that in everything she would do as I advised or commanded, but
that she begged me not to command her to give an answer to
my question until the corpse of her husband should be buried.
That done, she would answer me. Considering these circumstances, I do not urge her until the said corpse shall be buried,
because I think it would rather produce an unfavorable impression. I have sent to Rome for a brief, in order to try
whether she could thereby be persuaded to bury the corpse

sooner. When it is buried, I shall again speak with her, in order to know her intentions with respect to a marriage; and if I find her inclined, I shall not permit that it be with any one except with the King of England, my brother."

The corpse of Philip was an obstacle to nuptial comfort, so that Henry pursued this match with his left hand, while he reached for Margaret of Austria with his right. Margaret would be as good as Mad Juana. Margaret was desirable and good looking. But she was also forceful and clear-minded. She knew exactly the kind of match that was being offered her. An elderly bargainer was eyeing her, as a broker buys a diamond, and as he salivated over the jewel in his scaly hand, Henry had no notion of the scorn that was stirred by his lidless gaze. He was a King. He had trained parliament to walk at his heel. He had weeded out the Yorkists to clear his title. He had bred his family by a woman whose motto was "humble and penitent." Little could he conceive of the figure he cut before these sparkling and passionate women, who, like Margaret and Marguerite, were the civilized beings of royal Europe. And yet the obstacles they raised were hardly so real as the indecisions of the avaricious man himself.

XIV

Yet he negotiated. And the most brilliant incident in all his negotiations was struck off by a young priest. To his court there had come a chaplain of no particular account, a tall blond man in the early thirties, Thomas Wolsey of Ipswich, son of a butcher and cattle-dealer. He said mass every day before his Grace in his private closet, and so was brought in contact with his master, but naturally by his position as chaplain this Wolsey or Wulcy gained no prestige. Wolsey, however, was fully aware that he was at the head-spring of power in England, and his was a nature marvelously alert. A good priest in the early morning, he became a courtier with breakfast, and "gave his attendance upon those whom he thought to bear most rule in the council, and to be most in favor with the King." One of those quick, hardy, energetic beings whose wills are flogged by unseen whips, he made himself useful to Bishop Fox and to Lovell, he showed them how "meet and apt" he was, and he gave them velvet deference.

The King had a message for Margaret's father, about which, in his usual way, he felt out Fox and Lovell. It was not merely his letter, it was a question of the right messenger. The two elderly councilors commended the excellent chaplain in one breath. Henry sent for him, told him to go to Flanders with his dispatch, and added his instructions.

This was the moment for which the chaplain had lived. He left Richmond at noon. He caught the barge at Gravesend at four. He came to Dover the next morning early, snatched a boat to Calais, was there in three hours, departed incontinent, and by night was with the Emperor. Maximilian, the last of the romantics, sent for him at once. Wolsey, bright with desire, keen with hope, won from Maximilian a yes to everything, and without an instant's delay, reached Calais by night, Dover by ten in the morning and back to Richmond by night. There he slept on it.

When the King caught sight of him the next morning, stepping from his bedchamber to hear mass, he cried, "Why have you not passed on your journey?"

"Sire," answered Wolsey, "if it may stand with your Highness's pleasure, I have already been with the Emperor, and dispatched your affairs, I trust to your Grace's liking.

"But the messenger I sent after you?"

"I encountered him, Sire," said Wolsey. "And I made bold, your Grace, upon my own discretion, to dispatch the same. And for as much as I have exceeded your Grace's commission, I most humbly crave your gracious remission and pardon."

Henry, rejoicing inwardly and showing no surprise, said: "We do not only pardon you thereof, but also give you our princely thanks, both for the proceeding therein, and also for your good and speedy exploit." Whereupon, with his mind twittering with excitement, Wolsey tried to say mass.

This was a feather in the councilors' cap. With such gravity and eloquence did Wolsey tell his story to the council that his smartness, and especially his speed, left them gasping. He was promptly made dean of Lincoln, and then the King's almoner. His career had dawned.

XV

It was less fortunate with Catherine's friar, Fray Diego. The closer Henry drew to the Hapsburgs, the more sternly he viewed Catherine. They began to say that Catherine's confessor meddled in politics. "I swear by the life of your Highness," protested Catherine to her father, "which is the greatest oath I can make, that this is not the case." But the court listened sardonically. The Spanish friar too figured in an incident. The King had told his daughter Mary to wait for Catherine to ride to Richmond. As young Mary waited, the friar came to Catherine and said, "You shall not go to-day." That night, as the friar knew, Catherine had vomited. "But I am well," she said, "I do not wish to stay here alone."

"I tell you that upon the pain of mortal sin," he said, "you do not go to-day."

The Princess contended that she was well, but Fray Diego persevered so much that the Princess, not to displease him, gave in.

Every one who had seen Catherine at mass and at table reported this incident to the King, and bemoaned the fact that poor Mary, attending Catherine, had had to wait two hours. King Henry himself, angry with Catherine, doubly infuriated by her asking to see her marriage contract, snarled at her that the confessor was her lover.

"He permitted himself to be led so far," Catherine quivered to her father. But the old peasant could not bend her. Only he could starve her. "In the house of the King," she said bitterly, "they would not give meat to any one, even if he were dying."

The Spanish nobles hated Catherine's rebellion, yet from the advent of her confessor she was not the same pleading exile. At the bottom of this nature was the tough self-conceit, the obstinacy and obduracy that are always produced by frustration in thick tenacious souls. Only a response to her loyalty could elevate a character like Catherine's, and only sunshine could sweeten it. She had ached too long for the surety of marriage with Henry. Her seven years of cold shadow at the English court did not sap her principles or make her vulgar or nimble. They simply fortified her stubborn belief in herself and her animal suspiciousness of things different from herself. She became like a stone tower, with a door high and no windows. She was not indomitable like her brightly intelligent mother. She was implacable in passivity. To unpack her convictions, when they had been for so long driven inward, was beyond even her confessor. She had no resources beyond herself, no power to disarm or dissuade, no pliancy and no tact. She could not be besieged, but this was a nature that believed in itself, lived up to its word, and could not surrender. No sortie could save it, and no battering-ram destroy it. Catherine was immured in her own squat righteousness. She invited the environment to adapt itself to her, and if it refused, she stood the siege until her walls became her tombstone.

XVI

The youth for whom Catherine was intended had no longer the insouciance of a boy. Within a few years he had shot up into an amazing manhood, standing six feet, and with this height giving the assurance of power. From the elder Tudor, who sniffled toward the grave, the eyes of attentive Englishmen turned irresistibly to the younger. Here was a contrast between the scion and the sire.

Few knew better than the King's councilors how shrewdly he had reigned. The best of them had come with him from exile four and twenty years before. They had held by him from his upstart beginning. Had he failed, he would have been as ridiculous as a Lambert Simnel or a Perkin Warbeck, or as obscure as a Warwick or an Edmund Pole. But he had won through. He had cared nothing for showy adventure. He had chosen to follow the wending valleys, to choke himself in the daily dust, to make mean treaties and plan long intrigues and accept the dingiest peace, favoring commerce but bleeding his subjects through Empson and Dudley; with one free hand to take the booty and the other to smother legal protest, not so much a king as a sutler, or at best a pre-king. Yet in the pound of squalid hoofs and the grind of wheels he had heard music. The mule train had grown longer and longer, the weight of the treasure heavier, the dust sweeter. And if God were angry, the older Henry beat his breast, saying mea culpa, paid for a hospice, and ordered the most exquisite of tombs.

From such a wisdom they turned to the son. He was far different from this slippered father. They saw him in his games and sports, flushed with prowess in one contest after another, flattered by his companions, his purse open to make a wager or to toss largesse. Many eyes watched him, the cautious, the audacious, the fearful, the hopeful. Childhood was over, as his grandmother knew, but not surveillance. Was he headstrong? Could he be managed? Had he character? Had he brains?

No one, least of all his father, could mislike the bearing of the youth. He was in no sense confined by medieval limits. He stood on a higher vantage point and took in new landscapes. He knew at a glance the grim, gray page of his father's crabbed script. He turned rapidly to more illuminated pages, to gold initials and rose-hued borders, opening on the renaissance, touching on the new learning. But it was not merely gayety that attracted him. The day of tutors was over, but not the day of fresh accomplishment. He had ravished the French manuscripts that his father had given to Caxton. He knew his Malory, his Froissart. He gleaned the lesson of older courts. But courtliness for him was the fine binding of a life of statecraft, and this statecraft meant mastery, mastery of his body, mastery of his mind, mastery of his council, mastery of his culture. With an eagerness almost nervous, and a youthfulness almost comic, he touched life at every side. While he looked back with amusement and scorn on the limitations of his father, his father's generation could not decide whether his progress was dizzy and superficial or dazzling and impressive. He was visibly perfecting himself, both for society and for the monarchy, but not until he turned with brightness on any one whom he sought to please did his full possibilities reveal themselves, like a spring landscape suddenly lavished with sun. Then his bodily vigor, his odd restlessness and uncertainty, his actual physical shiftiness, came into unison and a persuasiveness began to exercise itself with a charm at once personal and shy. This charm could waver against opposition. It could run forward and draw back, if the prospect were not favorable. But Henry possessed it. He could even, on occasion, spend it gloriously. It was physical in the candor of his eye and the comfort of his smile, but it was as well an inner animation, the animation of a young soul that expands in being comprehended and acknowledged. Then he became more than the young prince who is preening himself in the mirror. He became the inner personality of his England, the soul to whom England assented, the keeper of its conscience, the guardian of its interests, its actual king.

And for this kingship, Henry was not unprepared. Though one could never tell how like his grandfather Edward he might prove, with his sumptuous body and his lively eye, and though he had admitted Compton and Brandon to his intimacy and was gay with the Boleyns, his attentive grandmother Margaret Beaufort could see in the very easy vulgarity of these contacts a sort of provision against their absorbing him. When he lifted his head quickly, all alert as a quick-eared animal, it was in response to a question of statecraft, a word as to the papacy, as to the judiciary, as to the Star Chamber. And in religion, which meant everything to the Venerable Margaret, he was as dutiful as a child. He was definitely pious. He took to ritual with a positive zest. If his mind was acquisitive, it was not skeptic or uncertain. At seventeen or eighteen, it was more than usually conservative. Outside statecraft and sporting, it was well pegged down.

But one glance at the young prince, the picture of health, ready to sink his white teeth into the sweet juicy peach that life was handing to him, could only arouse the expectation, the happy or unhappy expectation, of a change. His father had acquired; he would spend. His father had narrowed; he would widen. His father had closed; he would fling open. Between the old man and the young, there was a silent, an implicit, resentment. How far he would go in disbursing the heaped-up gains of the miser, no one could foretell; but Henry VII, his rusty leaves still clinging in withered profusion to his blighted branches, could only seem a finished chapter when one turned to the young Henry, verdant and abundant, tipped with the folded bud of promise and rich with the sap of youth.

XVII

Up to 1509, Henry VII remained master. Catherine's stubbornness had only the effect of deadlocking Henry and Ferdinand, and creating passion. In 1508 Ferdinand and Louis and Pope Julius II had come together for the simple festival of carving up Venice, and this exploit heightened Ferdinand's tone. He wrote that either young Henry should marry Catherine or he would come with an army and chastise the English. This threat did not settle the matter, as the antique Henry was still brooding over his own remarriage. But there were other plans for him: in 1509 death took him by the ear, and he rejoined Elizabeth the Good.

When he had felt death approaching, he had become frightened. He was only fifty-two. He had gone on a pilgrimage to Our Lady of Walsingham and to Thomas of Canterbury; he had planned the Savoy hospital for a hundred sick out of the vast hordes who had no hospitals. As he lay dying he had gasped to his attendants that "if it pleased God to send him life, they should find him a new changed man." But his tuberculosis was too far advanced.

He expired April 21, 1509. Not till May 9, however, did they move him from Richmond to Westminster. The interval was not too long: a wax image of him had to be prepared, robed in state, that was to lie on the coffin during the funeral, holding the ball and scepter in its wire fingers, and afterwards to stand among the waxworks at Westminster Abbey; the black cloth of gold for the chariot had to be procured; the choir and the clerks had to be rehearsed; grandstands had to be erected in London for the little children who were to hold wax tapers; the Mayor had to order his black robe; great families in the shires had to be given time to come, bedsteads and all, and to bring with them their mourning for the funeral and their bright clothes for the coronation, banners, "pendents," arms, genealogies—the apparatus of royal exit and royal entrance had to be organized for an appreciative world, and meanwhile young Henry must withdraw to the Tower so that rejoicing for a young King should not trip sorrow for the old.

On his death-bed Henry VII had quavered prudence to his son, making him promise to marry Catherine of Aragon. He left an endowment to pay for masses for his soul as long as the world would endure—which, according to the computations of Christopher Columbus, would be 155 years.

The funeral was regal. It reached the expectant capital through Southwark, passing the parks of noblemen, the new mansions of wealthy merchants, the jolly taverns, the bawdy quarter, the little graveyard of nameless women. At London Bridge the Mayor received the funeral, attended by the city companies, and from every arch and hole in London wall crept curious cut-purses and scallywags, mingling with honest boatmen from gate and wharf, stout carters and their housewives, bronzed and brawny mariners. Away from Thames, toward the great Gothic St. Paul's, the proud procession mounted. Everywhere the houses were candle-lit, and through the narrow, glowing channel of these dense streets the mourners mumbled and chanted behind the chariot as it rocked over broken ways. Boys' thrush-like voices, clerks' jackdaw voices, rose and fell in a multiple jargon that was mellowed by the vault of heaven. Thousands of soft-shod attendants pattered in rank on rank behind the corpse with its waxen effigy, while the flare and fume of six hundred torches moved with the chariot and cast dancing shadows on the rapt Londoners' gaze.

That generous heart of London had no reproach for the dynast who was going to his grave. Not yet an empire within an empire, but already the aspirant to a soul, London could view its king with equanimity. Now he had upon him the mantling dignity of death. Eager, sober, illuminated faces peered through the glow at the endless pathos of the common fate. The white-hued messenger, the burly brewer, the cobbler, the pinched tailor, the blacksmith, the tanner, the hooper, the surgeon-barber, the German merchant from the Steelyard, the French embroiderer, the Flemish weaver, the stonecutter from Italy, the thronging Cockney apprentices with their sharp-cut

noses and rapid tongues, were welded together, hot and palpitant, into a receptive and wondering throng. Even in death the
monarch held supremacy.

While multitudes poured on the heels of the winding
cortège, now a blare of sonorous Latin, now a flare of fuscous
red, St. Paul's opened its wide arms to receive the body of a
king. Gradually the waves of life were gathered to its bosom.
Gradually in the distant thoroughfares under Tower Hill and
near the Thames the spring twilight resumed its peace and
these streets lay pensive in emptiness. A fresh air came from
the meadows of Finsbury. The evening light, a dim blue crys-
tal, bathed once again the deserted houses. Blue shadows
washed the black-beamed walls. A star rose over a thatched
roof. At St. Paul's they would be praying. To-morrow at Westminster the great officers of state would break their white
wands and cast them into Henry's grave. . . . And when all
the kings were buried, the month of May would still come of an
evening and whisper eternity in a London street.

BOOK TWO

Henry and Catherine

"Princes do not marry for love: they take wives only to beget children."

GATTINARA

I

HENRY VIII had come to the Tower of London. While the old King lay in his coffin amid a blaze of candles, in the hush of death, the young king moved away to the center of excitement. At the moment it hummed, but it only waited for the funeral to be over to break into glorious acclaim.

The acclaim would be national. The whole realm outside the council throbbed with Henry's youth. A system that had revolved with many a strain around the person of the father had suddenly shivered into release, and swung into rhythm round the son. It was the rhythm of national hope, national pride, national energy. Some whom the elder Henry had been using might expect to lose their holds; but these would be few. The vast part of Englishmen who were conscious of a political change felt that with the father's death an amnesty could indeed be declared, a stale will made vibrant and a jaded heart refreshed. It was the change from age to youth. Waves of welcome rolled toward Henry from every quarter that felt, and sought, appreciation. The soldiers, the scholars, the priests, the courtiers, the people, parched during a grudging reign, were thirsting for this dispensation, and gave themselves to it even before the chief herald cried aloud, "Vive le Roy Henry le Huitième!"

The youth on whom all this hope was centered, and to whom all this power was attributed, had joined his councilors in the Tower. He had come there, as all the kings came there, to prepare for his coronation.

The White Tower housed him. It was not a festive residence. Though it had been made gracious by eager hands, with fresh straw on the floor and tapestries on the walls, the banquet hall garnished and the council chamber made sweet, these thick walls knew secrets that no tapestry could hide. The past peered darkly from ceilings and high windows, dripped itself into moments of silence and flowed into little pools of red remembrance under the thoughtful eye. Here Henry's boy uncles had been murdered for his granduncle, their bodies hidden under stairs that he trod. Below these windows Warwick had been beheaded by his father. Here his grandfather Edward had ordered Henry VI to be slain. These were memories that skulked in the Tower. Yet their savor, too pungent to be allayed, was drowned for Henry in the intoxicating incense. He had come to the Tower as to a monarchical sacrament. Its gloom and baseness, stealthy with assassination, laden with treachery, sharp with torture, was bearing in its muffled bosom something besides crime: it spoke of emergencies that had been seized white-hot and dreadful dangers that had been surmounted; it held the ax of authority in readiness, the weapons of the kingdom, the first and last resorts of monarchy in peril. It was grim, but it was also reassuring. It was foul and it was fair. The heady mixture of its horror and glory tingled in Henry as the new and marvelous wine of power.

With this he glowed. He had not come to Moloch to promise it fresh victims. No one had less desire to look into its blood-shot eyes. Yet it was under this sinister roof with its shadow cast lightly on his boyish hand that Henry was opening his virgin page.

II

He stood among his councilors, the tallest of them all, broad-shouldered, hot-looking, heavily perfumed, lightly sweating, courteous to every one, yet grading his courtesies as befits a king.

The council that gathered about him, chosen by his sage and dauntless grandmother, was in reality his cabinet. It did not take so simple or so enthusiastic a view of the new monarch as did the outside world. These were the elders; wary, seasoned men who had been accustomed to the father, to his circumspect pace, his shrewd calculation and dry wit. Most of them were soldiers but some of them churchmen on parole. Margaret Beaufort had not gone to the Old Nobles. She had picked among tried Tudor adherents, and she had sown in Henry the suspicion of the Old Nobles that she had learned before Bosworth was fought and Richard III killed. No one could doubt the loyalty of this cabinet; the day of civil war was over. But the day of national wars was not over, and everything turned on finding the drawbridge into Henry's will. He was a splendid adolescent. But when a boy of eighteen becomes the richest man in England, one of the richest men in the world, the goal of every adventurer, the magnet of every schemer and every dreamer, the arbiter of fortune, there is bound to be a conflict of policies. This conflict could not be hidden from Henry. Yesterday he had been, perhaps, a mere boyish prince; but to-day he was the head of the nation. With the least stir about him, a prompt and wide alertness was noticeable. His ears were open, his white eyelashes flickering. He was preternaturally aware.

But he was not aware in any confusion of mind; already he was the young master weighing his world.

The men who judged him most shrewdly were the soldiers. No one of them had any special influence with him, and he did not commit himself, but one glance at his beautiful physical condition, his glowing complexion, his open yet ordered smile, his fair-haired radiance, would make any man say, "Here is the making of a soldier!" And those who knew him best could be sure that he was furnished with a few simple massive prejudices that would narrow their problem. Though speakingly Norman in body, he despised the French like any English schoolboy. He had the boy's religious feeling for sport. He feared women. He knew himself, in the old phrase, to be "upon the square." He was ready to worship, and identify his ends with, God. Out of this material a soldierly ambition could be created, and a soldierly future made.

Yet the youthful king was not transparent. If he possessed the power that was attributed to him on every side, it was not showing itself in any fury of conviction. The soldiers knew that he had been buoyant and vigorous from childhood. The prelates knew that he had been fitted to be Archbishop of Canterbury when his father first spotted church revenues. Which was the core of Henry's being?"

At the moment he could hardly have said. He could feel that England thirsted for him and this generously stirred him. He knew that his people wanted a monarchy quite different from that which his father had provided; he knew it the better because he wanted it himself. He had loved his mother, but the meanness of his father's rule had humiliated him. He had hated his sly meekness. He had disapproved of his covetousness. He had suffered under the unpopularity that came from Empson and Dudley. He had fretted and chafed under the backwardness, the provinciality, the stuffiness of the English court. This was no secret. To plant Henry VII in that lyrical tomb in Westminster Abbey would relieve no one so much as his son, who wished for magnificence and cordiality, who wished to fling down the barrier and lead the grand procession. A miser, it has been said, is a weir across the stream that stops the current. For Henry the weir had crumbled, and he stood ready to unleash the golden stream.

III

It was the moment for which Catherine had longed day and night. She was now twenty-four. On his death-bed, Henry had urged his son to complete their marriage, and everything depended on the council. So far as Catherine was concerned, the young king knew that she asked nothing better than to marry him, and for himself, feeling instinct to be of minor consequence, he would not postpone. The difference in age would not be altered by the running of time. He knew that Catherine had been married to his brother, and he knew that the arguments from Leviticus and from Deuteronomy had not changed since 1502, but the wedding had hung fire, Ferdinand was imperative, the French were in Italy, coronation was at hand.

The council was divided. The soldiers did not fumble their decision. Surrey, a stout warrior of the old school, the tough and able Poynings, Shrewsbury, loyal and level-headed, old Lovell, Darcy, Wyatt, Marny and Herbert dropped their noble metal into the scales against their habitual enemy France. Bishop Fox of Winchester had always favored the marriage, while Ruthal of Durham, insignificant except for his immense wealth, would side with the majority. Only the Archbishop of Canterbury demurred. He was a friend of France, believing in the father's policy of economy and peace. He had been active for the crown before Henry was born, a skillful and weighty negotiator who cherished the relicary of St. Thomas, while he could be a mild patron of Erasmus. He stood out against the marriage and disputed the papal dispensation. But Warham was not Hercules, and Warham was overruled.

Urged by his instinct, by his positive sense of the real forces in his council, Henry went to meet the opposition when it had been isolated. It was the first instance that he had encountered of those moral scruples that might conflict with policy, and he spared no pains to convince the Archbishop how much depended on loyal coöperation. He must have seen Warham privately. He knew his own mind so clearly, argued so naturally, imposed himself so sweetly, that the Archbishop did not have the heart to stand out against him. When he deferred to his master's will, Henry clenched it by asking him to perform the ceremony himself. Once more Warham yielded.

With the disregard for public expectations that was excused by his mourning but that sprang from an odd obliqueness, Henry arranged for a secret wedding. He took Catherine to their favorite chapel of the Observant Friars, and there, the world excluded, was united to her by Warham in the first days of June.

For Catherine it was no sacrifice of self. Though it was a wicket-gate by which she entered the long promised land, her marriage to Henry found her vindicated and happy. She looked up to him with pride, she looked down on him with love. He seemed to her young, flexible, and touchingly immature. And if her marriage had been secret, the coronation would not be secret. Into every detail, Queen Catherine plunged with sparkling eyes and busy hands.

IV

Among the men of the New Learning there existed fraternity in its best sense. They had breadth, wisdom, gayety, innocence of spirit, and strange and gallant independence. They welcomed Henry extravagantly. Linacre had taught him Latin grammar (in six weeks). Erasmus had corresponded with him. John Colet counted on him for the Greeks against the Trojans. Bishop Fisher could see in him a joyous change from the older monarch, who had been contented with a groveling realism, a tinkling chronicler and dancing bears. And Thomas More hailed him in a poem that he had encrusted with jewels and inscribed on vellum.

But Catherine's chamberlain Mountjoy, who wrote instantly to Rome to urge Erasmus to hurry to England, could speak of Henry with more than happy anticipation. He could speak with knowledge.

Henry had abruptly opened his heart to Mountjoy, confessing his want of learning. He knew his Latin fairly. The Consolations of Boethius was at his bedside. He had studied theology. He had escaped from Duns Scotus to Aquinas. But this path that Erasmus was mounting bewildered him, and a gust of youthful depression swept over him as he reflected on the abyss between himself and the scholarly.

"I wish I was more learned," he told Mountjoy.

Mountjoy would have none of it. "We do not desire this of you, Sire, but that you should welcome and cherish those who are."

"And why not," answered Henry meekly, "for without them we should scarcely exist."

This conversation Mountjoy reported to Erasmus. "Oh, my Erasmus," he wrote in the *style noble*, "if you could see how all the world here is rejoicing in the possession of so great a prince, how his life is all their desire, you could not contain your tears for joy. The heavens laugh, the earth exults, all things are full of milk, of honey and nectar! Avarice is expelled from the country. Liberality scatters wealth with bounteous hand. Our King does not desire gold or gems or precious metals, but virtue, glory, immortality. . . . Make up your mind that the last day of your wretchedness has dawned. You will come to a prince who will say, 'Accept our wealth and be our greatest sage.' "

Erasmus took little time to make up his mind. He was a European who spoke no English or Italian, who used Latin as the tongue of his humanism, and whose life was being spent to give the classics to the printing press, to give liberal ideas to educators, to mold civilization through the mind. A frail and slender man, he had extraordinary nervous force. He went on his work forming allies, spending energy, fighting gayly for truth, taking offense easily, creating ahead of his age and far beyond his resources the mode of the good European. Serving no particular master, he had no particular income. Though the best-selling author in Europe, he made little from his books. He had worked his way to Rome as the guardian of two rich boys, giving to them and to the son of the King of Scotland—a juvenile archbishop—the first claims on his attention. His travels were irksome, yet in spite of sensitive health and broken routine, he labored without cease, and met everywhere the humanists who valued him. He came to Rome, beyond doubt, in the hope that here as priest and savant he would find the soil for his fruition. "The wisdom of the scribe cometh by opportunity of leisure."

It was a brilliant Rome. Bright wits, gracile cardinals, beautiful courtesans created a dazzling society that set its heart on "old gold, young girls and short masses." Christ was well lost for an epigram. The Pope, Julius II, was a grizzled hero, smoking with battle, hating the French who had hollowed his Michelangelo statue into a cannon. Erasmus was most welcome because he could charm at dinner tables. But Erasmus was not a dessert. His gayety was serious. His comedy was freighted. He had a mind that without being revolutionary could never fit into a beautiful Latin vase.

He stifled, and he did not suffer in patience. He felt nostalgia for a new world, the kind of world he had discussed at Cambridge with Thomas More and Colet and Linacre, Latimer and

Grocyn. This present Europe, mad with war, sick with hate, gay with recklessness, aroused in him the tragi-comic philosopher, born idealist and illegitimate.

When his old friend Mountjoy summoned him, he hearkened. He hastened North to a financial background, to "Octavius" and the Golden Age.

V

But Henry's favorite courtiers did not wave aside the precious metals in the name of virtue and immortality. Mountjoy went too fast. These courtiers had long smiled at schoolmasters. They had another ideal for the prince. Into his head they endeavored to put "a certain greatnesse, with that princely sumptuousnesse and readinesse of courage, and unconquered prowesse in armes, that should make him beloved and reverenced of all men, in such wise that for this in especial he should be famous and notable to the world. . . . He ought to be full of liberality and sumptuous, and give unto every man without stint, for God, as they say, is the treasurer of freeharted Princes; make gorgeous banquets, feastes, games, people pleasing showes, keepe a great number of faire horses for profit in warre, and for pleasure in peace: Haukes, houndes, and all other matters that belong to the contentation of great Princes and the people."

So felt Brandon and Compton, the companions of Henry's pleasures as prince. So felt Thomas Boleyn. These were the men with whom the Prince of Wales had been jousting and fencing, wrestling and pole-jumping, hunting and gambling. These were the gay guardsmen who said, "Teacher, I'll beat you if you beat me," and who believed that "learning is a great hindrance and displeasure to a nobleman." Bastard, fool, rogue, mope—these were the naughty words they heaped on their tutors. But who more excellent than they with a hound or a horse? From the beginning they had provided Henry with

amusement and themselves with fortune. They admitted no
weakness, stood pain, stood fatigue, opened no book except a
stud-book or a betting-book, and blandly called themselves
stupid. Their minds shone with perfect clarity in a little space.

They loved direct experience, loved soldiering, took no man's
word for anything, and for the good things of life had a competent appetite. They welcomed the new king no less than the
intellectuals, and perhaps understood him better.

VI

The coronation came on St. John's Eve. Very tall, very fair, admirably proportioned, Henry was a capital horseman. He rode
in state from the Tower to Westminster, the anointing spoon in
Warham's hand to spill chrism on his head. A robe of crimson
velvet furred with white ermine fell from his shoulders. His
coat was raised gold. His placard shone with rubies, great
pearls, emeralds and diamonds. Catherine, demure in white
satin, "beautiful and goodly to behold," her hair loose in token
of her virginity, was borne on a splendid litter. Nine children
in blue velvet jaunted on great coursers to represent Henry's
possessions—England, Cornwall, Wales, Ireland, Gascony,
Guienne, Normandy, Anjou and France. It was a parade that
filled the eye, a spectacle from a fairy tale, a pageant out of
wonderland.

At the glorious sight of Henry, the people surged with hope
and pleasure. He had begun his reign by arresting the cruel
bloodsuckers that his father had employed, and yet out of the
chrysalis of his father's thrift he was opening golden wings.
The people could not but rejoice at this profusion of treasure,
this money to spend and to spare. They had come through
hard times. They wanted to be able to count on their king, to
have security, to have safe roads to travel by, a chance to sleep
sound and breathe easy, to reach his ear, to gain his heart, to
gallivant with him and love him. Long was the story of skinflint

monarchs—the seared memory of Louis XI in his old felt hat
with eleven apostles outside and the financier within; of
Cosimo de' Medici with his pawnbroker's three balls; the
flitting shadow of Maximilian with hardly a shirt to his back;
of Ferdinand sardonically stroking his doublet and boasting
that it could still outlast three pair of sleeves. It was not in this
mean and narrow direction that Henry was facing, but toward
magnanimity, toward the sun. He was joining the renaissance,
catching the rhythm of the new Europe, hailed by the courtiers
as a model, by the intellectuals as an ally, by the merchants as
a patron.

The newly crowned king, with his queen by his side, looked
on this loyalty with emotion. No one existed to dispute that he
had come to a power absolute enough to be reckoned almost
Oriental. His was no longer an England of Magna Carta, a
strong regiment of nobles and squires, a confident church and
a stalwart general opinion. It was no longer in its essence a
country of jury trial, of parliament, of order and balance. This
was not hidden from a few simple troubled people or from a
handful of unknown lawyers who puzzled over human liberties
in the inns of court. But Henry appealed to the instincts of his
people; he looked like a man, he looked good and shrewd and
ample, he delighted their native craving for force and energy
and he reassured stupidity. His very body said that he would
give them continuity and guarantee them continuity. And this
confidence that he created in the multitude did not fail to return on him and exalt him.

These first days were not without silent pledges and fine
raptures. He inherited an England that had been shorn of
greatness. That England looked to him and acclaimed him. He
did not phrase his response in words, but in bursts of liberality.
It showered from him like sunshine on little leaping waves.
With Catherine near by, he was grand enough to open his heart
and his purse to Reginald Pole, whose brother his father had

killed, and whose grandfather his grandfather had killed. Empson and Dudley he did not spare, but their goods he bestowed
freely. On the edge of this benevolence stood his chaplain Wolsey, ready to be his almoner. Wolsey would soon have a noble
mansion, with orchards running down to the Thames.

VII

For a short time the festivities were suspended on account of
Margaret Beaufort. She died with the coronation, worn out and
fulfilled. Catherine's sway was deeply respectable, and she and
Henry owed much to his grandmother. They were starting, in
any event, as pious as two palmers. Even on the days he went
hunting, Henry heard three masses, and sometimes five on
other days, though these five masses could be obligingly tele-
scoped. Every evening in the Queen's chamber he heard vespers
and complines. Catherine had been accustomed, with Spanish
rigor, to spend six hours daily in divine communication. Under
her royal robes she wore her habit of the Third Order of St.
Francis. She prayed at midnight, at five in the morning; and already the heir she designed for Henry was the temporal object
of her devotional life. But the youth who modeled himself on
the parfit knight, who headed his early letters "Jesus is my
Hope," and who aimed at "piety, valor, courtesy, prowess, the
gifts of poetry and eloquence, and dexterity in the management
of the horse, the sword, the lance and the bow," a blend, that is
to say, of Jesus and Hector—was not always on his knees in
devotion.

He cared too much for life, for the gorgeous toy of monarchy, not to play with it like the adolescent Gargantua. This
aroused and quickened the pulse of every gentleman. It drew
out every noble family that had social art; it excited the old
ones to adapt themselves and the new ones to assert themselves. And in the thick of it was this kingly young king. He
was eager to shiver a lance with any of his courtiers, to argue

with any of his doctors, to design a coat of arms, to be an expert
in heraldry, to decide on precedence and on hereditary claims.
He was eager to be known as the romantic cavalier. He took a
childish pleasure in the more violent forms of dancing, in immense leaps and pirouettes. The whole world gasped with admiration when Henry gamboled and cavorted, snapping his
heels high in the air. When he rode before the ladies, he made
his mount prance and career, rear and capriole. His prowess in
the saddle brought him showers of compliments. And he was so
insatiable in his desire to impress and to dazzle that he turned
from theological disputations and triumphs in the ring, to the
composing of hymns and the singing of his own lyrics. Henry
was enough his father's son, enough a Welshman, to have a real
taste for music. He wrote two masses, and he sought out the
best lute-players to teach him and to play to him. His energy
did not halt at this: he wrote ballad and verse.

And in all the masques and pageants in which the opening
years of his reign abounded Henry's was the craving, the insistence, the fancy. His was the taste most gratified by these
singular attempts to put into form the unsatisfied instinct for
drama and play-acting. His hand was heavy and his invention
flat, yet it was another tremendous effort to defy the law of
gravity and to rise into the mood of the renaissance. Through
these early years the middle age hung on like a ragged fog after
the sun had risen: cold formalities clung to status and clustered
around privilege: the barren rules of the grammarian, the
mysteries, the elaborations, the incantations, the suffocating
gloss, the infinitudes of pedantry and preciosity, hampered
the movement and veiled the light of reason. But out of this
fog, ostentatious and half liberated, strode Henry and his royal
procession.

The coin amassed by his father gave the happy illusion of
inexhaustible wealth. Two centuries before the Bank of England came into being, Henry had in his own keeping the im-

mense real wealth, the actual treasure, by which self-assurance is fortified. He was the creditor of his own court, a banker and money-lender. Next to the church he was the greatest land-owner in England. He had a vast number of manors, forests, rivers, mills, fisheries, ports, markets, towns and mansions. This meant that he had an army of servitors who wore his harness and fought under his banner. His absolutism loaded legality in his favor with the weight of his precious metal. He had the natural support of men of property. It was not the noble who loved him so much as the "new men." The new men saw in him one of themselves. And while he was regal in his state and in his manner, he blossomed first of all as the prince whose gold was invincible. His wealth was the plain advertise-ment to his subjects, lay and clerical, noble and common, that he was as much above other Englishmen in fortune as he was above them in station and prowess. This did not offend his subjects. They felt that as he was big, they were big; as he was wealthy, they were wealthy; as he could rule, they could rule. They identified themselves as kinglets and reveled in his supe-riority.

In so intimate a group as Henry's, where he was the domi-nant figure, where all the young beauties and the gallants around him were only too anxious to please, and where the older hands were themselves reluctant to interfere with spar-kling and high-mettled youthfulness, the life of the court had to choose between Venus and Mars. The courtiers and the maids of honor were together during banquets which were novel and costly. Sometimes the women sat in the gallery, but in general the men and the women sat alternately. The air was festal. Religion, in so far as it was active, drilled the court: the body groaned with long kneeling and weary standing at attention. Yet these penitential services explained how feasts could be so royal in reward. The men who survived were not the pale Arthurs: they were the heroes of the joust, the tilt, the archery-butts and the carousal. A round of continuous entertainment occupied the buoyantly venturous company: outside were the burgesses of London, who gathered for the public spectacles to be diverted and amazed. Sycophants who picked among the leavings, artisans who titivated and regaled the court, hucksters who rejoiced at such fluid prosperity, and beyond them still further the workaday Jack and Jill, sober or merry, sweet or grim, to whom the King was as rare as the coin on which he was stamped, for whom the mere sight of his gala attire was so intoxicating that he was jostled and stripped of ornament, who lived their struggling days in swarming streets, jocund and plucky in the filth and stench, and who, like the tortoise that is skinned alive for its shell, were by their very toughness to found the wealth of England.

It was hard for any one, even Henry, to believe that a court could be so splendid. At the sight of his gold trappings the visitors pressed near, not believing it possible, but Henry smilingly allowed them to see for themselves, and these chains and bits proved to be that marvelous magnet, solid gold. England's gold elbow nudged Europe in the ribs. Everything that could be gold was gold, the ewers, the pitchers, the handles, the brocades, the pantaloons, the curtains, the tassels. Henry's "spears," a select company, were trapped in cloth-of-gold. Up to now Portugal and Burgundy had been the most dazzling courts in Europe, but England obliterated them. Henry was proclaimed the best-dressed sovereign in the world. When he gave a banquet, butcher's meat was left to the base-born gluttony of aldermen, except pork stewed in broth and venison with sour cream; swans and peacocks, cranes and seagulls, flew from the sky to the royal table. Hippocras, malmsey, the "fulsome" wines, flanked these condescending birds, and luxury decreed jellies and sweetmeats of every shape and size. The revel became an institution. The Howards, the Bryans, the Carews, the Guilfords, the Boleyns, Seymour, Brandon, Compton, Sandys, appeared and reappeared. As the art of conversation did not allure these knights, every banquet flowered into gambling and dancing, frolic and charade. Bowls of ducats would be passed to the guests, thousands of pounds, so that they could amuse themselves at dice. The costumes of the masques, themselves elaborate and ingenious creations, were bestowed on the courtiers and their ladies. No group could have had higher spirits, shown merrier faces, or carried more stimulants.

Such a court, so rich, so free, so full of nature, at the same time so overwrought, and so emulative, was bound to tire of sport and to demand the outlet of war. "He was young and lusty," said a visitor, "disposed all to mirth and pleasure, and to follow his desire and appetite, nothing minding to travail in the busy affairs of his realm." Such a king, with a sword in his hand, could hardly grow old in peace.

VIII

It was not, of course, rare instinct that decided the tone of Henry's court. It was also the pattern of his time. Those who were in the trade of being kings did not improvise their conduct. Nothing was more discussed, down to its tiniest details. It had come as a tradition from Persia or Arabia, by Spain and Portugal, by Urbino and Mantua, by Dijon, by Paris, by Madrid. In England they were dancing to the flute, the harp, the violetta and the fife. At Urbino they were saying, "All instruments with keys are full of harmony, and the music with a set of violes doth no less delight a man, for it is very sweet and artificial." Henry's accomplishments and amusements were not his own by temperament, but by training and profession. He was ardent in them as the leader of the profession. He did not play football, because no gentleman played the filthy game. But he wrestled because "wrastlynge is a very good exercise in the begynnynge of youthe." He did not ride a mule, God forbid, but he knew "that a gentilman do lerne to ride a great and fierce horse whiles he is tender and the barwnes and sinewes of his thighes nat fully consolidate." Henry consolidated his thighs according to Elyot. Like any man who masters his trade young, he did it as well as his trade union could make him. In England at the moment, elegance in manners was rather like elegance in language—rich, but impure and uncertain. It was partly the tradition of Chevalier Bayard, partly of Castiglione's courtier, and a little of guzzling Gargantua. The older families, the Percys, the Staffords, the Poles, had their own idea of Henry's breeding, though they considered Catherine of Aragon a thorough gentlewoman. But the myth of Henry's personality had started growing, and he was already trying to live up to it. The best men found themselves competing with the worst men to work on him. Every force in England had been set in motion to capture him. And when, in the duet between the man and his myth, Henry had the misfortune to sing a false note, propaganda at once drowned it in the accompaniment.

Catherine, however, knew him for what he was. As she stood by him, "rather ugly than otherwise," looking steadily out with her prominent, fixed blue eyes, she scanned the jeweled nobles, the silken prelates, the gay-clad ambassadors, the "handsome damsels of sumptuous appearance," for those who would make the best of her young husband. Her own hope, to give him an heir, was destined to a terrible disappointment within a few months. Her first child was still-born. To her father she wrote, "Do not be angry with me, it is the will of God." But the disappointment she caused him she could not measure. She was well aware of the pretty faces around him, and yet she had the best grounds for feeling he was happy. His politics and her politics walked together, keeping perfect step, and it was not in her nature to fear to enlist him for her father. On the contrary, she had openly made herself Ferdinand's ambassador.

Henry had not been king six months, before he proved that he chimed with Spain. From Ferdinand and Maximilian he had received the fatherly encouragement that his ardor required, and Pope Julius had bestowed on him the Golden Rose, odoriferous with musk. These attentions met his wishes. The alarming victories of Louis XII in Italy had agitated every soldier about him, and recalled no less the dangers from an overbearing France than the historic mission of reconquering Normandy and Guienne.

It was at this moment that Louis XII, a tired warrior, answered a polite English letter that had reached him, speaking of friendship and peace.

The young king tossed his plume.

"Who wrote this letter?" he flared at the envoy. "I ask peace of the King of France, who dare not look me in the face, much less make war on me!"

With these words Henry strode out of his reception chamber, leaving the French abbot bowing to the air.

It was Henry's own crude declaration of policy: he would link himself with Spain and Germany and Pope Julius, to repress the "savage tyrannies" of France.

Catherine could credit herself with a part in this harmony. A more personal disharmony she was forced to manage. Those who made it their business to go about the palace insidiously spying out every unwatched movement came to her with the news that Compton, egged on by the King, was carrying on an intrigue with one of Buckingham's married sisters. The other sister, devoted to the Queen, soon informed Catherine how much for himself, and how much for Henry, the hearty Compton was acting. The Duke of Buckingham, a feather-headed man, attacked Compton out of hand, while Catherine, advised by her friar and adopting the high Spanish style, stormed Henry about his boon companion at the same time.

Henry's anger was controlled. He did not defend Compton

too strenuously, but in very little time the Buckinghams were all sent from court. Catherine's confessor, who had survived the marriage, was also marked down. In the presence of a little group of friends, Henry one day sent for him. "You are a fornicator!" he assailed him. The courtiers assisted with pleasure, not unwilling to believe that friars are naughty. In spite of strong protests and a defense that rumbled for months, the friar was returned to Spain.

Not a gesture was lost on a single maid of honor who demurely held Catherine's skein of thread for her, or on a single esquire of Henry's body. But Catherine held her head high. She counted on the heir she would give Henry, and on a glorious union of English and Spanish arms.

IX

The early days of the reign shone with humanism. Henry had not overlooked Thomas More. He had made him undersheriff of London, in place of Dudley. More was also busy at the bar, and he was living in Bucklersbury, in the heart of the city, a near neighbor of John Colet, who was no less busy with the founding of his school at St. Paul's. These two staunch friends gave the warmest welcome to Erasmus on his arrival from Italy. Erasmus came charged and flashing. He had seen Rome. He had seen the mighty swashbuckler, Pope Julius. He had dodged Maximilian's hundred thousand man-killers who had just poured into the plains. Amid shouts of laughter over the plight of his faith exposed to the Italians, his purse to the bandits at Dover, his stomach submitted to the inns of Germany, he moved both More and Colet with his story of the hideous wounds that were scalding Europe, body and soul. It was not simply the cicatrice that the Borgias had laid across the face of Italy, the massacre of seven thousand at Capua that still vibrated, the waste and pillage and pain of common people. It was not simply St. Peter's, ready to devour millions. It was the way men were poisoning their own minds. Men were mad. The future had not been so black for six hundred years. Only in the shelter of Henry VIII's England would he dare to tumble out this candor in such untrammeled words.

They listened with the curious deference of the more modest and less critical Englishman. Write it, they begged him, write it. He took a week and wrote it. He called it "In Praise of Folly." More seized it from him like a disciple and sent it abroad to be printed, not trusting it to the young printing presses of London.

What stirred these men, in their different ways, was the prospect of the happier day before them in England. More was naturally sanguine. Colet was older and more narrowly concentrated on church reform, Erasmus more detached and ironic. But all three agreed on the moral genius, the heroic validity, of Christ's teaching, and the very blindness and hypocrisy they saw in Europe made them passionately anxious for healthy outspokenness. They were not courtiers. Yet they could not help feeling they must have influence. Colet and Erasmus were both in the confidence of the Archbishop of Canterbury. They were both free to go to Lambeth. They knew and admired John Fisher. Wolsey, of course, they could only regard as a most able politician. They had no hope of the soldiers in the council, but they saw in its every bearing the choice that lay before the young king, who gave such proofs of accessibility and goodwill.

The danger of militant nationalism aroused Erasmus. "It is the duty of a prince," he wrote plainly, "to seek the public and not his own private advantage." But he saw Folly guiding the princes. "They think they fill their position well if they hunt with diligence, if they keep good horses, if they can make gain to themselves." He satirized the dynasts, drunk with power, as if he were the ghost of Marcus Aurelius.

The book that Erasmus published had its parallel in a ser-

mon that Colet preached, save that Colet burned with a re-
former's practical zeal.

Five years before Luther opened his lips, Colet stood up before the assembly of half the church—the convocation of Canterbury—and said, " 'The Church, the spouse of Christ, is become foul and deformed.' 'The faithful city is become a harlot.'
'She hath committed fornication with many lovers.' 'All things
that are in the Church are either the lust of the flesh, the lust of
the eye, or the pride of life.' 'The priests give themselves up to
feasting and banqueting; spend themselves in vain babbling,
take part in sports and plays, devote themselves to hunting
and hawking; are drowned in the delights of this world; patron-
ize those who cater for their pleasure.' "

This was a true celibate speaking, and a man who had spent
his own substance to found St. Paul's School. "Covetousness,"
he told his clergy, "mother of all iniquity." "From thee come
burdensome visitations of bishops; from thee corruptions of
law courts, and those daily fresh inventions by which the poor
people are harassed; from thee the sauciness and insolence of
officials."

"The magnates of the Church," he asserted, "are busied in
vile and earthly things, and in their stead vile and abject persons meddle with high and spiritual things."

"The root of all spiritual life—charity itself—is extinguished." "We are troubled in these days by heretics—men
mad with strange folly—but this heresy of theirs is not so
pestilential and pernicious to us and the clergy as the vicious
and depraved lives of the clergy."

"Consider the miserable state and condition of the Church,
and bend your whole minds to its reformation!"

Colet, as he had foreseen, did not escape the consequences of
this lance-thrust. He was charged with heresy at the instance of
the Bishop of London. But he did not reply to the feeble
charges, and his friend Warham rejected them with contempt.

The young King sent for him. He told him privately that he approved of him, that he was to continue attacking the corrupt morals of the age, that he was not to hide his light in times so dark, and that no one would be allowed to meddle with him.

x

But Erasmus, who attacked the State, did not fare so well as Colet, who attacked the Church. In spite of Mountjoy, who had married one of Catherine's lovely Spaniards, the sage was not admitted to the presence. Perhaps Henry could not feel at home with him in Latin, or perhaps he did not feel he could say to him as a later king was to say to a later sage, "You must catch the spirit of my calling." That spirit, in any case, was moving Henry to Armageddon.

Catherine and he had had a great happiness. Their first son was born at the beginning of 1511, and called Henry. But their happiness was daunted in six weeks. The child died. This misfortune did not estrange Henry, and he even turned with relief to the grand program of the Holy League. The veteran Ferdinand had been persuading him that the wicked French were defying Christ in the person of Pope Julius, and Henry was feeling his way to a Holy War. He approached Ferdinand. He approached Maximilian. The truth was, Ferdinand was promising himself Navarre, and he easily promised Henry Guienne. Guienne is that noble region of Southwest France that, together with Gascony, stretches from Bordeaux across the whole river-bed of claret, and runs down through smiling plains toward the Pyrenees, curving round and bending into Bayonne. It had come by marriage to England with Henry II, and a young full-blooded monarch could ask nothing better than its recovery. Ferdinand showed that it would be adventurous, high-principled and inexpensive. It had the air of a bargain, and attracted Henry as feasible.

A great English expedition was accordingly sent to Pasajes, the gullet of San Sebastian in the north of Spain.

But if you eat cherries with your superiors, the Danes say, you get the pits in your eyes. Ferdinand had no idea of helping the English. He merely wanted them at San Sebastian as back-stop, while he pushed on into Navarre for himself.

The English commanders were on a hot griddle. Their expeditionary force could not advance on Bayonne without Ferdinand and could not advance on Pampeluna except as Ferdinand's puppets. They had arrived with a beer thirst, which they slaked on much red wine and Basque cider. They got diarrhœa. They hated the climate on account of the inconsiderate heat and the vehement rain. The natives raised prices on them. They in turn demanded higher wages from their tormented officers. They cried for beer. The officers wrote home to Henry. Henry, completely misunderstanding the situation, and still trusting his father-in-law, wrote a violent letter telling Ferdinand to cut their throats.

But it was too late. The warriors chucked it. They would not remain beyond Michaelmas "for no man." They shipped home without leave, willy-nilly, home to their hearthstones and their mugs.

Henry was indignant and furious. He wanted to have their blood. But his council persuaded him that this would be to admit the offense, so he smothered his wrath, and announced publicly that they had come home by his orders and Ferdinand's consent.

With the malice of old hands dealing with a new hand, the Europeans sniggered. The French published a satiric poem, which Thomas More hotly answered. Maximilian's daughter, Margaret, ventured to think that the English might have forgotten how to fight through lack of practice. It gave her, she said, "the qualm of a little melancholy about her stomach."

XI

The failure of this expedition was the first public check that Henry had received. It touched him on the raw. He had been made ridiculous, the thing he most hated in the world. He had played low, and lost. Angry with the cunning Ferdinand, he now decided to play high. In combination with Maximilian, who had failed in Italy, he planned to enter on his martial career in person by invading northern France at the head of a vast army, while Catherine as regent was to hold from thirty to forty thousand men to resist Scotland. It was an unprovoked war, a sort of aggressive self-preservation. After Guienne, it accepted France as an enemy.

This frank policy found the council divided. The soldiers favored it but not the prelates. And the division could not be healed.

This was Wolsey's chance. Ever since the seventh Henry died, his fingers had itched to grasp the helm. He was Henry's canon of Windsor, and Henry had bestowed on him the fine mansion that had belonged to Empson. He was the youngest man in Henry's council. With Henry, he was not the priest in cassock: he was the man of worldly experience, the one cleric who did catch the spirit of Henry's calling and at whose house the King could be free.

A glance at the future cardinal revealed a churchman of big energy, a man of histrionic imagination. Wolsey dreamed untiringly of the rôle that England might play on the grander European stage. Exactly twenty years older than the King, reading his appetite for power, knowing in detail the resources and potentialities of the island, scorning the fact that England should be reckoned ninth among European states, feeling within himself a boundless fund of health, the personal grip of realities and the strength to tame and ride them that make constructive genius, and possessing in passionate degree the hatred of a stupid noble caste that had been so jealous of a priest's place in England, Wolsey asked nothing better than to become Henry's right-hand man.

The council included strong obstacles in jealous churchmen. It included Warham, a stick-in-the-mud whom he would set aside. It included Fox whom he had won previously. It included Ruthal who would sing "treble to his bass." These priests would not employ the soldiers: but Wolsey would employ them. He was ready to give them their fill.

There was one enemy. Thomas Wolsey was a commoner. He could feel in old Surrey, and in his eldest son, that sort of antagonism which makes men bristle. Wolsey knew that in these bleak, insolent Howards with their flat cheeks and long chins he would be dealing with the most stubborn tradition of the conquerors' blood. The Howards had in their hearts the icy core of pride. This jewel they preserved by hard courage, grim zeal, smooth habit and level-eyed contempt. They did not shine, they glinted. And no corruption was too deep or treachery too inhuman for the pride they lived to conserve. Wolsey could perhaps use the Howards, but only in so far as he could outplay them, for theirs was a vigilance which knew neither rest nor generosity, and which had in it the tenacity that does not acknowledge change. The reason for this inexorable tenacity was adequate: the Howards were the most deeply instinctive of all the great families in whose medium the royal or papal principle swims. It is not their lot to change, but to transmit intact the germ-plasm of an established order, and nothing short of revolution or extermination can shatter such families. The stiffness of their clay is such that they frame the royal portrait not only for the world at large, but, much more important, for the royal order itself.

It was in conflict with this basic function of the Howards that Wolsey found himself pitted. He was willing to let their legend swell. He was a priest, they were soldiers. He wore the cloth, they carried the sword. But when the Howard frame came to narrow the royal portrait to their stupid limits, as in its tenacity it must, then Wolsey would risk a struggle that would drain the last drop of his blood. It would be a struggle between change and rigidity, between upstart and aristocrat, between England the sower and England merely the harvester. Life, crude and generous, flung the son of a butcher into this fierce battle with the sons of more soldierly butchers. In this high conflict, everything turned on the caprice of the jealous instinct of the young autocrat. And to this Wolsey appealed.

He took his fate in his hands. At Greenwich Wolsey waited dry-mouthed for Henry, his eyes strangely luminous and sparkling. Few men were more capable of high excitement than this priest, for all his solid frame, and he alternately scowled and smiled as thoughts streamed through his mind like clouds in a storm current. He grasped the chair-back to steady himself, one eye drooped as he looked down. The game was in his hands, but was he mighty enough to play it? He had already entertained the King in his house, laughing and lewd. Into the balance he was ready to cast everything, his mistress, his honor, his health, his peace, so long as this career could be opened to him. He saw it begin where he stood, and mount dazzlingly, until his galloping heart told him that it was lost to sight. Bishop, archbishop, cardinal, pope, with Henry as emperor of the Holy Roman Empire, and England master of Europe. This dream made Wolsey clench the big muscles of his determined jaw. He reminded himself of the control he must practice. Once, at a fair in Hampshire, he had lost his head and the quarrel that followed had landed him in the stocks. The memory of that vileness froze in him as he thought of the man who had humiliated him. He would make him smart for it. But could he master Henry?

Wolsey was of the conquered English breed. The ultimate

passion gleamed in him, the passion of seeking his own authentic will; but he hid its difficulties behind his confidence in manipulating Henry. He did not set himself outside this master. Inside him he would work his destiny, as Henry's brain and his steersman. On steersmanship he would stake everything.

He was admitted to his King. In that warm baritone of his, Wolsey unfolded his plan in the manner of the schools from which he had never escaped. How should a King conserve his power if he divide it and let it fall at once on divers inferior persons? Secrecy in business is the life of council, and yet how preserve it with many heads? Contradictions in council are of their nature, yet it is unsafe to believe one side and impossible to believe both. "Why not choose some one, who, being disinterested, may have no passion or thought but to serve your Highness?" "Kings must never descend but by steps. The more orders are under them, the higher still they stand." "When your Highness hath occasion to acquaint your councilors only with some part of your meaning, what instrument can be so apt as a favorite?" He can guard and divulge the secrets. Through him the people can address their suits. But would not his Highness be at the mercy of his favorite? "Sire, let me say, I should never advise your Highness to see by his eyes or hear by his ears only. That were to keep you in too much darkness and subjection. Set watch on him secretly. Thus shall your Highness take order not to be deceived. Have three or four confident persons, not yet of the body of your council, with whom separately your Highness may advise. Only, if any thing be determined, let your favorite still be the chief actor in the execution.

"Neither will I presume to nominate myself; only I will crave leave to say thus much, that when your Highness would out of your own election think fit to use my own best service, I should not doubt but so to establish and conserve your Highness's authority, as to make you the greatest and happiest prince living. Neither should I fear to fall, when any benefit may grow to your Majesty thereby."

For the young King, hampered by a council, impatient of crowds and delays, wearied by mediocrity, hot in his will and quick in his temper, this offer of Wolsey's was seductive. Not an inch did it invade him, yet it begged to share the real burden. It claimed no title, assumed no confidence. Wolsey was saying, "You are the master, you must be saved at all costs. Give me the drawbridge, and if I fail you, fling me into the moat."

Henry could trust this suppliant, who looked him in the eyes and talked to him quietly. There was no censor here. He could unroll his map to Wolsey and not fear to hint his mind.

If he stood up and laid his hand on Wolsey's arm, the older man's mobile face must have revealed in quivering intensity that he had found his master, that his foot was in the stirrup, that he could mount. He could with heart-felt gratitude kneel and kiss his master's bejeweled hands.

XII

War was in the air. On Good Friday, 1513, Dean Colet preached before the King, and he preached of war. But it was of the victory of Christ. How, he asked, could a man who loves his brother thrust his sword into his brother's blood? Wicked men, out of hatred and ambition, go to war, and few undertake a worldly war, except from hatred and ambition. The Christian ought to fight and conquer under the banner of his Heavenly King. Instead of the Cæsars and Alexanders, he ought to follow the example of Christ his Prince.

The Dean had hardly retired to the Franciscan monastery that adjoined the Palace at Greenwich, when he received word that the King wished to talk to him in the monastery garden.

Henry, with customary curtness, dismissed his attendants: he wished to talk alone. He met Colet with perfect friendliness, telling him at once to be covered and at his ease. He came to the point.

"I did not call you here, Dean, to interrupt your holy labors," he said, "for of these I altogether approve, but to unburden my conscience of some scruples that by your advice I may be able more fully to do my duty."

The Dean, ascetic and concerned, listened to the young King as they paced the monastery garden. It was still wintry, toward the end of March, but at that moment of the year when England first promises spring. The trees are leafless, but the bushes glisten, the birds dart and flicker, the broken soil is glinting, the earth suspires, the human body itself is enclasped by hope and gladness. In the keen open air, their faces tingling with its piquancy, the King unfolded his scruples as he walked. He was the man of action, seeking guidance. That day he had gone on his knees around the Station of the Cross. Now, manly and simple, he needed to be put right. He had approved of Colet's sermon. He had agreed with what he had heard of hatred, of ambition, of the wickedness of war. But did the Dean intend to declare that there could be absolutely no just war?

The fleet already had its orders to sail. The Thames that buoyed it was running by this garden. Henry touched on the war and divulged his motives. The French were clearly schismatics. Louis had called a schismatic council at Pisa.

Did Colet think for a second of Pisa and his own memories of that city and of Florence? As a young man, burning with curiosity, questing Plato and Plotinus, he had gone to the Florence of men who had given all to follow Christ, the Florence of Savonarola who had withstood the dying Lorenzo il Magnifico. But if his mind went to Savonarola, it returned to St. Paul's. This was not a garden of olives. Under the clear blue eyes that Henry bent on him, Colet moderately explained. He did not maintain that all war is unlawful to the Christian.

The garden path turned, and with it turned Henry and Colet. The King was glad to find that the Dean had not intended to declare absolutely that there could be no just war. He and the Dean were in agreement. But lest the raw soldiers should go away with a mistaken notion, and think that he had really said that no war is lawful to Christians, would Colet take the occasion to explain himself more clearly in another sermon?

Colet could only assure his Grace that he would explain. The talk lasted an hour and a half. The young King, at last taking Colet's arm, brought him into the Palace. In the center of his courtiers, he drank the Dean's health, and, embracing him warmly, promised him all the favors that "a most loving prince" could grant.

Dean Colet withdrew.

"Let every one have his own doctor," cried Henry in his jolly voice, "and let every one favor his own; this man is the doctor for me."

XIII

The war was in sight. Dean Wolsey, the Master Almoner, stood on no ceremony. He discarded the priest to reveal himself a rough-shod organizer with a stinging will. Into his hands he gathered the reins of somnolent England—army service, transport, ordnance, budget, sanitation. The war to him was the manipulation of a national economy. He created a national workshop. He raised and spent sixty million dollars. If there was no wind for the windmills, he foresaw watermills, since biscuit there must be. He controlled bake-houses, breweries, founderies, tanneries, smithies. He planned for pilots and surgeons, hutments and docks. He ordered dry cod, ling, cheese, beef and bacon. Trinity House and the College of Physicians were, in a sense, his war-babies. He personally signed contracts for everything from twenty-five thousand fat oxen for salting to the hire of fourteen mares to haul a culverin. This work told

on him as an irascible, imaginative man. Fox urged him to pull
up.

But it was not in this impetuous nature to spare itself. Wolsey worked with the fury of an artist. He did not stop to eat.
When he finished the task in hand, it was time for him to dash
through his religious office and go to bed. That he had a life-
force, the warm urgency of the creator, a jet of reckless and
spendthrift imagination, was clear even to his enemies, though
they believed it was by witchcraft and necromancy he prevailed over the King.

Henry took this war as the most glorious of his many games.
He went down every day to the docks, to hasten the fleet. He
bought himself a whistle, an enormous gold whistle with jewels
as big as warts, and hung it on a thick gold chain. On this instrument, "He blew near as loud as in a trumpet, or clarinet,"
to the consternation and delight of his marines. As Supreme
Head of the King's Navy Royal, he dressed "galley-fashion,"
in a vest of gold brocade, reaching to the middle of the thigh,
breeches of cloth-of-gold and scarlet hose. He had the guns
fired for him. He had his portrait painted on the deck of a man-
of-war. The gallant little ships multiplied—the *Mary-Rose*,
the *Mary-John*, the *Mary-George*, the *Peter Pomegranate*, the
Dragon, the *Lion*, the *Anne of Greenwich*, the *Barbara*, the
George of Falmouth. A little boat was called after Erasmus.
And Henry, remembering that this was a holy war, had his
great guns cast in the images of the apostles.

XIV

Henry was twenty-two years old and he was off to the wars. It
was the action that he had wanted. His quarrel with France
was "God's Quarrel." Not only had his enemy Louis an "undisguised lust for dominion," not only had he favored "detestable schisms," not only had he broken poor little Venice, amid
horrible atrocities, but Henry craved to defend the Church, to

"free it from the savage tyranny of the King of the French, who is the common enemy of all Christian princes;" and also he craved "to recover the realm of France, his very true patrimony and inheritance, and to reduce the same to his obedience." Scotland, too, had been interdicted by the Pope. The haughty and arrogant Scottish King had spoken impiously and shamefully "against the sovereign pontiff, the head of our religion." The Scots, "deluded by the French," could not possibly be granted peace. In short, as Henry puts it, it was a "just, holy and somewhat necessary war."

We have the men, we have the supplies, we have the engines of war—these were Henry's open arguments. If we should spare the French King now, when he is "almost overpowered," he would soon be puffed up with pride and ambition. "We must teach him by force of arms to know himself," Henry wrote to the Vatican.

Louis XII, indeed, had almost been overpowered. He had won at Ravenna, but to suffer a crashing defeat soon after. He had barely dragged himself to Paris, when this new war confronted him. War was his trade. In itself it was no more horrible to him than midwifery to a midwife. But it was the younger King who still saw war as glamorous and could feel, as Montaigne, that "there is no profession more pleasant than the military, a profession both noble in its execution (for valor is the stoutest, proudest and most generous of all virtues), and noble in its cause: there is no utility either more universal or more just than the protection of the peace and grandeur of one's country. The company of so many noble, young and active men delights you: the ordinary sight of so many tragic spectacles; the freedom of conversation, without art; a masculine and unceremonious way of living pleases you; the variety of a thousand several actions; the encouraging harmony of martial music, that ravishes and enflames both your ears and souls; the honor of this occupation, nay, even its hardships and difficulties, which Plato holds so light that in his Republic he makes women and children share in them, are delightful to you. . . . 'To live, my Lucilius, is to make war.' "

No doubt Henry felt this enthusiasm for war. He was buoyant with a good conscience, superb in style and grandly prepared. And, having executed his prisoner Edmund de la Pole under the noise of departure, he left his capital to the encouraging harmony of martial music, his armor shining, his plume waving, his steed prancing, and Maximilian waiting to reënforce him with eight thousand German spears.

Catherine and Henry parted with all loving solemnity. The sails that bore the young warrior to Calais were cloth-of-gold, and twelve "trappers" filed ahead of him into Calais, laden with his shining personal trappings. He looked like St. George-Hercules. One hundred priests accompanied him to his first High Mass and Benediction.

Like an old campaigner, Henry began to make his rounds, riding about of a wet night. "Well, comrades," he said cheerily, "now that we have suffered in the beginning, fortune promises us better things, God willing." He practiced archery in a sunny garden, cleaving the mark in the middle and surpassing every one in stature and personal grace. The Emperor Maximilian, who received a hundred thousand crowns in advance, had arrived in the humblest of black frieze, in mourning for his second wife. His landsknechts, hardy ruffians, looked exactly as Dürer had depicted them. Maximilian took the line that he was but a common soldier, and he saluted Henry as his son, his brother and his King. There was much entertaining in richly decorated tents in front of Terouanne, a town that incommoded Maximilian's adjacent territory. King Henry had perhaps twenty thousand men with him, though he and Wolsey had given out figures ranging up to sixty thousand. The twelve great siege guns created rare interest; one of the guns, St. John, took its military baptism by falling into a pond; a hundred workmen were sent to probe it out, but failing to set a guard they were attacked by the skirmishing French who killed or wounded most of them. This was the biggest feat of arms of which the French could boast. They refused to lock arms. They frankly ran away at the Battle of the Spurs, thus adding to the reputation of the *gens d'armes* as "hares." Chevalier Bayard, as noble a human being as ever gave a model to Cervantes, fell into English hands. Henry was greatly excited. He was gallant and courteous to his prisoner in a pleasant interview, and he told Bayard how much he regretted he could not catch a glimpse of the heir to the throne, Francis, who was hovering somewhere in this evasive war. Bayard presented Francis' excuses. After a hundred days or so, Terouanne, the "doghole" as Cromwell afterwards described it contemptuously in the House of Commons, succumbed to Henry. He had quicker results with the virgin city of Tournay, which fell to him in a week, Wolsey being on hand to have the income of the bishopric bestowed on him.

This was, in truth, a nervous campaign. Henry wanted to go into action "afore his horsemen" but "his council persuaded him the contrary." As Wolsey knew and as the French knew, a decisive battle would be too serious. It was warfare such as the Chinese had patented several thousands of years before the Christian era. Every participant in it was feinting, and it could not afford to become real.

Henry and Maximilian could have advanced on Paris, since the Swiss had thrust in as far as Dijon, and Louis had no reserves. But neither Maximilian nor Louis cared to try conclusions. Maximilian had mopped up the border, and that was enough for him. Louis XII knew that England was again significant on the map. By not rasping the English, by not breaking their wounds, by running away, and by acting on the knowledge that both Ferdinand and Maxmilian were seeking peace behind Henry's back, Louis was looking to the future. Luckily for

Louis, the English had no one with the least pretensions to be considered a general.

Henry's preference was for war .He wanted to knock out the French. But Maximilian diverted him to Lille, where his daughter Margaret and his grandson Charles were waiting to get acquainted with Henry.

Since Henry's young sister Mary was soon to marry Charles, this visit to Lille was gorgeous in the extreme. Màrgaret of Austria was a great lady. Two such cavaliers as Henry and Brandon attracted her immensely, and perhaps because his sister Mary was infatuated with this handsome "fellow" Brandon, Henry set himself to striking up a match between him and Margaret. "Why won't you marry him?" was Henry's jovial refrain. Margaret was enchanted with him, but she shirked the match. She had been married twice already, and had had enough "infortune" of that sort.

"One night at Tournai, being at the banquet, Brandon put himself on his knees before me," she told her father, "and in speaking and him playing, he drew from my finger the ring and put it upon his own, and since showed it me; and I took to laugh and to him said that he was a thief, and that I thought not that the King had with him led thieves out of his country." Henry had to be summoned to explain to his beaming comrade that "larron" was not a term of endearment, and that she could not let him keep a ring that was too well known. He assented, but filched it again, and Margaret let it pass, little knowing that her gallant had two wives living, and was the apple of Lady Mary's eye. The interlude, however, was in the proper key of the whole sumptuous invasion, which had at last to be terminated on account of September rains.

Meanwhile, with Henry on the loose, Queen Catherine made a manful regent, thanking God to be ready for the Scots. "My heart is very good to it," she wrote to Wolsey, "and I am horribly busy with making standards, banners, and badges." But she confided to Wolsey her anxiety for Henry's safety. "I thank God ye make me sure of the good heed the King taketh of himself to avoid all manner of dangers." "I shall never be in rest till I see letters often from you." She who had mended Henry's nightshirts was concerned for his health, his pleasure, his comfort, so glad that in the sage company of the excellent Maximilian and with his good counsel, "His Grace shall not adventure himself so much as I was afraid before."

But this anxiety she forgot when, with throbbing pride, she could give him the bloody news of Flodden. James IV had no council that kept him from leading his horsemen. He had mishandled Flodden and was killed, with scores of earls and barons and ten thousand Scots. The Spaniard in Catherine emerged stout and boastful. She exulted, dispatching by hand a torn surcoat stained with James's blood. "To my thinking," she proclaimed, "this battle hath been to your Grace and all your realm the greatest honor that could be, and more than if you should win all the crown of France." She thought to send James's corpse itself, "but our Englishmen's hearts would not suffer it." She extolled the "great victory that our Lord hath sent your subjects in your absence."

Catherine's tone, "alone I did it," was not warranted to soothe her Henry. She had James's body to show for home prowess; Henry could only exhibit Tournay and the pleasant Duc de Longueville. It was not the way to dispose him to pull with her father.

XV

Flanders mud had made war impossible, and Wolsey, long familiar with the Channel from having lived at Calais, directed the return of the army with masterly skill. Henry's homecoming in October was triumphant. He had captured towns and made prisoners. He had collected tribute. He had reëstablished the English reputation for arms and handled his forces without a hitch. His own glory mingled with that of Flodden, which had been won by the Howards, but which, as Bishop Ruthal declared, "all believed to have been wrought by the intercession of St. Cuthbert, who never suffered injury to be done to his church unrequited."

The men from the shires, recruited from sixty to sixteen, had behaved cleanly and seriously as citizen-soldiers, and now there were bonfires on the green, toasted apples, free beer, the church bells pealing gladly and hearts gladly beating. The girls at Lille had run out to Henry with garlands, but it was sweet to be home, to pass under triumphal arches and ride to an unfeigned welcome. Catherine's ardor was radiant. "Love for the King," wrote a Venetian, who saw in Henry the avenger of Venice, "is universal with all who see him, for his Highness does not seem a person of this world, but one descended from Heaven."

The descent from Heaven, unfortunately, is very hard to stop once it gets started. And in spite of public rejoicing Henry was in a false position.

He had gone into this unselfish and holy war on the supposition that it would continue until he had humbled France. And in the meantime Pope Julius had died on him. He had been hailed on his return in heroic strain. "Let all other Christian princes take example by this unconquered king," wrote one enthusiast, "and be prepared to pour out wealth and blood as he had done in defense of the Church, to gain both from God and man the same reward for their labor." These were the eulogies that whetted Henry, and this was the tune he wanted to hear. His ambition had been fired by his taste of war. Instead of returning assuaged in the fashion of old war-horses like Louis, he was conscious of something amiss both in the war and in himself. Once more he wanted to measure himself against the enemy and the world, to test his manhood and prove his stamina, to keep on playing. Officially he did not consult astrologers, but he was influenced as a martial chief to learn that the Turkish Tyrant was destined to be conquered by the King of England. Parliament met in a war fever on his return, voted him a great subsidy, and he began "incredible preparations" for renewing the campaign.

Maximilian, who had been playing this game for forty years and who had tested Henry's sense of proportion by seriously offering to resign and name him Emperor, was soon to declare that "if Ferdinand does not put a bridle on this young colt, he'll become impossible." He and Ferdinand were old stagers. Their feeling about the Pope was not that of Henry's pious grandmother. Their feeling about war was wholly unsentimental. They served propaganda, of course, but not to themselves. They did not think it necessary to believe in their own public pretensions. What was Henry's game? Did he suppose that they would go on to Paris? Ferdinand had secured Navarre. Maximilian had cleaned up Flanders, and collected 120,000 crowns from Henry. Neither Ferdinand nor Maximilian saw the need to prolong the war in the present state of Europe. And in place of the late Pope, who had been a Genoese with crows to pluck and eagles to tame and whose motto was, "From the barbarians, Good Lord deliver us," there had come the suave son of Lorenzo il Magnifico, who wanted to build St. Peter's and pursue a peace policy and who sweetly asked Henry to desist from avenging him. Maximilian did not want to fall foul of Henry, but he could not take him seriously.

His daughter Margaret, however, had got her own personal impression of Henry, and she urged her father to make a friend of him. "Monseigneur," she wrote to her wily sire, "unless you give him cause to the contrary, he will help you both with his person and his money, without deceit; for I assure you that there is no hypocrisy in him, and, therefore, he should be treated in a like manner, and the promises made should not be broken."

They were already broken. Henry's allies, Maximilian and Ferdinand, had both left him in the full stride of his war preparations and made secret truce with Louis for a year.

It was a base betrayal, and it came at a bad moment.

XVI

No sooner was Henry back in England than he had to face ugly news. Catherine had been pregnant, but her hopes had to be forfeited by September, the third cruel disappointment of their married life. Nor was this all; he himself fell ill soon after his return. "The King of England," one report said, "has had the fever, and his physicians were afraid it would turn into pustules called the smallpox (variolæ)." "Henry of England," ran another rumor, "has had a fever; the physicians were afraid for his life, but it ended in the smallpox." It was a disease, apparently, that he had brought home with him from France. It may have been completely cured, or it may have reappeared as the chronic ailment from an ulcerous leg which is first mentioned two years later, and which was to afflict him until his death. This ailment was to give him a frantic personal interest in liniments. He became his own apothecary, made up the most elaborate ointments, ground magic pearls into them, and was treating his friend Will Compton's ulcer, which appeared in 1514. But by February, this time, Henry recuperated. "He is now well again, and rises from his bed, fierce against France."

Hardly was he on his feet, beginning to prepare for war in good earnest, when one of the messengers to arrange about the ransom of noble French prisoners came to him in secret. He had been sent by Louis; he spread before Henry the absolute proof that Ferdinand "did but deceive him."

The rage into which this threw Henry brought out a side of his character that was as yet unknown. It was the anger of any man who suddenly learns that he has false friends, but the vehemence it created, the spleen it aroused, passed beyond the terrible wrath of the good-natured man who has been traded upon, into something that indicated funds of another species of anger almost too deep to explore. This golden, manly youth could glower. His anger ran like a red spark, eating into blackness, his whole nature at once darkened and on fire.

"Henry was very bitter against Ferdinand," the word went to Spain. He "swore he was betrayed; and lamented such an opportunity had been lost for crippling the pride of France. He says that Ferdinand had induced him to enter on the war, and had urged the Pope to use his influence for that purpose; that he had been at great expense; assisted Maximilian; had taken Tournay; and had reduced France to extremities; and now, when his enemy is at his feet, Ferdinand talks of peace. He will never trust any more."

The provocation that Ferdinand had given him was flagrant, but it produced illusions in Henry. He forgot he was one of three allies; he forgot the great battle in Italy, for which Venice paid the Swiss, that had crippled Louis and sent him limping home. He saw himself as one combatant who by taking Tournay had reduced France to extremities. France was not at the feet of all three, she was at *his* feet. This illusion of primacy, no doubt, Maximilian had done everything to pamper. He and Ferdinand had pretended that their one idea was Henry's personal enhancement, and, in joining with them for the sake of the Pope but with his eye peeled for his own conquests, Henry had glossed over Ferdinand's universal reputation for being shifty and crooked. Now, with the undeniable proof of Ferdinand's roguery, Navarre in Ferdinand's pocket and a truce concluded without consulting him, Henry could hardly contain his rage. And worse than being treated like a puppet by his own father-in-law, was to feel balked at a moment when the delicious fruit of victory was falling ripe into his mouth.

Henry's pique and disappointment did not pass away after

the first smart. Whetted by Wolsey, he began to search in his
heart for every possible means of revenge. He no longer feared
to reconcile himself with Louis, the "savage tyrant." That was
a simple first step. But how to punish Ferdinand? He was only
puzzled by what means he could lay hands on.

The nearest was his wife. Catherine might hardly seem game
for robust manhood, but his self-esteem had been outraged by
her father, and Henry had grievances in reserve. He poured his
wrath on her, knowing she was Ferdinand's partisan, and just
as unwilling to face the truth about her father as he was to face
the inwardness of his alliance with her father. Her position, in
fact, was not strong. From the first, seeing Henry's amiable indolence, she had treated him as Ferdinand's own. With the
"vain and boastful custom of these Spaniards," she had written
to her father in the first years, "these kingdoms of your Highness are in great tranquillity, and show great affection to my
lord and myself. The time is spent in continual feasting." It
was the picture of Henry as a guileless inheritor of rich kingdoms that Ferdinand could call his own. The feast was now
over. But to have her father's treachery thrust at her, to have
Henry's expenditures and sacrifices and services and conquests
so described to her face that she could only retort with Flodden, exposed between the young husband and his somewhat
older wife the concealments, decent and indecent, of a marriage
made for profit. Between them there was the darkest of fail-
ures, hers to bear a healthy child, his to procreate one. It was
their humiliation as dynasts and Catherine could not deny it
within. From the beginning she had been hurt by this lamentable fact. So had he. Their first still-born child had been looked
on with horror, with a feeling of infamy. "Never had a pauper's
brat, conceived in shame and born in penury, been hidden from
the sight of man more stealthily than this daughter of a line of
kings." Now, betrayed by his wife's father, Henry forgot
tenderness, he taunted his wife with her still-born children. She

was pregnant again, but in the frenzy of the moment he did not spare her. She fought back, meeting upbraiding with strong and stinging reproaches. She knew that "yong men be wrapped in sensuall love." He stabbed back at her that they were not really married, and that he could throw her off.

"It is said," wrote a Venetian in Rome in August, the Vatican having sharp ears in England, "that the King of England means to repudiate his present wife, the daughter of the King of Spain and his brother's widow, because he is unable to have children by her, and intends to marry a daughter of the French Duke of Bourbon."

In the midst of this rancor, a son was born prematurely, due, the Spanish said, to Henry's brutality and Catherine's alarms.

XVII

His big-bodied vigor was now reined in. He saw Ferdinand, Maximilian, Margaret, the boy Charles, Catherine, the whole Spanish-Imperial connection, in a red light of anger. Wolsey seconded him. Mary was betrothed to Charles, and Henry had actually been planning for the nuptials at Calais in the spring. It was an alliance which the landed nobles welcomed, as all their leaning was toward peace with the Flanders that took their wool, and all their habit was for war with France. But Wolsey could play on the suspicion of his nobles, which Henry inherited. The break with Ferdinand was exactly the chance Wolsey longed for. He now proposed to steer his young master into a brilliant peace.

The Duc de Longueville was brought into the game, a "prisoner of war" who could play good tennis and win heavy stakes from Henry. King Louis's wife had just died. Why should not the French King marry Mary? This would secure peace, provide a tribute, make an alliance. It would avenge England up to the hilt. It was a piquant and surprising proposal. It turned the tables on the hoary sinners. It showed them how far they could trifle with England. Henry saw in it a deed more eloquent than words.

But this reversal of policy, which sounds so cold and reasoned, was not arrived at by Wolsey and Henry in cold reason. It was only a few months from the time when Wolsey had prepared the war and Henry had gone out in full panoply to defend the Church and punish a schismatic, knowing Louis to be excommunicated and himself to be an instrument of "God's quarrel." He was now agreeing to force his young sister to marry the savage tyrant, and by doing this to outrage his natural allies. How did Henry make so violent a change?

His change was prompted by that mixture of pride, resentfulness, panic and suspicion which was surcharging the dynastic nightmare. Venice, as strong a power as England, had been broken in one convulsion. Navarre had just been wiped out. Burgundy had been obliterated and the armor of Charles the Bold actually offered for pawn to Henry himself. The world in which Flodden and the Day of the Spurs were fought stood half in honest daylight and half in madness, and at any moment the warriors who went out in vainglory might be swept by hysterical fear. St. Cuthbert might keep whole masses of Scotsmen out of action. The memory of Agincourt might suddenly flick the bravest Frenchmen. Men were at once fierce and credulous, forgiving and harsh. It was in the bluntness bred by fear that Henry had executed his trussed prisoner Edmund de la Pole before leaving London. It was, on the contrary, in the kindness of fellow-feeling that he had exclaimed after James's death at Flodden that it was "a heavier penalty for his perfidy than we would wish." Henry's feelings were nervous, gusty and spasmodic. He had not the phlegm of a soldier, though he could risk his neck in violent sports. He had gone to France with a huge army, sending six thousand men in advance of him, fetching nine thousand himself, and spending a paltry week at the front. He was just as afraid of the French as the French were afraid of him. The Don Quixote in him was ready to charge the fuller's mills that groaned in the night; the Sancho Panza in him quivered in infantile fear. He held Te Deums, took the sacrament, wore relics, and conjured the evil spirits. He looked placid and implacable, but he lived in a world of enormous bogeys with Maximilian and Ferdinand at his back. When they deserted him, with France towering over him, he lost no time to throw himself into a defensive union.

To confess such infantility to himself would of course have been impossible. He was twenty-three years old, a plumed knight. The guise in which Henry appeared to himself was monarchical. He saw himself as all the people around him saw him, a young ruler who had been called on by God to fulfill his mission. Just as Wolsey could turn to the Summa and give him the sliding-rule of supernatural values, so Henry could turn to dynastic politics and give himself his own natural values. Those natural values, for him, were supplied in part by experience, and in part by theology. But his mission in life was simply to be a dynast. And he saw himself not unfavorably in that gorgeous rôle.

His vanity was not overweening. He soon knew that Wolsey was a man of far wider vision than himself, and he was big and shrewd enough to admire the springing quality of Wolsey's mind, even though, young as he was, he could see clearer and quicker than Wolsey on certain points. He doubtless comprehended that he had a hot and ugly temper, was impulsive and dangerously violent. His path twisted often enough for him to catch his profile in expressions that he sometimes canceled for handsomer ones. He could fairly tell himself he was open-minded and broad-minded. He really listened to Wolsey when they argued Thomas Aquinas. He genuinely disapproved of such bigots as Fitzjames, the Bishop of London. He could see himself as just and staunch and fearless in dynastic policy, and, within the narrow circle of those whom he could afford to trust in politics, he could believe himself to be a straightforward and candid man. He knew, as we all know, how he appeared to the outer world. He felt strong enough to enjoy being unbending. He was manly by upbringing, and took a natural pleasure in the sensation of sheer power. He deferred only to God. With God he was scrupulous. To God he humbled himself. In God he trusted, and thus took the weight off his spine.

But what Henry could not see was that, cast by birth for the rôle of dynast, he was converting it into the rôle of consummate egoist. When the outer world crossed him and gave him a smaller value than he craved, his retort was an instinctive and personal one; he became outraged and outrageous, self-willed and righteous. He stiffened in a desire to impose himself on the outer world and compel it to see his value. Inheriting a trade consecrated to ambition, he was making it a personal protest against the accusation that he was not manly, a doubt that inhered in his own impoverished heart. He had not the love of other people that gave the humanists their serenity, though he tried to buoy himself with the humanists. The sweet and genial temper he had inherited from his grandfather Edward he was complicating with a morbid sense of danger, with a mistrust as quick as that of any craven; he was bullying and blustering to assure himself of strength.

This had its pathetic side, though Henry was unaware of it. With men like Maximilian, he was stiff and pompous, putting on his masculine front. With women, on the contrary, he was appealing. They are not obliged to pretend that they are not sometimes frightened, and they detected in Henry the shyness and immaturity that his male exterior belied. Margaret of Austria was touched by it, and became his partisan against her father. With her he had expanded and been natural. "He passed three days in her company and the many fair ladies that attended her; when, remembering himself that it was time to visit his army, he takes leave of the ladies." The ladies paid their return visit to Tournay. Once again he and Brandon and his other squires went to Lille to the ladies, where in a great room paved with black squares of polished stone, mounting horses shod with felt, a joust of amusing novelty was held. "After which the lords and ladies danced all night."

Might Henry have found the ladies to his liking? If he did so, he had a confessor to put him *en règle*. He was never un-principled. If the facts of his behavior did not agree with his principle, he rearranged the facts to suit the principle. And he was ready to hector any one stoutly who would not subscribe to his version of the facts.

This stoutness of principle baffled Ferdinand and Maximilian. They did not understand the boy. He was of a different breed.

XVIII

Henry's sister Mary was a passionate young thing with pretty features. She had been ready to marry young Charles, whose picture she kept on display, and she would submit to marry old Louis; but, when Louis died, could she marry "as me liketh for to do?" This she asked her older brother with an expression unhappy, helpless, tearful, such as one sees in her portrait. He knew she loved Brandon, whom he had made Duke of Suffolk, and he gave his royal word to her. Then he had his trump-card.

Louis was no longer a schismatic. He had patched up his difficulty with Pope Leo. And Pope Leo had already sent a ship from the Tiber to the Thames, loaded with Agnus Dei, ham, sausage and wine. He now sent Henry a sword, and a conse-crated "cap of maintenance." These insignia, a Gog and Magog sword and the cap a canopy of purple satin a foot tall, enor-mously wide with ermine tails, were meant to be seen, not worn. Henry arrived at St. Paul's on a courser in a checkered gown of purple satin and gold, "a jewelled collar worth a well full of gold," a cap of purple velvet, and an admiring multitude of thirty thousand. He was attended by his nobles who "bore such massive gold chains that some might have served for fetters on a felon's ankles." On being presented with the papal emblems, and no one daring to tell the young master that these were mere tokens, Henry donned the cap which covered his whole face, and, girding himself with the sword, made the solemn tour of St. Paul's.

This was in June. In July the trump was played; Mary was married by proxy to Louis. Luckily for herself, she had never seen her future husband, "an ancient man, infirm and sickly," gouty, pockmarked and scrofulous. The ceremony was performed in the noblest style. "The bride undressed and went to bed in the presence of many witnesses. The Marquis of Rothelin, Longueville, in his doublet with a pair of red hose but with one leg naked, went to bed and touched the princess with his naked leg. The marriage was then declared consummated."

For Catherine, who had built everything on the alliance with her father and Maxmilian, this was a most crushing blow. But she went with Henry to see the girl sail to France, Suffolk as her escort. And at the water's edge, the girl whispered to Henry to remember his promise. He said he would remember it.

In Brussels, meanwhile, the boy Charles was brought to his council, to learn from his elders that he could not marry Mary. This council, pro-French, was not sorry to break the news.

He was only fourteen, but he did not lack an aunt who had a sense of his importance. He appeared before his council in cold anger.

"Well, am I to have my wife as you promised me?"

"You are young, but the King of France is the first King in Christendom, and, having no wife, it rests with him to take for his queen any woman he pleases."

The boy, so reported a Venetian, saw from a window a man with a hawk. He called a friendly councilor. "I prithee go buy me that hawk."

"I know that hawk," the councilor said. "He is a young bird and does not yet know how to quarry; he is not a bird for your lordship."

"I prithee go buy it."

The councilor hesitated, and Charles exclaimed, "Come with me!" descended, and came back with the hawk. He seated himself in a window and began plucking the live bird.

"Sire, what are you doing?"

He continued, and in his own time he answered. "You ask me why I pluck this hawk; he is young, you see, and has not yet been trained, and because he is young he is held in small account, and because he is young he did not squeak when I plucked him. Thus have you done by me: I am young, you have plucked me at your good pleasure; and because I was young I knew not how to complain; but bear in mind that for the future I shall pluck you."

Margaret felt as surprised and mortified as Catherine at this revengeful diplomacy of Henry's. "The penance," she flamed, "is too great for our offense towards England." She felt hurt and tricked and took to her bed. She had no idea that when the world crossed a man so friendly and kind as Henry, he could hit back with such savagery.

In the background was Wolsey, who saw in this grand maneuver his first chance to prove that England was the pivotal state in Europe, able to effect a complete reversal of European policy in a few months.

XIX

Mary had barely alighted in Paris, when her husband began to sink. He could not "sufficiently praise or express his delight in" his young bride. He had brushed away the English matrons who proposed to stay by her, only overlooking a few little maids of honor like Mary Boleyn, and he made himself at once gallant and fatherly. His bride was just the same age as his daughter Claude. But the new flight was beyond his strength. The change from veteran to cavalier, which obliged him to nod through odes and to sit through feastings and to dine at the dissipated hour of 6 P.M., was too much for the weary *Père du Peuple*. From a couch he watched the jousts in the rue St. Antoine, where his son-in-law was resplendent, and there he mournfully gazed at Francis: "This big boy will ruin everything." With the old year he closed his eyes forever.

XX

In the very week Louis lay dying, worn out with war-fatigue and disease, Henry was sending him proposals for another war against his own late ally. His fury with Ferdinand had not lessened. He carried it to the point of secret proposals that they were to oust Ferdinand from Navarre, and then he himself was to have Castile. It was to be a further punishment for Ferdinand's backsliding, and a vehement proof that Henry was no longer in leading-strings to his wife or his wife's father.

This was precisely the kind of politics that Erasmus had feared. His own work at Cambridge had been blighted by the war: he had been starved out of wartime England. "What madness it is!" he had exclaimed. "The wars of Christian princes begin for the most part either out of ambition or hatred or lust, or like diseases of the mind. Consider also by whom they are carried on: by homicides, by outcasts, by gamblers, by ravishers, by the most sordid mercenary troops, who care more for a little pay than for their lives. . . . In our times it is the people who build and improve cities, while the madness of princes destroys them. . . . In this hurly-burly of human affairs, in the confusion of so many leagues and treaties, who cannot make out a title to what he wants? Meanwhile these wars are not waged for the good of the people, but to settle the question, who shall call himself their prince."

Erasmus did not stay silent when he learned at Basle, where

he had gone to see his Greek Testament through the press, that
the rancor of Europe was increasing. His heart was whipped by
the hypocrisy of statecraft, by the "splendid lies" that gilded
monarchy, and by the plight of the people. Life had been unsafe in England during wartime, but it was doubly unsafe on
the Continent, with "black bands," marauders, brigands like
Von Sickingen ready for "inhuman private warfare," and the
law defied and impotent. Erasmus depicted the kings as eagles
who fatten their eaglets on the flesh of innocent birds. "How
terrible are the threats of princes, even uttered in jest. . . . At
this scream of the eagle, the people tremble, the senate yields,
the nobility cringes, the judges concur, the divines are dumb,
the lawyers assent, the laws and constitutions give way;
neither right nor religion, neither justice nor humanity avail."

Royal intermarriages, royal leagues, he treated with a scorn
no longer mischievous but passionately direct and scathing.
"When princes conspire together to oppress and exhaust a
commonwealth, they call it a 'just war.' When they themselves
unite in this object, they call it a peace. . . . The office of a
prince is called a dominion, when in truth a prince has nothing else to do but to administer the affairs of the commonwealth."

Not from the esthetic renaissance, to which beauty alone
was holy, but from Northern conscience steeped in classic
sanity sprang this clear, reproachful voice. It was poignant but
never desperate, strong in feeling but unready to invoke the
violence that abdicates reason, and so limpid and natural that
it worked to loosen authority through the seams of men's prejudices and the fissures of their faith without creating any actual
schism. Erasmus, indeed, remained a Christian, and he believed ardently that if Christ spoke to pious and open hearts all
might be saved. "I wish that even the weakest woman should
read the Gospel—should read the epistles of Paul," he said.
"And I wish these were translated into all languages, so that

they might be read and understood, not only by Scots and
Irishmen, but also by Turks and Saracens. To make them
understood is surely the first step. It may be that they may be
ridiculed by many, but some would take them to heart. I long
that the husbandman should sing portions of them to himself as
he follows the plow, that the weaver should hum them to the
tune of his shuttle, that the traveler should beguile with their
stories the tedium of his journey." So spoke the Christian
humanist, yearning from the kings to the peoples. He had
voyaged to England, hungry to enlist Henry in his faith, which
was the great antique tradition of universalism. During the war
he had gone unheeded, and the merest churl now seemed to him
more promising than any prince. Yet he still thought of Henry
as good, with "remarkable courtesy and unruffled temper." He
still hoped to sway him. He still counted on the good example
of England.

XXI

But Henry's temper was not unruffled at the beginning of
1515. The fine edifice that he and Wolsey had erected had been
based on a poor, broken life, and with Louis's death it collapsed
ignominiously, leaving them out of position, out of pocket and
out of countenance. Louis's death confirmed Henry's innate
feeling, that you can never rely on a Frenchman, but he was
forced to draw in his salient and to deal with a young Cæsar
whose popularity with his people was boundless.

That long-nosed youth had soon come to Mary, sequestered
in her dark room by royal etiquette, and he had glittered at her
with gallant speeches that made her tremble. He proposed to
discard Claude and to keep her—not only her, of course, but
her dowry of two hundred thousand pounds and her jewels. It
was worthy of Mary's own father. Virtually a prisoner, the
little girl could only write to Henry, "your Grace is all the
comfort I have in the world." "I am very ill-diseased with the

tooth-ache and the 'mother' withal [hysteria], that sometimes I wot not for to do!" Friars came to her in the dark room, sent by Wolsey's enemies in the council to say how wicked he was, to say he trafficked with the devil. Every one's object, including Henry's, was to keep her for a new dynastic marriage, with Maximilian perhaps or with Savoy. She got no letter from Henry.

But Suffolk arrived, to negotiate with Francis, and like a child she clung desperately to her brave Englishman, and swore that now or never would he marry her. Suffolk, afraid of his master, tried to postpone, but the young girl had the urgency of a Tudor; she shamed her lover into secret marriage, and then both of them laid their fate in the hands of Wolsey.

"The Queen," wrote Suffolk to Wolsey, "would never let me be in rest till I had granted her to be married; and so to be plain with you. I have married her heartily, and have lain with her, insomuch I fear me lest she be with child." "I was lyke to be ondon," in his own spelling, "if the matter schold coume to the knollag of the Kyng me Masster."

Wolsey threw up his hands. But these were all children to this masterly man, and he wrote straight to Suffolk: Henry "took the same grievously and displeasantly," "ye have failed to him which hath brought you up of low degree," "ye put yourself in the greatest danger that ever man was in." To escape, to placate Henry, it would be necessary to offer him Mary's dowry, to take over all the expenses of the French marriage, to pay, pay, pay.

Suffolk had no pride. All he wanted was to escape from Paris, this "stinking prison." "I am obliged to you, next God and my master," he told Wolsey. And he wrote obsequiously to Henry, offering his body, knowing he might be put to death or in prison or be "destroyed."

Henry had given his word to Mary that after Louis she might marry as she "liketh for to do," but his displeasure, shared with the council, was unlimited. The pleas of Francis had to be added to the sisterly coaxing of Mary, and Mary's coaxing had to be rewritten by Wolsey to give it more humility, with promises from Suffolk to relinquish dowry and jewels, and to bargain with Francis for better terms, before Henry would melt to his best friend.

And yet Henry's real anger was not with Suffolk and Mary, whom he reinstated. It was over the trick that fate had played him. A rival Cæsar had dispossessed his sister, and was already saying to himself the dazzling words, "Beyond the Alps lies Italy."

XXII

Francis was champagne incarnate. To expect him to compress any ambition now that his father-in-law was dead was to invite a champagne cork to go back into the bottle. This vivid and sparkling prince, long-legged, long-nosed, quick-eyed, quick tongued, had the most galloping and vaunting desires. He was not *chaste et pur*: he was a little ventricose, and he had an eye that ignited with facility. To him women as such were attractive, and most women responded to his attraction. He had that effervescent energy, that amber fire, that delicate and teasing art, that piquancy which carries through exaltation and the headache, through a black gullet back to exaltation. No king was ever better endowed than Francis to lead the dance of chivalry. But if he were a soldier as venturesome and lithe as any Frenchman, he was not the traditional French noble.

"The Frenchmen knowe onely the nobleness of armes," it was lamented in Italy, "and passe for nothing beside: so that they doe not onely set by letters, but they rather abhorre them, and all learned men they doe count very rascalles, and they thinke it a great villainy when any one of them is called a Clarke."

This was the reputation of Louis's generation, the same as that of England's noble barbarians. But Francis would be a son of the renaissance. "If Monseigneur de Angoulesme have so good luke," said Giuliano de' Medici, "that he may succede in the Crowne, the glory of armes in France doth not so florish nor is had in such estimation as letters will be, I believe. For it is not long sins I was in France, and saw the Prince in the court there, who seemed unto mee besides the handsomeness of person and bewtie of visage, to have in his countenance so grat a majestie; accompanied nevertheless with a certain lovely courtesie, that the realme of Fraunce should ever seem unto him a small matter. . . . Among other things, it was told me, that hee highly loved and esteemed letters." So Pope Leo's ambassador quoted Pope Leo's brother. So he praised "the greatnesse of courage; prowesse and liberalitie that was in him."

It was not as a copartner in these goodly attributes that Henry now greeted Francis; it was as a rival. His own handsomeness of person and beauty of visage, his own courage, prowess and liberality, his own love and esteem of letters, were dully impaired within his bosom by the rising of this younger star. Henry had fed on the honey of the immortals, and he had seen himself as radiant. But gods are jealous. With each syllable that rejoiced in Francis and that reminded him of himself in comparison, a drop of pain distilled in Henry's heart. As a child he had been the second in the family. He had been the younger son. This new resplendence in France was too near to him. He suffered.

XXIII

The new situation made Henry restless. He fidgeted with his mind and with his body. He went to a morality play by Henry Medwall, no doubt tedious, and he got up in the middle of it and walked out. He simmered with impatience in dealing with ambassadors. He could not wade through details. "Writing is to me somewhat tedious and painful," he said, allowing Wolsey to draft long letters in his name. Reading, even, was impossible. He went to the country as soon as possible, flinging himself into sport, getting up at four or five in the morning and hunting till nine or ten at night. The demure, sober and sad clerks from abroad who saw this aspect of him could not believe he was serious. "The King is a youngling who cares for nothing but girls and huntings, and wastes his father's patrimony."

But while Wolsey did his best to enable them both to dispense with the council, Henry did not defer for a second on anything that concerned his vital prestige. He was willing to let Wolsey make him Emperor, if Wolsey could; but meanwhile he did not propose to relinquish an ounce of his power. This he grasped with that obstinacy of his which rooted in his instinct of self-preservation, which was consequently violently unreasonable and violently suspicious, and had in it the primary Tudor strength.

The Church, unwittingly, came into conflict with Henry on this dormant but mighty instinct, and Wolsey had warning that in these home waters he could never be Henry's pilot.

A small local episode started the trouble. One day, toward the end of 1514, it was announced by the clerical authorities that a prisoner of theirs, one Richard Hunne, had committed suicide by hanging himself in the Lollard's Tower at St. Paul's. An immediate storm rose over this disclosure. Richard Hunne was a burgess who read the forbidden Bible. He was a freethinker. He had annoyed the clergy by refusing on the death of his child to yield up the customary fee of the winding-sheet. He held on to the winding-sheet, was imprisoned by the clergy and tortured by them. The citizens had been angry at his arrest: they were infuriated at the news of the good man's death, and a coroner's jury, hot with suspicion, declared that Hunne could not have hanged himself as claimed, and that he had been murdered by the clergy. The Bishop of London was aimed at, the very bishop who had hit at Colet and tried to suppress him. This bishop retorted that the jury of citizens were "false, perjured caitiffs." The body of Hunne was proceeded against for heresy by the enraged clergy, condemned and publicly burned. It seemed like their triumph, especially as Henry and his council could not confirm the suspicions of the coroner's jury. But the citizens were convinced that these reactionary clerics had been murderers in the Lollard's Tower, and the whole question of priestly privilege was at once raised before parliament. It soon ceased to be a clash between London pride and canon law: it swelled to the issue of a clerk's right to be tried for civil offenses by his own clerical tribunal. In this case Henry had the strongest opinions. He had always seen for himself that "religion bears the greatest sway in the administration of public affairs, and is likewise of no small importance in the commonwealth." He summoned all the parties to Blackfriars to review the whole question.

In the Church, the Church which Thomas More and Colet and Erasmus criticized so freely, Henry envisaged the biggest rival to his own domestic power, and in his present mood he sharply resented its usurpations. He was a faithful child of Holy Church. His God was the mysterious being, alone greater than himself, "by whose goodwill he might rise." The root of primitive religion, "the sense of absolute dependence on something not himself," was in both Catherine and Henry. But this did not mean that the Church as a domestic institution filled him with humility. The Church in England had two-thirds of the votes in the House of Lords, owned one-third of the land, and possessed an income two and a half times that of Henry himself. Its roll call reached the huge figure of between thirty and forty thousand persons. Henry's mind was never inactive where his personal power was involved, and he surrounded himself with his own lay judges to declare whether or not a clerk could be summoned before a lay tribunal. It was a trial of strength. The lord chief justice, well aware of Henry's royal feeling, of the citizens' feeling, and of the feeling of the nobility, definitely asserted the supremacy of the crown. It was England, not Rome, which was final. And the clergy were declared guilty of præmunire, or asserting papal jurisdiction in England.

Wolsey, on his knees, tried to keep his loyalty to his priesthood while serving his King. But young as Henry was, and persuasive as Wolsey was, the King's will was adamant. In his foreign policy he had gone forth as a champion of the Church, but in his domestic policy, the King clashed with Wolsey, with Bishop Fox, with the Archbishop of Canterbury. The old rights of sanctuary, the "benefit" of clergy to be tried for civil offenses in canon courts—these assertions of sovereignty that had been contested on and off since Thomas à Becket, stirred Henry in the core of his being.

"Wolsey kneeled before the King, and assured him that the clergy had no intention of doing anything prejudicial to the crown."

Henry retorted, "The Kings of England have never had any superior but God alone. Know well, therefore, that we will ever maintain the right of our crown and of our temporal jurisdiction."

Such a victory, not for the citizens who clashed with the clergy, but for the friar who had taken the side of the crown against the clergy, did not lead Wolsey to resign his office. Where Warham and Fox, acknowledging the tendency that Henry revealed, soon resigned their places in his council, Wolsey ignored it with superb effrontery and still used Henry to help him to be made a cardinal.

XXIV

For Wolsey was essentially the sanguine manipulator, and his eyes were flashing at the prospects in Europe. He gave leash to

his imagination. He had talked at length with Pope Leo's secret
envoy, Canossa was certain that Leo was anti-French and so
leaning on England that he would at once send Wolsey his
cardinal's hat. This was the sort of tangible proof of power that
always excited Wolsey, and his belief in a new league, with
England as the nuclear point of it turned the less sanguine
Henry back to thoughts of Maximilian and—even Ferdinand.
Wolsey had to go lightly as yet, so far as father-in-law was concerned. But all was possible. The young husband saw that he
had gone too far in his first anger. Catherine forgave him. They
had a reunion of heart.

Pope Leo did name Wolsey as cardinal within a few months.
He sent the hat, the supreme symbolic hat, by an ordinary
messenger. But this was not Wolsey's way. He had the messenger detained outside London, dressed in the finest silk, met
on Blackheath by a solemn procession and proudly conducted
to Westminster.

"The hat was then placed in state on a table, with tapers
around it, before an empty suit, and the greatest duke in the
land was compelled to make a curtsy to it."

So it was reported at the time. But this was not puerile
vanity on Wolsey's part, it was his deliberate and joyous
method of magnification. By trumpeting his importance at
home, he impressed all Europe with his right to be considered
one of the few living statesmen fit to make, to hold and to turn
the balance of power. "If you wish to gain mankind," Maximilian told Charles, "you must play at a high stake." So Wolsey understood.

XXV

While Francis was preparing to descend on Italy in the summer, certain ambassadors of the Republic of Venice left his
presence for London. Both Henry and Wolsey looked on this
visit as a golden opportunity to impress the Venetians and to

lure them from France. They had been entertained at Paris en route for England. Now they should see what England could do for them and what England was like, even if they had voyaged from their own great city, as populous in 1515 as it is today, bathed in indulgent light and radiant in Istrian marble, the jewel that no rival had ever ravished and that swam amid mankind's destructive enmities, a water-lily of such opulence and sweet glory that to dazzle a Venetian ambassador away from home would be like casting eyes on an exile from Venus, a Venus rising from the sea.

The Venetians came suavely. They themselves were oligarchs, members of the three thousand who ruled the Republic, who transmitted that organism against every enemy and every principle. They came as old masters to crude new ones, destined in truth to supersede them on the sea, and who, in their own imperturbable juvenile arrogance, thought of the Venetians as damn fishermen.

Venetian policy in regard to France was exceedingly simple. Their existence had always depended on the transit of their goods, and since the old days when their neighbors on the mainland had made them pay through the nose, they had long sent out sly and powerful tentacles in every direction, to smooth their way. These tentacles Pope Julius and his allies had cut in 1510. Maximilian had nipped Verona for himself. The Venetians had, however, so riposted on Louis in 1512 that he had altered French policy, wisely concluding that he could have no power on the plains of Lombardy except in league with Venice. Until Venice recovered its Verona, therefore, the entente with France suited both their interests perfectly. It was this entente that Wolsey and Henry wished to shatter, while the Venetians, on the contrary, desired England to be friends with France. They favored especially Francis's descent into Lombardy, hoping it would be so hot for Maximilian that he would drop Verona from his paws.

But first they had to see the court of England, and to judge of it for themselves.

Early on a March morning a lavishly decorated barge came to bring them to Richmond, two hundred nobles and grandees traveling on the same barge. On arriving, to keep them from growing faint during mass, they were served with bread and wine. Then, through chamber after chamber hung with gold and silver tapestries, three hundred halberdiers in silver breast-plates and pikes at attention—"by God," said one of the Venetians afterwards, "they were all as big as giants"—they came into Henry's presence to be received.

He was leaning against his throne when they entered, the handsomest potentate they had ever set eyes on, young and glowing, his complexion very fair and bright, his auburn hair combed straight and short and "an extremely fine calf to his leg." To his right were eight noblemen dressed like himself. To his left were the prelates in their white rochets. On seeing them the King immediately moved toward them, smilingly gave them his hand to kiss, and then lovingly embraced them. They were overcome, but not so overcome that they could not observe the canopy of Florentine cloth-of-gold, "the most costly thing I ever witnessed." As for Henry's apparel, even before breakfast they took an instant inventory of it—purple mantle lined with white satin, train "verily more than four Venetian yards in length," doublet of slashed white and crimson satin, cap of crimson velvet, mantle held by "a thick gold cord, hung with large glands entirely of gold." They took it all in. They were especially smitten with his jewels. They wrote home to the Seigniory, that he had one thick gold collar with St. George in diamonds, another gold collar from which hung a round diamond, "the size of the largest walnut I ever saw!" "A most beautiful and very large round pearl" was trickling from the diamond walnut. He had, in addition, an ornamental dagger in a pouch of cloth-of-gold. "And his fingers were one mass of jewelled rings!"

This glory, satirized next year in More's "Utopia" was not confined to his Grace. The noblemen were gorgeously appareled. Ten heralds with tabards of cloth-of-gold, and six attendants each carrying a gold scepter, made the Venetians murmur admiringly. So satisfactory was their appreciation that Henry himself, "showing himself, by my troth, most affable," "chose us to see the service of the courses, contained in sixteen dishes of massive gold with sixteen covers."

And gathered round Henry in silk and cloth-of-gold was the pride of England. They were of a younger and fresher race than the Venetians, half of them bordering on the illiterate, blunt-natured and tight-skulled. But they were men of a master class. They bore themselves like soldiers. They had that clear glance, that fine vigor and bodily resplendence, which showed how indomitable they felt themselves and how, in their own measure, they had wile and heroism. One or two of them would later visit Venice, and command family portraits from proud Venetian brushes. A score of them, perhaps, already knew what a sonnet was, though all of them knew what a musket was. A few of them had the bright comedic mind that Henry hated. Some of the toughest of them, like old Wyatt with his forthright soul, or foul-mouthed Surrey, would have crisp-nerved sons. The rose-brick house of Compton Wynyates showed that taste could exist in them, though the outer shell of their natures was like their own armor, made for resistance, made for self-protection, and with a brutal notion of law and order that was costing two thousand executions a year. They were man-killers, broad-shouldered, thick-necked, full-chested, regarding it as their prime obligation to eat well, drink well and yet look well. They thronged round Henry as their natural leader, no guild in London or no clique in the Vatican forming a tighter corporation. Here was blue blood dashed with red blood, the possessive refining the acquisitive; and Henry both possessive and acquisitive was their appropriate king.

He was even more their king than some of them guessed. Here was Sir John Seymour, whose daughter Jane was now a prim little child of five; Sir Thomas Parr, whose daughter Katharine was still too young to think of her first marriage; Sir Thomas Boleyn, ever-assiduous, father of Anne, now eight years old; and Edmund Howard, whose girl Katheryn was not yet born. On the outskirts of the coruscating crowd, a lesser mortal, stood John Blount, soon to be a knight, whose daughter Elizabeth would also be Henry's. Four of them, Seymour, Parr, Blount and Boleyn, had been in France under arms with Henry and were well accustomed to sights of blood. On this fair morning, under the costly canopy from Florence, stood the arbiter of their destinies. Neither Edmund Howard nor Thomas Boleyn could have imagined the drama of their children, but if they had, if the scroll could have been unrolled, their own inmost desires were still realized by standing in this company. They were on the royal barge, the rest of the world was loyally floating them. Bloody the scroll might be, but it was a scroll of national honor and achievement. For that, even if mutilated, they would brandish the stumps of their hands.

Such a sincere love of power, of money power and of martial power, was in essence like that of Venice, less tempered and refined as yet but possessing the same oligarchic tenacity, the same genetic energy, and the same total lack of scruple. This did not, however, impede the worship of God. The whole troop poured into the church, dutiful as children, early on the March morning. After a grand procession, the most serene Queen watching them, high mass was "chaunted." Henry's choir boys sang like angels, "voices really rather divine than human." "As for the counter-bass voices, I don't think they have their equal in the world." And Henry listened to them, no less than the Venetians ravished in his inmost soul.

XXVI

The Venetians had not been fêted enough. They were bidden again for May Day, coming to Greenwich at "a very early hour indeed," seven in the morning.

Henry loved May Day. "On May Day, in the morning," said one of his citizens, "every man would walk into the sweet meadows and green woods, there to rejoice his spirits with the beauty and savor of sweet flowers, and the harmony of birds, praying God in their kind." This was the feast that refreshed Henry's spirit. And the Venetians rode out into the country to meet the King.

A triumphal car, full of singers and musicians, drawn by griffins with human faces, headed the happy procession, followed by hundreds of the King's guard, all in green.

Henry, dressed entirely in green velvet, "cap, doublet, hose, shoes, everything," met them graciously, curveting on the bright bay horse that had been sent to him by the Marquis of Mantua ("So ho, my minion!"), "performing such feats that I fancied myself looking at Mars."

But the praise of the Venetian ambassadors, seated in Henry's arbor, did not reach the tenderness in his young heart.

"Talk to me awhile!" he said abruptly, in the arbor. "Tell me," in French, "the King of France, is he as tall as I am?"

"Your Grace, there is but little difference."

"Is he as stout?"

"No, Sire."

"What sort of legs has he?"

The Venetian wrinkled his brow. "My lord, he has spare legs."

"Look here," said Henry, opening his doublet, showing his

thigh. He watched the Venetian, and he cried, "And I have just as good a calf to my leg, too!"

He added, "I am very fond of this King of France."

They returned from Greenwich in jolly procession, the musicians singing, the trumpets sounding, and Gog and Magog, the pasteboard giants, grimacing deliriously from their car. The King rode proudly at the rear, followed by the Queen with her twenty-five damsels, while thousands on thousands of the London May Day crowd pushed and panted after in the golden dust.

Then Henry changed to a new handsome gown of green velvet, with a new collar of cut diamonds, and gave his Venetians audience. A dinner "served with incredible pomp," succeeded their "proper good breakfast" in the bowers. After dinner the lustral bowls refreshed them, and then "the trumpets blew to the field the fresh young gallants and noblemen gorgeously appareled with curious devices of cuts and of embroideries, as well in their coats as in trappers for their horses; some in gold, some in silver, some in tinsels, and divers others in goldsmiths' work; goodly to behold."

In the grassy palace court, they held the joust. The young King, prodigious in energy, was quickly in the saddle, every window crowded with admirers. It was the center of all that was courtly in England, each window and each balcony swift with glance and word. It was not a bull fight, as it would be in Spain or Italy. It was sport with something of war in it and always the thrill of danger. The air was suddenly pierced by the sharp silver crackle of the trumpets, as if they themselves were breathless with excitement, and tingling like iced wine. The drums made every heart beat fast. With a rush, the caparisoned chargers, ten a side, flashed blindingly to the barriers, a proud shock of steel and lance, of skill and weight and nerve, spilling color and tossing light. Over thirty times the feverish trumpets shrilled, the drums hammered the heart, and Henry like a thunderbolt ran his course, shivering many lances and capsizing William Kingston, horse and all. This hot game kept on for three vibrant hours. Then, taking off his helmet, Henry "came under the windows where we were, and talked and laughed with us to our very great honor, and to the surprise of all beholders. After this he went to disarm, and in the meanwhile we visited the Queen."

The Venetians had good cause to hate the Spaniards, but the ambassador was a sage diplomat of long experience, and he addressed Catherine in his best Spanish, which pleased her immeasurably. She seldom heard that music. "She commenced talking with me about Spanish affairs, and about her mother, making me all possible civil speeches." Her mother was still vivid to her in her isolation, though it was eleven years since Isabella had died.

But Henry's triumphs at the jousts were for Catherine. They were reconciled.

XXVII

Henry did not believe that Francis would cross the Alps. "By God," he said to the Venetian ambassador, "he gives the French poor reason to love him, running thus, at the very commencement of his reign, into the toils and charges of war." Henry spoke from experience. "He is a Frenchman," he warned the Venetian, forgetting that he married his sister to Louis, "and I cannot say how far you should trust him." And he added in frank outburst, "I'll confess the truth: his dread of me, lest I should invade his kingdom, will prevent his crossing the Alps. My belief is, that if I choose, he will not cross the Alps, and if I choose, he will cross."

Francis had started as these words were spoken. He and twenty thousand men crossed the Alps from Barcelonnette to Salazzo over a track which they had to follow almost on their hands and knees. This was one of the most dashing, one of the most hair-raising, one of the most indomitable exploits that ever lifted the heart of a young warrior. It ended in a battle no less marvelous, September 13 and 14, the victory of Marignano.

It was not in Henry's power, so sick was he in his jealousy and his consciousness of his own empty début, to hide his chagrin at Francis's personal bravery, his sweeping victory and royal entrance into Milan.

"It seemed, to look at him," reported the French messenger, "as if the tears would burst from his eyes, so red were they from the pain he suffered in hearing and understanding the good news and prosperity of my master."

"Has he concluded the Concordat with the Pope?" Henry demanded.

"Yes, Sire."

"I know better than you do. The Pope has yet to ratify. Where is the Emperor Maximilian? What is he doing?"

"I have no news of him, your Grace, but I hear he seeks the friendship of my master."

"I know where he is," Henry blurted, "and what he is about, and as for his seeking the friendship of the King your master, the contrary is the truth."

He stopped. Then he asked, "How many Swiss fell?"

"About twenty thousand, your Grace."

"Twenty thousand! Not more than ten thousand. I have heard from people present at the battle, the rear-guard were never engaged. They did not strike a blow. Not that I am sorry for the Swiss, they are nothing but villains, not half as good soldiers as the Germans."

XXVIII

The depths that were stirred in Henry by Francis's triumph were not lessened when he heard of the Concordat. At the moment Francis was on the crest of the wave. He was everything his mother could call him, "my glorious son and triumphant Cæsar, the conqueror of the Helvetians." The crown of this victory was the meeting with Pope Leo at Bologna in December. The Pope did not allow Francis to kiss his toe; he rose and embraced him. "The Pope, Leo X, had the mien of being a very honest, worthy man. He was very fearful, did not see clearly, and was fond of music. He sang mass every day in great pomp and triumph, all the French princes assisting him. He gave the King a beautiful True Cross a foot long, to be carried in procession on the anniversary of the late battle. They took their meals mostly together; were often closeted; and after eight days, parted with mutual promises of friendship and peace."

And what did Francis and the son of Lorenzo il Magnifico talk about? Leo found in the victor of Marignano a young Cæsar of great and supple charm. They discussed the disposal of the Sforzas of Milan—whom Leonardo da Vinci had honored in equestrian bronze not so long before. The reigning Sforza was to be pensioned with a cardinalate. They discussed Italy, the Empire, the fortunes of the Medicis and the French or Gallican Church. Leo promised to support Francis for emperor on the death of Maximilian, and Francis promised to go against the hostile and advancing Turk. Incidentally he arranged with Leo the Concordat by which his royal absolutism and the absolutism of the papacy made common cause in France. In return for Francis's undoing the democratic work of the Councils, the Pope conceded to the French King the immense patronage of the priories, the bishoprics and the abbeys. This gave Francis an increased supremacy, and he went home to browbeat his parliament. "I'll make the parliament trot after me as I do my Council," he menaced their committee. The Concordat was no mere occasional treaty, such as Francis now

signed with a flourish on every hand, with Charles, with Maximilian, with Henry VIII. The Concordat was germinal; it
drove liberalism into irreligion.

It meant that Francis need never drive out the papacy to
make the Church his creature. It was a compromise between
two absolutisms.

And meanwhile Francis stayed at Milan as the conqueror,
fêted and flattered, consorting with the highest and the lowest, taking his keenest pleasures in disguise with the Venetian
Coppo as his comrade, a gentleman nimble with the tongue and
the dagger, who was only separated from Francis when it was
discovered that he was also nimble with poisons.

XXIX

While these triumphs were in progress, Wolsey was feverishly eager to counteract Francis. This was the signal for Ferdinand to reënter, bearing gifts. He sent Henry a very valuable
jeweled collar, two capital horses caparisoned, and an extremely rich sword. Some said he wanted to borrow money on
these objects, as he had never been known to make a gift.
Others said that Ferdinand had lost his mind. But these
frivolous interpretations were cut short when word came that
the Catholic King, hunting to the last, had died in a little village in Spain, in January, 1516, aged sixty-three. At the
moment, however, the news could not be broken to Catherine.
She, who had suffered so many disappointments, had at last,
on February 18, 1516, successfully launched a child into the
world. This was the Princess Mary, who was to be known
to history as Queen Mary Tudor. Her godparents were Wolsey and the Duchess of Norfolk (Surrey having been made
second Duke of Norfolk after Flodden). The prudent Venetian
ambassador hardly knew whether to leave flowers or a wreath
when he learned that the baby was a girl. He visited Henry,
and on murmuring to the father that a man must resign him-

self to the will of God, "who distributes his favors as he pleases," Henry buoyantly declared, "We are both young: if it was a daughter this time the sons will follow, by the grace of God!"

XXX

The death of Ferdinand meant that Catherine's nephew Charles would be King of Spain and would have Naples. This brought back the very words of Ferdinand at the beginning of the century. "Should the King of France gain Naples, which God forbid, he would be sole monarch of all Italy; and if Italy were to be joined to France, it is easy to see the peril in which all other princes would be placed, over and above the injury which would accrue to us from it." With Ferdinand dead, his antique policy still dominated England, and Wolsey and Henry had only one thought, to weaken France.

Erasmus had described the Swiss returning home from Marignano, "ragged, gaunt, disfigured, and wounded, their ensigns torn, their festal songs turned into funeral dirges." But what of the power of money, and ten thousand landsknechts sent into Lombardy? Wolsey would find the money for Maximilian to strike at the French.

The Venetian ambassador came to Wolsey in alarm. He had heard that coffers of money were on their way to Antwerp, and bills of exchange had been drawn.

Wolsey listened to him most attentively and patiently for a quarter of an hour of pained inquiry.

"I will speak to you with all sincerity and truth," he answered, "and will tell you what becomes a cardinal on the honor of the cardinalate," putting his hand on his breast; "it is true that the King has remitted moneys to Flanders which will reach Germany and perhaps Italy, for two purposes: in the first place, for the purchase of inlaid armor and other costly furniture; then again, certain needy princes have pledged a quantity of very fine jewels, which we hope to obtain at no great cost. Whoever told you that this money was to help Maximilian lied in their teeth."

The Venetian listened with gravity. He had dealt with many Orientals. And he wrote to the Seigniory, "The Cardinal aspires and aims at nothing save to obtain profit for his Majesty, with whom he maintains himself in great repute."

But in earlier candor Wolsey had complained bitterly that the French King paid no attention to Henry, and that he himself, the "author of the peace" with Louis, "contrary to the opinion of many of these lords in the council" would "destroy his own fabric" if Francis were so arrogant. So the Venetian went to "these lords" over whom Wolsey had exulted to him. He asked Norfolk and Warham and Ruthal whether Maximilian was being subsidized. They assured him there was nothing in it. Warham gave his oath on it.

Wolsey took the offensive with him. "You are certainly very bigoted in the faith you place in this King of France of yours." And so did Henry. "Domine Orator. I love you very much, and much do I love your lords. But know you are deceived. The King of France is negotiating peace with the Emperor to your exclusion. Think, now, how you are circumscribed. I have chosen to warn you, that you may open your lords' eyes."

"I thanked his Majesty for so loving and important communication," said the weary Venetian; "it has seemed fit to me to mention the whole to your Sublimity, because I deem the words of Kings worthy of consideration; not indeed that I believe anything he told me, being of the opinion that it proceeds from these two ambassadors from the Emperor and Spain, who aim at drawing money as leeches do blood."

The Venetian was right. But he found that it was not merely the Emperor and Spain that wanted blood. Wolsey, he wrote in good Venetian slang, must be cured of the jaundice before he can let the Venetians bring wine from Candia into England;

and the cure for jaundice was difficult for a Venetian. "It is not our custom," he noted, "either to give or take bribes."

Maximilian had no such scruples. He was once more taking English pay. He was being subsidized so well that he pumped and pumped until he had got to the very pebbles and grit. Then under heaviest pressure he set off at last for Lombardy with thirty thousand men. But Milan was not yet in his hands: while Wolsey had shown finesse in dealing this underhand blow to the French with whom England was still allied, he merited the anger of his older colleagues for using so cranky a weapon. Maximilian was incalculable. After dawdling and halting, he came in full force to Milan in March, but lo, the night before the attack, he declared he had a dream: two old men of the tribe, Charles the Bold and another, had appeared to him, bathed in blood, and warned and implored him not to go into action relying on his Swiss. Instantly the good Emperor heeded his friends from the other world: he wheeled his entire forces around and melted like a wraith. It was not known whether Charles the Bold had winked at Maximilian during this impressive vision, or whether a messenger had come out from Bourbon or the Venetians to say that a price would be forthcoming for Maximilian's own towns in Lombardy, but within a year he did accept 200,000 ducats for Verona.

Thus the Holy Roman Emperor gathered his pennies. He had no more shame in profiting by the occasion than he had in bribing others, and soon he was seeking the Electors of the Empire to induce them to promise their votes to his grandson, Charles, as his own successor. "Mon filz," he said to that heavy-lipped Hapsburg, "vous ales trumper les François, et moy je va trumper les Angloise." My son, you go fool the French, and I'll go fool the English.

XXXI

Before it was known that Maximilian had failed before Milan, but when the news of his stealthy advance could no longer be hidden, Sebastian Giustinian, the Venetian ambassador, went again to see Henry.

Henry had been somewhat indisposed for three days, and he received Giustinian alone, in a private chamber.

Henry no longer tried to disguise his feelings. The Emperor, he said with a certain gloating humor, is now between Verona and Milan, and the French are on the run. "So that," said the King laughing, "you see how you stand!" If France should win, Venice would be despoiled. "If she loses," he repeated, "you know how you stand!" While uttering these words, the King seemed to exult and "moreover, to wax somewhat warm."

The Venetian thought to explain why Venice sided with France but Henry interrupted him, saying, "It was not necessary for you to abandon your friends, some of whom could and would have aided you," alluding to himself. "There could be no necessity soever for making you have recourse to such perfidy," and this he uttered with some indignation, "becoming rather pale in the face."

"Perceiving him more irritated than I could ever have imagined," reported the Venetian to his masters, "and more openly hostile to France, I thought it time to appease him." He thereupon spoke of Venice's many indebtednesses to powerful England.

"You speak the truth," Henry said, "for I have done more for you than my father ever did, or any other prince who may have been your friend."

More mollifying words followed from the Venetian, but Henry was not mollified.

"Be assured, Domine Orator," he said outright, "that I have now more money and greater force and authority than I myself or my ancestors ever had; so that what I will of other princes, that I can obtain."

"When saying this, he seemed to be wroth; so I told him that I who was on the spot, knew this, as I perceived the kingdom to be the most powerful; the great plenty of its money; the endowments of his Grace; and his extreme authority with all the princes of Christendom, whom I see all prostrate themselves before him as the justest of refugees; but yet greater than either his power or wealth did I deem his justice, benignity, and clemency, which I was sure would never fail such a friend as Venice. I besought him, therefore, to persevere in his amicable intentions, and to hold the Seigniory as his most devoted ally.

"In uttering which expressions," adds Giustinian, "I bowed myself with all submission down to the very ground."

The word "perfidy," however, rankled in the Venetian breast. And he went to Cardinal Wolsey with it.

Wolsey said, "You must have deceived yourself and misunderstood its application. His Majesty did not vituperate the perfidy of the Seigniory, but the perfidy of the King of France."

"Pretending to be convinced," reported the Venetian, "I let it appear that I was satisfied. The nature of the times, most serene Prince, requires this, in observance of an old proverb, which enjoins our kissing the hand we are unable to cut off."

XXXII

It was not Henry's habit to explode to outsiders. Red-tempered as he easily became, and pushed by powerful impulses to overbid and overreach, his tightened mouth showed capacity for cautious repression, and many visitors recorded how amiable and courteous they found him. But with the good Venetian he had been thrown off his guard. Few men are benign when they are in acute physical pain, and this was one of the first periods in which he was laid up by his ulcerated leg, the horrible agony of it announcing itself with a clang. Lying there,

hot and goaded, with his nerves set on edge, he already thought
of Milan as captured, and his animosity against Francis made
him burst with his triumphant news.

Henry's grudge against Francis was deeper than politics.
The French King had a succession to his crown even more precarious than Henry's own, having received it in an indirect line
from Louis, who himself had received it indirectly. Yet in spite
of this precarious succession, in spite of a mother and a sister
who adored him, in spite of prudent advice such as Henry himself had obeyed as a warrior, Francis had led over sixty thousand men into Italy, and gone into the thick of the fight time
after time. It was no use minimizing it. This was the old kingly
tradition, the *noblesse oblige* of Maximilian, Ferdinand, Louis,
Julius, James IV. Francis and his compeers had fought like
"infuriated boars." They had withstood the best shock-troops
in Europe, and when the sun declined on the second day, with
fourteen thousand Swiss corpses cast into one grisly pit by the
victors, Francis had knelt on the field, and Bayard, the noblest
man in Europe, the man for whose death his very enemies
would weep, took his sword and named the young king a chevalier. It was this that set Henry's heart quivering with un-
nameable emotions. He had never seen a real battle. His father
had been canny and he himself was pushed by his canny ances-
try to methods that could hardly be termed glorious. He was,
in this very instance, paying Maximilian to fight for him. But
while Henry's intelligence pounced on the practical method,
and while he could make blunt decisions in council and hold
obstinately to his opinion, and could warmly assure himself
that the man who was dashing and gallant and devil-may-care
would tempt his providence, he was still young enough to feel
the pointed reproach of a neighbor so audacious and free. He
knew himself to be timid in warfare, to be unwieldy with
women, to be overemphatic, to be clumsy. His flesh encumbered his spirit. He was burdened by his uncourtly size. These

were the things, more than any statecraft, that churned and lashed his soul.

The mere sight of Giustinian, therefore, had been too much for him. Out broke his crude jubilation over the trick he was playing on Venice, a kind of heartless and malicious and yet boyish desire to crow. But the thought of Venice and Milan brought up Marignano and Francis, and the darker feelings that prompted Henry, the anger and rage and envy that smoldered under his desire to be triumphant, led him to the bluster that made the Venetian feel he must soothe and propitiate.

To propitiate Henry, however, took stronger meat than the soft words of a diplomat. Henry feared and distrusted Francis. Scotland alarmed him. The Duke of Albany had sailed there from France and had driven away Henry's sister at the behest of the Scots Estates. The Scots had no right to act with the French, the English council felt, no right to act with any one outside the English. "Unless the King of France reinstate the Queen," they said, "we shall not brook it, and shall wage war on your King in every possible way." That accounted for the ships that Henry was constructing and took care to exhibit to the Venetian. Wolsey lamented that Queen Margaret, with her sultry body, had hurried into a new marriage after Flodden. He "would have resigned the Cardinal's hat," he declared with the alcoholic valiance of the sixteenth century, "or lost a finger of his right hand, to have married Margaret to the Emperor Maximilian." But Margaret was a simple, ripe organism, who had looked among her courtiers with heavy-lidded eyes. She was already tired of her second husband. She would soon choose a third. She had none of her brother's combative ambition. Scotland to her was a mere connection by marriage.

But Albany was not to be borne. Francis's nonchalance was not to be borne. "He never writes hither," shouted Wolsey to the Venetian, "he does not impart any of his secrets!" Nothing was to be borne but a concerted league against France.

Behind this pressure, with its bearing on Verona, was the constant artful incitement of that old Iago, Maximilian. He had studied Henry in 1513. He had detected his weak spot. He saw that he was self-deceived, violently crediting the worst of the French and already jealous of Francis. Maximilian's sheering away from Milan could not have been explained to any veteran like himself, but he soon made it plausible to Henry and Wolsey. Out of his hat he kept tempting Henry that he could produce for him the rabbit of the Holy Roman Empire, and though Henry suspected a trick, Maximilian could see from his popping eyes how much he wanted the rabbit. If only more money were forthcoming, he impressed Wolsey, a little more money, he could wipe out Francis in Lombardy. His old cupidity appealed to their young cupidity. Under cover of fantastic and elaborate promises, the dangling of a gold crown and an iron crown before Henry, he extracted chests of weighty ducats. And during this hugger-mugger and mystification, all of it based on Francis's "vast ambition for empire," Maximilian and his grandson were thick as thieves with French agents, Charles insuring Naples at the cost of calling Francis his lord, paying him an annuity, and promising to marry a French bride; Maximilian arranging to get tangible florins for Verona.

XXXIII

Henry did not dissimulate his fear of Francis, and Wolsey repeated the same tune in his own rousing voice. It was a duet in which the conductor was invisible, but for three years the baton was Maximilian's.

Whenever the pro-French Giustinian brought Henry startling news of the Turk—and the Venetians, who had "eyes and ears everywhere," could tell that Europe was not to be spared—Henry "seemed to take small heed." Already in 1516 the Venetian was saying, "But Syria is of the greatest importance.

If he routs the Soldan and takes Egypt, if he conquers Persia, it will mean an immense increase in territory. I perceive no safeguard against the ruin of Christendom!" The Turk left Henry quite cold. Two years late, Giustinian told him the news from Hungary, which "his Majesty seemed to hold in as small account as if they had related to the affairs of India." But when it came to France or Italy, it was utterly different. There the King was all ears and all nerves. And, prompted by the Emperor, he sought in every way to break down the Venetian belief in Francis's honor and good faith.

"You are certainly very bigoted in the faith you place in this King of France of yours," sneered Wolsey; and, pointing at a crucifix on an altar in his room, he dramatically swore by it that he had positive proofs of Francis's duplicity.

Henry employed direct tactics. "I warn you, he always keeps behind the door the staff with which to cudgel you." "He aims at your ruin." "By God," laughing grimly, "they will plot to your detriment."

When Giustinian had proof that Francis was not betraying Venice, he fetched it to Henry. Henry was "stricken with great astonishment, saying and repeating to me several times, 'How can this be?' "

He almost suspected Maximilian, but since he was believing what he wanted to believe about Francis, he could not listen to reason. He betrayed his thoughts. " 'Verily, the Emperor has been deceived by the King of France, and I know how'; uttering this, however, with great hesitation."

Giustinian inquired what this deceit could be.

"I do not know for certain," Henry's white eyelashes reproved, "but I suspect it; and things uncertain ought not to escape the lips of a king."

Francis's "vast ambition for empire," was the fixed tenet, and in a few weeks Henry was saying to Giustinian that he *knew* Francis had negotiated with the Emperor and Spain:

"They negotiated against you expressly, expressly, expressly, expressly! I have this from one who was present, and who knows but he was a Frenchman!"

He was not a Frenchman, as Giustinian soon learned. Verona was returned to Venice, in spite of oaths on the crucifix, and the velvety Giustinian came back to press Henry on the subject of general negotiations for peace.

"I told you not to imagine such a thing possible while the French throne is filled by one utterly faithless, who boasts of meaning to do what is far from his thoughts, all for the sake of obtaining money and realizing his schemes."

Not aware that in unjust suspicion a man dips into himself for the colors he is painting, Henry continued, "I cannot trust any one, for each endeavors to deceive his fellow; nor do I see that there is any faith in the world, save in me, and therefore God Almighty, who knows this, prospers my affairs."

After much in this strain, "censuring the treachery of others, and lauding his own loyalty," the genial Henry added, "placing his hands on my shoulders, and laughing, 'I know that now you have got *your* territory, you care nothing about these things but only thank God that you are out of great danger.'"

Because of the Venetian's unshaken faith in Francis, as well as his calm benevolence, Henry could not let Giustinian alone. Sometimes he was somber, but at other times he was free and sincere, which Giustinian liked.

"How is it possible for any one to trust him?" Henry frankly asked about Francis.

Giustinian urged that "there are those who never cease exciting either sovereign, in order to foment discord," hinting at Maximilian.

Henry thereupon "drew me nearer to him, and also took my secretary by the hand, a gest which he repeated several times in the course of the colloquies, saying,

"'Shall I give you manifest proof of the deceit of this King of France? He tells everybody that he means to march against the Turks, by way of Italy,' single-handed, but once in Italy he'll subjugate it.

"To which I replied that this was a most ingenious and sage discourse, presupposing that the King of France had ever said he would go single-handed against the infidel.

"His Majesty again said, 'Shall I *prove* to you that this King acts solely with dissimulation? I know for certain that he wishes me worse than he does the devil himself, yet you see what kind of friendly language he employs toward me. . . .' "

Giustinian answered Henry in his soothing fatherly way, saying that as Henry's "chief object was to be loved, and not to be hated," and as he was so excellently disposed to all, so he must believe that others are similarly inclined to him.

" 'Let me ask you this one question,' retorted Henry. 'If the King of France acts sincerely by us, why does he not have justice administered to our subjects? . . . Then again, who could put up with his choosing to send the Duke of Albany into Scotland, where my nephew is King, and the title of the Kingdom is mine, for I style myself King of England and of Scotland? . . . True friendship forbids one friend to do that which may displease his fellow. I am King of this island, and am perfectly satisfied; and yet it seems to me that I do not do my duty thoroughly, nor govern my subjects well; and if I could have greater dominion, nay, upon my oath, if I could be lord of the world, I would not, as I know that I could not do my duty, and that for my omissions God would judge me; whereas this King,' and immediately Henry's voice changed and roughened, 'this King is a greater Lord than I am; he has a larger kingdom, and more territory, and yet he is not content, but chooses to meddle in matters which appertain to me, such as Scotland, but this he will never accomplish, for I have more money than he has, and shall have more troops whenever I please.' "

Giustinian heard the baying bell in Henry's voice. "I might have alleged two arguments," he told his Seignory in reporting this interview, "but I was aware that such a rejoinder would have stung him to the quick, so I avoided it, and turned the conversation." He did so by the most human means. He made a little love to Henry. He explained that publicly, "where the links are equal, there ought to be parity of affection," as between the Seigniory and France and England; but "I myself individually, from my knowledge of the character, sincerity, wisdom, and other rare endowments of his Majesty, had become incomparably more partial to him than to the King of France."

Henry intimated that he knew this. And so, he said truthfully, "I speak freely with you."

XXXIV

While Henry was blurting and Wolsey thundering, the tide of diplomacy had silently turned. Francis's new treaties and new alliances had multiplied behind the scenes, and even as Wolsey was saying to Giustinian before the Spanish ambassador, "You are in a very perilous position, but guard yourself more against the Christian Turk than the real Turk," Wolsey was actually planning a treaty with France himself. Once safely alone with Giustinian, he stopped acting and said in the most tranquil of tones, "If I perceive the King of France to mean well toward his Majesty, and administer justice to our subjects, I will at any rate conclude this union," adding, moreover, "The King of France has now got a son, and his Majesty here has a daughter—I will unite them!"

This decision had limped. Long before Henry and Wolsey closed down on Maximilian, deciding to "dissemble wisely this past and shut the King's purse in time coming," the whole of Europe had rearranged itself around the freshly gilded dome of French primacy. While Wolsey had been sending money to bribe Charles's council and Henry had been saying, "The Pope is mine," the Pope had already made terms with Francis. In trying to play France false, England had itself been played false by Maximilian, and it had cost about a million and a half crowns.

The older magnates of the Church had thoroughly disapproved of the adventure; it was monstrously expensive, England could not stand it, it was useless to continue alone, with a navy only half ready and war economically unpopular. It looked as though Wolsey were heading for disaster, and Henry heading with him.

When Maximilian's dupery could no longer be hidden, Henry wrote him furious letters which, however, the moderate Cuthbert Tunstall got him to keep back. And when Wolsey, resilient as any showman, turned round to propound "universal peace," the older churchmen were elated. Bishop Fox wrote to Wolsey, "It was the best deed that was ever done for England, and next to the King, the praise of it is due to you."

XXXV

With "universal peace" Wolsey came into his real element. He was at home with Latin, the language of internationalism. He was at home with universals, the language of his Church. And he was enough of a clerk to prefer peace to war.

He was not, indeed, an internationalist like Erasmus. Studying Henry's combative ambition every day, seeing its kinship with that of armored barons like Norfolk and Suffolk, whose brains fumed with rich prejudices and who crashed the mailed fist as the decisive argument, Wolsey was as pityingly contemptuous of the pacifist-idealists, on the one hand, as he was of these blunt-minded bullies, on the other. "I would not have you muse upon the moon," he barked at a disputatious agent of his, "but to go straightly and wisely to my matters." These "matters" were not spun of Platonism, and Wolsey smiled at Plato.

If peace did not serve his purposes, war might answer them. It made little difference to Wolsey. But while he had been willing to use gold and steel, he was at heart a churchman and preferred churchly methods, seeking, through the adroit manipulation of his royal master's prejudices, to turn the rivalries of Europe to profit and importance.

Under any circumstances, it was a rôle that called for audacity. To fill out a grandiose scheme for a country so small as England, giving it European influence and redounding fame while at the same time satisfying a master whose self-esteem made urgent demands, required more grasp of their office than any of the older magnates could supply. Neither Fox nor Warham could lead Henry. They had not the effrontery. But Wolsey had subservience as well as effrontery, and while he spoke to Henry as if Henry owned him, he behaved to the world as if he owned both Henry and England.

This domineering manner had its effect. Outside the Pope and the King, he was no respecter of persons, and his brusqueness in handling men gave the impression of unlimited power. He frankly outraged the Archbishop of Canterbury, who shook with anger at his presumption. He infuriated the old stock of nobles, sending Northumberland, Buckingham's son-in-law, to the Fleet for daring to have too many men in livery—having hundreds in livery himself. No one was safe from his hectoring. He shamelessly intercepted dispatches and broke the rules of etiquette. His bad temper, his "extreme vehemence and mental excitement," were as notorious as his gusts of honest jocularity or his calculated inaccessibility. But these excesses, these caprices, were not the result of a temperament out of hand. They were sparks from the anvil he was hammering.

His anvil was Europe. Bringing to statecraft the great theatrical tradition of the Church, he saw it far more as an affair of stage management and as a huge game to be aligned and negotiated than as a drama of moral or social import. Whether he was improvising a war or a "universal peace," building a palace or a college, toying with dukes or popes or emperors or sultans, Wolsey was not interested in the third or fourth dimension. He was interested in frontage and façade. He saw life as the speculator sees it, his brain foaming with projects of unrivaled picturesqueness, his spirit endowed with an endless fund of enterprise, as ready to embark on a new equity or a new method of taxation as on a new dodge to be papal legate or even a dodge to be pope. Perhaps he would have been the architect of a state if he could have afforded to, but the first charge on his resources was Henry's suspicion and Henry's vanity, and he soon developed the candid nature of the wrecker. If he were obliged to lure Europe on the rocks, it seemed to him a simple necessity, so long as the wreckage were washed up at Henry's feet. He appeared, of course, to be busy with the "balance of power." But while he had the energy to make England a diplomatic clearinghouse, and to take his percentage, it was not the activity of a statesman. It was the activity, glorious and impudent and incalculable, of a dazzling promoter, an opportunist high-spirited and superb.

His show, which was now commencing as "universal peace," was to continue for almost a decade, with three concurrent wars to diversify it. And in the center of the European ring, cracking his whip and wearing the red hat, was to loom this magnificent Cardinal. Through the hoops of paper that he would hold up, paper treaties and paper alliances, paper bulls and paper dispensations, one crowned head after another would leap with becoming and creditable agility, and one royal betrothal would follow another, with little debonair princes and princesses alighting like butterflies and balancing on his ecclesiastical hip. But this gorgeous entertainment, which would have its box office attached to it and a heavy price of admission, its zoo and its cage of diplomatic monkeys, could only come to a happy end if the young proprietor were to content himself without including the papacy in the circus business. A great deal would depend on the young proprietor, with his tight little mouth and heavy jowl. Something would depend on the weather.

Meanwhile, Wolsey had the air of a genuine catalyzer. He was gathering Europe around him. One could hardly believe that he would leave only a memory of palaces and golden oranges, a memory of gingerbread and circuses, a ring of trodden grass.

XXXVI

He was at the moment extraordinarily mobile. Almost every day he fulfilled his religious duties, keeping his mistress modestly in the background, and every day he swept to his court of equity where, without being versed in the law, he gave open, forthright hearing to rich and poor alike. He defied envy, despised rivalry, insulted pride, mocked precedent and ignored yea-and-nay. To do this as an upstart, having no mortise for his tenon except Henry's favor, revealed the degree to which he was living in the present, serving its exigencies, working inside the Tudor monarchy and the Medicean papacy, completely illuded by the wealth of the one and the grandeur of the other.

A career like this required cash. So long as he did not have to provide it himself, the King cared nothing where Wolsey got it, and Wolsey got it wherever he could. He stood at the crossways of every negotiation, and he openly demanded his perquisites. Sforza bribed him for prospective help in restoring Milan. Charles soon promised to pension him. His claim on Tournay was to be compounded for an annuity. He expected valuable presents at New Year's, as the King did, and he took all the gifts that his court of equity brought him. The Pope gave him the right to suppress certain small monasteries, which would enable him to erect Cardinal College at Oxford. To have a bishopric fall vacant in England, or in Spain for that matter, was likely to arouse his cupidity. To admire a ring or a jewel was his way of suggesting a present. He asked for a hundred Damascene carpets from the Venetians. And within a few years this needy cleric had bedecked his Hampton Court where he entertained so superbly that even the Venetians were awestruck. This grandeur, costing Henry's rivals a great deal and costing Henry nothing, was, in effect, a ransom growing under Henry's eyes. No priest outside Italy had sought to found a dynasty, so that Wolsey was a eunuch to Henry, even if he had a son and a daughter. His wealth was not imbedded in a powerful family. Unlike Buckingham's in England, or Bourbon's in France, it was not an intimidation to the royal master. It was a gem that threw reflected light on the master, a gem that flattered and invited him.

A certain conflict, unfortunately, was unavoidable in Wolsey's pursuit of money, but no man fought more ferociously to have his way. There was, for example, the bishopric of Bath, worth ten thousand ducats a year. It had been the perquisite of an Italian, Cardinal Adrian, who was a friend of England's at the Vatican. But in May of 1517 Adrian fell into disgrace. As he was chatting with another Cardinal named Petrucci, Petrucci happened to see a Vatican surgeon go by, and he remarked, "That fellow will get the College out of trouble." Being a member of the College of Cardinals, Adrian asked how, and Petrucci explained that "that fellow" who was treating Leo's fistula, was going to put poison in it. The notion of so new and so simple a solution of removing a pope was too much for Adrian: he burst out laughing, shrugging up his shoulders. It was, however, no laughing matter in the eyes of Leo. He had Petrucci tried, and executed in the Castel Sant' Angelo. In the height of his rage he interviewed Adrian, fining

him 12,500 ducats. Adrian was so afraid of further consequences that he bolted for Venice, which received him almost
too kindly.

The revenues of Bath were immediately given to Wolsey by
Pope Leo. As Adrian's partisans, the Venetians were agitated,
and sent word to Giustinian to persuade Wolsey not to take it.

The King scouted the idea of intervention. "I understand
this matter better than you Venetians," he told Giustinian.
Bishop Fox believed it was hopeless. "We have to deal with
the Cardinal," he said, "who is not Cardinal but King, and no
one in this realm dare attempt aught in opposition to his interests."

Wolsey was beside himself. While Giustinian's secretary
asked for an interview, he "held a cane in his hand, and kept
gnawing it with his teeth." "Your master has dared to give
letters and to canvass against me," he roared, "at the request
of a rebel against his Holiness."

Giustinian ran to see him. He was kept waiting three hours
and then refused audience. Two days later he did see Wolsey,
but he had to fight hard with this "wind in his teeth." His defense was broken into by "rabid and insolent language." "Go
on, write to the State to proceed in favoring rebels against me,
for she'll see what victory she'll gain." This rebel-poisoner,
"who also poisoned Pope Alexander," was not spared. Giustinian pretended not to hear most of Wolsey's "asperity" and
insolence. A month later, still "with a troubled countenance
and bent brow," Wolsey visited disfavor on Giustinian. "Considering the love I bore you!" he reproached, "I should have
expected such an injury in the world from any other person
rather than from you."

At long length, however, the Venetian overcame him, "without provoking any deviation on my part beyond the bounds of
discretion. After a while my gentleness overcame his arrogance."

"Domine Orator," Wolsey said at last, "I own myself vanquished, and receive you as that very good and dear friend that you have always been to me." He gave him his hand to kiss, and he embraced him. And he kept the ten thousand ducats a year.

XXXVII

While Wolsey fought so desperately for his Oriental ostentation, what about the "natives"? What about the common people and the new Bible, the virus of the New Learning?

Wolsey was a man of action. His nervous force as a negotiator, his skill in managing Henry, stood him in good stead when facts wore a regular badge or livery. Unrecruited notions, however, the awkward squad of unconventional and unreceived ideas, the medley that becomes a revolution while beginning as a brawl—these he averted from. A brawl to him was only a police problem. He disciplined the brawlers.

So, while the "universal peace" was being formulated, he had to deal with the London apprentices.

With the perspicuity of apprentices, they chose to break out under a government that had a clear field and both hands unoccupied. Theirs, however, was not statecraft. It was fury. Theirs was a London of a thousand trades, a London of goldsmiths, silversmiths, armorers, blacksmiths, pewterers; of girdlers, loriners, saddlers and cutlers; tylers and plumbers and masons and plasterers and glaziers and painters; of fellmongers, curriers, leathersellers, skinners, salters; of pinners on London Bridge, of wireworkers and spurriers; fletchers and bowyers and stringers for warfare; joiners, cordwainers, printers; of tapsters and brewers and ale tasters; sausage-makers, butchers, victualers, chandlers, grocers, vintners, porters, water-bearers; cappers and purcers, mercers, clothiers, haberdashers; weavers and fullers and dyers, shearmen, drapers and tailors; and a myriad other employments that were slowly forming a "wide middle class of opulent traders and comfortable craftsmen."

But this process was not smooth. The cost of living had risen high in 1517. Wolsey had got rid of parliament in 1515 and let the council substitute for it during eight years. According to sympathizers, "the poore English artificers could skace get any lyvinge; and moost of all the straungers were so proud that they disdained, mocked and oppressed the Englishmen." "The foreign artificers," according to the opposite view, "in general much surpassed the English in dexterity, industry and frugality." And they were powerful. The Flemings, who had the technique of weaving, were close on five thousand. The French artisans comprised another colony. The Italian bankers, silk importers, makers of fine swords and armor, workers in wood and stone, were rich and numerous. The Hanseatic group of the Steelyard, who were bringing over iron, leather, timber, nails, tar, tables, chests, rope and wax, were jealous as monopolists and unpopular as human beings. It was one of the features of an agricultural country, still predominantly peasant, that in spite of a growing middle class, the capital city should be thronged with aliens. In Florence there were no horizontal barriers to shut out the 'prentices. The whole city pulsed with the life of the artisan: it was a creative commune. In London the things of beauty, the things of fine craft, were increasingly alien, and the English folk had no communal efflorescence, no joy in the artist, no passionate life such as Bruges and Ghent and Lyons and Nuremberg and Venice. It was an impoverished soul, and these servants of the merchant class, two thousand of them, incited by a popular preacher, goaded by poverty, led by one Lincoln, threatened the strangers that on the first of May they would cut them to pieces and sack their houses.

Four Englishmen showed their natures in this crisis of the Evil May Day of 1517. When the riots were foreseen, Surrey

came as a soldier to kill the rioters; Wolsey was the man who
saw to it that Surrey was forewarned; Thomas More, late
under-sheriff, came out to parley and reason with the mob, and
Henry, who had been advised of the approaching trouble, kept
his distance. "Having received news that the Londoners were
in arms, and committing great outrage upon the strangers, he
got up at midnight, and took the field with a good number of
persons, and sent messengers to London, announcing his coming with a large army; though, in reality, he never quitted
Richmond."

The 'prentices killed no one, but they frightened every one.
Gibbets were erected all through the city, forty were "cruelly
hanged and quartered," "so that it is horrible to pass near" the
city gates. Four thousand troops in armor dominated the approaches, while hundreds of the workers were flung into prison.

Then Henry appeared in angry majesty. Eleven days after,
in full pomp, he came with Cardinal and council, mayor and
aldermen, Queen Catherine, Queen Margaret from Scotland,
Queen Mary, now Duchess of Suffolk, to a high dais in Westminster Hall. "The King commanded that all the prisoners
should be brought before him. Then came in the poor young-
lings and the old false knaves, bound in ropes, all along one
after the other in their shirts, and every one with a halter
about his neck, to the number of four hundred men and eleven
women."

The Cardinal pleaded for them. The King refused. On hearing it the prisoners fell on their knees, crying, "Mercy, mercy!"
The three queens, Catherine, Margaret, and Mary, were so
moved that they too fell on their knees. Henry still refused,
but turned to Wolsey, and the Cardinal, now in tears, assured
the King that henceforward the prisoners would be his obedient subjects. At last his Grace yielded. "And when the Cardinal
told them this," the Venetian declared, "it was a fine sight to
see each man take the halter from his neck, and fling it in the

air; and how they jumped for joy, making such signs of rejoicing as became people who had escaped from extreme peril."

That they had escaped from extreme peril was certain; that they had revealed the existence of revolting unhappiness was also certain. In spite of so many happy signs of a new world, such a free display of wealth and national strength, such a proud new navy and gorgeous pageantry, the condition of London was backward and frequently savage in its misery. And, as always happens in lands where the contrast is so terrible, the oscillation was between dearth and orgy, between extreme luxury and hideous squalor.

Men like Thomas More could not read Plato or think of the golden mean without regarding England as a commonwealth brutal, barbarous and lamentably unprincipled. And even the most complacent were shaken with fear when the London apprentices revolted.

Neither the executions nor the pardons, however, ended their protest. In September, again, they were threatening vengeance. London was terrified. Three thousand "householders and public functionaries were in battle array," and the ringleaders were arrested. The Venetian ambassador, who reported these things, asked to be taken home.

What complicated this sullen revolt, and deepened its horror, was the dance of death that had begun in London. The "sweating sickness" was raging. "This disease makes very quick progress, proving fatal in twenty-four hours at the farthest, and many are carried off in four or five hours. The patients experience nothing but a profuse sweat, which dissolves the frame, and when once the twenty-four hours are passed, all danger is at an end." "Very few strangers have died, but an immense number of the natives." It was a filth disease, reported by Osler as still occurring in the nineteenth century, but extremely virulent in Henry's reign.

Henry met it with the same discretion as he had shown on Evil May Day. He withdrew himself "with a few of his attendants to a certain remote and unusual habitation, in consequence of this malady." Wolsey stayed in London, sickened of it three times, and at last recovered. Henry's pages and his Latin secretary caught it and died.

XXXVIII

Henry's state of mind in 1518 was that of a war-weary young ruler. He had just escaped the dangers that threatened him from internal unrest. He now set about evading the dreadful problem of the Turk.

To bind the Christian nations in "universal peace," Pope Leo projected a war. This was the war that the Vatican had so often discussed, the war on the Turk.

The Turk was no fantasy. Indisputable word came through the Venetians from Cairo, from Aleppo, from Damascus, from Alexandria, from Joppa, from Beirut, of the appalling progress the conqueror had been making, with his twenty thousand Christian janissaries and his hundred thousand troops besides. Russia and Venice were both secretly suing his favor, and it would not be so long until the next Sultan, like a force of nature, would begin to advance on the whole Eastern flank of Europe, eating his way with a silent remorselessness that would at once terrorize and paralyze those that were near enough to observe it. It was a military danger of the first order, so huge that men would be powerless to resist it. It would advance with the zeal of a forest fire, shooting its tongues of death into Hungary, licking the coasts of the Mediterranean, enveloping the islands, baring plains, denuding mountains, dropping its brands on the roofs of cities, roaring across chasms of heroic pygmies who opposed it, and burnishing with sinister beauty the whole arch of the Eastern sky. It would not be Christendom which would save Europe, but the mere cooling deluge of circumstance, the drizzle of misadventure, which would convert smoke and flame to charred and sodden desolation.

Hardly palpable in France, impalpable in England, the scimitar already shimmered with bright menace on the horizons of the Empire, and Pope Leo thought the danger sufficiently imminent. Francis, the Most Christian King, was in agreement. Maximilian, the Holy Roman Emperor, wanted it financed. Charles, the Catholic King, looked on the crusade as his special mission. And Henry asked the Vatican to equip him for it by giving him a title like Apostolic, or Orthodox, or Defender of the Faith. This was as early as 1516.

Before Europe could be saved from the Turk, however, its dynasts had certain preliminary victories to achieve. Pope Leo, a sick man who spiced his existence with Tanagra and Gorgonzola both, had been disconcerted by two things. One was the eruption of Martin Luther in Germany. The other was the plot to poison him in the Vatican. Francis had his own preoccupations. His pungent mother had never been jealous of his wife, but she had become jealous of his mistress. There was good reason; Francis was airily bestowing the three highest commands in the French army on his mistress's brothers. He was dispossessing the most seasoned and faithful veterans for such dashing sprigs as Lautrec, Lescun and Lesparre, harebrained youths who were later to bring disaster to himself and the French army. And while Francis and Leo were so engaged, the young Charles, borrowing his expenses from Uncle Henry, had gone to Spain with his Flemish council to subdue a revolution, the Flemings taking their wives with them to select, superintend, and bring home the loot.

This was the spirit of peace as the dynasts interpreted it; and once Henry was sure that the French were planning to descend on the English coast only to ask for Mary's hand in marriage, he entered into this same spirit with ardor. Since

1511 he had been dabbling with war. He was now twenty-six years old. He intended to take his relaxation. He had Wolsey to work for him, and even to think for him, while he sank back into the post-war frame of mind.

XXXIX

She was a girl of seventeen. But this was not to be an affair like that which reverberated at Blois, in social acceptance and openness, the troublesome woman having a full share in her royal lover's existence. This was to be a respectable affair, and when Henry was finished the Cardinal would produce a little husband for her, his own ward in chancery, a rather soft-witted but quite docile young lord. It would aggrieve Catherine, privately, but it would not impair that precious idealism to which Henry clung, the sacredness of the marriage vow. "Who does not tremble," he would write in the midst of it, "who does not tremble when he considers how he should deal with his wife, for not only is he bound to love her, but so to live with her that he may return her to God pure and without stain, when God who gave shall demand his own again."

Henry was unusually good-humored and good-natured, unusually gay. The glittering pageants of 1517 and 1518 found him happy in his attendance on Catherine, all the more so because she was a mother and because Ferdinand was gone. But the thing that helped him most to behave charmingly to his wife was his discovery that he had charms for another woman. The gayeties with which the reign had commenced were repeated with higher color and fuller sumptuousness, gold baudekin, horses barbed with silver chainwork, trappings "half of gold embroidery and the other half of purple velvet, embroidered with gold stars," enlivening the spectacle of joust and parade.

When the peace-seekers arrived, they saw Henry in all his glory. "Between the courses, the King and the pages, and the other cavaliers, performed marvelous feats, mounted on magnificent horses, which they made jump and execute other acts of horsemanship, under the windows where the most serene Queen of England and the Dowager of France were, with all the rest of the beauteous and lovely and sumptuously appareled damsels. Adjoining was a chamber occupied by the Cardinal and all his gentlemen and attendants; the ambassadors were likewise there, including myself. The King performed supernatural feats, changing his horses, and making them fly rather than leap, to the delight and ecstasy of everybody."

In the morning his courtship was equine. It became musical in the evening. "In the centre of the hall there was a stage on which were some boys, some of whom sang, and others played the flute, rebeck and harpsichord, making the sweetest melody. The banquet being ended, the King and the guests above mentioned betook themselves into another hall, where the damsels of the most serene Queen were, and dancing went on there for two hours, the King doing marvelous things both in dancing and jumping, proving, as he in truth is, indefatigable."

It was not merely in the saltatorial that Henry carried on this courtship. It was in the sartorial. He wore "stiff brocade in the Hungarian fashion." He "was dressed in white damask in the Turkish fashion." He "wore royal robes down to the ground," while "all the rest of the Court glittered with jewels and gold and silver, the pomp being unprecedented."

The girl was English, Elizabeth Blount, one of "the damsels of the most serene Queen." Like so many girls of good family she had come to court at twelve, a little maid in waiting. At sixteen or seventeen, when she arrested the King's fancy, she was already one of the principal figures in masque and banquet, one of the inmost circle of the royal household, living under Henry's observation, curtsying to him, smiling to him, dancing with him, chatting with him, and fluttering in his consciousness like the scent of a tea rose or a cornfield radiant by the sea. These ravishing damsels, blonde or brunette, were no novelty to Henry. The royal palace saw them appear and dis appear with a delicious provocativeness, and the courtiers never disguised the hunt for their favor nor the pride of their conquest. Henry was not above consulting his favorites as to how to run his quarry down, and a bold pleasantry could at any time disquiet the damsels when his Grace, putting his head together with Francis Bryan or Nicholas Carew or William Compton or Suffolk, made one of those sly remarks that seem so irresistibly amusing to a group. That his jokes won their laugh before it was earned was as certain as the happy flush that mounted his cheeks. Henry stood before his vasty fireplace in dominating body and spirit. His dogs could tell by his royal stand whether it was wise to be near him. If he laughed, they turned on him a grave liquid look and set their tails in prudent motion. So did the courtiers. And as he expanded, the tide of expectation ran warmly up every courtly rivulet and creek. The damsels, set apart by custom, listened from their cluster near Queen Catherine to the meaningful laughter of the men, and speculated in their private souls on their place in the sun. Even Cardinal Wolsey, brilliant in his entry, deep in his vocal dignity, grand in his presence, could tell by a word caught edgewise the tilt of his master's mood. If it was prickly, the Cardinal soon departed in a cloud of conscientious preoccupation, but if it was propitious, no one dispensed more leisure, had more fluent appreciation, lifted the mood higher than the Cardinal, with his speedy wit, his hearty freedom and courtesy, his vivacious observation, his reverberating mirth.

It was soon clear to Wolsey, surveying his Prince, that a maid in waiting was elect. He at once approved. The girl's father was at court, one of the King's Spears, and was promptly made Esquire to the Body.

The Blounts were an old family connected with the Mount-joys. Their part in the court was like that of the tiny goldfish whose mouths open and shut sympathetically while the bigger goldfish are actually being regaled. They were a fighting stock, from the Welsh border, gentlemen and gentlewomen, like the Pastons. "War and law went hand in hand. . . . The very love-making has more of business than of love in it; politics mainly consist in doing the best for oneself and one's family; parents are harsh and brutal with their children; guardians look upon their wards almost as chattels to be bought and sold." In times of peace they bred children and acted as squires, played and hunted, shot and drank deep. Whenever a war came, the head of the family donned his coat of mail, took down his lance, gathered his twenty or thirty retainers, and rode off behind his knightly standard with his head high in the air. Their courage on the field was stubborn, and they dreamed of loot as a dog dreams of bones. Sometimes, if their retainers grew too unruly, they strung a man from a tree. When the war was *à outrance*, as could happen, they cut throats, killed babies, finished the wounded, raped the women, according to the note of "licentious soldiery," Blaise de Monluc testifying that the licentiousness reeked with reality. Yet the Wars were never deserted because of their lawlessness. Soldiers might fall on a defenseless town like jackals on a stricken horse; boys who had never shaved might be sent to silly death by laconic veterans; gallantry might be craftily bled by the cynical; and yet the glamour was eternal. The Wars were a medley of heroism and crime, roguery and hardihood. Even if in the end it was the silken knight who made the finest courtier, the man in the field kept the illusion of his Prince. The old soldier, gnarled with war, was no more fit to bend the knee than his hoarse voice was ready to lisp a compliment. Only a king who was himself a soldier could read in these veterans the volume of their romance. Henry, a knight in his own courtyard, but hardly a captain, left this tradition behind.

But luckily for the Blounts the ways of the courtier could be learnt by men and women of good family. Bessie Blount's portrait has not been kept, nor has one word of hers passed into history, but to judge by her family she was not the blonde of soft old gold but the Norman-English red gold limned with a brush dipped in sunlight. In ten years she was to be a statuesque matron, but now she was glowing with invitation. She had in her voice the throstle note of the English countryside. She danced and sang "most excellently" in all the court masques and mummeries, and one may imagine that she loved Henry before he ever saw her, that she fell when he sued her with the soft silence of a petal. Had she borne no child to Henry, this maid in waiting would have left no imprint on the swept sands of history. But she was not destroyed by him. She had the peasant standard of her time and class. The lovely girl of the sixteenth century trusted not in men's "honor" and never talked of being "ruined." At nineteen Bessie Blount was sent to a priory where her child was born, fortunately of the right sex. He was christened Henry Fitzroy and taken away from his mother to be brought up in semi-royal privacy.

And word reached Catherine that her husband was at last the father of a boy.

XL

The year of this courtship saw Henry at his affable and gracious best. The realm, "our Lord be thanked, was never in such peace nor tranquillity." The plague, indeed, infested London, but Henry went to Abingdon, where people, as he said, were not continually coming to tell him of deaths, as they did daily in London. His happiness with Elizabeth overflowed to Catherine. He took pleasure in the fact that his wife was once more going to have a baby. And he took pleasure in Mary, now two years of age. It was as an adoring father, in 1518, that he paraded his child.

"His Majesty," said the Venetian, "caused the Princess his daughter who is now two years old, to be brought into the apartments where we were, whereupon the right reverend Cardinal and I, and all the other lords, kissed her hand, formally, more than to the Queen herself."

The moment the child cast eyes on Memo, the organist of St. Mark's, who was a treasure of Henry's court, she leaned from Henry's arms, calling out in English, "Priest! priest!" and he was obliged to go and play with her.

"Domine Orator," exclaimed Henry, "by the Eternal, this little girl never cries!"

"Sacred Majesty," said the ambassador, "the reason is that her destiny does not move her to tears; she will even become Queen of France."

This was not the only bond of a tender marital kind. While the King was in love with Elizabeth, he had never been more cheerful or more liberal. So long as he pursued his war policy, he had not been able to bring Thomas More to court, but one of the first men to whom he and Wolsey turned when the tide was running toward peace was the author of "Utopia," and he used More as one of the diplomats to talk of selling Tournay back to France. Cuthbert Tunstall and Richard Pace were friends of the New Learning; Henry brought them close to him. He accepted from Erasmus a present of the book written for young Charles, "The Christian Prince." At Abingdon, when he was avoiding the plague, he let More and Pace induce him to tell Oxford that the students "would do well to devote themselves with energy and spirit to the study of Greek literature." A preacher who abused Greek in his presence he publicly rebuked. "That spirit is not the spirit of Christ, but the spirit of foolishness," remonstrated Henry. The preacher apologized.

"I am not very hostile to Greek letters," he said, "since they are derived from the Hebrew."

It was the moment when Martin Luther had just proclaimed himself, and when Thomas More was constantly at Henry's elbow. As soon as the King had done his own devotions, says More's son-in-law, it was his custom to send for More "into his private room, and there some time in matters of Astronomy, Geometry, Divinity, and such other faculties, and some time in his worldly affairs, to sit and confer with him, and other whiles would he in the night have him up into the leads [the roof] there to consider with him the diversities, courses, motions and operations of the stars and planets.

"And because he was of a pleasant disposition, it pleased the King and Queen, after the Council had supped, at the time of their supper, for their pleasure commonly to call for him and to be merry with them."

While he was cultivating More, Henry was also discussing with Wolsey the heresies of Martin Luther, and he soon made up his mind to break a lance with the German. This, too, was occupying him at the beginning of "universal peace," but he laid it aside as his affair with Elizabeth progressed.

It could only be taken as a tribute to Catherine's influence that Henry had persisted in his dealings with Maximilian and had kept flirting with the notion of the Holy Roman Empire. The peace policy, unfortunately for Catherine, could no longer be reconciled with her desires. She had the chagrin, in 1518, to learn that Tournay was to be sold to the French for 600,000 crowns, infinitely less than it cost to conquer, and in addition, as a result of Wolsey's cleverness, that her daughter Mary was really to be betrothed to the French dauphin.

This was a return to the Anglo-French alliance that she had detested. It brought Henry and Francis together. It was anti-Spanish, anti-papal and anti-moral. Catherine avoided the gorgeous festivities that Wolsey was arranging for the French visitors. She shunned Henry's younger companions, who were conspicuously under French influence. She frowned on his gambling with them and sporting with them, especially as he was losing as much as six or seven thousand ducats in one evening and carousing more than was good for him. She deplored the betrothal of her daughter, aged two years. It was not in her power to prevent it, but at least she could discountenance it. And she could regard Wolsey as her arch-enemy.

The "French set" certainly were completely anti-Catherine. And Henry, who turned at one moment to his loyalty to Catherine and his repute as "demure, sober and sad," was drawn the next moment to these "young minions"—"youths of evil counsel and intent on their own benefit, to the detriment, hurt and discredit of his Majesty."

"During this tyme remained in the French courte," says the contemporary Hall, "Nicholas Carew, Fraunces Brian, and diverse other of the young gentlemen of Englande, and thei with the Frenche Kyng roade daily disguysed through Paris, throwing egges, stones, and other foolishe trifles at the people, whiche light demeanour of a Kyng was much discommended and gested at. They return to Englande and are all Frenche in eating, drinking, and apparel, yea, and in Frenche vices and bragges, so that all the estates of Englande were by them laughed at; the ladies and gentlewomen were dispraised, so that nothyng by them was praised but it were after the Frenche turne, which after turned them to displeasure, as you shall here."

The displeasure, so far, was only Catherine's. But in January, 1519, Maximilian had a stroke of apoplexy. Out in the Tyrol, where he hunted the chamois, as he had so long pursued everything that was fleet and elusive, this singularly unconventional emperor died. A scamp, a romantic, a true aristocrat, Maximilian left a vacancy in the empire that he had never regularly filled. The election would be held in Frankfurt in

June. It concerned Henry, as a prospective candidate, to give up his gay friends and prepare for the descent of the Holy Ghost.

XLI

"Then was there foure sad and auncient knightes put into the Kynge's private chamber, whose names were Sir Richard Wingfield, Sir Richard Jernyngham, Sir Richard Weston, and Sir William Kyngston: and divers officers were changed in all places."

This was a shake-up that the imperial candidacy demanded. Wingfield, Jerningham, Weston and Kingston were strait-laced gentlemen of the old school. But it was not in this way alone that Henry was making character. In 1518 Pace had written to his old friend Erasmus, "The kindness of the king towards you increases every day, and he is very often speaking in your praise." More, as Erasmus knew, was now in the King's service, receiving a handsome salary and given a "magnificent present." And Erasmus himself had been offered fine quarters and six hundred florins a year by Henry and Wolsey. These he could not accept, but on the eve of the imperial election, when his friend Pace was in Germany as Henry's agent, Erasmus sent out letters from Antwerp that were the warmest testimonials to Henry's character, one of them being addressed to Henry himself. "The King's court has more men excelling in erudition than any academy." "The erudite stand round the royal table." "He delights to be surrounded by these, rather than by young men lost in luxury; or by women; or by gold-chained nobles." "The King there, himself not unlearned but with most piercing talents, openly protects good letters and puts a silence on all brawlers."

These tributes, which suggest that Pace or Thomas More had urged Erasmus to write them, were especially intended to depict Henry as an exemplary husband. "Who among private persons," wrote Erasmus to him six weeks before the election, "is more observant of the laws than yourself? Who is more uncorrupt? Who is more tenacious of his promise; who more constant in friendship; who has a greater love of what is equitable and just? What house among all your subjects presents such an example of a chaste and concordant wedlock as your own? There you find a wife emulous to resemble the best of husbands."

And, as if these laudations were not enough, Erasmus three years after his scathing denunciation of war, demanded mellifluously, "Who is more dexterous in war than Henry VIII, O bosom truly royal, O lofty mind, worthy of a Christian monarch! Although no king is better furnished with all the means of war, yet you apply all your study, and all your powers, to make the peace of the world."

Erasmus laid it on thick, though what he said had plausibility and perhaps a tincture of sincerity. His tribute to "chaste and concordant wedlock" missed the birth of Henry's illegitimate child by about a month. His tribute to Henry's efforts for the peace of the world missed the greatest of wars by several years. It was, however, the moment when Ulrich von Hutten, himself the Don Quixote of Lutheranism, was under the wing of the most corrupt churchman in Germany, and Erasmus had forgotten "In Praise of Folly," and his own austere friend John Colet. He was to cry bitter tears within a few months, when Colet died.

But Henry was not being put forward for the Empire, Wolsey told Pace. He might, however, be drafted. "Say," Wolsey instructed Pace, "say that I without any great labor exhort and encourage the King to his election, purely out of his desire to promote the welfare of others."

Charles's aunt Margaret was not so coy. She pledged all of Antwerp to the Fuggers of Augsburg, who advanced the necessary bribes. It was her diligence and her foresight, her willingness and her ability to corrupt the Electors, that completed the work begun in 1517 by Maximilian, and gave all of Spain and Austro-Germany to the taciturn Charles, aged nineteen.

XLII

Henry's amorous interlude was over. With the imperial election of June, 1519, every European value had changed. Charles, who had been a low black suit, had passed by this election into imperial "no trumps." Francis, on whom everything had seemed to pivot, found himself suddenly wondering what help he could get from a partner; and Pope Leo and Wolsey were scrutinizing in a happy light every knave and every king in their hands.

This was the moment that the tired Giustinian was released from his labors in England, and, decorated with a gold chain that he was allowed to turn over to a grateful but frugal Seigniory, stopped for a few days at Paris to pay his respects to the French King.

Francis gave him a hearty welcome and demanded the English news. He asked first of all, "Does he mean to maintain the peace?"

Giustinian answered that not only did Henry mean to maintain it but that he would wage war with all his might on whomever should be the first to violate it. The King, he said, and yet more the Cardinal, "who considers himself its first author and promoter, have peace continually on their lips."

With this Francis was gratified. He next proceeded to "catechize the ambassador, item per item, about the King personally," whom he extolled to the utmost. And then he asked, "What sort of statesman does he make?"

Giustinian would rather not have answered. "For to bestow praise on this score would be impossible, while to blame appeared to him unbecoming."

Francis pressed him. "He at length said that King Henry

devoted himself to pleasure and solace, and left the cares of the state to the Cardinal."

Whereupon King Francis rejoined, "By my faith, the Cardinal must bear his King light good will, for it is not the office of a good servant to filch his master's honor."

Giustinian no doubt let this go by. But his extreme politeness did not veil from him the sad fact about Francis, that the King and his mother "were more unpopular all over France than words could express." *Le roi champagne* was an expensive luxury, and his mother, knowing her son, was fighting every one for every sou. "Intent on hoarding, for the purpose, it is said, of aiding the King in the event of sudden need."

So the sage Venetian observed with fidelity, adding of Francis's consort, "The Queen of France is so universally loved, that it is impossible to describe or imagine greater affection."

XLIII

Francis was dimly aware that he was unpopular, but his life was being spent in weaving a daisy chain of festivity, each daisy a *fête champêtre* that cost a prince's ransom. He, and three thousand with him, moved at the gallop from one château to another, to invent gayety, to escape boredom, to discover a new illusion. But he was not oppressed by the approaching conflict with Charles. Knowing his latent resources and Charles's weakness in Germany and poverty in Spain, he fully believed himself the stronger and affected to despise his young rival. Yet he could not rely on the Pope. The restoration of the Medicis to Florence, the marriage that had already seen the birth of Catherine de' Medici, the sanction of Urbino for a Medici, the plan for chasing Charles from Naples—all this was no link with a Pope who had inherited the papal states, was thinking only of adding to them, and looked to a Medicean dominance in Italy. It was, quite clearly, a new game. But the victor of Marignano felt he was ready for it, and at last began to see the full value of the alliance with England which threw him into Wolsey's arms.

For several years Wolsey had been talking of a gorgeous love-feast with Francis, in which he was to bring the two young kings together, and Francis was to expose to him "the secrets of his soul."

Charles, however, was now Emperor, and once more he was asking Henry to advance him some money, 150,000 ducats, as he was on his way to Spain.

It was the situation for which Wolsey had maneuvered: Charles and Francis were both courting England. What could England not glean from this headlong, this disastrous rivalry?

For a man so fertile as Wolsey, who had seen to it that it was laid on England to maintain the peace, and who had therefore a vested interest in this rivalry, the chances of selling English friendship appeared magnificently high. If Francis wanted to hold them, he would have to put up something better than Guienne and Normandy. If Charles wanted to be the success-ful suitor, he would have to pay with the triple crown. Henry as well as himself savored the gigantic possibilities. Francis had just named his second boy "Henry," in honor of the King of England. It was symptomatic. And Charles, plunged into the utmost difficulties with the Spaniards, with the great Ximenes dead, and embroiled in every province, was willing to leave everything, to entrust the seething country to his old tutor, Adrian of Utrecht, if only he could reach England before Henry met Francis.

It was May, 1520. And although everything was ready for the Field of the Cloth of Gold, Henry and Wolsey would have liked to postpone it, on account of Charles, but unfortunately Queen Claude was soon to have a baby and further postpone-ment would demand sincere explanation. The clumsiest of juxtaposing was therefore inevitable: Charles had to hurry to

England, only to reach there five days before the love-feast of Picardy. His Aunt Catherine was enchanted to see him. Suffolk's wife, Mary, to whom he had been betrothed (as well, indeed, as to Claude, Renée, Charlotte, Louise and five others) waited palpitatingly to gaze on the Emperor, whom she had been obliged to forswear for the sake of a guttering King. It was a visit too crowded, too hurried, too complicated, for the business that was pending, and the Emperor thought it well within his dignity to be still on hand for Henry after the approaching month-long festival of the Field of the Cloth of Gold.

XLIV

The name itself is dazzling. The reality, in that June of 1520, was of a sumptuousness inconceivable. It cannot be said that these amazing spectacles were without a touch of fancy. When Francis and Leonardo da Vinci had met one another at Bologna in 1516, brought together by Leo, and the spark of mutual recognition had leaped from the old man of superb and curious vision to the gallant and perceptive youth, it could not be forgotten that for many years Leonardo had lent himself to devising the extravagant and soaring ceremonials of the Sforzas of Milan. These were ephemeral, like the decorations by Velasquez on the Isle of Pheasants, like the gestures and movements of great actors, like the voices of great singers, and the songs of birds. Leonardo was dead, in 1519, but the Francis who was joining in this present spectacle had shown by the passionate delight with which he had brought Leonardo to France, and the ardor with which he and the man of genius had conversed, that he was not a mere lover of puppetry. He seduced Leonardo from Italy, but he had bought the Mona Lisa, and honestly paid for it four thousand florins. There was an impulse of crass yet natural ostentation, of crude yet positive grandeur, of sheer royal magnificence, in these outdoor parties that included thousands of sparkling participants and invited the weather to keep smiling for a month. Such magnificence, unfortunately, was promoted by Wolsey against every economic principle. Martin du Bellay noted dryly that "many carried on their shoulders their mills, their forests and their meadows." Only by the wars that were adumbrated, only by turning towns into shambles and living men into carrion, could this sunburst begin to see knighthood in pocket once again. A hundred Mona Lisas could have been commissioned, a hundred Erasmuses relieved from cadging and begging for half a century, out of one petty morsel of this Cloth of Gold. But no reason except reason of state urged Wolsey to such incredible extravagance. He saw politics theatrically, accustomed to vast, stinking, miserable hordes of common people who knelt on the tombstones of their forebears and breathed the smell of corpses, while the chant of angelic voices rose through clouds of incense, and light was poured like jewels into uplifted eyes. The Field of the Cloth of Gold was the last throe of churchly ceremonial: and long years after would Manchester shake its salt-and-pepper head over this lamentable orgy, which was indeed lamentable, and which even before it happened made the alarmed Francis inquire if Henry could "forebear the making of rich tents and pavilions."

The approaching pageant meant much to Wolsey, as the golden frame of high politics. He felt at last that he had Europe at his feet, and this he revealed by a vast good humor. He was no staid diplomat: when he was annoyed, he exhibited "a troubled countenance and bent brow"; when he was elate, he skyrocketed. "Come and ye shall be welcome," he cried to the Flemings, "ask and ye shall have, speak openly and freely and we shall say Amen to whatever you require." His high spirits became even obstreperous. "The blind old man," he called the myopic Pope, who was forty-five. "Blind men need a guide," he laughed, and tapped himself on his silken bosom.

Such a man tries to carry his victory with a high hand, and

Henry took the same lofty line. "I will do all I can to smooth
the difficulties between the two sovereigns; for if it be not
done now, I have very little hope of its being done hereafter.
However, I trust that God, who knows my good intentions, will
further our wishes. I desire to establish peace in Christendom,
and gain some opportunity of doing honor to God, and promot-
ing the Faith by turning our united arms against the Infidel."

This did not impress Charles's cynical agent. "If you think
that the English here will labor for us, out of pure love for our
smiles and our good looks, and turn a deaf ear to others, certes,
Monsieur, you will find yourself very much mistaken." "There
is no doubt," he admitted, "that the French interview is
against the will of the Queen and of all the nobles, though
some may already have 'tasted the bottle.' " A little refreshment for the Cardinal might help, he suggested, "but it must
not be less than five thousand or six thousand ducats a year,
or he will not esteem it." Charles made it seven thousand.

The rendezvous could only displease Catherine. When it was
first discussed, Henry had told Sir Thomas Boleyn that he
would not cut his beard till he met Francis. "And I protest,"
declared Francis eagerly, "that I will never put off mine, until
I have seen the King of England." Catherine, however, did not
propose to see this beard-growing competition indulged in
honor of France. Every day she severely complained to Henry
that she did not like his beard. At last, having "daily made
him great insistence, she desired him to put it off for her sake."
And Henry shaved. When Francis's loyal mother heard of this
breach of international agreement, she went to Boleyn. "She
axed me," wrote Boleyn, "how the King my Master had put off
his beard." He told Louise the situation. "But their love," he
asserted, "is not in their beards, but in their hearts."

Yet Henry, at the last moment, had gone back to hairi-
ness. He was as Giustinian had left him, "on hearing that
Francis wore a beard, he allowed his own to grow, and as

it is reddish, he has now a beard which looks like gold."

At Canterbury, Henry suggested the little Princess Mary to Charles, "to tarry for her and, when she is ripe, marry her." And then, with this idea planted, though Mary had the Dauphin's ring on her baby finger, he set out for the great rendezvous.

The Field of the Cloth of Gold was nominally a festival which included every kind of knightly tournament and kingly courtesy and civility, but in effect it was a religio-political circus. The general public had ample warning that they were not to be admitted, and the French threatened to hang any one who came within six miles. The magnet was too powerful. In a day when every court was still simple enough to have its jugglers, its tumblers, its minstrels, its clowns and its zoo, the attraction of such a meeting for every sort of townsman and yokel, vagabond and rapscallion, thimble-rigger, fortune-teller, joker, cut-purse, songster, beggar, huckster and peddler, was beyond the power of even a proctor like Wolsey to suppress or even regulate.

It never occurred to the thousands and thousands of excited spectators that this gorgeous show was the prelude of a European war which would last thirty-eight years and cost half a million men. What they beheld under a dry sunlight that gave charm even to their prosaic plain, was the miraculous, windowed palace a hundred yards square set up by English glaziers and joiners, the big enclosure for the lists with grandstands built around it, the 2,800 white tents of the English, alive with knightly pennons and standards, the French pavilions (with the spangled canopy that seems to have served in 1518), the gold statue of St. Michael on a pinnacle, and the hundreds of French tents that flashed and glistened with every breath of wind.

The crowd could not know how reluctant Buckingham and

Abergavenny and Dorset might have been to come amongst the French, whom they heartily despised. All they took in was the intoxicating jingle and rustle of Henry's arrival with four thousand in his retinue, Catherine with twelve hundred in her retinue, and Cardinal Wolsey with his stalwart archers and his graceful ushers, fifty solemn giants carrying gold maces with knobs as big as a man's head, and a scarlet bearer carrying a crucifix with precious stones. Hardly less interesting to the commonalty would be the bleating sheep, 2,200 of them, the 800 spring calves, the 340 beeves, and wine in such profusion that the antique fountain could spout claret and hippocras for a month. If the world in general had no part in this resplendence, they enjoyed it from afar, they caroused and sprawled and frolicked and danced while Francis and Henry met each other, took each other's measure, and strove for position.

Riding forward in the fresh and sparkling morning, at the signal of cannon shots, the two hosts that descended into the wide plain so resembled the finest martial array on either side with "cloth-of-gold, cloth-of-silver, velvets, tinsins, satins embroidered and crimson," standards waving, lances flickering, that a tremor of apprehension and panic suddenly ran through the more primitive noblemen.

"Sire," blurted Abergavenny, "stop! I have been in the French party, and they be more in number—double as many as ye be!"

"Sire," growled honest Shrewsbury, "whatever my lord saith, I myself have been there, and the Frenchmen be more in fear of you and your subjects than your subjects be of them. Your Grace should march forward."

"So we intend, my lord," replied the King.

The officers took his nod. "On afore, my masters!" they cried, and the two companies, the pride of England and the pride of France, advanced toward each other, until, at a signal, all halted except Henry and Francis.

The Kings spurred their great coursers and rushed together at the gallop. They had the world, and the eye of the world, to themselves. Henry in silver and gold, Francis in gold and jewels, reined in and uncovered simultaneously, embraced, spoke their word of greeting, dismounted, embraced again, and walked to a little pavilion, while the retinues, now set loose and laughing, mingled together, the English inviting the French to refreshments, crying, "Bons amys, Francoys et Angloys, bon courage, good luck, have a drink."

Henry at last could see the King about whom he had been so curious. Francis was much his own height, "a goodly prince, stately of countenance, merry of cheer, brown colored, great eyes, high nosed, big lipped, fair breast and shoulders, small legs and long feet."

And to the French eyes Henry was kingly. "Le Roy d'Angleterre est moult beau prince, et honneste, hault et droit; sa manière douce et benigne; un peu grasset, et une barbe rousse, assez grande, qui luy advient très bien."

This rendezvous, as Henry took it, was above everything a tournament. It was a chance to display a wealth, a virility, a prowess and a skill that the French could hardly have realized beforehand as the distinctions of Tudor England. The revenue of England might be only 800,000 ducats, where that of France was 6,000,000; the population of England might be only three million where that of France was fourteen million; but the Field of the Cloth of Gold could show that the King of England, his nobles, gentlemen, squires and knights were of a formidable pride that could no more than be rivaled by any other power. Where Charles was content to go abroad in Flemish woolens, Henry wished the French to behold and to admire, and his small eyes flashed as he rode to the joust, where he soon knocked his opponent silly, and was to kill one of his own mounts through sheer exhaustion. The chronicles of Froissart, which Lord Berners was to translate for him, gave Henry the pitch for the lordliness that was to impress his neighbor Francis; and to thrust at the French with an expenditure that they could hardly parry was to his mind a memorable magnificence.

He was right. He dumbfounded the French. But Francis was ready to be impressed. He was afire with the decision that war between himself and Charles was unavoidable, and that now was the time to strike. He knew it was vital to win Henry. Believing that the betrothal of the Princess Mary to the Dauphin was still valid, feeling convinced that Henry could have no objective in France outside the Pale, and thinking it unnecessary to study Henry's interest as he had studied those of the "brittle and variable" Leo at Bologna, he allowed himself to come forward not as a political trader but as a mere courtier. He did it exquisitely. By nature an artist and a lover, he threw himself into the conquest of his English brother with that natural verve, that dandyish gayety, which made Henry for the moment live up to him. Early in the morning before his Grace had stirred, Francis arrived with a page and, defenseless, walked through the guards, strode into Henry's room and roused him. "I am your valet," he cried, warmed Henry's chemise himself and gave it to him when his naked Majesty arose. "And I am your prisoner," responded Henry, fastening his collar on Francis. The present was accepted, and a bracelet offered instantly. It was the homage of King to King.

They deferred so long before either would be so rude as to kiss the book in chapel before the other, that Catherine and Claude had to ignore the book and kiss one another instead. Though the minuet was not yet invented, Henry and Francis went through their paces from castle to castle with rhythmic punctilio, and from the ranks of the maids in waiting who observed their Kings with glowing loyalty, a slight sapling of an English girl, no longer a child, and yet scarcely old enough to be in the world, watched Henry with big eyes and grave white face—the little English girl who had been with the French princesses for two years, slim Anne Boleyn.

The French were compelled to admire Henry's dexterity and aplomb. "He is a marvelously good bowman and strong. It did one good to see him!" But there was a moment when Henry, in the exuberance of his triumphs in archery, turned to Francis as they entered the tent for refreshment, in front of Catherine and Claude, seized the long-legged Frenchman by the collar, "Brother! I will have a wrestle with you." It took Francis off his guard. In the abruptness of the assault there was a real tussle, a twist, and Henry was thrown to the grass. He rose purple with rage. The ice had crackled. On every face was depicted the nervous fear in which this love-feast had so far been suffered, and before Henry could begin again, all were summoned to the table by their ladies.

It was the tension of the coming struggle. In an hour that called for patience, Francis chafed at uncertainty. He did not dissimulate. He sought to woo Henry, to create a bond with him, to pledge his loyalty. But though Henry had laughed at the beginning, "I will not put 'King of France' while you are here, for that would be untrue," his affability in resigning this formal boast of the "righteous inheritance" did not signify any personal bond whatever. He hurried from Ardes to his post-mortem meeting with Charles, and Francis could only hope that he might influence Wolsey.

XLV

These French! The great interview had not brought Henry and Francis together. The Frenchman, at close range, had proven even less intelligible than from England. He was malapert where Henry was proper, making jokes about Catherine's Portuguese brother-in-law as the "King of Spices," the "Grocer King"; and jousting in funereal black with a ribald motto, where Henry would decently call himself "cœur loyal." But

worse than this grating flippancy, which had recently made him
send Bonnivet to England with instructions to "chauffer" the
English damsels, was his sudden capacity for a mad Quixotic
seriousness, as when he had shed three million crowns in pursuing the Empire, and had plumped Sir Thomas Boleyn "hard
by the wrist with one hand, and laid the other upon his breast,
and swore to me by his faith, if he attain to be emperor, that in
three years after he would be in Constantinople, or die by the
way."

This he could say feelingly, towering over little Boleyn, but
when it came to winning Henry and Wolsey he shrank back to
smiling, wary particularism, talking grandly, but never talking
business, never baiting his line with anything that *proved* his
sincerity—wine, for example, or salt, or alum. He had studied
to win, but had not entered into practical habits of thinking.
He had chosen his flies prettily, "the blandishments of the
handsomest women of France." But he had not suited his flies
to the fish.

When Henry and Wolsey were free to talk it over, they held
themselves down, but they brimmed with everything they had
learned. War was certain, as Francis made clear. They had
keenly observed Bourbon, his "constable," whom Francis had
slighted and who showed his sallow temperament in black and
fiery glance. They had seen the "Trinity"—the choleric Louise,
the liquid-eyed Marguerite, the demure Claude. They had in-
spected Francis' nobly proportioned mistress. The saucy Bonnivet, de Longueville, the Bellays, the young war lords—these
they had scanned. And Wolsey had looked into the secret of
Francis's soul, to share with Henry, while Henry, a cold breeze
blowing from the Sierra Nevada of his spouse, had yet caught
and held the warm consoling glance of an English girl, Mary,
senior daughter of his old friends the Boleyns.

While Henry's head simmered, Wolsey's whirled. What

course to steer between the champing French King and the glum young Emperor? Delay was all the better because Francis was so eager. But what to do?

The love-feast had worked no miracles. A Venetian had daily noted, "These sovereigns are not at peace. They adapt themselves to circumstances, but they hate each other cordially." So much was unchanged.

Certain links, however, bound England to France. There was the yearly annuity, until a million was paid. Wolsey got his 12,000 livres for Tournay and 2,800 for good will. Norfolk, Suffolk and Shrewsbury got 1,750 each, Fox, always a good friend, had his 1,050, and even Lovell and Compton had smaller annuities. Outside Richard Wingfield, the imperial side were paying few gratuities, except to Wolsey, though Charles was a heavy personal debtor. So far the honors rested with France.

But friendship with France could lead to a rupture with Spain and Flanders, which would destroy the export of wool. It was England's one important article of export, the basis of its wealth. Nearly one hundred thousand pieces of woolen cloth, to say nothing of raw wool, were going to Flanders— there was free entry of cloth into the Netherlands, at the expense of the natives and for political insurance. What could France offer as against that?

The papacy? Leo was incurably ill, and it was not so long since Francis had made the direct offer to Wolsey, before the imperial election. Not even Henry knew the extent to which this had been discussed.

But if Francis had one violent Roman faction in his pay and could deliver fourteen cardinals, Charles had seventeen or eighteen to dispose of. Even here he was preferable to Francis.

And Catherine, forced by twelve years' marriage to be self-effacing, had flared out "as one would not have supposed she would have dared to, or even to imagine." Her one treasure was her child, and to see her married into the French court aroused her to desperation.

At Gravelines Charles was faithfully waiting. He came with them to Calais to hold an extremely intimate conference; and he left Calais satisfied.

Henry thereupon instructed his envoys to tell Francis that Charles had striven to alienate him, striven to make him seek Milan and to take Mary away from the Dauphin. But these assaults he had successfully defended his virtue against, "dearest brother, confederate and compeer."

"Take good heed what ye do with Henry," Bonnivet soon advised Francis, "and not to trust too far."

XLVI

The atmosphere was undeniably tense. Outwardly there was peace. The Turk was quiet since Selim had gone dripping to his Allah, and Soliman the Magnificent had not yet imbrued his hands. But a tremor ran through every nation, spitting its electricity in each casual contact, shooting its signals, creating its marvelous illusion of the inevitable, and drawing to its bloodbath every land from Stockholm to Peru where a handful of Spaniards, penning the helpless into their sheepfold and undaunted by the example of Selim, would kill, until their arms would fall, a ten thousand of the mild, the bleating, the unbelieving innocent, to whom they were about to introduce the Jesus of Love. Selim's drug was opium. The mandragora of the Christians was a lustrous metal in which Wolsey had draped his diplomacy, lit up his monstrance, heightened his chasuble, gilded his tabernacle and lifted his sacramental chalice. Europe had expropriated the wicked Moors and scattered the wicked Jews, its eyes fascinated by this new mirror for its imaginings. The bloodbath was not its lure, as one said of Selim. What young Europe followed was the gold mirage. And in front of its fierce mercenaries strode its consecrating cardinals, its Wolseys and its Schinners and its Medicis, the tataratata breaking through the music of the mass, the swords clashing against steel breastplates, the ashen lances bristling, the blazon of war on these uplifted Christian visages while, to the cleaving of the trumpet, priesthood shook out its arm and held aloft the pride of the cross.

But earthly princes could brook no insolence. Bourbon was the wealthiest noble in Europe. Buckingham was the wealthiest noble in England. If Bourbon survived for the moment it was not for lack of resentment. Resentment caught Buckingham, like a noose thrown from afar and bringing to its knees an elegant and high-stepping animal, whose defenselessness does not alter the desirability of its pelt.

Wolsey had bullied the Duke of Buckingham, and Buckingham had retaliated by spilling water on his shoes. He came of a proud and petulant line. Northumberland was one son-in-law, Norfolk's son another. He was stiff and brittle. Talking to his chaplain or his steward, he had spluttered indiscreetly. Wolsey warned him, which increased his indiscretion. He was angry, for Catherine's sake, over the love-feast in France. He took a high tone, and a servant whom he had just discharged reported him to Wolsey, who told Henry, who sent for the servant. One accuser named another. A monk, who had things from God direct, was brought to book. He admitted having made prophecies that Buckingham "should have all." Buckingham had elsewhere said that "if ought but good come to the King, he should be next in blood to the crown." These dark words were from 1514.

It was a case that came straight into Henry's hands. Buckingham knew as little of the surrounding climate as one of those French vegetables which grow under a glass bell. But Henry was the surrounding climate: at this instant loaded and mad with tension only needing Buckingham to proffer one sharp

point to splinter and destroy him. With the suddenness of a
nature long surcharged, Henry summoned Buckingham, who
cantered up to London without apprehension. He could only sit
down unexpectedly, and ask for a cup of wine, when he was
ordered to the Tower to await trial. The witnesses were already
in the Tower, and men with heavy jaws and thick hands were
pressing the juice of evidence out of them, drop by drop. All
was ready by May 13, 1521, for the opener ways of justice.
Buckingham came before a jury of his peers, the Chief Justice
on hand to advise them. War was in the air. The very name of
treason made men quail. The accusers had been coached for
three weeks, rumor and oath and boast and wild prophecy becoming a labyrinth too deep for mortal man. Buckingham had
no counsel. With a stertorous breathing behind them, unheard
yet palpable, they found their peer guilty.

Old Norfolk, crying the while, pronounced verdict on the
traitor, who defended himself in few words.

"You have said, my lord, as a traitor should be spoken to,
but I was never one. But, my lords, I nothing malign for what
you have done to me; but the eternal God forgive you my
death, and I do. I shall never sue to the King for life; howbeit,
he is a gracious prince and more grace may come from him than
I desire."

Buckingham's "gracious prince" did not lift his finger.
Catherine tried to plead, but encountered such a sense of outrage that she bowed to it. The executioner on Tower Green did
his duty with a woodman's ax.

XLVII

The Buckingham trial had an amazing effect on Henry. He
could not digest. He could not eat. He took to his bed. On the
day before the execution Fitzwilliam wrote to Wolsey that the
King had been "sharply handled" by a fever; but "such
moderation, abstinence and diet hath been used by his High-

ness, that the fever and disease is totally departed." He was able to be up, by the time that Buckingham was dead.

Henry's sense of outrage at Buckingham's conduct had borne all before him. Those like Catherine who knew how good-natured he could be, how benignant, could hardly understand the gust of resentment with which he had shaken when he heard of the Buckingham "conspiracy," and the ruthlessness with which he had pushed the trial to its end. But they had forgotten how he had pounced on Buckingham's brother as the first act of his reign, and how he had waited for the least move of those noble rivals whom he feared. Once Henry thought of himself as deceived, or believed himself menaced, he lost his placidity, and shed every trait of his mother, "humble and penitent," whom he resembled when things were going well with him. He who appeared tolerant and smiling and lordly, his eyes twinkling and his heart expanding, looking down from a genial height on the littler folk around him and shining with the sun of splendid spirits, suddenly contracted, hardened, bristled, his mind sharp, his movements abrupt, his strategy instinctive, his force crushing, so that he seemed like a different man. The moment that he felt himself to be in danger, his robustness passed from large geniality into bitter self-preservation. With Henry this was no normal instinct, governed by reason and backed by courage. It was a crafty instinct that threatened to monopolize his character. It could become morbid, and it could learn, with the facility of all morbid traits, to speak to him in the purling language of his rank, the noblest tones of his country and his religion.

Sometimes his desire for security made him downright timid. He could never master his terror of the sweating sickness. When people around him were dying, he thought only of his own safety and he fled from the stricken without shame. He had little pity in him, but much self-pity. He could be pusillanimous as when he faced Evil May Day from the safety of his

palace at Richmond. He was nervous in anticipation of treach-
eries, and it led him to unusual measure of self-protection. But
so far it was his first impulse to seek security by rushing against
his enemies. Those who thought him soft or easily imposed on,
those who said abroad, "he is under Wolsey's thumb," did not
understand the silent repugnance with which he took any slight
or any restraint that was put on him. Had he been really in-
dolent, had he been content to divert his senses and amuse his
nerves, he might have floated down the stream with scarcely a
ripple. But the Tudor blood was tart, very different from the
serene fluid that had left untroubled his grandfather Edward's
lax brain. Henry was born restless. He took the lead physically.
Where Francis loafed in bed all morning, Henry was up at
dawn. He still thought nothing of spending the whole day in the
saddle, and no sport was too arduous or dangerous for him. He
wielded the two-handed sword. He nearly lost his life pole-
vaulting. He had dangerous falls from his horse. He jousted
with brutal vehemence. He was vigorous, active and excitable,
with a stout endurance and a tough muscular strength. He
hunted and shot with gusto. Slaughter did not disgust him. He
enjoyed the baiting of bears and bulls, having no trace of the
squeamishness that distinguished Thomas More and Erasmus.
He could even laugh at the plight of the hunted and watch
without pity the fate of the weak.

But Wolsey understood that this stoutness of body was not a
proof that Henry had stoutness of heart. If the foundations of
the Tudors had been more stable, or his childhood more settled, the King might have feared rivals less. As it was, he was
unsteady at the center of his power, with little faith and incessant suspicion. He was not able, like his father, to become the
watchman of his own inheritance, merely frugal and acquisitive.
Henry's shallow reserve of tranquillity went with too strong a
sense of his own value. He was combative, emulative, competi-

tive, qualities of force and energy, and Wolsey knew that he demanded from life a positive vindication of the personality that he hesitated to endanger and expose. A gentler man would have taken to drink, to damp his fires. A heroic man would have mastered his nerves. A humbler man would have accepted his rating. But Henry's inordinate sense of his own value absorbed him, and drove him to circuitous and sinuous ambition. Pushed by his demand for power, and his anxiety for self-preservation, he set no limits to his desire for distinction on the Continent or his fierce apprehension of danger at home. This sincere concern for himself, inch-deep in fat flattery as a general rule, made him act with a sudden savagery when he came into discordance.

Yet Wolsey, to hold him, had stimulated his ambition. He had urged him to pursue Guienne, Normandy, Castile, Scotland, Milan. He had fanned his wish to be Emperor. He had fed the notion that it was Henry who had elected Charles. But the pupil could go beyond the master when aroused. He had consented to the execution of Empson and Dudley at the beginning, and he had secretly dispatched Edmund de la Pole. Now he had sent Buckingham to his grave without a hitch. It was a triumph for his ego, but, as Wolsey was soon to recognize, a dangerous one. For all that this ego demanded, in order to treat his fellow-beings as mere objects, was the assurance that he could subdue discord with the complicity of his subjects and the approval of God.

Those few who already knew "The Prince" might have seen in the killing of Buckingham an act of devilish calculation. This was not to know Henry. The Italian and the Englishman were poles apart. To Machiavelli there was one thing sacred, human experience, and he schooled himself to consider anything that could muster human behavior. But Henry was of a tenderer mind. Blood-curdling as his abrupt act might seem to the nobility, unsentimental as he might appear, hard as he might press on his advisers to broaden his scope and give him elbow room, he still clung to neat medieval sanctions, and he still jealously barred out disreputable acts.

To admit turpitude as possible to himself was as little likely to occur to Henry as to send an army out of England headed by any one less than an earl. He might take to his bed, but it was in the birth-pangs of a new moral conception. He demanded official license. He sought the process of law. He required the theologian to shoehorn his conduct into a moral category, and the judge to outfit him legally. It was the rule of his morbid being to "row one way and look the other."

Buckingham's case had therefore been a moral episode to him. He had matched himself not only against the old nobles but against the due order of law. He had issued defiance to a caste and to a tradition. He had won. The law had discreetly crumbled under the accused peer. Norfolk had wept, but he had said "Guilty," and no one had stood up to Henry. Though the trial had given his nerves an ugly shock, he could arise purged and gratified by the clean result. His will was moral; his will was law. He lifted his head, victor and champion.

XLVIII

It was the same Henry, combative and insecure, who, up to the actual trial, had been writing a book. He had early been outraged by Martin Luther; Luther had attacked his Mother! "Would to God my ability were equal to my good-will," he wrote, "but I cannot but think myself obliged to defend my Mother, the Spouse of Christ."

His Mother was the Church. The Church was built on a rock, and Luther, its Prometheus, stirred in Henry an emotion so sincere that he could not restrain a desire to crush the rebel. It was "The Babylonian Captivity" that made Henry want to vindicate the seven sacraments. He did not, like Luther, see the sacraments as the devices of a human institution to hold its members by the most solemn ritual, taking them as they came in by baptism, holding them from month to month by penance and communion, catching them as they married by matrimony, nailing the priests by holy orders, ushering them out of the institution by extreme unction, and only needing, for perfect discipline, a sacrament of the tithes. These inventions, part of "captivity" to Martin Luther, who thirsted for direct divine experience, were to Henry the very essence of religion. He reviled Luther. A serpent, a plague, a mad and raging dog, an infernal wolf, a "trumpeter of prides, calumnies and schisms," "turns the name of the most Holy Bishop of Rome to that of Antichrist." "What a great member of the Devil he is," exploded Henry, "who endeavors to tear the Christian members of Christ from their head!" "This monster," he deemed him, "this Fratercula." He could not but believe that Luther was a man of low life. "Loss of faith comes from loss of morals." "He strives to breed discord."

So far did Henry go in pleading for the Pope's authority that even Thomas More demurred. "I think it best that place be amended," More ventured to suggest, "and his authority be more slenderly touched."

Henry smiled. "Nay, that it shall not: we are so much bounded to the See of Rome, that we cannot do too much honor to it."

More was enough lawyer to remind Henry of præmunire. But the King insisted. "Whatsoever impediment be, we will set forth that authority to the uttermost, for we receive from that See our crown imperial."

His real reason for exalting the Papacy, he did not admit— that he hoped to see Wolsey elected to it. If he said, "All the faithful honor and acknowledge the sacred Roman See for their Mother and supreme," it was because Thomas Wolsey would be the Holy Bishop, and fulfill his promise to use the Papacy to "contribute to your Majesty's exaltation." Only this could set aside the good doctrine that "the Kings of England in times past never had any superior but God."

Henry's "Assertio Septum Sacramentorum" was a declaration that he would uphold the papacy against all comers, especially when Luther "makes the Pope a mere priest." As he wrote his book laboriously, he consulted Fisher, Pace, Edward Lee, Stephen Gardiner, Tunstall, Wolsey. The Spanish declared, "All the learned men in England have taken part in its composition." Thomas More he most depended on, both for theology and for Latin. "By his Grace's appointment, and consent of the makers of the same, I was a sorter-out and placer of the principal matters therein contained." So More declared many years later. But for the present the "aureus libellus" was Henry's. He was proud of it. He wanted the Pope to see it, to read it, and to give him a title for it—Apostolic, Orthodox, Faithful, Glorious, Angelic, Defender of the Faith, or perhaps even Francis's title Most Christian.

The neatness of Henry's universe was never so well shown as in this book on the seven sacraments. He was one of those lucky men, who, having read St. Thomas and discussed the Summa with his Thomists, could spread out the verity. He had labored on this task long enough to familiarize himself with the Holy Fathers, and, ignoring his own nature, and his own conduct, to roll out the edifying truth. He was now thirty years old, at the height of his intellectual pride though by no means at the height of his intellectual power. To smite Luther in the name of Holy Church gave him a sensation of moral integrity. He sent two presentation copies to Rome, sheepskin underneath but covered with cloth-of-gold, to be laid at the feet of the Pope.

The English agent at the Vatican was Mr. John Clark, a faithful old dumb-waiter or lazy-susan, to whom nothing was so sacred as a platitude and nothing so deserving of respect as "commonly received opinion." Clark brought Henry's book to the Vatican with breathless unction, and he was allowed to deliver an address himself, as he presented it in full consistory. It was not long since Leo, "the double Florentine," had given his approval to Machiavelli, the least self-deceived of Italians. But the intellect is no match for the instinct. So simple an Englishman as John Clark, immersed in practicality and incapable of self-criticism, could speak far better for Henry than any Machiavelli, whose rejection of "commonly received opinion" depends on acute sensitiveness to good and evil.

Clark enjoyed telling the Pope anew what sort of poisonous serpent Luther was. "This man," he said with pious horror, "this man institutes sacraments after his own fancy, reducing them to three, to two, to one; and that one he handles so pitifully, that he seems to be about the reducing of it at last to nothing at all. O height of impiety! O most abominable and most execrable villainy of man!

"What intolerable blasphemies, from an heap of calumnies and lies, without any law, method or order, does he utter against God, and his servants, in this book!

"Socrates, a man judged by Apollo's oracle to be the wisest of men, was by the Athenians poisoned for disputing against the commonly received opinion they had of God, and against that religion which was at that time taught to be the best on earth. Could this destroyer of Christian religion expect any better from true Christians, for his extreme wickedness against God?"

Pope Leo thanked Mr. Clark for his most "brilliant discourse," and for Henry's readiness to aid the Holy See "with sword and pen." "We all but welcome Luther's crime," he said with his charming smile, "since it is the occasion of your noble championship." He took the beautiful book in his hands, and, running his short-sighted gaze along the two lines that Wolsey had composed for Henry as a dedication, he nodded with the greatest pleasure, and read aloud three times:

Anglorum Rex Henricus, Leo Decime, mittit
hoc opus, et fidei testem et amicitiæ.

Henricus.

"It was beautiful to hear with what exultation the Pope and
cardinals broke out into praises of Henry."

But Germany as well as Italy had its look at Henry's book.
The Assertio, as it was called, reached Martin Luther almost
immediately after he had openly defied Rome. He had long
reviled Thomism as the scum of stale theological platitude, and
he saw in Henry's lucubrations the driblets of that stagnant
pond. Into a short pamphlet he gathered a volume, not of
argument but of such low and hearty vituperation as was native to the swarming miners' village where he had first learned
to battle for himself in slack-heap and kennel. The fact that
Henry was an earthly prince excited in him an exuberant glee:
he hurled stink-pots at him with a vehemence that showed the
broad monkish kinship of himself and Rabelais. The royal
answer was not direct. It was entrusted to Thomas More. Those
who have read this exchange of swarthy insults must conclude
that More was vulgar without being funny.

One man alone seemed to dissent from the performance
which earned Henry the title Fidei Defensor.

"O good Harry," broke out Henry's court fool, "let thou and
I defend one another, and let the faith alone to defend itself."

XLIX

While Henry was finishing his book against the rebel, which
showed how his sense of authority had been stimulated, the
duel between Charles and Francis had advanced from secret
diplomacy to open clash of arms. It was the sequel to the Field
of the Cloth of Gold, the natural outcome of Wolsey's policy of
"universal peace," and he prepared in the summer of 1521 to
collect his dividends on the approaching war.

Four years this European war was to last, which already lifted its thunderheads on the horizon. It found France free in 1521; it was to encircle it and leave it entrammeled. Those words of Louis, "ce gros garçon gâtera tout," were to be vindicated to the full; and in the tracks of Louis's own Italian adventure Francis was to drag his people near to ruin.

This war would not be fought by conscript armies. The stubborn blond Swiss, the German veterans, the Gascons, the spring-heeled Basques, mercenaries from Wales, mercenaries from Naples, reluctant Flemings, yeomen from England, new German Protestant lancers, Spaniards of unparalleled daring and ferocity were to dispute each field in Picardy, in Lombardy, in Burgundy, into Provence and across the Pyrenees. While the Christians were thus waging war to dismember a dangerous France, the Turks were to take Belgrade and Buda, carrying on their campaign to the ravaged outskirts of Vienna. It was to be a combat of sieges and raids, of intrigue and conspiracy, of suspicion, delay, indecision, treachery and resentment. And when it came to its end in a French disaster that was to be the sardonic obverse of Marignano, the peace that was to follow would be a mere breathing spell for beggared Europe until enough assets and enough infants had been matured to continue the bout of dynastic competition.

Three smart thunderclaps announced the war. The lord of Sedan struck into Luxembourg for Francis: Lesparre invaded Navarre for him: and in a few months Bonnivet would seize the bold knob that commands the southwest corner of France, Fuenterrabia.

"God be praised," exclaimed the young Emperor, "that I did not begin the war, and that the French King wishes to make me greater than I am. In a little while either I'll be a poor emperor, or he'll be a poor king of France."

The French capture of Navarre was as easy as carving a melon; in fifteen days it was finished, with no incident more memorable than the wounding of a young Spanish cavalier, St. Ignatius Loyola, as he later came to be called. But such a capture was empty. "He has taken a kingdom from me," cried Charles, "but I will have my revenge." He had his hands full, with Spain fighting the Cortés, yet no difficulty could deter him from this duel. There was something about Francis, something in the least rumor and least accent of him, that made Charles stiffen. The man who had contested the Empire against him he regarded as revolting and despicable. His emotions jostled so hard in the narrow passage with which nature had provided him that they left the young Emperor pale with anger.

"I know your master does not love me," said Francis to Charles's provost; "no more do I love him. I am utterly determined to be his enemy, and deal with him by all such means as I see fit."

To the English envoy he reported bitterly that Charles had declared, "he would leave the King of France in his shirt."

L

From the first outbreak the antagonists turned to England. But it was not Henry they solicited, it was the Cardinal. "Mon bon ami," wrote the French King, "bon et vrai ami." "Monsieur le Cardinal, mon bon ami," the Emperor addressed him. "Mon fils," cried Margaret from Brussels.

These endearments were met with the calm voice of mediation and arbitrament. So well had Francis prospered in his invasion of Navarre that at first he regarded anything less than open alliance as an injury; but Navarre being snatched out of French hands with a celerity only more marvelous than its first early feebleness, Francis perceived the immense dangers and uncertainties of the great conflict and put his case in Wolsey's hands.

It was the strategic position that Wolsey had bargained for—umpire of Europe. He was superseding the Pope, who hated him. Commanding the gorgeous paraphernalia which had now become his tool-kit, Wolsey shipped to Calais in August, to decide the merits of this vast international dispute.

To come into this rôle of arbiter was what he had been imagining since 1518. What he had prepared at Dover before the Field of the Cloth of Gold, and what he had devised with the Emperor and Henry in the close conference at Calais, was exactly the dénouement before him. He had the two competitors in the hollow of his hand. But arbitrage was not the climax of his statesmanship. To mediate would be impossible. To arbitrate would be a sham. What he planned was to falsify the scales so that England would gain maximum. He needed to retard French action long enough, by the otiose methods of which he was master, until the hour would come for the payment of the next French installments. By that happy hour, the palaver having been sustained in the noblest manner, "so full of melancholy, with a flap afore his eye," he could then withdraw and pronounce in favor of the Emperor, England by that time having got its six thousand archers in readiness, and having raised the necessary funds for entering on the war on the right side.

Charles was at Bruges. Greedy of every instant that meant delay in his preparations, he begged Wolsey to leave Calais to come to him. It taxed Wolsey's dissimulation. He persuaded the French, however, that he could prevail on Charles in a private interview infinitely quicker than by long correspondence. The French agreed, and the arbiter was received at Bruges with every honor and deference.

Wolsey rapped his knuckles on the counter. His price was threefold: the papacy for himself; Mary to wed the Emperor; and all French pensions and annuities to be made good.

These terms he advanced, "sometimes with sharp words and sometimes in pleasant manner." England, as soon as its work of mediation had worn threadbare, would be ready to join the war to the extent of 10,000 horse and 30,000 foot.

The imperials debated every inch with Wolsey for a fortnight. Charles was just in his twenty-first year, and had been barely two years elected to the Holy Roman Empire. He was fresh from the Diet of Worms, where he had clashed with Luther. Wolsey was very favorably impressed by him. He admired especially the cool, deliberate manner in which he did business. That business was obliged to include the prosecution of heresy, Luther having been excommunicated and the Pope having accepted the ambling white hackney from Charles as his vassal in Naples. To please the Pope, Wolsey gladly agreed by treaty to pursue in Henry's dominions "all and each who seem to think badly on the Catholic faith."

The French were driven from Milan just as Wolsey was concluding his secret treaty against them, and going home with his ambidexterity not yet disclosed.

Henry was delighted with his able servant. "By God," he said, "my lord Cardinal hath sustained many charges in this his voyage," and he rewarded him with the rich abbey of St. Albans.

Only one difference had occurred between the King and the Cardinal, of any moment. It had seemed to Henry, fresh from getting rid of Buckingham, that the best way to begin hostilities against Francis would be to carry out a "secret devise" he was enormously proud of. This was for himself and the Emperor to make a joint surprise attack and thus provide "for the destruction of the French King's navy." This bit of strategy had somehow not commended itself to Wolsey. Henry yielded. Even without it, he saw the path clear to his "righteous inheritance."

LI

Pope Leo's right-hand man was his handsome cousin, Cardinal Giulio, an illegitimate Medici. Giulio had been running the military affairs of the papacy, but Leo's heart was deep in it, and when the news that the French had lost Milan was brought to him in the evening at his lovely villa, he flung open the windows to the fresh autumnal air and leaned out to respire the great dream of Lombardy in the hands of the Medicis.

It was a fatal moment; the chill he received clung to his gross body; he returned to the Vatican only to be suddenly congested in the middle of the night, gasping in strangulation. His fat cardinal-buffoon was the solitary creature near. In vain he lifted Leo. In vain he called, puffing in terror, begging the Pope to say a word, to repeat God's name after him.

Leo had died, leaving a deficit of nearly a million ducats at the Vatican, and in Germany the deficit of Luther.

This was the moment for Charles to square his account with Wolsey.

"Move the imperial troops now in Italy to Rome," urged Wolsey, and so control the conclave. But it was too sudden, too hurried. The election was a mad scramble. "The cardinals brawl and scold." "Devils in hell," one ambassador called the cardinals. Their hell was to decide on a Pope. No Medici, the elders decided, never the sinuous Giulio de' Medici. Wolsey's name came to light, and he received seven cursory votes, but the battle was always between Giulio and the anti-Medici. At last the name of a complete outsider, Adrian of Utrecht, was offered. He was distant and unknown, Charles's deputy in Spain, a "barbarian heavy with age, whose reputation for simplicity and holiness, however, cast a lunar rainbow on minds desperate with fatigue. He would please Charles and hold against Luther. They elected him.

It was a betrayal of every vested interest in Rome. Leo had sold offices to over two thousand revenue-seekers. The Vatican was honeycombed with indulgence and indulgences. So angry was the populace that the cardinals could not step a foot out of shelter.

Adrian Florentius, the new Pope, was a conscientious Dutchman, short, stout, and florid. He was no one's henchman. He had avoided delaying to meet Charles, and he arrived in Rome with a Flemish housebody, and a man-servant to whom he gave a ducat every evening for the next day's provender. To the Roman populace he was unintelligible, a bonze, a strange and somber pilgrim from some desolate and sunless hinterland, a graven priest at whose coming the doors of the Roman banks, and the doors of the Belvedere, seemed instinctively to have closed.

Adrian took one look at the Laocoön. "Heathen idols!"

But his homespun honesty was out of place. The cardinals balked him. The office-holders resisted him. He was called a miser because he refused to lavish Church money. He was derided as a plebeian because he listened to lower appointees. Alexander's debauchery, Julius's impetuousness, Leo's extravagance and double-dealing—anything seemed better than this dull honesty. The Italians hated Adrian, and they destroyed him. Within a year he was beaten. "When his Holiness arrived, he was stout: now he is thin, pale and his eyes are rheumy." He lasted less than two years.

LII

In the spring of 1522 Henry had several attacks of conscience. The first was personal and private. He consulted his confessor Longland about his relations with Catherine, who could no longer bear children. What was disclosed, under the seal of the confessional, could not as yet be known. Only Mary

Boleyn, perhaps, could have inferred the result, but it stayed private, so far as the great world was concerned.

Conscience was not reserved for private life. The English at Francis's court were soon hurrying from Paris, among them a gay black-eyed girl, Anne Boleyn, who had been three years at the French court and was now fifteen. And a formal declaration was made to Francis by the English ambassador: Henry "felt it in his conscience" that he must declare against the French.

"As I lose him once," retorted the voluble Francis with passion, "I make a vow that I will never win him again so long as there is breath in my body." He "would never again confide in any living prince."

Henry and Wolsey were untroubled by this outburst. Adrian's election had been forgiven; the court was scintillant with the most gorgeous visit it had yet arranged; Charles had arrived with two thousand retainers, coming to England with a fleet of a hundred and eighty ships.

The splendor did not impress every one. One laconic visitor declared that English cooking "was as bad as possible." He found his lodgings bad and dear. He thought the jousting "not very splendid." He discovered that the accommodations were wretched in small villages, to which some of the two thousand retainers were necessarily allotted, and that provisions cost too much. He spoke plainly of "the small bad horses they had bought in England," and he noted that "the embarkation of the troops was very badly managed."

Officially, however, all was pompous and glorious. The central figure was the young Emperor. Charles was a blond, extremely serious and suffering from adenoids, bad teeth and anemia. Only his blue eyes, vivid in that white mask, and his pinched aquiline nose, bespoke the intensity of his methodical and conscientious existence. He had dominions, it was boasted,

on which the sun never set: and his motto was "More Beyond."
To obey impulse, like the incalculable Maximilian, was the
last thing that this tired youth desired. To neglect his work for
sport, for wine, for love, for song, was impossible to his driven
nature. Yet, quiet as he was, his armature as invisible as it was
impenetrable, he had humility only before God. He was a stoic,
however, in whom the bay-leaf of humanism had been omitted
and the religious faith of Mad Juana, finely minced, had been
included. It was misleading that he had the moral envelope of
another emperor with Spanish blood, Marcus Aurelius, since
where Marcus Aurelius had really striven to form an adequate
moral alphabet for an emperor, this young man was too sagacious to employ any but the current alphabet.

He knelt to his aunt Catherine. She glowed, behind that clear
complexion of hers, to show him Mary, now six years of age,
who was to marry him. Charles's steady eye revealed no secret
as he greeted the child who was his intended. He had not himself invented the system by which diplomacy required a prince
to promise to marry his client's daughter as a sort of grace
before meat. But it was not in Charles's nature to break
abruptly with anything, even insincerity. So he lived up to his
aunt's foolish faith in him, and kept in the dark that other
niece, whose father was the King of Spice, whom Spanish sentiment favored, and who would bring him a dowry of a million.

Mary, he assented, would be his bride, and Mary's father
was happy with Charles. Somewhat more fleshly than at the
interview of 1520, the avuncular rôle brought out everything
large and gracious in Henry. He smiled over his nephew. He
liked Charles. They were kinsmen. And now they were heart-
felt allies in a war against the natural enemy.

But even when the French herald brought the news which
Henry and Charles received together, and even when the English herald (white with fear, said Louise, absolutely white with
fear) gave the news to the French King and his mother at

Lyons, the great war could not get into its stride for a year. It began with raids of the border type, a specialty of the Howards. Surrey landed with seven thousand men near Cherbourg and bombarded Morlaix; "the town was quickly sacked and burnt, and a rich booty carried to our navy." The booty was valued at 800,000 ducats. Boulogne impeded operations in the other direction, thus recommending itself for capture. The campaign had a nuisance value, and was abundant in loot, but it had no military value. The great push would come in 1523.

LIII

For a "great push" in a great war with a great goal there must be corresponding sacrifices. The figure, as Wolsey estimated it, was not stupendous; it would be 800,000 pounds. This, for a country of three million, would be about sixteen million pounds of modern money. To raise it in a hurry would entail hardship, but for this price England would certainly regain its foothold in France, perhaps by good luck obtain Normandy and Guienne, and in addition install an Englishman in the papacy. On paper, and within a hundred years or so of Agincourt, it was a brilliant prospect for conjunction with the Emperor, especially since Francis and his mother had become bitterly unpopular, were fighting tooth and nail with both parlement and treasury, and were, as England had the best reason to know, about to be confronted by one of those revolts which when a Buckingham even breathes its possibility costs him his head, but when a Bourbon decides on it entitles him to a bride from the Emperor and financial aid from Henry.

An immense difference existed at this period between French and English absolutism. The nobles of France and the lawyers of France could contest the road with their monarch. Even when Francis knew that his greatest noble was conspiring to rend the kingdom apart, and even when the proofs were complete and Bourbon had escaped to become the open lieutenant of the Emperor, the parlement refused to find true bills, refused to hurry the investigations, turned a deaf ear to Francis. Buckingham went from his Tudor garden to his Tudor grave within a month. Francis spent six months of futile bluster, saying, "I command you to get their confessions," "I insist that you torture them to make them speak," without budging the legal gentry, their powers of absorbing his protests equaling the power of their black robes to absorb light. St. Vallier, the old man who told how the Constable had won him and how he had tried to dissuade the Constable next morning from a terrible crime against France, how they had mingled tears until Bourbon remembered Francis's mother and her venom because he would not marry her—this St. Vallier was to be tortured but seemed too elderly to be tortured; was to be executed but only got as far as the scaffold; and owed his life, some said, to the pleas of his daughter, Diane de Poitiers, and others said to Francis's irresolution—but at any rate he died in his bed a decade later, somewhat arrested in his development as a conspirator but not headed off so summarily as Buckingham.

Wolsey imagined he could attack the Englishman's pocket in the same summary manner. The parliament of 1523 was called, and he planned to come down to it and tell it what to do.

Sir Thomas More was named speaker by the King. The author of "Utopia" was not a rebel; he was not a pacifist. He told the Commons that it was their duty to support the war and to agree to a tax of four shillings in the pound. But when Wolsey began to thunder, and said he would "rather have his tongue plucked out of his head with a pair of pincers" than move the King to be content with less, and wished to lay rude hands on the Commons as he had laid rude hands on the papal nuncio, threatening him with the rack, Thomas More then showed that he too, like the parlement of Paris, had manhood in him. And it was manhood without alloy. "It shall not in my mind be amiss," he said in his sweet way to his Commons, "to receive him in all his pomp, with his maces, his pillars, his poleaxes, his crosses, his hat, and his great seal too," but insisting on the privilege of the Commons when strangers are present, in a "marvelous obstinate silence."

This was an effective silence-strike. More went on his knees to the intruding Cardinal, and explained it. Wolsey retreated. And Henry, who studied nothing so much as the habit of public bodies from convocations to law-courts, marked that Wolsey's whip and Wolsey's spur were unpopular horsemanship.

A bullet-headed man with a lean, lipless mouth and a twinkling eye, made a good speech against the war. His name was Thomas Cromwell, a commoner. To invade France, he argued, was uneconomic. He quoted the old saying, "Who that intendeth France to win with Scotland let him begin." His speech was plain, practical and massive. It touched on war and peace, riches and poverty, "truth, falsehood, justice, equity." The light of two o'clock, clear and hard, beat down on the dusty velvet of Wolsey's war-policy. Cromwell good-humoredly showed its worn elbows and its seedy seams. He exposed it, though wholly without rancor—not so much rancor, at any rate, that Wolsey could not promptly take so able a critic into his employment.

France, however, had to be invaded, even for less than 800,000 pounds. Under the persuasion of his council, Henry was not to lead the army, and Wolsey gave up his own original plan of acting as general. Suffolk was given the command. Henry was convinced that the best way for the English to help the Emperor might be to make sure of Boulogne for themselves. So Wolsey might have agreed. But word arrived that Pope Adrian had expired. Margaret, Charles's aunt, soon prevailed on Wolsey to take an imperial view, sending the English army forward to capture Paris. Henry reluctantly agreed, insisting that his soldiers be allowed to compensate themselves by loot and brigandage, as otherwise they could not be disciplined. So it was arranged.

LIV

In spite of his successful diplomacy, Henry was not satisfied with his allies. They all wanted money from him. They wanted it at the moment when he was hardest pressed in England. And they did not live up to their obligations.

On paper the conquest of France was easy enough. Bourbon was to begin by acknowledging Henry "his supreme and sovereign lord making oath and fidelity as to the rightful inheritor of the said crown of France." Legality thus assured, the Duke was to escape to Burgundy where an army of German landzknechts was ready, whom he was to lead back into France. Charles, besides repaying the money that had been lent him and supplying the French pensions due to Wolsey and the rest, was to cross the Pyrenees at the head of his forces, while the English and the Flemish troops were to cross the Somme and converge on Paris. While France was thus to be invaded from three sides at once, Francis was not to be on hand. He was to have departed at the head of a huge army into Italy.

This plan of 1523 was too smooth. Francis started for Italy, but delayed out of suspicion of Bourbon, who was compelled to escape to the South. Charles was penniless. He could not repay Henry. He crossed the Pyrenees, but merely took a couple of towns. The French held Bayonne. The landzknechts crossed the Meuse but were driven back. A number of the Bourbon conspirators were arrested. And everything finally depended on Suffolk, who advanced on Paris without opposition.

LV

Meanwhile the Pope was dying. Wolsey who awaited this good news in London was hardly less avid for it than the Cardinals in Rome. As his Holiness neared his end, "many of the Cardinals committed the greatest cruelty ever heard of. When the Pope was dying they importuned and pressed him to confess how much money he had, and where it was hidden. They did not treat him like a Pope but like a private man who is on the rack. The Pope swore he had not one thousand ducats." The Spanish ambassador adds that he himself drove the Princes of the Church away, but as they retreated they stole papal tapestry, jewels, silver plate and vestments.

Such shamelessness was not surpassed by Wolsey. He told Henry how "unmeet" he was to so high and great dignity, but he planned the bribing of the Cardinals. "The young men," he told his agent, "for the most part being needy, will give good ears to fair offers." "Great dexterity is to be used." "You have ample authority to bind and promise on the King's behalf, as well gifts as promotions, as also large sums of money to as many and such as you will think convenient."

But bribery was not enough. The dominant voice in this election was Charles's.

Charles had seen at Bruges what sort of "impartial" arbiter Wolsey was, and he knew what sort of Pope he would make. He therefore played a double game. He sent Wolsey copies of the instructions he was dispatching to Rome, urging his election and virtually commanding it. But at the moment he ordered his messenger to depart for Rome, he told his authorities at Barcelona to abstract these orders. His own candidate, to whom he had been paying a pension, was Cardinal Giulio de' Medici. Giulio had been Pope Leo's adjutant, and he was credited with vast ability. It was he who proved to the late Pope that he had been treacherously deceived by his adviser, the pro-French Cardinal Soderini. He had even induced the honest old Dutchman to go in with the Emperor at the end. Adrian in his last months had even threatened Francis with excommunication, which Francis had parried rather brutally. The brandish of excommunication, it was known, had made the Duke of Urbino's hair stand actually on end. But Francis's scalp had not this contractile power. He was more troubled by excommunicating Bourbon from France than by being excommunicated from Rome.

The new papal election was essentially political. It began, as usual, with solemn ceremony. Bribery was to have no part. The thirty-nine cardinals were confined to their cells, knowing that if they did not come to a decision within four or five days, the proctors would reduce their diet to the choice of one dish, "all roast or all sodden," and if they continued too long without naming a Pope, they would find themselves prisoners in their cells, living on bread and wine.

Yet for over a month they could not agree. The mere rumor that Wolsey, another "barbarian," was being considered brought the sea of the populace raging around the Vatican; only reassuring words spoken by one of the conclave from a balcony saved the Cardinals and induced the growling mob to retire. Wolsey was too young, too remote, too unknown, to have any chance at the papacy. The papacy was the perquisite of the Italians.

As the deadlock frayed tempers and manners, Cardinal Colonna, "a man of hasty and very proud temper," and Giulio's bitter enemy, came to him and reproached him with being a dog in the manger.

"What will you give me if I support your candidate for a turn?" asked Giulio, who knew that Colonna would support an Italian cardinal, a mild imperialist of fine character.

The older man, spokesman for the eight "old" Cardinals, believing that he could count on all the French votes, promised, "I'll lend you the same number of votes that you lend me."

Giulio "gave him instantly a bond under his hand," promising to make him chancellor and to give him "his most sumptuous palace." He did so, aware that he could withhold four French votes. The mild imperialist was tried, and failed. And so angry was Colonna with the French for going back on him that he went to Giulio de' Medici. "*You* kept your promise," he said, "and now I'll give them a Pope they did not bargain for."

Thus, after a conclave of fifty days, Giulio de' Medici was elected, his illegitimacy being wiped out to suit the election rule. He called himself Clement VII, and he was about forty-five years of age.

When the news of his failure reached Wolsey, the English troops had passed Montdidier and had crossed the Oise. They were within reach of Paris.

LVI

Wolsey's defeat for the papacy saw one of those swerves in English policy for which Henry did not seem to be prepared. While he had actual reënforcements ready, the army that had advanced within thirty miles of Paris was speedily withdrawn, and it took a long time for Henry to be sufficiently mollified to seek Suffolk and the other commanders.

But Wolsey was at no loss to explain. Every one knew there had been "fervent frost, so that many a soldier died for cold." "The season of the year," he sent word to the Emperor, "was so frequent with extreme cold, and other sore weathers, that neither man nor beast could longer endure marching in the field; but died daily and nightly, on both parts, in great numbers for cold: and divers lost their fingers, hands and feet, being frozen dead upon their beds, and some daily cut off."

So the retreat was accounted for. But the imperialists regarded the Cardinal with mounting distrust. "A rascally beggar." A man of "very base nature." "His intentions are evil." And even neutrals recorded general suspicion. "This man," wrote Guicciardini, "though of a very low extraction and despicable blood, found means to gain such an ascendant over the Prince (Henry), as to make it evidently appear to every one that the King's orders, without approbation, were of no significancy; and, on the contrary, whatever orders he issued, even without the King's knowledge, were punctually executed."

The Italian, who was in the thick of affairs himself, understood that Wolsey was playing for peace at the beginning of 1524. "He ambitiously coveted and expected that the King his master would be constituted umpire of all differences. And, as he knew his authority in settling the articles of peace would have the greatest weight, he pleased himself with the thought of making his name glorious throughout the universe, and intended at the same time to establish his interest with the King of France, to whom he had secretly inclined."

While Wolsey could entertain peace for reasons of state, the intellectuals still demanded it for reasons of humanity. The Pope, however, and not Henry, was approached. This time it was not Colet, who was dead, nor Erasmus, who was at last in his home at Basle with his good books, good open fires and good Burgundy. He was too deep in controversy with Luther on the subject of free will, and too discouraged with violence everywhere, to recur to his strictures on the dynasts. Thomas More was equally handicapped; he was in office. But the voice of Ludovico Vives was raised, the Spanish-born humanist, whose plans for poor relief were showing such amazing social insight. Vives was in Louvain, where Erasmus had been living previously, and he wrote to the Pope his outspoken protest against the human waste of the European war:

"I wish," he said, with deep feeling for the people, "I wish all princes could pass some part of their lives in a private station, that they might know the wants of their subjects; and from suffering themselves, learn to pity those who suffer. But, educated amid regal pomp, they have little feeling for the calamities of others.

"They think it nothing that for a petty quarrel, or from vain ambition, fields, villages and towns should be laid waste, a population consumed and even nations subverted.

"Who can see without groans, or hear without tears, the crowds of the aged and of infants rendered homeless, and weeping about the churches: their property taken away by military violence, even of their friendly armies, and, what is still more intolerable, destroyed and burnt before their eyes."

Vives did not mention the plague, but already it was raging in Italy. Fifty thousand were to die of it in 1524 in Milan alone. The war was scourging Europe, and no outcome of it was in sight.

LVII

But the cause of European peace was not entirely forlorn so long as peace could profit any one statesman. By negotiating with Charles at Bruges, Wolsey had striven to make sure of the papacy for himself, and of a French key position for Henry. The Papal election had exposed the worthlessness of Charles's promises: it had deeply embittered Wolsey and headed him toward peace.

It was easy for him, with his great prestige, to present the war in a new light to Henry, to show him how little help he was getting from Flanders or from Bourbon, what great expenses he was incurring, and what selfishness the Emperor was capable of. No one was more ready to believe in other people's selfishness than Henry, and when the dream of conquering France was induced to fade in his mind, and the chance of compromising with the French was skillfully enlivened, war began to look less remunerative than a favorable peace. Wolsey was sanguine that the French were in such straits that they would concede an enclave, while he and Henry could at any time, as moral referees, find a reason for demanding that the Emperor stop fighting. It was not a bad position. War preparations on a grand scale had been postponed to 1525, and Wolsey planned to dwindle association with Charles unless victory became cheap.

His disappointment was not confined to non-conductivity.

When the imperial ambassador came to see him about the subsidies which Henry had promised, Wolsey gave him a broad-
side. "The Emperor is a liar," he said, "a liar, observing no
manner of faith or promise; the Lady Margaret is a bawd;
Ferdinand, the Emperor's brother, a child, and so governed;
and the Duke of Bourbon a traitor." This luxury of epithet
was not lost on the ambassador, and it was reported. But Wolsey cared nothing. He knew the Continental opinion that Pope
Leo had once expressed: "The King of England is not a powerful prince; the geographical position of the kingdom enables
him to be troublesome only to the King of France." This being
the dire truth, Wolsey did not propose to waste any courtesy
on a potentate who had failed him in the biggest scheme of
his life. He let the French understand that he was ready to
treat with them; and soon his confessor, Lark, was housing a
secret agent at Blackfriars, Louise of Savoy's maître d'hôtel.

This secret agent, a Genoese, arrived toward the end of June,
1524. Wolsey was meanwhile made aware that Charles had a
magnificent plan with Bourbon which promised startling success; Marseilles was to be besieged, and Charles counted on
England to make a diversion in the North. The capture of
Marseilles was to precede an advance on Lyons, when Bourbon
was to push on, and Henry to be crowned at Rheims. Wolsey
listened, but collectedly. The capture of Marseilles could only
mean an open path for Charles between Spain and Italy without any corresponding advantage to England. He received
every pledge that Bourbon was giving, but he did not propose
to rush money to him, or land 14,000 English except when he
saw fit. He was still an ally, but an ally sticking his finger in
the ground to smell where he was.

LVIII

The summer attack on Marseilles was really formidable.
Twenty years before, such artillery as Bourbon's would have

carried the day, but in this period new ways of attack had instructed new defense, and such works had been devised, such redoubts and bastions, such clearance of the approaches, whether gardens or houses, and such radical destruction of sheltering buildings in advance, that the citizens, braced on the crest of the amphitheater that is the noble site of their city, could count on making Bourbon pay for his shameless invasion of France. Every sort of women, young and old, had joined the men in digging the trenches. The finest churches had been leveled, and the famous dead at Marseilles had been disinterred, to be borne inside the city as a pious preliminary to its protection.

While the siege was beginning, deputies went to Francis to ask his help. He was in camp near Avignon. The rogue in him was just as alive as ever. His wife Claude dead only a few weeks, he had found time to try to ingratiate himself with the daughter of the mayor who received him; and his reputation was so terrible that she had destroyed her looks with acid. But this cavalier exigence of his did not make him neglect the Marseillais. He sent them encouragement and help, promising to arrive with his army in short order.

A bizarre comedy played itself before Marseilles. The dour Bourbon shared leadership with Pescara, a brilliant soldier of Spanish extraction, married to Vittoria Colonna, of whom it had been said by a well-informed Italian that there was not in Italy a man of greater malignity or less faith. Bourbon ran to his fellow-general when he heard the explosion of a shot from inside the city, which killed a priest saying mass in their midst. "What was that?" "That," said Pescara, "was the burgesses, no doubt, bringing you the keys of the city." When Bourbon, after eight hundred cannon shots, had made a jagged breach in the walls, he was ready to climb into the city. Pescara addressed his Spaniards. "The table is beautifully laid," he said. "If you want to sup to-day in Paradise, hurry up. If not, follow me to Italy, which has no one to defend it and is going to be invaded."

The Spanish, the Italians and the Germans declined in turn to step into Bourbon's breach. Unable to impose his will on allies to whom he was fatally committed, this proud and unfortunate man was forced to keep pace with Pescara in his retreat. They took to the Corniche by which they had come, covering up to forty miles a day. Francis, his great army at last prepared, pressed on their heels, and before they could do more than hurl themselves into Pavia, was himself in the plains of Lombardy, and once more with his hand on Milan.

LIX

The fiasco of Marseilles changed everything. Nothing could have been more confusing for Henry, for Wolsey, for Charles, or for the new Pope, than this utter failure of Bourbon to get his clutch on the gorge of Provence. The young Emperor was so sick he contracted the ague, a quartan ague. Henry and Wolsey behaved like dubious lawyers with a watching brief. Pope Clement, who had been so resourceful as Leo's lieutenant, found himself completely lost as Pope, the second in a tandem compelled to act as leader. He could not conceal his timidity, his dubiety, his flurry, his nerves. "The Pope," it was noted by the Spanish envoy, "is beyond all measure afraid of the French." He dreaded a catastrophe. He communicated his panic to the Venetians, who had gone in with Charles. He listened to the Viceroy of Naples, who reported that Charles had no money. In December, when the French King had left plague-stricken Milan and was planted before Pavia with his huge army, bottling up the imperial forces, the best that Clement could think of doing was to make secret peace with Francis, uniting the Venetians with him, hiding his terror of the consequences with Charles, and holding his head. Wolsey had reason to rejoice.

This condition of intense strain and panic, high temper and wild rumor, was confined to no particular camp. Francis had managed to leave his own country only by giving his mother the slip; "he had passed the mountains in the hope to win all with a visage"—that is, at a stroke. He set about diverting the flooded river that protected Pavia on one side, and his impatience to strike home, when this proved impossible, cost him thousands of lives. The word that Charles was "very feeble and nothing apt for the war" carried surmise to the farthest point in England; but as it seemed evident that Francis had the upper hand, and as news crept out from Pavia, where Pescara and de Leyva were in control, that "provisions begin to be scarce and the soldiers dispute among themselves whether horse flesh or the meat of the beasts of burden which they brought from Provence is the better food," Wolsey felt no hesitation in congratulating Henry on his own policy of playing it both ways. Should the Emperor win, he said to Henry, we can point to our manifold services; and should Francis win, we have been friendly to him as well. It was meant to convey to Henry that he could have a happy Christmas. But it claimed much.

Charles, however, was not without consoling news. The Abbot of Najero wrote full of resounding confidence from Italy: "His captains in Italy are confident that the King of France will lose his credit and his army, and finally either be killed or made prisoner, as has been predicted to him by astrologers and prophets." "All, from the highest officer to the lowest soldier, are sure of victory." The Abbot would hear of nothing else. He communicated his faith to Pace, who sent the word home to England.

Francis had over thirty thousand troops to confront Bourbon's army hastening to the relief of Pavia. He himself had superior forces, was full of plans, and full of gayety. In the park where he was encamped, outside the walls, it was so cold that the highest officers came into his kitchen to warm themselves; and a chicken cost nearly one hundred dollars. But Francis was sanguine. He had boasted that he would take Pavia or die, and he intended to keep his word. His older generals pointed out the risk to him; young Bonnivet laughed at them, and the King laughed with Bonnivet. He was at once madly occupied with his projects for the attack and busy with his diversions. He danced and entertained, marveled at the morbidezza of the Italian women, and caught glimpses of glorious blue in the bisque winter sky.

Charles wrote forebodingly to the Pope. He was a lover of peace, he said. He lived at peace with Francis, and had he continued to do so he would have obtained great advantages for himself; but Pope Leo had persuaded him to make war on Francis, and as Clement had been at the head of affairs of state during the reign of Pope Leo, it was he who was personally responsible. Yet though he preferred peace to vengeance, he would prove a hard adversary. He was not feeble. His illness did not prevent him from mounting very unruly horses. Those who did not stand by him would repent their perfidy. "They will weep one day." And the severest punishment is reserved for the Venetians.

"I shall go into Italy," he menaced later, "taking my revenge on those who have wronged me, especially on that poltroon the Pope. I will carry out my designs, even if it costs me my crown and my life."

So hung the balance as Bourbon hurried to the rescue of Pavia, and Francis carried on the siege, with the Pope facing both ways, and Charles himself in distant Spain, listening to the feverish excuses of Clement and pushing himself, anemic and melancholic, to thoughts of universal dominion.

Wolsey, meanwhile, had forced the French negotiations so hard that the imperial ambassador in London was furious and scornful. His letters to Charles did not spare Wolsey's character; but the Cardinal knew their tenor, had his dispatches seized by the night watch as by accident, opened them, summoned the ambassador before the privy council, and denounced him in outrageous terms.

The antagonism he drew out by this lawless act he exposed to Henry as malignance, and he induced Henry to promise to meet the French envoys openly on March ninth.

LX

The ninth of March, at an early hour in the morning, Henry was fast asleep. A messenger arrived at Windsor, straight from the Lady Margaret.

"I must talk to the King without delay," he declared. "I bring him news from beyond the mountains that will rejoice his heart."

He was a man of authority and his word carried weight. The King was waked up. He knew who the messenger was by name, flung on his night robe, and told them to bring the post to him.

The messenger was brought to his room, handed Henry his dispatches and saluted him.

The King nodded. "What are my good friends doing over the mountains?" he asked.

"Sire, if you read these letters you will see clearly in what a state they are."

The King opened his letters, began to read them, and as he read them began to cry for joy.

"My God," he said, falling on his knees, "I thank you. You have sent me this news that I badly needed. You know and understand all."

He stumbled to his feet. "My friend," he cried to the dispatch-rider, "you're like the Angel Gabriel, who announced the coming of Jesus Christ. This news tells me what I ought to answer to the French on what they are asking me, which has weighed on me terribly; and the news is such that I won't have to make any answer to them."

Henry called to his squires. "Wine for the post!" He drank to his health. "And did you see the King of France in the hands of the Viceroy of Naples, as this letter testifies?" asked Henry with open eyes.

"I helped to disarm him," he admitted. "He was on the ground. His horse was on top of him. The men who surrounded him were going to kill him, when one of Bourbon's men recognized him, and ran for the Viceroy. The Viceroy ran up, and kissed his hand. The King of France handed the Viceroy his sword, and the Viceroy gave his own sword to the prisoner. He was wounded, in the cheek and in the hand, but only slightly. As he lay on the ground, everything that could be taken from him was taken by his captors, every plume of his helmet."

"How did you leave the army?"

The messenger told him. Ten thousand French slain. Only fifteen hundred imperialists slain. Bonnivet dead and many nobles with him; the rest of the French nobility captured, except Alençon.

"And Richard de la Pole?" asked Henry.

"The White Rose is dead in battle."

"Did you see him dead?"

"I saw him dead, with the others."

"God have mercy on his soul! All the enemies of England are gone. Give him more wine. Entertain him well."

LXI

Francis's downfall was the hard sequel to his audacity: it thrilled Henry to the marrow. He and Catherine had followed the campaign with intense eagerness. They had scoffed together at Francis slipping away from his mother, and Thomas More had made jokes to Henry about it. Catherine had been bitter over the retreat from Marseilles, which was ignominious, and she told Henry how glad she was the Spaniards had at last "done something" during the period of pin-pricks before Pavia. But the defeat itself was on the grand scale: it eliminated the most galling of rivals. And for the Queen it was a crowning Spanish triumph.

She needed this fillip. She was now forty years of age, indifferent in health, and receding into the background, becoming a mere official fixture in her young husband's life. He was restless and manifestly under the whip of his instincts. Catherine knew too well that her handsome maids in waiting found disturbing favor in his eyes. She sat knitting, counting her stitches, watching him, yet seeing no more than it paid her to see. Her real compensation was Princess Mary, whose welfare and education engrossed her and who was as devoted and dutiful a child as any conscientious mother could wish. Ludovico Vives had come to Oxford, and he had continued the lessons in Latin that Catherine herself had initiated. Mary, besides, had some of her father's extraordinary talent for music. Their interest in the child, at any rate, the parents had in common. But they also had Charles in common; he was engaged to marry his cousin Mary. After many anxieties, many rebuffs and humiliations, Catherine could see the road opening to this marriage. It was the proudest political future her Spanish heart could desire.

Henry was still radiant when the Flemish envoys came to see him on the heels of the good news. "Now is the time to devise for the Emperor to have his, and for me to have mine," Henry told them. "Not an hour is to be lost." He was full of plans. He would pack the French negotiators home. As early as May he would take a great army into France in person. He ordered public rejoicing throughout the country. "In the city of London were made great fires and triumph. The Mayor and aldermen rode about the city with trumpets. Much wine was laid in divers places in the city that every man might drink. On Tower Hill the ambassadors of Rome, Flanders and Venice had a great banquet in a goodly tent, and as they returned home all the streets were full of harnessed men and cressets attending on the constables." On Sunday Wolsey celebrated high mass at St. Paul's and Henry gave another banquet at the Bridewell, more wine tuns being opened in the streets.

The project of carving up the fallen enemy, however, ran at once into tedious and prosaic detail. Many of the council saw danger in Charles's predominance. Henry's proposal to help himself to Normandy, Guienne, Gascony and Anjou was received in damp diplomatic silence. The Flemish and the Spanish did not hail him as King of France, and with his sharpening political tact, he soon perceived that this line of action would prove costly. Wolsey, on the other hand, was ready to find money for the great spring push. He went at it with steam and bluster. He did not dare assemble parliament but he could render up a third of his own revenues and ask for general contributions half the size of his own under the name of an "amicable grant."

The English people had no wish to spare France, but in 1523 they had yielded their fleece and they were close-shorn after these four years of broken trade. No grant, amicable or hostile, could possibly be extracted from them. All that Cromwell had said in the last parliament was proving true. The commissioners found no response to their pressure. Sir Thomas Boleyn was man-handled in Kent. The rich promised to do their best, but the humbler clergy and the common people were obdurate and inconvincible.

"Sirs," Commissioner Wolsey berated the citizens of London, "resist not and ruffle not in this case, for it may fortune to cost some their heads."

The Mayor of London could not answer for his citizens. "If I enter into any grant," he said wryly, "it may fortune me to cost me my life."

Wolsey was incredulous. "Your life! that is a marvelous word. For your will towards the King will the citizens put you in jeopardy of your life?"

The citizens in general gave signs of it. They gathered in the stricken weaving towns particularly, four thousand of them coming together in one district, armed for fight. The new Duke of Norfolk tried his hand at getting an "amicable grant" from them. "Small, spare of stature, hair black, astute, prudent, liberal, affable, associates with everybody," Thomas Howard had much experience of rough work in France and in Scotland. It was this consummate emergency man who rode out to meet the workers that were ready to fight the King's commission, and he demanded their captain.

One John Green, a man of his own years, spoke out in naked words. "My lord, since you ask who is our captain, forsooth his name is Poverty for he and his cousin Necessity have brought us to this doing."

It was the truth, and Green's arrest could not change it. The lesson of the Comuneros in Spain was not lost, nor the rumors of the wild Anabaptists from Germany. Henry could well understand popular rumblings and he adroitly changed his tone. "The King openly declared that his mind was never to ask anything of his commons which might sound to his dishonor or to the breach of his laws. He was sore moved that his subjects were thus stirred, and said, 'I will no more of this trouble; let letters be sent to all shires that this matter may no more be spoken of. I will pardon all that have denied the demand.' "

Wolsey concurred. England, he told his flock, must now treat with France. They heard him bitterly. The people had never implicated their King, but they viewed their base-born fellow-subject with dark resentment. "All people cursed the Cardinal, as subverter of the laws and liberty of England." "Now here is an end of this commission, but not an end of inward grudge and hatred that the commons bear to the Cardinal."

LXII

More than the amicable grant had collapsed for Wolsey. The pale young Emperor had taken the news of Pavia undemonstratively, though the Abbot of Najera had blown a fanfare: "Your Majesty is from this day in a position to prescribe laws to Christian and Turk according to your pleasure." The last thing, in fact, that Charles was consulting was his pleasure. He was of a serious temperament, north light in his methodic brain, and he accepted Pavia as a merciful and astounding dispensation of Providence. If he was Cæsar, "lord of the world," his sense of heavy and almost exclusive responsibility was guiding him. He was Atlas, the Quaker brother of Prometheus. "He most sincerely thought the subjection of the whole of Christendom served 'as well the interests of the house of Austria as the interests of God and his church.' "

The orchestra he had been conducting had been desperately unruly, but Pavia had lightened matters up. He soberly fell on his knees and thanked God. But if he did not indulge his temper, if he did not rage and splutter when he heard that Wolsey had called him a liar and hectored his ambassador, he still had a memory for injury like the Pope's mule. With Francis his prisoner, the insubordinations that had been inflicted on him by the Pope, by Venice, by Wolsey, by the Moors of Valencia, as well as by Francis, were brought to the surface, fresh and chilly from the depths of his pride. Charles was not vindictive. He did not use politics to avenge these injuries. But he energetically used these injuries to help his politics.

It was, indeed, at his suggestion that Wolsey, with rough humor, had outraged the Venetians by interning their galleys and taking their guns in order to ply them to the war. This Charles did not care to remember. He did not remember that he had been perpetually in arrears with England and that he had never fulfilled a single pledge to Wolsey regarding the papacy. Wolsey had been "mon bon ami" up to Pavia. Now he became an outsider. Charles did not propose to share the benefits of Pavia with the man who had held back during 1524—

the man whom Gattinara described as "the most rascally beggar in the world and the most devoted to his master's interests." Charles's hauteur combined Germanic phlegm with Spanish obduracy. He did not quarrel with England, but within three months he reduced the temperature of the alliance below the point where it could, except between snakes, be effectively amorous.

LXIII

For a European of Wolsey's sweeping imagination, at once bold and dramatic, this contemptuousness was impossible. The reproval of Charles, as he saw it in his speculative mind, was natural and inevitable. Charles no longer needed England: so England might as well make the best of it, look to the future, and balance the account with France.

And the French plight, as Wolsey had foreseen with the keenest divination in England, was nothing so tragic as appeared. The young cock had been trussed, but there emerged his mother, "ma mère," as Wolsey addressed her, a "femme de vertu," indomitable and unscathed. Louise of Savoy loved her gallant son, but she herself was as shrewd as a concierge. She heard great rumors of sixty thousand English to invade Picardy, but she did not flinch: she knew the state of European finances; she knew that the Emperor could not pay the victors of Pavia; the Flemish were cleaned out; Wolsey reclaimed in vain the 500,000 crowns from Charles; and the price of peace had been under discussion between herself and the Cardinal for six months. Robertet, the spider of French statecraft, old, rich, indefatigable, was noiseless at her side. Her secret agents were busy. Attrition, not contrition, was bound to bring the dynasts to their senses; she had to rally her country in this black hour, and she was steady, deft and cool.

In Italy, besides, the Emperor had his difficulties. The French had been hated, especially for their tyranny in Milan. They were held to be "by nature arrogant and self-conceited," politically underhanded, and their King "by nature as much deficient in deeds as he is redundant in words." But Charles suddenly appeared far more formidable. "To be left a prey to the Spaniards, who for their cruelty are most hated of all nations," shot fear into the Italians. The Pope especially was in terror. He swerved and trembled like a needle too near heavy metals. "The Emperor, whom he now feareth above all earthly things," was sending minatory letters. By June Clement was in panic. "His Holiness is of late fallen into such fear and so discouraged and incowarded that the world marveleth thereat."

He first thought to unite Italy. The instinct to expel a foreign body was powerful. For a moment, even dashing Pescara, in rage with Charles's coldness, had listened to the appeal for an Italian "Prince." But the plot passed like an unholy breath through Pescara's soul to be revealed by him, in fatal temerity, to Charles. He was dead in a few months, from drinking water, the Italians innocently said.

Charles had one human bond with England that he could not repudiate and remain punctilious. This was his engagement to Mary. But he was resourceful. His Cortés at Toledo had been told to request him to wed Isabella of Portugal. He had previously reminded Henry of his sacred pledge to Princess Mary. He asked for her immediately, at the age of nine, and with the exorbitant sum of 600,000 ducats. The refusal of this outrageous request left him free to marry the Portuguese, who was to bring him a million ducats with which to pay his soldiers and hold Italy.

Charles's marriage with Isabella required a papal dispensation, which Clement did not dare delay or refuse. It was evidently what Charles desired, and in a few months he married Isabella: it ended every pretense of real friendship with England.

LXIV

Wolsey had taught his master something in politics in ten years. He was, of course, a priest. He had the great Roman inherit- ance. In Milan—whose cathedral, half-German and half-French by construction, is the symbol of jealous and emulative influ- ences—he saw "the key and gate of Italy," and in Italy he saw the destiny of Europe. "Italy," he said to his master, "is the true seat of Government, to the scepter of which the whole world will be subjected." So he had striven for English leverage there, even by bidding for the papacy and combating any absolute control. Even when he himself was refraining from helping Charles by a diversion in the North, he was vehemently abusing Clement for making peace with the French. Wolsey knew too well that any overwhelming victory would nullify the impor- tance of England, and destroy its pretensions to be the honest broker. He did not veil from himself or from Henry the auda- city of his own policy or the humble fact that "this your realm is in an angle of the world." But when his audacious policy was brought to nothing by a battle which eliminated the broker, he still could lead his master to go against his heady prejudices. He could now make him see that France must counter the Emperor and England add its weight to France as Pavia had decided. It was not an easy or natural conclusion for Henry, but the failure of the "amicable grant" helped him to see it. And Wolsey could show Charles in such a bad light, especially when Mary had been rejected, that Henry's next step was secure. To head him in the right direction—that was Wolsey's art. To head him, and to head him off.

The first public sign that a new policy had been born came in the middle of June, 1525. Henry brought his six-year-old boy to court, and amid the most pompous and impressive ceremony made him Duke of Richmond, the title his own father had borne. It was a signal honor, crushing Catherine's pride and

darkening Mary's prospects at home. The King treated the
child as his male heir, and began discussing alliances for him.

The bearing of this act on Catherine did not immediately
become apparent. Henry was acting with far greater astuteness
and far deeper intention than when he had flung himself
against her father a decade before. But he was not overlooking
the least fraction of the prestige of which Charles had cheated
him. He had begun life with a Spanish policy. He had be-
friended and helped with money and harbored and entertained
and cultivated this young man who now extinguished his generosity, like sand blown into a living field. There was no explosion of feeling in 1525, as there had been when divorce was
bruited in 1514. But Henry had been hurt by Catherine's
nephew. Every commitment he had made suddenly became
like a grain in a powder-train. What catastrophe could he plant
at the end of it? Once Henry was primed, he had no mean gift
for reprisal. The peace with France, which Wolsey had foreshadowed, was concluded in August. France staunchly refused
to concede Boulogne, but it pooled all the old and new obligations into a promise to pay two million crowns. Wolsey himself
was given 100,000—about two million dollars of modern money.
It was an enormous donation, and a little while after he thought
it well to turn over to Henry the lease of his palace at Hampton
Court.

But these harmonious dealings with France, at last made
public, included subtler and finer projects that could not be
divulged. The doctors had told Henry that Catherine could have
no more children, and Wolsey had never favored Catherine or
Catherine's conservative friends. Francis's sister Marguerite had
become a widow. Whether Wolsey had been talking with
Henry, or had imbibed the notion from Jean Joachim, Louise's
Genoese agent, whom he had close by him for months, or
whether the bright idea had come into his own head, would be
impossible to say, but in the very beginning of 1526, when

Francis was still a prisoner and when Marguerite was fresh from visiting him, old Robertet charged Warty and Jean Joachim to make overtures to Wolsey on the marriage of Marguerite to Henry himself, "in case he was going to have his marriage with Catherine annulled."

The overtures must have come from Francis himself. They were made to Wolsey at the end of January, 1526. He answered hesitatingly. To annul the marriage with Catherine would be a political decision of the first order, involving Charles and the Pope. Wolsey raised the question of having this marriage and the marriage of Mary to the Duke of Orleans, which had been submitted at the same time, considered with that of a closer alliance, and having them made conditions one of the other. The French diplomats had no power to agree. They proposed to ask France for further instructions.

LXV

At the Alhambra Catherine's fate had first been decided by her parents. She was almost an infant when her bridegroom had been chosen for her, the Spanish ambassadors inspecting the baby Arthur, first dressed, then naked, then asleep. The motto of the transaction had been put in bald words by a bald diplomat: "Princes do not marry for love; they take wives only to beget children." Out of human instinct and decency the boy Arthur declared that he had never felt so much joy in his life as when he beheld the sweet face of his bride. That was at the beginning of the century. Now Catherine's fate was once more being weighed in political scales in the same city of Madrid. Why not annul her marriage? Why not break this bond with the Emperor and Spain? Her sweet face was already heavy and worn. She had had ten years of miscarriages. But she had failed in her mission. "Princes do not marry for love; they take wives only to beget children."

Francis was offering his sister over the counter to Henry. He was himself ready to marry Charles's sister for reasons of state. Eleanor was not beautiful. "Her thinness was so excessive that doubts were raised as to whether she was at all fit to be married." But she had served very well already for one political marriage, in Portugal, and Francis was ready to take her on, though she had been earmarked for his Duke of Bourbon.

Charles had some tenderness for Eleanor. When she was a young girl, he had deprived her of her lover, as Henry had deprived Mary of Suffolk. Now he was older and more lenient; he gave her her choice, a Duke or a King. She chose the King. He compensated Bourbon with Milan. The bargain concluded, Charles drove over his prisoner to show him his new wife, the emaciated Eleanor. She danced for Francis, who pronounced himself charmed.

The captivity in Madrid, however, had impaired Francis's notions of felicity and charm. From Marignano to Pavia, he had undertaken to behave as a gentleman. This he had tried to combine with his pursuit of the prizes for which the dynasts were competing, a pursuit which was no less passionate because incompetent. Had he won Pavia, he might have covered his insouciance with glory, but now, in defeat, the tinsel had scaled off. It was no game that a gentleman could play, and Francis had done his best to die.

He had spent a bitter year. He had been locked up in a fat-walled room. There he had sickened. There he had changed clothes with the Negro coal-boy and tried to escape in smudge. There he had divided the sacred wafer with Marguerite on the eve of death, and had been brought back to life by her tenderness. There he had sworn on the true cross, the Bible and his honor to give his royal jailer everything he implacably insisted on—his ancestral duchy of Burgundy, Navarre, Naples, Milan, Genoa, and innumerable oddments, to give up Charles as his "vassal" in Flanders, to take Eleanor as his spouse, and to send his two small boys to take their turn as hostages in the bleak, drab, dingy cell in Spain. This was the "concordia" of Madrid. "I will call myself a coward and a scoundrel if I do not keep my oath," said Francis. Before he signed he had taken his fellow-countrymen to witness what he regarded the treaty as in no manner binding.

"Lâche et méchant," Charles commented.

"Lâche et méchant," Francis reiterated.

The acrid comedy was played to the end. On a barge in the Bidassoa, which was anchored exactly in the middle, the exchange of Francis and his sons was made with a symmetry that persuaded itself it was justice. Claude's children had time to kiss their father's hand. They then blinked into Spain from which their royal sire was bounding away.

"I will take off the mask," he declared once he had galloped to Bayonne, to greet the English envoys. The English were his salvation, his only hope. "Henry is my father," he announced, "I am undyingly grateful to him. The Cardinal is my grandfather!" And his grandfather Wolsey wholeheartedly committed himself to the canonical opinion that Francis was not obliged to observe the treaty of Madrid in any way. He had taken the oath under compulsion and under duress.

Francis's gratitude for Henry's restraint while he was in prison was, in effect, the presage of his new alliance with England. Outside the Turk, for whose friendship he had made a bid, it was an alliance on which his future depended. And Henry accepted and cherished it. He had turned his face from Charles.

Meanwhile the idea of annulling his marriage had entered into Henry's mind. It was, as yet, an infertile idea, because Marguerite d'Angoulême did not choose to oust a wife of such long standing. Her marriage to Navarre was settled. But Henry fed on the prospect. Any political marriage could be annulled.

He had forgotten that only Pope Clement could annul marriages and that his Holiness was discouraged and "incowarded" and now feareth the Emperor "above all earthly things."

BOOK THREE

Anne Boleyn

"*I am as brown as brown can be,*
My eyes as black as a sloe;
I am as brisk as a nightingale,
And as wild as any doe."

THE BROWN GIRL

I

THE executioner's ax is an unsociable tool. The shedding of
Buckingham's blood, legal and orderly as it was, was not an
incident discussed at royal banquets, but it had sent cold
shivers down noble spines. In the inner hearts of the Norfolks,
the Shrewsburys, the Poles, the Exeters, the Northumberlands,
there was always a deep respect for Catherine and her right
Catholic and royal line, but these people believed themselves
to be of better blood than the Tudors. The feeling that the
king was rather an outsider, which is habitual among nobles
and which underlay Buckingham's offense, was now met by a
sudden, formidable, pitiless retort, and however Henry might
laugh and chaff in future, a ghost would haunt the feast, to
warn and to remind.

Henry felt this himself. Until the Field of the Cloth of
Gold, he and Catherine stood close enough to the older nobles.
After the execution, dastardly as it could not help seeming, the

humor of the court changed involuntarily. He found himself thrown less with his queen and her sober intimates, and more with the younger group who were far from sharing the grave, feudal tradition.

This junior group centered in the Boleyns. Though Lady Boleyn was Thomas Howard's sister, Surrey (as he still was) always held off from them, and had the gruff soldier's view of the mincing courtier's ways. Surrey's wife, moreover, was Buckingham's daughter, a Catholic grandee, one of Catherine's trusted friends. The actual Boleyn set was younger, brighter, bolder, and in a sense cheaper. There had been many Howard sisters, who meant little to their foul-mouthed brother, and they had married a series of knights, so that the Bryans and the Wyatts and the Boleyns and the Ap Rices were all cousins. The break in the manners of the gloomy baronial hall showed in this gay and talented crowd. Henry, who liked to unbutton, christened one-eyed Francis Bryan "the vicar of hell," and this Francis Bryan and Thomas Wyatt and George Boleyn had all been to Italy and France and come back with a zest, to disport themselves not as heavy soldiers and councilors but as courtiers, as chevaliers, as poets. It was a transition from the religiosity of the older families, and, around the greensward of the court a first warble of the bird-song of the Elizabethan renaissance. These were not, perhaps, the nightingales, but they were the starlings; they had listened to the Italian sonnet and the French lyric, and, in this mild English February, they were trying to capture the refrain.

If there was anywhere that Henry was at home, it was not with his castellated wife but in the easy bosom of this group. They admired him. They owed their advancement to him. They lived in his smiles. They lapped him in those little wavelets of praise which make such an exquisite music to mortal man. But in this lake of approval, which buoyed Henry, there was a special island, private and guarded, where he was partic-

ularly at home. By making Thomas Boleyn the treasurer of the
household and employing his son George as an envoy and giving a small place at court to William Carey, who was married
to a daughter, and having the other daughter as maid in waiting and her mother as lady in waiting, the enlacements were
so multiplied between Henry and the family that it was perfectly natural, so far as the gaping world was concerned, to
keep the elder daughter, Mary Boleyn, near him, and to pay
many visits to the treasurer at Hever. When Mary was about
to have a child, which caused a smile, it was supposed that
Henry would relax his attentions to the Boleyns. On the contrary, he kept on seeking the pleasant seclusion of the castle in
Kent, where he could count on the obsequious cordiality of the
father and the silent favor of the mother. But the attraction
could not be Mary. And the only other attraction was Anne.

II

Why the court should have smiled at these intimacies requires
a retrospect to account for the Boleyns.

The family was noble without being exactly ivy-clad or moss-
grown in the nobility. It was held against Thomas Boleyn that
his grandfather had earned his living in wool and silk. This
gentleman, who then spelled himself Bullen, had made his
fortune as a mercer, becoming Lord Mayor of London, and
his station in life compared not unfavorably to that of his contemporary, Henry's Welsh ancestor, who was consoling Henry
IV's French widow, and founding the Tudor family. The rising Bullens were not content to be mercantile. The Lord Mayor
annexed a daughter of Lord Hoo and Hastings; and their son,
a wealthy man, married an Irish girl, Margaret Butler, daughter of the Earl of Ormond.

By these two lustrations of the mercer's blood, Thomas
Boleyn, Anne's father, could almost have been reckoned an

aristocrat, yet the stain of a gainful occupation is visited on the children of the ennobled, even unto the third and fourth generations.

Thomas Boleyn, however, being a serious and dutiful man, took up the climb. He looked higher than a Hoo or a Butler, and he was favored by fortune. The Duke of Norfolk backed the wrong horse when Richard III and Henry VII raced for the throne, and he was lucky not to lose his head as well as his fortune and his dukedom. He was, notwithstanding, a great breeder, and he begot many children. When Sir Thomas Boleyn came along, with four family places in full view (Blickling in Norfolk, Hever in Kent, a place in London and a Hoo mansion in Middlesex), his gilt-edged stock was a fair exchange for a marked-down Howard. They married and bred, and of their children three came to maturity, Mary, George and Anne Boleyn.

Before passing to the children, the father and mother should be regarded. Thomas Boleyn and Elizabeth Howard look at us silently and enigmatically across four hundred years. Thomas's picture was drawn by Holbein after he had become Earl of Wiltshire and Ormond. Holbein, one of the most veracious of historians, shows us a man still fresh and upstanding, dressed and barbered so beautifully as to proclaim the ambassador-earl. It is a cold face. The eyes, a little weary, have a direct but stony expression. They look toward a master. Under a mustache that has been much stroked and silkened, the mouth is that of a weakish and even meanish man. A massive nose shows that this creature proposes to survive, but his low brow suggests that the survival will be prudent rather than brilliant. And yet it is not a bad face. The man is not sympathetic, but he is dapper and stylish; he is limited but he is reasonable. Such men are as necessary to diplomacy as doorknobs are to doors. They must be suave, smooth, hard and solid. They must fit the palm of their master. A soul in such a man would be needed if he had to mold policies, but for one who is essentially a subaltern it would be incongruous.

His wife is a mystery. Elizabeth Howard cannot be depicted with any certainty, at least on the basis of the facts known. She cannot have been much older than the King. She was to die the same year as her husband, 1539, soon after her boy and girl were executed. This event did not unseal her lips, so far as we know. She is mute, and in some way tragic. She is even more tragic because of the rumor that she looked kindly on Henry when he was Prince of Wales. It is not impossible that as a young matron she appealed to Henry at seventeen. Thomas Boleyn, at any rate, was one of Henry's first appointees. He was a squire of the body from the beginning.

The three children, in whose veins mingled the blood of Boleyn and Howard, were born at dates not yet certain or verifiable. One may assume 1503 for Mary, 1505 for George and 1507 for Anne Boleyn.

True to the hard custom of the sixteenth century, Thomas and Elizabeth Boleyn did not rear their children at home. Had Boleyn been a mere squire, he would have placed Mary and Anne in the home of another squire or perhaps in that of a nobleman, to "learn" them manners and accomplishments. But, being a nobleman, Boleyn aimed higher. It chanced that in 1512 he was sent on a mission to the kindly Margaret of Austria, whose palace at Brussels was rich in decoration and treasure, and he was permitted to dispatch Mary as a little maid to Margaret, to be tucked under her own wing. This was the beginning of the child's career outside the home. She was only aged nine!

But a finer opening came within two years, on which Boleyn seized with shameless eagerness. He secured his elder daughter as one of the group of girls who were to accompany Mary Tudor to the dazzling French court. So he sent to Brussels at once, blurting his joy to Margaret of Austria as if she ought to be glad of this French marriage that was a direct insult to herself and her father, and yet being at once allowed to reclaim his child to place her in the princess's train. The little girl's immaturity was in her favor. When Louis swept away the cluster of Englishwomen who disputed his privacy, Mary Boleyn was so young that she was allowed to remain. Within a hundred days, Louis expired, but this did not alter Thomas Boleyn's wish to have his child at the French court. The new queen, little Claude, was only seventeen, and she accepted *la petite Boullain*. It was not a position of great intimacy, since Queen Claude gathered around her about three hundred girls, but as the French court was the most elegant and polished that then existed outside Italy, and had already the understanding of conversation and polite intercourse, which ameliorates the human barbarian and mellows the religion of power, Thomas Boleyn was keenly alive to its advantages as a finishing school.

Himself ambassador to Francis after the new friendliness of 1517, he asked permission to bring his younger daughter Anne as well, when she was coming on eleven or so, and he even assured Anne by letter that she would know the queen and that the queen would talk to her.

Anne, in a letter written in a rag-doll French, acknowledged this glorious prospect with bated breath.

Boleyn's two damsels, then, lived at the French court when it was at its most scintillating. They were sixteen and twelve when their cousin Francis Bryan and his compatriots were roystering with the King through the streets of Paris in disguise, throwing trash at the citizens in the rôle of gay, roving blades.

In a fine and flourishing world like this, full of thrilling young men, swift changes from place to place, the outpouring of national wealth in a flashing stream, a continuous parade and excitement, with the glamour of Marignano cast over everything, the education of these sisters went along lines not at all prescribed in the books of etiquette. Mary Boleyn was four years the elder. She was a light-hearted and easy-spirited girl, the sort of being who is soon in intimacy with men, knows the morose valleys between the heights of their ardor and the heights of their disdain, and is aware that she must inveigle or humor the beast, or be beaten. She had not much iron in her nature. In the long letter to Cromwell that reveals her character so well, there is liquidity, an April-like glisten and quiver. But it is without calculation. She was one of those ingratiating yet simple women to whom it would never be of great importance to say no, who are pliant and sweet, who cling like ivy and are as easily detached.

With the dry realism of the French mind, this girl who yielded to the happy moment came to be classified as a "ribald." Francis recalled her in later years as a "hackney," or as his "mule." It was an era of gentlemen who kissed and told. Mary Boleyn's reputation was gone before she was seventeen, and she was all the more reproached because she had not collected on her investment.

Her willingness to be loved was a direct warning to the younger and far more intelligent sister. No one could have better shown Anne the pitfalls of court life, or seemed more like the Idle Apprentice.

Mary went home in 1520, with the English contingent from the Field of the Cloth of Gold. She was then a wisp of passion, fresh and winning, and it was in view of her French reputation that she caught Henry's eye. Henry was not a man of adventure, either in regard to warfare or to women. He was cautious unless armored. His relation with the Boleyns was sufficiently intimate, however, to bring Mary into full notice. Almost immediately after her arrival home she married William Carey, who was given an insignificant office in the household and a small fortune; and soon she began an affair with Henry which went on until 1526.

Thomas Boleyn profited heavily. Henry's enjoyment may be measured by the pains he took to advance the complaisant father. By the spring of 1522 he was treasurer, and when the spoils were distributed after Buckingham's execution Boleyn expanded from Hever in almost alarming dimensions, steward of Tunbridge, keeper of Penshurst, bailiff of Bradsted. The King plied him with new stewardships up to 1525, then, defying Catherine completely, he made his six-year-old illegitimate son the Duke of Richmond and honored Boleyn on this occasion by creating him viscount.

The question of personal dignity does not seem to have arisen in either William Carey or the new Viscount Rocheford, probably because it did not arise in Mary, or in Henry, or even in Catherine. Catherine dimly appreciated by this time that her husband must either live as a celibate or establish a liaison with some woman at Court, or else divorce her and remarry. She often said things to show that she thought Henry was weak and easily led astray by designing females, but she accepted his nature as something that could not be changed. And she preferred Henry's furtive affairs to the flamboyancy with which Francis had paraded the large lady who towered over Queen Claude. Poor Claude's chapter, however, was closed. She had just died, at the age of twenty-five, having given birth to seven children.

The lessons that swarmed in the situation both in England and in France were not lost on the younger Boleyn's adolescent mind. Until war was foreshadowed in 1522, she lived on at the court where the one most intense preoccupation was the art of woman's relation to man. The new generation of women were in revolt against the medieval female. They did not sympathize with the rôle of Anne de Beaujeu, Isabella the

Catholic, Catherine of Aragon, even Queen Claude. They were moving from prayer books to the Heptameron. Not being of a heroic mold, they played with love, they saw the woman as mistress rather than the man as master, and they cared more for diversity and multiplicity than for the rigid self-possession and massive maternity of the old school. The renaissance was vibrant and many-colored. It had new values, new audacities, new freedoms. Anne was saturated in French courtly life and she could never again take the stiff, slightly bucolic, view that distinguished the heavier English nobility. She tried to understand this fine art of man and woman in which, at a high distance above herself, Marguerite d'Angoulême was already finding such exquisite and troublous inflections. Anne's young head was possessed by subtleties of which Henry could have no clear idea, and which, without rebuffing him completely, would eventually force him to explain to her and to himself the meaning he gave to "love" and the nature of his intentions.

In 1522 when the young Mary was deeply his mistress, Anne Boleyn returned to England. No statecraft or solemnity weighed her first appearance. She danced into English history, a laughing girl. Among the many feasts that Wolsey arranged for Henry at his sumptuous mansion where Whitehall now stands, one of the most famous in luxury and pageantry took place on the eve of the second French war; and among the unknown maids of honor who flashed on the courtier's gaze and held his eye and won his applause was this flame-tipped, inviting girl. She was fifteen. It was the age on which the satyr and the idealist then agreed as the most delicately provocative in womanhood. In the poems of the early sixteenth century, written under Southern influence, the virgin of fifteen is sung both tenderly and lasciviously. It was the moment that appealed to the imagination of very simple men, and especially toward the end of these exuberant feasts, when everybody was a little drunk, did the vision of dewy youth seem almost irresistible. A maudlin sweetness would rise in the male and mingle with his amorousness. Avid yet unsteady in his pursuit, he was no match for the butterfly that flew beyond him. In the sober morning after, the grave damsel struck him into horror at his previous temerity and subdued him into lyric love.

But Henry did not as yet see this young Boleyn except as a political pawn. He was dallying with Mary. He wanted Anne to marry an Irishman. The Irish, as usual, were a nuisance and a confusion. They kept breaking into the graceful arrangement of life at inopportune times, like a drowned wretch who humorlessly leaves the sea to come dripping into the festival. Thomas Boleyn had a claim on the Ormond estates through his mother, and this claim was violently contested by a wild young Butler in Ireland, whose extermination would unfortunately cost more than it was worth. It was a case for compromise. Wolsey and Henry both agreed that the simplest way out would be to marry Anne Boleyn to this firebrand and unite the two families forever. She would then, in time, be Lady Ormond. She would live at gray Kilkenny Castle, watch the Nore flowing by for her amusement, go to thatched Dublin for the parliament, and whenever there was a coronation or a royal wedding in London, she could, if times were quiet, take sail for England. It would be a change from Paris! Anne Boleyn declined it with a shudder. She preferred to be a maid to Queen Catherine, a spinster, a nun, to marrying this red-headed James Butler. She would remain at the English court and enjoy life as it came to her.

III

It came to her soon, in spindling young Percy, the son and heir of the Earl of Northumberland. He was one of Cardinal Wolsey's pompous household, and whenever Wolsey visited the court in his regal state, Percy wound his way to the Queen's chamber, "and there would fall in dalliance among the Queen's maidens."

He was a quick, highstrung youth, and he and Mistress Anne Boleyn chatted together with much vivacity. From vivacity they passed to seriousness. He and the black-eyed, leggy girl had found each other, and were so in love that it could not be hidden. Not a glimmer had Percy of the imprudence he had committed till one ominous evening when, on returning with his master from court, he was curtly told that the Cardinal was waiting to see him in his great gallery. He found Wolsey not alone, but with the servants of his chamber. There was icy silence when he entered. Wolsey, grimly dignified, turned on him in his most superb and scornful manner.

"I marvel not a little," he said, addressing him before every one, "of your peevish folly, that ye would entangle yourself with a foolish girl yonder in the court, I mean Anne Boleyn.

"Do ye not consider the estate that God hath called you unto in this world? After the death of your noble father, you are most like to inherit and possess one of the most worthiest earldoms of this realm. It had been most meet and convenient for you to have sued for the consent of your father on that behalf, and to have made the King's highness privy thereto; he would have matched you according to your estate and honor, whereby ye might have grown so by your wisdom and honorable behavior into the King's high estimation, that it should have been much to your increase of honor. But now—" Wolsey measured him with disdain, and Percy, every eye on him, hung his head.

"Now behold what ye have done through your wilfulness! Ye have not only offended your natural father, but also your most gracious sovereign lord, and matched yourself with one, such as neither the King nor yet your father will be agreeable with the matter.

"I will send for your father," Wolsey proceeded coldly, "and at his coming he shall either break this unadvised contract, or else disinherit you forever."

Percy, his lip quivering, waited for the storm to pass, but Wolsey was inexorable. "The King's majesty himself," he lowered, "will complain to your father on you, and require no less at his hand than I have said. His Highness intended to have preferred Anne Boleyn unto another person, with whom the King hath travailed already, and being almost at a point with this person, although she knoweth it not, yet hath the King, like a most politic and prudent Prince, conveyed the matter so that she, I do not doubt, will be right glad and agreeable to do as he arranges."

The pressure on Anne alarmed the youth. "Sir," he broke out, all weeping, "I knew nothing of the King's pleasure therein, for whose displeasure I—I am very sorry. I considered that I was of good years, and thought I could choose a wife as my fancy served me best, not doubting that my lord my father would have been rightly persuaded. Sir, though she be a simple maid, and having but a knight to her father, yet is she descended of right noble parentage." Percy stopped crying. "By her mother she is of the Norfolk blood," he explained eagerly, "and of her father's side lineally descended of the Earl of Ormond, he being one of the earl's heirs-general. Why should I then, sir, be anything scrupulous to match with her, whose descent is equivalent with mine when I shall be in most dignity?" He thought his point made, and he added, "Therefore I most humbly require your grace and your especial favor, and also to entreat the King's most royal majesty most lowly on my behalf in this matter, the which I cannot deny or forsake."

The Cardinal lifted his hands. "Lo, sirs," he sneered, "ye may see what conformity and wisdom is in this willful boy's head."

He pointed at Percy and shouted ferociously, "I thought that when you heard me declare the King's intended pleasure and travail ye would have relented and wholly submitted yourself, and all your willful and unadvised act, to the King's royal will."

"Sir, so I would," quailed Percy, "but in this matter I have gone so far, before so many worthy witnesses, that I know not how to avoid myself nor to discharge my conscience."

The Cardinal's drooping eyelids lifted for a second to consider the covert apology. Then he resumed his thundering manner. "Think ye that the King and I know not what we have to do in as weighty a matter as this? Yes, I warrant ye. Howbeit," he darkened again, "I can see in you no submission to the purpose."

Percy's face became utterly miserable and imploring. "Forsooth, my lord," he said in heartrending plea, "if it please your grace, I will submit myself wholly unto the King's majesty and your grace in this matter, my conscience being discharged of the weighty burden of my promise."

The Cardinal drew a deep breath. This young man's will was broken! "Well, then," he said in a mild voice, "I will send for your father out of the north parts, and he and we shall take such order for the avoiding of this your hasty folly as shall be by the King thought most expedient. And in the mean season I charge you and in the King's name command you that ye presume, not once, to resort into her company, if ye intend to avoid the King's high indignation."

He nodded to Percy who bowed deeply, then rose up and went into his little room.

Against the Cardinal, the King, and his own father, Percy hysterically planned for victory. But Northumberland, the Magnificent Earl, disembarked at York Place, spent a long while in secret talk with the cardinal, then, after a cup of wine with him, took his leave, walked to the end of the gallery and, sitting on the waiters' bench, spoke to his son before the servants.

"Son," he barked, "thou hast always been a proud, presumptuous, disdainful and a very unthrift waster." On this note, as arranged with Wolsey, he continued at great length. Percy was ungrateful, light-headed, disloyal. He had almost ruined his father. Only the almost divine mercy and goodness of the King could pardon him. To the assembled courtiers and servitors Northumberland explained what a prodigal this was, what a waster. He mentioned that, however, he had other sons, "more choice of boys who, I trust, will prove themselves better." "Yet in the mean season I desire you all to be his friends, and to tell him his fault when he doth amiss."

With that he took his leave, snapping at the boy, "Go your ways, and attend upon my lord's grace, your master, and see that you do your duty." And so the Magnificent Earl of Northumberland departed, with a whole skin but a sore one, and went his way down through the hall into his barge.

In due time Anne Boleyn got word that her young friend was engaged. He was to marry a Talbot, one of the Earl of Shrewsbury's daughters. He was to go from court, and to complete this marriage, and he was not to see her again.

IV

For a girl of Anne Boleyn's age, and mettle, and vaunting spirit, this first encounter with the world of brute ambition, and the religion of power, was more than she could stand. She had given her heart to this proud, presumptuous, light-headed boy, who would be the most powerful noble in the North of England, and all her friends knew it: now she was commanded to leave the court, and sent home again to her father for a season.

Another girl, awed by her elders, might have bowed her will, but Anne Boleyn's was a passionate nature, and this outrage on her personality filled her with fury. Her love was shattered. Her pride was revolted. Her name was cheapened. It was not the King she blamed for all this, but the man whose broad shoulders took the burdens of the King. Every brutality that Wolsey had inflicted on young Percy, before a host of witnesses, recoiled on her. From a girl of fifteen she passed to hard young womanhood, never to forget what life could do to her, never to forget what it meant to have "but a knight to her father," and never to forget the cold and arbitrary fiat of his Grace the Cardinal.

Her white face sallow, her black brows bent, Anne Boleyn spent months at Hever, consuming her wrath until it was like sulphur in her blood. She had set her heart on Percy, and he was riding the Marches, to marry a Shrewsbury. Her love for him whirled into contempt and bitterness. And as she suffered, he suffered. He was physically sick. He could not stand his new marriage. After two years his wife left him. His father's death gave him one of the most worthiest earldoms of the realm, and he was one of the most unhappiest of men.

It was many months after Percy's exile before "Mistress Anne Boleyn was revoked unto court." She left England to become a maid to Margaret of Austria, like her sister Mary, and, after Pavia, passed most of her time at Hever in Kent. One of her neighbors was Thomas Wyatt, the poet, her first cousin. Wyatt had several of the qualifications of a court poet; he was young, he was sweepingly handsome, he was high-spirited, and he was unhappily married. In the period that succeeded Percy, Wyatt saw much of Anne, found the young girl cool but evocative and disturbing. Did she invite his love, this slim thing? Half unwilling he pursued her, with the somewhat acrid passion of a divided man. If one peers through the bull's-eye window of Tudor spelling and Tudor translation, one gets the mood in which Thomas Wyatt was to sing an enchantress who had drawn him and escaped him:

> *Who so list to hount: I know where is an hynde*
> *But, as for me: helas, I may no more.*
> *The vayne travail hat werid me so sore,*
> *I ame of theim, that farthest cometh behinde*

Yet, may by no means, my werid mynde
Drawe from the Der; but as she fleeth afore
Faynting I folowe. I leve of therefore:
Sins in a nett I seke to hold the wynde.

Who list her hount: I put him oute of dowbte:
As well as I: may spend his tyme in vain.
And graven with Diamonds with letters plain:
There is written, her faier neck rounde abowte:
Noli me tangere for Cæsar's I ame
And wylde for to hold: though I seme tame.

"Cæsar's" diamond necklet was soon to girdle Anne.

V

It was in 1526 that "Cæsar" first really saw her. She was then a girl of nineteen.

Henry so far had moved with the shining tide, not questioning or not driven to question his own longings. But these stretching years of marital quiet, of endurance or acquiescence, did not alter the fact that he was an incompletely married man. And now, without willing it, he reached the crisis that so often arrives; he looked out and saw a new and wonderful possibility from which he was debarred. Full-blooded and always under the pressure of desire, he supposed at first that this was another pleasant polygamous episode, but as it proffered itself to him it broke in on his heart that he had never been in love before. A man of the slowest imagination, but incredibly tenacious when fully aroused, Henry combated this vision at first, which was natural. But his body had spoken, and his heart had spoken, he had listened to the fairy music that once on some far-off Celtic hill must have stirred the soul of an ancestor, and when it had penetrated his being, all the powers of earth and heaven could not divert him from his course. How he would pursue this course, when he came to another crossroads, was not yet decided. But for the moment he had opened his eyes on the plight of the incompletely married man.

At the beginning, the spring of 1526, Henry did not foresee much difficulty in winning Mary's sister. There was always love-making at the English court. On dry days a man could hunt, but on wet days, when the fun of tossing arrows over a screen or laying bowls or incessant gambling had brought satiety, there was a swift glance to be caught, a kiss to be garnered, and an adventure to be tried. The royal troupe was no different from a theatrical troupe or a garrison town. The number of casual relationships was high, there was a quick spark between the feelings of the dame and the instinct of the squire, yet always the admitted seriousness of the uninvited baby and the frightful prevalence of disease. Henry's casual relationships seem to have been continual. Yet he remained incomplete, and as he grew older he was too abundant to be satisfied with trivialities.

With the facility so usual in a man of power, Henry toyed with the idea of this curtseying, glancing girl. Unemployed in his affections for Mary, he amiably scanned Anne. And then a surprise greeted him. The atmosphere of Hever, hitherto one of serene complaisance without current or ripple to it, became keen with the presence of a living will. There was something of the Howard, after all, in Anne Boleyn, something of that grim grandfather who had fought for Richard III, and made a bold speech to Henry's father and won Flodden to the grief of Scotland and carried himself, scars and gnarled endurance, well on to eighty years. Anne Boleyn was mistress of her own body. Even if Henry's eyes followed her into the Queen's chamber, even if he came riding to Hever to see his treasurer on only one excuse, the girl might seem tame, but, as Wyatt had said, she was wild for to hold.

VI

The master of England was checked in a desire that was over-powering him, and this for the first time in his career. For seventeen years he had swum along as King of England. Of recent years there had been much in Wolsey's leadership to irk him, but on the whole he had gladly given himself to that dynamic personality and to his ambitions to make him a European power. This sort of thing, however, had not gratified Henry. He had consented, he had been acted upon, but it was not his inner will. The thing that most affected him in life was narrowly personal. It was his failure to beget an heir. In 1510 a still-born daughter had been born. In 1511 came a boy who had died in seven weeks. That boy had been christened Harry. In 1513 there was a still-born son. In 1514 there was another. In 1516, at last, a child was born that lived, but it was Mary, a girl! Again in 1517 there were miscarriages, and in 1518 another child still-born.

One thing was certain to Henry, his wife had failed him. These miscarriages, these humiliations, these horrible repetitions, had accumulated for Henry till they seemed to him almost a sign from heaven, a judgment of God. His marriage was cursed. It was inescapable. And it was not less inescapable since the changes in Europe in 1525 and 1526.

Henry could con a fact without lifting his eyes to it, and behind the figure of poor Catherine he could see her growing political uselessness. He had married her because of England's weakness in sight of France. To reconquer France had been his dream. But the defeat of Pavia had at once disarmed the French nation and made Charles mightily independent of English favor. It was a deadlock in European affairs, a lull in Wolsey's programme, and for the first time since his marriage this incomplete husband was politically freed from his dynastic wife.

She was worn out. "Howebeit," wrote Thomas More, a dozen years before, "the husbande to put away his wife for no other faulte, but for that some myshappe is fallen to her bodye, this by no means they [the Utopians] wyll suffre. For they judge it a great poynt of crueltie, that anye bodye in their most nede of helpe and comforte, shoulde be caste of and forsaken, and that olde age, whych both bringeth syckness with it, and is a syckness it selfe, should unkyndely and unfaythfullye be delte withall."

But Henry was no Utopian. When Anne appeared at nineteen, he was thirty-five, and Catherine was a sick and saddened matron of forty-one. The young girl was of the slender, swaying figure that is like a daffodil on its stalk; Catherine was squat, white and dropsical. Anne Boleyn had a clever pointed face, quick expression, long, fine fingers, and was ready on the instant with a witticism or a peal of laughter; Henry's wife never laughed, seeing that she was the heavy and rather torpid Spaniard, immersed in saints' days and expert in indulgences, grave in her communication with servants and rustling with her crucifix and keys. The girl of nineteen was partly of Irish blood, black-haired, with lively searching eyes, and a sense of mischief uniting with a strong sense of romance; Catherine had prominent, watery blue eyes and was of a Gothic blondness, her mainspring being her rectitude, her suppression of the irregular self and her submission to duty. She submitted. She had never been frivolous and she had never been temperamental, she was as honest and slow and faithful as her royal Greenwich barge. In the twenty-five years she had spent in England, her one thought had been of Henry. Not being of æsthetic urgency, her serpent of fidelity had swallowed up all the other serpents, and the devotion she gave him had the full semblance of love.

She had, it was true, really married him in the course of dynastic duty. Had Arthur survived, Catherine would have marshaled her fidelity and her devotion with the same cruel thoroughness, and entombed him under the same mound of obligation. Had Arthur become king, she would have watched that fat younger brother Henry with sheer apprehension, waiting for the moment when Henry would attack *her* husband and undermine his interests.

Catherine was not, in any light sense, a person; she was the wife and mother, a link in the long chain of racial continuity, based on the throne, backed on the Church, rooted in the family, a block of institutional granite set in her weak human flesh and her quivering nerves.

Anne Boleyn was neither grave nor principled in this tragic sense. Where the Spanish wife and mother, slow as oil, had sacrificed all the play of personality and the witchery of change to racial continuity and sedentary salvation, the English girl had not yet arrived at uterine preoccupations. There was in Anne Boleyn what there was never in Catherine, an exciting climate of change. Catherine had never been young, though she could be extremely tender and loving. But this crisp rival was sparklingly young. And few things cause such a pang of emotion in the mature man as the high-spirited young girl who is arrested by him. Under her audacity, he feels a frailty, a plea for sympathy, for understanding, even if pride denies it and courage avoids it. Her soul is like her body, a little angular and fragile, and the very stride of her freedom is not assured. Anne came under Henry's loving eyes when she still seemed untied and uncommitted, her very light and slender person declaring she was unattached, and her big black eyes cleaving untracked waters and leaving behind a sea-fire in the heart of the male.

VII

A male like Henry, posed between a wife of forty-one and a charmer of nineteen, behaved as you would guess him to be-

have. He fell head over heels in love. And as he was stirred to
his depths by Anne Boleyn, tossed out of his habit by the surge
of his feelings and swept into currents the like of which he had
not conceived and the strength of which carried him in wide
and baffling semicircles, he changed the course of his nation
in battling for his life. He did not set out to be the champion
of the state against the Church. It grew out of his predicament.
Since we are all but tiny wheels fitting into wheels of an order
not visible to us and barely apprehended, there were times
when the astonishing discordance between Henry's acts and
the larger operation of human consequence about him sent a
shiver of anguished protest into the tragic spaces; but these
shrieks did not dismay Henry or divert him from his obedience to his massive instincts. Henry's loyalty to his instincts
is, in fact, the only loyalty of which he can be accused. But it
would be a brave man who would imagine that he stood condemned on that account. In few things, at any rate, was he
more touchingly human than in this discovery of Anne Boleyn.
It was his supreme flight, the curvet of a winged bull. He
sprang high and fell leaden, rebounding into history with that
shocking force of a completely sincere catastrophe. And out of
this catastrophe, in exceeding pain, were born two more or less
legitimate children, Queen Elizabeth and the Church of England.

It is a long way from Cranmer and Latimer, Fisher and
Thomas More, to the obstinacy of a girl of nineteen. Anne
Boleyn's refusal to accept the rôle of Henry's mistress uncon-
ditionally changed the course of English history. If ever a slip
of a girl owed it to the established order to satisfy her lover by
a union outside the bonds of matrimony, this was a clear instance; and cardinals and ambassadors and blood relations
and the Pope were soon beside themselves with eagerness to
learn that this chit would remain simply Henry's mistress.
Her father grew weary of her obstinacy. Her uncle Norfolk

resented her ambition. Her sister could not understand Anne's rigorousness. But she was not a coquette nor a wanton. She was a high-spirited, high-handed girl who made this marriage a term of her being and who, in spite of this, delivered herself to ruin.

VIII

When a whale is harpooned, he seeks madly to escape, and as he flies through the water he trains with him the bold little creature who, greatly daring, has flung the fatal weapon.

Henry could not believe at first that he had been dangerously smitten. She liked him. She felt affection for him. Yes, she even admitted "indissoluble affection" for him. He went away from Hever, conning these words.

"The uneasiness of absence is already too severe for me," he wrote her. It would be "almost intolerable" if she had not admitted that she felt affection for him. But affection? He examined the word. On its face it gleamed. On the reverse, it glowered. And what did he hear? That she and her mother, in the end, had decided not to come to court. A cry of outraged protest burst from Henry, which showed that the harpoon had pierced him, or, as he delicately called it, the dart.

"I have never committed any offense against you," he raged openly, "and it seems to me a very small return (*bien petite retribution*) for the great love I bear you, to be kept at a distance from the person and presence of the one woman I most esteem in the world."

These hot words, this snort of anger and lashing of the tail, did not free the mighty lover. So long as the question of Mary, and what had happened to her sister, and what now lay between her sister and Henry, and between the Queen and Henry, was present in the mind of this proud girl, she was incapable of accepting Henry. This he knew. It was against these implacable facts he raged. A woman, the custodian of this order of private sincerity, had stood to her demand for candor. Henry was intelligent. He knew that Anne was right. And, with the tactics of the badly hit and much hurt, he was trying to lay on Anne the responsibility of giving him up.

"Consider well, my mistress," he wrote her, "how greatly your absence grieves me; I hope it is not your will that it should be so; but, if I heard for certain, that you yourself desired it, I could do no other than complain of my ill fortune, and by degrees abate my folly; and so, for want of time I make an end of my rude letter."

This threat, so comically idle, would have provoked the sardonic laughter of Francis Bryan, "the vicar of hell." More and more heavily Henry floundered in the net. He wanted to acquire her without facing where he stood with Mary, and with Catherine. But Anne was alluringly, defiantly cool. She had her sister's example before her. Henry stirred her deeply, but she asked him to consider what he meant by these great words, these sighs, these tumultuous assurances of eternal and infinite love.

The egoist in Henry died hard. But neither he nor she was cynical. Neither was greedy. His soul, vulgar and purblind though it was, was completely engaged. In absolute agony of spirit, he sat down and wrote her the sort of letter that a man of his great shrewdness and ceaseless cunning could only write when torn by the uncertainty of love. He had really found the woman he wanted. He was bewitched, obsessed, infatuated. And he wrote her at long last in the sincerity of his heart:

"By turning over in my thoughts the contents of your last letters, I have put myself into a great agony, not knowing how, whether to my disadvantage, as I proved in many places, or to my advantage, as I understood some others; I beseech you now, with the greatest earnestness, to let me know your whole intention, as to the love between us two.

"For I must of necessity obtain this answer of you, having been above a whole year struck with the dart of love, and not yet sure whether I shall fail, or find a place in your heart and affection.

"This uncertainty has hindered me of late from naming you my mistress, since you only love me with an ordinary affection, but if you please to do the duty of a true and loyal mistress, and to give up yourself, body and heart to me, who will be, as I have been, your most loyal servant (if your rigor does not forbid me) I promise you that not only the name shall be given you, but also that I will take you for my mistress, casting off all others that are in competition with you, out of my thoughts and affection, and serving you only.

"I beg you to give an entire answer to this my rude letter, that I may know what, and how far, I may depend.

"But if it does not please you to answer in writing, let me know some place, where I may have it by word of mouth, and I will go thither with all my heart.

"No more for fear of tiring you.

"Written by the hand of him who would willingly remain yours,

"H. Rex."

This letter, urgent and sincere, was Henry's last word. He was willing to give up Mary Boleyn, to give up Catherine, to root them out of his heart, if Anne would give up herself, "body and heart," to him.

The girl was in agony. Though Henry was in love with her, she could feel behind the palpitating words his brutal desire for certainty, his possessiveness, his blunt offer of a bargain.

In this perplexity, so sure of him and yet so intuitively aware of what he could be like, so aware of what men could be like, Anne read and re-read his letter to find some way of postponing. He was a lover, but he was also an assailant, he demanded her surrender. And he demanded it, though he was committed to her sister and bound to his wife. If only he were free! If he were free, Anne told herself, she could perhaps love him. She could give herself to him absolutely, entirely, forever. There was about Henry this radiant feeling of strength, of good nature, of appealing warmth, he was her master and her king. Possessed by this picture of him, the girl sat down to reveal that he, and he alone, would have her heart, but it could not be until he determined to be free. It was at once a love letter and an answer to an ultimatum; and to convey more than her words could, she sent him a token.

Henry's answer was joyous. The uncertainty under which he had collected so many of his emotions—the child in him, the coward, the dependent, the suspicious one—now was thrown off in the glorious assurance that she did not belong to Wyatt or any one else, and that she would soon be his.

And first, of course, in the shy, pompous manner of the sovereign, he must acknowledge the token, with due regard to its value. Henry was nothing if not a public man.

"For a present so valuable that nothing could be more (considering the whole of it) I return you my most hearty thanks, not only on account of the costly diamond, and the ship in which the solitary Damsel is tossed about; but chiefly for the fine interpretation, and too humble submission which your goodness hath made to me.

"I think it would be very difficult for me to find an occasion to deserve it, if I was not assisted by your great humanity and favor, which I have sought, do seek, and will always seek to preserve by all the services in my power: and this is my firm intention and hope, according to the motto, *aut illic aut nullibi.* [Either here or nowhere.]

"The demonstrations of your affections are such, the fine thoughts of your letter so cordially expressed, that they oblige me for ever to honour, love and serve you sincerely, beseeching you to continue in the same firm and constant purpose; and assuring you, that, on my part, I will not only make you a suitable return, but outdo you in loyalty of heart, if it be possible.

"I desire you also, that, if at any time before this I have in any sort offended you, you would give me the same absolution which you ask, assuring you, that hereafter my heart shall be dedicated to you alone; I wish my body was so too; God can do so, if he pleases; to whom I pray once a day for that end; hoping that at length my prayers will be heard.

"I wish the time may be short, but I shall think it long till we shall see one another.

"Written by the hand of the secretary, who in heart, body, and will, is

"Your loyal, and most assured servant

"H, no other 〈ⱭB〉 seeks REX."

This letter, which begins in the public spirit and ends in the private, showed how passionately Henry was in love. When he began, it was a king writing to a humble subject; he ended as a man writing to a woman. This man was not a poet. Even with the strongest of currents sweeping through his soul, he never became lucent. He moved slowly and heavily, clouded with a thick wash of mother earth. But no lover could be more truly solicitous, or more whole-heartedly sincere.

When he wrote himself, "Your loyal and most assured servant," or, as he actually wrote, *"Votre loyal et plus assuré serviture,"* he felt the gulf between his words and his impulse, he felt a bursting desire to convey to Anne the love that absorbed him. He sat tied in his seat before his clumsy "rude" letter. None of his loutish flights of fancy could possibly have satisfied him, and somewhere in his soul, perhaps inherited from his grandmother Margaret or perhaps his mother Elizabeth, there was a little clear spring of pure aspiration, a pang of loveliness.

One can imagine the sturdy, heavy-breathing man, his face ardent with suppressed fire, his fingers grimly determined, his body muscle-bound, his soul yearning. Thus many athletes have wrestled by candlelight with the desperate longing to master their dreams. Thus soldiers who have toyed in jocular fashion with many wenches have become as children again in this first timid excursion into candor. Henry, the athlete and the captain, could at times escape into the courtly and become the stately sovereign, but a painful gaucherie, a tremendous sheepishness, overwhelmed him when he sought to be tender. He sighed and heaved in this torture of the spirit, and at last, with melting heart, he traced on paper the symbol of that very aching organ, and in it he wrote the initials of her who filled it, A.B.

No longer was he the monarch and she the subject. He was a yeoman in the greenwood, and in the flesh of the beech tree, itself so noble, he was carving his heart and enshrining the name of his true love. This little sketch of his heart, he set inside the pledge of double fidelity, "autre——ne cherce," "seeks——no other," and this symbol his name embraced. It was his Valentine. And beyond it, above it, was the opposite of his whole being, the vision of a creature so infinitely finer in grain, so like a vapor that interpenetrated him and that yet he could not grasp, so ravishing and so intangible, that he seems to be stretching out his hands to embrace her body, saying to her in so many words, as if he were playing blindman's buff and ached for physical certainty, "Oh, to have you in my arms, in my arms!"

IX

Henry was ardent. Once he had really the physical proof that Anne loved him and wanted him, he was as good as his word. To obtain a divorce he would need to set the church in action: that meant Cardinal Wolsey and Archbishop Warham, the *legatus a latere* and the *legatus natus*. It would need setting aside Catherine and his daughter Mary. With the appalling heartlessness born of a new love, Henry saw no reason to spare Catherine, and he saw no difficulty in speeding a divorce. For, having discovered that Anne Boleyn could be his, Henry had begun to seethe with conscientious scruples.

There is no hotbed like a burning desire. A little cold scruple that has wintered in snowy peace as if in its pious grave needs only to be breathed on by the south wind to become imperious. So it was with Henry after his long life with Catherine. The minute Anne became a certainty, his conscientious scruples began to rumble within him. Humor and self-criticism were not Henry's strong points. He believed more in dignity and censorship. He did not think it funny that his scruples rose from their pure slumber at the back of the cage and came bristling forward at the thought of his immoral marriage to Catherine, lashing their Old-Testament tails and fluffing out their Divine-Law hair. Henry's hungry conscience roared for meat. He wanted a divorce, and on the loftiest grounds imaginable.

For this, Wolsey and Warham would be his servants. Wolsey was his machine, and Warham, as he knew, had always opposed his marriage to Catherine. It was a sanguine and resolute lover who sent for Wolsey to disclose these thrilling plans in the May of 1527.

x

This was to prove the crucial moment in the lives of these two men, and Wolsey, for once, was not prepared.

He was not an old man in years, being fifty-five, but he had ceased to command that marvelous flexibility which so often wears out its man of genius. Wolsey was no longer the tireless captain who takes the bridge himself in every difficult hour. He was beginning to yield to his age, to give himself to vast armchair schemes, to bold and high-flown projects that had in them a luscious ripeness of imagination. Henry had been so ductile, Wolsey had found him so easy-going, that it had never occurred to his servant to ponder on this new liaison. First the mother, then Mary, then Anne,—he viewed it with the lenient, slightly bored cynicism of an old hand, rather disliking Anne, "that foolish girl yonder in the court," because of her father and her uncle, but he took her no more seriously than any other maid in waiting.

Besides, Henry's marriage to Catherine was a fixed fact, it was the keystone of a whole political system. Much as he himself had disliked it, Wolsey knew that for twenty years the conduct of England had been built around this existing marriage. It was a serious thing. The trade with Flanders, the desire to add Boulogne to Calais, the negotiations with Bourbon, the navy policy, the attitude toward the Vatican, the indignation with Luther, the essential friendliness with Charles against Francis—all that had inclined and colored the mind of England from 1509, involving two wars with France, had been insensibly but steadily promoted by the irrefragable reality of Henry's marriage to Catherine. It had cost England millions and brought it into serious debt. It was the central commitment around which everything turned, the loyalty to which the good English people had been educated, and which was now nature to them. Both as statesman and as churchman, Wolsey looked on this marriage much as the boatman looked on London Bridge.

And now came Henry in high courage, ardent and babbling, taking Catherine out of the accustomed family group and substituting for her the great-granddaughter of a Lord Mayor of London. It was a proposal that made Wolsey jump in the air.

It was not Spain that frightened him. He had no illusions concerning Spain. He had no loyalty to Charles and no patience with Charles's English stalwarts, the so-called imperialists. From the day that the cold-blooded Charles had behaved so treacherously about the vacant papacy, Wolsey had hated him, and this hatred had drawn the Cardinal closer to the French than Henry wanted or liked. Influenced by a resentment that was sometimes stronger than reason, and by pensions that he needed, Wolsey had even been tempted at times to undermine his master's policy and to twist his instructions. It was the duty of the older man to proportion his pace to the slower and stupider course of his master, but from 1522 the impatient Wolsey had adjusted this difference in the working of their minds by increasing his sophistry and proportioning his version of the "facts." Considering the strength and arrogance of his nature, the sharpness of his insight, the boldness of his imagination and the quickness of his wit, he found it easier in his supple career as foreign minister to act first and palaver with Henry afterwards, always regaling Henry with the most sumptuous flattery. But here, in spite of his subtlest care to play with the French around the Spanish, the king had gone miles ahead of him, and, with a prince's bluntness, had made a political decision of the first magnitude.

It staggered Wolsey. It was a decision that did not pay heed to the most elemental political facts. He groaned inwardly. What about the difficulties of the Vatican, with Luther ravening and the Anabaptists raging, with the Turks ripping up Hungary, with England bled of money, with Charles and Francis still capable of being manipulated and England throwing away its leverage?

Wolsey, swept off his feet, flung himself on his knees in tears, and with all the anguish of a statesman whose instinct has been at fault and whose imagination has been so dormant that he has allowed his life work to be endangered, for longer than a long hour begged, implored, cajoled and wooed his master to give up his incredible dream.

His master broke his pleas. He might as well have asked Parsifal to give up the Holy Grail. It was he himself who had educated Henry to be ruthless and daring, to sacrifice the Venetians, to kill Buckingham, to deceive Francis, to sanction himself as arbiter when they were using this prestige to cover the dagger of underhand war. Now Wolsey's pupil had a purpose more dear to him than any political principle, the purpose of his own delight.

On what ground could the veteran, even with a torrent of words that no gesture could stem, dissuade this headstrong pupil? Wolsey literally wrung his hands. The cool day would come when this slow brain, now stirred to music by his singing blood, would once again be as sober as a usurer's. But now, how radiant it all looked to Henry, how different the stained glass from the plain glass! Wolsey, who so often had contrived this sort of radiance himself, dragged himself from his aching knees, a beaten mortal. He had not been battling with Henry alone, whom he knew like his hand, but with the invisible host of the ideal—Henry as the beau chevalier. This chevalier was to gain the world for his mistress, and for the first time Wolsey, sardonic and incredulous, found himself listening to a language, the very sound of which was as unreal as a lyric from a bull.

It was this that Anne Boleyn had foreseen. She knew that the only remarriage conceivable to the cardinal would be remarriage with a French princess for reasons of state. That he could understand! But what she had suffered from Wolsey gave edge to her mind. She had finely coached Henry to be ready for the violent discordance that Wolsey would be bound to reveal, and she had forewarned him how firm he would have to be, and how clearly he must prescribe Wolsey's course of action. This

Henry had faithfully performed. He gave Wolsey his orders, and Wolsey, agreeing to get in touch with the Archbishop, kissed his master's hand.

XI

In the dead of night the lord chancellor communed with his bruised spirit. He viewed himself with gruesome candor. What till now had seemed fertile invention suddenly seemed like the maudlin ooze of faculty decaying. He had failed to forecast Henry's course of action. This knowledge twisted in him like the discovery of a fatal disease.

But how could he be so obtuse? He a statesman! Could a man call himself a statesman who did not estimate the influence of love? By God, he had better imitate Henry and consult sorcerers and astrologers. Wolsey was too intelligent for these fripperies of his master, and yet the pit of his stomach gave him the dreadful news that he had lost his hold on that primitive will.

The Cardinal breathed the heaviest sigh of his life as the glorious tapestries and gorgeous vestiture and furniture of his apartment faded from his eyes with the quenched chandelier, and he lay awake to think of the stark outlook before him. His luxury. Bah! He had given Henry Hampton Court two years before without a second thought. These were counters in his game, like his silver crosses, his copes, his cardinal's hat, his aim at the papacy. What he confronted was a change in the very center of things. Henry in love meant Henry under a new domination. Anne Boleyn as queen meant that Henry would revolve in a new orbit, an orbit in which the woman would be central, and both the papacy and its Cardinal superfluous.

Like all men of his creative temperament, Wolsey spent his life imagining obstacles and sketching the means he would take to overcome them. The defeat that robbed him of his sleep was that cruel surprise, an obstacle he had not imagined. His nervous indigestion, always his torture, destroyed the one chance he had of recuperating after this cursed interview, and, while he tossed in desolation, Henry, a little mile away, no doubt smiled in the happy dream of Anne's entwining arms.

For a brave spirit, however, the morning is seldom so gruesome, and Wolsey gathered himself to join Warham in summoning Henry to a secret and solemn tribunal where, on Henry's revealing his gnawing conscience, his horror at having suddenly discovered that for eighteen years, he had been living in sin with Catherine, the two dignitaries, as prearranged, undertook to save him from this predicament. Catherine was to know nothing of this salutary work until it was an accomplished fact, and then Henry was himself to hit her on the head with it, as one kills the stalled ox. Then he could marry Anne Boleyn.

But the church dignitaries, Wolsey and Warham, had not undivided responsibility. They were serving two masters, Henry and Jesus Christ. Much as they wanted to aid Henry, they owed it to their Master in heaven to acquaint His vicar on earth with the act they projected, and to produce its ratification. To give weight to their act, they decided to enlist all the bishops, so that England would be irresistible at Rome, and Henry's heir by Anne declared fully legitimate. If Henry wanted his heir to come undisputed to the throne, among the Poles and the Suffolks and the Norfolks, he would need the full and ceremonious sanction of Mother Church. That would delay the remarriage proceedings a little, but it would double assurance.

XII

This was the precise moment chosen in history for Mother Church to be stricken low, and this by the very hand of the man who, four years before, had been suborned and armed by Henry.

On May 5, 1527, when Wolsey and Warham began the proceedings that led to the Vatican, the Vatican itself was already in view of the most terrific gang of bloodcurdling adventurers who ever came to kill, steal and rape. At the hour when Henry was protesting that he had never been married to Catherine, these warriors were pointing out the towers and domes that were a chorus until one caught the skeleton dome, the great solo of St. Peter's, and they held their breath, marveling and vibrating, at the sight of this gleaming city in a lazy blue haze, procumbent by the Tiber and stretching itself in graceful indolence on seven hills, with its open vineyards, its gardens with tall cypresses, and its sun-yellow defenseless walls.

Two days later, as Henry plumed himself on his adroitness and sat back in happy ignorance, these cutthroats girded themselves in the cold morning mist to begin the Sack of Rome.

Vesuvius never erupted so savagely as did the Lutherans and Neapolitans and Spaniards who, pent up for months in the growling fury of their hunger, their squalor, their rags and skin-coverings, their frustrated arms that killed no enemy and won no booty, at last burst from under the feeble command of Bourbon and, flinging aside every restraint of discipline and every pretense of military purpose, poured in their hot and lavish multitude over the walls and into the panting streets of Rome. In swift and rustled silence, like flames licking the footsteps of the terrified Romans, these scabrous marauders raced into the city in every direction, killing every citizen they overtook, cleaning the streets of life, and then, amid single shrieks and piercing cries, that were soon to become a clamor and a roar, invading the fountained courtyards and the broad-doored palaces, slitting the throats of the seniors, dragging out the nuns, vamping prelates into the alleys, chastising and unfrocking monks, chasing priests like dogs, seizing armfuls of vestments and chalices and ciboria, denuding the altars, tossing gold and silver plate from palace balconies, heaping hand-carts with glistening and radiant treasures, piling up the booty with wine and viands, lashing the terrified cardinals to mules and stripping virgins and matrons with mad and malignant laughter, releasing in a carnival that was to palpitate for five scorching days and to smolder out for eight pestilential months in all the knavery and tropic lasciviousness of the Neapolitan, all the brutal swinishness of the German, and all the keen and unassuageable cruelty of the hireling Spaniard. The long sunny afternoon of the æsthetic renaissance had ripened Rome until it hung in loaded sweetness over its golden walls. For years its veins had been plumbed with rich intoxication. It had grown into a presence so magnificent and so opulent that it seemed like a tree pendulous with indescribable blossom and humming with innumerable bees. Its very domes, swollen and pointed, were laden with promise to a world that in this high defenselessness could only see an indulged and drowsy cupidity. With a rancor in which lust mingled with rage and hate with righteousness, the troops of Bourbon broke like the thunder-storm which disrupts the sultry day.

From the Vatican itself to the Castel Sant' Angelo, which was Rome's Tower of London, the Pope and his intimates scurried at the first alarm. They ran by a hidden exit from the house of God to the house of the emperors, their hearts liquid with fear. From the grand eminence of this fortress, which lifts itself like a Hercules over the pygmies, Benvenuto Cellini potted Bourbon on his scaling ladder, precisely as Falstaff with his own hand killed Hotspur, but this triumph of marksmanship and coincidence did not prevent Pope Clement from becoming a helpless prisoner, cut off from Christendom by a ring of fire.

And it was to this Pope, the servant of the emperor's servants, that Henry the Eighth was sending for permission to divorce the emperor's aunt.

XIII

The situation was monstrously difficult for Clement. Ever since the defeat of the French at Pavia, he had foreseen Charles's dominance in Italy, and the papacy sought the same balance of power in the South as England sought in the North. The treaty of Madrid, relentless as it was, drove Clement to the French, but the French were thinking only of themselves at this crisis, and Clement was intensely grateful to the English, who in an hour of utter depletion had sent him thirty thousand crowns. Between Charles, who was the upper stone, and Francis, who was the nether, the Pope was caught in his temporal sovereignty. He had not the power to resist them or to escape them.

Few popes deserve more pity than Clement. Coming to the papacy after such gross padroni as Alexander, he had the misfortune to seem relatively feeble. Alexander VI had carried gross appetite to the Lateran. He was a strong and shrewd animal, wallowing in the papacy like a rhinoceros in the warm mud. But the Medicis were unlike the Borgias. They were Florentines, urban and urbane, natively fastidious, lettered, exquisite, the descendants of brigands whose enterprise had been subtilized into banking and distilled into diplomacy. Alexander with his arm around his daughter, guffawing from the papal balcony at the stallions and the mare, had a very different temper from Clement who saw red only when his drunken Lorenzino had decapitated a marble antique.

Clement was now under fifty. He had been faithful to his cousin Leo X as chancellor, when the finances of the Vatican were tubercular, and the office to which he was elected was no less diseased. He was a handsome man with a sensitive face, brilliant eyes, quiveringly alive, with a suave, caressing, ingratiating soul, who hoped by imparting his difficulties to excite sympathy and thus escape them. He lied, intrigued, temporized and played for position. He never went out to meet a

difficulty. He never fought. The head of an institution eaten
out with corruption and crippled in resources and prestige, he
inherited Martin Luther and Zwingli, the Valois and the
Hapsburg and the Tudor, the domination of Italy by the
Spaniards, the downfall of the Medicis, and now the Sack of
Rome.

With councilors at his elbow who were at last awake to the
danger, who loved their subtle institution and knew their world,
to whom opportunism became an instinct as perfect as Giotto's
for the circle, Clement peered in alarm for a chance to squeeze
through. To their wise whisper he leaned his ear, and so, hated
and derided by his enemies, without a trace of purism or
heroism, he guided the quaking papacy through the iron gates
of the Reformation.

While the Pope was still expostulating with Charles,
Henry's agent rode into Rome to solicit Clement's good offices
about "the secret matter." This agent, incidentally, was not
of Wolsey's choosing. Anne and Henry thought they would be
cleverer than the Cardinal, and they had dispatched Henry's
old secretary, Knight. He was an amateur, sent by amateurs,
and instead of looking at his business from the standpoint of
the Vatican, he exposed it in all its verdant simplicity, mentioning Anne Boleyn by name. What he sought, though not in
clear words, was a dispensation for Henry to remarry a girl
whose sister had been his mistress. Henry and Anne were treating the annulment as a minor matter, a detail, a foregone conclusion.

But this was absurdly high-handed. The Vatican, as a man
like Wolsey always realized, was not merely a will that had to
be conciliated; it was the best-organized memory in the world.
If evolution pressed too hard, it could nimbly reorganize its
memory to suit evolution, but otherwise it reposed on the
broad imperturbability of precedent. It remembered, among
other things, the Babylonian captivity of Avignon, where a

French king, informed that the Pope is above prince and people, that "every human being is subject to the Roman Pontiff," had made the Popes political prisoners in a golden palace on a knoll by the Rhone. Clement had no wish to be exiled by Charles from the Italy where his family needed him. He had no wish to be conducted like Francis in 1525 to the sour seclusion of Madrid.

But England might leave the Church? The cardinalate weighed this possibility. England was a small and thinly populated island, wealthy enough but remote, swathed in fog, a wet country, with one cardinal, and only moderately literate. England might follow Germany and Scandinavia into the Lutheran error, but far worse than this estrangement at the present hour would be the actual captivity which the young emperor, tight absolutist by nature, could so easily enforce. It was not the sacred contract of holy matrimony that Clement was upholding. Clement was just arranging a divorce for Henry's sister Margaret, for a cause as light as thistledown. The papacy had dissolved dozens of marriages without a qualm, just as it had declared Clement himself to have been born in wedlock to suit the papal rule against illegitimate children. It was not principle that ruled this era. It was state necessity. Leo had worked against this very Charles as Emperor on the ground of his being ineligible, and then, in a fashion graciously unprincipled, had taken Clement's advice to bow him into eligibility on his election. State necessity—it had been pricked into Clement with the sword and the pike.

He saw Knight at Orvieto. The emperor's garrote still around his ears, he did not dare to give Henry's agent the power to wipe out the papal dispensation, which Henry desired for Wolsey and Warham. Not brave enough to refuse, he issued a quasi-release, with a clause referring it back to Rome. Knight, delighted with the handsome document, triumphantly sent it home.

XIV

Meanwhile Henry had to face Catherine.

The prospect of this interview unnerved him, but it was straight in his path, and he could not meet it by letter or by proxy. She was sharing the palace with him, appearing at his side in public, and behaving as his Queen. Already, in all probability, her friends had warned her of what was happening. There were no secrets in the royal household, where almost every room communicated, and every rustle on the straw drew a spying glance.

But Henry was a forceful man, and a religious. On his knees before his confessor, he had learned that God was his friend. He was fortified in what he was about to do by the explicit approval of the Almighty. Since he was in love with Anne and had already planned his divorce, God might not seem to have been called in except as a late consultant, but Henry had been forehanded; as early as 1523 his own confessor, Longland, had told him that to continue with Catherine would be mortal sin. The blight on his children, since of course a female child like Mary could hardly count—was not that conclusive? Except for the tiniest little pea of doubt under fifty-three mattresses of theology, Henry convinced himself. He went to confront his wife, opening and shutting his eyes, murmuring a prayer, consoling himself that he was obeying the will of God.

In her apartment he made his little speech. They were living in mortal sin. He would not appear with her in future. She must retire to some place far away from court. So he spoke, not unkindly.

Catherine heard the words. She broke into tears. These were the tears of a good woman who felt for her child and herself after years of life together. For the rest, she raised her standard before the enemy. The argument for their separation she was prepared to meet. She had met it in her own soul in 1502.

She, too, had her dynastic conscience. If his scruples were unfounded, there was no other reason why she should give up her place at court.

Henry was set back. He could not descend from his lofty scruples to give her his real reasons for sending her away—his love for Anne, and his desire for a male heir. Thick-headed and confused, he stared at her dumbly. Then he abruptly cut off the interview, asking her to keep it secret! Neither Anne nor his confessor had prepared him for a rival set of conscientious scruples.

XV

The grand issue between husband and wife was now joined, however, and on grounds that spread out in an alarming vista on both sides.

The nucleus of the issue was never admitted to be Henry's human desire to take a fresh young wife in place of a stale elderly wife. The whole medieval culture on which Henry based his moral existence, comprising his theology and his chivalry, his simple belief in godly and kingly authority, and his fiction of his own supreme dynastic significance, could not have survived in the raw air of such self-exposure. Henry really believed in himself as a morally superior man.

When you believe in yourself as morally superior, and at the same time do not scrutinize yourself, when you dispense with this scrutiny because you are a Defender of the Faith, a Knight of the Garter, a Knight of the Golden Fleece, and a vast number of other distinguished things making you an automatic gentleman, you do not descend from the height of your scruples, even though they are spavined, to the level of mother earth. You are knighted for all time. You do not accept yourself as a barbarian who, by calling natural intentions by plain names, may knowingly select the more delectable and the more exhilarating, the less cruel and the less beastly, if such can be managed. Henry never supposed he was a barbarian or could be cruel and beastly. He insisted with the utmost seriousness on these biting scruples about having married his late brother's wife, and having lived with his present intended's sister. These scruples were to become the whole contention between Henry and Catherine with Pope Clement agonizing as referee.

So was Catherine afforded a far better issue than she could have found in a mere human rivalry between herself and Anne. By taking Henry on his own terms, the resources of casuistry were not yet exhausted. In the next six years, step by step, Henry would be forced to deploy every regiment he could muster—to seek victory through the legates, the rota, the universities of Europe, the printing press, a proposed church council, the diplomacy of Francis, and a complete manipulation of his own ecclesiastics and his own parliament. And all this so that he could secure his divorce safely and soundly inside the Catholic Church.

Catherine, on her part, could marshal ambassadors and cardinals and magnates and the emperor to counteract through canon law and public opinion, papal tradition and papal expediency the onslaughts and concussions made by Henry. By the pride and iron of this woman alone, by her embodiment of a passion and a conviction, Henry was to learn that he must either give up the divorce or give up the Church.

What began as an amatory episode, was becoming a grandiose public question, a graphic vital choice. Rome shattered itself against sex. The will of the papacy to regulate through an instinct aroused another fundamental will. The Englishman was no less stubborn than the Spanish woman or the Italian prelate, and where on one side was the mother fighting for her inheritance, on the other was a man fighting for personal experience inside the rules. Seldom through a single struggle, however mighty, are the rules inflected, but once

Henry engaged himself to divorce Catherine, he pursued his end like a bull baited by dogs.

A lazy and luxurious character to begin with, and content to let things drift, he became bold, cunning, tireless, ferocious and yet capable of calculated inactivity, so that it meant little or nothing to him in the end to depose the papacy in England.

As the struggle proceeded, he ceased to be adolescent. His respect for law, which had the quality of deference at the start, became an estimate of force. He passed from a youth of barbaric ostentation and pomposity to a closely measured and intricately reasoned middle age. What had begun as a clash of personalities developed as a shock of vested interests, a war of institutions, a battle of lies.

Like monsters on whose heaving backs two rival pagodas had been reared, this King and this Queen were to affront one another, freighted with toppling towers. But the battle of Henry's conscientious scruples went beyond the normal. It became an edifice of figment erected tier on tier with the intention of supporting his cause and giving his arquebus the chance to sweep his enemy. Out of his love for Anne grew a divorce, which, to be valid, required an entirely new foreign policy, a new council, a new hierarchy, a new church establishment, a new chancellor, and, strangest of all, a new wife. And with these novelties the man himself evolved, if not a new nature, at least a nature alarmingly new in its assertion.

Not once but a hundred times he was to bend his head and crash with his full weight into rebellious circumstances. He was to pit his strength against the yielding yet ever-accumulating hindrance to his emotional demands. The bull-man had embarked on that most ambitious of all adventures, the grouping of world-facts around a personal desire. Henry willed it so. And as the pressures of an unfriendly if fearsome society resisted his will, he changed from a comparatively passive figure in the drama to an implacable creator, sparing no effort to ply the spirits he could not break, but requiring for his sustenance a laudatory fiction in ever-movable type of flesh and blood.

As his soul hungered within him for an assent that is only valid when paid in the free accents of independence and sincerity, this man who destroyed independence and withered sincerity, ached for the medicine he trampled underfoot. It was not the pattern of the North. It was the habitual pattern of the Near East, the Byzantine design. But in dominating the sphere to which God had called him this handsome and amiable youth slowly and irresistibly changed into the personage on whose lowering visage was written the judgment of psychological law. From a bland dominance that gave simple satisfaction to his face, he advanced to a wider power that brought with it an increasing bewilderment. He quaffed his glass and it sharpened his thirst. On this fact, toward the end, there came no illumination. On the contrary, there rose within it the mirage of sweet waters that were forever beyond reach. Henry's eyes searched the horizon in a gaze that was denied as it yearned, and that yearned because it was denied. He had entered the circle that turns on its pitiless self, and as he hurried in his traces, he encountered the reminder that this was not simply despair but despair mirrored in a mockery.

And yet, with the curious sovereignty in all human experience, this exercise in self-will was also to prove sovereign. Henry was an integer. Blinded, brutalized, bewildered, he gathered his heavy and corrupted body every morning for a renewal of the endless experiment. Bankrupt, it seemed he had entered into the labyrinth where men, weaving a new path, walk into their own wraiths and start with equal animosity in an opposite direction. But Henry held on his rounds. His possessions clutched by him at the end with the same abiding instinct that had ruled his cradle, he still remained a positive though distorted will. He remained a man. He was of the stuff of creative humanity. And as such he kept significance.

XVI

The Sack of Rome aroused the whole being of Wolsey. Once more he looked abroad, he saw the papacy cast in the dust, saw the Emperor meeting his triumph and the French forced to consider a new war. Weary though he was, he determined to go into action on the grand scale.

It was the last ambassade of the great cleric. Like a bugle of defiance, he marched out of Westminster, and, with liveried servants in black velvet and horsemen to the number of nine hundred passed through all London, over London Bridge, and on to impoverished Kent. "He rode like a Cardinal, very sumptuously," said his secretary, "on a mule trapped with crimson velvet upon velvet, and his stirrups of copper and gilt; his spare mule followed him with like apparel. And before him he had two crosses of silver, two great pillars of silver, and the great seal of England, his cardinal's hat, and a gentleman that carried his valaunce." With him he took a paymaster and barrels of money to pay Frenchmen to fight. So for the last time, he passed in solemn pomp before the unfriendly yet circumspect stare of London.

He was not deceived by his own show. As he knelt at Canterbury, the choir by his orders singing "Ora pro papa nostro Clemente," instead of "Ora pro nobis," he bowed down his head, the sweet voices melting him to sadness, and he did "weep very tenderly." Well might he weep for the papacy.

But this was a hidden moment. Braced by pride, he called his noblemen and gentlemen together to tell them the ceremony they owed to him on coming into France. "By virtue of my commission," he announced to them, "I must have all such service and reverence as is due his highness himself. Nothing

is to be neglected or omitted, and for my part ye shall see that
I will not omit one jot thereof."

In the same spirit, turning his back on universality, he advised his gentlemen how to dispute honor with the French.

"They will be at the first meeting as familiar with you as
they had been acquainted with you long before; be ye as familiar with them as they be with you. If they speak to you in the
French tongue, speak to them in the English tongue; for if you
understand not them, they shall no more understand you."

He caught sight of Ap Rice and he said merrily, "Rice,
speak thou Welsh to the Frenchman, and I am well assured
that thy Welsh shall be more diffuse to him than his French
shall be to thee."

Having enjoyed his joke, he added with becoming fatherly
gravity, "Let all your entertainment and behavior be according
to all gentleness and humanity, that it may be reported after
your departure that ye be gentlemen of right good behavior
and much gentleness."

This was his natural buoyant style, and Wolsey carried it
into his parleys. He completed the treaty with France, pledged
Mary's marriage to the Duke of Orleans, and reassured Francis and Louise as to his adherence. He admired and extolled
the architecture for which Francis showed such passion since
he had come back from Madrid. Without broaching the divorce
too directly, he hinted at a marriage with Renée, insisted that
if Clement was the emperor's prisoner a council of cardinals
must be appointed with himself at the head, a suggestion that
the French took rather tepidly and that somehow failed to at-
tract Clement. But it was one of Wolsey's usual feints, part of
his deliberate self-assertion and a constant effort to keep England European.

While he acted this ambitious part abroad, Henry was at
home sweating in his pursuit of the buck and his courtship of
Anne Boleyn. "I send you, by this bearer," wrote the royal

lover, "a buck killed late last night by my hand, hoping, when you eat of it, you will think on the hunter; and thus for want of more room I will make an end of my letter. Written by the hand of your servant, who often wishes you in your brother's place."

It was a courtship letter, and Anne responded warmly. Her point of view was changing. With the departure of Knight for Rome, the divorce loomed near, and there dawned on her the vivid prospect of being Queen of England. It dazzled her, as it dazzled her father, her brother and her uncle, and the young girl in her was quickly giving place to an excited, avid, energetic woman. Her brain, busy without being deep, was already teeming with plans. She had dispensed with Wolsey in her own mind and determined to let him know it.

No sooner was Wolsey back from France, than Anne's new status was brought home to him. His messenger came to the great hall at Greenwich with the momentous news that the cardinal had arrived and asked where it pleased his Highness to receive him. Anne, sparkling at Henry's side, spoke for the King herself without hesitation.

"And where else is the Cardinal to come but here where the King is?"

Every courtier heard her interpose, and looked at Henry. Without a quiver he seconded the imperious young woman. Yet once Knight sent his courier from Italy, and a glance at his document enabled Wolsey to pronounce it valueless, the lovers saw how ill-prepared they were to discard Wolsey. They were forced into his experienced hands.

Anne yielded to circumstance. Without understanding the shoals and sandbars that must handicap any pilot, and secretly ascribing every hitch in the divorce to the ill-will of the Cardinal whom she had good reason to hate, she still undertook to mask her enmity. She soon was writing letters excessively warm and profusely insincere. He meant more to her than any one

else on earth save Henry, she said, and she protested her love
for him. Wolsey, shrugging his shoulders, took her letters simply as weather signals. Feared by Anne, hated by Catherine,
he had been honest when he took God to record that he lived
to advance Henry's plan, but he alone knew the people he was
dealing with.

Now he went to the root of the matter. The man who had
been imagining himself Pope for ten years could act greedily,
which was his fault, but he was of European stature when it
came to the Vatican. He had the scope, the vision and the experience that this divorce demanded. Knight had blurted out
Anne Boleyn's name. Wolsey knew very well that Anne's reputation must long since have been besmirched by the imperialists, and that Mary Boleyn's ill-fame must have set its mark
on Anne. His first care, then, was to select two stout
churchmen to go straight to Clement, Gardiner and Foxe by
name, and their first task was to expound in the plainest word,
"the approved excelleut virtuous qualities of the said gentlewoman, the purity of her life, the constant virginity, her maidenly and womanly pudicity, her soberness, chasteness,
meekness, humility, wisdom, descent right noble and high
through regal blood, education in all good and laudable qualities and manners, apparent aptness to the procreation of
children, with her other infinite good qualities, more to be regarded and esteemed than the only progeny."

It was only four years since Wolsey had sneered at Anne's
plebeian origin. Now she was of descent through regal blood.
So he acclaimed her chastity. He would have declared her a
virgin or the mother of twins, as it chanced to suit the occasion.
Henry read Wolsey's testimonial with delight. He ordered
Gardiner and Foxe to stop at Hever, to show Anne these tributes to her purity, pudicity, chasteness and constant virginity.
"Darlyng," scribbled Henry in hot haste, "these shal be wonly
to advertyce yow that thys berer and hys felow be dyspecyd

with as meny thynge to compasse oure mater and to bryng it to
pas, as oure wytts colde immagyn or device. . . . Kepe hym
nott to long with yow, myne awn swette hart, wrytten with the
hand off hym whyche desyryth as muche to be yours, as yow
do to have hym."

XVII

A hard winter journey brought the envoys to the feet of their
Pope. They found his holiness in the hill-town of Orvieto, to
which he had escaped in disguise from the Castel Sant' Angelo.
"The Pope plieth in an old palace of the bishops of this city,
ruinous and decayed, where, or we come to his privy bedchamber, we pass three chambers, all naked and unhanged, the
roofs fallen down, and as we can guess, thirty persons, rif raf
and other, standing in the chambers for a garnishment. And as
for the Pope's bedchamber, all the apparel in it was not worth
twenty nobles, bed and all."

But Clement, stripped of pomp, was still the head of his
church. Admitting in his easy way that, while "the Pope has
all laws in the cabinet of his breast," God had not happened
to give him the key, he called in one adviser after another,
dark, tonsured men, who brought the English clerics into the
formal reception room of their minds. But Gardiner and Foxe
were dogged. They refused formality. And bit by bit began
real negotiation. "His holiness is cunctator maximus" [the
prince of delayers], reported the Englishmen, and they said,
"all the stop, difficulty and delay in this matter proceedeth
only of fear," fear of the "Spanyards."

Clement held court in his little bedchamber. For hours at a
time, his back to the bare white wall, he sat on a plain bench,
while on peasants' stools in a semicircle around him sat
Gardiner and Foxe and the learned men of the Vatican. They
spoke in Latin. It was close disputation, inch by inch, the
Englishmen pressing for the divorce-case in England, the

Italians retorting, and meanwhile a tradition being shaped in this tiny room that was to affect millions of the born and unborn, and to endure for centuries.

"We find in every man as great desire to further the King's matter as we can wish, as far as we can gather of their word, fashion and manner. And in that they assent not to our requests we can impute it to no other thing, but only fear." So spoke Gardiner. Yet there was perhaps more than fear. He tried to bribe Cardinal Pucci, as instructed. But from Pucci there came a glint of unmistakable tradition and purpose. He intended to be free and declined the two thousand crowns. "I could in nowise cause the said Cardinal to take one penny by no means." But the Cardinal's secretary took thirty crowns.

The Pope privately confided to Gardiner that, while he was persuaded of Henry's being in the right, the law must be observed; and when Gardiner hectored him at this, Clement "sighed and wiped his eyes," and looked most melancholy.

Weeks of negotiations bore fruit. Clement appointed Cardinal Campeggio to try the case in England with Wolsey, and, under extreme pressure, without daring to tell his cardinals, he agreed to give this legate a secret decretal or pronouncement, signed by himself, saying that the legate's decision would be final. The way was apparently opened for a speedy divorce in England.

XVIII

Meanwhile Henry was the ardent lover. Still living with his wife Catherine, and sharing the vast royal bed with her, he had Anne near him constantly or kept in touch with her by letter. The life he lived in those days was abundantly and glowingly active. He had seen the older companions of the council build up their families and pass out of the character of mere courtesans, but the new company of satellites had taken their place and he was even more at home with Harry Norris, Thomas

Wyatt, Francis Weston, William Brereton, Francis Bryan, George Boleyn. With them he cast dice, shot with the bow, hunted, galloped and hawked. He loved every sort of gambling. The day of the tournament was over, since he had hurt his foot and gone around in a black velvet slipper, but he was still up early in the morning, prompt at mass, restlessly busy all day, and ready at night for masque or banquet.

He spent most of his time from spring to autumn within a day's courier's ride from London, and he showed his extraordinary vitality by moving every four or five days from one grand house to another, the whole court moving with him like a humming swarm. He loved people, and he loved to be in the center of them. Around him, since he carried his business with him, hovered the privy council. As dispatches and commissions and petitions came out to him from London, he sent for his fellow-directors and discharged the nation's work offhand. He had one parliament in fourteen years, but it had proved too restive. Francis had declared war on Charles at the beginning of the year 1528, but since he could only afford to contribute in monthly installments, and since he was reverting to his father's canny views about peace and economy, he was content to deal summarily with commerce, law and order, heresy, discipline, passing on the tedious details to his able secretaries and sharing with Wolsey and the council what was worthy of royal attention.

But this routine life masked his great preoccupation. He was really concerned with nothing but Anne. And he soon had to suffer for it. In the summer of 1528 forty thousand people were attacked by the sweating sickness in London. Henry was thrown into alarm for the most precious person on earth. He wrote to her at once, disturbed and frightened. Few or no *women* are sick, he assures her. "I beg you, my entirely beloved," he writes in French, "not to frighten yourself, not to be too uneasy at our absence. For, wherever I am, I am yours, and

yet we must sometimes submit to our misfortunes; for whoever
will struggle against fate is generally but so much farther from
gaining his end; wherefore comfort yourself and take courage,
and make this misfortune as easy to you as you can, and I
hope very soon to have us *chanter le renvoye.*" And he rounds
off as usual, "No more at present for lack of time, but that I
wish you in my arms."

He was too sanguine. "There came to me sudden in the
night," his next letter breaks out, "the most afflicting news
possible." Anne had the sweating sickness, but a light attack.
He sent his own physician. "And I hope very soon to see you
again, which will be to me a greater cordial than all the precious stones in the world."

Henry was brave to encourage Anne, since he was scared
beyond words himself, and saw death before him. He hurriedly
made his will. His friends seemed to be going all round him.
Compton of Compton Wynyates, for whose ulcerous leg he had
once ground up pearls in ointment, died in a few hours. So did
Mary Boleyn's husband, Carey. Five in his own household
were attacked, including the "potecary." The plague pursued Henry, and, though he changed his residence almost
nightly, it came nearer and nearer.

XIX

A clever Frenchman like du Bellay made irreverent jokes in
the midst of this panic, but bluff King Hal made no jokes.
Were these sudden deaths a judgment of God on his boon companion, Compton, and on the complaisant husband Carey?
Henry had his uneasy suspicions. He prudently dined across
the table from his physician. Wedged in between this physician and his confessor, he walked in the narrow path. Every
morning he went to confession, received his Maker of Sundays
and holidays, and, declining to look deep into his soul, reassured himself with extreme moral punctilio. In these few weeks,

reiterating that he had no reason to be afraid, that he had not departed from rectitude, that his intentions and behavior were impeccable, he commenced to develop one of those fantastic fictions by which a man, closing his mind on the facts he does not approve of, insists exclusively on the facts that flatter his self-righteousness. This useful but exacting fiction grew on Henry. Far more cerebral than his genial grandfather Edward, whom he much resembled, Henry was more seriously self-willed and more sententiously religious. He needed a moral formula that would at once save him from the Judgment Day he dreaded, and give him the Anne Boleyn he loved. He was pushed toward moral pedantry. It was a strange development, which had only begun to be noticeable.

But, as it happened, Henry's freshened moral delicacy served Anne Boleyn at the moment.

Anne had complained to her lover about Wolsey. She had been urging a nun named Eleanor Carey, her sister-in-law, as the new abbess of Wilton, and Wolsey had rejected her. The case for Eleanor, Henry was obliged to write back, is very weak. "She that we would have had abbess," he explained, "had confessed herself to have had two children by two sundry priests, and furder since hath been kept by a servant of the lord Broke, that was, and that not long ago; wherefore I would not for all the gold in the world clog your conscience nor mine to make her ruler of a house, which is of so ungodly demeanor, nor I trust you would not that neither for brother nor sister I should so destain mine honor or conscience."

These were fine words, though spoken by the man who had seduced Carey's wife. But Anne did not want to touch on Henry's honor and conscience. She pointed out that Wolsey, against express orders, had appointed Eleanor's rival. Was Henry going to stand this insolence?

Feeling on so lofty a plane of honor and conscience, Henry undertook to castigate Wolsey. He wrote a letter of stinging rebuke, so stately that it was almost God-like. And Henry felt God-like when he showed it to Anne. "I pray you, my lord, think not that it is upon any displeasure that I write this unto you," he wound up superbly. "For surely it is for my discharge afore God, being in the room that I am in; and secondly, for the great zeal I bear unto you, not undeserved on your behalf. Wherefore, I pray you, take it so; and I assure you, your fault acknowledged, there shall remain in me no spark of displeasure; trusting hereafter you shall recompense that with a thing much more acceptable to me."

Anne sent Wolsey one of her sweetest letters at this juncture, but Wolsey understood too well what it meant when an absolute king mounted the high horse, which he himself had so often groomed. This letter from Henry was no longer that of one confederate speaking to another. The moral trump had been slipped into the old easy-going game. It was the king speaking to the subject, the chief to the dependent, and Wolsey labored under two fatal limitations; he was in the wrong, and he had never stood alone.

Painfully the proud Cardinal cringed before his young master. He admitted and deplored everything, "purposing, with God's help and your gracious favor, so to order the rest of my poor life that it shall appear to your highness that I love and dread God and also your majesty."

Such victories were not good for Henry.

XX

Henry in love was less afraid of Anne. He wrote to her in rich bucolic strain, as one accustomed to hard sport and of rude robust appetite, and of nerves dulled and mulled by copious wine. It was another story than with the more delicate souls that were already repelled by grossness and were drawn to the exquisiteness of Botticelli. In his early youth Henry had himself tried musical and poetic gambades, but his was not naturally the picked tune of Wyatt and Surrey and the other italianated Englishmen.

"Seyng my darlyng is absent," he wrote tenderly, "I can no less do than to sende her summe flesche, representyng my name, whyche is hart flesche for Henry, pronosticating that hereafter, God wyllyng, you must injoye summe off myne whyche he pleasyd I wolde wer now." From this outspoken warmth with its hearty sigh that flesh is flesh and love is love, Anne Boleyn did not shrink. She echoed her lover when he said with a pang, "I wolde we wer to gyder an evennyng."

Soon they were together, and their intimacy was complete. But Anne governed his passion, and, in spite of his urgency, which she soon came to share, she kept him docile and human. His yearning for her burst out the moment she was out of his sight.

"Mine own sweetheart," he said to her of a bright August evening, "this shall be to tell you of the great torment that I feel here since your departing, for I assure you me thinketh the time longer since your departing now last, than I was wont to do a whole fortnight. I think your kindness and my fervence of love causeth it, for otherwise I would not have thought it possible that for so little a while it should have grieved me. But now that I am coming toward you me thinketh my pains been half disappeared, and also I am right well comforted in so much that my book maketh substantially for my matter in loking whereof I have spent above four hours this day, which caused me now to write the shorter letter to you at this time, by cause of some pain in my head. Wishing myself (specially an evening) in my sweetheart's arms, whose pretty dukkys I trust shortly to kiss, written with the hand of him that was, is, and shall be yours by his will, H. Rex."

The "book" was his argument against his marriage to Catherine. In preparation for the coming of the legate Campeggio, he was rehearsing his case. With the legate in sight, and Anne assured to him, Henry was far calmer than his mistress. Through the Cardinal he had "got on" a lodging for her in London, to be near him, and he confidently told Anne that "there can be no more done nor more diligence used nor all manner of dangers better foreseen and provided for."

Yes, fumed Anne, but where *is* the legate? It was already September, 1528, and here was Henry in the country, the assuaged lover, writing such nonsense as "I think it long since I kissed you. Written after the killing of a hart at eleven of the clock, minding with God's grace, tomorrow mightily timely to kill another." But Henry had not forgotten the legate. "The legate which we most desire arrived at Paris, on Sunday or Monday past, so that I trust by next Monday to hear of his arrival at Calais."

Anne's impatience did not cease. A sharp letter from Henry, marveling that it was known they were to be in London and saying "lack of discreet handling must needs be the cause of it," brought from Anne the sort of spirited retort that always cowed him. Her defense was counter-attack, and Henry waited till he saw her to plead with her to be gentle. He found her fiery. He had much difficulty in soothing her, but at last she sent him word that she trusted him to keep pressure on this new legate and on her *bête noire*, Wolsey.

Henry felt immense relief. "To inform you what joy it is to me to understand of your conformableness to reason," he exclaimed, "and of the suppressing of your inutile and vain thoughts and fantasies with the bridle of reason, I ensure you all goods in this world could not counterpoise for my satisfaction the knowledge and certainty thereof." And then he made a little propaganda. "Wherefore, good sweetheart, continue the same, not only in this, but in all your doings hereafter, for thereby shall come both to you and to me the greatest quietness that may be in this world."

Here, for the first time, Henry struck the note with Anne

Boleyn that became almost plaintive in repetition. Let Anne put on "the bridle of reason." Let the Pope "pay due regard to my wishes." Thereby shall come the greatest quietness that may be in this world.

"And thus, for lake of tyme, sweetheart, farwel."

So closes the last of the seventeen precious love letters which the Vatican quietly purloined from Anne Boleyn. Sensuous and almost pathetically simple, they reveal the intensity of Henry's burning heart. They throb with sincerity and they say much of Anne's constant allurement. They reveal the completest intimacy. But what do they say of beauty, of tenderness, of gentleness? What do they say of loyalty? Anne might well wonder as to the course of this powerful passion to which she had surrendered.

XXI

At last the Roman legate was in London. Cardinal Campeggio was England's choice. He had been in England ten years before, drew an annuity as Bishop of Hereford, owed his palace in Rome to England, and was soon to see his young son knighted by Henry. But these were all minor considerations to the graduate of a very old school. He came with a full conviction that the cause was momentous. He knew how hot Anne and Henry were for the divorce, how Wolsey was forsworn, how it seemed to Francis and the Emperor. He had long since dealt with Luther, and had no illusions as to the security of the Church. Heavy with years and crippled with gout, he undertook his task with the utmost gravity. It was his ponderous habit to regard every cause *sub specie æternitatis*.

He learned with sorrow that Henry was immovable. "I believe," he communicated to Rome, "I believe that in this case he knows more than a great theologian and canonist." An angel descending from heaven, he sadly surmised, would not be able to persuade Henry that his marriage was valid.

But Queen Catherine? The old man ordered his litter and, accompanied by Wolsey, went to see Catherine. He recalled to her the ill-omened execution that had preceded her marriage. He solemnly suggested to her that, like the sainted (divorced) wife of Louis XII, she might withdraw into a convent at this latter end of her life, for the good of her soul. The Spaniard in Catherine flared out at the Italian. If Henry went into a monastery, she agreed, she would go into a convent. But she admitted no suggestion that she should recede. Though she be torn limb from limb, or die and come to life again, she was truly married, and would die twice for this opinion.

Wolsey on his knees to her left her absolutely untouched.

Catherine's courage so stirred the common people, that Henry was forced to counteract it, even though he had to send Anne Boleyn away. There was no press to inspire and no parliament to use, but he took his own way of molding opinion. He sent out commands to the bridewell, and there, to a notable gathering of lords, judges and aldermen, he bared his heart. His hypocrisy and duplicity were unmeasured, almost magnificent. He was happy in the affections of his Queen, he said, but he was obliged to satisfy his conscience. Here he was, married to a woman of most gentleness, of most humility and buxomness, yea, and of all good qualities appertaining to nobility without comparison, and yet the censor of public morals (Wolsey) had raised this horrible specter that they were living in sin. If Catherine were only his lawful wife, Henry swore that there was "never thing more pleasant nor more acceptable" to him. But he recalled the Wars of the Roses. He dwelt on the succession to the crown. He feared for the worst. And he asked his loyal auditors to tell their friends how things really stood, and to join with him in praying that the truth might come to be known.

Having sown the seed, Henry was eager to have the matter come to trial, especially as Campeggio had with him the Pope's secret permission to give judgment. But Campeggio moved with the weightiest deliberation. By the foresight of the Vatican, he, and not Wolsey, was the presiding legate, and when news came in February, 1529, that Pope Clement was mortally ill, the presiding legate suspended action.

It was a gamble. For a few weeks Henry and Wolsey let themselves dwell on the gorgeous prospect of an Englishman as Pope. Orders for lavish bribery were sent to the English agents at Rome. But Clement's fever abated, and he slowly recovered, allowing the legates to depend on their commissions as still valid.

As the spring of 1529 advanced, it became impossible for Campeggio to hold back longer. While the war of 1528-9 had been going in favor of France, the papacy might have hoped to indulge Henry, but Lautrec was dead, the French army had melted away like hailstones, and Charles and Clement were to arrange terms at Barcelona. A real peace between France and Spain was at last to be negotiated by two sane human beings, Margaret of Austria and Louise of Savoy—the last great act of their lives, since both were soon to die. With this peace in sight, Clement regretted his secret pronouncement, and, even though Henry had seen it, he sent private word ordering Campeggio to burn it. It was therefore with full knowledge that Clement was becoming an imperialist that Campeggio and Wolsey opened their court at Blackfriars.

XXII

It was the month of June, 1529. Henry had been used to spending his Junes in the tiltyard, in all the splendor and thrill of the tournaments. This was a tournament not less thrilling and splendid, in a great chamber by the Thames, and every courtier in England, new blood and old, quivered with the terrible excitement. It was a tournament between a king and a queen, a man and a woman; on it hung the fate of Catherine, the fate of Anne and Henry, and the fate of the Cardinal. Not since Augustine had stepped on English grass nine hundred years before did the link with papal Rome come to such a trial, and with it the spiritual culture and evolution of the English people. Henry and Catherine were no longer persons; they had become the representatives of two orders, one a national dynast and the other the liege of an older obedience. In this hall of Blackfriars, below the dais of these two scarlet-clad priests, the King and the Queen made this last joint obeisance to the power of ecclesiastical law.

"King Henry of England, come into the court!"

"Here, my lords!"

"Catherine, Queen of England, come into the court!"

Without a word of answer to the court, Catherine, rising from her chair, walked round until she was before Henry, and, kneeling down at his feet in the sight of all the court and the assembly, despite his efforts to raise her, she spoke in broken English.

"Sire, I beseech you for all the loves that hath been between us, and for the love of God, let me have justice and right, take of me some pity and compassion, for I am a poor woman and a stranger born out of your dominion. . . .

"I loved all those whom ye loved only for your sake, whether I had cause or no, and whether they were my friends or my enemies. . . . This twenty years I have been your true wife or more, and by me ye have had divers children, although it hath pleased God to call them out of this world, which hath been no fault in me. . . .

"And when ye had me at the first, I take God to be my judge, I was a true maid, without touch of men; and whether it be true or no, I put it to your conscience. . . .

"It is a wonder to hear what new inventions are now invented against me, that never intended but honesty. . . .

"I most humbly require you, in the way of charity, and for

the love of God, who is the last judge, to spare me the extremity of this new court, until I may be advertised what way and order my friends in Spain will advise me to take. And if ye will not extend to me so much indifferent favor, your pleasure then be fulfilled, and to God I commit my cause."

With that she rose up, made a low curtsey to the King, and left the court. The crier called after her, and her attendant said, "Madam, ye be called again." "On, on," she said, "it is no impartial court for me. Go on your ways."

The King could see how Catherine had swayed her audience. With his voice warm and trembling, he rose to speak.

"She hath been to me as true, as obedient, and as conformable a wife, as I could in my fantasy wish or desire. She hath all the virtuous qualities that ought to be in a woman of her dignity, or in any other of baser estate."

His tribute paid, he turned to his conscience. Some words of the French ambassador had pricked his conscience. "These words were so conceived within my scrupulous conscience, that it bred a doubt within my breast, which doubt pricked, vexed and troubled so my mind, and so disquieted me, that I was in great doubt of God's indignation." Thus being troubled, "in waves of a scrupulous conscience, and partly in despair of any issue made by her, it drave me at last to consider the estate of this realm."

He "attempted the law," therefore, whether he might marry again, not of course "for any carnal concupiscence, nor for any displeasure or mislike of the Queen's person or age, with whom I could be as well content to continue during my life, if our marriage may stand with God's law, as with any woman alive." But it was his conscience, his wounded conscience, and he declared that all the bishops of England had granted the license he "axed" of them, to come to this court.

The bishops, seated in a decorative row, listened to these amazing words. Old Warham spoke, "That is truth, if it please your highness. I doubt not but all my brethren here present will affirm the same."

One ancient man, intensely spare, with burning eyes, said in a clear voice, "No, sir, not I. Ye have not my consent thereto."

The King glared and shook the paper in his hand. "No! ha' the—! Look here upon this. Is not this your hand and seal?"

The bishop, John Fisher of Rochester, raised his voice again. "No, forsooth, Sire, it is not my hand nor seal!"

The King turned to the bellwether. Warham turned to Fisher. Fisher insisted, "I said to you, that I never would consent to no such act."

The old Archbishop of Canterbury tried to assuage him. "You say truth. But at the last ye were fully persuaded that I should sign for you and put to a seal myself!"

With a scorn that must have scalded Warham's heart, the Bishop of Rochester retorted in a voice like a bell. "Under your correction, my lord, there is no thing more untrue."

"Well, well," broke in Henry, "it shall make no matter. We will not stand with you in argument herein, for you are but one man."

The forgery of Rochester's name and seal was not an auspicious beginning for Henry's case, but it was fairly launched, and needed only the proof that Catherine and Prince Arthur had really been man and wife.

Nearly forty noble witnesses were heard at Blackfriars. Their testimony bent the knee to the man who beheaded Buckingham. Prince Aruthur's age was no bar to consummation, since, as the Earl of Shrewsbury swore, he himself knew his wife, not being sixteen. The Duke of Norfolk also took the stand to swear that at the age of fifteen he himself did carnally know and use his wife. Sir Anthony Willoughby remembered Arthur's very words.

"Willoughby, give me a cup of ale, for I have been this night in the midst of Spain," after which he said, "Masters, it is good pastime to have a wife." Lord Fitzwalter had waited on Arthur at table, and he repeated his witticism. Anne Boleyn's father corroborated. Lady Fitzwalter said she saw the young couple in bed together, which was blest, and that she left them alone together. Certain linen sheets, that had been sent to Spain to Queen Isabella, were also produced and exhibited. And yet, on the other side, the Bishop of Ely testified that the Queen had often said to him "that she was never carnally known of Prince Arthur."

XXIII

The case went too slowly for Henry. He sent for Wolsey, on a hot day in July.

"Sir," said the Bishop of Carlisle, meeting him on the barge later, as he wiped the sweat from his face, "it is a very hot day."

"Yea," said Wolsey, "if ye had been as well chafed as I have been within this hour, ye would say it were very hot."

The tired Cardinal tumbled into his naked bed for his siesta, as was the custom, and was not in it two hours before a message roused him out. He must come at once to Bridewell, with Campeggio, to argue with the Queen.

Wolsey was outraged. He suspected Anne Boleyn, and he turned on Anne's father, whose eyes promptly "watered tears." "Ye and other my lords of the council are not a little to blame and misadvised to put such fantasies into his head. Ye are the causes of great trouble, and it will get ye but small thanks either of God or of the world."

Fetching Campeggio from his bed at Bath Place, Wolsey presented himself in the Queen's chamber of presence.

Out she came of her private room with a skein of white thread about her neck.

"What is your pleasure with me?"

"If it please you to go into your private room."

"My lord, if you have anything to say, speak it openly before all these folks."

Wolsey began in Latin.

"Nay, good my lord, speak to me in English, I beseech you, although I understand Latin."

"We came to know your mind, and to declare secretly our opinions and our counsel to you, which we have intended of our very zeal and obedience to your grace."

Then she thanked them, "But I was set among my maidens at work, thinking full little of any such matter. And will any Englishmen be friendly unto me against the King's pleasure, they being his subjects? Nay forsooth, my lords. But I am destitute and barren of friendship and counsel here in a foreign region, and as for your counsel I will not refuse but be glad to hear."

No counsel and no pressure moved Catherine. The summer drew to a close. Vacation time arrived. Campeggio, at last taking his courage in his hands, adjourned the cause, according to the order of the court in Rome.

This act was a thunderbolt. On hearing the words spoken, Henry strode out, while Suffolk, his face flaming, stepped forward. "It was never merry in England whilst we had cardinals amongst us!" He clapped his hand on the table.

From his judicial seat, Wolsey gazed on the man who had married Henry's sister. The prelate did not yield to the blustering noble.

"Sir," he said, in his deep baritone, "of all men within this realm, ye have least cause to be offended with cardinals. For if I, a simple cardinal, had not been, you should have had at this present no head upon your shoulders."

XXIV

For all this just answer, the failure of the legatine court was in itself a schism between Clement's Rome and Henry's England. Wolsey knew how many councilors would gather round the King to incite him to the wildest actions. He had every reason to fear for himself. He had every reason to fear the night crow, as he called Anne, and Suffolk's outburst startled him as the hunter's halloo would startle any quarry.

His first concern, now as always, was the man who had ridden into the country with his mistress. Could he make Henry wait on Rome, and, if not, would Henry turn against him?

Anne Boleyn's resentment was flaming. The legates' court had been a bad experience for her. She had had to scurry ignominiously from London, and to submit to Henry's half-hearted and double-faced pose. The collapse of the court seemed to her to be entirely Wolsey's fault. With tongue already barbed, she attacked him to Henry, urging the King to see how useless it all was, and pleading with him to burn his boats and marry her at once.

As usual, Henry shirked the pain of taking a positive position. He now had less reason than Anne to hurry action. He knew how many of his courtiers hated Wolsey, but he was not certain that Wolsey was culpable. It was a crisis in which he instinctively went slow. He needed time.

The Cardinal in fact was not to blame. Campeggio was immovable, and Clement obdurate, not because they were moral heroes, but because the control of Europe had passed into one man's hands. Wolsey had met and studied Charles V, and he appreciated what this control would be like—"right cold and temperate," but grimly firm. If only Andrea Doria had not been driven to Charles by Francis's utter stupidity, or if only, with Clement's underhand support, the French had taken Naples: but this was spilt history. Francis had failed, Charles gripped Italy, and the Treaty of Cambrai (in which Wolsey had not had a finger), confirmed it. Clement was soon to crown Charles with the iron crown at Bologna, and to see a Medici gladly marry Charles's illegitimate child.

Wolsey understood the deadlock so well that he could not help being frightened. If he were to placate his "serpentine enemy," Anne, he must outwit Charles, and he had no power to do it. The skill with which he fabricated new schemes had deserted him. He could only imagine ill omens, and fabricate pictures to which his poisoned body gave hideous color, pictures of humiliation, terror and ruin.

Henry, meanwhile, slid round Anne's demands for Wolsey's head. He too knew Charles. His warm tributes to Catherine were for the nephew's ears, and if Wolsey were to go, who would manage Europe for him? Henry's own anger was with distant Rome, and he was especially wrothful with the deceitful Clement. When he was pressed and irritated to condemn the Cardinal, his eyes flittered uncomfortably. Some day he might sacrifice Wolsey, whose wealth and pensions would be worth having, but this conflict was ungrateful to him. Under his good nature, which was ample, there were two apprehensions: the apprehension of the cute practical man who, as a dynast, knew by instinct the dangers incipient in dynasty, and who therefore wanted to keep agents of strong head and ceaseless vigilance to aid him; and the more furtive apprehension of the credulous man which came from his vague timidity and fear of the unknown, the mysterious laws of "conscience," that Wolsey himself had instilled into him. Being sure of Anne, who was now traveling with him in the Midlands in the season when he dodged the plague and hunted the hart, he was bent on working out a divorce which would keep him safe with Charles, safe with the Vatican, and safe with God. He was still very much under the influence, if not under the power, of Wolsey; hence, inexpressive, not committing himself, tight-mouthed and seeming weak, he went on his summer peregrinations, with Gardiner, his secretary, and Foxe, his almoner, near at hand.

XXV

At the manor where Gardiner and Foxe were staying there happened to be a priest whom, in the old days, they knew well at Cambridge. This was a quiet man of their own age, Thomas

Cranmer. As they had much to tell their friend about being in Orvieto to see the Pope, and as they were aware of his extreme tact and discretion, they opened up on the divorce and on the puzzling question of the next offensive.

It was one of those vital conversations in which intelligent men, warmed by mutual admissions, advance their inmost views and prepare future opinion in the intellectual laboratory. Cranmer was clearly an able man. Though far away from court, a don and tutor and divine, he had given no little thought to church politics, and, like many Cambridge men, he had followed Lutheranism closely enough to have had his private opinions run far ahead of his actual professions as a priest. He was of a later vintage than Wolsey. He and the King's men talked to the point, especially about the power of the papacy. How could its authority be checked and modified at this instant? A great strength against the papacy, Cranmer musically suggested, would be the voice of enlightened opinion. To secure this opinion, he gently hinted, Henry ought to build up his case and appeal to the universities. The theologians of Oxford and Cambridge, of Louvain, of Paris, of Bourges, of Padua, of Bologna—the mass of such orthodox opinion, given the deviousness of the papacy and Charles's wholesome fear of the Lutherans, ought to unsettle the Rota and permit a verdict in Henry's favor.

Cranmer was a man of polished expression, and his views were weighty and novel. The men from London were as impressed by his feline reasoning as Lovell and another Fox were once impressed by the filed tongue of Wolsey. Both Gardiner and Foxe had been sufficiently entangled by the Vatican logicians to welcome any adroit flank movement, and, still enthralled by the persuasive art with which Cranmer had woven his argument, they went with it to their master.

Henry at once grasped it. "By God," he cried, "that man hath the right sow by the ear!" But who was this divine? He must be sent for, he must be seen.

It was reasonable he should be seen, the occasion crying for a new man. The older bishops were in balk, since they could not serve Henry without disserving Rome, and Wolsey was incapable of a movement away from Rome. What was badly needed, therefore, was a judicious, resourceful man, reputable in theology, fertile in ecclesiastical devices, and ready with an array of legal and political and constitutional lore that would favor an orderly divorce, soothing Henry's conscience while challenging the papacy.

Cranmer's mind was open in this direction. A dynast seemed to him quite natural, but he was a long way from thinking that the power of the papacy was natural. If Wolsey's generation had been born into the glories of the papacy, his had been born into its scandals, into biblical discovery, into the national state and the new learning. But Cranmer was not in the least an enthusiast, which literally means "possessed by God." He was a casuist and a theorist, a man without pugnacity, a Northern edition of Pucci or Simonetta. For the peaceful transition of the church, as distinguished from the vulgar Lutheran revolution, Cranmer's metal was of just the right alloy.

Henry was still immersed in the mood of Rome. He did not see at once how valuable a man this would be. But the ability to say one thing and mean another is a necessary alternative to heroism in periods of change, and as the difficulties of change thickened around Henry, he gratefully woke up to the treasure that he had in Thomas Cranmer. With Wolsey there had been a check on his preferences. With Cromwell there was to be a rasping character. With John Fisher there was a simple heart. With Thomas More there was Platonic irony. But with Cranmer there was at once a high purpose and a deep receptivity. He was muscle without bone, with a discreet yet powerful capacity for insinuation. Left to his work as a divine, this made him no more pliant than any cardinal. But in Henry's special predicament, needing a moral batman, a man to keep his conscience in order no matter how hardly he used it, the rôle of Cranmer had to be double; it had to be institutional, and it had to be personal.

The success that he was to score with Henry personally was a thing by itself. Where Wolsey had been Henry's male partner, Cranmer was to become a sort of cathedral wife. His gentle and somewhat don-like temperament could accept it, though henceforward, in this nobly submissive rôle, his life was to be a series of little moral surprises. He was often to discover, with some dismay, that his lord and master was bringing off some unexpected dénouement, like a beheading. This was to fill the new Archbishop of Canterbury with meek astonishment. He would never reproach Henry; but he marveled at the people, in whom he himself had been so blindly mistaken, who dared outrage Henry. And having the sweet milk of obedience in his veins, and having espoused his master, he sometimes, without profaning obedience by the use of reason, ventured to conflict with his master, not as a humane man, but as the devoted and wifely architect of the post-papal Catholic church. For this object which enveloped Henry, he could show decision, imagination and courage. It is a nature often found in academic circles, in which the blood meant for the human fiber is fed into the brain, and the result is a moon of a man, without heat, without independence, extremely sensitive and luminous, and yet longsighted and punctual in his loyalty to his own concatenations. This mind that housed an oubliette as well as a prayer book, that lent the alembic of religion to distill one political opiate after another, that included a cupboard of theological skeleton keys—this mind had its own curious integrity. It was a beautiful instance of the definitely cerebral man, forced, in middle age, into action. Distrusting himself in action, hating punishment, and avoiding the crudity of conviction, Cranmer ran in endless circles before he was brought to bay. But in the end, cornered like so many of the people whom he had so bloodlessly pitied, he showed that he valued something more than logic, he touched the hem of Socrates' garment, and was burned to death rather than continue to revolt his intelligence.

If the corkscrew could be credited with the wine that it opens, Cranmer was a hero.

XXVI

But while Cranmer was still a mere deviser of propaganda, Campeggio and Wolsey were to the forefront of Henry's mind, the cardinals of Rome. They came into Northamptonshire to take leave of him, the courtiers slyly wagering that there would be a scene. But Henry was most gracious, in spite of Anne's frank sallies of opinion and girlish headshakings; and the reason of this open-handedness was just round the corner. He was sending word to have Campeggio searched at Dover and to have the Pope's secret decretal taken from him: on his being then pushed out of the country, Wolsey would be left legally competent to give his legate's verdict alone.

The customs officers bullied the old Italian, ransacked his belongings, but instead of the stolen love letters, and the decretal (long since burned) they found a sorry heap of old clothes and rags and bandages that he was taking home to have washed. And he had none of the bullion that Wolsey was supposed to be expediting for safe keeping to Rome.

Irate, he departed. Henry gave the fatal signal. Within a week Norfolk and Suffolk came to Wolsey to demand the great seal. Wolsey as a last move requested a written order from Henry, and Henry who had hoped to keep out of it gave his written order. He also sent private word to Wolsey that he must have York Place, the grand Westminster mansion on which Anne had set her heart.

Wolsey collapsed piteously. Faced with the writ of præmunire, which accused him of asserting papal jurisdiction in England, he feared his ruin; but after his first tragic breakdown he began to use his flurried brains. Parliament had been called, for which Norfolk had in great part made the nominations. There could be no hope for him from the parliament of burgess and baron. He could appeal to the law courts, but victory would infuriate Henry. Why not strip himself of his pretensions, of his possessions, of his pride, and save his mortal skin? Knowing Henry, he believed that his one hope was to arouse in him the moral apprehensions, the "remorse of conscience," he had always harped on; so, with tears and lamentations, Wolsey pleaded guilty.

It looked as though he had no more to fear. Henry smiled on him. He sent him a ring by Sir Harry Norris, which, on seeing, Wolsey flung himself from his mule and knelt in the mud. He would uncover himself to thank God. The ribbon of his hat tied too tight, he tore it open, and with bared head, tears streaming down his face, he thanked his God, while "gentle Norris," ashamed to stand before him, knelt in the mire opposite him, and embraced him. He gave Norris his own amulet, a bit of the true cross. What could he send his master? His eye alighted on his fool. He commanded his fool to go with Norris, that he might pleasure the king. The fool, at home with Wolsey, howled refusal, and it took six tall yeomen to make Comus leave Wolsey for the king.

The world was cheated of its prey. When London heard that Wolsey was leaving York Place forever, no less than a thousand boats full of men and women "waffeted" up and down in Thames, waiting to see him taken to the Tower. "I dare be bold to say," writes his usher, "that the most part never received damage at his hands."

The news of his dismissal was honey to Anne Boleyn. She opened her wings and, like a young bride, soared with her lover to see their future home. They examined York Place as if it were a new toy, and found it richer and more exciting than they could have expected. The velvets, satins, damasks, caffa, taffeta, grogam, sarcenet, in whole pieces and all colors, lay high on big tables. The richest suits of copes that had ever been seen in England, made for Cardinal College, were shown with cloth-of-silver and cloth-of-gold, while on the tressels was set "such a number of plate as were almost incredible."

The empty house at Esher to which Wolsey retreated was a prison in comparison. On one hard-bitten citizen this descent in the world bore heavily, and "the tears distilled" from the eyes of Thomas Cromwell as, prayer book in hand, he stood on the cold October morning and gazed out of the great window at the desolate winter before him. "I am like to lose all that I have worked for all the days of my life," he said lugubriously, "for doing of my master true and diligent service." But must it be so? The resolute jaw said no, no. "Thus much will I say, I intend this afternoon to ride to court, where I will either make or mar, or I come again."

XXVII

Of all the Thomases, More, Wolsey, Cranmer, Wyatt, Boleyn, Howard—this Thomas Cromwell was the readiest by nature and by circumstance to see the cold reality of power. He had a peeled eye and a hard face. Life to him was no philosophic interlude, no theological way-station, no unfurnished junction between Nowhere and Somewhere: it was a fight with poverty, a fight with necessity; it was a mixture of hell and kriegspiel. His father had been, like Wolsey's father, a commoner, only much more on the breaking edge of lawlessness, a brawler, a scallywag, in trouble with his neighbors and the bailiff, drinking too much, violent in liquor, rather scant in his manners. The boy had been blunted into ruthless egoism rather than exquisitely cultivated into it. He was not subtle enough to soften or disguise his ultimate acceptance of the rule of force and fraud. Prompt and vigorous, thick-set and inexhaustible, rapid of speech though scarcely moving his lips, and with a skin not merely impenetrable to insult but actually resilient, a hide of bristle and rubber, and even humorous in his blunt realism—this merciless son of Mother Earth, with his bullet head, his cold eye, his plebeian hands, his glittering enjoyment of the inevitable—this ruthless climber was yet the only man human enough to dry his useless tears with the back of his hand and say to his master, "Your poor servants hath taken much more pains for you in one day than all your idle chaplains hath done in a year. For my part, I will give this towards the dispatch of your servants." He voluntarily pooled his big contribution to the servants thrown out on the world. "And now let us see what your chaplains will do." While Wolsey bemoaned, Cromwell devised. He never supposed that his master could escape the human wolves by the artlessness of raising the white flag.

Cromwell knew the privileged class well, but from their under side. He had been trained in the back-rooms of the money-lender and the usurer, in the stinking and cringing offices of the underling, the sunless alleys, the black passages, the musty corridors. In every dualism there must be dirty work, and every toughened aristocratic dowager who took a good look at Thomas Cromwell could say, "There is my man." He would be the man to act as go-between, to pay off the wench in trouble, to force through the liquidation, to browbeat the timid, to break down the evasive, to clean up the débris of orgy, ill-nature and extravagance, to push the resourceless to the wall. But united to this uncommonly valuable coarseness, there was a diamond edge. Though a layman, he possessed a cynical knowledge of the clergy second to none. He had been employed by Wolsey to suppress monasteries. He understood the church establishment in its whole plump and defenseless organism, and knew it to be as rich in resources as it was poor in spirit. While Cranmer was to converge on the Church from the side of discipline, Cromwell was to converge on it from the side of property. All that remained for Henry was to find courage enough to put the nut and bolt in this admirable shears.

Men like Thomas Cromwell swim up the sewer to power. By the very fact that they do the dirty work, the nerves that they spare recoil on them, and they are reviled. Though Cromwell was to supersede Wolsey and to serve Henry's direct purpose far better, he jarred on Henry from the first, and he jarred on the council. They needed to feel honorable, and Cromwell dripped of the unspeakable. So long as he was the right man, only a contemptuous glance could be interchanged at his expense, but he lived under sufferance among councilors who were gentlemen— who had been initiated into power by nice experience, first by a stoical upbringing as children in which the imagination had been clipped into line like a hedge, next by a religious training in which a class is sanctified by emotional associations with God, king and country, and finally by an exposure to strain only after a long process through the shrewd and servile care of tutor, butler, groom, sergeant and parson. Cromwell was a battering-ram. He had the brute value of a wrecker. He could do work of gross demolition with an imperial crowbar in hand. But this descendant of the Saxon who went to work for his Norman masters seemed to them like a troll with an evil twinkle, like a stunted giant. He lived in open sin with the law of Nature. Henry, who loved music, had heard strains of music in Wolsey, but when he turned to Cromwell it was to a tuneless servant. For Cromwell there was no *magnum mysterium* in life, no delicacy in the education of atoms through long spells of time by which a grace is mellowed in mountains, and a tone in violins, and the very words that men speak are molded and made affectionately melodious. Cromwell was parvenu. He did not walk in the midst of putridity, like Wolsey, with a perfumed orange in his jeweled hands. His was the guilt which, once he had stripped the monasteries and clothed the courtiers, was even deeper than Wolsey's and never forgiven.

But it was not evident how parvenu was Cromwell until he mounted to the very top. At this juncture he was as bland as he knew how. He nudged Wolsey to give annuities to several of Anne Boleyn's needy courtiers. He winked at Norfolk and got a seat in parliament. He made so strong a bid for Henry's favor that within the year he was his secretary, and all this time he was doing his best to smooth the downward path of his late master.

XXVIII

The Cardinal's enemies controlled the new government, Norfolk and Suffolk at the head of the council. Sir Thomas More, disregarding at last the words he had given his alter ego in Utopia, "that philosophy hadde no place amonge kinges," had descended to act his part in the play in hand. "If evil opinions and naughty persuasions cannot be utterly and quite plucked out of their hearts, if you cannot even as you would remedy vices, which use and custom hath confirmed: yet for this cause you must not leave and forsake the commonwealth: You must not forsake the ship in a tempest because you cannot rule and keep down the winds."

The parliament was opened by More in a speech against Wolsey, and a bill of attainder was promptly introduced. This was a bill in which the suppressed emotions of a decade found relief, and which burst from the medieval hearts of the insulted and injured. During his high career, Wolsey had been singularly reckless of the pride and self-esteem of other men. In hastening on his way, he had spared neither time nor fortune, he had ridden roughshod, flayed council and convocation, monks and parliament. The methods did not exist by which ordinary folk could punish him, but he was now to pay for his overdraft on human tolerance by an outburst of such animosity as is bred only by violated pride. While he had kept Henry's favor, these feelings had brooded; now they leaped into savage release. The bill of attainder against Wolsey is a howl of ferocious anger, human indignity seeking to rend its author to pieces.

It began with protest against the Cardinal's "high, orgullous, and insatiable mind." It frantically accused him of giving the King syphilis, "the same lord Cardinal knowing himself to have the foul and contagious disease of the great pox, broken out upon him in divers places of his body, came daily to your grace, rowning in your ear, and blowing upon your most noble grace with his perilous and infective breath, to the marvelous danger of your highness, if God of his infinite goodness had not better provided for your highness. And when he was once healed of them, he made your grace to believe that his disease was an impostume in his head, and of none other thing." He impudently said and wrote, "the King and I." He bullied the council, "so that he would hear no man speak, but one or two great personages, so that he would have all the words himself, and consumed much time with a fair tale." He compelled Sir John Stanley to marry "one Lark's daughter, which woman the said lord Cardinal kept, and had with her two children. Whereupon the said Sir John Stanley, upon displeasure taken in his heart, made himself monk in Westminster, and there died."

This bill, in its thick detail, was not Henry's case against the Cardinal. It was the outpouring of those who felt that he had monopolized the King. It was not one mind, but a rabble of minds: Thomas More crying against the outrage of monasteries suppressed for his two colleges, Norfolk and Suffolk raging against his cursed presumption, Catherine's friends denouncing his behavior as legate, and the henchmen clamoring about his greed, his loose life, his highhandedness, his graft. No document could have better concentrated on the hatred of an upstart and a usurper. Fifty years earlier, these men, knife and sword in hand, would have trooped to Wolsey's bedside and killed him in the night. Now they sought by process of law to slay his character and flatter the King. The first name signed to the rancorous, infuriated document was that of Thomas More, lord chancellor.

Could Thomas More and the passionate men who accepted Lord Darcy's indictment have imagined for one moment that Henry would welcome it? The practical man in Henry could accept a definite charge of overt treason such as condemned Empson and Dudley to death, or Pole, or Buckingham. The irrational man might be aroused by some occult charge that gratified his conscience if at the same time it served its turn. But such an indictment, breathing fire, raking up stale grievances, discussing public policy, debating royal motives, could only spring from a utopian desire to relate public conduct to private and Christian morals. Henry instinctively resented this course, which at its best would lead to revolution, and at its worst to inquisition. He was a manipulator, not a zealot. He was a public man, not a Galilean. He frowned on the whole inquiry. Under his sanction, Cromwell at once emerged in the Commons, and pushed the indictment into the shade where, in the chill of royal discouragement, it soon wilted into oblivion.

York Place, however, was a tangible reminder to Anne Boleyn that Wolsey was gone. Though it belonged to the bishopric of York, Henry took it, the judges not daring to follow Wolsey's pregnant hint "to put no more into his head than the law may stand with good conscience." There was no apartment for Catherine in this palace, and Henry, gay and expansive, commanded a banquet for Anne, where he gave her precedence over the duchesses of Norfolk and Suffolk. In a circle where precedence is like a quotation on the stock exchange, this act alone was enough to sow hatred, but Henry's large geniality was unlimbered. He had got rid of the Cardinal. He embraced his Anne before his guests.

XXIX

As 1530 opened with Charles's coronation in sight, Henry and Anne decided to bid against Catherine herself for the emperor's favor. Since the Duke of Norfolk said he did not know enough

French to go on this errand, the only other diplomat available
was Anne's father. Thomas Boleyn had just been made Earl of
Wiltshire and Ormond, so he was obliged to go, French or no
French. While he started for Bologna, to chip at Charles's hard
head, Norfolk sent word to Wolsey that if he did not at once
leave Henry's vicinity, and go North to York, he would "tear
him with his teeth."

"Marry, Thomas," observed Wolsey to Cromwell, who
brought him this message, "then it is time to be doing, if my
Lord of Norfolk take it so."

But that Henry had a "prick of conscience" was clear. He did
feel a sentiment about Wolsey. Hearing he was ill at Christmas,
he had sent tokens of friendliness, and had asked his sweetheart
to join him in sending a friendly token herself. Anne impul-
sively took her gold tablets from her wrist and dispatched them
to the Cardinal. The King went further: a pardon arrived in
February, with certain goods legally restored. At last Wolsey
withdrew, a chastened spirit, departing North to the noble dio-
cese that from a decade's neglect of ministration was a field of
brambles and weeds. The new council was left frankly in control, with Cromwell in the offing.

The divorce was Henry's steady, and Anne's passionate, preoccupation. Living in a state of mental and sexual tension, the
desire for some kind of result was beginning to be like the longing for a big "push" in trench warfare. Anne's father was savagely abused by Henry for his failure to impress Charles at
Bologna, and young Francis Bryan at the Vatican was in actual
dread of Anne's wrath. The only advance was Cranmer's progress with the theological propaganda. It was going to cost a sum
equal to a million dollars, but the viscous flow of scholastic opinion was moving with dignity and somber restraint toward the
Vatican. It was slow work, and Anne, not too certain of Henry,
and definitely uncertain of most of the council, could not keep
from outbursts of temper. One of the recipients was the choleric

Suffolk. In his anger the imperialists believed that Suffolk had told Henry that Anne had been Thomas Wyatt's mistress. The Spanish rumors were usually blistering, but if Suffolk said it, Henry showed remarkably little sign of being a jealous man.

XXX

Wolsey was in York. The divorce had passed out of his mind, but he could not forget his own dismissal and his pallid exile. The habit of power was in his blood. As he settled local disputes with elaborate art, he could not help reflecting on the stage he had quitted, and his pride, stained by the concessions he had made in panic, kept urging him to that glorious return, that sunset entry, which is the most compelling dream of the de-throned. All that was pompous and grandiose and pretentious seemed to come uppermost in him in his thoughts of Europe, and the ever-sanguine cloud-builder lost his habitual judgment. He solicited the French, who had already sent back Jean du Bellay and who naturally were cultivating the Boleyn party on the principle of *cherchez la femme.* He solicited the imperial-ists, who hated him and who were cultivating Norfolk and Suf-folk. From the imperial ambassador to Catherine, from her to the Duchess of Norfolk, then to the duke and the King, there was one of those secret slips by which enemies interchange in-formation mutually advantageous. And when Wolsey's Italian doctor gave him away, the evidence of high treason, which al-ways touched Henry to the quick, was in Norfolk's craving hands. It was a very sketchy treason, but the aging Cardinal had overreached himself at last.

One afternoon late in autumn young Northumberland, who seven years before as Percy had loved Anne Boleyn and yet had been broken, arrived unexpectedly with a troop at the door of Wolsey's lodgings at Cawood, outside York, and barred the stairs. Wolsey, hearing commotion, asked who was come, and on learning it was Northumberland left his dessert to greet his

guest with open arms. With a flow of courteous and apologetic
and hospitable words, he led him upstairs. When the welcome
and the bidding to dinner ran itself out, pale Northumberland
tremblingly laid his hand upon the Cardinal's arm and, "with
a very faint and soft voice," said, "My lord, I arrest you of
high treason."

The Cardinal, silent for a moment, drew himself up to take
his highest tone, but, one of Henry's close favorites coming in
the door, he read his fate and submitted. He parted from his desolate household, blessed the crowd that collected, and, very different from the swift courier who had plied for Henry VII, began the final pilgrimage.

It was not a bloody end. In the English November, so monot-
onous and decaying, when the daylight itself is dispirited and
the trees drip such great tears, the elderly man, his body broken
like a battlefield, rode slowly with his guard toward London. At
one halting-place a new official took over the task. This was a
big, serious man, Kingston, the constable of the Tower, and
with him twenty yeomen of the guard. Wolsey cried out at this:
he could not hide its meaning. But his host, a man near to
Henry, said that the King was friendly, the King had goodwill,
the King meant him no harm. Some of the yeomen, once his
own, he greeted by name and questioned them paternally. They
wondered to see their old master so feeble and so gaunt. It was
in a wintry nightfall, stripped of charity and burdened with
cloud, that he reached the town of Leicester. Servants with
many torches came out from the abbey. As he fell from his mule,
he said in his deep melancholy voice, "Father Abbot, I am come
hither to leave my bones among you."

He lay, mortally sick, in his darkened room. "Who is there?"
—"Sir, I am here," answered his usher.—"How do you?"—
"Very well, Sir, if I might see your grace well."—"What is it of
the clock?"—"Forsooth, Sir, it is past eight of the clock in the
morning."—"Eight of the clock? That cannot be. Eight of the

clock, eight of the clock, nay, nay, it cannot be eight of the clock: for by eight of the clock ye shall lose your master: for my time draweth near that I must depart out of this world."

But a message had come from Henry to Wolsey. Kingston marched in with it, his brow puckered. The King wanted to know what had become of the ready money on hand, the fifteen hundred pounds.

Wolsey paused awhile. "Ah, good lord," he said bitterly, "how much doth it grieve me that the King should think me in such deceit."—This was the distance they had traveled from the pageant of youth, from the Field of the Cloth of Gold. "It is none of mine," groaned Wolsey, "I borrowed it of divers of my friends to bury me, and to bestow among my servants. But if it be his pleasure to take this money from me!"

A day and a night passed. He asked for broth in the morning. After a spoonful he turned his haggard face to the usher. "Whereof was this cullis made?"—"Forsooth, Sir, of a chicken."—"This is a fast day! I will eat no more."

He confessed. The big solemn Kingston arrived in his room. "With the grace of God," remonstarted the constable, "ye shall live, and do very well, if ye be of good cheer."—"Master Kingston," he answered indulgently, "my disease is such I cannot live. I have had some experience of my disease. There must either ensue excoriation of the entrails, or frenzy, or else present death: and the best thereof is death."

"Nay, Sir, in good faith, ye be in such dolor and pensiveness, which maketh you much worse than ye should be."

The dying man reflected on this cold consolation. It was death or the Tower. And then, his voice hollow with spiritual pain, he pronounced his own epitaph in lamentable words:

"Well, well, Master Kingston," he said, "I see the matter against me how it is framed: but if I had served God as diligently as I have done the King, he would not have given me over in my gray hairs. Howbeit, this is the just reward that I

must receive for my worldly diligence and pains that I have had
to do him service; only to satisfy his vain pleasure, not regarding
my godly duty. Wherefore, I pray you with all my heart, to have
me most humbly commended unto his royal majesty; beseeching
him in my behalf to call to his most gracious remembrance all
matters proceeding between him and me from the beginning
of the world unto this day, and the progress of the same: and
most chiefly in the weighty matter yet depending [the di-
vorce]; then shall his conscience declare whether I have offended him or no. He is sure a prince of royal courage, and
hath a princely heart; and rather than he will either miss or
want any part of his will or appetite he will put the loss of one
half of his realm in danger. For I assure you I have often
kneeled before him in his privy chamber on my knees, the
space of an hour or two, to persuade him from his will and
appetite: but I could never bring to pass to dissuade him there-
from. Therefore, Master Kingston, if it chance hereafter you
to be one of his privy council, as for your wisdom and other
qualities ye are meet to be, I warn you to be well advised and
assured what matter ye put in his head, for ye shall never put it
out again.

"And say furthermore, that I request his grace, in God's name,
that he have a vigilant eye to depress this new pernicious sect of
Lutherans, that it do not increase within his dominions through
his negligence, in such a sort, as that he shall be fain at length
to put harness on his back to subdue them. . . ."

Wolsey's excitement had so aroused him that he poured out
his inmost mind until, his powers failing, his voice went suddenly weak and infinitely weary.

"Master Kingston, farewell. I can no more, but wish all things
to have good success. My time draweth on fast. I may not tarry
with you. And forget not, I pray you, what I have said and
charged you withal: for when I am dead, ye shall peradventure
remember my words much better."

"And even with these words," says Cavendish, his usher, "he began to draw his speech at length, and his tongue to fail; his eyes being set in his head, whose sight failed him."

He died at eight o'clock.

At four in the morning of the next day, the monks buried him in Leicester Abbey. His faithful secretary then took horse and rode straight to Hampton Court, where the King lay. "And perceiving him occupied in shooting, thought it not my duty to trouble him: but leaned to a tree, intending to stand there, and to attend his gracious pleasure. Being in a great study, at the last the King came suddenly behind me, where I stood, and clapped his hand upon my shoulder; and when I perceived him, I fell upon my knee. To whom he said, calling me by name, 'I will,' quoth he, 'make an end of my game, and then will I talk with you'; and so departed to his mark."

The secretary saw him after the game, Henry now attired in russet velvet furred with sables. It was still a question, not of the dead Cardinal, but of the living fifteen hundred pounds. The secretary revealed its custodian. Henry closed the interview. "Let no man be privy," he said, "for if I hear any more of it, then I know by whom it came to knowledge. Three may keep counsel, if two be away; and if I thought that my cap knew my counsel, I would cast it into the fire and burn it. Your year's wages is ten pounds, is it not so?"

"Yes, forsooth, Sire, and I am behind for three quarters of a year."

"That is true, for so we be informed. Ye shall have your whole year's wages, and a reward of twenty pounds."

So fell the curtain on Cardinal Wolsey.

XXXI

Even in exile Wolsey had drawn men's minds to him, and even as he declined in power, his shadow lengthened across England. No one could fill the Cardinal's place, Henry reproached his council. The new House of Commons was well in hand, burgesses and squires who had no objection to sending up a stiff bill to the Lords against the graspingness of the clergy at the very moment that they wiped out £150,000 of the King's debts. This, however, was marking time: and national policy was bound to limp so long as the Cardinal had life.

But after the lonely pilgrimage that ended at Leicester Abbey, it was as though the whole world began to march at the double to a rattling tune. He was dead. He was buried. It was an end. It was a beginning.

The Boleyns were shameless. So high were their spirits and so happy their prospects that they gave a banquet, and the crown of it was a farce, Cardinal Wolsey Descending to Hell. It was not exactly a chivalrous farce, salting and peppering the enemy when he was safely dead, but it relieved strong feelings, and it so tickled Norfolk's sense of humor that he had it put into print. The French ambassadors were shocked by its vindictiveness, but the French ambassadors had neither been balked nor been frightened by this overwhelming man.

Anne, in particular, did not conceal her glee. To Catherine's partisans, who were determined to see Anne as wicked and to magnify her bad temper and to call her naughty names, there was something revolting in the exultation that danced out of her over Wolsey's ruin. But Anne was young. She did not pose as meek or long-suffering. Her ideals were undisguised, and if her courtship was irregular, she did not think it nearly so irregular as the "marriage" that bound Henry. Who believed Catherine's story that she had never been married to Arthur? In the lively, malicious circle of which Anne was the center, few shreds of dignity or even decency clung to Catherine's cause.

Henry pursed his lips and lifted his eyebrows when too much was said against Catherine. She had been his wife, and therefore in a sense made holy. But Anne was relentless, partly because she had the high spirit and tenacity of youth on trial, but also because she was intensely personal in her judgments and continually checked in her ambition. She never flinched before the sneers of the older courtiers or the anger of the mob. Instead, she looked for allies and the means of counter-attack. Far from pillowing Henry, she held him to the course that her bold mind had sanctioned—to drive against the Vatican, to send Catherine away from court, to establish herself on a throne no less proud than that of the Queen she was displacing. Henry faced both ways; Anne faced one way. And it was through her that Cromwell, cap in hand, walked on tiptoe into the vacancy that Wolsey had left in Henry's will.

Henry had no intention of accepting another tutelage, and certainly not from Cromwell. When he held the knave in playing cards, he laughingly said he had a Cromwell. He even cuffed and abused this new secretary of his, with the round head and the ruffian-like look. But it was no agony for Cromwell to endure these humiliations. He thought he knew Henry. He brought him a policy. The King might curse him, but Cromwell was at his elbow to point out the region they must conquer, to explain the disposition of forces, to account for the reserves and the field army, and to plan the action. So long as he had Henry's ear, Cromwell cared nothing about Henry's manners. He gave the King a policy at once plausible and insidious, temporizing and yet thick with tendency, a flexible but ever-wary and ever-encroaching program that spread out in every direction and for its kernel had the gratification of Henry's egoism.

The two men who knew Henry best had always foreseen the perils of such an adviser. One was Wolsey, who had counseled several public men against it. The other was Thomas More, who, turning his candid eyes on Cromwell himself, said in his dry way, "Master Cromwell, you are now entered into the service of a most noble, wise and liberal prince; if you will follow my poor advice, you shall, in counsel-giving unto his grace, ever tell him what he ought to do, but never tell him what he is able to do; so shall you show yourself a true faithful servant, and a right worthy councilor. For if the lion knew his own strength, hard were it for any man to rule him."

To tell this to Cromwell was telling a jackdaw not to build in chimneys. Henry's self-will was the very material that Cromwell proposed to work in. Immeasurably dangerous as it might look to Wolsey and More, it was far too tempting not to be exploited gorgeously. Cromwell came to it at a moment that actually salaamed to him.

XXXII

Boleyn partisan though he was, Cromwell viewed the divorce as quite secondary to his own main object. He had one scheme in view: to carry out on a grand scale the dispossession of the church of Rome. No man was better fitted to do it. He was not in the least timid. He was not superstitious. He was not scrupulous. And he rightly regarded as poltroons the men who for long years had fattened on the bishops' meadows and the abbots' gardens of England.

What elated Cromwell was the contemptible weakness of the enemy. Wolsey himself had induced it. The oak whose spreading arms had sheltered the church in England had slowly fallen to earth, and Cromwell knew from hard experience how open the landscape was, how cleared the field that had been held by a real authority and a personal magnificence, how headless the mob that remained. Though Wolsey at the end had tried to build up clerical education, he more than any one else had secularized the bishops and made the church subservient to the prince. He had preserved the link with Rome, canon law, the joy of paying annates and Peter's pence, the joy of upholding the house of Medici, the pleasure of submitting to probate dues and mortuary gifts. But what would England lose if this episcopal tie that bound the English church to the Vatican, were cut to-morrow? What would Henry lose? Cromwell's eyes snapped. It would make Henry the richest king in Europe. It would make the state indomitable. It would subdue Scotland and Wales and Ireland by solidifying power in England. It would make Anne Boleyn queen.

Without the Reformation on the Continent, of course, it would not have been possible for Cromwell to think that he could grapple with the Church. But the fires that purged Germany, the vibrant conflict that was raging in Switzerland and was to cost Zwingli his life this very year, the quickening of the religious spirit everywhere that had nerved men to challenge authority, created the political mood in which sweeping changes can be made. And yet it would not be necessary to stir the hearts of the common people; this could be a bloodless legal reformation from the top, in which headship of the church could be transferred from the Pope to Henry while emotional upheaval and hot heresy and the riot of illiterate opinion could be repressed with a fatherly if not papal hand. Cromwell knew his England. He understood the Church. Could he persuade the prince?

Henry was in no easy frame of mind. He took no fanciful view of the difficulties before him, being shrewd and sensible, but unknown to himself he had that heightened sense of difficulties that comes from keeping contradictory ends in view. He wanted at the same time to combine a good conscience, political advantage and romantic love. This was a combination of motives that suited neither Anne nor Catherine, and it led to painful scenes. On Christmas Eve, humiliated by his open devotion to Anne, the queen upbraided Henry for the scandal he was giving. His retort to her was most characteristic: he boasted to her that there was nothing "wrong" in his relations to Anne, but that he was keeping company with her in order to learn her character, as he was determined to marry her. This he announced with no suspicion of its oddity, and equally he could not see why Anne should be resentful because he went on allowing Catherine to treat him as her husband, to attend to his comforts, to make his shirts, to arrange for his laundry, and to dine with him alone.

But Cromwell perceived Henry's oddity. He saw his capacity for hotly defending any flattering fiction, and he saw that on this masculine vanity Henry could be nursed into asserting his will. All his life the King had lived in the ocean of papal universality. He considered that his throne was derived from the Holy See, and, through the Holy See, from God. But warmly as he had espoused the cause of the Church from the beginning, Clement's failure to meet him halfway had cut him to the quick. By reverence, by habit, by innate conservatism, he was allied with Catholicism; but how could the papacy clash with the Defender of the Faith? A kind of incredulous anger had burst in Henry at this maddening opposition to his will. If that was the way the papacy was going to treat the Defender of the Faith, simply because Catherine was an aunt, then it remained to be seen on what grounds its authority really stood.

XXXIII

While Henry wrestled with moral justification and wounded pride, Cromwell sharpened his knife. In the Church two aging men were the custodians of tradition. Of these Fisher was negligible—a thin pure flame of idealism—and Warham was a dignified, glum man in whom a prudent inertia was slowly becoming a heavy resentment. All the strong men who were coming up—Cranmer, Gardiner, Stokesley, Longland—looked on Warham as an encumbrance. The loyalties on which he could count as Archbishop of Canterbury, the power he thought he represented, even if Tonstall and Gardiner were prelates, were like the rusted guns of an obsolete fortress. It was the national state that won these new men's allegiance; and Cromwell proposed to guide the state.

Had the common people of England been stirred, one way or the other, Henry might have frowned down Cromwell. But the people of England, peasantry for the most part, were not as yet consciously involved in the religious struggle. They were still too near to the civil war, or too deep in the local scheme of existence, to lift high out of their obscure and burdened life. The gentry and the nobility were their focal points, not the nation; and whether they were bitterly unfriendly or happily dependent, buying or selling, chatting at the alehouse or following the plow, playing forbidden football, shooting the bow, dancing or churching, they were cut off from national political expression. They lived on a fixed class level, and yet under pressure not galling or intolerable. Their church cried for reform. The common clergy were badly educated and menial, the monks and the nuns were frequently unstrict, their numbers were swollen no less than their wealth, and the King made courtiers and councilors out of the best of the bishops, though expecting them to subsist on the revenues of the church. If the new men were coming up, it was not out of the heart of the people; Gardiner and Cranmer and the others were heads first and hearts afterwards, while the Latimers could only preach the new order if their stomachs were strong enough to digest the King. Hence the mastering of the Church reduced itself to sheer statecraft. As Henry talked over the coming parliament, Cromwell laid the problem in the King's well-cushioned hands and made him glint to attack it. It was not a struggle between the new learning and the old learning, between the new patriotism and the old allegiance. It was not an attempt of the people to throw off moral paternalism. It was an attack on the foolish who confused the Pope and the Catholic Church, who willfully refused compliance to their royal master—a day's sport in which the hart were in the grease season, vulnerable, defenseless, frightened, and paled in.

XXXIV

Convocation and parliament both met early in 1531. Convocation, the assembly of the clergy, had every reason to expect a message from the King, and they were not disappointed. The heavy weapon that had crushed Wolsey, the weapon of præmunire, was leveled at the assembly: could they deny that they had asserted papal jurisdiction in England? It was a declaration of war. The clergy offered to pay a fine of 160,000 crowns. Henry refused to accept it, swearing he would have 400,000 crowns or confiscate their bodies and their goods. In their panic they assented. But when they sent their submission on his terms he refused it: unless they would accept him as Supreme Head of the Church.

In two audacious moves Henry and Cromwell had the convocation cornered. The Pope's nuncio put in an appearance, but was chased away in fear; "they had not the King's leave to speak with him." Summoning all its courage, the assembly tremulously agreed that Henry was head of the Church, "so far as Christ's law allows."

This assertion of sovereignty over the Church, and this tacit submission of the clergy, was a masterly counter to the Pope's declaration that Henry must plead at Rome. "It is not intended to infringe the authority of the Pope," said Henry caustically, "provided his Holiness will pay due regard to me; otherwise I know what to do."

The victory over the clergy, qualified though it was, was an encouragement to threaten parliament with the same præmunire, but the Commons could be used to do almost anything except fine itself, and as Cromwell and Henry had no wish to lose prestige, they decided to climb down. The next enemy was

Catherine. Henry put it to his council to go to her in a body, at nine in the evening of June 1st, 1531, to see if they could break her. She answered, with her long knowledge of the man himself and unshaken faith in her cause, that Henry was her sovereign, and she would serve and obey him; but as to the spiritual realm, it was not pleasing to God that she should so consent or the King so intend. "The Pope," she said, "is the only true sovereign and vicar of God who has power to judge of spiritual matters, of which marriage is one."

If this was Catherine's belief, and if Henry went on genially living under the same roof with her, Anne Boleyn's position would be unbearable. She knew that Catherine understood Henry and could almost prevail on him, and she learned that the King's friend, Sir Harry Guilford, had openly shown his sympathy to the Queen. She spoke so sharply to Guilford that he resigned from the court, and she spoke so vehemently to Henry that he was forced out of his natural hatred of the unpleasant. Already in spring he had complained to Norfolk that Anne berated him in a way to which he had never been accustomed, but now he could no longer shilly-shally. He wrote to Catherine in July, one of his ugliest letters, referring to her marriage with Arthur, showing his anger at her obduracy, and telling her she must join Mary at Moor Park, and must be gone from Windsor before he and Anne returned. It was the curt end of their personal relations, though before many months she was to receive orders to separate from her daughter Mary, so as to prevent conspiracy, and in October she was obliged to parley with another powerful deputation.

The case for divorce was still monopolizing Henry's mind. A boat-load of books on theology had been rowed to Windsor, he had delved into the conciliar question, the question of sovereignty, and while Anne pined for action, he worked patiently at a tortuous pamphlet, called *A Glasse of the Truth*.

The question, he and Cranmer agreed, "is tossed and turned

over the high mountains, labored and vexed at Rome, from judge to judge, without certain end or effect being very perilous for his highness, and much more dangerous for us his poor and loving subjects." "If a man be excommunicated because he doth that is good, or will not do that is ill, the sentence of excommunication is none."

In the mere thought of marrying thy brother's wife, there is a vileness, a sort fault, contamination, abomination, execration. "I marvel that Christian men do not tremble to hear it, and much more fear not wittingly to do it, or advisedly to continue in it."

"The Church of God hath his foundation set upon a firm and steadfast stone of truth and faith, and not upon the mutable and willful pleasure of Peter's successors."

As for Catherine and Arthur, the "noblest men of this realm" knew them both "to be of competent age, fit, apt, and prone to that natural act; bedded together at sundry times, living at liberty, in one house being," with no witness to the contrary but the Queen on her own behalf. In urging this, Henry has no motive but a public motive. "Our most loving Prince's true endeavor is much more for us than him."

"Wherefore methinketh the King's highness and his parliament should earnestly press the metropolitans of this realm (their unjust oath to the Pope notwithstanding) to set an end shortly in this, and to take a greater regard to the quieting of his grace's conscience and this realm, than to the ceremonies of the Pope's law; for, by God's law, they are bound to the obedience of their Prince, and to seek also the quietation and peaceableness of this realm, which ought to be regarded more than any man's law. . . . Rather ought we to obey God than men."

This was Henry's case. It did not go without an answer. Henry's cousin, Reginald Pole, of the same mind as John Fisher, himself prepared a book that was to bring reprisals in its train. But Catherine's friends despaired of mere pamphlets.

They believed that Henry could not be withstood by Fisher and Warham, since parliament had a hunger for church property. The Pope and the emperor alone could save Catherine but while Clement was freshly indebted to Charles for the restoration of the Medicis to what was now the throne of Florence, Charles was frantically busy with the empire, facing the Turks on the front and the Lutherans behind.

XXXV

Theologically Henry could not stand completely still. The divorce, which had prompted him to clash with the papacy, had opened his mind to the Reformation. Though he really wanted to keep inside the Church Catholic, in spite of Cromwell, he could not help despairing of Clement. For a moment he actually thought of marrying Anne and taking the consequences. This was the advice that Francis gave him, and Jean du Bellay and the Pope himself. How, after all, could the emperor retort? Could he demand that Clement excommunicate him, which would weaken the Church by another schism? Catherine would frantically protest, and the emperor would be enraged, but the storm would blow over and Catherine retire to a convent.

Anne was furious. She expostulated with Henry over the endless delays. She was growing "old." Her reputation had been injured. Why did he not end the futile campaign for a divorce? Jean du Bellay shrugged his shoulders. The vast theological arguments, the insistence that the divorce be transferred from an ecclesiastical tribunal to a lay tribunal—it began to seem ridiculous to the logical Frenchman.

But it was not wholly ridiculous. With that restless, nervous look that went with his uneasiness, Henry was beginning to see the larger possibilities of Cromwell's plan for besieging and blockading the Pope. Bit by bit and day by day he occupied himself with the fine movements of what was unwittingly to become an elaborate and conclusive campaign.

So long as Wolsey was in power, the young King had not molded policy. To tell the truth, he had sacrificed his impulses by walking on international stilts. With the escape from his mentor, which came as he reached his zenith, he instinctively went back to the Tudor method of building up his strength at home. In this Cromwell was completely at one with him. If he were entrenched at home, with every natural resource gathered round him, he need not care three straws for the papacy or for excommunication. No less canny than his father, he calculated with rapid brain his real strength. It was not to depart from orthodoxy. A sincere horror filled him at the thought of anything radical. It was simply to organize the country so that he could vindicate his own course of action. Henry needed money, the discovery of the Americas having reduced the purchasing power of his own fixed revenues of silver and gold. But what attracted him most, in the program with which he now bustled, was the possibilities of legislative power. He had parted company with Wolsey on far more than foreign policy. No longer fearing anti-clericalism, which made Wolsey shun the Commons, Henry meant to use parliament to the limit. The works of theology that he studied embodied the medieval notion of Pope and emperor, but he was getting ready to contest this notion, should the Pope continue to balk him. Cromwell, avoiding the sore topic of Luther, encouraged his independence. He had the greatest hopes of parliament, and Cranmer never cast a doubt on Henry's innate gift for divining and interpreting the law of God.

XXXVI

The split with Rome, it was borne in on Henry, would have to be accomplished with infinite care so as not to wake the sleeping people.

Having no preoccupation with the Deity, Anne's friends took the blunt view that Wolsey's death had not been enough and that it was Bishop Fisher who was blocking the divorce. One day, by the hand of his cook, the bishop's soup was poisoned, killing a dozen of his household, and a beggar woman who was in the kitchen, without reaching the bishop himself. Henry detested this mad attempt at direct action; he did not propose to poison or be poisoned. With a sudden gust of anger, he forced through a law that poisoners should be boiled alive. And, as the cook confessed his guilt, he was legally boiled alive.

The unpopularity that even Anne's father feared was by no means chimerical. The recklessness of her party was now antagonizing so many elements that the tide began visibly to set in Catherine's favor. Though Archbishop Warham mournfully assured the Queen that "the anger of the King is death," not a few English men and women were increasingly ready to brave his anger and to stand out against the change. Henry's coldness to his daughter Mary was discerned as unnatural. The attempt to legalize divorce by lay tribunals ran at once into the religious prejudices of both lords and commons. Lord Darcy, one of the stoutest men in England, took part against the King and won the day. As 1532 dawned a momentous year for Anne Boleyn, Clement sent a solemn rebuke to Henry. He ordered him in the plainest terms to send this woman from his bed and go back to his wife. Anne herself had to fly from an irate mob of thousands of women. Even Warham, now very ill and coming to the end of his tether, set his hand to a written protest against encroachments on the church. Two monks, one after the other, preached violently in Henry's presence, sparing no words. If words could dissuade Henry, he would never marry Anne.

But Henry was a wary and experienced stalker of game: he proceeded on a course which was admittedly "very cunning." Drawing as close to France as possible, for the sake of pressure on the Vatican, he caused parliament to increase its anticlerical legislation. The papal tribute of annates, or the first year's revenue of benefices falling vacant, was suspended, so that he could at any time deprive the Pope of this revenue and yet depict himself as shoved by parliament. He restricted benefit of clergy, and he clipped the wings of canon law. Then, announcing to a parliamentary committee headed by the speaker that his priests were only "half Englishmen," because they took an oath to the Pope, he outraged even partisans like Gardiner by exacting the most abject submission from convocation.

As Cromwell hoped, Thomas More could read the stars in their courses. He had taken office on an express understanding, "first to look unto God, and after God to his Prince." He had conducted it with simplicity and vigor, scrupulously honest, searchingly impartial, refusing the golden bowl of grateful litigants and the five thousand pounds offered him by anxious convocation. Holbein lived with him in the home that Erasmus described so glowingly. Henry himself came there, to court an honest man. Now More sent for the Duke of Norfolk, who found him in his little chapel, next to his house in Chelsea, a surplice on his back and singing in the family choir. As they went to the house, arm in arm, Norfolk remonstrated.

"God body, God body, my lord chancellor," he said, "a parish clerk, a parish clerk, you dishonor the King and his office."

"Nay," More smiled, "for serving God, the King's master?"

On the plea of ill health, he begged humbly through Norfolk to be allowed to give up the great seal. Henry, who had always respected More, parted with him in the most princely style, without a word of open reproach.

XXXVII

When More resigned as lord chancellor, Cromwell was his real successor. It was symbolic. The reasoned soul withdrew. The appetite grinned and snatched his office. A man who asked to live and let live gave room to the more predatory animal.

But in this resignation of 1532, where the kind and sensitive and honest human being, who loved the common people, made way for the selfish and grossly immediate Cromwell, there was far more than the triumph of a ruder will. Cromwell, harsh as he was, was a creature of the new world that was being born in blood and agony.

Thomas More believed that the things he valued in life could best be preserved by the papal system. Seeing through it and around it as he did, mocking and salient as he was, he took the mellow conservative view of human nature, though he was too noble, even for his own system, to be an inquisitor. To an ideal he was wedded. He now gave up the world, and was turning to those starry nowheres on which he had always smiled.

The world that saw him resign had divorced his ideals though it had not had time to organize its hypocrisy. It had forsworn the medieval universe and had not yet accepted the discipline of humanism. Base, foul, rude and brutal, snarling in its naturalism, yelping in its statehood, it sought to hide its shame in satin and to glorify its obscene vanity by sticking a diamond in its shirt front. But this new world, trying hard to swaddle itself in a state religion that was to clothe its cannibal politics, had yet within it the robust ardor and humor that Rabelais was chanting, medieval in form but in substance the shout of a rebirth, rebirth of the man once more completed, the soul reunited with its body, the individual breaking loose from his Father Pope and his Mother Church, and seeking to be creative and responsible.

It was this rebirth that More declined and that the broad humanist in Erasmus accepted. But both of these great men had their eye on that hypocrite interloper, the dynastic national state. They could see the godly garments of which the Pope had stripped himself in his scramble for power, and they could see the dynastic hand, with its dirty finger nails, creeping forward to steal these garments one by one. And soon the national state, Plato in one hand and Machiavelli in the other, was to parade itself with the new priesthood of diplomat and secret agent, cabinet minister and assassin, admiral and press-ganger, conscript will and conscript intelligence, rearranging on a new system and with clownish variations of Monarchy and Republic the whole sanctified wardrobe of the papal religion.

Armed with self-righteousness, more compulsive than any priesthood, with privilege in their most intimate tissue and casuistry eating out their instinct for the real, these new nations that superseded the Europe of Pope and emperor came into power. The religion of Christ, to which Erasmus gave his mind and More his heart, remained a fashionable synthesis, while the greater working synthesis to which man broke his way in the Renaissance was crowded out of direct social expression by the dynastic state.

But even these piratical pharisees who succeeded feeble universalism were gradually increasing through commerce the means of self-direction in myriad human lives. The slavishness of Merrie England, and of Golden Spain, especially from the Black Death onwards, implied a system of docility and exploitation that could not be endured forever. As each man became heritor of the widening world, he was forced to rend the bondage of the ghoulish England that Utopia described. The conflict was inherent between a religion worked into class patterns and hierarchy, and a life of audacious trial and error, free experience and material experiment. What Thomas More resigned went deeper than the lord chancellorship. It was the pain of sanctioning the error in Henry and Anne. But revolting as it must have been to so wise a man, a man so richly and sweetly endowed and so aware of the radiant possibilities of human existence, to witness the dispossession of Catherine, yet the Henrys and Annes could refrain from trial and error only by continuing to immure themselves within the vast complacent stupidity which, like stony arcades around an empty square, hummed with the eternal bead-telling of Catherine's iron monogamy and her obedient medievalism.

XXXVIII

Anne was very preoccupied in the week that Thomas More resigned. She was planning a "night gown." Thirty-two Flemish ells of golden arras had been delivered to her at the king's expense, and Henry had just paid the money that she had lost at bowls. She had been out hunting with him in green and a feathered hat, her arrows slung before her, and by her side the sprightly French bishop, Jean du Bellay, on whom she had pressed the gift of a hunting suit with a hat, a bow and arrow, and a greyhound. Henry had, as usual, recompensed the watermen who waited on her to Durham House, and to her dancing man Mark Smeaton he had allowed shoes, hose and buskins. But the orange pies, the quinces, the capons, the strawberries from Hampton Court, the lantony cheeses, that gave the "Lady Anne Rochford" delectation, the greyhounds and the white falcons that he bought to amuse her, were of no interest in her reflective eyes beside the new cloak she was ordering, and especially the fine dress for her evenings with her King.

Fourteen yards of black satin, for the cloak, at eight shillings (now eight pounds) the yard. A yard of black vellute for its edging, with two yards and three-quarters to line the collar and the vent. The vellute at thirteen and fourpence the yard, while for the lining satin and the Bruges satin something less. John Malte was asking only five shillings for his own labor.

The "night gown," as she called it, or the evening dress, as we should call it, John Malte was to make to match with even less regard for expense—fourteen yards of black satin, lined with buckram and black taffeta and bordered and edged with the same black vellute.

The frail skeleton of Anne that was disinterred in 1876—how very different it must have appeared in its fleshly whiteness, and the fleshly whiteness in this inhuman black resplendency! As her headdress was scintillant above her black hair, and her black

eyes alive with strange fire; as those quick hands expressed themselves in their transparent ivory against the voluminous deeps of
her cloak; as her cloak fell from her shoulders and those fine and
sinuous arms freed themselves from the rippling waterfalls of
satin; as the stones with which Henry had decked her flashed
into the dense and perfumed air with spiteful green and frosty
blue and dizzying white and fires as red as serpent's eyes, each
gesture a sibilant cataract of tumbling ebony and a play of living sparkle—the hot heart that throbbed in Henry's great body,
the flood that was dammed in him, must have surged at this vision of sable and snow. Anne's body, svelte and white, half-
sheathed in this ostentation of voluptuous blackness—it must
have gathered itself into such a picture as the renaissance adored
to paint, one of the least official yet most indubitable of historic documents. The fate of England here depended on a
woman's power to enamor a King, nothing more or less. As
Anne's lips laughed, as her eyes spoke, the irony of this tremendous battlemented "night gown" must have made Henry forget
for a few hours the theological stoneslingers and catapults and
scaling ladders and giant petards of moral warfare that he was
laboriously collecting against the papacy, and reminded him
that here was his fate—the woman publicly forbidden to him, a
being of palpitant white fire hidden in its jewel case of satin.

XXXIX

When two people are so self-concerned, when they are plunged
in a purpose that immerses and suffuses them until everything
and every one outside it leaves them impatient, the last thing
that has reality for them is another's loss. Anne had no heart for
any one but herself and Henry. She had already estranged Suffolk, Guilford, Norfolk, even her own father. She was intoler-
ant and almost intolerable. And when she and Henry learned in
August, 1532, that Warham, who had done his best to serve

both crown and papacy for half a century and more, was dead at last, it seemed the most welcome act of his career.

Who would now be Archbishop of Canterbury? Gardiner was the strongest man in sight, but he was not pliant. Both Henry and Anne wanted a blade that would bend. Cranmer was the man. If Rome would appoint Cranmer archbishop, a great stronghold would at last be in the right hands.

Cranmer was in Nuremberg, cultivating Lutheran opinion. Like many an intellectual of forty-five who leaves his desk for the world of sight and sense, the good priest had been attacked in a weak spot, and had, in fact, committed an indiscretion. Without quite meaning to, he had been deeply charmed by the niece of Hosmer, the German divine he was visiting. She seems to have been a warm, confiding, infinitely adoring Nuremberg girl. Cranmer, dulcet himself, had not resisted her, and the two sweet natures had commingled. It must have been a pretty idyll, after years of flat Cambridge, hand in hand on the heights, looking down on the rich red town. But for a tonsured priest, it was admittedly awkward. Hosmer, lifting his eyes from the problem of consubstantiation, thought that marriage was indicated. Thus the Reverend Father Cranmer took unto himself a wife. But when word came to him from his master, who firmly believed in celibacy (for the clergy), that he must come home to be made Archbishop of Canterbury, Cranmer's pleasure was blended with modest confusion. To explain how it all happened in Nuremberg, in the land of fluid thought and Rhenish wine and schwärmerei, made him draw in his breath a little. With Margaret left behind him, he came sidling to Henry, a journey of three weeks drawing itself out to seven.

While the susceptible cleric was still abroad, Anne and Henry had put their heads together to some purpose. Anne had reached the limit of her endurance, and Henry of his postponing, so they connived together on a magnificent way of breaking their unpopular news to England—to do it from a distance and indirectly—to compel the courtiers of every type to come forward and go with them on a state visit to the court of France. It was a triumph of Tudor shuffleboard. In October, the King and his bride-to-be would visit Francis and the French at Boulogne. Francis would return the visit at Calais. It would implicate everybody, the councilors in especial being unable to evade, every one of them being a French pensioner. If all went smoothly, the marriage bells would ring across the Channel.

XL

The courtesies of this amazing visit led to serious bickerings. Henry began by demanding precedence over Francis. This was scorned. He then asked that the French King should not be accompanied by that Spanish wife, Charles's sister, whom Francis had taken after the treaty of Madrid with the patriotic words, "I'd marry Charles's mule, if necessary"; the lady that Anne desired to sanction her visit was Francis's proud sister, Marguerite. Marguerite had strong Lutheran sympathies, and openly admired Henry, but since she was frankly disgusted by the hypocrisy of the divorce, she did not find herself well enough to meet Anne Boleyn. Not to seem wanting in courtesy, however, the French tendered as hostess the Duchess of Vendôme. But Anne had lived at court long enough to know that this was presenting a splendid though somewhat tarnished veteran as the equivalent of herself, a lady of almost spotless reputation. She told Henry to decline the Duchess of Vendôme. The difficulties of being unconventional conventionally, as Cranmer would agree, were almost hopeless, even for the matched ingenuities of French and English. But Henry was of the most stubborn power when it came to pushing through an arrangement that would commit both courts to Anne Boleyn. He grimly demanded the court jewels from Catherine, who painfully parted with them. He let it be known that quite colossal sums were to be spent on gems for the French courtiers. He wished Francis's two sons, restored from the prisons of Spain, to be brought to meet him, and he planned to bestow on them the receipts for war loans that France had not yet repaid. If Francis would come in full pride, would later intercede with the Pope and avert excommunication, while securing the divorce, Henry was willing to call him his brother and to pledge perpetual amity. And so, on terms mutually satisfactory, the love-feast was arranged.

The two Kings had traveled far since the Field of the Cloth of Gold. Still handsome, though more portly and less athletic, they had sobered from youthful cavaliers into something like astute business men. The emotions that had rippled the interview of 1520 were now broadened and flattened. Francis had shaken hands with compromise; Henry, who had been jealous of Francis, longed only to have his warm support against the frigid Charles.

While Anne remained at Calais, Henry rode forward with a gorgeous troop, resolved to be agreeable. One thing he had firmly stipulated before leaving England, that on no account should he be chaffed or teased. Jean du Bellay had written to the Grand Master from London, "Especially I beg you to bar from the court two kinds of people, those who are imperialists, if there are any, and those who have the reputation of being mockers and waggish fellows (mocqueurs et gaudisseurs) for it is indeed the one thing in the world most hated by this nation." Sure of being taken seriously, Henry expanded. He had brought a company of trained theologians with him, including some rabbis to interpret Leviticus for the French. He assured Francis of his honorableness in suing for divorce. He took pains to visit a number of shrines of Our Lady. He left a wake of largesse behind him. He lost great sums in betting with the right people. And he and his squires escorted Francis and the French court to Calais to greet Anne Boleyn.

Anne's status had been elevated in the eyes of her own people in September, by her being created Lady Marquis of Pembroke, and endowed with an annuity. Sulky though the older group still remained, she was admired and championed by the younger group that now thronged happily around her—Harry Norris, Francis Weston, William Brereton, Francis Bryan, Thomas Wyatt, Edward Seymour—and Henry encouraged their friendship, and drew them into a circle.

Queen by a side entrance, Anne Boleyn glowed as she received the homage of France. Francis paid her his personal court for several hours. The facility with which he assured the Pope that he discouraged this marriage did not impede his meeting the Lady and freely encouraging her. Anne, he knew, was his best ambassador in England. He had no love for Catherine. All he really asked was to see this marriage accomplished with smoothness. He himself was going on to the Riviera, where Pope Clement was to meet him, in order to celebrate the wedding of his second boy, who had been engaged to Princess Mary, to the juvenile Catherine dei Medici. This was Francis's second buttress against Charles.

Francis was no longer a confident man. Dashing as he was, he rather dreaded the generous fire of youth by which he had been so badly burned. His adventures, too costly, had wasted his spirit, leaving him morally languid, a graceful and prudent Epicurean. He did not like this dubious recognition of Anne Boleyn, *mais que voulez-vous?* The two courts intermingled, danced and feasted and smiled.

Anne's victory was almost formal. She had been paraded as Queen. She had found the one ally who could prevail on Pope Clement. Henry assented. The lovers went back to England in high excitement, their marriage a fact if still a little lacking in form.

XLI

In the proud confidence of security, a great dinner was arranged by Anne Boleyn for the end of February. Two days before, as the courtiers stood around in the grand hall, gossiping about the King's affair, coquetting and making their pretty speeches, the hangings were parted and the Lady herself swept into the hall.

Amid curtseys and bows, she found herself near her still brooding admirer, Thomas Wyatt, and, with her black eyes alight, she burst out, "Lord, I wish I had an apple! For three whole days now I have had a mad desire to eat apples."

He looked bewildered and she laughed outright. "Do you know what the king says it means?"

His stare made her laugh so that several turned toward them, at which she laughed the more. "He says it is a sign that I am with child!" Here her mirth so overcame her that the whole group, Wyatt included, listened in pained amazement.

"But it isn't true; nay, it isn't true!" In a folly of laughter she turned and flew out, leaving every one astounded and ashamed.

While this bit of gossip was spreading, with the lips of certain courtiers curled in disdain, her guests came for her banquet to Whitehall, and here the rumors thickened. Henry was no fonder in attendance than he had been many times before, but he was pointedly outspoken. Showing the sideboard armored with plate and gold that must be costing Wolsey several centuries in Purgatory, he hailed Anne's grandmother, the old Duchess of Norfolk. "Isn't that a great dowry? Isn't she a good match?"

This could only mean that they were just married, or just about to be married. But who had married them and when? Anne was conspicuously adding a panel to her skirt. She said to Norfolk that she would be going on a pilgrimage to Our Lady of Walsingham, where Our Lady's milk was preserved, if she were not really to have a baby. The friendly, the unfriendly, the amused and the scandalized, wondered how the Church could have been persuaded to marry them. Cranmer, after all, was still waiting to be confirmed by Rome. In spite of every warning from Catherine's friends, the Vatican had yielded to Henry's threat that he would withhold the payments of annates, and the royal chaplain was in a single stride being duly sanctioned as Archbishop of Canterbury. But a month was to elapse before he was consecrated, and in that Lenten period the sparse table was much enlivened with speculation.

Catherine's friends were eminently concerned. If Anne bore a child inside matrimony, however that could be arranged, it meant that Princess Mary would be disinherited. And if Mary were disinherited, and the crown passed to the child of the concubine, then England would be lost to Catholicism.

These forebodings were confused by Henry's behavior. He was paying the most polite attentions to the papal nuncio. He opened parliament with the French ambassador on his left hand, and the gratified nuncio on his right. Was he, after all, going to disown Anne? Anything was possible.

When the papal bulls were in England, toward the end of March, and the actual day of Cranmer's consecration arrived, it looked as if the Catholic Church were to score a victory and the lady in Nuremberg to lose a husband. But the future primate of all England was something of a celestial thimble-rigger. He was at once indebted to the Vatican for his ratification and alive to Henry's dictum that "to follow the Pope is to forsake Christ." So he called in a group of trusty witnesses and swore an oath before them, that, no matter what else he might say or do, he put the King before every one. At the altar he turned to these witnesses and reminded them what he had said was sincere, that everything else was an empty formula. Then he vowed himself to the papacy before the altar, renewed his oath of celibacy, was anointed, and celebrated mass.

Henry had held his breath. He had every reason to fear that

some hitch might occur in these delicate and nimble proceedings, and he did not dare let the Vatican suppose what was up the primate's voluminous sleeve. But once Cranmer was safely consecrated, the path was smooth. As primate he had been made competent by act of convocation and act of parliament to pronounce a legal divorce. The Pope would dispute it, but Henry had a case that he could argue before Charles, before Francis, and before the English people. What he was doing had the color of the law.

XLII

Catherine's friends were convulsed by the hint of these developments. The one man among them who had immunity was Chapuys, Charles's able ambassador, and he went straight to Henry. Speaking as a Catholic, he insisted on the respect that the King owed to God.

Henry could not quarrel with Charles's envoy, but he was not at all shaken. "God and my conscience," he said from his sturdy height, "are on perfectly good terms."

But Princess Mary ought now to be married, Chapuys insisted. She was sixteen and she ought to provide for the succession by having children.

Henry met the veiled inquiry. He replied that he would have children of his own.

Since the Spaniards were reporting Norfolk as saying that "the expected child will be weak, owing to the father's condition," Henry's infected leg being already troublesome, Chapuys had the coolness to ask if Henry could be sure of having children.

Henry answered testily, "Am I not a man, am I not a man like others? Am I not a man? But I will not let you into my secrets."

His secrets, however, were already open. Since parliament had reluctantly empowered the primate to pronounce divorce, and since Anne was crying for the finishing stroke, a deputation headed by Norfolk waited once more on Catherine, this time to demand that she relinquish the title of Queen. The tactics were two-fisted—the open request and the shove, the renewed request and the harder shove, a soft gesture alternating with an ugly menace and actual threats of pain and penalty, all with appropriate ducal and episcopal circumstance, and in the proud name of the King. But Catherine was not Henry Algernon Percy. In spirit she was a Queen. She yielded nothing. Let them promise, let them threaten, she stood her ground. At the end Norfolk blurted out that it made no real difference, as the King and Anne had been married more than two months.

Sometime in January, it then appeared, between dawn and breakfast, in a corner of York Place, the wedding had taken place. Some said that Rowland Lee was the priest, others a monk named Brown. Cranmer denied that he had done it. In any case, the fact and the date of January 25th were generally accepted, only the more gallant chroniclers taking note of Anne's condition and setting it as far back as November.

Whatever royal ceremonial had so far been neglected in Anne's retinue was now assiduously arranged for, trumpets crying her approach, Norfolk's daughter bearing her train, and Henry moving around among the malcontent courtiers and inviting them to go forward and salute their Queen.

XLIII

It was the hour that the law-abiding party had secretly feared. But what could they do to avert it? They had trusted to events while Henry was shaping them. They had chosen to believe with Catherine that Henry, "for all his bravado and obstinacy, would listen to reason." But while they dreaded to try conclusions, and the Pope drew the "leaden sword," the supposedly mean-spirited Henry had moved forward behind Cranmer and Cromwell.

Catherine herself was in fever. She was unwilling to strike. She did not ask for war against Henry. "A war," she cried to Chapuys, "I would rather die than provoke." But she did ask, and count on, moral aid from the papacy. "I am separated from my lord, and he has married another woman without obtaining a divorce: and this last act has been done while the suit is still pending, and in defiance of him who has the power of God upon earth. I cover these lines with my tears as I write. I confide in you as my friend. Help me to bear the cross of my tribulation. Write to the emperor. Bid him insist that judgment be pronounced. The next parliament, I am told, will decide if I and my daughter are to suffer martyrdom. I hope God will accept it as an act of merit by us, as we shall suffer for the sake of the truth."

Such anguish moved Chapuys. He did write to the emperor, and, being no believer in moral aid from the papacy, he begged Charles to send an army.

"Forgive my boldness, but your majesty ought not to hesitate. When this accursed Anne has her foot in the stirrup, she will do the Queen and the Princess all the hurt she can. She boasts that she will have the Princess in her own train; one day, perhaps, she will poison her, or will marry her to some varlet, while the realm itself will be made over to heresy. A conquest would be perfectly easy. The king has no trained army. All of the higher ranks and all the nobles are for your majesty, except the Duke of Norfolk and two or three besides. Let the Pope call in the secular arm, stop the trade, encourage the Scots, send to sea a few ships, and the thing will be over. No injustice will be done, and, without this, England will be estranged from the Holy Faith and will become Lutheran. The King points the way and lends them wings, and the Archbishop of Canterbury does worse. There is no danger of French interference. Francis will wait to see the issue, and will give you no more trouble if the King receives his due."

This letter of April, 1533, Charles received and pondered like the man of phlegm he was. He could valiantly take the field, as he had recently shown, but he could not be a knight-errant. He had to repulse the Turks in Hungary and to encounter them in the Mediterranean. He had to deal with the Protestant princes in Germany, whom Francis was supplying with cash. He could not attempt to go against England without risking the same sort of national obduracy as he had early encountered in Spain, or without risking a war that would deliver Flanders to the Anabaptists. His sense of proportion was inflexible to merely passionate appeals, and he was so encumbered and over-laden that to assume one more duty might be to lose his grip on all. He soberly pitied his Aunt Catherine. He was the partisan of Princess Mary. But he was compelled to write Chapuys, "Wait and see."

Mary even more than Catherine was to suffer by Anne's ac-cession. She was just the age at which her unhappy mother had set sail for England. Reared strictly and gravely, taught Latin at Catherine's knee, instructed by the Spaniard Vives as to the rôle of woman in the world, and given a contempt for every-thing frivolous and meretricious, she was one of the most serious and bleak of young women. The ambition of both her parents had been to stuff her with certain accomplishments, useful and ornamental, and Henry had delighted to trot her out before the visiting ambassadors to play the spinet or orate in Latin. But she was her mother's child. When coarse words were spoken before her by Henry's boon companions, he was astounded to see that she did not understand them. She took a stark view of Henry's desertion of Catherine, and from 1527, when Anne Boleyn passed from maid in waiting to wife in waiting, Mary had been devoured by her mother's cause.

Already too rigid, the little girl became further contracted in this dire preoccupation. Catherine had God on her side, virtue, justice, constancy, and Anne was a wicked woman, and her child would be the child of sin. This story in primary colors was burned into Mary's brain. The roots of her nature absorbed corrosive certainties and coiled and crisped in the venom of a family feud. Understudy of passions that shake the strongest adult, the poor child began to hate and to seethe before she was half mature, her face taut with righteousness before it had learned to smile or to answer or expect kindness, to love or to be kissed. The grill of self-defense was always before her eyes. Her mother gave her that dreadful yet irresistible heirloom, a holy war. Mary deplored her father and detested the strange woman, by turns vehemently indignant, stiffened in pride, and quivering in misery. The old lessons of Torquemada were retold, with Lutherans as the Jews and Moors. In this world Catholic England was to be her heritage, Heaven in the next. She was to pursue her joint heritage with brain compressed and her heart a furnace of conviction.

Narrow as her conviction was, and premature her fervor, this intensity was soon to be heightened. For Cranmer, primate of all England, had at last held his court at Dunstable, four miles from Catherine's retreat at Ampthill, and there, in her scornful absence, delivered his verdict in good legal order, pronouncing the royal marriage null and invalid, according to Leviticus, and divorcing the most serene Lady Catherine from the most illustrious and most powerful King Henry VIII. This could only mean that Catherine, "the Princess Dowager," as she was now to be called, had never been married, and that Mary, instead of being heir to the throne of England, was an illegitimate child.

XLIV

The divorce issued by legal English authority was a happy moment for Anne Boleyn. Now, in all the handsome pride of youth, she was ready to cross the formal threshold of her ambition.

It was an exquisite scene into which she was entering as the new Queen. Surrey's lyrical outcry had depicted Windsor, "the large green courts where we were wont to hove, with eyes cast up into the Maiden Tower, and easy sighs such as folks draw in love. . . . The stately seats, the ladies bright of hue; the dances short, long tales of great delight; . . . the palm-play, where, despoilèd for the game, with dazzled eyes oft we by gleams of love have missed the ball and got sight of our dame, to bait her eyes, which kept the leads above."

This was the Tudor setting. In its suavity, and its dialect of beauty and love, the younger courtiers found a spirit very different from that of their immediate elders—the sneering Norfolk, the bullying Fitzwilliam, the florid Suffolk. Those men were gluttonous for power, but this was the theater of a hope and an enchantment. A Frenchman, with delightful complacency, was to say of Anne, "At Claude's court she became so graceful that you would never have taken her for an Englishwoman, but for a Frenchwoman born." In this gracefulness, there was the accent of her Renaissance upbringing, and the lilt of her heart.

She was indeed no longer the fresh youngster who had returned so gayly from France, nor was she the pensive maiden to whom Henry had pleaded. For six years, almost alone in her purpose, she had used her wiry will to drive Henry faster and farther than his imagination wished to travel—to depose his Queen, to break with Clement, to unite with France and to pledge the hope of his dynasty to the heir now carried in her womb. Henry had warily followed her. Such audacity, energy, recklessness and nervous impatience had cost a price, especially as she was illumined by no certain moral conviction nor companioned by a trustful man. The fight had frayed her spirit and hardened her heart, but no one—not Charles, not the Pope, not the nobles, not her faint-hearted father, nor the mass of the English people—had been able to arrest her progress. She had flown the barrier and leaped the weir. And the spirit that had braved so much, the something hard and ringing and dauntless in her, rose anew to the triumphant hour.

Her coronation glistened in the most tender of light, May sunshine in England. From a sky that was gently brilliant, fair wisps of aërial vapor enhancing the virginal blue, there floated an air so fragrant, so tender, so subtly warm, that a world with little love for Anne Boleyn could not help opening its small-paned windows and letting in the pleasant rustle of a festival in preparation. The streets of London were strewn with fresh gravel. The houses hung out their silks and embroideries. They draped linen, and to the linen they pinned flowers. The whole town moved as with a single expectation—messengers running to and fro; boat men and bargees hurrying to the river; fond parents with little round-eyed, round-nosed children, burdened for an outing; cavaliers in jingling chain and metal aclank; bigwigs bustling to their places; young girls as dewy as morning and fresh as roses; and only Thomas More calmly at home in his old robe in Chelsea garden, musing on the artful invitation to come and give countenance that he had rejected and the twenty pounds for a new suit that he had quipped about and offered to keep.

Anne went by water from Greenwich to the Tower of London. Kingston, "the tall, strong and comely knight," received her at the water and escorted her to her special apartment. It had been a glorious entry into London, salvo after salvo maddening the pigeons, the windows near the Tower actually shattered in the noise. The Thames had never been so embossed with strange and marvelous barges, or paraded in such color or vibrated to such string-music as danced and chanted for her in kind piquancy by the hour. All England accompanied Anne, and her night at the Tower was decked with flowers.

The next day saw her procession go slowly from the Tower to Westminster, a stream of glinting gold and satin between banks of arras, of velvet and brocade. Those who hated Anne noted signs of popular coldness: the people did not cheer, they did not salute freely, they resented her taking a gift of a thousand angelots and not distributing it as queenly largesse. The Hanseatic merchants laughed too grossly. The Spaniards gritted. Anne herself was reported to have said that "the city was well enough, but she saw few heads bared," and Anne's jester cried to the crowd, "You must have the scurvy, you are so afraid to uncover." But these discords did not spoil the effect of a ceremony so superb and solemn. The next day it lasted for ten long hours, ending in a banquet at which Anne was fêted, personally attended by noblewomen who held up a ladylike white cloth before her when she wished to spew. Henry from a balcony watched this triumphant royal feast. It was the fine ribbon to that great seal which Cranmer had affixed to her, not with the heavy crown which swayed her little neck, but with the lighter crown that had been made for her, setting it on her lifted brow with his archiepiscopal hands.

XLV

Only till September was Henry obliged to wait for the birth of his heir. To his own way of thinking, he was not a superstitious man, but he was reassured that so many people could promise him it would be a boy. Astrologers and soothsayers and witches came forward in the many gatherings where he touched humpbacks and healed children: these weird and wise people lifted up their red-rimmed gaze to him, swore it would be a boy, and fumbled away with his spontaneous royal reward. He asked his physicians the same big question: they agreed with the sorcerers. Henry believed in his modern physicians, though he could not discard the more ancient lore, nor despise his religion. In 1531, during the plague, he had paid a good price for some precious relic water, "a tear which our Lord had shed over Lazarus, preserved by an angel who gave it in a phial to Mary Magdalene." Also he purchased "a phial of the sweat of St.

Michael when he contended with Satan." If he had been saved from plague, who could tell but it was St. Michael's sweat or Our Lord's tear that had saved him? In the present crisis men maintained that the jewel called aëtites, found in an eagle's nest, or else the skin cast off by a serpent, applied to the thigh of the one that is in labor, makes for a speedy and easy delivery. Was it forbidden to use charms as well as relics, when Anne and he had many enemies, and when enchantments, invocations, circles, witchcraft, soothsayings "or any like crafts or imaginations invented by the devil," could so easily be invoked by the enemy to bring harm to mother or child?

It was not in level and sober mood that the heir was expected, but in a stew of high excitement, half hysterical and more than half alcoholic. Anne imagined or perhaps realized that Henry's exaltation made him too friendly to her maids in waiting. Such things happen, and who knew better than she how inflammable he was? But even the week before her confinement her reproaches only made him lose his temper. He did not wait till they were alone. "You close your eyes, as your betters did before you!" he flared at her. "You ought to know that it is in my power in a single instant to lower you further than I raised you up!"

For two or three days after that scene he had not addressed her. He was under too great a strain. God was about to signify His approval or disapproval, and Henry's normal human feelings about Anne were complicated by painful uncertainty and perplexity. The birth of a healthy son had become to him the measure of their joint worth. When he loved Anne in his first ecstasy, he had warmly supposed that she could complete him: but now he knew that she must give him a son to complete him. She was a means to this end. A daughter? What security, what dignity, what glory could a female give to a nation of men? A daughter would mean the shame of Englishmen.

On September seventh Anne was delivered. The sad truth

could not be hidden: the heir was a girl. Officers and yeomen, butlers and pantry-boys, passed the word with hand to mouth. Once more, like stealthy oil on water, the flat news spread that this great masculine Henry had failed of his desire. Her name would be Elizabeth, after Henry's mother and Anne's mother. The imperialists, like good Christians, revelled in the disappointment: and no one felt the disgrace of Elizabeth more than the father.

But when Anne opened her heart to him and confessed her own grief and misery, Henry melted. He took her in his arms and said fiercely, "I would rather beg from door to door than forsake you!"

XLVI

The birth of a daughter weakened Anne Boleyn's position. Her enemies were encouraged, and believed it was not too soon to detach those who only stood by her because of fair weather.

Thomas Cromwell was flying his hawks in the open fields, a few days following Elizabeth's birth, when he was quietly joined by Chapuys. Charles's ambassador did not care to have listeners, so he chose the deaf open spaces for asking the secretary whether he was ready to turn against the new régime.

As was his wont, Cromwell listened attentively, with lips compressed and eyes of steel. Then he shook his head decisively. In a few straight words he made Chapuys understand the situation. It was not at all that he was wedded to this régime, or that he resented the inquiry. He spoke as one realist to another. But the time had not come to abandon Anne Boleyn. It was too soon, things were "too fresh," Henry's love was still too impetuous and ardent.

This was not mere cynicism on Cromwell's part. If Anne Boleyn counted on him as an ally, and if he made it appear that he was devoted to her interests, only a fool could suppose that his alliance was personal. He had no sentiment about Anne, about Catherine, about Princess Mary. He took with the calmest indifference the palaver of the French or the approaches of Chapuys. So long as Henry loved Anne Boleyn, Cromwell would no more touch her than a good steward would touch the pet lamb with a silver bell around its neck. But all lambs make lamb chops, and Cromwell was not a vegetarian. His political purpose was single: to build up Henry. And if Henry came to need this dish, Cromwell was the man to serve it to him.

This coldness came from the very core of Cromwell's being. He was not a fanatic who ignores the everyday world. He was not a mere philistine, who ignores everything else. He was a cold-blooded man of action with the prime quality for success: singleness of purpose joined to a wide practical vision. Knowing that supremacy was Henry's obsession, though Henry did not quite understand how to obtain it, Cromwell had the confidence in his own ability to give him supremacy while calming the scruples and lowering the dangers and placating the suspicions that upset the King. The fact that Henry was imperious, was liable to change and backslide, did not disturb Cromwell for a moment. He was not a man of unsteady nerves. Nature had given him the useful cortex of a plebeian—of the turnkey, the lunatic attendant, the best of thick-set public guardians. But he was setting about his chosen task of establishing Henry as supreme over church and state with the ruthless ability of a legislative engineer. While Anne stood in Henry's favor, he included Anne in the specifications. Personally, he wanted to see Princess Mary regarded as born "in good faith" and therefore legitimate, because that gave England one more asset in the market of dynastic marriage. But if Anne and Henry proposed to make mincemeat of Princess Mary, Thomas Cromwell stood ready, book in hand, to note this item of mincemeat on his general list of things to be catered for. He did not waste his energy fighting for Mary. His master was always right.

Such a man did not let his eagerness for results make him

headstrong. But Anne Boleyn had no such knowledge of the world, or no such thick skin. With her usual directness and the presumptuousness that came from her confidence in Henry's favor, she set out without waiting a moment to impose her baby Elizabeth on England. Her animosity had been quickened rather than tempered by her disappointment as to the sex of the child, and she demanded forthwith that the stubborn half-sister Mary be declared illegitimate and compelled to act as a maid to the infant.

Henry was with her. He was incensed with Mary for siding so completely with her mother, which reflected on his conscientiousness, and he was intent on establishing Anne Boleyn. He agreed to the humiliation of Mary. But he sniffed danger in the air. He knew that, so far, the English people had not been won to Anne Boleyn, or given any good reason for preferring a daughter by Anne to the older daughter by Catherine.

Henry worked in the medium of men. The popular temper which Anne Boleyn defied, he respected. One Sir Thomas Jakson had been arrested a few months before for saying, "the King's grace had lived with the Queen's grace, not after the laws of God, but in adultery with her grace, and so doth now still continue, putting away from him his lawful wife." He said maliciously that "the King's grace should first keep the mother and after the daughter, and now he hath married her whom he kept afore and her mother also." This was in Yorkshire, "the last place God made," but loose tongues were wagging all over England. Another "lewd and naughty" priest, Sir James Harrison, was soon to be arrested for declaring, "I will take none for Queen but Queen Katherine; who the devil made Nan Bullen, that whore, Queen? for I never will take her for Queen and the King on his bearing." So the priests and people were thinking and talking. Henry did not bow to this prejudice, but he was acutely aware of it, and he felt increasingly uncomfortable.

"Of the good success of this our cause," he had written to the

Pope at the beginning of the year, "dependeth the surety of our succession, and thereupon ensueth the rest, peace and tranquillity of all our realm."

Now that the child was a female and a weaker card with the people, the "cause" became doubly pressing. It was well enough for Anne to storm and for Cromwell to go ahead with his policy of alienating sovereignty from Rome; but Henry did not abandon his own stolider and simpler notion. That was to compel Clement to tell the English people that Anne Boleyn was their legitimate Queen. While the nobles remained imperialist, and the people remained Catholic at heart, Henry had more to gain by dominating, than by separating from, the papacy. He had agreed to Cromwell's policy, but it was not his own real preference. He knew that Cranmer's decree of divorce had so infuriated Rome that his excommunication had been agreed on; but he still had so much faith in putting pressure on the vacillating Clement that he sent his best councilors to Francis. Francis was on his way to Marseilles to meet Clement: at that interview, late as it was, he could turn the screw on the papacy and have the divorce and the marriage made regular. Henry was sanguine: he thought it was all in Francis's hands.

XLVII

But the forces that were inherently opposed to Henry were enormous. In a short time quite unfavorable news was coming from Marseilles, which aroused in him a fury at once infantile and terrific. Gardiner wrote that the Pope stuck to his guns. "Henry became pale with anger and crushed Gardiner's letter in his hand, exclaiming that he was betrayed, and that the King of France was not the true friend that he thought. He continued for some time to swear at the Pope, and could not regain his equanimity."

Francis was not the culprit. At his interview with Henry a year before, he had promised to work on Clement. When Henry had suggested that he give his second boy to Clement's niece, he had scorned the idea. "I'd rather throw my son in the fire and watch him burn, than consent to so low an alliance." So he had said. But as a matter of fact he had come round to this alliance as a counter against Charles, and it was this approaching marriage that enabled him to argue strongly for Anne and Henry. He knew of course that the sword of excommunication had already been unsheathed by the Vatican, but he knew also that such swords have their scabbards, and if Clement held the sword in one hand, he always nursed the scabbard in the other.

Clement, however, was not feeling amiable. He was no longer the suave, verdant man, with wonderful eyes. He was now long-bearded and gray-faced, suffering from a disease of the stomach that made him often irascible. At Bologna he had been seeing Charles, who, to placate Germany, was proposing a distasteful general council. This meeting with Francis was more to his liking, since it brought his niece Catherine dei Medici within a fair distance of being Queen of France. He had wanted to perform the ceremony at Nice, but it was too frightfully hot, and his doctors had said Marseilles in October. Even so he had arrived in great warmth after a bad passage, and he now had to sleep in the garden. His ablest cardinals were with him. It was the visit of a prince rather than that of a priest.

The English interests had at first been entrusted to Norfolk. But Norfolk had gone white at the news of the excommunication, so it was Gardiner and Bonner who had come to Marseilles to look after Henry's affair, and to try to make the Pope relent.

Clement was personally angry with Henry. He had heard that after the coronation men dressed up as cardinals had paraded the streets of London on horseback holding prostitutes or else buffoons on the croup. This incensed him. He dealt curtly with Gardiner, and he waited for Henry's submission.

Bonner brought him the hot answer from the King of England that he wrote after crushing Gardiner's letter, and when Clement heard Henry's big, blustering words, he simply boiled. Henry too threatened a general council! As these words were read, Clement "was continually folding up and unwinding of his handkerchief, which he never doth, but when he is tickled to the very heart with great choler." Chafed as he was, however, he contented himself with ironic ejaculations such as, "How true!" "This is a good one." "O good Lord!" "Ah, a worshipful process and judgment."

The big, long-nosed Francis came in as Henry's appeals were being heard. He turned his back on the English bishop and chatted and laughed merrily with Clement for three-quarters of an hour. They parted with "great ceremonies," Clement seeing him out, Francis demurring.

It was then Francis's turn to blow the English up. "As fast as I study to win the Pope," he said, "ye study to lose him. I went to the Pope to take a conclusion in your matters, and, when I came there, I found one making the intimation, which, when the Pope had told me of what sort it was, I was greatly ashamed that I knew so little in it. Ye see the effect of all your desires. Ye require a general council, and the the emperor desireth, and I go about to bring the Pope from the emperor, and you to drive him to him. Ye have clearly marred all!" Wringing his hands, he wished that rather than a deal of money he had never meddled in the matter.

The Marseilles interview closed the door of the Vatican in Henry's face. Anne Boleyn was in no way disturbed. She still believed in the French. She had feared to see the divorce re-opened, and she cared nothing for reconciliation with Rome. But Henry took it differently. He was at once resentful and defiant, angry and brooding. He glumly foresaw trouble in England, while Anne blithely spurred him on against Catherine and her friends.

XLVIII

The year 1534 found Henry embattled for Anne. Not visibly weakening because of the opposition of the Vatican or the feebleness of the French, he went ahead with his decisive program. Certain Lutherans of the humbler sort had been put on trial for heresy and burned to death, but this did not keep his passionate anger with Pope Clement from lending itself to the boldest counsels of Cromwell. Parliament had yielded without any upheaval on the succession; the crown was now settled once and for all on Anne's children, and Henry loyally sided with her in all the personal insistence that she spent on making Mary knuckle under.

The Act of Succession was the builder's wreath on the new house that she and Henry were founding, but there was a sequel to it of a punitive kind. Thomas More, whom Henry had so often honored and whose wit and quaintness had so often delighted him, who in the old days used to take him and Catherine up on the leads and tell them about the majestic laws of the new science of astronomy and point out to them the rhythm of the stars—More was arrested, and with him the fiery old bishop, John Fisher. These two men, the grand pillars of the Catholic tradition, did not quarrel with parliament for passing a law as to the succession, but when the law took on itself to imply that Cranmer's divorce decree was valid, neither More nor Fisher could honestly subscribe. It was like Cromwell and Henry to lay this oblique trap, just as it was like More and Fisher to walk into it with open eyes. Now they were in the Tower, hostages in the war with the Vatican.

These were victories, but Anne was not content with them. Conscious perhaps of the deep and inherent difficulty of her rôle as Queen, she demanded a harder offensive and even more sweeping victories. She was wild enough to say that if Henry went to see Francis in June, and she were left as regent, she would find a good reason to put Mary to death.

This violence was not made any the less by Henry's irritability. Though he kept loyal to her in public act, it daunted him to feel that wind and tide were dead set against him, and while he stuck to his course he let a dangerous resentment well up in him. The woman for whom he believed he had made these great sacrifices—he could not view her romantically. He began to see her in the hard, flat light of the long matrimonial afternoon.

So fine a test of adroitness had not so far been visited on Anne. Hers was a naturally saucy and open spirit that made her believe in herself and her capacity for anything; to bridle herself was certainly not natural to her. She did not believe that Henry was tired of her, and she told herself that all he needed was more courage and more audacity, to crush the enemy.

This was her one way of carrying all before her, but it ignored the dangers of her position.

She was the young wife of a divorced man. When she was Henry's mistress, she could point to the harness that galled him, and stir his imagination and his self-pity to discard the wife whom he did not love. But in marrying him, in herself becoming the institutional wife and taking on the great obligations of publicly satisfying him as the Queen of his subjects and the mother of his children, she was running capital risks. She had avoided, certainly, the crass fate of a mere pensioned mistress like Elizabeth Blount, or the haggard end of a Jane Shore, as bare as a gleaned field. But in stepping into Catherine's shoes, she had really stepped into Catherine's shackles. Worse than that, she had created derangements on her own account. And Henry might at any moment transfer his entire debit to herself as a sanguine young partner who had glibly promised to work miracles.

Henry was not a subtle man. He missed the secret solace that
Anne had given him as mistress. She had left a warm vacancy,
which he felt like the absence of an accustomed stimulant to
which she had educated his nerves, and it was instinctive with
him to turn to a new admirer, in whose eyes he could swim as in
the ether. He had only to look to find them.

Within a year of her coronation, Anne could see how troubled and restive Henry was, but she did not at once believe she
had a rival. The news of it was picked up by Chapuys, who
wrote it to cheer the emperor. It was fetched to Anne herself by
her brother's wife, Lady Rochford, whose gift for prying was
considerable. Who the girl was, how far it had gone, how long
it would last—these were all minor details beside the detestable
fact that there was a girl, a very self-effacing one, but a member
of the anti-Boleyn faction.

What was Anne to do? She knew that if Henry were taxed
with this diversion, no one could be more truculent or bellicose.
He had the fixed idea that he was a loyal and conscientious
man. But if he were distrusted and pestered, if he were watched
and spied on and checked up and generally treated as if he were
not conscientious and loyal, he could naturally be driven into asserting himself. Was he not a man like others?

Confronted with this little rift in their union, Anne acted
drastically.

Henry had been planning to cross the Channel to cultivate
his brother Francis, but Anne told him that she was again with
child. This was the best news he could have. As the mother of
an heir, she could give him a great and lasting satisfaction, and
with this happy prospect before him he stopped trifling and became the loyal husband. So, to share his Queen with his subjects, he gave up the idea of leaving her—and of endangering
Princess Mary's life—and set off with Anne on an open summer "progress" through the Midlands.

XLIX

Anne's bold method with Henry might have worked if fortune had favored her, but she encountered unexpected obstacles. She had not lost her influence on young Northumberland. He had recently fallen foul of one of the most Catholic of the Northern nobles, Lord Dacres, and he had managed to secure Dacres' indictment for treason. It looked like a good hour for such a trial. The year before Cromwell and Cranmer had laid Elizabeth Barton by the heels, and as a long list of Catherine's sympathizers had been listening to the lurid prophecies of this hysterical "Nun of Kent," it had been thought well to condemn her and burn her to death. But Dacres was tried by his peers, and if there was anything that could overwhelm the terrible memory of Buckingham's fate as a treasonable peer, it was hatred of Anne Boleyn. To every one's amazement, the Lords had the courage to acquit Dacres. Such a defiance was unheard-of in Tudor times. Henry and Cromwell could not help realizing that Anne's ascendancy was wholly inacceptable.

Just at this anxious moment, Anne's elder sister Mary did the one thing that a charming widow of four or five years' standing cannot readily explain. She gave signs of being about to become a mother. Anne and Henry, from the glassy height of their self-interest, were furious with her, and drove her straightway from court. All the Boleyns and Norfolk disowned her. It was only to Cromwell, who took in every one's misfortunes on usurious terms, that Mary Boleyn could safely address herself. The man in her case was now a gentleman usher named Stafford. "One thing, good master Secretary, consider: that he was young, and love overcame reason. And for my part I saw so much honesty in him that I loved him as well as he did me; and was in bondage, and glad I was to be in liberty; so that for my part I saw that all the world did set so little by me, and he so much, that I thought

I could take no better way but to take him and forsake all other
ways and to live a poor honest life with him; and so I do put no
doubts but we should, if we might once be so happy to recover
the King's gracious favor and the Queen's— For well I might a
had a greater man of birth and a higher, but I ensure you I could
never a had one that should a loved me so well, nor a more
honest man. I had rather beg my bread with him than be the
greatest Queen christened."

Mary's plight, that of a woman saved from shipwreck with
not a stitch or a stiver, called in vain to a sister's heart that was
already sore.

In September, Anne had to admit to Henry that she was not
going to have a child. With elemental simplicity, he rebounded
into his flirtation. Anne's anger at this renewal of an affair with
an enemy made her try to order the girl away from court, but
Henry retorted with a brusque countermand, savagely reminding Anne that she derived her authority from him alone and
telling her to remember where she came from. His tone was beyond all reason exasperated. Anne met it by using the venomous
Lady Rochford to drive the girl away underhandedly, but this
so enraged Henry that he gave full rein to his temper and sent
Lady Rochford to the Tower.

The handicaps inflicted on a polygamous man by a tyrannical wife were, however, only one cause for his being irascible.
While Cromwell was pushing him along the path from Rome,
and was nursing parliament into declaring Henry the supreme
head of the church in England, the French were beginning a
most ugly maneuver—to renew the old proposal of a match with
Mary. It was true that Clement had physically broken down
and had at last died in September. The Roman populace
showed its rankling remembrance of the Sack of Rome by in-
sulting and stabbing his corpse. The new Pope, a Farnese, sixty-
seven years old, who was yet to outlive Henry, took the name of

Paul III; he was far more disposed to be friendly to Henry than Clement had been. But this change for the better at Rome was counter-balanced by Francis's evident determination that it was unsafe not to work with Catholicism and Charles. Francis had tried alliances with the Turk and with the German Protestant princes. But he wavered at the challenge to absolutism that flashed out in Germany from time to time. He was suddenly alarmed of heretics. For this reason, and in view of Henry's anti-papal tendency, he began proposing a French husband for Mary, and telling his envoys to turn a cold shoulder to the Boleyns. It was a new turn in the eternal diplomatic wheel.

Anne had everything to fear from it. So long as Francis stood by her, so long as he did not betray her by joining with Charles, she could always hope to manage Henry. But how could she manage Henry if Charles and Francis and the Pope were all opposed to her?

England could not draw back from its offensive against the Vatican. With Fisher and More in prison, and the Act of Supremacy in Cromwell's doublet, an access of Catholicism on Francis's part was calculated to flurry Anne. But the chance of losing Francis was infinitely less immediate to her, and less evident, than the chance of losing Henry. How stinging that was, she showed at a state ball in the beginning of December. She was talking to the visiting French ambassador, no friend of hers, when Henry left them to fetch another French envoy. Suddenly, without any apparent reason, she began to laugh in her most wild, immoderate way. Conscious of his own hostility and extremely irritated with her in any case, the Frenchman asked heatedly, "Does Madame see something funny about me, or what?" Anne laughed without answering. Then she controlled herself and begged his pardon. "He went to fetch the admiral," she gasped, "but he ran across a lady, and she has made him completely forget what he went for!"

L

Before his arrest, and during the height of Cromwell's drive against the papacy, Thomas More had fallen in with his old friend Norfolk.

"By the mass, Mr. More," said that laconic sinner, "it is perilous striving with princes, and I would wish you somewhat to incline to the King's pleasure. For, by God's body, Mr. More, *indignatio principis mors est.*"

If the privy council had any pious motto, it was this: the King's displeasure is death. "Is that all, my lord?" More parried. "Is there in good faith no more difference between your grace and me, but that I shall die to-day and you to-morrow?"

More's humor had a slight quiver in it, yet it was deep and shrewd and stoical. As he had grown older with the King, and as he had implicitly refused to fortify Henry in the lies that Henry wished and needed to believe, he had seen how the temperature had fallen and how the kingly smile had frozen. He had word that it was only by the councilors going on their knees and talking of him, Thomas More as a European figure that the King had been persuaded not to seek to entwine him in the poor lunacies of the Nun of Kent; but this was a mere halt in the march of their conflict: More stood for a certain order of reality that thwarted Anne and Henry, and by long and sad experience of Tudor methods, dating from his own father's imprisonment by Henry's father, he could but shake his head when his favorite daughter Meg had rejoiced over his temporary victory. He knew his Henry too well.

He was startled, just the same, when the word had come to him that he was to appear at Lambeth. With his eyes down and his heart heavy, he silently took his place in the boat, his son-in-law Roper with him, and the four servants rowing him from Chelsea to Lambeth. "Wherein sitting still sadly awhile, at the

last he rounded me in the ear and said, 'Son Roper, I thank our
Lord, the field is won.' "

In the maneuvers that followed More's arrest he held his
poise. It seemed at first that his "discreet qualified answers"
must baffle all attempts to corner him. With More, as with Catherine, Henry tried his arts of seduction and will-breaking, but
where Catherine always met demand with inflexible refusal,
Thomas More took Cromwell and Norfolk and Suffolk and
Audley sportively, let them say their say, and then humorously
turned them upside down. Of all the logic-choppers on Henry's
side, the only one who could chop finer than himself was Cranmer. More admitted that this myopic cleric could see distinctions invisible to a merely human eye.

But the conflict between Henry and Thomas More was a
conflict of civilizations, a conflict of principles, a conflict of
wills. A new ferment, that of nationalism and commerce and
the possibilities of economic individualism, was beginning to
work in society, and was breaking up the medieval mind.
Thomas More had been a humanist, as had John Fisher; he had
criticized Rome until he saw that it was in danger of falling
and in its collapse dragging down the precious spiritual tradition of a society governed from above. But when this danger
was present, when the alternative to the papal religion of
Christ, which Luther assailed, was the willfulness of Henry and
the horde of evil and ruthless instincts that Cromwell stabled
and hunted with, then More forgot his zeal to reform the
Church in a greater zeal to love his Master, to praise him and to
serve him.

As a young man he had married an elder sister rather than
pain her by asking for the younger sister, who had really won
his heart. As an old man, he now chose in the same spirit of ab-
negation between humanism and papacy—he turned his back
on the lovely younger daughter, and to the elder daughter gave

his hand. Where Cromwell had seen the Church as lazy bones layered like those of a filthy beggar encrusted in one infested garment piled on another, Thomas More dreamed of the Society that the Church had adumbrated. And where Cromwell had rebounded from his sojourn in Italy into his shark's grin at Christianity, his belief that Christian love was still a phantom and that the imponderable and the intangible and the impalpable are mere connivances by which princes exalt humanity while picking its pockets, Thomas More cared so little for his own pocket that he spurned this vulgarity, beholding the passion and torment of Christ as still winning no other recompense than the blows and sneers and spittle and revilement of mankind; and that mankind so trivial that it still cast away the salvation which was its true destiny for a few trinkets of giddy splendor or a few hours of idle wantoning.

Such convictions as Thomas More maintained were the bitterest gall to Henry. While he used Cromwell, he morally despised Cromwell: he himself professed an ordered conscience and Christian love no less than his ex-chancellor. But from More he could not gain the inner deference that his conscience ached for. More refused him the pinch of incense. Hence the long imprisonment in the Tower was marked by deprivations and hardships, constant prickings and offers of compromise, attempts to intrigue him into argument and to inveigle his mind.

But this was one man to whom the King was not Messiah, a man who had moral courage and a lucid soul. He dryly pointed out the character of Mr. Rich, afterwards Lord Rich, who had tried to trick him into constructive treason, while "trussing up his books" and in "familiar secret talk." He argued as former lord chancellor with knowledge of legal and moral values to which the King himself had long since testified. But the verdict was foreordained. More heard it upstanding, and speaking of the one who had held the clothes of those who stoned Stephen to death, he said to his judges, "Though your lordships have now in earth been judges to my condemnation, we may yet hereafter in heaven merrily all meet together to our everlasting salvation."

On his way to the Tower, his daughter Meg was on the wharf, and as she saw him land, she ran through the guard that with halberts and bills were round him, "and took him about the neck and kissed him." She followed him and once more broke in and embraced him. Next day, with a coal, he wrote her the hour of his execution. It was to be St. Thomas's eve, "a day very meet and convenient for me. And I never liked your manners better, than when you kissed me last. For I like when daughterly love and dear charity hath no leisure to look to worldly courtesy."

Henry sent him a last message: "that at your execution you shall not use many words."

More thanked the messenger, and besought that Margaret might be present at his burial, to which the King assented.

As the messenger, Sir Thomas Pope, broke into tears, More comforted him. "Quiet yourself, good Mr. Pope, and be not discomforted. For I trust that we shall once in heaven see each other full merrily."

He dressed in best apparel, changed to plainer dress to please Kingston, and left an angel of gold for his executioner.

As he was led to the scaffold, so flimsy that it gave to his weight, he said to the lieutenant, "I pray you, I pray you, Mr. Lieutenant, see me safe up, and for my coming down let me shift for myself."

Then he knelt and was executed.

His head was impaled on London Bridge, but this indignity was unbearable. Margaret came in the night, and, mounting to the spikes, bore away in her loving arms the pitiful token of Henry's will to be supreme.

LI

Thomas More was not the only man executed. While he and
Fisher were in the Tower the monks of the Charterhouse were
called on to acknowledge Henry as supreme head of the
Church. They refused. Of those who did not go to Tyburn,
some perished in the plague-ridden dungeons of the Tower, and
others, chained to pillars and left without enough bread and
water, died of starvation and neglect. The three priors who were
condemned to death as treasonable adhered to their treason:
they were lifted from the gallows half-choked, their abdomens
cut open, their bowels dragged out and cut off, and were further mutilated after death. This was at Tyburn, in the presence
of Anne's father and Henry's sixteen-year-old son, of Norris and
Suffolk and Norfolk. The counterpart of these executions was
the burning alive of nearly a score of Anabaptists who had come
from Holland thinking that Henry was still in league with
them. Such acts were narrated with much horror in Paris,
though it was only a few months since Francis and his children
had marched round in a chanting procession while several Lutherans were burned to ashes in front of Notre Dame.

John Fisher's end was more humane. As he was held in the
Tower, the new Pope was foolish enough to name him a Cardinal. "I'll send the head to Rome for the cap," said Henry with
ferocious humor. But the old bishop was not tortured. He was
quickly and mercifully decapitated.

And these seemed trying experiences to Henry. Still of the
Catholic faith, though not acknowledging the Bishop of Rome,
he took greatly to heart the opposition of these papists. The
name of the Pope had been eliminated from divine service and
prayer-book, but it remained on the lips of men who had perhaps not studied the question to the same effect as Henry, and
certainly had not been thwarted and humiliated in their di-

vorce. He was harassed, short-tempered, brusque and defiant. If the world intended to attack him, he proposed to defend himself. "I'll prove the truth of the prophecy," he said, "that I would begin my reign as gentle as a lamb, and become more raging than a lion!"

No one could have had greater sympathy for him than Anne Boleyn. So far as the Catholics were concerned, she had seen or heard nothing to incline her in their favor. She was described as a "goggle-eyed whore" in public. Time after time she was derided and reviled, and even in official imperial correspondence she was called the Concubine, while her daughter was always named the Bastard or the Little Bastard. When she had clashed with Norfolk after Christmas, he had stormed out of her presence muttering, "The big whore!" Her opponents taught the court idiot to say, "Anne is a ribald, the child is a bastard." These vilenesses had no power to injure her, but they were like a curtain of summer lightning on the horizon, sizzling around her nerves and presaging storms.

Had she been absolutely sure of Henry, she would have been able to throw off these insults and to retort with energy. But she was at last painfully uncertain. The first six months of 1535 had brought home to her the brutal truth with which Henry had taunted her: it was he who had raised her up, and it was in his power to set her down. In his moods of self-sufficiency Henry so openly ignored her angry disapproval of his affair with the demure maid-in-waiting, that she had connived at throwing her own pretty cousin, Madge Shelton, in his way, in order to distract him from the enemy camp. This had succeeded, but it was a desperate remedy.

She tried every other means of holding him. Finding him still grappled with theology, she equipped herself to help him. She read the new books for him, marking with her thumb-nail the passages he ought to digest, and groped with these for him in

the vast desolate twilight where the gray monsters who live by
sucking the life blood of religion writhe in their chimeric and
unending war.

These attempts to create a mutual life were not too successful.
Henry's physician had told Princess Mary's physician that the
only way of getting Henry to listen to reason was to have him
fall a little ill. This Anne was discovering. But she did not know
the worst: he had already gone to certain of his most faithful
councilors to feel out their opinion on the advisability of his
getting rid of her. How about divorcing her, he had hinted. If
you do divorce her, he was told, you must take back Catherine.
The very thought of this had silenced him. But for him, within
two years of marriage, the strategy of a new divorce was think-
able. Alone with his complications, like a miser with his avarice,
Henry could detach from himself this young woman whose
initials he had cut into his heart, and he could ask: why should
I not save myself by getting rid of her, in the midst of these endless difficulties, these frustrations, these thwartings of my will?

But he forgot this temerity when he knew that John
Fisher had mounted the scaffold and that he had actually drawn
blood. He came to Anne Boleyn, a little frightened, big-eyed
and simple, sensitive for himself in a way that bordered on the
humble. And Anne Boleyn rejoiced to be able to console him.
She ordered a banquet, with play-acting and mummery. She
spent herself amusing the master, her smile nervously ready and
her gayety assured.

LII

It is only bit by bit that a man like Henry comes into a situation
really desperate. He is powerful, to begin with, and active in
the assertion of his forces. His manner is so confident, his presence is so robust, his health so vigorous, that his fate seems
anxious to live up to his jolly and rubicund reputation. In a
world where credit is half the battle, and where the appearance

of prosperity is itself halfway toward the fact of prosperity, the national monarch who has the air of a magnificently successful innkeeper, a man who recommends his own good cheer by looking as if he always enjoyed it, cannot convince any one that he is not the soul of good-fellowship, with his heart at least as big as his stomach.

Look at that plump beaming face, and the merry jowls, and the twinkling eyes, and the glowing golden hair. Even if Henry shaved his poll after the recent executions, and had his beard cut shovel-shape, it could not convince the world that he was anything but an Old King Cole, a Bluff King Hal, the sort of man who eats a baron of beef and says Arise, Sir Loin; the sort of man who cuts off his wife's head, ha-ha, out of a big, jovial, exuberant good humor. Off with her head! Off with the next one's head! The more, the merrier.

But this great bouncing King Hal, this prince of good fellows, who was to divert himself by doing to two wives what so many men have never been able to do even to one wife—this Boniface among Kings is one of the most fatuous of illusions. This big-faced, little-eyed man, whom Holbein has immortalized, is not a healthy soul, who went through wives as some men go through socks, with a kind of hilarious destructiveness. Henry did not lead a life like a barn dance, where one girl after another was slung into his embrace and slung out again. Rabelais, in whose kind arms a du Bellay was to die and go to Thélème, might have invented this grand, ruddy, pot-walloping, trilling and trolling Falstaff of a Henry. Otherwise he never existed. He is the myth of the eternal school-boy who goes by the picture on the cover.

Henry did look good to the public eye of his times. He was a man of open manner and gracious fellowship who needed the sunshine of approval, and he carried with him the magnet of a facile imagination. But in spite of his geniality and gorgeous style, in spite of monarchic prestige and buoyancy, he had con-

trived within two years of Anne's coronation to plunge himself
and his country in the thick of an inextricable jungle. Shrewd
as he was in regard to his own people, fertile as he was in expediency, he had taken a spur that left the broader track, and he
found himself in strange depths of undergrowth and dripping
silence, where a sallow light was shed on him.

The situation was disquieting beyond words. In the spring
Charles had set sail for Tunis, while the Anabaptists were up-
roarious in Flanders, Paul III was still friendly, the Lü-
beckers were still beckoning to Henry and offering him the crown
of Denmark, and Francis was chirping for an English-French
marriage. But before the summer had passed, the scene had
shifted and Henry had to face a very different world. The death
of More and Fisher had revolted Europe. The emperor said he
would rather have lost the best city in his dominions than such a
councilor as Thomas More. Francis, who was of the Renaissance
more than Henry or Charles, understood the turpitude of executing this creative humanist. The Vatican was so flown with
anger that Henry's excommunication was poured in hot metal
into the antique mold.

These were not material injuries, so far, but word now came
from Tunis of so glorious a success for Charles's arms that when
Henry and Cromwell received it, they looked, Chapuys said,
like dogs who have tumbled out of a window. As if to add to
this brave and adventurous victory, which shone toward Europe
like the gleam of a far-off, silvery, single-handed crusade, the
dangerous Anabaptists were overthrown in the Netherlands by
Charles's resourceful sister Mary. This was not all. The Germans, who had been flirting with Henry and promising him
Denmark, were empty-handed and defeated and like to lose
their heads. On the news of Charles's victory, Francis prepared
to fly his flags for the conquering hero until he could gather his
resources and recruit his arms. The outlook for Henry was there-

fore singularly unfriendly on the Continent, and he had to turn for comfort to home.

But England had no comfort to give. The absorption of Wales was certainly proceeding. The supremacy of the Church was accomplished and already the Vicar General was practicing his old hand on suppressing a few of the weaker monasteries. But the people were not happy, the spies reported unfavorably, the moral tone was not good. Lord Darcy, Lord Hussey, Lord Bray, the Marquis of Exeter—all these crusted Catholics were constantly in touch with Chapuys, exchanging tokens, whispering passwords, and conspiring behind gooseberry bushes in the garden. They were not formidable, but they were busy as gnats. And to spirit Princess Mary out of the country, to pass her into the hands of her first cousin the emperor, was the romantic and perilous maneuver against which Henry had to guard.

He had to be on guard against cruder maneuvers. For years he had gone nowhere without a locksmith, whose first work in a new house, even for overnight, was to put bolts and bars on his bedroom door. Every night the straw of his bed had to be shaken and searched for the hidden dagger—not a great aid to merriment.

In addition to these worries and suspicions, the good people said it had never ceased raining since Thomas More was beheaded. The crops had failed. Trade with Flanders was paralyzed. There was no money in the treasury. The notion of calamity was circulating, and Anne Boleyn was reaping a new harvest of muttered curses and black looks.

LIII

Anne's spirit drooped. She had times of being combative, but more frequently of being listless. She wrote, in answer to a friendly letter from Marguerite d'Angoulême, that she had only two wishes—to give birth to a boy and to see Marguerite.

Her wish for a boy was not impossible of fulfillment, but while she could hold Henry long enough to woo him to this end, she had the chagrin, the humiliation, the shame of his contemptuous infidelity. Henry had given up Madge Shelton, and was now known to be busily cultivating the good graces of that retiring young woman who had been in the same relation to Anne Boleyn as Anne herself had been to Catherine. Hence he included in the "progress" of 1535 a place in Wiltshire called Wolfhall; there Anne could once more study with the politest acidity this rival on whom Henry was lingering.

She did not seem like the choice of a lewd or dissipated man. Jane Seymour was four years younger than Anne Boleyn, the daughter of a good county family who had a spoonful of royal blood in their veins from the times of Edward III. The father was Sir John Seymour. Jane was the very reverse of her former mistress: where Anne was sparkling, she was still; where Anne was challenging, she was meek. By a motion not of the warm blood but of the aching heart, Henry had taken to this Wiltshire primrose, after his marriage to an equal. Here in this gentle presence, her pale eyes vibrating uncertainly to Henry, the nerves that Anne had entangled by her sweeping ambitions were one by one relaxed and mellowed in the consciousness of adoration. The music might be simple, the range limited, the instrument rather warbling, but there was something in its loving kindness that dissolved into Henry's veins.

She was only twenty-five, and the King of England had condescended to her. Jane had a little, precise mouth, which, like the snap-button of a reticule, closed down on the very thought of impropriety. But her ears received the wistful tenderness for her and for himself that welled up in the afflicted heart of the great lover. Jane garnered that sigh as a primrose the first confidence of a premature bumblebee. She was maidenly, sentimental and fortunately inarticulate. As her brother Edward had served with the emperor, she probably thought that Anne was in truth a concubine. She, unlike Anne, was a well-bred lady. She must have pitied Henry for falling into the clutches of this wicked woman, and believed him to be misunderstood.

But Chapuys at once saw in her another Concubine.

"She is the sister," he later wrote a friend, "of a certain Edward Semel, who has been in the service of his majesty; she is of middle height, and nobody thinks that she has much beauty. Her complexion is so whitish that she may be called rather pale. She is a little over twenty-five. You may imagine whether, being an Englishwoman, and having been so long at court, she would not hold it a sin to be still a maid. At which the King will perhaps be rather pleased . . . for he may marry her on condition that she is a virgin, and when he wants a divorce he will find plenty of witnesses to the contrary. The said Semel is not very intelligent, and is said to be rather haughty. She was formerly in the service of the good Queen [Catherine], and seems to bear great good-will and respect to the princess."

In the opinion of other experts, she was not a virgin. But Chapuys' letter, omniscient as it sounds, possibly has only the value of folklore. A diplomat who believed in any woman's chastity at an unfriendly court would be ordered to see his oculist. Jane Seymour, however, assumed a virtue if she had it not, and Anne Boleyn was unable to drive her out of Henry's mind.

But so far this was not a conflagration on the part of the husband: if Henry and Anne quarreled, there was still a certain rude reality about their feelings for one another. Anne was soon looking forward once more to giving him an heir.

LIV

Of all the barbs in Henry's flesh, the worst was Catherine. With Charles and the Pope fully occupied, it still exasperated him, but with Charles returning from Tunis as the greatest military power in the world, and with the Pope so angry over Fisher and

More that a chorus of cardinals could not drown his tremendous cries for Henry's destruction, the emotional annoyance of Catherine's obstinacy merged with him into a practical fear. At the beginning of November, no doubt quickened by Anne, Henry burst out to his confidants in the council, "I will not remain any longer in this trouble and fear and suspicion that the Queen and the Princess are causing me. You must rid me of this in the next parliament, or by God I will not wait any longer to provide for this myself."

So violent was Henry that some of the councilors could not help showing their terror.

"This is nothing to cry or make wry faces about," Henry jumped at them. "If I am to lose my crown for it, I will do what I have set out to do."

These heated words, promptly retold by a councilor to the Exeters and thence to Chapuys, could have only one effect on Catherine. She had been too many years Henry's wife not to form her own conclusions as to his character. She had always been to him like a repressive though loving mother, and even while she had cared for him and held him to the mark she had noted his weakness and insincerity. Having watched him since he was a boy of ten, she regarded him without awe: he and his advisers, she said, are like sheep to those who appear like wolves, but lions to those who are afraid of them. But impossible as it was for her to give in to him, or even to be reached by his threats, she appealed desperately to the Pope and to the emperor for the justice which she believed they could secure her.

It was an attitude calculated to drive Henry wild. Though it was his adjustment to Anne that occupied the center of his being, he had not got rid of Catherine simply by leaving her. There she was, the First Wife, even when he turned his back on her, like the eternal river in an old map that goes rimming the circumference of the world. Catherine had not been disposed of. Liberally pensioning her on thirty thousand crowns (since

Henry could hardly withhold her fortune), imprisoning her as a dowager princess at Kimbolton, withholding her daughter and Chapuys and the whole of the society friendly to her, Henry had failed to make her acknowledge the tiniest validity in the divorce. She had never lowered her cause to bitter personalities, but, deeply and implicitly a Catholic, she judged Henry as another Catholic, and she took the break in her life as a moral calamity that involved Henry with herself. All his crude propaganda concerning herself and Arthur, all his threats and imperious messages, she disregarded in her positive way. She was essentially the wife of long standing who refuses to be put aside on technical grounds by a man who insists that he too is deeply religious. Isolation, imprisonment, torture, martyrdom—nothing could make this Spanish woman subscribe to the hoax of his "conscientious scruples" that Henry wanted to foist on her, on his country and on himself.

There was something still a little juvenile in Henry's dread of Catherine. In March he had refused to let her see Mary when the girl was sick. "With her daughter at her side," he said credulously, "she might raise an army and take the field against me with as much spirit as her mother Isabella!"

His least word about Catherine and Mary was repeated and dilated by the imperialists. On hearing of his menaces in November from the excited Exeters, Chapuys wrote to the emperor that he feared the worst. But Charles had something else on his mind. The French claims to Milan had for some years been lulled by his niece Christine of Denmark having married Sforza: these were now revived by the death of Sforza without issue. And where Francis felt his ache for Milan stir in him like an old, insensate love, Charles felt himself moved in his viscid depths by his personal hatred of Francis. This emotion blunted him toward Catherine. "I cannot believe what you tell me. The King cannot be so unnatural as to put to death his own wife and daughter," he wrote Chapuys. "The threats you speak of can only be designed to terrify them. They must not give way, if it can be avoided; but, if they are really in danger, and there is no alternative, you may tell them from me that they must yield. A submission so made cannot prejudice their rights. They can protest that they are acting under compulsion, in fear for their lives."

When Francis protested that he had acted under compulsion in signing the treaty of Madrid, Charles had called him wicked and a coward. Now, himself the sole human being to whom his aunt could appeal, he gave her excellent reasons for acting *"lâchemont et méchamment."*

But these current ethics, Chapuys believed, held life no more sacred than promises. From time to time Cromwell had hinted to him that perhaps, after all, if Princess Mary were out of the way . . . It looked as if Henry or Anne Boleyn was considering the use of poison. Princess Mary believed this herself, and so Chapuys kept writing to his master. He had no clear proof, but he was immensely suspicious.

LV

Then at the end of December Chapuys learned that Catherine was seriously ill, and he hurried out to Greenwich to see Henry.

He found him in the tiltyard, in the thick of his courtiers. Henry was as affable to him as only Henry could be—and Chapuys agreed with Wolsey and Thomas More and Catherine that this was really a lovable and cordial person.

With his arm around the ambassador's neck, as he used to put it around Thomas More's neck, Henry walked up and down with Chapuys. Why did not Charles write? Francis was burning for war, and he might be forced to listen to him, but he wanted to act honorably and openly with Chapuys. "I am an Englishman," he confessed, "I cannot say one thing when I mean another."

Yes, he went on, still cordially linking Chapuys, Madame

was ill. "I do not believe she has long to live." And he added, "When she is gone, the emperor will have no further excuse for interfering in English affairs."

"The death of the Queen," answered Chapuys soberly enough, "would be of no advantage."

He received permission to visit Kimbolton, but as he reached his barge, Suffolk brought him back to Henry, who announced in very matter-of-fact tones that he had just received word that the Queen was *in extremis,* and that he would hardly be in time to find her alive.

But Chapuys, having asked that Mary be allowed to see her mother, and Henry saying "No," and afterwards, "I'll think about it," went at once to Cromwell for his pass to see Catherine, and then took horse for Kimbolton, some ninety miles north of London.

He reached there after a day and a half's journey, on New Year's morning, 1536.

Catherine was desperately ill, but not actually dying. It was a great event for her, who had been cut off from every one except her Spanish confessor and a physician and a few attendants, to be now able to see her nephew's trusted representative. He was brought to her ceremoniously by the royal officers—whom she had not allowed into her presence for a year—and, weak as she was, she gave him her hand to kiss, and said what a consolation it would be to die in his arms, and not to depart "like a brute." Her condition she did not disguise. She was taking it with her bravest equanimity. But she had not the force to entertain him and she sent Chapuys to rest after his long journey until the afternoon.

The physical state in which she found herself was not discussed by them. Catherine was only fifty years of age, but she had lived in the greatest anxiety and anguish for at least nine years, and she had all the symptoms of cardiac dropsy. She had not been sleeping more than two hours for the six days preceding Chapuys' arrival. She had had violent pains in the stomach, flatulence, vomiting and general weakness. Her years indoors, her dietary, her history of ill-health before all could go far to account for her breakdown. But now, with her most faithful and able partisan by her bedside, she talked only of the great struggle that she and Mary had waged, and of the terrible delays, the suffering, the souls who had gone to perdition perhaps because of her own affair. Chapuys consoled her like a diplomat, holding out the hope of action by the French and by the Vatican.

And now a human surprise came for Catherine. When she had sailed out of Corunna over thirty years before, one of the young Spanish beauties who had accompanied her—Henry VII had stipulated they must be beautiful—was a girl who later had married Lord Willoughby. Always loyal to Catherine through those first penniless years, through her matronly career, through the separation and through the divorce, she had sought in vain for the necessary written pass from Cromwell to visit Kimbolton. His failure to accommodate her had not stopped her. She arrived from London at night, knocking at the gates in the wretched winter weather, and, pretending that she had broken down, begged for God's sake to be let in by the fire. The mother of the Duke of Suffolk's wife, this charity was granted her. In the going and coming of Catherine's people and Chapuys' and the royal guard, she slipped upstairs to the bedside of her Queen, and there she was allowed to remain, to see out a mortal destiny.

This Spanish friend's coming, and Chapuys' coming, had put great heart into Catherine. She slept better. She let him send for his jester—one of his servants—whose quips made her laugh. And primed to move for a better house for her, Chapuys thought her well enough to bid her adieu and return on January 4th to London.

She kept better till the afternoon of the 6th, then actually

was well enough to sit up and do her hair. After midnight, however, she became worse. She wanted to hear mass, but refused to
let her chaplain infringe the law, which she cited to him in
Latin, to say it before the canonical hour. At four o'clock, however, her wish could be gratified: the candles were lighted, mass
was said. She devoutly received communion and prayed at
length, afterwards asking her household to pray for her soul and
to beg God to forgive her husband.

Then she called her physician. He had been told by Chapuys
to ask her, in this solemn hour, to repeat that she had never had
physical intimacy with Prince Arthur. But as Catherine told
him to take a letter, he neglected or omitted to trouble her. The
letter he wrote down for her as follows:

"My most dear lord, king and husband,

"The hour of my death now approaching, I cannot choose,
but out of the love I bear you, advise you of your soul's health,
which you ought to prefer before all considerations of the world
or flesh whatsoever. For which yet you have cast me into many
calamities, and your self into many troubles. But I forgive you
all; and pray God to do so likewise. For the rest, I commend
unto you Mary, our daughter, beseeching you to be a good
father unto her, as I have heretofore desired. I must intreat you
also, to respect my maids, and give them in marriage, which is
not much, they being but three; and to all my other servants a
year's pay, besides their due, lest otherwise they should be un-
provided for: lastly, I make this vow, that mine eyes desire you
above all things: FAREWELL."

It was Catherine's last word to the great unmanageable male.
His carnal nature, the troubles that had sprung from it in his
life, and the calamities in her own, his duty to God, his duty to
"our daughter Mary"—all these simple verities she repeated

with her last breath as she had never failed to do in life. It was
the threnody of her strong and stubborn character. Everything
had been done to break down that character and make her yield
to circumstance, but while she had accepted Henry's infidelities
to herself she was too much the daughter of Isabella and the
daughter of Spain to pretend with Henry that he was sincere.
Catherine met this pretense with an honesty stronger than
death. And yet her honesty had not been enough. To cut
Henry's instincts to a purely formal pattern, to overlay them
with charity and forgiveness of another formal pattern, had not
equipped her for that strange human adventure she had lived—
the adventure of the mismated woman. But to confound her
own reason, her own little masterpiece of the institutional lore
which she had just nobly uttered, she gave a cry from her
starved and cheated heart that was like a gush of agony, "mine
eyes desire you above all things." He had spurned her. The poor
woman at death's door had been hurt to the heart. The desirable
man, she had lost him. It was as if for an instant she had
glimpsed the open door to that great cage in which she had
groped all her devoted, artless, tactless, righteous life.

But she did not die humiliated. She had left Spain at sixteen
but she had brought it with her, and now, on the brink of what
she believed to be eternal salvation, she was Spaniard enough to
take the pen and in a fugue of pride, brave, desolate and magnificent, signed herself for the last time: "Katherine, Queen of
England."

The news of her death galloped to London. It aroused in
Chapuys a furious zeal to know if in truth she had been poisoned. The royal officers had taken over the body, but a humble
official—to wit, the candlemaker—was called in to embalm her.
He said the only abnormal organ was the heart: it was completely black, black all through, with a round black growth attached to it. Whether this indicated crime, or a cardiac disease
resulting in dropsy, or cancer of the heart, no one could say:

but Chapuys believed that she had been done away with by poison in tiny doses.

If Henry had poisoned her, which remains a surmise, the more evil crime had been to postpone it for nine years. But in truth, toxin from outside or inside, dropsy natural or artificial, the woman's life had been poisoned.

When Henry received the news, he was touched for a moment. Then he exclaimed, "Praise be to God, we are delivered from all fear of war. The time is come for me to manage the French better than before because in wondering whether I may now ally myself with the emperor, they will do all I want."

True to his contention that Catherine was never his wife, Henry dressed in yellow from head to foot, with a white plume in his yellow cap, and he did not let her death interrupt the winter festivities for an instant. With the baby Elizabeth in his arms, just as he used to carry the baby Mary in his arms, he went around the grand hall showing her to every one in the highest spirits, while the lute and the fife and the viola and the harp were playing and the courtiers were dancing.

Anne Boleyn was apparently not with Henry. She had been left alone a good deal by Henry in these early months of her pregnancy. On hearing the news of Catherine's death she was reported as saying she rejoiced. Her father and her brother only regretted that Mary had not kept her mother company.

LVI

In the first days after Catherine's death, Anne had companioned Henry in gay yellow. But as one word after another fell from him, as her eye traveled round the circle, the glow somehow faded out of her keen personal triumph and she took a more subdued tone. Henry in middle age was basically a political animal, and this kind of animal is seldom safe when he once has had blood on his tooth. The zeal with which Henry began to address himself to the emperor brought it home to the acute young woman that if his pulse had been left admirably steady by Catherine's death, his brain had become sharply excited. Before Catherine's death there had been two lives between Henry and any remarriage: now there was only her own. If she bore him a son, she could count herself safe. But if her pregnancy did not result in satisfying Henry? If she disappointed him, and he turned against her? With Jane Seymour, who was now at court and receiving presents from him? With Princess Mary? The hilarity that had once been so misguided after Wolsey's death was no longer in Anne's temperament: but even her tamer rejoicing sobered down. She sent for her brother George and her closest friends. She was reported by her enemies as depressed, uneasy, agitated and in tears.

Her first attempt was to please Henry by mollifying Mary. Anne's cousin Lady Shelton was told to assure the girl that if she would stop being obstinate and would behave like a good daughter to her father, Anne would be the best friend she ever had, another mother to her, would do anything she asked, and if Mary came to court she need not bear her train but could walk by her side. This, Lady Shelton urged on the bereaved girl with "warm tears." Mary answered, wholly in the fashion of the mother she had just lost, that she wished for nothing more than to be the most obedient daughter in the world, if it did not conflict with her honor and conscience. But she could not forswear the principles for which More and Fisher died.

Anne gave it up. "Go no further," she wrote bitterly to Lady Shelton. "When I shall have a son, as soon I look to have, I know what then will come to her. Remembering the word of God, that we should do good to our enemies, I have wished to give her notice before the time, because by my daily experience I know the wisdom of the King to be such that he will not value her repentance or the cessation of her madness and unnatural obstinacy when she has no longer power to choose. She would acknowledge her errors and evil conscience by the law of God and the King if blind affection had not so sealed her eyes that she will not see but what she pleases.

"Mrs. Shelton, I beseech you, trouble not yourself to turn her from any of her wilful ways, for to me she can do neither good nor ill. Do your own duty towards her, following the King's commandments, as I am assured that you do and will do, and shall find me your good lady, whatever comes.

Your good mistress,

ANNE R.

This dispirited letter was the prelude of a terrible misfortune. On January 24th Norfolk burst in to Anne to say that Henry had fallen off his horse so heavily that at first they thought he was killed. On January 29th, Anne gave birth to a dead male child.

Those who had seen Henry when Elizabeth was born had kept an impression such as thousands of doctors and nurses could reconstruct—the hour of waiting when the impatient, over-wrought, imperious father, his face set hard, marches up and down like a wild animal, waiting for the delivery of his heir, the heir that will be and must be a son. Himself still a handsome animal, if wild—great, supple, though beginning to thicken and sag a little, walks endlessly while those who nervously watch him wonder why this son delays so long in being born.

A cry, a shriek of anguish, comes through the door. His heart bounds, "My sweetheart, you suffer!" There is silence, an interval, his sleeve is plucked, a word is spoken.

He shouts, "A daughter? Me. Me! A daughter?"

A feeble voice barely makes itself heard, calling his name.

"But Christ, this to me! To me! A daughter! I would prefer a son blind, deaf, crippled, but a son! Imbecile, anything, but a son! You—I married you to have a son, and you have given me a daughter. You make filth of me. You give me a daughter!"

"Do you not wish to see your little daughter?"

"My daughter, my daughter. You old devil, you witch, don't dare speak to me." With a brutal gesture, he breaks out of the room.

This is the way that males of Henry's kind are reported to behave, in the naked hour of egoism, but in the present case we have a few of the actual words that Henry spoke when Anne was now prematurely brought to bed.

Anne must have cried. He came in, and standing over the defeated woman, he said, "I see well that God does not wish to give me male children."

She tried to answer him. It was the news of his fall, she said. "It is because I love you so much more than Catherine did that my heart breaks when I see you making love to others."

"When you are on your feet," he answered, "I will speak to you—"

"I was seduced into this marriage," he muttered to a confidant, "and forced into it by sorcery! That is why God will not permit me to have male children. That is why I want to make a new match."

LVII

In the early part of 1536, following her accident, Anne Boleyn was definitely aware of Henry's neglect. She no longer had Lady Rochford to spy for her, since that hardy lady had not been on the best terms with her husband and had gone over to Mary and the imperialists; but even without her Anne had cute and serviceable friends. Her sister Mary had come to her when she was in trouble. Her cousin Madge Shelton was one of her maids, while Thomas Wyatt's sister was another. And her brother George Boleyn, Lord Rochford, a decisive character who had turned from his early fame as a galloper-poet into a convinced Lutheran and able ambassador, was some one for her to rely on who had a clear head and a discerning eye. She was still unpopular, all the more so since Catherine's death, but she was the mother of Henry's child, the reigning Queen, with a curt tongue and a temper. Even Henry did not venture to defy her outright or to plan any startling intrigue.

But under the normal life of the court, where ceremonial was always elaborate, with amazing simplicities and crudities intermingled; where gallantry and gayety, jousting and dancing, still made up the currency of the gilded day; where the life of Greenwich and Hampton Court and Whitehall saw Cromwell's shaven poll and glittering grin rather than the forgotten rotund splendor of Thomas Wolsey; the tragi-comedy underneath was shuttled by certain passionate and even distempered human beings, bathed in that marvelous conviction of their own huge importance, which impregnates humankind.

But Henry was carrying it to excess. His self-esteem had been swelling for some years, and now it was in the state where almost every one was afraid of him, and where the sycophant gained a ludicrous advantage. It stood to reason that negotiations with the emperor should follow on Catherine's death. No one saw this clearer than Cromwell. He had hardly waited till the six knights had carried Catherine to her grave in Peterborough before he had sent for Chapuys. But Henry was creating difficulties, behaving unmanageably, acting like the sorest of bears. His enemies said that his ulcerated leg was beginning to hurt him, and crude remarks were made about his condition. But this did not alter the practical consequence for his courtiers. It increased the problems of Anne Boleyn.

Curiously enough, it improved Jane Seymour's chances. While Henry was indubitably attracted by her, and had made her brother Edward a gentleman of his chamber, as once before he had made George Boleyn a gentleman of his chamber, the girl either was instinctively so coy or had been made so discreet by the example of the lady she had waited on, that she gave to Henry the response most likely to impress and placate a much-ruffled man.

He sent her a purse of gold and a courtly letter. She kissed the letter but handed it back to the messenger. Falling on her knees, she told the messenger to kneel to Henry, beseeching his grace to consider that she was a gentlewoman of good and honorable stock without reproach; that she had no greater wealth than her honor; that for a thousand deaths she would not wish to impair it; and that if he wished to make her a present of money she prayed it would be when God would send her a good offer of marriage.

It was sweet and humble and cooling. Its tone was the very tone of Henry's own mother. He was touched by it. He thereupon turned Cromwell out of his rooms in the palace which connected with the royal suite by a private passage; there he installed Jane's brother Edward and his wife, and there, in the presence of these witnesses of good and honorable county family, Henry had the pleasure of receiving the homage that is like balsam.

Anne Boleyn had never given this homage to her husband. She might scintillate among her courtiers, and they might laugh at her pert comments and delight in her black eyes. But this was that French influence, the spirit of mockery and waggishness. Henry cared naught for mockery and waggishness. He liked a good story, a hearty laugh, an honest practical joke: but what he liked best of all was the unsullied modesty and deference of a pure good woman.

LVIII

The emperor sought to come to terms, now Catherine was dead. Henry sent for Chapuys at Easter time, and the imperialists were enchanted to see their prime man at Greenwich. They even forgave him for bowing to Anne Boleyn.

But negotiations with the emperor could not go ahead without affecting Henry's break with Rome. Cranmer was horror-stricken. Was Henry going to undo all the magnificent work that had already been put in on the supremacy? He preached a sermon in full excitement, which brought down on his knuckles the marker of the Supreme Head.

Cromwell, though the lay Vicar General, could see no reason for not weighing the pro and con of any movement back or forward. He was fully alive to the political advantages of a deal with the emperor, and he was even ready to suspend his work in liquidating the monasteries if it could be shown to him that it would pay to have a reconciliation with Rome.

The mere hint of such treason on Cromwell's part aroused all the old fire in Anne. She had never minced matters with Cromwell. She had told him she would see his head off his neck when he had clashed with her on a former occasion: and now, with Chapuys actually received at court, Anne lost no chance of reminding Henry of all that he had endured during the agonizing six years of the divorce suit when Charles backed up the "great Devil" Clement.

Chapuys' visit to Greenwich was the fatal event for Anne. It started the most passionate conflict, in which Cromwell was to learn the full fury of that lion whom, against the advice of Thomas More, he himself had lured and whetted into being. Cromwell so far had held his own preferences in check. He had always deferred to Henry. Good as his intelligence was, he had always controlled his vivacity and waited for his master's voice. But even with his training and experience and conviction, he was too human not to become furious when he saw Henry tactless and overbearing with Chapuys.

Henry and he almost came to blows. When Chapuys set before the King the conciliatory and reasonable offers that Charles was making, Henry began to show the temper that made Francis say a year before, "He treats me as if he were my master!"

"We gave him the imperial crown when it lay with us to dispose of it," boasted Henry. "We gave him the money that alone enabled him to quell Spain."

Chapuys tried to soothe him, but Henry would not be soothed. "He had shown nothing but ingratitude," he shouted, "stirring the Bishop of Rome to do us injury. If he will express in writing his desire for us to forget his unkind doings; or will declare that what we consider unkindness has been wrongly imputed to him, we will gladly embrace his overtures; but as we have sustained the wrong we will not be suitors for reconciliation. As to the Bishop of Rome, we have not proceeded on such slight grounds as we would revoke or alter any part of our doings, having laid our foundations on the Law of God, nature and honesty, and established our work thereupon with the consent of the Estates of the Realm in open and high court of parliament."

So Henry said, and so he instructed his ambassadors to say to Charles. He blurted to Chapuys that Milan and Burgundy belonged to Francis, and that he had always done his part and more than his part. He wanted no favors. He insisted on white gloves.

Calling over Cromwell and Audley to the window where he and Chapuys had been speaking, he repeated his diatribe. Chapuys stood aside. In a moment Cromwell made such scathing remarks that Henry lost his temper and retorted. Their voices rose. They both began to lose their heads. Then Cromwell, mastering himself, said he had to have a drink. Completely out of breath, panting and snorting with anger, *"romphant et grondissant,"* he sat on a chest out of sight in a corner, to collect himself and cool off.

But this was no whim on Henry's part, as Cromwell soon learned. The full privy council, on their knees to Henry, implored him not to reject the imperial alliance on a question of punctilio. No, he told his councilors, he would sooner lose his

crown than admit that Charles had cause to complain of him.
These were his terms.

So firm an attitude as this, with its bold intention of driving
the wedge between Charles and the papacy in the hour when
Charles was acting to demolish Francis, could not but prove
that Anne Boleyn and her party were keeping alive Henry's
rage against Rome.

Cromwell felt sick. He was furious with Henry for not aban-
doning the quarrel with the papacy. He knew him too well not
to know that his statecraft was based on his wounded ego; and
he knew that this wounded ego could never be freed from
French influence until Anne and her brother and all who hated
Princess Mary were suitably dealt with. But how could this be
contrived? He must be turned against Anne Boleyn so that he
could be induced to deal with Charles. It must be shown to
him that the Boleyns were treasonable.

Cromwell could not risk seeing Henry until he had a scheme
—until, in his own words a month later, he could manage to
"*fantasier et conspirer*" the right thing.

Cromwell was sick for several days. When he emerged on
April 22d, he had made up his mind.

LIX

On April 30th, one Mark Smeaton was asked to Cromwell's for
dinner. Though he had been at court for three or four years,
Smeaton was still indicated as "no gentleman." The son of an
artisan, like Cromwell himself, he had come penniless to court,
but by his gift as a music player and his elegance as a dancer he
had found favor with Anne and Henry, had been amply rewarded, and was apparently a mobile, pleasant, sentimental
youth. To be asked by the Secretary to dinner at Stepney must
have seemed a signal honor; we may imagine that he leaped
lightly from his boat and arrived merrily at the Secretary's door
in the blithe April forenoon.

But the entertainment to which he was bidden was a grim one. He was shown into a room with Cromwell sitting at the far side of the table, and when he sat facing him two men came up soundlessly and stood behind him. This was not an ordinary dinner.

The Secretary had delved into many lives. He had examined papists and Lutherans, priors and abbesses, monks, nuns, traitors, debtors, the broken and hounded, the suppliant, the defiant, the alert, the terrified. He had faced Thomas More, the Carthusians, the Brigittines. This child of pleasure that now sat opposite him on the edge of his stool, looking into his eyes was as formidable as a paralyzed rabbit. How did he pay for that ring he was wearing? Who gave it to him? How much did that doublet cost? Where did he get it? What else did he get? When? How much? What did she say? Come. Have you no answer? A look to the soundless men. A harmless rope on Mark Smeaton's damp ringlets. The rope tightened by a stick. What else? A nod. Tightened again. Sterner and louder questions, with thinning lips and knuckles rapping. Questions shouted, and beads of sweat on Smeaton's trembling lips. But had she yielded to him? She had. She had. How often? It must have been— Yes. Yes. Anything. Well, confess. Names. Who else? You are lying.

How Smeaton was plied and tortured was never officially known, but it was told by one of the agitated household to a sympathetic Spanish merchant, who wrote it down at great length in his chronicle: and this story of Mark Smeaton's little party with Cromwell gives the first link in a fatal chain.

He was taken upstairs after this experience, flung into a room till further notice, and locked up. Then Cromwell sent a message to Henry.

LX

Six days before he had invited Smeaton to his house, Thomas Cromwell had gone with all his accustomed briskness to the

King and asked for certain extraordinary powers. He said he wanted a commission to be appointed of Henry's most trusted councilors, together with some judges, to make inquiry as to every kind of treason, "by whomsoever committed," and to hold a special session to try the offenders. Norfolk, Suffolk, Audley, Wiltshire, Fitzwilliam, Sandys, Paulet—Henry appointed the tried and true.

Now, in 1535 Thomas Cromwell had thought it expedient to cut off the Law Reports, a muffling of the voice of English legality which the most sinister statesmen had not ventured upon during two hundred and fifty years. Parliament, that still had a voice though mainly for repeating its exercises, had gone out of session early in 1536. If he found the treason he was thus empowered to look for, he could count on coping with it. He could not have asked for a clearer field.

He was aided, moreover, by the perfect network of secret service that he had woven between himself and the favor-seekers since 1533. When Cromwell spoke, a trap in every important establishment noiselessly opened, and he received the gleanings of the underground. No man was better prepared to lay back his ears and revert to the jungle. He was no longer social man. He had the stealth, crouch, cat quickness and economy, the lightning spring and the steel claw that rips the jugular vein. A velvet footstep that said nothing, an eye bright with blackness, he moved with the impressive agility of the beast.

This man did not announce what his object was, what his method was, who his victim was. He had whipped away Mark Smeaton on April 30th. His hunt had only begun.

May the first was Henry's favorite festival. All his courtiers were round him for the tilting at Greenwich. Twenty years before he was foremost in the saddle on May morning, but now it was the younger men, Harry Norris and Lord Rochford, who entered the lists and met the challengers, while Anne and he sat in the galleries to applaud and to reward.

Some time at night or early this May morning, the message had reached Henry from Cromwell. This was the moment on which the Secretary had counted, and the poison he had dropped was eating into Henry's brain. Henry had loved Anne Boleyn; he could be jealous of an injury to the love he had loved. He went down to the jousting. There in the gallery with him was Anne Boleyn, who had made him a cuckold.

His heavy, fat face quivered with insupportable rage at the rôle that had been thrust on him. Who was this woman who had dared to prefer other men to himself? His mind had for years held in suspension all the little glittering particles of suspicion that are carried to a jealous husband on the wind. This mote from Wyatt, that from Bryan, the word that had been spoken to Norris, the feeling that had been spread by silent smile and faint fastidious shrug by all the older nobility who had given their loyalty to Catherine of Aragon. What had the people of England called her? Nan Bullen, the Whore. That was a bitter word to a man to whom she had offered the injury of infidelity. Henry knew enough about his own court to believe that any suspicion could be true. He and Compton and Brandon had laughed often enough over the hot-handed pleasantries, the sudden flares, the urgency, the simple unending amorousness of all these warm-blooded young men and women. His court had surged with rich-lipped, sweet-spoken maids in waiting and their sparkling cavaliers. He himself had enjoyed this eternal gambol. They had been as happy as a harvest dance. They had drunk their wine and sung their song and gloomily, as Catherine had regarded it, it had circled around him in a gorgeous gayety. For himself there had been no lack of intimacy. The French-women with their infinite knowingness had been so much more easy, yet so much less easily stirred. But now! Who could say what lay behind these yielding girls? Anne Boleyn he had wooed like any commoner. She had been shy with him. She had held him at a distance. She had so refused herself to him that he had gone on his knees to her and offered her the crown of England. And this was the woman who had betrayed him with every gamester in the court, who had laughed at him behind his back, who had lavished his money, spent his honor and boasted of his impotence. A sullen fury, full of a hideous congested righteousness, took complete possession of this maddened soul at the thought that a woman he courted so slavishly, loved so hungrily, so immeasurably valued as to marry and enthrone, should now have laughed at his feebleness behind his back with these loose-tongued, flippant courtiers, any one of whom could make her happy. Could make her happy, and had made her happy! Of that he was suddenly certain. "Faugh!" he snorted. But this was no game to ruin. As the jousts continued, with her friends in the yard below, Henry tightened his muscles. She spoke, and he did not hear her. She had not loved him. The delight she could squander on the least of men seemed to his lascivious mind so immeasurably sweet that her indifference to him goaded him to hatred. He hated every smile she had ever smiled. To cut her neck from her body could alone kill her smile.

Those hands had lingered in the clasp of young Smeaton. He had caught a glance, gay as a butterfly, that had fluttered to Norris. To kill her, to turn to clay those clinging arms, to fling naked in the earth those limbs he had adored, seemed to his imbruted mind too good a reward for her indifference. She had loved beyond him, and seen him as he was. This condemnation infuriated him. All that there was in him of ruthless, of terrible, of absolute, of thorough, congested into a resolve that was at once cunning and sinister. There was not a man in England who dared say him nay. He could count on Cromwell to see through what he had started. He could count on Cranmer, who was a sophist. He held Norfolk and Anne's father in the hollow of his hand. A savage joy possessed this heavy frame and radiated this skulking brow at the certainty that no man dared speak a word for this harlot. He had tried by all his arts to make England wed her, with himself. He had failed. The knowledge that he had failed had been the first uneasiness. But now, once more, he had behind him the solid walls of prejudice. It gave him strength. The world was with him.

He sat the tilting through. Grunting an unintelligible good-by to his consort, he ordered his guard, called to Harry Norris, and started to ride to his palace in London.

LXI

He acted abruptly. Riding knee to knee with this most intimate of his attendants, Henry, gray-faced and quivering, accused Norris of adultery with the Queen and told him that he had better confess, adding that if he confessed he might be pardoned. Norris, utterly surprised, took this shock as he took his jousting. He denied the charge. He declared he knew nothing against Anne Boleyn. He said he was completely innocent.

When they reached London, after this amazing tête-à-tête, Henry passed him into the hands of the burly, truculent Fitzwilliam. Fitzwilliam escorted him away, cross-questioned him, tried to get something out of him, left him under the guard and went back to Greenwich.

So far these two isolated arrests had made no stir. Henry's departure did not alarm Anne. She was accustomed to his going to London, to the proximity of Jane Seymour. But at supper, the musician Mark Smeaton was not in his usual place, and Harry Norris was gone. At ten in the evening she heard they were under arrest. It was rumored that Mark had accused her, and that Norris had been implicated for not warning the King. Anne had no official word. Madge Shelton, who had been so attractive to the King and then to Francis Weston and was supposed to be engaging herself to Norris, was one of the women in her company. She and the others could not but infer that something was afoot that concerned their mistress. Their mis-

tress had been extremely generous to many of the courtiers, as
well as in private charity. When the vague, ominous sense of a
net drawing about her began to awaken in them, and the shadow
of its filaments appeared to lie athwart her, the night passed in
hushed whispers and still, listening hearts.

A message was brought to Anne early in the morning. She
was to come before Norfolk, Fitzwilliam, Paulet and others of
the council here in their chamber in Greenwich.

What did they say to her? Her uncle presided. They told her
that she was to prepare to go by the barge to the Tower.
Smeaton and Norris, they declared, had confessed to adultery
with her. As she tried to answer, her uncle said "Tut, tut, tut,"
and shook his head at her three or four times. "I was cruelly
handled at Greenwich," she cried . . . "But I to be a Queen
and so cruelly handled was never seen!"

She sat to dinner. The whole court was silent. The master of
ceremonies who always came to her to say, "Much good may it
do you," forgot his greeting. Every one waited under strain for
the barge.

LXII

Just after two she went from Greenwich to the Tower. In full
daylight, with her uncle and two chamberlains and a guard, she
went up the river in the barge that used to be Catherine's.
Under many eyes that already were hard in curiosity, her grand
vessel came to its final stop at a low dark gate. The solemn Sir
William Kingston, who had been conspiring against her in
favor of Mary, stood to receive her as he had done three years
before.

In trepidation at the awful novelty, she faltered before him.
"Master Kingston, shall I go into a dungeon?"

"No, madam, you shall go into the lodging you lay in at
your coronation."

She gasped. "It is too good for me. Jesu have mercy on me!"

Unable to stand, she found herself on her knees, weeping. And then she laughed at herself for being on her knees weeping, and could not control her laughing.

In the lodging where she found herself, four unfamiliar matrons selected by Cromwell were ready to wait on her, under Lady Kingston. She asked that the eucharist might be exposed in her closet, that she might pray for mercy: "for I am as clear from the company of men, as for sin," she told Kingston, "as I am clear from the company of you, and am the King's true wedded wife."

She asked for her brother. Kingston knew where he was. "I left him at York Place."

But that morning they had been at York Place to arrest her brother. Before noon, he had already been brought to the Tower.

Anne had no comprehension that every word she uttered was being garnered and sent at once to Cromwell. Her excitement, wild and unguarded, mounted as each bit of news came through to her. She was living out the feelings that came to her, or rather she had become the mere æolian of her feelings.

"I hear I shall be accused with four men, and I can say no more but Nay—without I should open my body." Here she threw open her gown and she cried, "Oh, Norris, hast thou accused me? Thou art in the Tower with me, and thou and I shall die together; and Mark, thou art here too! . . .

"Oh, my mother, thou wilt die with sorrow!"

"Master Kingston, shall I die without justice?"

With his customary gravity, the bearded giant answered, "The poorest subject of the King hath justice."

Anne burst into laughter.

While these words were being spoken and noted, Henry at Westminster inclined to a light footstep. His boy, the Duke of Richmond, had come to kiss him good-night.

The sight of his son, his only son, brought tears of self-pity gushing to his eyes.

As he kissed the youth—Richmond was now seventeen—Henry sobbed, "You and your sister Mary ought to thank God for escaping that cursed and venomous whore who tried to poison you both."

LXIII

On the next day in the Tower, Anne Boleyn was plied with questions by Cromwell's matrons, the two Kingstons outside the door.

Only on the previous Sunday Norris had told her almoner that "he would swear for the Queen that she was a good woman."

"Madam," asked the matron, "why should there be any such matters spoken of?"

"Marry I bade him so, for I asked him why he did not go on with his marriage with Madge Shelton and he made answer he would tarry a time. Then I said, 'You look for dead men's shoes, for if ought come to the King but good you would look to have me.' And he said if he had had any such thought he would his head were off. And then I said I could undo him if I would; and therewith we fell out."

Her story of Norris led to Madge Shelton and then to Weston who, though a married man, was too attentive to Madge Shelton. She reproved him; and he answered he loved "me in her house better than Madge as his wife." "Who?" "It is yourself."—And she "defied him."

Her babblings were treasure trove for Cromwell. Unwitting, she began to reassure herself, and even dined merrily. Soon she supped. "I think the King does it to prove me!" she smiled.

"I would to God I had my bishops," she added later. "They would all go to the King for me."

While she kept up her spirits, Weston and William Brereton were added to those arrested, and the news conveyed to Anne. She was now quite calm. She spoke of Mark Smeaton. On the very Saturday before May Day, he stood in her round window, looking sad. She asked him why. He answered it was no matter. "You may not look to have me speak to you as I should do to a nobleman," she said, "because you are an inferior person."

"No, no, madam, a look sufficeth me, and so fare you well."

Her confidences were poured out with the facility of a woman whose whole life had become nervously fluid and unstable. She was even alive to her own miserable picturesqueness. "They might make ballads well now; but there is none but my lord brother that can do it."

"Yes, Master Wyatt."

"True. . . . My lord my brother will die."

Wyatt had also been arrested, and Sir Richard Page. This was May 5th. All of London was now aware that the Queen of England was to be charged with adultery. Meanwhile Henry was acting as if less than nothing had happened. His barge, gayly lighted, moved up and down the river in the evenings, and the music from it told the world of banquets, of dancing, of happiness and new love.

LXIV

The charges against Anne could now be framed into indictments. But instead of saying that she was a woman as avid for praise as any poet, living in an atmosphere of flattery and flirtation, and collecting compliments with the vulgar zeal of an adolescent, she found herself accused not only of adultery with four men and of incest with her brother but also accused of treason, plotting the king's death and destruction, and "often saying she would marry one of them as soon as the King died."

The true bills were promptly found by the grand juries of the counties where these crimes were believed to have been committed—Kent and Middlesex—and the commoners were sent for jury trial on the next day, May 12th, before the Cromwell commission at Westminster Hall. Anne and her brother were to be tried at the Tower by twenty-six selected peers on May 15th.

While these events were taking shape, only one unknown youth—a lawyer named Buckley—made any move to fight for Anne Boleyn. Her father was so subservient that he offered to go on the jury to try her. Cranmer was, of course, inexpressibly shocked. "I am clean amazed, for I never had a better opinion of woman; but I think Your Highness would not have gone so far if she had not been culpable—I loved her not a little for the love which I judged her to bear towards God and His Gospel." He wrote this letter, and then held it until he was put through a cold questioning by the Commission. He added a sagacious post-script, "I am sorry such faults can be proven against the Queen as they report." Anne had been his patroness. He had been made archbishop to legalize her. But was she not culpable? Might it not affect Henry's "zeal for the Gospel"?

The calculations that moved Cranmer's chicken heart may have affected the youth who was tortured, Mark Smeaton. A jury had been most carefully packed for the trial in Westminster Hall. Smeaton pleaded guilty to the charge of adultery. Norris and Weston and Brereton pleaded not guilty. None of them admitted treason. All were promptly found guilty on both counts and sentenced to death.

Anne and her brother could not be tried so expediently. By the time this ordeal came she had been two weeks in the Tower. The infidelities of which she was accused had been detailed in each indictment—one of them a month after Elizabeth was born and another a month before the disappointment of January 29th. The dates at which Henry's death was plotted were also fixed with equal definiteness and inopportuneness, if ordinary human motives were to be considered. But the trial turned on something besides evidence. Anne had become Queen of England through Henry's obstinate attachment to her and against the social, religious, class and personal feelings of most of her own kind and a great many of the common people.

Had her virtue been as unassailable as Wolsey once declared, had her defense been irresistible, it would still have been necessary to get rid of her unless her conduct at the trial created an enormous revulsion of feeling. She was indicted not for unchastity but for unpopularity: and Henry and Cromwell both felt that they could risk her conviction by peers who had been her steadfast enemies.

She and her brother, however, almost won the day. Even after her peers pronounced her guilty, Northumberland so ill that he collapsed, she was able to stand firm and appeal only to God. During the evidence, such as it was, she had been "unmoved as a stone, and had carried herself as if she was receiving some great honor." "Her face spoke more than words, and no one who looked on her would have thought her guilty."

"Her speech," said one outsider, "made even her bitterest enemies pity her."

She was led out, and her brother's trial followed.

Rochford's incest was based solely on the charge that he had once been alone with her for several hours. But he was charged with other things than treason and incest: with making fun of the King, with making fun of his ballads, and his dress; with saying something that could not be spoken of in court but could only be written down and handed to Rochford.

The young man had defended himself so vigorously and cleverly that listeners in the crowded courtroom were betting he would be acquitted. But he knew Henry and his peers, and when he was handed the piece of paper, he read aloud what he was accused of having said: "that the King was not able to have relations with his wife: that he had no virtue or potency in him."

To give voice to this scandal was the last defiance of a man who had no faith in the trial. And when he was condemned he coolly asked to be allowed to plead "Guilty," to avoid the confiscation of his property.

On May 17th, under Anne's windows in the Tower, the five men were led out to the block.

Her brother spoke with passionate seriousness to the public around. "Trust in God and not in the vanities of the world; for if I had so done I think I had been alive as ye be now.—Also I desire you to help to the setting forth of the true word of God." He did not and would not speak of his offenses. But he was no traitor. "And heartily I require you all to pray for me and to forgive me if I have offended you, and I forgive you all, and God save the King."

Weston, who had been revealed to his devoted family as a thoughtless gallant, unfeeling about his wife, now spoke humbly and penitently, but explicitly avoiding the cause for which he died.

So died Brereton. Smeaton did not change his plea: "Masters, I pray you all pray for me, for I have deserved the death."

Anne turned pale when she heard that Smeaton had repeated his confession.

"Did he not clear me of the shame he brought on me? Alas, I fear his soul will suffer for it."

The older man, Harry Norris, was alone in his hauteur and stoicism. He died with few words.

LXV

Anne alone was left. In all that Cromwell had written abroad to Gardiner he had spoken in holy horror of "abominations," "unmentionable things." But this woman had so far given no impression of guilt.

On the morning following her trial, Cranmer had come to the Tower. After her talk with him, she was elated, saying to her matrons that she would be allowed to go to Antwerp. But this hope, possibly based on some gentle insinuation of Cranmer's, was a pathetic illusion. He had merely come preparatory to a little handiwork for Henry.

The next day, on grounds not revealed but probably relating to her sister Mary, Cranmer held his court at Lambeth, declaring her marriage to Henry null and void. She had never been married to Henry, and therefore, you might say she had never been adulterous. But for her the time had passed for these sophistries.

She was now to die on the 18th. True to her court tradition, she had requested that her head should not be cut off by the common headsman who used an ax, but by any executioner who could wield the sword. This had been allowed, and the man had been sent for to Calais. But her request had deranged the hour appointed. She was up before daybreak on the 18th, at the hour of the freshest May bird-song, and when morning came she sent for Kingston to hear from her own lips after receiving the host that on the salvation of her soul she had never been unfaithful to the King. It was the declaration in the letter addressed to Henry, discovered among Cromwell's papers. "Never prince had wife more loyal in all duty, and in all true affection, than you have ever found in Anne Boleyn."

"Master Kingston," she said, on seeing him, "I hear say I shall not die afore noon, and I am very sorry therefor, for I thought to be dead by this time and past my pain." Kingston told her it should be no pain, it is so subtle.

"I heard say the executioner was very good, and I have a little neck." She put her long slender fingers around it, and her laughter this time was merry.

The hour of noon came and went. She had gained one more day. As evening drew on, she prayed at times, and then she chatted freely, saying she would be easily nicknamed—Anne sans-tête. And at this joke at her own lack of head, she laughed. Her laughter was no longer hysterical: she had returned to the quips so natural to her disposition. And there was one moment that showed how deep a change had come since the agony of her battle was over. She said she did not think she had been brought to this end by divine judgment, except for having been the cause of ill-treatment to Princess Mary—"and," quotes Chapuys, "conspiring to kill her."

Her last dawn, Friday the 19th, saw her awake. She had scarcely slept, but had prayed with her almoner and conversed all night. Kingston came to her early, gave her a purse of twenty pounds to distribute in the usual way as alms, and told her to make ready.

She came down to the little green where the platform with straw on it had been made purposely low so as not to have her seen from outside. No foreigners had been admitted but the English public had crowded in, with the councilors headed by Cromwell and Suffolk and Audley, and accompanied by the boyish Duke of Richmond. She was preceded by Kingston along the path, and followed by the four matrons. Her gray damask robe was cut low and trimmed with fur, a kirtle of crimson beneath. She wore a headdress embroidered with pearls, and a net to keep up her hair.

As she mounted the scaffold, Kingston handing her over to the sheriff, she knew that her executioner was one of those standing by her. Her voice nearly left her, but in a low monotone, she said that she had not come to preach but to die. What else she said was breathless and not clear. She kept nervously glancing behind her. She asked every one to pray for the King, who was so good, remitted her offenses to God, and asked forgiveness of all whom she had wronged.

As she finished her few words, she knelt down, while one of the matrons bound her eyes. "O God, have pity on my soul; O God, have pity on my soul; O God, have pity—" The stroke of the sword severed her neck: her little head rolled to the straw. At once the matrons lifted the trunk, her lifeblood still flowing. They gathered her broken body into a coffin, and they bore her to her brother's grave in the chapel. Thomas Cromwell had seen her to her end.

BOOK FOUR

Jane Seymour

I've lost my love, and I care not,
I've lost my love, and I care not;
I shall soon have another
That's better than t'other;
I've lost my love, and I care not.

FAR FROM THE MADDING CROWD

I

LONDON was tense on the morning of May 19. It was one of those moments in a city when every nerve is strained, when men say little and women talk low and even children are aware of something impending too large and vague for their small grasp. The boatmen on the Thames, lying on their oars, looked toward the Tower. Prentices walked slowly. An event that at first was welcome but that now was painfully threatening hung in the morning air.

At nine o'clock a cannon boomed from Tower Green. As its heavy sound rolled through space, many a citizen's wife stood suddenly still, listening to the silence in the wake of that solitary detonation. She with the bowl under her arm, he with his gesture arrested, adze or mallet lifted, did not need any one to tell them the meaning of this signal. It was the end of Anne Boleyn.

London had never accepted her as Queen. When salvoes had greeted her from the Tower three years before it had awakened no popular joy. She was displacing the rightful Queen. She was one of the Bullens, an imperious upstart, and there was something ruthless and violent in the way she had broken with tradition. But her abrupt fall, so tragic a change from pride to shame, had laid an icy hand on London. At first her humiliation had come gleefully, but while she lay in the Tower awaiting trial, the man who had made her Queen kept passing in his barge on the Thames on his way to his new mistress, and returning to his palace late at night, his vessel festive and brilliant and music sounding over the water. The London that had ascribed all blame to Anne Boleyn now muttered a new opinion of the fickle King. To utter it out loud was fatal, men were arrested every day for light words spoken on the ale-bench or in the inn parlor. But few women could but pity this mother who was leaving a child three years old; few men could but feel horror and awe of the unswerving power that struck her down. If she had given herself to her cavaliers, her dancing man, the older silent knight who admitted nothing, it was a terrible end to her hard splendor; her flight was over and her portion was death.

The goodness of the English people, their warmth, their inability to harbor enmity, their hatred of pain—all these rich qualities of their ample being were moved by the execution that was so grimly announced. Thousands of the common people had taken part in the drama; a few favored ones had seen her debarking at the Tower; hundreds had crowded into the trial where, in the thick of enemies who were her judges, she had stood composed and straight to meet condemnation; hundreds pressed behind the yeomen of the guard as the five men had been led out to die, fresh in their white linen shirts, and the populace could tell what had been said from the scaffold in the light silence of the morning as their last words ran out like

ebbing sand. Through blinding tears the people had watched
the headsman strike while their words still floated in the air and
their cheeks were still the color of life. In many a kitchen, in
groups that hugged together, men who had stood outside the
Tower, or even on the Green itself, could tell how Anne Boleyn
had looked and spoken, how the Lord Mayor and the aldermen
were present, how she had prayed, and how the executioner
from France had knelt to ask her pardon before he stepped behind her and swung his two-handed sword. Some said that he
had told her to look one way, while he had smitten her from
the other side. More declared that he had hidden his sword in
the straw until the very end. "Christian people," she had addressed them. Her voice was hardly louder than a whisper. The
young Duke of Richmond, pale as a ghost, had watched her
die. So had black Cromwell. It was in a narrow box that the
ladies had taken away her body. A few lucky ones could show
the dole that had been distributed in her name.

The feeling of the people could find no outlet. There was no
press. The preachers were Henry's. The parliament was his. He
was the arbiter of fate, the giver of rewards and punishments.
But as he went from the mistress he had just disowned to the
mistress who would be the next Queen, this London became
darkly unfriendly. No new coronation would be possible. His
bastard, the Duke of Richmond, could not be foisted on them.
Their loyalty was to Princess Mary, the daughter of "the real
Queen."

II

The same signal that had betokened Anne's death to London
came across to Westminster, where Henry had been astir since
early morning. He had not been waiting pensively to hear it.
In the middle of the night Cromwell had fetched the intelligence from the Tower, a written report from the faithful
Kingston, and Henry had decreed that the foreigners were not

to remain on the precincts and that Anne was not to speak much or long. This done, he must have slept for a few hours. He attended early mass, and as this was Friday he could not have taken meat with his golden bowl of wine. Breakfast over, he had plunged into the plans that crowded on him, knowing that his council would soon step from the scaffold to fetch him the last word of that "accursed whore."

Henry's mind, at such a crucial moment, bounded, flustered, darted and recoiled. It was no doubt the appropriate thing to murmur condolences, and Cranmer, who had seen Anne out and was to see Jane in, stood at his elbow waiting to arrange for to-morrow's betrothal, the proper lugubrious expression on his sagging face. Chapuys, Charles's ambassador, who had predicted Anne's downfall six months before, and who, on her arrest, had exultantly told his master that "I used several means to promote the matter, both with Cromwell and with others," and who had suggested an increase in emolument on the strength of it, sent the tactful word to Henry almost immediately—"Many great and good men, even emperors and kings, have suffered from the arts of wicked women." To thank God that the great and good King had escaped from the wicked woman was the cue. But Henry, immersed in details, did not care to linger on the morning's work. For several weeks he had been bombarded by suppliants who wanted Norris's lands and sinecures and Brereton's lands and sinecures. He was hearing from the widows who sought to excuse themselves, from the bishops who were pestering him about purgatory in the Ten Articles he was devising, from the sheriffs who were appointing trusty members to come up to parliament, from the French who were bargaining for an alliance and to-morrow would propose a substitute spouse to him, from Charles who was courting him, from the marches of Wales and the Irish Pale and the Scotch border, where Cromwell was organizing his sovereignty with iron hand. This immense host pushed on Henry, each brandishing its existence and begging his interest, swarming, thronging, elbowing, jamming, like the sick with the King's evil, who pleaded with their lord to heal them. The shot that rumbled to Westminster, the crack of Anne Boleyn's doom, was drowned in this courtly clamor, to which, this morning, he lent willing ear. His boast was nonchalance. Before she died he was openly saying he believed that more than a hundred "had to do with her." "You never saw prince nor man," observed Chapuys dryly, "who made greater show of his horns or bore them more pleasantly." Perhaps once during the day a pang might have suddenly skewered through him, the quiver of severed ganglia. But his Grace was hurrying to interpose a new arrangement of life between himself and his memory. He was to be freshly betrothed next morning. It was necessary to forget the drip of blood. He lifted his chin and ordered his barge; he was "taking water" to see his bride-elect.

III

Was the bride-elect already a mother-elect? That was the suspicion which only a few dared breathe. It was more than four months since Henry had blurted that he had been seduced by Anne's witchcraft and that he believed he might take another wife. This had followed Anne's miscarriage. Anne's "intense rage" at his infidelity had not been concealed, and while Jane Seymour had been coached by the Imperialists "by no means to comply with the King's wishes except by marriage," she had been brought to live in the palace, in rooms vacated by Cromwell, where Henry could come and go by secret ways. This compliance had been safeguarded by Edward Seymour's presence, just as Anne Boleyn's compliance had been safeguarded by George Boleyn's presence; but Cromwell, for one, did not pretend that Henry was faithful to Anne in recent months. He said to Chapuys in a "cold voice" with his eye cocked, "I believe

he will live honorably and chastely, continuing in his marriage,"
and as he said this he put his hand to his mouth and hunched to
conceal a grin. But why these months of delay in leaving Anne,
the hesitation, and then the violent haste? Why the marriage
with a nobody, who like Elizabeth Blount and Anne herself,
had nothing to recommend her beyond the possibility of pregnancy? Why at last a precipitate marriage without any bargaining for a bride with the French or with the Emperor? Why
execution rather than a divorce? Charles had written in March,
"If perchance the King of England should wish to marry anew,
you are not to dissuade it." Chapuys had sent a letter crossing
this which assented; he thought it would be a great thing for
the faith and for Princess Mary to break this marriage with a
Lutheran. But the new marriage demanded Anne's death to
clear the decks. So it was declared explicitly. And Anne's death
would have become doubly necessary if Jane were quick with
child. As for a child born in wedlock but conceived in January
or February, Cranmer and the Act of Succession could provide
for any such legitimization. All that Henry needed to urge him
into decision was to know that Jane Seymour could indeed become a mother. His mania was to secure a male heir. And the
one vengeance that Rochford had sought in the trial, even at
the risk of being tortured, was to declare that Henry was "without vigor or virtue." This was the only reprisal possible on Jane
Seymour's child.

In those odd conversations of the early spring between the
maidenly Jane Seymour and the conscientious Henry, she had
ventured to suggest to him that Princess Mary should be reinstated. "You are a fool," said Henry, according to Chapuys' spy,
"you ought to solicit the advancement of the children we will
have between us, and not any others."

Those children were already her title to queenship. And their
precipitate marriage, within ten days, without any decent prep-

aration, without a word to the public, without a chance for France or the Empire to treat the new Queen with becoming dignity, without anything more ceremonious on Henry's part than an order to change A into J, fairly implied that this new wife was not so much a person in herself whom he appreciated or valued as the female envelope of a guaranteed heir. Hence her shrinking presence, her quiet first months, her resolute retirement. Hence Henry's admission in a few months that he could not be a father, and hence the long interval from the date of marriage before Edward was born. Hence the urgent, the peremptory, reason for Anne Boleyn's elision. These things could scarcely be recorded or even hinted at. Chapuys' chat with Edward Seymour on the eve of Anne's arrest had no witnesses. The tiniest subsequent reflection on Henry's treatment of Anne Boleyn, the tiniest breath against Jane Seymour, was as much as a man's life was worth. "He was made sure unto the Queen's grace half a year before." The subject who said this was guilty of treason. His fate is not recorded.

Dr. Ortiz at Rome could assert in June that Jane was "five or six months gone with child" by Henry. But the free witness in this instance was necessarily remote, probably biased and more than likely credulous. The English Imperialists said no such thing. But the English Imperialists, on the other hand, were Jane Seymour's partisans. She was Princess Mary's best friend at court. As for concealment, it was a familiar game. Henry had been able to conceal the date of his marriage to Anne Boleyn, though a number of witnesses had been present. He was able to conceal the grounds for Anne Boleyn's divorce, two days before her execution, though a whole court was assembled. Sampson, his henchman, was continually with Cromwell during the four days in which Anne Boleyn's execution was being planned, and not a word of this connivance had been breathed except by Chapuys. To conceal Jane Seymour's condition at this period would not have been difficult. And yet nothing could have induced Henry to marry her so promptly as the knowledge that she was already bearing his child.

IV

Rumor, it must be agreed, had not taken long to distort the story of Anne's trial and twist it into legend. Dr. Ortiz knew by May 23rd that "in order to have a son who might be attributed to the King, Anne committed adultery with a singer who taught her to play on instruments. Others say it was with her brother." It was, in any case, foretold that this Anne would be burnt to death. At Paris on May 24th, the Bishop of Faenza was writing to Rome, "It is said that the King has been in danger of being poisoned by that lady for a whole year, and that her daughter is supposititious, being the child of a countryman; but these particulars are not known for certain, according to what the King [Francis] said to-day. The discovery was owing to words spoken by the organist from jealousy of others." Hannært at Lyons on May 26th was writing, "There is news from England that the so-called Queen was found in bed with her organist, and taken to prison. It is proved that she had criminal intercourse with her brother and others and that the daughter supposed to be hers was taken from a poor man." Melanchthon on May 29th wrote, "The reports from England are more than tragic. The Queen is thrown into prison, with her father, her brother, two bishops and others, for adultery. You will hear the whole thing from Bucer." Chapuys was hinting that Elizabeth was not her brother's child, or Smeaton's or the child of an unknown countryman, but the daughter of Norris. An absolutely circumstantial Portuguese declared by June 10th, "After her execution the Council declared that the Queen's daughter was the child of her brother." By that time Melanchthon had got his second wind and was writing sadly, "She was more accused, than convicted, of adultery."

While such rumors reverberated through Europe, Lady

Bryan, Elizabeth's guardian, could hardly know what to call the child. She poured out her troubles to Cromwell with the garrulity of a nurse.

"Now as my lady Elizabeth is put from that degree she was in, and what degree she is at now I know not, but by hearsay, I know not how to order her or myself, or her women or grooms. I beg you to be good lord to her and hers, and that she may have raiment, for she has neither gown nor kirtle nor petticoat, nor linen for smocks, nor kerchiefs, sleeves, rails, body stychets, handkerchiefs, mufflers, nor begens. All thys har grace's mostake I have dreven of as long as I can, that, be my trothe, I cannot drive it no longer.

"Mr. Shelton would have my lady Elizabeth to dine and sup every day at the board of estate. It is not meet for a child of her age to keep such rule. If she do, I dare not take it upon me to keep her Grace in health, for she will see divers meats, fruits, and wine, that it will be hard for me to refrain her from. Ye know, my lord, there is no place of correction there, and she is too young to correct greatly.

"My lady has great pain with her teeth, which come very sloyly, this make me give her her own way more than I would. I trust to God and her teeth were well graft to her Grace after another fashion than she is yet; so as I trust the King's Grace shall have great comfort in her grace. For she is as toward a child and as gentle of conditions as ever I knew any in my life, Jesus preserve her grace. As for a day or two at a hey time, or whansomever it shall please the King's Grace to have her set abroad, I trust so to endavor me that she shall do so as shall be to the King's honor and hers, and then after to take her ease again."

It was as the mother of Elizabeth that the last reminders were coming of Anne Boleyn. A bill was sent in for boat hire from Greenwich to London and back "to take measure of caps for my lady Princess, and again to fetch the Princess's purple satin cap to mend it." "On April 20th a fringe of Venice gold and silver for the little bed." On April 28th, two days before her arrest, red fringe to mend the harness of the Queen's mules, and "two leading reins with great buttons and long tassels."

Elizabeth, at three, was left without a mother. But she was not deserted. Jane Seymour had her in mind and felt pity for her banishment.

v

Jane Seymour was a gentlewoman. Her blank and somewhat sheeplike expression, with her porcelain whiteness of skin, might announce that she was docile, with the perfect orthodoxy of the sheep; that she would follow her husband's lead, bear his children in unbroken series, and wear his pearls. She might appear to be the ideal wife of whom a bearded Deity inspired the description in the Epistle to the Ephesians: "Let women be subject to their husbands as to the Lord; because man is the head of the woman as Christ is head of the Church . . . as the church is subject to Christ, so the women to their husbands, in all things." These words of kindly despotism Henry had ordered transcribed in the book that defended the sacrament of Marriage against Luther; and now he had found the ideal successor to the wife who had tied him to France, thwarted his politics, hampered his pride, clogged his curiosity, and interfered with his ambition. Already Jane had chosen her motto on the model of Catherine, who was "humble and loyal," and his mother who was "humble and penitent." Jane was "bound to obey and serve." But such exquisite appropriateness reposed for her on a solid base of her own breeding. She had been a maid in waiting to Queen Catherine; Anne Boleyn for her had been an interlude of infelicity; from this, by espousing her King, she was rescuing him. Many a gentlewoman had gone into religion in this spirit; to wed the Supreme Head seemed hardly less religious. The royal blood in her veins that had

filtered from Edward III through the charcoal of the Seymours
was no more than Anne Boleyn had a claim to; but Jane Seymour was not a hoyden; she guarded and revered her inheritance and was a funnel of tradition; not so much a human
being as the matrix of an heir, who, with discreet sedulity, desired to transmit the whole royal layette as well as the baby. She
conformed to Henry. Sure for her part that he could never
have really loved "that woman," sure that Mary should be reinstated, and that the future must repair the ugly present, Jane
lifted up her eyes to her lord and master with a heart that
echoed her device, "Bound to obey and serve."

The appalling insipidity of this devotion made Henry restive.
"Within eight days of the publication of his marriage having
twice met two beautiful young ladies, he said and showed himself somewhat sorry that he had not seen them before he was
married." But the Seymour obedience had implications, those
that her brothers Edward and Thomas gave, two young men
who accompanied her into royal favor. Edward Seymour and
Thomas Seymour had mettle. Edward had a visage like a clean
blade in a black scabbard. Thomas was a wild whipping rapier,
ready to brag and brawl, lithe, fascinating and extravagant. To
take raw ambition on an empty mind is always dangerous, and
Thomas would succumb to it; but Edward Seymour was a man
of noble quality. He framed his gentle sister as a Queen.

In a little church nestled in the country the following Sunday, this deferential girl went with Henry to mass. As they
crossed the field among the buttercups and varnished celandine
of a Maytime English meadow, a lamb might have raised its
head and tweaked its pink ears in wonderment. This was a vast
biped with the demure little biped floating beside him. In a few
weeks, the lamb could hardly know, he would be forty-five
years old, almost twice as old as his companion. The lover was no
longer uppermost in him but the benevolent potentate, at the
moment beaming, subdued and winning. Jane loved and feared

him. Jane was the port after the storm. He respired her inexperience and dependence. This was no passionate struggle with a
black-browed witch. This was Sunday morning in the heart of
the country, the lisp of spring and the whiff of hawthorn.

VI

Henry's ruses in advance of his remarriage were like the twist-
ings and turnings of a fox. Before Anne's execution he took
pains to declare that he had no desire in the world to marry
again unless "constrained" by his subjects to do so; and five
days after his betrothal to Jane he was telling the French that he
was at liberty. Even to Cromwell, who knew how "marvelously
scrupulous about his honor" Henry could be, this sort of palpable dishonesty seemed disgustingly stupid, and he did not hide
his feelings in talking to Chapuys. But Henry's ruses were seldom stupid. His visits to Jane, housed in a mansion where he
had the prevision to install his own cooks, could not possibly be
hidden from London. Long before June 4th "everybody begins
already to murmur by suspicion." But this softened the impact.
It reduced the shock by just the use of those fenders which
Henry had provided. On May 30th he and Jane were united
in that same Queen's Closet at York Place where he had been
married to Anne Boleyn. By Whitsuntide, June 4th, he and
the new Queen glided into the open, and the following Sunday the whole fashionable world thronged with them to Westminster Abbey, "almost a coronation."

To proceed by indirection, as Chapuys observed, was Henry's
artifice, though his nature was fidgety and impatient. When the
Imperial ambassador came to greet the new Queen, whom he
was allowed to kiss, and was telling her in his suave and politic
way that he hoped she would labor to obtain the honorable
name of "pacific," Henry, "who had been talking to the other
ladies, approached, and wished to excuse her, saying I was the
first ambassador to whom she had spoken, and she was not quite

accustomed to it." "I quite believe," Henry continued, "she desires to obtain the name of 'pacific' for, besides that her nature is
gentle and inclined to peace, she would not for the world that I
were engaged in war, that she might not be separated from me."

The war Henry had in mind was that which had once more
renewed itself between Charles and Francis. On the eve of
Anne's arrest he had been in fear of peace, followed by a General Council of the Church, in which the Christian powers
could be prevailed on by the Pope to invade England and dethrone him. To avert this danger, however, he did not adopt
Cromwell's policy of directly cultivating the Imperialists. Henry
had learned from Wolsey the supreme lesson of English diplomacy, that its place in the European seesaw is at the center.
Henry's craft was sovereignty, and as early as February he had
repeated to Gardiner, who was at Paris for him, the principle
that alone was sufficient to keep him from ever going back to
Rome. He told Gardiner and Wallop to remind the French
that, "if they cleave to Rome for devotion, they shall consider
the abominations that have grown from it—how they have encroached upon Princes who by God's word are heads and supreme ministers of justice in their own dominions." He "wishes
them to compare the advantages they have from England and
the Bishop of Rome, who is nearer his end than the other, and
when he is gone 'our realm shall still continue the same it was
and is.'" England, in other words, can be a better arbiter of
Europe than any Church with pretensions to be a military
power, if only because a hereditary monarchy is more stable
than a monarchy where the sovereign is elected by a college of
bribe-taking cardinals. England's rôle was not, therefore, to ally
itself with Charles or Francis but to keep its principle fluid and
to act as counter-balance and make-weight, never being caught
on the end of the seesaw but doing its dance at the center, swaying contra rather than pro, and always high-minded and impartial. This had been Wolsey's doctrine, though he had be-

trayed it by a real feeling for Rome, on the one hand, and a cynical acquisitiveness on the other. Henry's acquisitiveness was wholly subordinate to this dominating sense of sovereignty which made him "insist on plain terms touching the Bishop of Rome." He could be mean as the most grasping peasant about money. When Catherine bequeathed her robes and furs, Henry would not fulfill her bequests; he first "wanted to see what the robes and furs were like." Those she left to the Church he took for himself, saying the Church had more than enough already. He refused her body a hearse from St. Paul's, saying it would be "more charge than was requisite or needful." The older he got, the more he was stigmatized as avaricious, grudging, stingy and mean. But when it came to diplomacy he was not distracted, as was Wolsey, by actual bribes in money. And he did not run, like Cromwell, to connect himself with the strongest power. He was too devoured by his wish for power to negotiate with anything but power in mind.

Chapuys was irritated by this trait. "The more one shows a desire to do business with them," he said, "the more they draw back." "The more these people are pressed, the more they grow stubborn like donkeys." And he described Henry's intractability to the Emperor. "The King maintains an opposite opinion, both because his natural inclination is to oppose all things debatable, taking great pride in persuading himself that he makes the world believe one thing instead of another, and also to make your Majesty feel the more grateful if he come to declare himself for you."

This native resistance, so strong and imperturbable, did depend, however, on having power in the locker. Henry's anger at being opposed or disregarded made every one around him walk on egg-shells. Even Chapuys coached Charles, who was himself not without a superb temper. "This King's character should be taken into account," he hinted. He requires "the most gentle treatment." He recognizes no superior and would

not have any one imagine that he could be led by force or fear."
"Treat him," he begged, "with the greatest possible courtesy."

Charles listened, as he always listened to everything that concerned business.

As for Francis, he shrugged his shoulders. He did not care
quite so much about business as all that. He thought Henry
"the most unstable man in the world, and has no trust of ever
seeing any good in him."

Charles's sister, Mary, who had succeeded his aunt as Regent
in Flanders, viewed Henry and his superbness not without humor. A few days after Anne's execution she wrote to her brother
Ferdinand, the junior partner in the Hapsburg concern. "I hope
the English will not do much against us now," she said, "as we
are free from his lady, who was a good 'Frenchwoman.' I hear
he has already espoused another lady, who is a good Imperialist
(I know not if she will continue), and to whom he paid great
attention before the death of the other. As none but the organist
confessed, nor herself either, people think he invented this device to get rid of her. Anyhow, not much wrong can be done to
her, even in being suspected as naughty, for that has long been
her character. It is to be hoped, if hope be a right thing to entertain about such acts, that when he is tired of this one he will
find some occasion for getting rid of her. I think wives will
hardly be well contented if such customs become general. Although I have no desire to put myself in this danger, yet being
of the feminine gender I will pray with the others that God may
keep us from it."

VII

Mary of Hungary took this sprightly tone about Jane Seymour's
rôle, but Jane, gentle as she was, had no easy task even in the
one thing on which she had set her heart, her husband's reconciliation with his daughter Mary. To touch Henry on any
point of his conduct was like turning the simplest of door-

handles and setting off all the burglar alarms. Mary was his child, but she was also the child of Catherine, who had been a papist and who had defied him. Mary, Catherine, Rome, sovereignty, wish for power—the whole orchestra of bells went off clamoring in Henry's brain, and his ego came to the door, hot and glaring, to defend the actual power on which he was projecting his egoism.

Princess Mary was now a shriveled woman of twenty, living in isolation at Hunsdon. Ever since the age of ten she had been the burning partisan of her mother, and this grim apprenticeship to an injured parent had scoured away the bloom of her youth. Her face was not hard or bitter, but it was shorn of gayety, bare of charm, strained, pinched, narrow, with the martyr's hymn book almost visible or the War Cry in her mittened hand. Her body was dried up yet inflated, her color parched, her voice gruff. She had been branded as illegitimate by her father and her heart had never known its springtime or the expansion of hope.

She was not allowed to address her father, but within a week of Anne's execution she was prompted by her friends to approach Cromwell, the gangway to the King. "Nobody durst speak for me," she said, "so long as that Woman lived," but now she begged Cromwell for the love of God to be a suitor for her to the King.

Knowing how Jane Seymour revered Mary, Cromwell did approach Henry, and at first, with the expansiveness so natural to him, Henry sent her his blessing and permission to write to him. But before she could do so, or "come to his presence, which she desired above all earthly things," a breath of suspicion ruffled his mind, and in an instant all was changed. Everything that he had combated in the mother, everything that had made him break with Rome, was still alive in Mary—loyalty to Rome, dependence on Charles, reminder of his failure to beget a male, denial of the divorce, refusal to accept him as Supreme Head.

Once he recollected all she stood for—he had called her "my worst enemy" a year before—his quick mind pounced on the possibility of danger, with the Catholics and the Imperialists to rally round her and ensure her the throne.

Cromwell, chafing under the ungoverned irascibility of his master, could not meet his sharp inquiries or dodge the impatient repetitions that rapped like hard knuckles on his skull. The bulky Henry, all red hair and bull neck, was suddenly charged with virulent wilfulness, and he sent for Norfolk, whose hinges were well oiled with fear.

Norfolk and Bishop Sampson and Sussex were to go to Mary, one of those delegations of the council that her mother used to rebuff but that now would arrive with Anne Boleyn's short shrift fresh in every mind. They were to tell the girl that she seemed a "monstre in nature," willfully disobedient, ungrateful, disobeying her father and sovereign and arousing the indignation of Almighty God. They were, Henry told them, to recall his Majesty's "gracious and divine nature," his clemency and pity, his merciful inclination and his princely heart. They were to stress his just displeasure and her imbecility, and yet to depict him as ever ready to take pity and compassion on all offenders repentantly crying.

Such were their written instructions. Mary was just as ready for them as her mother used to be, and Norfolk just as brusque. But this time no offer was being made. She could hardly be a bastard, she was told, she was so obstinate. "If you were my daughter," Norfolk said, "I would knock your head against the wall until it was as soft as a baked apple." He called her a traitress and said she should be punished. But by whose motion and means hath she continued in her obstinacy? She refused to acknowledge Henry as Supreme Head of the Church. She had held to the position for which More and Fisher had died. Now she would have to make an answer in writing.

Mary was frightened. Still hoping to evade the issue, she

wrote to her father asking for his blessing, vaguely acknowledging her "offences," submitting to him in all things next to God, "humbly beseeching your Highness to consider that I am but a woman, and your child."

It was the first of June, two days after his new marriage, but Henry was in no melting mood. "The King, on hearing the report of the above commissioners and the prudent answer of the Princess, grew desperate with anger, which was for two reasons: first, for the refusal of the said Princess; and second, because he suspected that several of her attendants had advised her so to do."

While Mary waited in trepidation for an answer to her appeal to her father, he began to feel his rage mounting and to search for the proper objects of this rage. He knew very well that all the mastiffs and the bulldogs on whose fidelity he counted—Fitzwilliam, Kingston, Shrewsbury, even his cur Cromwell—were out of sympathy with his wish to degrade Mary. He abruptly told Exeter and Fitzwilliam not to come to the council. He ordered the strictest inquiries made. For six or seven days he had the council at court from morning to evening. The parliament was meeting on the 8th, but he had Cromwell go to the houses of certain titled ladies, he had Francis Bryan and Anthony Browne searchingly examined, the least remark looked into, and oaths rigidly administered. He was so angry, meanwhile, that Cromwell did not dare to see Chapuys, who had written a long letter to Mary telling her that, to save her life, she must dissemble and submit. "God," wrote the Savoyard, "regards more the intention than the act." Henry, like God, regarded the intention, and he glared so ferociously at his councilors that Cromwell "remained for four or five days," he said, "considering himself a lost man or dead."

At last Mary could not bear the suspense. She wrote Cromwell, "good Mr. Secretary," to know if her father had accepted her letter.

Her father, far from accepting her letter, had concentrated on her obstinacy in regard to her "conscience," in spite of his own proclivity in that respect; he swore "in a great passion" that not only should Mary suffer but Cromwell and Exeter and others. "In spite of the prayers of the Queen, which he rudely repulsed," according to Chapuys, "the King called the judges to proceed, according to law, to the inquest and first sentence which is given in the absence of the parties."

The judges demurred. If she refused to sign a submission, they said, they would proceed.

Cromwell now took it on himself to procure this submission, having convinced Chapuys that her refusal would mean her death.

The degree of her peril had less impressed Catherine's daughter than the problem of her conscience. "You will see," she wrote Cromwell, "I have followed your advice, and will do so in all things concerning my duty to the King, God and my conscience not offended; for I take you as one of my chief friends next his Grace and the Queen." But she added, with a burst of sincerity, "I desire you, for Christ's passion, to find means that I be not moved to any further entry in this matter than I have done. . . . If I am put to any more—I am plain with you as with my great friend—my said conscience will in no ways suffer me to consent thereunto." And she wrote to the King, putting her state and living in his mercy, "next to Almighty God."

Next to Almighty God! Furious at this insult, Henry rammed it at Cromwell, and he, betrayed into actual panic, sent a frenzied letter to Mary. I am ashamed, he cried, I am afraid. "With your folly you undo yourself." "If you do not leave all sinister counsels," he said, "I take leave of you forever, and desire you to write to me no more, for I will never think you other than the most ungrateful, unnatural and obstinate person living, both to God and your most dear and benign father."

This was an ultimatum, and at last Mary faced the array

against her—her father, her friend Cromwell, her advisor Chapuys, the council, the judges, not to speak of all the bishops and all the intimidated nobility. From the hour she received Cromwell's rebuke she fell ill. She crumbled. "The pain in my head and teeth hath troubled me so sore," she moaned, "these two or three days, and doth yet so continue, that I have very small rest day or night." As for writing Henry, she sent back Cromwell's version "word for word," without adding or minishing. "I cannot endure to write another copy."

At eleven o'clock at night on June 13th she signed the letter that went with submission, beginning, "Most humbly prostrate before the feet of your most excellent Majesty, your most humble, faithful and obedient subject which hath so extremely offended your most gracious Highness that mine heavy and fearful heart dare not presume to call you father." With this deference, terming him merciful, compassionate and "most blessed," she acknowledged him Supreme Head of the Church, disavowed the Pope as a pretender, and declared her mother's marriage "by God's law and man's law incestuous and unlawful."

"After the Princess had signed the document," said Chapuys, "she was much dejected, but I relieved her of every doubt, even of conscience, assuring her that the Pope would not only not impute to her any blame, but would hold it rightly done."

"She never did a better day's work," Chapuys told the Emperor, "for if she had let this opportunity slip, there was no remedy in the world for her."

The next day she was summoned before the King and council and orally repeated her submission.

VIII

Henry was not yet satisfied. Everything had been done to soothe him during the period of wrath. The new Queen had walked on tiptoe on the edge of his anger. For three or four nights, as dawn came over the Thames, five of Chapuys' men who played

instruments, went in a barge below the windows of the
King's chamber and gave him morning music, "to soften and
amuse his fancy." He was much pleased; but his mind was so
framed that when he had formed a suspicion it glared at him
like the eye of daylight at a man who is walking through a
tunnel, and he could not get it out of his mind. Mary was told
to court him, and she did so in language of almost ecstatic abasement. "Most humbly lying at your feet, my most dear and benign father and sovereign, I have this day perceived your gracious clemency and merciful pity to have overcome my most unkind and unnatural proceedings," etc. "My poor heart," she
went on, "I send unto your Highness to remain in your hand, to
be for ever used, directed and framed, whiles God shall suffer
life to remain in it, at your only pleasure."

An oriental potentate, one might suppose, would have been
content. "I beg you to receive it as all I have to offer," Mary
added, "I will never vary from that confession and submission
I made to your Highness in the presence of the Council. I pray
God preserve you and the Queen and send you issue." She
fawned. And she wrote Jane Seymour, five years older than herself, "to the Queen's Grace, my good mother," thanking her for
her pleasure in the reconciliation, and for her "most prudent
counsel."

So far as it went, this was good, and Henry took Jane with
him to visit Mary secretly, a sign of her being restored to grace.
"The kindness shown by the King," Chapuys reported from the
information of a spy in Mary's household, "was inconceivable,
regretting that he had been so long separated from her. He
made good amends for it in the little time he was with her,
continually talking with her with every sign of affection, and
with ever so many fine promises. The Queen gave her a beautiful diamond, and the King about a thousand crowns in money
for her little pleasures, telling her to have no anxiety about
money, for she should have as much as she should wish." Mary

expressed her thanks for this visit in a letter "prostrate at your most noble feet, humbly and with the very bottom of my stomach beseeching you to believe what I have professed." And if you have issue, "I shall as glady and willingly serve with my hands under their feet as ever did poor subject their most gracious sovereign."

It had the air, certainly, of submission. The letter that followed it up toward the end of July, saying "she would rather be a chamberer having the fruition of the King's presence than an empress away from him," left little to be desired. But the gnawing question of sincerity, of true inward consent, of perfect abjection, haunted the uneasy royal heart. Henry could not deny himself the final pleasure, the assurance that she whom he abased really was abased in love.

In August "the King conjured her to tell him if she had consented to his will cordially or with dissimulation, for he hated nothing more than dissemblers." Sometimes, he said to her, his councilors advised him to dissemble with ambassadors, but he would never do so, and he begged the Princess in this matter to show herself his daughter.

She consulted Chapuys, and "she replied to him as she ought, and will take good care henceforward to dissemble as is requisite, especially being warned by me of the danger she will occur doing otherwise. I think if she come to court she will set many things right by her good sense." She had already made a private protest for Rome, disavowing her submission, and she had told Chapuys she would never make any match without the express consent of Charles, though declaring "she would not care to be married at all."

Have you ever written to Charles? her father asked her suspiciously. Never, she lied to him.

By October Henry had forgotten his talk about never dissembling. He sent her two drafts of letters which he wished her to write to the Emperor, to the effect that, being better instructed by continual consultation of books and holy and learned persons, "but principally by the Holy Spirit," she "freely, willingly and without fear or restraint" had acknowledged and approved the statutes made by parliament declaring her mother's marriage unlawful and the King her father Head of the Church, and requested Charles to permit the truth to have place and not hinder it, in order that the King, "who treats her so kindly," may not have occasion to change toward her.

"The Princess," Chapuys informed Charles, "has charged me to write this to your Majesty to forewarn you of the said letters."

Meanwhile, "to soften the temper of the people," Mary and the child Elizabeth had been brought to court. "Madame Mary is now the first after the Queen, and sits at table opposite her, a little lower down, after having first given the napkin for washing to the King and Queen. And the Marchioness of Exeter gives the water. Madame Ysabeau (aged three) is not at that table, though the King is very affectionate to her. It is said he loves her much."

Henry's affection toward his children was a trait much commented on. He ceased to believe in the plot that had flurried him. As he had said to Francis Bryan, "All is one. Naughty bruits are soon blown."

IX

While the struggle to bend Mary was most intense, Henry turned to the business of manipulating the law-givers. On June 8th, he opened a hand-picked parliament in all his magnificence, and the chancellor Audley, a useful emollient, told the new body what its attitude was to be. It appeared that the King's Highness, their dread Sovereign, had just escaped the most appalling conspiracy. Audley described it eloquently. Dark dangers, "great intolerable perils," had threatened the King, and for one whose care and efforts were directed solely to the ruling of his subjects in peace and charity, "so long as his life endures," the hideousness of those who had threatened to deprive England of "the sure possession of these blessings," could hardly be palliated or disguised. It appeared that Anne Boleyn, "inflamed with pride and carnal desires of her body," had confederated herself with her brother Rochford, Norris, Weston, Brereton and Smeaton; "and so being confederate, she and they most traitorously committed and perpetrated divers detestable and abominable treasons, to the fearful peril and danger of your royal person, and to the utter loss, disherison, and desolation of this realm, if God of his goodness had not in due time brought their said treasons to light; for the which, being plainly and manifestly proved, they were convict and attainted by due course and order of your common law of this realm, and have suffered according to the merits."

Anne's flippant remarks to Norris had thus become "the fearful peril and danger" of Henry's person: and her guilt had been plainly proved "by due course and order of your common law." What this imported, evidently, was the necessity of doing extraordinary things to safeguard the realm in time to come.

Henry had already fulfilled his public duty. "Our most excellent prince, not in any carnal concupiscence, but at the humble entreaty of his nobility, hath consented once more to accept that condition (of matrimony), and hath taken to himself a wife who in age and form is deemed to be meet and apt for the procreation of children."

It remained for this new parliament to act with the prudence of Solomon, "with whom our most gracious King may deservedly be compared."

Anne's marriage being decreed unlawful, Elizabeth born out of wedlock, and Princess Mary still unreconciled to Henry, the parliament could only count as successor to the throne either Henry's boy the Duke of Richmond, or "the issue of the marriage with Queen Jane." Directed by Cromwell and Henry himself, an act was passed which renounced the sovereignty of the people and completed the illusion that the throne of England was Henry's personal and private property. Henry was given "full and plenary power and authority to dispose, by your letters, patent under your great seal, or else by your last will made in writing, and signed with your hand, the imperial crown of this realm, and all other the premises thereunto belonging, to such person or persons as shall please your Highness.

"And we, your humbled and obedient subjects, do faithfully promise to your Majesty, by one common assent, that after your decease, we, our heirs and successors, shall accept and take, love, dread, and only obey such person or persons, male or female, as your Majesty shall give your imperial crown unto; and wholly to stick to them as true and faithful subjects ought to do."

This act of succession was the fullest public acknowledgment that Henry had yet received of the tyrannical powers which he demanded. He could not control the physical weakness of his poor boy Richmond, who, married to Norfolk's daughter, had revealed himself "tysique," like Henry's own brother and Henry's father. Richmond had been spitting blood since Anne's execution, and by July he was dead. Henry publicly ascribed his sudden end to Anne's sinister machinations, and his angry suspicions extended to the Howards. Norfolk's brother, Thomas Howard, was thrown into the Tower for encroaching so much on Henry as to have married without permission the Lady Margaret Douglas, Queen Margaret of Scotland's daughter. "Seduced by the devil," it was said, "he aspired to the crown by reason of so high a marriage." To attempt marriages with royal persons without permission was at once decreed to be treason. Howard's imprisonment in the Tower, which finished him within a year, showed that Henry was not tolerating "presumption," and the Duke of Norfolk nearly followed his half-brother. Henry had not dared to parade the burial of my lord of Richmond, so he had entrusted it to Norfolk, who had discharged it in rough and ready fashion. So annoyed was Henry that Norfolk's fate hung in the balance for a week. The duke wrote to Cromwell "full, full, full of choler and agony." "When I deserve to be in the Tower," said this shark, "Tottenham will turn French."

No effective opposition to Henry appeared in parliament, to which the suppression of the monasteries meant the aggrandizement of the squires. The vileness of the religious was now an article of faith. In a country forty per cent or fifty per cent illiterate, with such slow communications, with such rigidity of class, such a recent tradition of civil war, and such apparent need of solidarity to resist invasion, it was practically impossible to create the frame of mind in which Henry could be opposed. His parliament was successfully "unitary." Had Henry antagonized the nobles as did Christiern II in Denmark, he might have fused the opposition against him. But he gained by the experience that had cost Christiern his throne. He watched those who had defied Rome in advance of him. He divided his spoils with his peers, his courtiers, his officials and his industrials. This was the price for which many leaders of the laity were brought to compromise. The work of suppressing the abbeys was further facilitated by parliament, and Henry turned with relief to the convocation of clergy that he had summoned at the same time.

As Supreme Head he had set Cromwell over convocation and Cromwell as Vicar-General had sent round one of his henchmen to open the work. It was one of great practical importance, and Henry had been laboring since early in 1536 to frame a new theological program. Purgatory was peculiarly in his mind. "The great object of the King," Chapuys had noted, "is to persuade the people that there is no purgatory, in order afterwards to seize the ecclesiastical endowments"—that is to say, the chant bequests, which were a form of fire insurance. This was purgatory in its economic aspect. But to uproot it roughly could only excite the resistance of the simple people who were used to purgatory, and Henry had been sorely troubled. In April he had soft-pedaled. He had ordered the preachers to avoid "new" opinions on rites and ceremonies, and he had decided to admit purgatory as formerly, "or at least a third place neither paradise nor hell, and confesses that prayers assist the dead." Thus the Defender of the Faith picked his steps. The essence was to rearrange Catholic dogma as a bordelure around regal supremacy, but not to upset too many prejudices in so doing. If the displacement of the Pope was calculated to give comfort to the Lutherans, and if the omission of four of the sacraments had the vague suggestion of radicalism, Henry's Ten Articles took care not to disturb the sort of thing that simple people hold by— the fast days, the holidays, the mass. By creating commissions to carry out Cromwell's injunctions, to mold the clergy and to take over the property of the monks as well as to collect subsidies, a flexible instrument was provided for popular manifestation. Meanwhile the fatigued and bewildered clergy felt more or less as Princess Mary felt. "As to my opinion touching pilgrimages, purgatory, relics, and the like, I assure you I have none but such as I shall receive from him that hath mine whole heart in keeping, the King, my father, to whose presence I pray I may once come or I die." Henry had become Pope, and without a College of Cardinals. The ribs of the new ship might be inserted by Latimer or Gardiner or Cranmer or Tunstall. The keel Henry was laying.

Consulting freely, compromising readily, hopping from one to the other alternative with nervous eagerness, taking into account every aspect of existing opinion and every gain or loss in reshaping it, he worked out with his own cunning brain the least radical revision that would best serve his aggrandizement. It was an audacious subservience of religion and religious dogma to the present needs of royalty. Henry juggled with penance, with the Sacrament of Extreme Unction, with the Real Presence, with marriage, as a modern party manager would juggle with the budget or the tariff. And he did not leave the final word to any of his helpers. The Ten Articles were the articles that he believed offensive to Catholic prejudices while most flexible for the growth of Protestant sentiment. His own preoccupation remained simple: he proposed to remain dominant as King of England.

While this project went forward with few hitches, the wealth of the abbeys flowing to Henry, parliament and convocation deferring to him and Charles invading Provence to no purpose, it could hardly be said that he had advanced any great length on his road as a moral arbiter. He wanted both to suspend his convictions in order to triumph as a politician and then, having triumphed as a politician, to resume his maidenhead. This curious duplicity did not add to his prestige in Europe but it gradually developed in him a cult of "moderation." He grew increasingly angry with extremists who insisted on pursuing their convictions. He could not understand why, when he had ten such all-round articles in stock, the heretics should go pursuing God to the left hand while the papists tried to hold to him on the right. Henry knew better, and Henry was angry.

Meanwhile rational Europe, trying to keep inflammable passion and mad peasant blood within decent bounds, had lost its great spokesman in Erasmus. He died in April. The torch of good reason was for the moment dimmed. Two firebrands, still obscure, were planning the conquest of mankind for a Christ of their own making, each asking his followers to immolate their reason and to bind their will. In 1536 John Calvin published his "Institutio." In the same year a Spanish Basque, to be known as Ignatius Loyola, was finishing the studies at Paris that underlay the Society of Jesus. Henry's "moderation," on the terms of his own dominance, would push half-evolved Europeans along the road of the modern state, while Calvin and Loyola, borrowing statecraft and rousing the lust of warfare with the breath of the Eternal, would stir in religion precisely the same appetite for earthly dominance. Beside them Erasmus might seem a fee-

ble creature, sitting by his open fire with a glass of Burgundy
in front of him. But Erasmus had made the New Testament
his labor of love. He was not a hero, like Loyola or Calvin. He
was not an "emperor" as Henry now called himself. He was only
a humanist. Beside him the Jesuits, affirming liberty and vowing
obedience, or the Calvinists, affirming predestination and applying the scourge, recalled very ancient priesthoods and glorious
savage instincts that cry from the caverns to be released even
if they must carry a Bible in their hand.

Yet the Galilean Jew could not have despised the humanist:
if he had rested by the fire with Erasmus, this book of the New
Testament on his knees, and a glass of Burgundy before him,
perhaps he might have raised those sad eyes to see that truth and
charity had lingered for an instant at Basle, finding an honest
welcome there, that the Word was still alive; that the arm of
the law and the methods of torture, to which his own thin
hands bore witness, were perhaps not the only ways to prize the
divinity in man.

x

While Henry went ahead with his Church policy, the Pope
sought everywhere for a weapon with which to counter him.
The Catholic King being at war with the Most Christian
King, he was constrained to try two preliminaries: one, to influence Henry by a moral appeal; two, to arouse sentiment
against him in England.

The moral appeal was entrusted to an Englishman, Henry's
own cousin, Reginald Pole, and it was sent to Henry in the
form of that book on the Unity of the Church for which
Henry had been asking his cousin.

Reginald Pole was a tremulously sincere man. He was the
same age as the Emperor Charles, born in 1500, and he had
proved his integrity during the divorce campaign by declining
the archbishopric of York and, with Henry's permission, return-

ing to his books on the Continent. He was a spare indoor man, high-nosed and scant-bearded, with a fine forehead, a big Adam's apple and a small chin. He was Quixotic in the extreme, but instead of reading Amadis, he had read Aquinas, to much the same effect, and having no Sancho Panza for ballast he was ready at any moment to ride down his ponderous cousin on the snorting Rosinante of his rhetoric. To complete the idyl, his friends hoped that the Princess Mary would be his Dulcinea, as he had not yet become so deep in orders as to be ineligible.

Like everything Quixotic, the attack was glorious. "During the twenty-seven years he has reigned," said Pole in pure honesty, "he has continually plundered his subjects, and if he was liberal in anything, it was certainly not in the things that make for the common weal. He has robbed every kind of man, made a sport of the nobility, never loved the people, troubled the clergy, and torn like a wild beast the men who were the greatest honor to his kingdom."

This, with epithets like Nero and Domitian, was intended to open Henry's eyes to his less apparent faults and to lead him gently to mend his ways. It was Reginald Pole's manner of falling in with the papal notion that Henry, with moral suasion, would return to the fold. "To think of a King of such talent," said Cardinal Contarini, "whose authority has so frequently upheld the Church, trying to rend it in twain!" The King, wrote the Pope's envoy at Paris, "seems to stand in some estimation as being rather good-natured." Reginald Pole was reckless enough to put this good nature to the test.

Henry gave no sign that the admonitions rankled. He sent word to Pole that he was "not displeased," and invited him to come home.

He wishes to make him a Cardinal, observed Chapuys, the way he made Fisher a Cardinal.

The mild Tunstall was dismayed. Your book, he wrote, "made me heavy in the heart." "Your bloody book pricketh me." The nobles, he commented bitterly, will not fail to nourish learning "when they see what reward the King hath of you."

His own family was aghast. His mother, a revered matron, received a plaint from Henry and sent her son a severe letter. His brother, Lord Montague, soared into stately eloquence, concluding with brotherly candor, "Learning you may well have, but doubtless no prudence or pity, but showeth yourself to run from one mischief to another."

The mischief was all the greater, in Montague's eyes, because he himself was one of the few Catholic nobles who did not lie to themselves about Henry.

The tone of these romantic medieval aristocrats in general was that of the reactionary everywhere—perfect fidelity to yesterday, perfect despair of to-day, perfect credulity about the morrow. A few were tinged with More's faith, the Catholicism that had universe in it. Most of them had the cult of privilege gone but not forgotten. But so conservative were they, and so willfully blind, that they chose to believe it would be enough to wave a halberd at Henry, the coward-bull, to drive him back to Rome.

Lord Montague was a mordant man who saw Henry as he was. "Wolsey had been an honest man," he said shrewdly, "had he an honest master." And "The King glories with the title to be Supreme Head next God, yet he has a sore leg that no poor man would be glad of, and he shall not live long for all his authority next God." "The King and his whole issue stand accursed."

Accursed or not, Henry's efforts to become a father were too often mortified. He was well enough to hunt, but as the summer wore on he seemed to have a disappointment: he said to Chapuys in September that he felt himself "already old and doubted whether he should have any children by the Queen."

His temper was trying. When Chapuys crossed him, he began to "chafe" and retort "half between the teeth." On hearing that the Emperor was treating with the Pope again, Chapuys "had not for a long time seen the King so angry."—"A great prince," mused this Savoyard, "who wishes things to be at his pleasure."

Few knew better than the supple Chapuys that they were not at his pleasure, because few were so thick in the confidences of the Catholic leaders. But whether those leaders or even the shrewd Chapuys had ever measured the force of the instincts that nourished Henry's policy could not be told until the two clashed arms.

XI

On October third, at an unseemly hour, two squires arrived breathless at Windsor Castle. They demanded to see the King. He was aroused: they had alarming news to tell him: a rebellion had broken out in Lincolnshire.

As they poured out their incoherent story, two others, who had escaped from Lincoln, arrived at breakneck speed to define the first: the "commons" were up, their beacons blazing, their bells ringing "awkward," their priests rushing hither and thither, their gentry forced to stand by them, the King's lieutenant not raising a hand, some of Cromwell's agents to seize the abbeys or make parish registers surrounded by the swelling mob and one of them killed with staves and another torn limb from limb. No leaders could be named, but a shoemaker, as in the Peasant Risings of Germany, was at the head and a banner had been brought forth as if for a crusade—a plow and a horn on it, a chalice and a host, and the five wounds of Christ. Every one caught at crossroads had been forced to dismount, to swear an oath For God, the King and the Commonwealth. Still declaring its loyalty, the whole county was seething—ten thousand had collected, perhaps twenty thousand, perhaps forty thousand. From Louth they had gathered, from Caistor and from Horncastle. They were moving on Lincoln. Sixteen thousand men armed to fight. It was only in Lincolnshire, but it might spread like fire on the wind.

Such news staggered Henry, his mind racing from apprehension to defiance. He seized from the two gentlemen who came kneeling to him the demands which the commons had forced them to carry, and he snorted with contempt as he read them—the abbeys to be restored, subsidy remitted, no more tenths from the clergy, the new land inheritance statute to be repealed, the heretic bishops to be deprived, villein blood banished from the council.

Instantly his brain seethed with answers, with retorts, with crushing arguments. "I would rather sell all my plate," he cried, "than these rebels should not be put down."

Chafing and pale, he called his council instantly. Much as it went against the grain, his best soldier, Norfolk, had to be summoned. Richard Cromwell (Thomas's nephew), Sir John Russell, Edward Seymour, now Lord Beauchamp, could join with hardy familiars like Suffolk and Fitzwilliam to take an army into the field. He would go himself, at the end of the week. He trembled with a sense of outrage, of intimidation, and of fury. His jowls shook. The irreverent Richard Cromwell watched him keenly as old Norfolk arrived. Henry greeted him sourly. However merry the Duke might appear, "the King is all the more dejected, and, as Cromwell's nephew said to-day, he was in great fear."

A shrewd woman would not have chosen this moment of fear and dejection to make an appeal to Henry. But Jane Seymour was instinctive. Throwing herself on her knees before him, she implored him to restore the abbeys, saying that this rebellion was "a judgment" for their putting down. He was furious. "How often have I told you not to meddle with my affairs? Get up!" And as she quailed, he referred to the late Queen. It was, indeed, the moment to sap his courage.

But he had resources. The long list of musters was already in the hands of his new secretary Wriothesley (Risley.) The polite fiction that Henry ruled simply by good will and had no force at his command, save a bodyguard of fifty upholstered beef-eaters or yeomen, was now openly laid aside. The Tower of London was an arsenal, and he could take his last stand there. The ruling class could recruit tenants and servants to handle the arms which, through Henry's foresight, they knew how to use. There were war veterans who had fought in Scotland, in Wales, in Ireland, in France. The recent executions that had cemented in blood the union of England and Wales—about five thousand in number—showed the temper in which the Lincolnshire rebellion might be repressed. Suffolk, aging though he was, could climb into the saddle in 1536 as he had in 1513 and 1523. It would begin rustily; the grind of untried artillery, the rasp of stiff carriages, the rattle of skittish hoofs on cobble and the lurching along broken roads with a halt every five miles while groats were spent on ale—this would take from the majesty of the army, but from seven to eight thousand could reach Lincolnshire within a week.

Henry seized the pen. "We have already sent out Suffolk with a hundred thousand men," he proclaimed, "horse and foot, in harness, with munitions and artillery, which you cannot resist. We have also appointed another great army to invade your countries as soon as you come out of them, and burn, spoil and destroy your goods, wives and children with all extremity, to the fearful example of all lewd subjects."

As to their demands, he retorted on his subjects as he had re-torted on Jane. "Ye have no grace nor naturalment in you." "We marvel what madness is in your brain." "How presumptuous are ye, the rude commons of one shire and that one of the most brute and beastly of the whole realm, and of least experience, to find fault with your Prince for the electing of his councilors and prelates, and to take upon you, contrary to God's law and man's law, to rule your Prince whom you are bound by all laws to obey and serve, with both your lives, lands and goods."

"Bound to obey and serve"! He had come straight from Jane.

But while Henry's anger gave quivering life to his phrases, the sounds that had clanged so crazily in Lincolnshire were carried on the wind across into Yorkshire, and the fires that had fumed in Lincolnshire leaped from one black beacon to another, blazing out in the deep night like a flare from the heart, and carried secret and palpitant from hill to hill all through that North which Henry had never seen, where his name was a pious echo, where his parliament was an evil mockery, and his agents base and truculent and detested.

Those beacon fires and those alarms ran like keen wild liquor in the veins of York. Sober fellows who held back were spurred by their women, "God's Quarrel." The gentry, the nobility, the commons rose as one being, and within a week the name of Robert Aske sprang from lip to lip as messages flitted to tense yeomen who dug in their heels and rode hard to rally kith and kin.

Suffolk reached Lincoln within a week. "I dare well say he would eat the rebels with salt," mocked Richard Cromwell. But the rebels of Lincoln, urged by an emotion, had resigned their plan to Providence, and Providence, seeing the squires in cautious retreat and the seven or eight hundred priests in flurry, left the commons to block the streets, heavy and limp-handed, while the King's army made its slow and formidable entry into Lincoln, a burnished machine of war.

The class that had played safe in Lincoln was ready to stake their lives in York. Robert Aske was of a county family and had made his mark in London as a lawyer. He had actually been on his way to London when the turmoil in Lincoln caught him and whirled him home. He was about forty years old, staid and serious. The passion of public law was in him and the Catholic tradition of Thomas More. He had watched Wolsey in youth, Cromwell in maturity. The renaissance had not touched him. The Reformation was heresy to him. He was an upright, Godfearing, earnest citizen, the sort from which Virginian gentlemen were later recruited, who desired no revolution but a condition of society based on confidence, on honor and on loyalty. If only the King would resume his earlier ideals, from which wicked men had seduced him, Robert Aske would be his man. One God, One King, One Faith. This was the tinder that the beacons had lighted and the church bells fanned. "It is a lamentable thing," said Chapuys in the summer, "to see a legion of monks and nuns who have been chased from their monasteries wandering miserably hither and thither, seeking means to live, and several honest men have told me that what with monks, nuns and persons dependent on the monasteries suppressed there were over twenty thousand who knew not how to live." It was these who had started the straw fire in Lincoln. But in laying his hand on the standing army of the parishes as well as the skirmishing friars, Cromwell had provoked the people to its depths, and in Yorkshire the aristocracy and the gentry, if they wished to control, were obliged to assume the lead.

Cromwell and his agents—"such as be not worthy to remain nigh the King"—were denounced forthwith. It was these "simple and evil disposed persons," not the King, who were spoiling and robbing and destroying the Church. And they had undermined parliament. "These parliaments were of none authority no virtue, for if they should be truly named, they should be called councils of the King's appointment, and not parliaments."

Against these outrages the people had risen. "This pilgrimage," the leaders declared in the spirit of crusaders, "we have taken it for the preservation of Christ's Church, of this realm of England, the King our sovereign lord, the nobility and commons of the same, for the punishments of heretics and subverters of the laws."

Robert Aske would lead his company to London on pilgrimage to the King himself, "to have vile blood put from his council and noble blood set up again; to have the faith of Christ and God's laws kept, and restitution for the wrongs done to the Church, and the commons used as they should be."

The collapse in Lincolnshire, where a hundred "ring-leaders" were already being delivered over to Suffolk, did not retard the movement in Yorkshire for an instant. And as Norfolk advanced toward the Don, to stop the pilgrimage, he knew right well that his own soldiers were only half-hearted and that the Pilgrimage of Grace would be able to cleave through him at its will.

XII

While Norfolk rode North, hard as nails, tough as leather, sixty-two years of age but limber in his harness, Henry simmered in London. He was at once outraged and perplexed. His instinct said, No quarter, crush the rebels, unconditional surrender, while his prudence said, Prepare, and his panic said, Back to Rome. As he hurried to raise a third army—the cost appalled him—he waited imperiously for Norfolk to take the brunt.

He had ordered his herald to York to cow the rebels. The herald, foolish man, was knocked over when he found York clattering with great open preparation, and the rebels four times as strong as the King. Robert Aske was surrounded by cruel fellows, "keeping his port and countenance as though he were a great prince." The herald did not try to hide his awe and wonder. "The said Robert Aske," he narrated, "with a cruel and inestimably proud countenance, stretched himself and took the hearing of my tale, to which he gave no reverence." The King's man, in truth, had been so overborne that he had fallen on his knees. Yet this stern Aske had stood him up, got back his stolen horses for him, ordered him not to be touched, and dispatched him safe and sound.

No object was too mean for Henry's pride, and he noted the herald. But meanwhile the pilgrims advanced. While Henry chivied Norfolk at one moment, he told him to hold off in the next. "We desire you not to give stroke till we can repair to you with our army royal." Norfolk heard his master but he cocked his eye at actualities. He saw he must treat with the Yorkshiremen. The King's stronghold in the rear had been purposely kept weak, and Lord Darcy, a roaring veteran of eighty, had yielded it to range himself with a host of other Northern nobles behind the banner of St. Cuthbert and the standard of the Five Wounds. Aske's forces came down to Doncaster thirty-four to thirty-five thousand men "well tried on horseback." The King's forces were somewhere between six and eight thousand.

Neither side wanted bloodshed, Norfolk made terms. "Inforced to appoint with the rebels," he said with his usual sincerity, "my heart is near broken." The terms were, first, a free general pardon, and second, a new parliament.

Henry had protested that his "honor" would be touched if he granted pardon without making horrible examples. At the same time he had provided Norfolk with written powers, telling him however to delay "as if to send hither to us" while he himself went on preparing. This doubleness Norfolk emulated. Fye, fye, upon Lord Darcy, he said to the King, the most arrant traitor that was ever living. He then tried to get round Darcy "for old love." "I advise you to take, alive or dead, but alive if possible, that arrant traitor Aske, which will extinct the ill bruit and raise you in favor of his Highness."

This, to the outspoken Yorkshireman, was repulsive. He was incapable of it. And yet, honest as the day, he was not candid. While he declared in one breath that his Heavenly King meant more to him than twenty earthly Kings, he insisted in the next that he was obedient to Henry and that "Old Tom has not one traitor's tooth in his head." The Pilgrimage, in other words, was not a rebellion, but a demonstration. It only sought by displaying its physical power to prevail on love. But the common people, who wanted a new order, had no such pacific ideal.

For the moment the physical power was too formidable not to have its moral effect. A free pardon was announced at Doncaster, and a parliament promised. Robert Aske, constitutional to the core, was exalted. He knelt for his pardon, tore off his badge of the Five Wounds, and ordered his army to disband like Norfolk's pending further arrangements.

Henry thereupon "conceived a great desire" to speak with Aske. "Come with diligence," he said, "and no man privy thereto." He will perform toward Aske and all others the general and free pardon already granted and trusts Aske, at his access, will, by his plainness and frankness, deserve reward.

Shall I go? Aske consulted Darcy. Go, said Darcy, and if he holds you I will rescue you from the Tower.

"Wade with him with fair word," advised Norfolk three months later, when he had decoyed Aske to London a second time, "as though you had great trust in him. This will make him cough out as much as he knows."

No man required such advice less than Henry. Unless off guard, he shone in interviews. Nothing had been easier for him in meeting Aske than to convey, plainly and frankly, his own simple desire to know the truth.

"I opened to the King the grievances of the country," Aske told Darcy proudly, "and his Highness gave comfortable answers how Norfolk would forthwith come down, and then the King himself, and have the Queen crowned and parliament held at York."

The King asked the honest man to write out in full the whole story of the Pilgrimage. Aske gladly complied. And before the pilgrims' leader left, Henry gave him the gift of a jacket of crimson satin, no doubt for New Year's Day.

Aske returned North on his safe conduct, without one line in writing but the assurance of his sovereign lord warm within.

It was a great Twelfth Day for Henry, the first anniversary of Catherine of Aragon's death. The niggardliness that was beginning to grip him in middle age was loosened for the moment, and for the moment he rose out of his psychic impotence. He spent a merry morning bargaining with a French jeweler. "I am too old for that." "You ask too much, I'll give you three hundred." He spent five thousand crowns. "I lost money on it," ruefully declared the jeweler. Henry was jovial. His arm around Jane Seymour, he rejoiced in a conspiracy overwhelmed.

And then in a few days, he bemoaned a "new tragedy." Two eccentric fellows, Bigod and Hallam, had struck at the King's forces again.

XIII

The moment Aske returned North, pledging the King's good faith, the people asked for confirmation of it. A wedge was thus inserted between the leader who had trusted Henry and those who distrusted him. The King's forces were strengthening, Cromwell and Cranmer continued in office, the promise of parliament was not redeemed. Then Bigod and Hallam struck out of hand, without Aske's consent, themselves driving the wedge between the impatient commons and the suspect gentry like Aske. In the northern tier of counties, at the same time, raiders and thieves abounded, lawlessness broke out and old feuds revived.

Norfolk thereupon returned in force with no word of parliament but with loud word of justice and the breach of faith. He went on progress as pacificator, Aske anxiously by his side. Out of the five thousand who thronged for exculpation to Carlisle he took seventy-four marked men and executed them by martial law. Scores of bodies hung high; the wives and mothers lifted them down in the dark of night, and groups of women dug graves and buried their men with their own hands. Henry clamored for more executions and for the punishment of these women. Norfolk shrugged his shoulders. Offenders since the pardon began to be gathered in, and then offenders in general.

With supreme skill, Norfolk induced Aske to go back to London, where he was arrested. Darcy and Constable went up, and were also arrested. Then the true bills came back to Norfolk, who, like a saurian of old race, seemed most at home in slime. With masterly ingenuity he divided the Yorkshire grand jury into two "quests." On one, he said, "I will appoint such that I shall no more doubt than of myself." On the other, "the best friends these men have." And, he added grimly, if these best friends will not "find" as the packed jury finds, then they may have thanks "according to their cankered hearts."

He took Aske's own brother, Constable's sons-in-law, Darcy's sons-in-law. "I appointed two quests," he reported on May 10th, almost a year after he and his peers found Anne Boleyn guilty. "I appointed two quests, twenty of the one and twenty-one of the other, and after declaring my mind to them, made them go to several places. They shortly returned and found the two bills of indictments sent from your Highness' Council true bills, without putting out or adding a word."

Several score of the Lincolnshire ringleaders had already paid for their explosion. They were simple folk and they died a horrible death, "hanged, cut down alive, disemboweled, and their entrails burned while they were still alive, and beheaded."

For weeks Aske was examined, to discover every filament of conspiracy possible. He was a massive simple man, above wile and above suspicion. He now blamed himself for having taken up arms, and he spoke up in every case like a pure soul. Trifles occupied him, such as paying his workmen. He had left the King's gift at the Cardinal's Hat in London, and he prayed to have his belongings collected and his debts paid. His family that had fled into woods and "holds," he humbly recommended to the King's favor. "Let me be full dead," he begged, "ere I be dismembered."

Lord Darcy was foursquare and not subtle. He had been the man who drafted Wolsey's indictment. It was still Cromwell, not Henry, he was "grudging" to procure all the noblemen's heads to be stricken off. "Yet shall there one head remain," he boldly declared in Cromwell's face, "that shall strike off thy head!"

The promise of a free parliament was forgotten in this trial, as well as the promise of pardon. Aske's reports, that Henry had asked him to write, were also forgotten. Cromwell, extremely busy, had little trouble in reading guilt into these "traitors' hearts." On Tower Hill, Lord Darcy was beheaded. Constable was taken to Hull. Aske was ordered by the King to be executed at York, where, as he said, Aske had been "in his greatest and most frantic glory." There, on a market day in July, he was hanged in chains.

Lancaster Herald, who had not maintained Henry's honor in the way he should, was executed the year following.

XIV

Norfolk was in fine fettle after the insurrection. He gloated over Constable. "He doth hang above the highest gate of the town so trimmed in chains that I think his bones will hang there this hundred years." He looked hungrily at the loot of the abbeys, when certain abbots went to execution, though he dispatched the gold to London. Norfolk's wife poured out her grievances to Cromwell; she had been deposed for Bess Holland, a washer in her nursery. She had been overpowered by her husband's orders. "They satt on my brest till I spett blod." Great and abominable lies, retorted the old soldier. When I come home I will lock her up! Meanwhile he was Cromwell's heartiest friend. If Cromwell will come down and lodge in Teshe's house, he may be sure of a welcome. "And if ye lust not to dally with his wife," Norfolk chuckled, "he hath a young woman with pretty proper tetins." Under this honey, however, Cromwell was warned there was a scorpion. He "did not bear so much favor with Norfolk as he thought he did."

Cromwell chuckled perhaps a little longer than Norfolk. He had drawn the teeth of the Imperialists. He had made Mary forswear herself, sacked the small abbeys and prepared to sack the big abbeys, outwitted the Catholics in the council, weathered the insurrection in spite of them, sent Darcy and Constable and Bulmer and Lady Bulmer and Bigod and Aske to execution; and if he had put abbots at one end of the rope, he put Norfolk at the other. Norfolk hated the Bible and Cromwell had opened half a dozen of them in St. Paul's. The Emperor observed that he was now drawing a French annuity, the Pope's agents were unable to make headway with Henry, while Reginald Pole, who was camped at Liè with a bag of papal gold, had the boat and no oars with which to row it. The strongest will in England was Cromwell's. He was the watchman at Henry's gate. He took toll on every rancor, every orthodoxy, every heresy, every preferment. He had spies at keyholes and behind tapestries. By his commissions he had turned numberless volunteers into heresy-hunters and informers.

Here was a triangle of forces of which the apex was Henry. He knew that Cromwell and Norfolk were hostile, but he held aloof. Cromwell was the one man in England to smash the abbeys, and so long as he directed that work, controlling the commissions and controlling parliament, Henry could not be so mad as to hamper him. But while Cromwell rose in favor and rolled in wealth, and while Norfolk protested loudly that he was no papist, the opposition between the two worked uneasily. It was a conflict in which great latent forces in England were summed up. So far, Cromwell had won, and, so far, Henry, in spite of his own dislike of the parvenu heresy and the parvenu manner, found himself inclined if not to Cromwell's side at least to

Cromwell's utility: he had only to consult his treasury to see that it was Cromwell, not Norfolk, who was pumping in the liquid gold.

The habit of the confessional still held in England, but Cromwell sat in the box, his hand stroking his smooth chin, his ear inclined, and every man confessing his neighbor's sins. Lucy was telling him a priest had declared that "Ember days were named after one Imber, a paramour of a certain bishop of Rome." Another brought word that a bricklayer was preaching the gospel in Whitechapel. A seditious person had said, "Pity the King was ever crowned." Another seditious person had said, "It was a pity Lady Bulmer should suffer." "It is no pity if she be a traitor to her Prince." "Let us speak no more of this matter," the hasty man withdrew too late, "for men may be blamed for speaking the truth." "If I had the King here!" one growler had thundered. Latimer sent word of a papist who, seeing the Virgin's statue stripped, said, "I trust to see the day that they that stripped her shall be stripped as naked." His Grace was not spared. Vile remarks were made about him week by week, his habits with women, his good cheer, his getting drunk. All this came to Cromwell, and to the vigor of his injunctions he continually added the emphasis of death.

XV

With the collapse of the insurrection Henry had had the best news of years, "the quickening of our wife, the Queen." The prospect of an heir whose legitimacy could not be brought into dispute raised his hopes after so many withering disappointments, and as early as March, 1537, two months after conception, there was a public Te Deum. It was not the fashion to keep such a prospect private. A gentleman, on the contrary, could well write, "Jesu make you in time a glad mother," or, "it may please your ladyship to recommend me to your little boy in your belly." Henry's "little boy" was the grand preoccupation

of the summer. The coronation at York, and the visit to the pacified North, were willingly given up lest some accident might
upset the outcome. "The Queen, being now quick with child,
she might be in danger from rumors blown about in our absence, and it is thought we should not go further than sixty
miles from her."

This solicitude, which was very deep, fitted in with Henry's
sedentary mood. He was only forty-six, but ever since his new
marriage he had slowed down, and with the intense relief from
the anxiety of the insurrection he had physically unbuttoned
and begun to eat and drink at his large pleasure. For the first
time those around him remarked how enormously he had
grown in girth. He had new companions beside the Vicar of
Hell—Sir John Russell and Edward Seymour, while other new-
comers, John Dudley and Thomas Seymour, were alert in the
narrow seas as the Emperor and the French King carried their
furious war into Flanders. There had been a rumor that "the
man with the great nose," Francis, had died of his complaint,
but as a gossip remarked, "he dieth oft, but he is not minded
to be buried." Henry's own chronic complaint had returned.
"To be frank with you," he had confessed to Norfolk, "which
you must keep to yourself, a humor has fallen into our legs, and
our physicians advise us not to go so far in the heat of the year
(as York), even for this reason only."

In these months, buoyed by the most personal of human
hopes, he abounded with good nature. Recently he had not
been very genial with his aging sister, Queen Margaret; "you
must not think merely because you are my sister," that money is
always to be forthcoming. He had declined to issue a safe-con-
duct to her son King James of Scotland, who wanted to take
home his sick French wife by land. And he wrote to Gardiner,
in the summer, "We would be very glad to have the said Reginald Pole by some mean trussed up and conveyed to Calais."
But these were the rigors of business: inside the council he

laughed at Pole with the other "wilful and selfish men." Cherries and peas came to Jane from across the Channel, the *primeurs,* and Henry tucked in delightedly. She had a fancy for quail: quail arrived by the dozen. Cranmer purled in his ear about new works on theology, and Henry thrust these on the bright young men, the Pagets and Wriothesleys or the Seymours or Parrs. "The King commonly hands over books which he has not the patience to read himself to one of his lords in waiting for perusal, from whom he afterwards learns its contents. He then gives them to some one else of an opposite way of thinking. After hearing all these criticisms he forms his own judgment."

Meanwhile he went hunting daily, leg and all. He "made good cheer the week following Robert Aske's execution." "The King," reports Russell, "riseth himself more like a good fellow than like a King, among us that be here, and, thank God, I never saw him merrier." A letter comes to him from Lisle defending himself against the pins for which deputies are the cushions. "His Grace laughed full heartily."

By nature and by predicament, Jane was not so merry, this hot summer. She was gentle and somewhat timid, and she was terrified of the Death. "They die at my gate," said Cranmer, "even at the next house to me." Then Jane begged not to see Cranmer. "Your ladyship would not believe how much the Queen is afraid of the sickness." Henry sympathized with her and thought it better for people not to come to her from the "smoky air." He did not hide that his consort was "somewhat afraid."

Her refuge was religion, of the old kind. Cranmer was discreetly troubled. He deplored to Cromwell that the Court ate fish on Fridays and observed holydays. "My lord, if in the Court you do keep such holydays and fasting days as be abrogated, when shall we persuade the people to cease from keeping them?"

To force Henry in these matters was unsafe. But part of this was a reluctance to disturb his consort. As October approached, he was increasingly attentive and within reach. If ever he prayed hard at mass, he now leaned forward, a great mountain of heaving sanguine manhood, and implored coöperation from the other Supreme Head. He was on the eve of completion and the verge of justification.

XVI

"By the provision of the living God," approval was signified of all things—the first divorce, the second divorce, the execution—on October twelfth at two in the morning, when Jane labored and brought forth Edward.

Incontinent after the birth, Te Deum was sung in Paul's, great fires, goodly banquets, shooting of guns day and night.

The baby was puny, but living, and Henry's heart was lifted into heaven. All those who had claims on the throne—young Exeter, the Montagues, the Suffolks, the Norfolks, the Douglases—were by this frail life debarred from infringing on the Tudors. This little blue Edward was born a conqueror and on this slim bridge Henry could imagine his name returned over Lethe and borne down the proud avenue of posterity. With the insistence on self that always marked his fierce but uncertain grip of power, he saw in Edward his mortmain, his grasp of posthumous fame—Edward who in his seventeenth year would, for lack of modern prevision, become ill and die, eruptions coming over his skin, hair falling off, then his nails, then the joints of his fingers and toes, until some said the Catholics had poisoned him and others said the Protestants.

Now he was the tiniest of human pilgrims, and Latimer, who was nothing if not laudatory, hailed him as a John the Baptist. By the simple act of being born this infant changed the center of national gravity: Henry gave place to him, Jane gave place to him, and the whole court grouped itself around him. The

Seymours, Edward and Thomas, swelled out their chests, becoming the uncles of the Prince of Wales. The infant would have precedence over the sagest of councilors, the stoutest of soldiers, over the Archbishop, the Chief Justice, the Chancellor. A morsel of puling ignominy, a shrinking inch-worm, he blindly and automatically became the lottery ticket on which a nation staked its fate, the inheritor of a dynasty whose crown alone at this instant would snuff him out like a ha'penny dip.

And the nation that was too rational to endure the idiocies of control from Rome proceeded at once to prostrate itself before the Unknown Dynast. Three days after his birth, all of them, Henry himself, the dukes whose entries had been scratched, the marquis who had been disqualified, Anne Boleyn's father who had been warned off, Princess Mary who was a selling plater, the Archbishop and the various bishops crying, "A John the Baptist!" and all the other tearful and joyful hearts, could congregate around the baptismal font to splash loyal tears in it as the lamentable little victim of this antique tribal rite was tossed and twisted in the fashion dear to Europe.

Baptism, at the moment, was a sacrament in good standing; and as Edward was given his dip in the healing waters, his mother, Jane, big-eyed with fever, her head throbbing with wild signals, her hands clasping brocade in cold perspiration, and a stream of noise, wrench, reek, chaos and infamous agony clashing through her body like cymbals shattering at her ears and nails scratching on window-panes, she half-saw and half-imagined the triumph of her life, while Death, raising and lowering its curtain, obliterated her and allowed her to recover, dipped her in its own waters, and lifted her in cold sweat to smell once more the holy candles and swoon again in the nausea of another black descent.

She lived nine days longer, till October 24th. Norfolk was with Henry in this crisis. In terse and sincere accents the Duke sent for Cromwell. Jane was dying. "My good lord, I pray you to be here to-morrow early to comfort our good master, for as for our mistress there is no likelihood of her life, the more pity, and I fear she shall not be on lyve at the time ye shall read this. At VIII at night, with the hand of your sorrowful friend T. Norfolk."

She died before midnight.

Henry was not to blame. "By the neglect of those about her who suffered her to take cold," wrote Cromwell officially to Gardiner at Paris, "and eat such things as her fantasy in sickness called for, the Queen is dead. The King, though he takes his chance reasonably, is little disposed to marry again." He had, however, "framed his mind" to be impartial to the thing. The French King's daughter Madeline might suit, or Madame de Longueville, "of whose qualities you are to inquire." "But the inquiry must be kept secret."

Henry himself wrote with dignity to Francis, "Divine Providence has mingled my joy with the bitterness of the death of her who brought me this happiness."

She had died, certainly, as she had lived, "bound to obey and serve."

BOOK FIVE

Anne of Cleves

"Squire Harry wishes to be God and to do whatever he pleases."

MARTIN LUTHER

I

WITH Jane's death, Henry had a glimpse of sorrow and it was a new and bewildering experience for him. She had become his companion and his habit, and he had no other family to lean upon. His older sister Margaret, a heavy and somewhat complaining woman, he had scarcely seen for years: whenever she wrote from Scotland, where she sat unwell and unhappy, it was to scold her son James and to worry about her property. His favorite sister Mary had died two years before, and his old comrade Suffolk had at once married again—a girl under twenty—which took him away from Henry. Suffolk, in any case, was stupid. Except his two girls, Henry had no other near relatives, and while Elizabeth at five was as sedate as a woman of forty, and while Mary was anxiously devoted, they could not cross the broad moat with which he had surrounded himself. He had no one as his friend—especially not a single woman—when the blow reached him "he retired into a solitary place to pass his sorrows."

He felt alone, but he was miserable alone—helpless in a large way, forlorn and full of dejection. The infant, of course, clutched at his heart-strings, and he was instantly charged with a fierce and almost maniacal determination to provide against any possible injury to this little mortal. Food, raiment, shelter—everything must be rigorously superintended. Look what had just happened to Francis's eldest boy, when Francis could not "make" another son. Henry had been bitterly suspicious that the Emperor Charles had had the Dauphin poisoned, and he now drew up the most stringent rules for safeguarding Edward from what he most feared and detested—the danger of poison.

Could he turn to Cranmer? From this he averted himself in his grief. Jane had not been reformed: and he would obey her wishes, arranging for twelve hundred masses in the City and founding a Benedictine abbey for her at Bisham. His piety exacted it. His own devotions deepened, as the solemn masses went on every morning while her corpse lay in the chapel at Hampton Court. To these melancholy obsequies Henry gave a wide berth, Mary dutifully undertaking to be chief mourner for him, but he doubled his own pious exercises in more cheerful surroundings.

For three or four days, perhaps a week, no one in the Privy Council or the Privy Chamber could help pitying the widower. Norfolk sent a note to Cromwell urging him to come to Henry. Perhaps not wisely, he said, but plainly he had exhorted the King to accept God's pleasure in taking the Queen, and recomfort himself with the treasure sent to him in the Prince, and "advised him to provide for a new wife." It was now for Cromwell to try his hand.

So the second of Henry's toughest councilors took over the task of consolation. While the gentle Tunstall at a distance feared he "might rub too sore upon a green wound," Cromwell steered his master toward the duties confronting him. Close observers soon had hopes that the King would not sink under his bereavement. "The King is in good health," wrote one of the Privy Chamber a week before the funeral, "and merry as a widower may be." Good health is much, especially when appetite attends it, and Henry was gradually passing from sorrow into numbness. As Norfolk and Paulet and Cromwell summoned the mourners, ordering more tapers than had been commanded for Henry's mother, and as Jane lay at rest during those three long weeks of obsequies in the chapel hung with black cloth and garnished with rich images, Henry was being helped to lift his imbedded thoughts to the tracks of matrimonial diplomacy on which they must soon revolve.

At five in the morning on November 12th, Jane was escorted on her last progress from Hampton Court to Windsor: there the mourners were "sumptuously provided for." After dinner she was "interred in the presence of many pensive hearts," and by noontime "all was finished."

At Jane's wake, in quick reaction after so quiet a reign, the King's heralds became highly "distempered," and so continued for several days. Clarencieux fell downstairs, but landed on Garter King at Arms and Chester, thus saving his neck. Somerset "would have ravished the maid of the house, and in struggling with her wrang her neck so that for a great space she could not get her breath." He, "who has three wives living," and all his life used dicing and naughty company, was particularly riotous. It needed Cromwell to restore the College of Heralds to grace.

II

So quiet was the widower during November that prejournalists jumped to the conclusion he was dead; and only when a few of them had been whipped naked through their towns, after having their ears cut off, was the certainty of his being still in full vigor made evident. Toward the end of November, as a matter of fact, he was "merry" supping with his old friend

William Kingston at Black Friars, and actively discussing brides with Cromwell. Being in no great hurry, he could afford to shop with the most minute scrutiny and calculation; and so, thirty years after he had watched his father picking over the matrimonial bargains and remnants, he himself, the Prince Charming that was, had come to the same maturity. But his father had been emaciated and hectic, Henry was full-blooded, and he was by nature more rash and obstinate. He had no qualms as a recent widower. He was free. He had no liaison. He could choose for political reasons. It was chess, in which he needed a Queen. He particularly consulted Cromwell, the European board on his knees.

A week before Jane was buried, the plans and specifications for a new bride were being actively discussed with the French ambassador, and these details, quite similar to those that Henry's father had been wont to dwell on, were forwarded at once to the French Court. They tickled Francis, whose sense of humor was *gras*. "Francis laughed greatly at the language used to his ambassador, saying that it would seem they meant to do with women there as with their geldings, collect a number and trot them out to take which goes best. He does not approve of his daughter being put in the row with the others."

But Henry, so recently sunk in gloom, was beginning to revive again. Why could he not solicit a French bride and an Imperialist one at the same time? And, if a French one, why not the very woman that James, his nephew, wished to marry? With the craft which seems so brazen to the people who suffer it but so matchless to its author, Henry pretended not to know why he could not have Mary of Guise. He sent a secret agent to probe Mary's mother and he made his ambassadors nip at Francis's heels. Mary's mother was attracted, but Francis, who knew Henry after long years, refused to be enticed into trying to meet his mind, and simply said, "Impossible." But why? Henry argued. Francis responded, firmly and politely, that he could command any one else in the kingdom but not James's bride. Checked in this particular game, the project of a French match was kept open, while Cromwell sent scouts into the Imperialist camp.

III

It was beyond doubt a good thing to have Henry eligible. Ever since Reginald Pole had been made Cardinal, "to spite and harm Henry," the immense danger was to be attacked as a rebel against the Pope. The danger did not seem pressing so long as Charles and Francis were at war. But no European war such as they were waging could go on forever. Francis had spent millions, and Charles, although he was scuppering Peru, could never hope to drain enough to support his hireling troops. Those Spaniards of his, who massacred every one over the age of eight and looted to the last eyelet, had proved costly in Provence. War in Provence, Charles found, was gnashing cinders. The fight was now languishing in Flanders. And as peace was brewing, Henry needed something—a matrimonial alliance if nothing else—to prop these dangerous powers apart. Otherwise, hinged together by the Pope, they might close on him.

It was not Cromwell's intention to wait for peace. He had no belief in England's ability to act as arbiter or hold the balance of power. That was Wolsey's policy and out of date. His own tendency, at times heavily disguised, was anti-papal, anti-clerical, anti-Imperialist and pro-Protestant. Cromwell was indeed the enemy of the old nobility, as Darcy had so grandly proclaimed. He was of vile blood, viler than Wolsey's. Life to him was a revenge on all the pretensions to which these proud and narrow egoists were lending themselves, and even in Henry he despised the puerilities of class. The men who served him were Bryan, Wyatt, Vaughan, Sadler, wholly emancipated from any adhesion to medievalism. He had allied himself to the Seymours out of cold-blooded calculation, and he had used Jane's devotion to Princess Mary to break Princess Mary's religious spine. His real partiality was for the Reformers, Cranmer, Latimer, Shaxton. To hound priests, to clear out abbots, to destroy relics, to explode the whole mythology and pathology of the medieval establishment gave him a definite and acute satisfaction. He was intensely secular. When necessary, of course, he could play the hypocrite, in the real meaning of the word: he could act a part. But he was not one of those imbued hypocrites, like his master, whose auto-intoxication makes them pharisees. Cromwell was a ball of muscle, supple and devious as a wrestler, and when he yielded it was to make his treachery count. His unique foreign contribution, from the start, had been to utilize those elements in Germany which threatened to do Charles the most harm. He had favored Wullenweber and Marcus Meyer, democrats who were droll playmates for Henry. He had done his best to work up the protestant connection. This was his answer, at bottom, to Imperialists and Vatican forces either in England or out of it. He was fighting with every possible arm, the Bible in the churches, the spy among the clergy, the assassin on Pole's heels, the agent-provocateur, the briber, the traitor in the abbeys and the torturer and the executioner in legal combat, to defeat the old order that disputed sovereignty with Henry. He saw in Lutheranism, especially as Cranmer and Latimer exemplified it, the right attitude of ecclesiastics to their civil master. It was not for nothing he was himself vicar-general.

Henry's next marriage, he therefore intended, should be of some use in this struggle to build up Leviathan, and to build it up against Cardinal Pole, against Bishop Gardiner, against Norfolk, against every one, even Henry himself, who might try to warp the state to comply with the Catholics. Henry and Cromwell had combined to tool parliament for shaping autocracy. But it was Cromwell who had done the iron work at the bellows and with the forge. Cromwell had hammered while Henry held the pinchers. Politic as he was, at no time did Cromwell, hard-headed and hard-hearted, really relax in the struggle with Rome.

IV

The French bride, it seemed at first, would receive the nomination. "It is yet unknown what his Grace intendeth," people were saying in December, "but it is judged she shall come out of France."

Hutton, the envoy at Brussels, could find no girl worthy of Henry. There was a girl of fourteen, "of goodly stature, virtuous, sad and womanly," who might do. "The Duke of Cleves has a daughter, but there is no great praise either of her personage or of her beauty." And there is "the Duchess of Milan who is reputed a goodly personage and of excellent beauty."

"I have little experience among ladies," the playful ambassador told Cromwell, "but I have written the truth as nigh as I can learn, and leave further judgment to others."

Still, he commended Christine: "The Duchess of Milan arrived here yesterday. She is sixteen years old, very tall, taller than the Regent, of competent beauty, soft of speech and gentle in countenance. She wears mourning after the manner of Italy." And he noted, shrewdly enough, "she resembles one Mrs. Shelton that used to wait on Queen Anne." Though so inexperienced, he sent further details to Wriothesley the same day, and he was clearly becoming an ardent match-maker. "There is none in these parts for beauty of person and birth to compare to the Duchess. She is not so pure white as the late Queen, whose soul God pardon; but she hath a singular good countenance, and when she chanceth to smile there appeareth two pittes in her cheeks and one in her chin, the wich becometh her right excellently well."

Henry took it in. This was Christine of Denmark, daughter of Christiern II, who had been deposed and was now in prison, a fiery autocrat, reared in a bookbinder's household, who had genuine social ideas, introducing Dutch horticulture into Denmark, proposing to educate the people, and combining this with a savage attempt to break the Swedish nobles that had sundered Sweden and Denmark and finally cost him his throne. He had married Charles's young sister. Their child Christine had been bestowed on Sforza of Milan whose death had just made the girl a widow. And now she was with her aunt in Brussels, her dimples in evidence.

Henry, however, was "so amorous of Madame de Longueville" that he himself pressed his suit to the French ambassador. "I am big in person," he urged, "and have need of a big wife."

V

January opened with Henry at Greenwich to greet his noble friends. "How doth my lord and my lady? Are they merry?" Face to face he could be genial, and could hardly resist granting favors. But as he stood there, leaning against the cupboard, Cromwell at his side to take in the New Year's gifts in cash, which were an important source of revenue, Henry's glance fidgeted among his callers, knowing every one and spotting everything. There was Anne Boleyn's father, now a limp old man. There was Norfolk's boy Surrey, bringing three golden bowls. Was Henry computing the value as his quick eyes ran over the great chamber, or was he "full of flesh and unwieldy," counting on the minute to sit down? A rugose bulk, deep in mourning at present, he was not climbing to dominance: he had reached there. He was on the great plateau of middle age, no longer troubled by sensibility, but a formidable working organism of pomp and power. "An old fox," the new French ambassador Castillon would call him. But a fox, for the moment, in his lair, a pet fox who looked as if he had never seen a chicken and naturally drew his noble England about him to make himself warm.

No one could really trust him. His own suspiciousness made his life perpetually restless. "Whom many fear," as Chapuys said, "must fear many." But even those who felt he was a fox, secretive, dextrous, canny, false and mischievous, a fox alert and twisting, never to be understood by mere intelligence but only by getting inside his red temper and his verminous soul—even they, plumbing his nature, sure of his inconstancy, could at any moment, just by listening to his own account of his large motives and simple attachments and genuine impulses, begin to feel shaken in their judgment and see in him an easy, great-natured and miscomprehended man.

If he was a fox, he could loop any trap in existence. Lord Montague might say to his servant, "Jerome, the King never made man but he destroyed him again with displeasure or with the sword." But even Montague, who beshrewed Darcy for "not plucking away the head," was himself ready to harp on "the knaves who rule about the King."

The gossip still ran that Henry was misled by Cromwell. In the inner circles, however, where Cromwell was equally detested, the truth of Henry's willfulness and Cromwell's subservience was at last admitted. A Younger Son blabbed it on the road between Ross and Wexford. "By God's Body, if the King take a thing in his head, neither my Lord Privy Seal ne the best Lord in England dare speak or move him to the contrary." George Paulet dilated freely on the miserable plight of Cromwell. "I would not be in his case for all that he hath," he opened out to the men riding with him, "for the King beknaveth him twice a week, and sometime knocketh him well about the pate; and yet when he hath been well pummelled about the head and shaken up, so it were a dog, he will come out into the great chamber shaking of the bush with as merry a countenance as though he might rule all the roast."

This was not hearsay from his brother, treasurer of the

household. Oh no! "I standing at the lower end of the chamber perceive these matters well enough, and laugh at his faction and ruffs, and then my brother and the Lord Admiral must drive a mean to reconcile him to the King again."

Those who heard Paulet, Cromwell's friends amongst them, pooh-poohed the young man. But he insisted. "The King calleth him villain, knave, bobs him about the head, and thrusts him out of the Privy Chamber." Incredulous smiles made the young man engrave his story deeper. Cromwell is a great taker and briber, he said, like his old master the Cardinal, but he spends it honorably and freely "like a gentleman, though he were none." But Crum's outlook was none too rosy. Every day he draws nearer death, "he escaped hardly at the last insurrection."

This was the word of a gadabout. Cromwell was Henry's right-hand man, and busied himself about procuring a new wife, but nothing was certain with Henry's temperament.

As Charles and Francis made truce in Flanders, Cromwell redoubled his efforts, with Norfolk excluded and yawning. The policy was, first, to profess lifelong amity with the Emperor, regretting the clouds that had obfusked their dear friendship, but now showing every willingness to take Christine of Denmark. This local anesthetic administered to one Catholic power, Francis was to be impressed that the Emperor was no friend, and that a French bride would be infinitely desirable.

Throughout the spring of 1538, with peace threatening, Henry was immersed in these bargainings. He sent his "Servant" Hans Holbein (thirty pounds a year was Holbein's wages) to Christine "to take her physiognomy." The likeness "pleased the King very much." But he kept up his pressure on the French to provide him with a partner. Castillon, an urbane Frenchman of nakedly bright mind, saw Henry's fears of being chastised by the combined Catholic powers, and brought his diplomacy

down to the level of the Halles. The old velvet manners of the
Venetian envoy, the ironic dignity of the Savoyard, turned
with Castillon into concise and stinging witticism, which Henry
could not afford to resent. Henry's apprehensions lest his French
bride should not be sufficiently beautiful or sufficiently pure the
ambassador met with smiling impertinence.

"Take the young one," he counseled Henry in regard to
Mary of Guise's sister. "She is still a virgin, and you would be
able to have her to your measure."

At this stage Henry could not punish Castillon. He laughed
and slapped him on the shoulder, but protested he had to hurry
away "to mass."

VI

Efforts strenuous, even brilliant, were made by England to impede the reconciliation of France and the Empire. But fatigue
was too deep in both camps. The Pope ably directed a truce and
in the height of Southern summer long trains of nobility and
royalty converged on Nice, amid a buzz of diplomatic and human excitement. It was, Bryan wrote home, "as if all the world
were gathered on a plum." The plum was brandied, and Bryan
spent much time under the table.

A full peace was too thorny to handle, but Pope Paul, helped
by Francis's Spanish wife, secured the truce for ten years. So as
not to offend the Portuguese, Henry was gravely informed,
neither Portugal nor England had been brought into it.

More important than the treaty were its makers. At first it
seemed impossible for Francis to face Charles, who had called
him a coward and had twice challenged him to a duel. But at
the foot of the enormous national interests looming above them,
their personal quarrel looked so small, so like rancor and trivi-
ality, that by arts at once soothing to pride and sobering to reason, the two Kings were at last so combed into unison that they

agreed about the middle of July to risk seeing one another.

Aigues Mortes, not far from the Marseilles that had twice saved Francis's life, was a place happily chosen.

The Emperor came from his fleet, and Francis went out to his ship in the luminous Mediterranean. As he stepped on deck, Charles was waiting for him: both uncovered and embraced three or four times. They were exceedingly polite. When Charles pressed his guest to be seated, Francis would not do so first until some one murmured, "You are the elder."

He assented. "I confess I am the elder—and the more foolish" (*le plus sot*). With that he sat down.

They talked cordially and separated with great embraces. At the next interview, where Constable, Cardinal, Queen, Princes and Princess were all present, there was so much embracing that Francis exclaimed "Foie de gentilhomme, c'est assez baise," and bowed so often, and kissed the Constable so much on the cheeks and ears, that the ice completely melted and "the spectators shed tears of joy."

After dinner on this second occasion, each took a ring and put it on the other's finger. Charles, who did not wear rings, raised his ringed hand and pledged himself not to draw his sword on *monsieur mon frère*. Francis, who still had *élan*, responded from his heart. They supped together on land for the final time, and "during the supper there was nothing but good cheer and mutual embraces with great joy."

VII

The reunion did not go to the roots of their rivalry. Charles was really ready to abandon Burgundy, but he had not the grandeur to say so, and Francis might forever have said good-by to Milan if the right move had been made. But though these contentions slumbered beneath, the meeting had a deep effect on both men. Besides the burden of rivalry, they had loaded themselves with hatred, and it appeased two weary spirits to be relieved of this monster and to embrace. The strain of seventeen years of ceaseless or almost ceaseless conflict had not unbalanced them; they were both tamed and sobered; and their sanity showed itself in the magnanimity of this meeting.

It had not, however, included Henry. And his fate was so much on his mind, and he suspected the worst so vividly, that he resumed his work of stirring dissension. But Francis told Castillon not to trouble repeating the insinuations about Charles, so that the ambassador could only report Henry on the alluring topic of a French bride.

Henry had proposed a sort of large house party, near Calais, with the flower of French womanhood of the right rank and age, assembled for inspection.

"Well, does he send me nothing of the marriages?" he asked Castillon.

Castillon replied that Francis could not consign the young ladies on approval, but that Henry should send some one in whom he trusted to report.

This aroused Henry. "By God, I trust no one but myself, the thing touches me too near. I wish to see them and know them some time before deciding."

The ambassador had to laugh. "Perhaps, Sire," he said, with that trick of clothing thoughts in words which sometimes makes them seem more naked, "you would like to try them one after the other, and keep the one you found the most agreeable. Is not that the way the Knights of the Round Table used to treat the ladies in this country in the olden times?"

To have it brought home was rough. Henry laughed and blushed, and then, rubbing his nose a little, he said, "Yes, but since the King my brother is so friendly with the Emperor, what amity am I to have with him? Don't you see that if I married on the Emperor's side he would prefer me to your master?"

The ambassador shrugged and smiled, "It would need a wiser man than I to answer that."

"By God, I will not act till Dr. Bonner is there," Henry broke off.

VIII

But to "marry on the Emperor's side" was scarcely easier. It was Hutton who had arranged for Holbein to portray Christine, and he had said that Mr. Haunce, "having but three hours space, hath showed himself to be master of that science, for it is very perfect." Hutton, unfortunately, had since died, so Henry's able secretary, Wriothesely, had gone over to woo Christine by proxy. He was, in general, a capital agent for Henry. He had just superintended the stripping of St. Thomas à Becket at Canterbury, which had netted Henry seven staggering chests of gold and jewels. But Christine was less inanimate than St. Thomas, and to garner the matrimonial jewel required the art of catching quicksilver. While Wriothesley was of an imperturbable spirit, with a manner highly varnished, a blend of cool bluff and right thinking, which, at a hint of distrust, could become a menacing moral indignation, he did not find the demure Christine a still-hunt like Canterbury. She probably did say, "If I had two heads, one should be at his Grace's service," and she may have said, "My council suspecteth that my great-aunt was poisoned, that the second was innocently put to death, and the third lost for lack of keeping in her childbed." But the one remark with which Wriothesley, brass in velvet, did proceed to tax her was, "that he would lose his labors, for she minded not to fix her heart that way."

Had she really used those words?

"Mr. Ambassador, I thank God he hath given me a better stay of myself then to be of so light sort." Not these words nor any like them, she said, and prayed to be so reported.

"And what is your real inclination?" he asked her, smiling.

At this the girl blushed exceedingly.

" 'As for my inclination,' quoth she, 'what should I say? You know that I am at the Emperor's commandment.'

" 'Yea, Madam, but this matter is of such nature, that there must be a concurrence between his commandment and your consent, or else you may percase repent it when it shall be too late. Your answer is such as may serve both for your modesty and my satisfaction; and yet, if it were a little plainer, I could be the better contented.'

"With that she smiled and again said, 'You know I am the Emperor's poor servant and must follow his pleasure.'

" 'Marry, then I may hope to be among the Englishmen that shall be first acquainted with my new mistress, for the Emperor hath instantly desired it. Oh, Madam, how happy shall you be if it be your chance to be matched with my master. If God send you that hap, you shall be matched with the most gentle gentleman that liveth; his nature so benign and pleasant that I think to this day no man hath heard many angry words pass his lips. As God shall help me, if he were no King, I think, and you saw him, you would say that for his virtue, gentleness, wisdom, experience, goodliness of person, and all other qualities meet to be in a Prince, he were worthy before all others to be made a King.' "

Christine had difficulty in greeting this manful effort. She smiled, and Wriothesley thought she would have laughed out, "had not her gravity forbidden it."

She at last controlled herself long enough to say that she knew his Majesty was a good and noble Prince.

But she affirmed nothing, and it soon became clear, as Henry himself put it, that the Emperor was "knitting one delay to the tail of another."

IX

Henry, in the autumn after the truce, became engrossed in the Turk. As Castillon came to see him, he found him buried in a map. It could not be hidden that Charles was exposed to at least one grave danger; and this was helping Henry.

In August Reginald Pole's weak young brother Geoffrey was suddenly taken to the Tower. He was put under pressure, and in two months he had said enough to make a case against his brother Lord Montague, his mother Lady Salisbury, the "young" Marquis of Exeter, and several others. It was not so much a conspiracy as the seeds from which a conspiracy might, by a valiant effort, be matured. Some letters had been hurriedly burned; that was strong evidence. The whole thing was a decoction of violent suspicion, brewed from the dribblings of Geoffrey Pole, who tried to commit suicide. The elderly Countess had been visited by the heavy, lurching Fitzwilliam, now Earl of Southampton. She admitted to him that she had warned her son the Cardinal to guard himself against assassination. In her house there were copies of papal bulls, but she scorned the accusation of conspiracy. Southampton was astonished at her courage: "we may call her rather a strong and constant man than a woman."

The trial was a blow aimed at the Catholics, inside and outside. Yet whenever Henry dug in his paddle on one side, he quickly checked with a stroke on the other. No sooner was the Pole clique arrested than he himself staged the trial of a "miserable heretic sacramentary," a serious young man who had been in university circles but was not in favor, "denying the very body of God to be in the said sacrament in corporal substance, but only to be there spiritually."

Henry arranged for the ordeal in his own hall at York Place. Surrounded by bishops, lords, doctors, judges, he arrived near noon, clad all in white, and seated himself on a "haut place," while Lambert was brought to the bar.

He was known both as Lambert and as Nicholson, and Henry first attacked him roughly on his having two names; then made him answer "yes or no," on the sacrament; "Mark well, you are condemned by Christ's own word"; and, having brow-beaten him regally, turned him over to Cranmer. In Cromwell's words, Henry showed "most high wisdom and judgment." "After the King had confounded him by Scripture," said one witness, "so that Lambert had nothing to say for himself, the bishops and doctors exhorted him to abandon his opinions, which his Grace did also; but he refused, and will have his deserts." The affair lasted five hours. In five days Lambert was burnt alive.

This was a pro-Catholic hors-d'œuvre to the anti-papal sentencing of Montague and Exeter, with the Countess held back for a later crisis.

When Exeter and Montague were beheaded, the credit was disputed. The French Ambassador wrote to Francis that Henry had told him long before that he would exterminate the house of Montague, but Hugh Latimer, the Bishop of Rochester, wrote to congratulate Cromwell. "Blessed be God of England that worketh all, whose instrument you be! I heard you say once after you had seen that furious invective of Cardinal Pole that you would make him to eat his own heart, which you have now, I trow, brought to pass."

Henry had long convinced himself that a few executions in good time were the best way to terrify and hold down his subjects. He was happy in the extreme at the outcome both in Lambert's case and in the case of the Poles. "They would have made foul work in England," wrote one cheerful gossip. "The King removed from Westminster on Tuesday, and, thank God, was never merrier." He had been banqueting every evening, not without bravado. Castillon, who saw no danger, could not fathom it. "I know no more strange and hypocritical persons than Cromwell and his master."

X

Henry had little to fear at home from exterminating Montague and the others. Outside commerce, which was already creating its Greshams, he held every avenue to a public career, and at the axis of these avenues Cromwell controlled for him. Henry could make or mar any fortune in the law, in the Church, in medicine, in literature, not to speak of the army or the navy: and he had already made many brilliant fortunes, from Wolsey and Norfolk and Suffolk and Wiltshire and Southampton down to such New Men as Cromwell and the Seymours, John Russell, Paulet, Bryan, Knyvet, Wallop, young Dudley, Sadler, Wyatt, Wriothesley, Audley and so on, including quiet accumulators like Cranmer and Tunstall. These benefices, however, were not bestowed on independent men, nor were they thrown around unthinkingly. When there was dirty work to do, such as procuring witnesses, serving on juries, hunting down papists or heretics, sitting in parliament or convocation, the test of perfect pliancy was upheld by the piercingly intelligent Cromwell. Sometimes a bishop made a fuss about giving up his town house to a new favorite. Sometimes a Gardiner was irritable over paying an annuity to Bryan. Sometimes, even, a widow refused to remarry on command saying, "my stomach does not lean there"; but generally speaking the King's will was God's will. People who wanted to get on might dislike it intensely, but they voted, dressed, ate, believed, got up and went to bed with the opinions and the persons that Henry and Cromwell ordained. And whenever Cromwell came from the Court to his own office, carrying a basket of grants, every one who had a son to promote, a daughter to marry, a mansion to procure, abbey lands to pasture, a stream or a boat or a mill or a dowry to acquire, a crime to expiate or a dispute to settle—every one, in short, who was hungry and wanted to be fed, broke into leaps, like seals at the zoo, when the keeper dips his hand in the basket. The noble names that star the chamber of history owed, as Wriothesley did not hesitate to say, their every scintillation to their Grace, his Master. From the first moment of a state trial the phalanx of New Men formed solidly behind Henry. "A traitor these twenty years," Wriothesley described Exeter to a sympathetic listener at Brussels, "he ever studied to take his master's place from him, and to destroy all his children." This was the unbroken front, and when a favorite like Nicholas Carew, who had been an intimate of Henry's for those same twenty years, and whose wife was a particular friend, ventured to marvel at the hollowness of Exeter's trial, this treason, from a man with confiscable wealth, was perhaps the meekest thunder that ever brought lightning death.

But loyalty at home, which is always gingered by state executions, was not so easy to reproduce abroad. Francis, it was true, in the cause of English friendship, was willing to reprove those clerics who had given tongue to horror and disgust; and Charles, admonished by Wyatt that Reginald Pole was a "traitor," allowed this fact to weigh with him when the Cardinal now hurried to Toledo as an envoy from the Pope. Yet all the diplomatic pressure and all the state machinery in France and the Empire could not alter the recoil from Henry. Charles, who was not easily electrified, immediately stiffened the terms on which his niece Christine should be given to Henry.

This ended the match with Christine, who was to have her useful career in Lorraine. And it gave Cromwell the chance to pursue a bride for Henry in those disputed border states which ran from Savoy up through Burgundy and Lorraine and Luxembourg to the other side of Flanders, where the young Duke of Cleves, nebular so far, had attracted and almost consolidated a few nuggets of border territory that made him capable of inflicting injury and therefore made him a "power." Anne of Cleves was the sister of this potential nuisance: Cromwell saw in her a good match for Henry.

The motive was clear-cut. But not till Henry saw Holbein's portrait of Anne of Cleves did he allow Cromwell to begin in earnest.

Meanwhile a nervous disorder seized England. Henry could

not persuade himself that he was not to be attacked, by command of the Pope, and the worst war scare of years led to a muster of national forces and panic preparations against invasion. The French ambassador was withdrawn. The imperial ambassador was withdrawn. The English ambassadors were withdrawn. And the claws of one lion's paw—the Cinque Ports— were bared and retracted in spasms of anticipation. It was, it afterwards appeared, that archaic hysteria known as the "mother." But if it did not give birth to a war it gave birth to a parliament. And it served to show that at the threat of invasion Henry could rely on the beastly inhabitants of Lincolnshire no less than every citizens' guild and company in London.

The war parliament of 1539 was necessarily a conservative parliament. It was summoned when three great facts were vividly in mind; one, the danger of invasion; two, the "recent divers and sundry detestable and abominable treasons to the fearful peril of his Highness's royal person"; three, Henry stabilizing the succession. The new symbol of the King was not the man who had executed Anne Boleyn: it was the loving father with a baby in his arms: "he hath gone to the Prince," said Richard Cromwell, "and there hath solaced him all the day with much mirth and with dallying with him in his arms a long space, and so holding him in a window to the sight and great comfort of all the people."

This was a slight attempt, it may seem, to correct the unhappy impression left by executions and rebellions, but it sprang instinctively from the heart of a man who knew his people.

So did his fresh religious legislation. The Ten Articles had gone too fast, and Henry wanted to slow down the popular pulse. Cromwell and the Council had brought "all things so to pass that your Grace had never more tractable parliament." With little danger, then, of subversive opinion, he had his "unitary" parliament with which to work out a more popular bill of fare. Cromwell would defer as he could later manipulate the administration.

Henry's fear of the Catholic powers was dominant, and the soldiers in the Council, led by Norfolk, could influence him more than Cromwell, who did not belong to their most jealous and arrogant caste. The religion of Mars is always archaic, and after long debate and wrangle, where Cranmer had the courage to fight in the open against Norfolk and Gardiner, the forces of the Old Learning won the day, but of course with Henry as Pope.

Henry was beginning to discover that the man who crosses religion on politics does a dangerous thing. Nothing whets the thirst for self-assertion like religion, and when the inebriated who want to domesticate the infinite by statute begin to force their fellow-citizens to save their souls and to use the power of the state to penalize opinion, it is extremely difficult to restrain them. But if ignorant and blood-thirsty idealists are kept severely in check, it is equally hard to keep the politicians' relation to the finite from sapping or smothering the religious man's relation to the infinite. In this quandary, Henry could do nothing more resourceful than plead for "moderation."

No one has more belief in "moderation" than the autocrat, because no one needs more to extirpate dissenters. In Henry's attempt to "abolish diversity of opinion," he accordingly laid all the onus for lawlessness and turbulence and pugnacity—detestable and disruptive forces—on those who could not show themselves "tractable." He became eloquent and almost tearful in his plea for love, meekness, reverence, obedience and humility. He deplored the uproar of human instinct, the lash of appetite, the rage of curiosity, the extravagance and jar of headstrong discussion. He wore the sheepskin of Erasmus, though his features emerged with a less gentle and pacific mien.

The Six Articles affirmed the Real Presence, communion in one kind, celibacy of the clergy, permanency of religious vows, private masses, auricular confession.

All clergymen, like Cranmer, became felons if they did not put away their wives. The penalties attached to the act were so ferocious that it became known as "the whip of six strings."

And as it went into force, to the disgust of the German Protestants, the Reform bishops, Latimer and Shaxton at the head of them, were induced to resign. A small pension came their way, but the tides swept over them, and but for the execution of the Countess of Salisbury during the furor of debate, and the execution of several stout abbots who held out against Cromwell, the reaction was complete enough to cut Henry off from all heretics and display him to Europe as no more a schismatic than Louis XII or Ferdinand or Maximilian.

XI

The bargaining for a German bride, even one merely a schismatic like Anne of Cleves, had languished during the summer of 1539. So long as the Catholic Powers were quiescent, Henry was lukewarm and Cromwell was on suffrance. But startling news came in the early autumn: Charles—who had lost his wife in May—had assented to travel through France as a short route to Flanders. This was not taken as a quite natural outcome of the reunion at Nice. It was taken as a move full of evil omen. The commotion in the English mind was furious. The reaction which had paralyzed Cromwell was violently reversed, and he was enabled to round off the betrothal of Anne of Cleves to Henry, arranging for the new bride to come to England. Not only that, but another enemy of the Hapsburgs, Philip of Bavaria, came rapidly to England, saw Mary, was proposed to her as a non-Catholic husband and lugubriously accepted by her. He had the temerity to kiss her before he went away with the news that he had a good *partie,* though technically a bastard.

While this was being cogitated upon in Bavaria, Anne of Cleves was busy with preparation. Meanwhile Francis, though seriously ill, was on his way to play gallant host to the Emperor, whose visit to France was replete with curious and amusing aspects. The English council was in panic. Was "this poor King" going to be destroyed? Henry was steadier than any of his councilors except Cromwell. He did not believe peace could last. The strength of the Protestant princes in Germany, of the Turk, of the French pro-Protestants, made it look as though the German marriage might prove a form of insurance which Francis could later sympathize with, even to the extent of attacking Flanders. His fourth marriage seemed to Henry sagacious as well as exciting.

XII

As the year 1539 drew to its close, Henry became actually impatient for his picture bride. Lucas Cranach, the painter at Cleves, had been too ill to do her, but "Hanze Albein hath taken the effigy of my Lady Anne and hath expressed her image very life-ly." And Cromwell had ventured beyond Hans Holbein, whose honest eye was his king. Cromwell had private letters which led him to advise Henry that Anne of Cleves surpassed Christine of Denmark "as the golden sun does the silver moon."

Henry was convinced. He wished his new bride to have the most honorable of receptions. He debated what high personage was worthy to greet her at Calais. He ordered his palaces done over, had ships newly decorated, arranged many details that recalled youthful ostentation and ceremony, holding himself ready to start from London to meet his bride and by beholding her to "nourish love." Already the alliance began to have that tinge of the sacrosanct which Henry could never help imparting. And while a number of delays bent back his hopes, they always seemed to rebound more vigorously. His life as a widower had, after all, been dull. He looked kindly on a fourth marriage. He

sent Fitzwilliam, the Earl of Southampton, across to Calais to
await the fair lady, Cromwell including his son for his own
reasons, while every stage of the journey from Deal or Dover to
London was dotted with members of the Council to do honor
and homage to the new Queen.

Anne, for her part, was equally excited as she set out with a
"brave equipage"—over two hundred—from the Valley of the
Rhine. She had reached and passed her thirtieth year without
ever dreaming that she could give up a mere Duke of Lorraine
to become Queen of England. To depart on this palpitating adventure, at the age of thirty-four, was to soar into a new world.
Hers had been the nestled life of a small German court, corseted
in an etiquette that took its tightness to be modesty and judged
the absence to be ludicrous if not indecent. This Anne had
none of the ·black-eyed audacities that had brought the other
Anne to ruin. The least bit pockmarked, unfortunately, "tall
and thin, of medium beauty, and of very assured and resolute
countenance," she made up in stancher virtues for what she did
not flaunt in charm. It had been difficult for Wotton to see her
face at all, owing to her voluminous head-dress, but when he
complained of this her homely chancellor had asked with gruff
good humor, "What, do you want to see her naked?" Wotton
had no desire to invade "the lowly and gentle conditions" that
he so faithfully reported to Henry. Her mother, he said, is her
guide: in manner, she is never from her mother's elbow. The
hatchments and cross-hatchments of Gelderland, Berg, Jülich
and Cleves were no doubt at the tip of her fingers. She occu-
pieth her time most with the needle. She can read and write
Low German but no other language. Nor yet she can sing
nor play any instrument, "for they take it here in Germany for
rebuke and an occasion of lightness that great ladies should be
learned or have any knowledge of music." But she hath the wit
to learn English if she put her mind to it. Another thing, very
consoling, she did not overindulge in beer.

With the stealth of years, undoubtedly, she had lost a little bloom. But while without dangerous coquetry she was brimming with anxiety to please.

Her arrival at Calais was delayed till well into December, owing to foul roads.

At Calais the winds and the tides held her back for another fortnight. She had never been on the sea in her life before, and Southampton contented himself with showing her the ships in port and arranging jousts and teaching her a game of cards called Cent—one of the games, as she requested, that Henry would be liking to play.

Southampton was one of Henry's men of all work. As Marillac described him, "he had long learned to bend to all winds." While he thus entertained the bride, he made amends by expediting the welcome news of her grace and good countenance, her "manner of a princess," her excellent beauty and youth. He did not know German, any more than did Henry, and Anne had *chevaux de frise* of gentlewomen around her, named Swartzenbrock, Brempt, Osenbruch, Loc and Willik. But she had a good interpreter in her chancellor, and she could beam and say "Ja, ja."

They approached each other, bride and groom, as though nature had designed to raise their expectations to the highest pitch. It was nearly forty years since Henry's brother Arthur had ridden out in muddy winter to receive his Spanish bride. Henry on the verge of fifty was almost as tense. He had decided, with the gallantry of a knight, to waylay her at Rochester, thirty miles or so out of London, and he came down in a barge with Russell and Anthony Browne for this personal, private view.

He had not forgotten a New Year's present—a set of sable furs—and he tremulously sent Browne before him to announce his coming. On seeing his future Queen, Anthony Browne was dismayed, the lady was so far unlike what was reported, but he returned with the discreet word that she was awaiting her lord. Then the King, with his two seconds, went to her chamber.

As he stood on the threshold, his jaw dropped, "marvelously astonished and abashed." Could this be she? He entered to embrace and kiss her, but "a discontentment and disliking of her person" so overwhelmed him that after mumbling twenty words he left her, too upset to offer her his present. Returning on the barge, he wrapped himself in silence. Then, "very sadly and pensively" he remarked with ominous weight "I see nothing in this woman as men report of her, and I marvel that wise men should have made such report as they have done." The remark made Browne quail: Southampton who had trumpeted her was his half-brother.

The next day the King approached his other aide.

"Do you think the lady so fair and of such beauty as report had been made of her?"

Russell answered, "Your Grace, I took her not for fair, but to be of a brown complexion."

Henry bent his brows. "Alas, whom should men trust? I promise you I see no such thing in her as hath been showed unto me of her."

He was "sore troubled." So was Russell, who could not wait to consult Browne. Lady Browne had also been in attendance on Anne, and she came home appalled. She told her husband that she saw in Anne "such fashions and manner of bringing up so gross that in her judgment the King should never heartily love her." Perhaps, since Lady Lisle had given her precious gold pick-tooth, which she had been using "these seven years," to the crude Duke of Bavaria, who was taking her quill pens for dental purposes, this and other little habits had varied distressingly since the two great branches of the Germanic race had bifurcated. Anne's costumes, too, were not precisely of the mode. The French ambassador wrote home that her gentlewomen were "dressed so heavily and unbecomingly, that they would almost be thought ugly even if they were beautiful."

The public, however, had no suspicions. Five thousand on horseback were marshaled on Blackheath "well conducted with marvelous silence and no confusion." Every one who had a gold chain put it around his neck on January 30th. All the merchants, directed by Cromwell in person, put on their new tunics of black velvet. At the foot of Shooter's Hill was a rich pavilion, with fires of perfumed wood, and through a lane of attendants three miles long Anne came to be publicly embraced and kissed by Henry, while Cromwell sweated with anxiety, looking "more like a post-runner than anything else, running up and down with his staff in his hand."

Could he be blamed? On returning from the first shock at Rochester the King had made no secret of his chagrin. How had he liked her? He retorted on Cromwell with the terrible words, "If I had known so much before, she had not comen hither. But what remedy now?"

It was the old tragedy of a pig in a poke. Cromwell said that he was sorry. On her entry to Greenwich, after the King had seen her to her chamber, Cromwell again waited upon his master privately.

"How say you, my lord?" demanded Henry. "Is it not as I told you? Say what they will, she is nothing fair. The personage is well and comely but nothing else."

Cromwell had no retort, "By my faith, you say truth." He brightened up, however. "Me thinketh she hath a queenly manner withal."

Henry answered heavily, "That is truth."

Marriage under such circumstances is uphill work. Henry's eyes began to race round his chamber. How could he get out of it? To "impark" the Emperor in Flanders, between himself and France, the Duke of Cleves and the Protestant princes of Germany, and so to force Charles to "yield without any making of war," was the reason for this marriage in the first place. But could he not pick a hole in the covenants through which he might escape? Cromwell, going "the back way" between Henry's council and Anne's ambassadors, found that Lorraine's discharge of Anne's pre-contract had been left in Germany. Here might be a loophole. Henry took his aggrieved tone. "I am not well handled." But the discharge existed, it would be sent for.

"If it were not that she is come so far into England," he feebly railed, "and for fear of making a ruffle in the world, and driving her brother into th' Emperor and the French King's hands, I would never have her; but now it is too far gone." This he said with such petulance that Cranmer and Cromwell were on tenterhooks.

The wedding was postponed, to Anne's alarm. Monday was spent in fluttering. But her commissioners were so accommodating, and she herself so willing to sign on demand and acquiesce on sight, that no new excuses could be thought of.

To the last, however, Henry showed himself amazingly peevish, even as Cromwell brought out the harness. "Then there is no remedy," he complained, "but to put my neck in the yoke!"

Cromwell soothed him, but so slackly did Henry prepare for the chapel next morning that he kept every one on edge. Would he have the courage to back out? Even as Cromwell came to say that he and Essex were ready to fetch the blushing bride, Henry made one final weak man's lamentation. "My lord, if it were not to satisfy the world and my realm, I would not do that I must do this day for none earthly thing." With that he went to the altar, scowling to the last, and Anne "demure and sad."

The morrow after the wedding, which, like most of Henry's weddings, was by Cranmer, Cromwell arrived twisting his cap with nervous eagerness, to know if the King liked her any better.

"Nay, my lord, much worse," growled his master savagely, "for by her breasts and belly she should be no maid; which, when I felt them, strake me so to the heart that I had neither will nor courage to prove the rest."

It was for this man the gentlewomen were afraid that Anne of Cleves would be too gross.

The gentlewomen were not themselves so very delicate. Some time a little later, four of them happened to be with the Queen, "they wished her Grace with child and she answered and said she knew well she was not with child. My Lady Edgecombe said, 'How is it possible for your Grace to know that?' 'I know it well, I am not,' she said. Then said my Lady Edgecombe, 'I think your Grace is a maid still.' With that she laughed; 'How can I be a maid,' said she, 'and sleep every night with the King? When he comes to bed he kisses me and takes me by the hand and bids me "Good night, sweetheart," and in the morning kisses me and bids me, "Farewell, darling." Is not this enough?' Then said my Lady Rutland, 'Madame, there must be more than this, or it will be long or we have a Duke of York, which all this realm most desireth.' 'Nay,' said the Queen, 'I am contented I know no more'."

The public knew nothing. A royal marriage was announced in church, and Anne of Cleves rejoiced every one who favored religious change. The union, in fact, was the crown of Cromwell's policy. In spite of Norfolk and Gardiner, who hated him, Cromwell had pushed his master along the road away from Rome, and while Henry had lingered out of stubbornness, his villain minister had never ceased to drive him toward independence. For Henry the abbeys had been drained, and that golden stream had turned the wheel of royal supremacy. The papacy had been demolished in England. Along with this, the Church on the Continent had been defied. Cromwell, rough and thorough, had satisfied Henry's greed for power and from the downfall of Wolsey to the German espousal, ten full years, he had forced the opposition to Charles. Without any dependence on the French, Cromwell had undertaken to cut out the one power on whom the Pope could rely, and, by his audacious and startlingly original move, had presented Henry with an enclave in Germany. Henry now had a spearhead which could be turned against Flanders or the German Catholic princes. It was a masterly innovation, even if it obliged the King to go somewhat against his nature. Cromwell, on the whole could congratulate his envoy Stephen Vaughan on the lady he had picked out, and Vaughan wrote back by the middle of January, "glad Cromwell found his judgment true of the Queen."

Henry publicly concurred. He told Cleves how well he liked the Queen's Grace; and Anne thanked her people for "having preferred her to such a marriage that she could wish for no better." The policy, at the beginning of February, was definitely settled. Henry was living with Anne at Greenwich. He brought her from there to Westminster by barge with all solemnity and triumph. A new generation, the Earl of Surrey conspicuous among them, were jousting and tilting. And Charles, it was revealed from Brussels, was so worried that he was unable to sleep.

XIII

But Cromwell's fate depended on one man in Europe at this juncture, and that was King Francis. Ten years before, perhaps, the bullet-headed parvenu might have been able to convince Francis, smarting under insult and disappointed pride, that his one enemy ought to be Charles and his one aim Flanders. While those ten years had carried them all down the stream of mortality, Francis had learned to play for safety, had become lusterless and flaccid. The old Trinity was dissolved, but he was now played upon by Marguerite, Eleanor and his deft mistress. His throat was eaten out by disease, and, with the severe conservative

Montmorency at his side, he proposed to temporize. The Lutherans had thought it clever to paste abusive placards against the mass on the door of his royal bedchamber; Francis, extremely susceptible on the score of sovereignty, could no longer be induced, even by his beloved Marguerite, to reopen his mind to the new choice that is heresy. The Anabaptists, on one hand, the cutting voice of young Calvin, on the other, had aroused in him the mockery that so often excuses inaction. He had embraced Charles at Aigues Mortes, and slack water was, for the time being, his policy. He was friends with Henry, friends with the Pope, friends with Charles. The old name of Milan made him prick up his ears but could not goad him. Charles's tart statement to Wyatt that he, an Emperor, could not be "ungrateful" to Henry because a superior could not be "ungrateful" to an inferior—a statement which made Marguerite demand furiously, "Does he think he is God?"—simply caused an instant's tenseness in Francis's deliquescent soul. All that the strident little vulgarian Bonner could do on Cromwell's behalf was to make Francis lift his shoulders and suggest that the impossible envoy be taken away.

With French amity undiminished, Charles would show Cromwell that Cleves could be a liability as well as an asset. The Emperor had come to Flanders by land, with Ghent in revolt and the Duke of Cleves claiming Gelderland. He had much to fear from the local upheaval against his taxes, just as he had real danger from the Protestant Princes and the Turk. But his hands were both free. He grappled Ghent by the throat. Having secured an abject submission which gave him a chance to disclose how lucrative and how coldly pitiless such a triumph could be made, he was in a position to give Cleves some out of the same bottle. By May, Pate was writing to Henry from Ghent, "I never saw him of better cheer, and that natural and not constrained."

XIV

While Charles passed beyond Cromwell's short reach, Henry became dangerously restive. He had married Anne under compulsion. There was no fun in it. This state of affairs was borne in on Gardiner and Norfolk.

Every one, even Cromwell, admitted Stephen Gardiner's ability. He was rugged, disagreeable and stiff-necked. When Henry made him bishop of Winchester, he had said, "I have often squared with you, Gardiner, but I love you never the worse as the bishopric I give will convince you"; useful Gardiner undoubtedly was; he had bullied Clement at Orvieto on the legality of the dispensation to Catherine. He was an aggressive and contentious councilor, but his pigheaded manner did not preclude a surly deference to facts, and his strong sense of prelacy was enveloped in a pragmatist's brain. Luther said he had two girls in men's clothes in his establishment at Lambeth. This was the favorite cudgel with which to beat popish prelates. But Gardiner was clearly no puritan: and Norfolk and he understood one another.

To make Henry "amorous" had long been the recipe that these politicians bandied about. Give him plenty of revenue, play on his suspicions, frighten him, make him amorous, and all could be devised. That was the recipe. Tormented observers like young Surrey, who had seen his own cousin die in the Tower because he had married Margaret Douglas for love, and had seen his own sister deprived by Henry of her dowry as Richmond's bride because she had not physically earned her dowry, took a romantic view of Henry's depravity, and hardly veiled their hatred of this Nero whose amorousness it paid to galvanize. "Loathsomely wealthy," withdrawn from danger, scornfully proud, clad in vice, mischievous, cruel, bloody, scourging the poor, piercing with his tongue the simple that can make no defense, the Henry that this young poet upbraided was nominally from the Psalms—an unnamed King "whose glutted cheeks sloth feeds so fat, as scant their eyes be seen." The heart wavers, he protested, that the Lord should suffer one who, armed with power, laden with gold, his eyes "drunken in blood," can "suck the flesh of the Elect and bathe them in their blood."

This repulsion and revolt the older generation could grasp; but Henry was King, he had to be disputed with Cromwell by tempting his appetites. Surrey's own father, the tanning of long hard years in his hide, was ready to use the only bait sweet enough to lure his master away from his evil councilor.

In February Norfolk's chance had presented itself. Known as a pensioner of France and the one man who could talk straight to Francis about "imparking" Charles in Flanders, he had been named by the council and Henry to go to Paris. This was his supreme opportunity to turn Cromwell's flank. He had talked to Francis and Montmorency as one gentleman and papist to another. He had revealed how he loathed Cromwell and loathed the Lutheran tendency. He had knifed Bonner, assured himself that neither Charles nor Francis had any intentions of attacking England, and came home with the dagger that could rip the gas-balloon of fear and suspicion by which Cromwell had been carrying Henry into the German Protestant camp.

At the same time a kinder music was played to Henry than that of the kettle-drummer and the thirteen trumpeters who had been sent over by the Saxons. At Gardiner's house in Lambeth, in the spring of the year, one of the young ladies of the court, Katheryn Howard by name, was invited to the most private of dinners and suppers.

Norfolk's father had brought eighteen children into the world, and Katheryn was the daughter of one of the poorer and obscurer half-brothers, Edmund Howard. She had doubtless been named after Henry's first wife. The mother dying young, Katheryn had been entrusted to the old Duchess of Norfolk, widow of the victor of Flodden and grandmother of Anne

Boleyn. This was a venerable lady in whose shambling and disheveled establishment the child had pushed up like a rose in a neglected garden, a glorious young creature of clear features, fine coloring, sparkling and bubbling life, endowed with feeling, with quick and capricious judgment, with zest, with abundance, with romping blood. She had never been bridled in mind or body. Like a fresh rivulet that renews its clarity and purity by tumbling over its bowlders in the sunlight, this vivacious girl had flung herself into courses of generous experience and darkling depth that might have cost her every touch of quality but instead had quickened and inspirited her, and made her brave. She had been born in the year 1523, during the European war. She was four when Henry divorced Catherine. She was ten when he married Anne Boleyn. She was fully seven years younger than Henry's girl.

This was the eternal vivifier, the young wilding, that whips stale blood.

Norfolk had no scruple in decoying Henry. Neither had Gardiner. They lent themselves to this pretty liaison just as readily as Wolsey had lent himself to the pursuit of Elizabeth Blount. Henry was older and less savory. He had his constitutional leg. But when the experienced man of his age is really stimulated by the charm of dewy youngness, when music that has slumbered in his veins for twenty years begins to chant entrancingly, when forgotten felicity turns once again its radiant and exalting gaze on the landscape of the soul and lifts into glowing color the gray that is blue and purple, the dun that is maroon, no man, even the coarsest, can fail to believe in his indwelling love. The sounding-line goes down, and instead of the muddy bottom, loses itself in depths where all is unspoken and indeterminate, where all is vibrant, illimitable and free. Henry's aging carcass, purulent as it was, contained within it the curious urgency that made him both viable and iniquitous. He still could desire completion. And to see a fresh human being like this girl of eighteen was to clutch at vivifying experience with feverish, greedy hands.

At first, she must have skipped away, her blood curdling. But to drench the repugnant with perfume was an act in which her uncle was not inexpert. The Bishop of Winchester, a consummate dialectician, could teach that the evidence of the senses can never be relied on. Henry's simplicity, when a desire possessed him, had disarmed even Thomas More. And when Katheryn, poor as a broken shoe, looked at night in her mirror her eyes could see the aura of a crown.

By May Henry had begun to quarrel with Anne of Cleves, though without knowing German. She was told to be more attractive to him; her angular cloyingness thereupon drove him to his barge and across the Thames. His gifts to Katheryn Howard were a sure index of coming matrimonial delinquency. Anne of Cleves had been forced on him solely by political necessity; and he, who was one of the arbiters of political necessity, had been given a prime motive to deal new cards.

XV

Thomas Cromwell was no less a general than Norfolk. On the right, pressing dangerously on Norfolk's own position, he had broken the thorough-going Catholics. The weak and friendless Anabaptists he had sacrificed ruthlessly on the left. During the onslaught of the Six Articles he had been obliged to let Latimer and Shaxton go smash, but in spite of Henry's hints and warnings—"I would to Christ I had obeyed your often most gracious grave counsels and advertisements"—he held himself ready at any moment to inflict vicious punishment on the enemy. Several judges were imprisoned. A papist banker was give short shrift and his goods confiscated. The papist deputy of Calais, Lord Lisle, was brought home to the Tower. So was George Paulet, his critic. For a year he had kept Gardiner out of the council, had crippled the Six Articles in administration, had supported Cranmer in orderly retreat, had saved his theological shock troops led by Barnes, had gathered in the golden grain of the abbeys, had scattered White and Black and Gray and Brown friars, had presented Henry with the heaped booty of the sacred shrines, and now, planted to do battle, was prepared for an offensive in which he would employ the heavy metal of the parliament.

His liability was Anne of Cleves. It was his business to know that Henry found her distasteful and Henry himself was complaining to him in Lent that he could have no more children. "She begins to wax stubborn and wilful," was another ominous announcement. To this was added a new lamentation in spring. Henry's conscience was beginning to operate: he was haunted by a fear that, owing to Anne's pre-contract, she was not his lawful wife. "I have done as much to move the consent of my heart and mind as ever man did," he protested to Cromwell, "but the obstacle will not out of my mind."

The enormous danger of a collapse in this German marriage was all too plain to Cromwell. He had built everything on it, and on Henry's stability in it. But as the news could not be disguised that Germany was no asset, that the Pope was infinitely more concerned with disciplining Germany than England, that Charles had no intention of attacking England until he had first handled his Protestant Princes, and that Francis was as calming to Norfolk as James in Scotland was amicable with Sadler, Cromwell saw that the whole commitment was irksome and that he must now reckon with the excessive mobility and inconstancy of Henry's temperament. His German fortress was built on a bog. How to buttress it? What outworks or fieldworks possible? The supreme treachery of Henry's native substance, its viscous mass, its responses to pressures that were sometimes material, sometimes mental, never loyal or human, gave Cromwell that clang from the pit of the stomach which tells a man he must now brace himself and fight for his life.

XVI

Cromwell had plenty of brains and hardihood. He took the offensive. By an audacious move he had Barnes go to Paul's Cross, in front of the great Gothic cathedral, and deliver a scurrilous harangue against Gardiner. Gardiner, however, was no man to take this blow kneeling. He promptly and savagely hit back. Henry intervened. On Henry's orders and with Cromwell's assent, no doubt, Barnes ignominiously recanted, and in a few weeks was to go to the Tower. Cromwell's enemies on the council were hopeful of his downfall and gleefully informed the French ambassador that he was done. But the new parliament was his tool, and, though he had gleaned every penny from the abbeys, one fabulously wealthy institution remained—the Knights of St. John—and to expropriate them could placate Henry. A coup so brilliant restored Cromwell's ascendancy. He was immediately created Earl of Essex, which cost Henry nothing, and on the crest of this triumph he did not hesitate to compel the arrest of Sampson, Bishop of Chichester, close to Tunstall, who still held to the Old Learning, like a hen against a sunny wall.

Sampson's arrest was doubly daring because it was he who had joined with Cromwell to cook up the case against Anne Boleyn. Cromwell pursued him in spite of Henry's own recent pious manifestations, his communions, his two masses on feast days, his crawling on his knees on Good Friday. And five other bishops, Cromwell grimly declared, would follow him.

Sampson was in terror: he inculpated Tunstall. Cromwell's audacity was richly rewarded. He gave Sampson's rôle at St. Paul's to Cranmer.

But the hunt was up. If Sampson had papal leanings, Crom-

well's party had Lutheran leanings, and not all the hints from
Henry could keep them inside discretion. Gardiner and Norfolk
had not been idle in parliament. Their side had revived the debate on religious tenets, with Henry engaged. To the outsiders
it seemed that Cromwell was holding his own, with Lisle and
Wallop threatened, with Barnes and the other haranguers near
release. But those who knew Henry's unconquerable revulsion
from Anne, his native fear of the radicals, his old scar from
Luther, his fresh amorous life, and his ineradicable disdain for
the blunt commoner who sat with him as a knight of the Garter, could calculate that Cromwell's one escape would be by the
causeway which led from Anne of Cleves to a new Queen—a
Queen, as Norfolk could grin, who would do very little for
Thomas Cromwell.

XVII

In all this conflict from the middle of May to the beginning of
June, Henry had never gripped in. He was watching it with
the narrowed eye of a trader, knowing that whichever side was
cornered would have to sell its hides to him below the market
price.

On June seventh that rising young statesman, Wriothesley,
came home with Cromwell to Austin Friars. It was plainly his
mission to discuss the thing which troubled Cromwell, that the
King liked not the Queen, nor did ever like her. "Some way,"
suggested Wriothesley, "might be devised to relieve the King."

Cromwell pondered. "It is a great matter," he said. But he
tightened his lips and said no more. He had the suggestion to
offer the King's secretary.

The next day Wriothesley, who had once been Cromwell's
man, but who was now his own man, gave up hints and came
straight to the point. He asked my lord to "devise" some way for
the relief of the King, "for if he remained in this grief and
trouble they should all one day smart for it."

This was a *mot d'ordre*. The man who had got rid of Anne Boleyn must get rid of Anne of Cleves.

Cromwell nodded and nodded. It was all true. "But it is a great matter," he reiterated, "a big business."

"Marry, I grant," ejaculated Wriothesley impatiently, "but let the remedy be searched for."

"Well!" said Cromwell, and then brake off from him.

The remedy indeed! They were proposing to him to get rid of Anne in order to clear the path for Norfolk's niece. A sea of bitterness mounted to his writhen lips. Men who struggle in this sea load the air with curses. To be so strong, and yet to drown.

XVIII

That day Henry made his decision. He gave Wriothesley letters to draft in secret that declared Cromwell had been counter-working his aims for the settlement of religion.

Two days later, the tenth, the privy council met at Westminster to attend parliament. A gusty day, as they passed to the palace for dinner the wind blew off Cromwell's bonnet. Instead of doffing theirs, as was the custom, the others remained covered. The newly made Earl and Great Chamberlain scowled about him. "A high wind, indeed," he sneered, "to blow my bonnet off and keep all yours on."

During the dinner in common, this separation held. No one spoke to Cromwell. In a body he saw them leave for the council chamber, while he stayed behind in a window of the palace, to hear his petitioners. It was near three o'clock when he rejoined his colleagues.

He found them already around the table and as he chided, "You were in a great hurry, gentlemen, to begin," starting to take his seat, Norfolk called out in ringing tones, "Cromwell, do not sit there. Traitors do not sit with gentlemen!"

At the word "traitors" the big door opened: in marched the

captain of the guard, six halberdiers behind him. He strode to
Cromwell and took him by the arm.

Cromwell was on his feet. Casting his bonnet on the floor in
rage, he wheeled on Norfolk, his eyes blazing.

"This is the reward for my services!" he cried. "I am a traitor.
On your consciences, am I a traitor? I have never thought to
offend his Majesty, but since this is my treatment, I renounce all
pardon. I only ask the King not to make me languish long."

"Traitor! Traitor!" voices exulted.

"Be judged according to the laws you made." "A single word
is high treason."

Every man on his feet, the chorus yelped wildly at the fallen
minister. As the captain took him, old Norfolk, lithe as a cat,
snatched the order of St. George from his neck, his bitter mouth
reviling Cromwell's villainies, while Southampton, heavy and
choleric, tore away his Garter. At last he was rescued from the
council chamber and thrust by a back door that opened on the
water into a boat that awaited them. So, in black and heaving
silence, he was rowed to the Tower.

XIX

Henry's first care was to secure Cromwell's wealth. When fifty
archers came to Austin Friars in the evening, London suspected
that the minister had been overthrown. The inventory was
rapid. Only seven thousand pounds in sterling was in the house,
with plate (including crosses and chalices) of about the same
value. These movables were taken to Henry's treasury in the
night.

The curt procedure that Cromwell had himself so often applied made his death a certainty. This he knew. But no sooner
had his blood begun to cool and nature to take counsel with
itself, than his body seemed to cleave to life. The accusations of
treason that he had so often ratified, his bold eye racing down
the lines, his jaw firm and muscled, his hand ready with a signa-

ture, now ceased to be the hard machinery of a game of power and became instead the fangs and sinews of malevolence. This process with flat head and beady eye that now undulated toward him in the long and friendless night seemed infinitely venomous and infinitely personal. He was in coils so sleek, that the *virtu* of which Machiavelli had spoken to him fell from him like fancy dress, and he stood out of his borrowed robes naked as a foundling. Here he was within the walls where young Mark had shrieked, where Anne had spanned her throat, where Geoffrey Pole had tried to kill himself for shame. No one knew better than himself the pit into which he had fallen. But Cromwell was a man of simple clay. In the army of the imagination he was non-commissioned. Persons to him had meant nothing, status had meant everything, he had sent women to the fire and chuckled at dangling abbots and screaming friars, with no more pity for these creatures than the invincible Juggernaut which he had tended. But when he had passed one night in the Tower, one night away from his great engine, his hands empty, his head heavy, his habits broken, without a friend or a penny in the world, he was then ready to turn for mercy to his Juggernaut with a plea that was heart-wrung and servile.

Henry had invited him to excuse himself. Cromwell flung himself prostrate. If it were in my power, he quivered, to make you live forever, God knows I would; or to make you so rich that you should enrich all men, or so powerful that all the world should obey you. To me you have been most bountiful, more like a father than a master. I ask mercy where I have offended, but I have done my best, no one can justly accuse me of having done wrong willfully. I acknowledge myself a miserable sinner toward God and your Majesty, but never willfully. Desires prosperity for the King and Prince. "Written with the quaking hand and most sorrowful heart of your most sorrowful subject, and most humble servant and prisoner, this Saturday at your Tower of London."

To excuse oneself to Henry was to accuse oneself. Having let
Cromwell go to the Tower—"a very narrow place," as Marillac said, "from which no one escapes unless by a miracle," Henry
was incapable of reversing himself or of regurgitating Cromwell's wealth.

Two men owed much to Cromwell: one was Thomas Wyatt,
who would have helped him if he could. The other was Cranmer. But Cranmer was a weeping willow. He was amazed! He
was grief-stricken! "I loved him as a friend," he wrote to Henry,
"and the more for the love he seemed to bear your Grace. And
now, although glad that his treason is discovered, I am very
sorrowful, for whom shall the King trust hereafter?" It was as
Marillac shrewdly said of Cranmer, "who dare not open his
mouth."

But no one could have reversed the aspirant to Katheryn
Howard. Already he was feeding his indignation against the
man he had doomed, trying hard to believe that Cromwell had
planned to marry Princess Mary, lending himself to every story
from Norfolk and Gardiner, feeding his mind on phrases and
rumors, larding himself with appropriate prejudices. The indictment was sent to parliament, drafted with the usual class
rancor. "The most detestable traitor that has been seen during
the King's reign," though "raised from a very base and low degree by the King." Being "a person of as poor and low degree as
few be" within this realm, he had yet said publicly, "I am sure of
the King"—"and it is detestable that any subject should speak
so of his sovereign." He was a "detestable heretic," had dispersed
"books which tended to the discredit of the blessed sacrament of
the altar," and, in defense of Barnes's preaching, had held up
his dagger saying, "I trust if I live one year or two it shall not lie
in the King's power to resist or prevent it if he would." Bribery,
extortion, malversation—these were subordinate to his religious
offenses. He was to suffer as a heretic and a traitor. His death,

Norfolk told the French ambassador, would be the most ignominious in the realm.

When Francis heard the news, he thanked God. "Norfolk," said Francis, "will be able to remember what I said of it when he was last in France." No puishment could be too *"méchant"* for the evildoer. Montmorency, a devout Catholic, said it was a real miracle: God had inspired Henry.

The Emperor was not so fluent. "His Majesty, nothing moved therewith outwardly, only demanding, after his manner, "What! Is he in the Tower of London and by the King's commandment?" Such was the volubility of a slow player.

XX

But Henry had one further use for Cromwell. Now that the choice was no longer between Anne of Cleves and Katheryn Howard, but between death by the ax and death by half-hanging, evisceration, castration and torture, would Cromwell help Henry with his evidence in a case for divorce?

Cromwell had regained his hard sense. He said he would. Everything Henry wished him to testify, he testified in writing, in answer to specific questions but amplifying from day to day to please his master. At the end of this testimony, however, his heart could not refrain from bursting out, "Written at the Tower, this Wednesday, the last of June, with the heavy heart and trembling hand of your Highness's most heavy and most miserable prisoner and poor slave, Thomas Cromwell." And then, in a yelp of pure anguish, "Most gracious prince, I cry for mercy, mercy, mercy."

His cry was unheard. Henry's one aim was to detach himself from Anne of Cleves, and Cromwell's postscripts did not concern him.

A small committee of select men—Suffolk, Southampton and Wriothesley—paid a little call on Anne of Cleves shortly after

Cromwell's arrest. Henry had sent her to Richmond and failed to follow her.

When these trusty men entered, Anne of Cleves fainted. She thought her hour had come. Knowing her state of mind, they gently brought her to. They advised her that if she yielded gracefully she would be treated with consideration. She would become a pensioner and receive a certificate of honorable discharge, declaring that she was leaving Henry in the same state in which he had found her.

On this level, her position was strong, and Anne went down to it with perfect dignity and good sense. Divorce, by mutual consent, had no horror for her, relieving her from an intolerable strain. She had apparently no objection to Henry as a person, she in fact seemed rather to like him; and on one point she was almost distressingly clear, she infinitely preferred England to her own remote province. Perhaps the prospect of sitting at home at her mother's elbow, plying the needle, had lost a little of its virginal charm. In any event, only six months away from Cleves, and knowing the prying eyes she would return to, she was absolutely finished with it. At the prospect of remaining in England on favorable terms with the status of an ex-wife, Anne's spirits rose sky-high. She was not a romantic woman, and Henry had not aroused in her bosom any sentiments more exalted than those of self-preservation. But in a trying corner with a man of extremely dangerous instincts and proclivities she kept her head not only magnificently but literally. She did not propose to have her brother assault Henry and avenge her honor. So she wrote to him. She did not propose to have any one stir Henry up. To step aside for another woman did not agitate her. It was like leaving a hotel where her rooms were wanted, and where the proprietor was able to show there was a flaw in her lease. The terms of compensation, even, she did not discuss with any asperity or vulgarity. Slack-breasted she might be, which hurt her in the eyes of those who saw women as hackneys, but she was by no means slack in her judgment and intelligence. Her figure did not please Henry, but she had her own view of Henry's figure. She had seen his leg. He seemed to her at once a little comic and a little repulsive, and she separated from him with an alacrity that another man might have resented.

But Henry could not conceive that it would be a relief to Anne to get rid of him. The negotiations went through smoothly and pleasantly, with all the archbishops and bishops, both houses of convocation, working out a divorce on the ground that Henry had not given the marriage his hearty consent—excellent human doctrine, and good papal doctrine in the case of powerful and wealthy people. So serenely did it work, and so happy was Henry to have his own way without friction, that he gave Anne a most admirable settlement. She was to have four thousand pounds a year; two manors, Richmond and Blechingley, having splendid houses and great parks: hangings, plate and furniture, of course: the most exquisite clothes, jewels and pearls: and to be known in future as the King's sister, having precedence over all ladies in England, after the Queen and the King's children. It was hard on the taxpayers, but otherwise felicitous. Anne hardly knew herself. She was spied on, and her letters opened, but her skin was reasonably thick and she was engaged in no conspiracy. Marillac viewed her with a wrinkled nose, and wrote to his Constable within a few weeks, "As for her who is now called Madame de Cleves, far from pretending to be married, she is as joyous as ever, and wears new dresses every day; which argues either prudent dissimulation or stupid forgetfulness of what should so closely touch her heart."

Her brother's pride was touched. He received the news angrily. But he had not the power to do anything, and was he not Henry's brother now, instead of his brother-in-law?

At the first hint of the new divorce, Francis said, "Oh,

Jesus!" Hearing that parliament had petitioned for it, Francis exclaimed, "What, with the Queen that now is?" Then he fetched a great sigh and so spake no more.

Once the marriage was declared null by the bishops, and the separation confirmed by parliament, there remained nothing but to interrogate Cromwell on certain funds not accounted for. This disposed of, and Henry ready to go to the country for his honeymoon with his bride of eighteen, further delay was unnecessary.

XXI

Cromwell's end was prescribed for the morning of July 28th. Not fifty years old, powerfully built and sanguine, his execution would be like felling an oak in full leaf. He was taken from the Tower to Tyburn, on account of his low-class origin. Hundreds of his former servants and retainers thronged the cross, and a thousand halberdiers were on hand to keep order. His last words had been chosen in full awareness of the Catholic freshet under Norfolk and Gardiner, and he uttered select Catholic sentiments in a cold voice. But his self-possession, demoralized so long as he looked to Henry for mercy, was restored to him in the face of pitiless death. A Spaniard chronicled that as he beseeched the "good people" to pray for him, he noticed Wyatt among the gentlemen and said, "Oh, gentle Wyatt, good-by and pray to God for me." Wyatt could not answer him for tears and Cromwell, "who was a very clever man," quickly said out loud, "Oh, Wyatt, do not weep, for if I were not more guilty than thou wert, when they took thee, I should not be in this pass."

The English chroniclers declare that at the crucial moment the executioner (either drunk or nervous) was guilty of blundering. The Spaniard, however, notes no accident: the head leaped from the body with a single stroke of the ax.

BOOK SIX

Katheryn Howard

"The Rose without a Thorn"

HENRY VIII

I

CROMWELL went to death on July 28th, 1540. Though Henry had spoken angrily and contemptuously of him and had shut his ears to cries for mercy, his mind was too good not to see that there was no real guilt against himself: the thought of execution was disturbing. It was, of course, the outcome of circumstances which he himself had created and by which he had profited hugely. But moral bookkeeping was a tortuous task with Henry. While he had yielded to the death struggle between Cromwell and Norfolk, and now sidled away from the Protestants, he still nursed a hidden grudge against those to whom he was yielding. To please the Seymours, if nothing else, he kept Cromwell's son Gregory in fortune, and he retained his nephew Richard in his Privy Chamber. Thus, in his own heart, he disputed the capital sentence of which at the same time he proposed to enjoy the fruits.

One of these fruits was the new wedding. With his need for benumbing his nerves, Henry arranged it for the day that

Cromwell was to be beheaded. As that stout citizen, black brow and gray face, set out on the road from the Tower to Tyburn, an animal on the runway to the cleaver, his master Henry was at Oatlands, a private mansion not twenty miles away, to be united to his fresh young bride.

The rose without a thorn—that was the tribute Henry had inscribed on one of the countless jewels he gave to Katheryn. And as he gazed at his new choice, his eyes revealed that this was a union unlike the others. Catherine of Aragon had been the serious matron whom he perforce respected: Elizabeth Blount had been a ripe young goddess who submitted to him: Anne had been hard ambitiousness: Jane had been the perfect demure consort. There had been other affairs, like Mary Boleyn, casual and capricious. But this new choice was unreserved. "The King's Highness did cast a fantasy to Katheryn Howard the first time that ever his Grace saw her." And all he had heard of her—from her grandmother the old Duchess, from her companions, from Lord William Howard—made him value the "jewel for womanhood" he had luckily lighted on. He had himself chosen her device, "No other will but his," and this possessiveness beamed from him. He was like a collector who has brought home a treasure in faïence, not the most precious material but the gayest and the most vivid. "He is so amorous of her he cannot treat her well enough." He could not, in public or in private, keep his hands off his acquisition. "More than he did the others," he affectionately caressed her.

The object of these caresses was physically the rose without thorns which Henry desired. She was very small and well-rounded with a delightful open expression, vivacious, graceful, quick to dance, giddy, gay, imperious. She had dressed herself and her ladies in the French style, and her hazel eyes and auburn hair gave her the coquettish brightness that enchanted and elated her royal husband.

But she was scarcely the delightful toy that Henry surmised.

Six years younger than his daughter Mary, she touched in him the vibrant double chord of lover and protector: he saw her in his own amplitude and her submissive inexperience. But she could hardly be expected to share this glamorous autumnal haze. A rose though she was to him, she was far more like a plump and fleet young doe who turns on a rich pasture her vernal eyes. She could respect this corpulent personage, but he was less a fellow-being than a glorious circumstance that had endowed and enveloped her. She could not really think of her magnate as that marvelous creature, a man.

Katheryn was a juvenile delinquent. Though she had not been exposed, like her cousin, Anne Boleyn, to the licentious influences of the French, she had contrived without them to travel rather fast at home. In the great establishment over which the wealthy old Duchess of Norfolk presided there were enough girls to constitute a boarding-school, but it was a boarding-school of full-blooded and high-spirited youngsters with no religious training, no lessons, no mental interests, no discipline. When the old lady was safely in bed in the evening, the girls' dormitory (the gentlewomen's chamber, as they called it) was artfully opened by a key that Katheryn had stolen, and into her own chamber came "the light young men." These were favored kinsmen or poor relations, attached to this establishment as pages or gentlemen. The general level, naturally, was set by the older couple or two whose presence was buzzed among the dozing gentlewomen. The ducal youths brought delicacies with them from the table. They had exciting midnight suppers, and as the nights lengthened into indolence and luxuriant silence the young men lay on the beds with the girls and their attendants, in the medley of an emotional hot-house. It was what older people call "dangerous" but for warm and amorous young people with no idea in life but their adventure, it must have been throbbing and wildly pleasant. An immense amount of love-making, bickering, whispering, gift-giving, promising and reproaching went on in these covert visits to the dormitory while the old Duchess snored gently upstairs, possibly dreaming about her stepson Thomas and his similar behavior with the laundress Bess Holland.

Romance was in the air. Margaret Douglas's affair with young Howard was romantic. So was Anne Boleyn's with Thomas Wyatt. So was young Surrey's with Geraldine. It was the age of a dethroned Pope and the Heptameron. The effect on Katheryn, who was strong and adventurous but neglected and illiterate, was to plunge her into love at thirteen. It had begun before these parties. A young man, Manox, was appointed with another youth to teach her the spinet; the radiant little girl enamored him and he managed to see her alone and caress her. The Duchess came on them: she gave Katheryn a blow and drove away her teacher. Soon this first affair went out of the girl's mind with the advent of Francis Derham, a young gentleman "of a poor house" related to the Norfolks. He was one of the leading spirits in the midnight parties. He began by lying on bed with a chaperoned Katheryn, in his doublet and hose, but he and Katheryn soon fell in love. From hose and doublet between sheets to the naked bed was a certain transition. Their affair stretched from fourteen or fifteen to eighteen, a rainbow of delight. They excused their hot pulses by talking of marriage and they were intimate in the huddled and feverish fashion of rather promiscuous, desperately serious, highly lascivious and intensely passionate youth.

Manox was a cad, however, and his failure with Katheryn induced him to concoct a letter to the Duchess, which he piously laid in her pew. It advised her to swoop down on the dormitory, late at night. Acting on this advice, she did storm the gentlewomen's chamber and discovered the group gorging on dainties. She later found Katheryn and Derham "in arms kissing." To aim a blow at Derham, to strike at the girl, to hit Joan

Bulmer who was standing by, and to show how offended she felt, seemed the limit of the Duchess's resources as a mother superior. Lord William was more furious with Manox than with his niece. He gave the knave a piece of his mind, while the tittle-tattle he ignored. "What mad wenches! Can you not be merry among yourselves but you must then fall out?" He did not believe because Derham "used to haunt her chamber nightly" that the misrule was tragic. The old lady's sole weapon was the testy grumble of a toothless dowager. "I warrant you if you seek him in Katheryn Howard's chamber ye shall find him there." When, on Henry's suddenly favoring the girl, who seemed charged with mischief and vivacity, young Derham cleared out to Ireland, to try his hand at piracy, the old lady shook her head; and when he returned she half-approvingly pointed him out, "This is he that ran into Ireland for the Queen's sake."

But the young pirate's hold, by that time, had been broken. Shortly before Katheryn was appropriated by Henry, she had gone from the Duchess at Lambeth to reside at court where she dashed into place among the brilliant waterflies. The girl's own mother had been Jocosa Culpeper of Kent, and one of Henry's brightest favorites was a youth called Thomas Culpeper. It was Thomas who looked after Henry's leg, perhaps, to see that the physician's orders were carried out. He had slept in Henry's huge bed from a boy, upheaved his master in the morning, amused and undertook commissions for him, and was one of the most privileged gentlemen of the Privy Chamber. Henry heaped him with stewardships and sinecures and tossed him an abbey, which indicates that the young dandy had made himself agreeable. One extremely ugly story was hinted, but Katheryn Howard did not see a ruffian in Culpeper. She saw a man of her own people, her own age, her own inclination. When she was waiting on Anne of Cleves or Princess Mary, she had

made up her mind, quite frankly, to "try him." Her marriage to
Henry brought her higher and yet nearer to Henry's *"compagnon de lit."*

On the edge of Henry's vision, there may have been a flicker
of all these "doings." But he had sought guaranties that Katheryn was as good as she was beautiful: the Howards warmly
assured him that she was irreproachable. She was reputed for all
the freshness that a man of Henry's age would relish. They
"commended her pure and honest conditions." And the old
Duchess who had ridden with Anne Boleyn at her coronation,
comforted herself by mumbling of Katheryn, "She cannot die
for what was done before!"

The girl herself, pursued around and through the flame, had
singed her wings, but she was of sweet and abundant nature, of
invigorating temper, and of the impulse unusual among the
Howards to give herself rather than to acquire. The love of joy
was in her. The past, however, is hard to shed in a blackmailing
world. Joan Bulmer had not hesitated, with demure but meaningful insistence, to ask that she should be brought to court.
Young Derham soon came back from ravishing the Irish coast,
and, warned by Katheryn to "take heed what words you speak,"
was made a swaggering usher of the chamber to the Queen.
Meanwhile the whole Howard family, her two young brothers
and her two young sisters, went up in fortune and favor. Katheryn could hail the row of them from the royal box, and give
them the reversion of bounty, and buoy up the whole young
indigent tribe. Henry had to repress her a little. But this profusion of her destiny she seems to have longed to share, and her
impulses were generous not merely for the young Howards and
the Bayntons and the Arundels. She passed on things Henry
gave her—dogs, jewels, odd things—to such recipients as Anne
of Cleves. Henry watched this exuberance with the internal
groan of a man who has become abstemious in these matters. But
she even had it in her heart to ameliorate the human havoc

that he caused through his vindictiveness. She was sensual in the grand English pre-Puritan sense—"endowed with feeling."

Rather the contrary, that is to say, of Henry himself, whose liberality of feeling gave credit with the open hand, and retained the art of legal seizure in the other fist. At forty-nine, as Holbein has preserved him in the superb portrait at Rome, Katheryn's bridegroom was a solid Magnifico. Though he shuffled to the altar, obliged as a rule to help himself with a long stave on account of his leg, he presented himself before Bishop Gardiner not as an inert or sagging mass but as a pyramid of defensiveness. There was in the eyes that living twinkle, half-humorous and half-malicious, which may be as kind as dew or as cruel as broken glass. With ears laid back, fists doubled, feet widely splayed, the shoulders built out with velvet and the stomach at anchor, this was a ponderable man, square and imperturbable—until one viewed the face which gave his firmness the impressive mobility that a swiveling gun confers on a bastion. Through long years he had learned to plant himself in his own sort of genial island independence, and, with one eye wide open and the left narrowed, he looked at once crafty and debonair. But this free and good disposition which diffused itself from the unembarrassed Henry was not unlike the insouciance of his feathered bonnet: he could whip it off in an instant, and there, hard and bald, was the high skull, the convergence of all his smooth and receding policies on that one point, the apex of a pyramidal egoism. It was a strange climax for a nation's policy based on great lines of loyalty and obedience.

II

Henry's vigilance for the future was social and political. He had not forgotten Anne of Cleves in his new wedding, and he promptly invited her to join the Queen and himself at supper. Anne came palpitating to Hampton Court, where now, as later, she was received by her young successor with the "utmost kindness." She tried to kneel, but Katheryn would not have it. And Henry, who bowed to her and kissed her, used the occasion to file away every existing claim and polish off Anne's final renunciations.

If Anne was only too eager to buy peace, having her own life to lead, the King found others who contested his will, on the score of religion. Here he became stern. He had seriously considered what, in the way of religious opinion, would be just and proper all around, and he accordingly enacted the right opinion in parliament. Every subsequent retort and disagreement he regarded not as an attack on himself but as an attack on what is just and proper: and it was easy for him to sign death warrants on such high principle. So two days after Cromwell's execution six "doctors" were executed—three hanged, and three lashed to one stake and burnt to death.

"It was wonderful," said Marillac, "to see adherents to the two opposing parties dying at the same time, and it gave offense to both. And it was no less strange to hear than horrible to see, for the obstinancy and constancy respectively of both parties, and the perversion of justice of which both parties complained, in that they had never been called to judgment, nor knew why they were condemned. . . ."

This was a Catholic who poured out an astonishing letter to his King on the essential injustice of these executions. The Protestant, Hilles, wrote to Bullinger in the same strain. They were not justly condemned, he said. "But, to say the truth, people did not inquire much, as it is no new thing to see men hanged, quartered, or beheaded, for one thing or another, sometimes for trifling expressions construed as against the King."

"The papist Abel" was one of these victims. He had been locked up years before for denouncing Catherine of Aragon's divorce, and was "almost eaten up by vermin in a filthy prison." Another who suffered was Dr. Barnes, whom Henry had employed as envoy when cultivating the Lutherans but who had since had the temerity to attack Gardiner. These were the last executions for the moment as Henry was flying the plague and had inaugurated group executions out of his new habit of spring-cleaning the Tower.

It was a habit that revolted Katheryn Howard. With the audacity of her youth, she set herself against her husband's killings. But Luther gave no hope of his contemporary in the pamphlet that he devoted to his friend Barnes.

"Das juncker Heintze wil Gott sein und thun was in gelüstet." "Squire Harry wishes to be God," he diagnosed the disease, "and to do whatever he pleases."

III

But it was in amiable egoism that Henry enjoyed Katheryn Howard. He renewed his youth and set him on the strait and narrow path to beauty. The autumn of 1540 saw him again in the saddle. As three hundred a week were dying of the plague in London, he betook himself with his consort to the country. Though it was believed that he had waxen fat, had become "much more corpulent," he saw no reason for ceding to the enemy: with that readiness to dispute sovereignty even in his own flesh, he was bravely determined to give Holbein the lie.

"This King," Marillac said by December, "has taken a new rule of living. To rise between five and six, hear mass at seven, and then ride till dinner time which is at ten A.M. He says he feels much better thus in the country than when he resided all winter at his houses at the gates of London."

At Woking he was all day in the fields with his hawks; for months nothing had been spoken of "but the chase and banquets to the new Queen." Such a round of gayety brought with it an irruption of high spirits so that commands had to be given "for sober and temperate order in the chamber of presence." But while the Princess Mary held aloof from one whose coming had meant Cromwell's downfall, and while Katheryn was offended because "Mary did not treat her with the same respect as her two predecessors," the New Year brought a chance for conciliatory gifts; and no one could deny that Katheryn had "completely acquired" her husband's mellowing favor.

This was the more flowing because he had sent Gardiner and a hundred gentlemen—"all in grey with great gold chains on their necks"—abroad to woo the Emperor. That melancholy widower was supposedly in the market for a bride and much was being done "to move the Emperor to marry Mary." Toward the French, Henry gradually cooled off. These people "are weary of peace," sneered young Marillac, "and would irritate mankind in order that they may not have a single friend at need." They were preparing, at any rate, for the inevitable breach between Charles and Francis by fortifying Calais and bracing the Scottish border. It was the return to the old policy that Cromwell had combated. Cranmer, in aphelion, did not oppose Henry; rather he chided his German uncle-in-law for the sins of Lutheranism—allowing princes to have concubines and approving of usury and, the bitter pill, permitting the bigamy of Hesse. These signs were not lost on the French, but the French merely re-enforced their smiles. Marguerite kept asking Henry for his picture: she and Francis sent him pasties of wild boar, which had been made and seasoned and "sayed" under their own very eyes.

IV

Weak as water, Cranmer had water's power of insinuating itself and its gift of transmitting force. Where Cromwell had offered a solid front that Gardiner could smash, Cranmer divided and yielded with a surface that could only quiver and tremble obsequiously. But his commotion never really changed him: he always returned unruffled to the political and theological persuasions that his intelligence cupped and retained. Henry felt this consistency in him and had a sneaking admiration for him.

The archbishop was always ready to see a whale when his master said, "Methinks it is a whale." The Real Presence, celibacy, three, five or seven sacraments, carnal concupiscence, precontract, treason—Cranmer could see any or all of them when Henry affirmed them in the right voice. But whether he agreed or faintly demurred on the immediate proposition, the Primate mutely kept the purpose of a national church before him, and by ways as sinuous as they were elastic and buoyant, he nibbled toward his destined end.

This purpose Katheryn did not promote, and as she was an obstacle to the national church, like all Howards, Cranmer could not accept her. Her uncle Norfolk's views on the Word of God were terse. "I never read the scripture," he said with finality, "nor never will read it: it was merry in England afore the new learning came up: yea, I would all things were as hath been in times past." Cranmer, who heard these syllables as a pent-up scheme of irrigation might hear its dam quaking at the base, could afford to say nothing at the moment. For the moment he flowed round Katheryn with the sibilance and undulation of his nature. So long as she might supply Henry with an heir, he could not antagonize her. But Cranmer was a supple adversary whom any young woman of nineteen might well have dreaded. At present, however, he was as meek as the sea in moonlight purring as its little white paws are fribbling at the shore.

V

The reactionaries were busy undoing Cromwell's work. The new year, 1541, soon saw the arrest of Wallop the ambassador to France, Thomas Wyatt the ambassador to Spain, Sadler the ambassador to Scotland, and various other gentlemen tinged with anti-papistry. These opinions Thomas Wyatt had the audacity to defend, and Katheryn had the valiancy to plead for him. Her simple impulse to send warm garments to the old

Countess of Salisbury in the Tower was not nearly so impolitic as her advocacy of Wyatt. But in this instance, her fascination for Henry counted in an emergency. She won as against her own promoters. It was helped, of course, by Wyatt's and by Catholic eruptions in the North. The dehorsed ambassador had gone to the Tower in the utter ignominy that the Bishop of London, Bonner, had wished for him: hands bound like a criminal, for all his "visage stern and mild." But Thomas Wyatt was one of those tameless Englishmen whose tongues are nakedly and dangerously truthful when unsheathed. His defense was outspoken, even in regard to Henry, though it showed a sort of soldierly loyalty. At bay at the moment when Katheryn was sweeping to Greenwich by the Thames, meeting a splendid re- ception from the people and the Tower guns saluting, she had the spirit to try a "great intercession" for Wallop and Wyatt. "At the great suit of the Queen," it was written by the Privy Council to her uncle at Paris, the King yielded where he had angrily resisted Catherine on Buckingham and Jane Seymour on the Pilgrims. It was almost the only case in his whole career where he felt strong enough to be weak—that is to say, merci- ful.

He pardoned, though on condition that Wyatt confess his "guilt" and take back his wife—the sister of a lady whom Henry much admired. Wyatt, who "quick could never rest," did not stand on formality. He escaped the block, to the surprise of every one, even if the "hammers that beat in that lively brain" and the still quicker hammers that beat in that lively heart were to be stilled by natural death the following year.

The mood of mercy, however, came for Henry in his own re- action against Gardiner's failure with the Emperor. The world was betraying his mellow mood. In spite of his big expenses for defense, his ramparts at Dover, Portsmouth and Southampton had just crumbled. In spite of his big efforts to become shapely the banquets had undone the early rising, the fistula had closed alarmingly and "he is very stout and marvelously excessive in drinking and eating, so that people with credit say he is often of a different opinion in the morning than after dinner." In spite of his dream of making a son, Katheryn was not yet pregnant. It was an unkind world. He mirrored it by his own sourness. He spent Shrovetide "without recreation, even of music." He stayed in Hampton Court "more a private family than a King's train." He abused his people, saying "he had an unhappy people to govern whom he would shortly make so poor that they would not have the boldness nor the power to oppose him." He abused his Privy Council that, "under pretence of serving him, were only temporizing for their own profit, but he knew the good servants from the flatterers, and, if God lent him health, he would take care that their projects should not succeed." He abused, finally, those who had devised Cromwell's death. "On light pretexts," he violently asserted, "by false accusations, they made me put to death the most faithful servant I ever had!"

This was the fitful volcano that Katheryn had to live on. But while she soothed him with whatever endearments are suitable to a King who has a fistula and who is marvelous excessive in drinking and eating, calling him her wolf or her little pig or whatever, her own inmost mind was busy for other reasons with the approaching royal progress to the North.

VI

After long delays through June and the almost treasonable behavior of the weather, it was at last deemed possible for Henry and the Queen to proceed to the North. It was five years since Lincolnshire and Yorkshire had revolted. Norfolk and Suffolk, rusty perennials, took command of the immense and impressive cortège with which Henry was going to receive the penitential welcome of his subjects. The company numbered four thou-

sand to five thousand, and in case the penance should falter, it
included war-horses and artillery. Henry had invited his
nephew, the King of Scotland, to come to him at York. This
was the underlying object of his progress. But, before he left, to
remind the papal cardinals of his power, Reginald Pole's
mother (aged seventy) was beheaded, as well as Leonard Gray,
five years deputy in Ireland. Young Lord Dacres was also
hanged for the murder of a game-keeper; his property, as the
Council said, "will be very profitable to the King."

As the journey went forward, with every sign of public
loyalty and devotion, an extraordinary little drama of private
disloyalty was being enacted under Henry's unseeing eyes.

Katheryn had taken into her service Lady Rochford, the disillusioned widow of George Boleyn. This woman had played a
dubious part in her husband's affairs, but had managed to crawl
back into the court circle, and was now at the young Queen's
elbow. A year of the royal marriage had elapsed. There was no
heir, and no sign of an heir. And if Lady Rochford's connivance had never been employed with Katheryn's cousin Anne,
it was now certainly proffered for Katheryn. She was in love
with Culpeper. Lady Rochford, either out of the wish to gratify
her mistress, or else out of a natural aptitude for acting as a
procuress, began to make it possible for the two young people
to be together, sometimes with Culpeper poised at the head of
the back stairs, ready to spring downward; sometimes with
Katheryn and himself together in her chamber; and once with
the two of them for a whole evening hidden in a "vile place" that
heard the young woman reveal her loneliness for him, her exigence for him, her eagerness to compromise herself, and the accursed spite of Queens.

The young courtier was not instantly persuaded, but he was
in love with Katheryn: these were extremely tense and brittle
interviews.

"Jesus! Is not the Queen abed yet?" asked Katherine Tilney,

a gentlewoman who had been with her mistress in the Derham days. This was at Lincoln, at two in the morning.

Marget Morton, who had been waiting up, answered, "Yes, even now." The rendezvous had terminated at two.

Katheryn seemed to think that a love affair was "secret" if it were not deliberately announced at Paul's Cross. At Greenwich, at Lincoln, at Pomfret, at York, her "secret" interviews were contrived, with half a dozen of her women discussing them, and "in every house seeking for the back doors and back stairs herself." She was still the young girl fooling the old Duchess, but she seriously admonished Culpeper when he went to confession not to "shrive him of any such things as should pass betwixt her and him: for, if he did, surely, the King being supreme Head of the Church, should have knowledge of it."

"No, Madam, I warrant you," laughed the young cavalier.

Lady Rochford, who, with the Queen, let him in the back door, had learned nothing from her experience before, and "provoked him much to love the Queen."

Master Culpeper was no cyclone. But Katheryn knew her mind and she did not fear to scribble him a note, one of those tremendous Alpine struggles with the pen that are possible only to illiterate people who are climbing to their star.

"Master Culpeper," she wrote to him in August, "I heartily recommend me unto you, praying you to send me word how that you do.

"I did hear that ye were sick and I never longed for anything so much as to see you.

"It maketh my heart to die when I do think that I cannot always be in your company.

"Come to me when Lady Rochford be here for then I shall be best at leisure to be at your commandment.

"I do thank you that you have promised to be good to that poor fellow, my man, for when he is gone there be none I dare trust to send to you. I pray you to gyve me a horse for my man, for I have muche ado to get one, and therefore I pray send me one by him: and in so doing I am as I said afore; and thus I take my leave of you, trusting to see you shortly again.

"And I would you were with me now that you moutte se what pane [might see what pain] I take in writing to you.

"Yours as long as life endures.   "KATHERYN.

"One thing I had forgotten, and that is to speak to my man. Entreat my man to tarry here with me still, for he says whatsoever you behyw [order] he will do it."

It was a great effort: she might truly ask him to see what pain it cost her.

And while Culpeper folded away these simple lines, the King was busy with sport, helping to kill two hundred stags and does, "as near as if they had been domestic cattle," or seeing his arbalists taking in two boat-loads of dead swans. He and the Queen were busy receiving public homage, the Archbishop of York kneeling in penance for the insurrection of 1536 and Robert Constable, still in chains over the gate at Hull, where Norfolk had hoisted him, grinning a sardonic welcome to Henry and Katheryn.

VII

They were to be home by the end of October. But before they arrived Cranmer had been visited by a man called John Lassells. This was an underling at the Court, a stanch Protestant, who had never accepted the downfall of Cromwell, "so noble a man which did love and favor" God's holy word. Lassells was an early example of the stern and sincere Puritan. A year before, September, 1540, he had recited Norfolk's words about the Scriptures. "Let them alone and suffer a little time," he had darkly foreboded, "they will overthrow themselves!" But in the meantime, he had come upon a revelation that he imparted to Cranmer. He had been conversing with his sister Mary, who

had been a nurse with the old Duchess during the Derham period.

"Why not sue for service with the Queen?" quoth John Lassells.

"I will not," Mary answered, "but I am very sorry for the
Queen."

"Why?" quoth John.

"Mary," quoth she, "for she is light, both in living and conditions [behavior]."

"How so?"

Mary then revealed to her stalwart brother that one Francis Derham had lain in bed with Katheryn between the sheets
an hundred nights, and moreover one Manox knew a private
mark on her body.

John Lassells, Cranmer said, came of himself to him, and he
"being much perplexed," consulted Audley and Jane Seymour's brother, Hertford. The three men, anti-Gardiner and
pro-Cromwell, were of one mind. That Manox knew a privy
mark on the Queen's body, and that Francis Derham had slept
with her, was clearly something of which Katheryn's husband
ought to be apprised. And Cranmer, being an Archbishop, was
the man to do it.

VIII

The royal couple did not know what sort of reception Cranmer
had waiting for them. They arrived South at the end of October, happy to be home. But on reaching Hampton Court the
childlike eagerness of home-coming was soon disturbed. Henry's
sister Margaret was dead intestate: trouble. His boy Edward,
fat and unhealthy, had a fever: anxiety. And then Cranmer
drew near him "sorrowfully" during mass on All Souls' Day and
handed him a paper.

The day before the King had been felicitating himself on

Katheryn. After receiving his Maker, he had directed his ghostly father to make prayer and give thanks with him for "the good life he led" and hoped to lead with her. She was indeed the rose without a thorn.

Then he perused the story that soft Cranmer "had not the heart to tell him by mouth."

He read it, scanned it, turned it over. His first feeling was that of a man who had accepted some one unquestioningly. He had never in his life been less suspicious or more genial, and he felt it must be a forgery. Incredulous, he sent for the Archbishop. Cranmer stood firm. Henry began to be a little troubled. Three or four days he spent with the councilors he could trust, directing them to find Derham and Manox, Lassells and his sister, and make prudent inquiries. He wanted neither a break nor a scandal. The Queen, meanwhile, was told to stay in her chamber: and her musicians were sent off, saying, "that it is no more the time to dance."

On November fifth, about midnight, Henry sat in with the taciturn Southampton, the clear and frosty Russell, obedient Anthony Browne, and the resourceful Wriothesley. On Sunday morning Norfolk came out: he had been questioned at Exeter Place so as not to bring Henry the plague. He and Audley met the King at Hampton Court and dined "at a little place in the fields." That night Henry hurried secretly to London. The Council assembled at midnight and did not disperse till four or five A.M. All of them, even the grim Norfolk, now betrayed the heavy trouble that was brewing. The confessions were soon arriving. Lassells' sister Mary was crushed like quartz by Southampton: Manox, mentioned by Mary, was taken to Lambeth and peeled by Cranmer and Wriothesley. Derham was arrested, ostensibly for piracy, and taken to the Tower. Wriothesley handled him. Marget Morton fell to Anthony Browne. And Cranmer, Norfolk, Audley, Sussex, and Bishop Gardiner were deputed to undertake Queen Katheryn.

Everything, so far, related to what would later be called her "abominable, base, carnal, voluptuous and vicious life" before she met Henry and before she "led him by word and gesture to love him" and "arrogantly coupled herself with him in marriage." Henry's own pure life, and his own part in the coupling, which every one believed to have antedated the marriage, were not in question. It was not he who had tainted her blood but she who had "tainted the royal blood." It was not he who, by his scruples and his caprices and his political maneuvers, had sapped the foundations of marriage: it was she who was criminal. Light himself, but stern for others, Henry watched and waited.

Cranmer had been preceded by Norfolk in catechizing the Queen, and as the uncle had got nothing the Primate had purposed to begin by dilating on her demerits, then declaring the justice of the laws, and, lastly, signifying the King's mercy, to extract her confession. But this was unnecessary. Some word, some gesture, suddenly brought home to the young woman, not yet twenty, the catastrophe into which she had plunged herself. "Her state it would have pitied any man's heart to see," reported Cranmer. She was so in anguish that "for fear she would enter into a frenzy," Cranmer began straight off with the promise of mercy: and "this sudden mercy," meeting the conscience that was already coming out to surrender, completely broke her down. She launched on her confession, her life before marriage. The scene prolonged itself into twilight and after. The Angelus came to their ears from the chapel to her chamber at Hampton, with the graven face of the Archbishop emerging from the laden shade by candlelight. The girl fell into another "pange," "Oh," she cried, "about this time Master Hennage was wont to bring me knowledge of his Grace."

Cranmer had no clew to Culpeper. He did not touch at all on her married life. His one thought was to see if divorce could be grounded on a contract with Derham. There was no contract, Katheryn said, but she admitted carnal knowledge. Cranmer heard the sobbing admission. He wrote it all down and she put her hand to it. Then the grave and reverend Primate departed.

Her own sister was married to Edward Baynton, who was in attendance on her. When she divulged to the Bayntons what had just happened, they saw better than she the ruin before her. A message followed to Cranmer saying that what Derham had done was by force.

IX

The story, so far, was one of Manox and Derham. When Wriothesley came from the Tower to the council, to piece Cranmer's document with his own, there could be no shadow of doubt that Lassells' sister had been absolutely justified. Derham had confessed that he had known Katheryn as she had described.

The King had chosen his young bride for personal reasons. He heard this revelation not as a man of power, in whom the passion of power and the apprehensiveness of power were uppermost. He heard it as a very simple human being.

A deep silence came on the council as the disclosure of Katheryn's blemish was made, a blemish that could never be hidden and that secretly pleased every one who had seen a target in her temperament.

It was a long time before Henry could utter his sorrow. He sat there, feeling old, his heart "pierced with pensiveness." Then he began to cry. It must have moved every one. "And finally, with plenty of tears, which was strange in his courage," he opened the heart that had been wounded.

X

This was the indulgent Henry that Katheryn had known. And had she been behaving properly during her marriage, she might have escaped being sent to a nunnery for life. But the past treads on the present. Lassells' sister had cited the chamberer Tilney at the Duchess's. Tilney was hunted up and she mentioned Marget Morton: Morton named Culpeper.

"I never mistrusted the Queen," exclaimed this woman, "until at Hatfield I saw her look out of her chamber window on Master Culpeper after such sort that I thought there was love between them."

This was the thing Katheryn had feared, but not for herself. Before she could warn Culpeper to save himself, he was caught and sent to the Tower.

As the council reported the scandal in a graphic letter November 11th, to Paget at Paris, they wound up significantly, "Now you may see what was done before marriage. God knoweth what hath been done since."

XI

Norfolk's thin lips curled bitterly. He first told Marillac that his niece had "prostituted herself to seven or eight persons." This was out of his imagination. Later he said that only Derham was clearly proved. He told Marillac of Katheryn's state. She "refuses to drink or eat and weeps and cries like a madwoman, so that they must take away things by which she might hasten her death."

Her uncle felt no pity for her but the deepest pity for Henry. He spoke with tears in his eyes of the King's grief, who loved her much, and of the misfortune to his own house in her and Anne Boleyn. Henry was so grieved, he said, that he proposed never to take another wife.

But even the Culpeper disclosure did not turn Henry against Katheryn. He did not see her again, but his heart was not hard. He bowed to the catastrophe and Chapuys learned about this time, November 19th, from sober Southampton that Henry "would show more patience and mercy than many might think—more even than her own relations wished, meaning Norfolk, who said, God knows why, that he wished the Queen was burned." She was, however, sent from Hampton Court to be shut up in Syon, "a late nunnery near Richmond," guarded by four women and some men. And Henry was to go for five or six days to the country "to relieve his mind."

Chapuys, whose asperity had not been softened by years and who incidentally suggested to Charles that when Anne of Cleves had a drop taken she was not so different from Katheryn, admitted Henry's grief. "This King has wonderfully felt the case of the Queen, his wife," the old sinner said, "and has certainly shown greater sorrows at her loss than at the faults, loss, or divorce of his preceding wives. It is like the case of the woman who cried more bitterly at the loss of her tenth husband than at the deaths of all the others together, though they had all been good men, but it was because she had never buried one of them before without being sure of the next; and as yet this King has formed neither a plan nor a preference."

XII

With the two young men in the Tower and Katheryn at Syon, there was no chance for her to warn Culpeper. The ministers continued their invaluable police work. The girl's past had been scavenged in every "foul detail," as Marillac put it, and it did not lose in official narration. A dozen servants had been examined. The Lord Privy Seal was told to "pick out from Wilkes" anything that might trip up Lord William Howard. Wriothesley wrote with zest to Sadler, "My woman Tilney hath done us good service." And he triumphantly learned that Derham had once said, "An the King were dead I am sure I might marry her." This was volunteered by another youth. "And no torture," exclaimed the minister, "could make him confess this before."

The extraordinary eagerness to hunt down every bit of evidence was due to the fearful and exciting possibilities of treason and conspiracy. The old Duchess of Norfolk had not only hidden her money-bags, fearing Henry's avidity, but had broken into Derham's coffers and destroyed ballads and letters. This raised the ogre: she, her son, her daughter, and nine servants were quickly rounded up. The divided council were watching Henry as two sides watched a football and they intended to be thorough.

Derham and Culpeper went to trial on December 1st, before a special commission at Guildhall. Katheryn's young brothers and Culpeper's relations thought it better to show their indifference by riding about London, while Norfolk, one of the judges, took it on himself, during the trial, to laugh and jeer. Katheryn's signed deposition was read, pleas of "Not guilty" were soon changed to "Guilty." The story had no new aspect. Derham admitted complete intimacy, justifying it as an engagement. He was sentenced to death at Tyburn, to be hanged, cut down alive, split open, his bowels burnt, and finally killed by beheading. This terrific sentence was also passed on Culpeper.

"Gentlemen," he pleaded, "do not seek to know more than that the King deprived me of the thing I love best in the world, and, though you may hang me for it, she loves me as well as I love her, though up to this hour no wrong has ever passed between us. Before the King married her, I thought to make her my wife; and when I saw her lost to me, I was like to die, as you all know how ill I was. The Queen saw my sorrow and showed me favor, and when I saw it, tempted by the devil, I dared one day while dancing to give her a letter, and received a reply from her in two days, telling me she would find a way to comply with my wish. I know nothing more, my lords, on my honor as a gentleman."

Norfolk's sneer showed how he felt.

"You have said quite enough, Culpeper," Hertford commented, "to lose your head."

Ten days of renewed cross-examination followed the death sentence; but no further admissions could be had from them. Derham begged that the extremity of his judgment should be remitted but "the King thinks he has deserved no such mercy." The council, however, sent word that Culpeper was "only to lose his head."

On December 10th, the two young men suffered at Tyburn as decreed.

Till the trials were completed Henry was calm, but as the council strummed on his nerves day by day, each bit of evidence being submitted to him, he suddenly burst out before them into such a storm of grief and rage, calling for a sword to slay Katheryn, that they gripped their chairs and thought he had gone mad.

"That wicked woman!" he cried, his face tumid with hate and his eyes boiling. "She never had such delight in her lovers as she shall have torture in her death!"

These expressions exploded from him in the middle of a conference. All of a sudden he broke down and began to cry. She was to have been the wife of his old days. His ill-luck in meeting with such ill-conditioned wives was the thing with which he upbraided his ministers. "I blame my council for this mischief!" In a paroxysm he started up and called for horses. No one knew where he would go.

But where would he go? England is an island. His council were willing to do anything, to pass any law, to invent any device, that might protect their master from "the lightness in a woman" which Francis had just written to deplore. To see him ride away in this wild fashion alarmed them: they did their best to make him forget his grief. But he insisted on escaping. "He is gone twenty-five miles from here," reported Marillac, "with no company but musicians and ministers of pastime."

The master's departure did not mean, however, that he had lost touch with his council. He had received a sharp lesson from the public when he committed Anne Boleyn to a criminal death. This time he showed the most masterly comprehension of the art of preparing public opinion. He himself superintended every single detail of the case against Katheryn. The young men were tried in full public. Grand juries everywhere that he and Katheryn had been on progress were invited to return true bills. Every minute direction as to Katheryn's detention under Edward Baynton (who had been such a good bloodhound in the Boleyn case) came from Henry himself, down to her apparel and her decent style (but "no cloth of estate"). Lady Rochford was set to spy on her, though herself under condemnation. A most complicated set of questions to be put to the Duchess of Norfolk was shrewdly revised and pointed by the King. He had his eye, moreover, on her tangible assets, which were seized and reported to him. But where he had in the earlier crisis rushed the execution of Anne Boleyn, he was now carefully placing the responsibility on his tractable parliament. Henry had made costly mistakes and fed hostility: he had reflected and mastered his lesson.

The council were well trained to carry out his work. In these sparse days of Advent, they did not fast too arduously: one day and another they had salmon and flounder, sole and turbot, white herring and bacon herring, gudgeons and pike, shrimps and baked eels and oysters, beef, mutton, veal "marybones," rabbit, snipe, plover, larks, crane, quail, geese, peas, beans, onions, cherries, strawberries, pippins, oranges, pears, chestnuts, pomegranates, and all the other food and drink that go to support the labor of statesmanship. They were on the whole a team of ample and hearty men. They had little grudge against the old Duchess and not much against Lord William. They probably rather enjoyed the fact that the Duke thought it the better part to retreat to Norfolk like a wary campaigner. The surly willingness of Gardiner to take his share in running Katheryn to ground could scarcely have been lost on any one of them.

The extraordinary report that the King's good sister Anne of Cleves had just made him an uncle "for the King is informed that she had indeed had a child and imputes a default in her officers for not informing him," must have stirred urgent and amused curiosity. The rumor stopped, at any rate, the English-Cleves-French alliance, and paved the way for that reunion with the Emperor to which the world was again tending.

But for obvious reasons the council was left in control. Henry had gone away with his ministers of pastime. He was once more a man of sorrows. He seemed to turn his back on the fearful quandary, and to leave Katheryn to ministers of state and ministers of grace.

XIII

She was now cut off at Syon till parliament met in the middle of January. During the first weeks a feverous madness overwhelmed her, but gradually, with the verve of a girl under twenty, she recovered her spirits.

She could hope for nothing from the Howards. Norfolk had written to Henry of "the abominable deeds of his two nieces," fearing "his Majesty will abhor to hear speak of one of my kin again," but shrewdly reminding Henry of the small love that his stepmother or his nieces bear him, and praying for a comfortable assurance of that favor "without which I will never desire to live."

This was an appeal that Henry could grant to the best soldier in his realm. Katheryn, however, was of a new generation. She could ask nothing of Henry. She made no appeal.

"Very cheerful and more plump and pretty than ever." So Chapuys reported her at the end of January, saying she was just as careful about her dress, and just as willful and imperious, as when at court. But her cheerfulness had depths. She expected to be put to death. She said she deserved it. She only asked that "the execution shall be secret and not under the eyes of the world."

This acceptance of her fate seemed to arise from her wealth of feeling. She could not excuse her own insincerity. She had given Culpeper tokens of her love: she had wanted to give him herself: and, still living in her young imagination, she felt in a sense she was giving him her life.

For the elders whose imagination had long been paved for the pursuit of power and the responsibility of the state, the solid men who ate the larks instead of listening to them, the spontaneity that had ruled Katheryn was impossible. She was too young to understand the complex laws of self-preservation and not old enough to apprehend the dangers of sincerity. Even Henry, who had cried so much, was returning to social solace, and planning a huge banquet for young people, with bevies of fresh girls, nearly fifty of them, to entertain and distract him. Southampton had credited his master with the inclination, so magnanimous but so intolerably expensive, of indulging his feelings. But, his tears dried, Henry was employing a cheaper method of soothing his nerves. Katheryn had not lived long enough to master these economics and was even willing to take the consequences of her dishonesty.

When word came to her that both Lords and Commons had passed the act of attainder and that the King would allow her to plead before parliament, she did not ask to defend herself. She submitted entirely to the King's mercy and owned that she deserved death. She was resigned, or thought herself resigned.

But when Sir John Gage came out to Syon, a blond-bearded man with mercilessly direct eyes, to tell her to pack up and make ready for the Tower, an anguish wrung her nerves. At the actual moment for leaving, as she came to it, her body recoiled, her hands clenched, she fought back and said, "No, no." But the barges were ready. Engulfed in sobs she went down to embark at Isleworth. By the time she had reached the Tower, however, her cheeks in the fever of excitement, she had captured her composure. Southampton was first in a great barge, with other councilors; Suffolk with his men came last in another great barge; and she in a small barge with a few ladies and guards. The lords landed first: then Katheryn, in black velvet: "and they paid her as much honor as when she was reigning."

Gage was the new governor of the Tower, since William Kingston's death. Lady Rochford had been out of her mind, off and on, since learning she was to be condemned, but she had at last come to her senses and was with her mistress. Katheryn again broke down in the Tower, on the afternoon of February tenth. Culpeper had been here before her. "She weeps, cries, and torments herself miserably without ceasing." To give her leisure to poise herself and "reflect on the state of her conscience," her execution was deferred for a few days.

This was on the Friday. On Sunday, towards evening, Gage came to her and told her to prepare for death, for she was to die next day.

That evening she asked to have the block brought in to her, that she might know how to place herself. This was done, and the young woman made trial of it.

When she came to the block the next morning, February 13th, it was set on the spot where her cousin Anne Boleyn had been executed. The council, except her old uncle, had collected in the shiver of the winter morning, with the trees bare, the stars hardly gone out, and the air wraithed with the nearness of the Thames. A large number of people had gathered at the scaffold.

She spoke a few breathless words. A Spaniard heard them and wrote them.

"Brothers, by the journey upon which I am bound, I have not wronged the King. But it is true that long before the King took me, I loved Culpeper, and I wish to God I had done as he wished me for at the time the King wanted to take me he urged me to say that I was pledged to him. If I had done as he advised me I should not die this death, nor would he. I would rather have had him for a husband than be mistress of the world, but sin blinded me and greed of grandeur; and since mine is the fault, mine also is the suffering, and my great sorrow is that Culpeper should have had to die through me."

At these words she could go no farther. She turned to the headsman and said,

"Pray hasten with thy office."

He knelt before her and begged her pardon.

She said wildly, "I die a Queen, but I would rather die the wife of Culpeper. God have mercy on my soul. Good people, I beg you pray for me."

Falling on her knees she began to pray. Then the headsman severed her bent neck, and her young blood gushed out in a terrible torrent. Lady Rochford was then brought to the block, but, before she was led out, her mistress's little body, covered with a black cloth, was lifted up and borne to the chapel, where it was buried near Anne Boleyn.

BOOK SEVEN

Katharine Parr

"It is one of the best Bonds, both of chastity and obedience, in the Wife, if she thinke her husband wise."

FRANCIS BACON

I

WHEN an aging man begins to cry in front of his colleagues, he presents a touching spectacle. He may be bad but he is bewildered. He finds life difficult. And even those who have detested and feared him can hardly help lending him their handkerchief and lowering their eyes.

Henry's fifth marriage had gone wrong, as his fourth marriage had gone wrong, and his second and his first. Whatever doubts his loyal subjects had secretly expressed in all the earlier cases, they were able to say, *"This* time we are sorry for him." And they were sorry for him, sorrier than for Katheryn Howard.

Henry looked badly. When he was married to Katheryn, as Holbein showed, he was still plumped with pride and had September richness in his body. Suddenly, as with a cruel hand, he was stricken in years. He was only fifty, and that was not old; Warham and John Fisher reached seventy, Pope Julius reached eighty; Michelangelo was still alive and would go on nearly till ninety. But dejection of spirit opens the door to age, and Henry was submerged in dejection. He came down to parliament, and the members looked at him with amazement. His face had lost its sanguine tint. In repose it became lusterless and heavy, as if the gold had turned to pewter. His features sagged. A puzzled look, deepened by the transverse furrows of the forehead, seemed to say, "So this is life!" Love was finished for him. Rejuvenescence was postponed, at least till the next world. The world that had laid happiness in his lap had taken it away from him. A grille, the grille to the garden in which he had walked so royally, and through which he could still see its blossoms, had closed in his face.

It daunted him, and his people felt with him. All the details of Katheryn's attainder, even the signing of the documents, were taken out of his fumbling hands.

The parliament, in fact, showed how this new Henry touched the public heart. Audley had compared him to the connubial Solomon after Anne Boleyn's execution. He now referred to him as King David. David, he said in the opening speech, had sought neither honor nor riches but understanding and wisdom. At this tribute to his Most Sacred Majesty, every peer rose and bowed to the mature David. But though Audley, bending to the floor, assured parliament that these gifts of wisdom and understanding had been bestowed on Henry in large measure, he only waited till the King had withdrawn to dwell with severity on the lightness of woman.

The Adams thereupon legislated against the Eves, for Henry's protection.

Hereafter it should not be treason, it should be lawful, to reveal any lightness of the "Queen for the time being." Any lady courted by Henry should be bound, under pain of death, to declare in good time if she could be charged with misconduct. "An unchaste woman marrying the King shall be guilty of high treason."

Parliament was only thinking of deceitful woman when it tied this lifebelt on royal David. Wearing it, he might go out on the stormy sea again.

But what of courtship, under such circumstances? All the damosels of the court had known Katheryn Howard. Most of them were suspected of "modern unrest." The middle class that was studying the Bible saw wickedness in its cockatrice splendors and coupled "idolatry and adultery." Bishop Latimer would tell them in a few years at Westminster that they lived in the thick of "adultery, whoredom and lechery." He would accuse them of marriage for "pleasure and voluptuousness." All this affected the young women around Henry. "They stood off," says Lord Herbert, "as knowing in what a slippery estate they were, if the King, after receiving them to bed, should, through any mistake, declare them no maids."

It was the end of dalliance. Heavy impurity was leading to heavier puritanism.

In this very month Marguerite of Navarre was saying to Paget at the Louvre, "I must needs love that Prince for sundry causes; I should have been once his father's wife, and I should have been his wife, and he and I be both of one opinion in religion, for neither of us loveth the Pope."

But suppose Henry had courted Marguerite. Was it not true that Bonnivet, in his choicest nightcap and his perfumed nightshirt, had one night let himself into the sleeping Princess's chamber by a trap-door, and "the first intimation she had of his arrival was to find herself in his arms?" Being a "strong woman," she boasted, she made good use of her hands and nails. He tried to stuff the quilt in her mouth, but as she found he was doing his best to dishonor her, she cried to her dame of honor and Bonnivet made his escape, scratched and bitten.

She was warned by her dame of honor in wise words not to recount this story, it sounded so suspicious. But had she been bound, under pain of death, to disclose the same to the King or some of his council, it could only have aroused brutal doubts that could never die.

Since 1536 Henry had always kept in view the possibility of executing an unfaithful spouse. His eye glinted with it. It was the reason he gave in 1536 for not marrying an alien. But now, even at home, he had armed himself with legal artillery: courtship was narrowed down to the bullet-proof women.

II

He felt that he must show the world that he had risen above his affliction. Katheryn was executed on a Monday: on the following Sunday he gave a banquet to his council; the next day he dined his men of law; on Tuesday morning he went from room to room at Hampton Court, ordering the chambers for the young ladies; and that evening "he made them great and hearty cheer."

It must have been a banquet with curious undercurrents of feeling. He was in "his pleasing mood." He shone. But the thought of his next marriage could not be kept out of people's minds. He swam in the ripple of salutation, the fine wave of courtesy, but the former man was there, the man who had married young women of the court like Anne Boleyn and Jane Seymour and Katheryn Howard. And this presence, glittering, obese, his face a suet yellow in the candlelight, his red beard sparse, his smile tight, his thick gaze sparkling, his hands broken out in jewels, and the obsession of overwhelming power behind his courtliness, must have sent strange vibrations, fierce and macabre, down these young spines. As his eye ran round the pretty creatures, a ray falling on Lord Cobham's gay daughter, on Lord Lisle's stepdaughter, on Southampton's niece, it was as if the connoisseur would once more, with surer touch, name the masterpiece. As he passed, short of breath, abrupt, high-voiced, quick-eyed, he left a churning wake of intimate comparison and speculation.

But it was misleading. He was changed. In rising above affliction he had not really recovered his spirits. The blow that
Katheryn had dealt his confidence had sunk into his being and
gone deep. He had made her his Queen, rained jewels on her,
caressed her, displayed her; and no anger, no death-stroke, could
cancel the knowledge that he had never won her. He had held
her, yet his hands were empty. He was the elderly magnate who
could buy the young woman's body but who had never touched
her heart. At first he had not believed it, but she had proved too
honest to save his feelings. His defeat could not be disguised.

In his tired body there was no longer the evident malice
that had made him kill the Boleyns. That malice is another
aspect of strength, and Henry had lost potency. It was no longer
personal love that stirred him at fifty. Chapuys watched him.
"Indeed, except that he frequents ladies' company for mirth, as
a man nurtured among them, he seems not to think of a new
marriage. He has been low-spirited ever since he heard of the
late Queen's misconduct."

But when Chapuys, in order to lure him to the Emperor,
said he himself would submit to punishment if he abused the
trust he invited Henry to give him, he "saw the King's face ex-
pand and his eyes glitter." Submission he could still appreciate.
Political submission had not yet disillusioned him. As age shut
him out from the earlier experiences of sport and love, he was
all the more open to seek political prowess, uniting force to its
subtle sister fraud.

III

When Henry stood in the garden of Greenwich with his council this spring, a matron curtsied to him and presented a petition. She was the widow of Northumberland. She came to
say she had no living.

He looked at her bill and he looked at her. She was the

daughter of Shrewsbury. He heard her very gently, and "bowed down upon his staff to her."

It was twenty years after he and Wolsey had broken Percy. This woman before him had been married to Percy, who always hated her because he had been cheated of Anne Boleyn. And Henry in the end had weaned Percy's lands away from him for debt and sent his brothers to die in the Tower.

"Madam," he asked gravely, "how can your ladyship desire any living of your husband's lands, seeing your father gave no money to your husband in marriage with your ladyship, or what think you that I should do herein?"

She looked up to him with that pleading which is so loaded with submission.

"What it please your Grace."

He pondered. "Madam, I marvel greatly that my lord your father, being so great a wise man as he was, would see no direction taken in this matter in his time."

He gazed at the widow. He may have sighed. "Howbeit, Madam, we wolle be contented to refer the matter unto our Council."

He turned to Tunstall and Anthony Browne and gave Tunstall her petition.

"I beseech your Grace to be good and gracious to me."

He heard her. "We wolle." And he was.

And this sort of leniency developed in him. Dozens of small provocations that used to make him furious were now chuted away. The old Duchess of Norfolk and her brood were released in the spring and summer of 1542, and a few of her possessions were restored. Mary Boleyn's husband Stafford had been one of the witnesses against Katheryn Howard; he was a rewarded courtier. Young Norris was granted property. Though Dudley had been executed for conspiracy in 1510, his son was in high favor. All Henry asked was submission. As long as courtiers like

Paget expected him to "use towards me the part of my God, as indeed I take him for my God in earth," Henry was ready to act the part of God, even unto mercy.

"When he takes a fancy for a person or a thing," said Chapuys, "he goes the whole way." Had he God's power to fix on the heads he took off, he might even have had Cromwell walking with him in the garden at Greenwich.

His increase in mildness came in part from the ease of mind which he felt when Charles and Francis were going to war again. But it came also from the judgment, the authority, the temper, that had ripened in him.

He could even admit why he had married Anne of Cleves. "You had me pushed into a tight corner," he told Marillac, "but thank God I am still alive and not so little a King as I was thought."

The powerful resentments that sprang from doubt and insecurity had been allayed by that happy escape. If he was not wholly bland, if his spleen was sometimes not discharged simply because one red glance made every one give in, he had learned to brag less, to measure danger, to forestall it. He insisted that "this is a realm of justice and of no persecution of them that be good." He tried to exact straightforwardness. "We do naturally hate all compass and dissimulation." He tried to snuff out feuds that threatened discipline. "The King will suffer no man to give unsitting language to his meanest groom." He had built up forts and coast defenses. He had the North of England under control. He was receiving Irish "savages" and sending them away English noblemen. He was thinking and planning ahead for the Welshification of Scotland. The Henry of his last phase had come to his maturity; he was an astute, a unique politician.

IV

The politics he now played were a combination of Cromwell and Wolsey, and his hands were full with them in 1542. Tight in the center of his nature was the encysted hatred of the Pope. The truce of Nice, devised by the Pope to bring about a Catholic mood in Europe, a general council, and a restored power that would chastise the Lutherans and especially Henry, was something which Henry never believed would last. And as he haggled over the terms of marriage between Mary and Orleans, precisely as his father had haggled over the terms of marriage between Arthur and Catherine, he was really calculating his own part in the next European war.

The war was due. The French stood "like a deer upon a laund," knowing not which way to take; and Henry, the still hunter, waited with his eye on the deer and his heart in his trigger finger.

The man that had once played the cittern and written music was now examining boat designs, making suggestions for redoubts, drawing plans of turrets, sketching a cart that could grind corn as it rolled along the road. And every germ of an idea that he had was at once magnified by loyal technicians, unless they were cocksure Portuguese whom he kicked out, or hard unflattering Italian engineers.

The love-feast of Aigues Mortes had bound Francis and Charles together for four years but Charles had made a weak attack on Algiers in 1541, and the sight of his failure revived Francis's craving for Milan. He had sent ambassadors hotfoot to the Turk, and when those ambassadors were murdered by Spaniards near Pavia, the truce of Nice lost its tholepin and Catholico and Christianissimo started to put on their gloves and go after the belt again. Both of them came soliciting Henry, but as he advanced in years he gained in cunning. He managed Chapuys and Marillac so adroitly that each of them was persuaded he would stay neutral.

Though Europe was to stink with the corpses which this insane rivalry was to pile up, it is impossible to write of it with respect. The statecraft of Europe was still the statecraft of the barnyard. Every summer, as Erasmus pointed out, nature planted a kick in the English stomach, called the plague, to teach it elementary hygiene; but instaed of learning the lesson the heroes stood their ground and the poltroons fled, while the commissioner of sewers was really a commissioner of sea-walls and defense. And war, which lived on the vital lie of virility as the plague lived on vital excrement, was accepted with the same shrewd belief that secrecy and dishonesty were as unavoidable as sewage and perfume. Everywhere, as Erasmus foretold, when he saw the dynasts putting on their national warpaint, the play of instinct would be untrammeled. Sweden, Denmark, Poland, Germany, Bohemia, Hungary, the Balkans, Persia, Syria, Egypt, Italy, all north Africa, Spain, France, Ireland, Scotland and the England that never did, and never shall, lie at the proud foot of a Canute or a William, had seethed with war and armament from 1509 till 1542, with India and Peru and Mexico and Canada added, while only the clerks kept pleading for creative evolution as against evolution by war-dance and explosive shell.

But the sweet joys of pursuing the neighboring power were now beginning to be blended with stirring war within the neighbor himself, in the name of religion. And the dynast was in motley, half of him national and Catholico or half of him national and Protestantissimo.

In France Calvin was stimulating the Huguenots to war. In Scotland Henry was stimulating the Word of God men. In England it was the Emperor's agent who was hissing on the Pope-Catholics against the Anglicans. In Germany both Francis and Henry had encouraged the Protestant princelings, while Francis, half extinguished under Pope Paul, still stuck up a hand to wave on the Turk. The counter-movement in each nation, the movement toward uniform belief, called for the burning of boys of seventeen who believed in consubstantiation or strong-minded women who were drunk on the New Testament. In Spain the Inquisition was working in the marrow of Spanish intelligence like a disease of the spine. All for Christ. All for gentle Jesus. It made a situation that attracted political genius as a theater disaster attracts undertakers.

And what made Henry so remarkable was the skilled response he now made to his instinct, the handsomest of printing on the flimsiest of pulp.

Henry had learned, what no King in Italy or even in Germany had learned, to conduct the national band. That was his triumph. The manager in politics, whether he is a great autocrat or a leader in a public-house, has to lure the effective egoism; under his baton according to the music inherent in them, bound by their volume and their tone. He was doing this in 1542, and he was doing it as he had never done it before. While he was rehearsing his brasses for the next war, and ruling the kettledrum for his work at Tyburn, he had no intention of leaving the religious accompaniment to chance. He was perfectly aware of the feud between Gardiner and Cranmer, but he did not propose to let the burly prelate with the gorgeous Catholic cello drown the first violin, who could not avoid a whine in his otherwise exquisite Protestantism.

There had been a time in Henry's green days when he thought more of the score than of the playing. Now, willing to carry on the traditional symphony that his father had played before him, he was supremely concerned with his team. In his thirties, no doubt, he had referred everything to his conscience. But for seven years he had not mentioned that accusatory organ. It was gone, like a diseased kidney, and he was managing surprisingly well without it, finding, like most executive mankind, that (so long as the banks carry you) it is best to leave your moral worry to pressure from outside.

The pressure from the Pope was indeed in his mind. The pressure from public opinion he never neglected. Hence he was blending Cranmer and Gardiner, Wriothesley and Audley,

Norfolk and Hertford. If to-day he was obliged to sacrifice a handful of sacramentaries, to "make terrible examples of them," he was ready the next day to jail one of Gardiner's agents. So long as Catholic sentiment was strong in the country he would keep Gardiner at his elbow; but he loved Cranmer the more because he was faithful and labile.

Chapuys viewed Henry dryly. "Like the Florentine who had a sermon preached against usury that bankers might abstain from it and he himself profit by it," Henry constantly reproved dishonesty in others. He called Francis "Judas." He let Chapuys come in to talk to him as he lay distended in his private room, "à la domestique, en robe de nuit."

"Judas non dormit," he smiled to the old Imperialist. And in truth he could not pretend any longer that he would not fight Francis. His nephew in Scotland, the red-headed, square-built James, had married Francis's daughter Madeleine and then Mary of Guise. That gave England a French front on land in the North as well as on the coast in the South. Henry had gone back to the adage around which Cromwell had built his famous speech in 1523: "Who that intendeth France to win, with Scotland let him begin."

This was the only condition of civil order that Henry could really orchestrate, because it sprang from the center of his nature. A civil order founded on force and fraud.

v

The men who come to the top at a given hour in society are seldom the only men, or even the best men, available. They are the notes that the master-mood picks out and that the hour itself strikes.

Now that it had come to subduing Scotland, as the first move against France, Henry did not need Erasmus-men or Copernicus-men. His chief justice had cobwebs on him. His "singing men" were to be tried for heresy. Hugh Latimer was pensioned to be silent. Hans Holbein, paid thirty pounds a year with three subtracted for taxes, would die of the plague next year and be thrown into an unnamed grave like any other servant. It was no time for anything but power and the ministers of power. Henry needed men of force and fraud.

Among the first he found the great cart-horses of royalty, the solid practical heads who gave to the service of their master a sober and massive obedience on which he could always count. They ranged through Suffolk and squat Southampton and Anthony Browne down to John Russell and John Gage. They could all write their names. They were soldiers and sailors, and it was on soldiers and sailors that Henry reposed his ultimate intentions.

A good deal of heavy clay seemed to have been admixed with them, since Lovell and Poynings and old Henry Wyatt and Darcy had given the models at the opening of the reign. But they were indigenous and they were beamed like oaks. They grew and spread, formidable because of their slow imaginations, their thick wills, their truculence and their umbrageous tenacity.

Yet a little literacy distilled into these men and dreadful things happened. Stable and routine themselves, they bred hot-tempered, willful, adventurous children whose voluble and original, not to say eccentric, expressiveness carried them fast to the Elizabethan mood. Thomas Wyatt, George Boleyn, Nicholas Carew in young days, Edward Howard, Leonard Gray, Thomas Seymour, Henry Howard, Wyatt's son, were lean and vibrant versions of their fathers' breed. They were not so much bulwarks as flying buttresses, but they managed by sheer daring to translate their illiterate forebears into something that raced and rhymed.

These were men on whom England could count for force. Henry's fraud was hardly less plentifully manned. It had a ductile leader in Cranmer when it came to divorces. It had a soft agent in Tunstall on the Council of the North, a powerful servitor in Roland Lee, and two supple and resourceful secretaries in Wriothesley and Paget. A man like Sadler could turn his hand to soldiering or negotiating. So could Dudley, who became Lord Lisle.

But the rarer men transcended their caste. Norfolk was more than a fearless soldier. Though too contemptuous to play statecraft with the new pieces made in Germany, he was by birth a man who could rule janissaries and brisk in the palace courtyard, know the secrets of the council and the harem. He created nothing, exploited everything. A tough-minded and patient adversary, he had a "busy head." He had matched wits with Wolsey and Cromwell, and defeated them in the privy chamber.

On this noble plane, however, Edward Seymour, the Earl of Hertford, was a match for Norfolk. He was also a soldier and he was uncle of the King to be. He had youth on his side, a mind open to Protestantism, a fierce and desperate desire to create a social order with which Norfolk could neither cope nor compromise.

Gardiner and Bonner were plebeians, just as Cromwell had been plebeian. But they were kin with the soldiers. They added to the natural stoutness of their type a rather special loud and pugnacious note. This extreme positiveness, this excess of the instinct of self-preservation, which made them snort like tugs against opposition, gave them the enormous blunt and concentrated power of tugs in every enterprise. Even as much as the soldiers they were charged with energy and made for work. An amazing capacity for brute effort, indeed, marked this meaty generation. Well or sick, these men never shirked the mountains of labor that ambition imposed on them. Norfolk stuck to the saddle when he was fluid with disease. Wriothesley reeled in fever when he interviewed Mary of Hungary and Christine. Southampton was to die in harness, not a word of protest from him. Lord Poynings held up his funeral, so to speak, to scribble a last memorandum. If Chapuys did business when he could move nothing but his tongue, as Marillac bitingly noted, the same fortitude marked a right hardy gentleman like Suffolk.

The incentive was tangible. It was public honor based on private property, two delicious things. But though they whiffed these as mice whiff toasted cheese, their native quality stirred them to do an infinitude of disagreeable and even odious things, to curb their sensibilities, to rule their preferences, and to assuage themselves by sugaring their kisses, their tears and their wine. They weltered in sentiment and sweltered in action. The ordered spaces of intellectual honesty and measured conduct and humane self-knowledge were as deserted as Oxford and Cambridge, which graduated about 360 bachelors of art in the next six years. The mind was the poor relation, the sizar, of these sturdy bodies, which had to be stroked and decked and ordered and stoked, exercised and disciplined, and God Save the King.

Brains could be bought and taste could be hired. Not merely the military engineers and the gunners could be imported, from whom secrets could be gleaned of vast importance while the mind pretended it was too dull to learn them, but the painters, the musicians, the sculptors, could be condescendingly set to work, along with the fine cooks and the costumers, since it was foreigners who did that sort of thing and had had their palate cultivated by the renaissance. Thus art, shy in the North since Gothic spent its impulse, could blow on its cold fingers. The nobility in view was now the military order, strengthened by Henry with churchly revenues. Henry spent the shrines on war as he would spend most of the schools on war. The educator was a deaf man tolling a muffled bell. The death of Thomas More had left Henry's council without its humanist; and that chair passed to the Audleys and the Wriothesleys.

VI

Henry scarcely troubled to hide his intentions about Scotland. The fig-leaf of diplomacy did disguise aggression. Scotland, it seemed, was trying to conquer England. But his best soldiers were in the North, and he revived his antique claims to that thistly realm.

One incursion failed in August, 1542. The Scots caught five hundred prisoners at Haddon Rig. But this angered Henry. And Lord Lisle exalted the duty of incursions. He wanted to see the Marches extended. It would be an acceptable deed before God, he said, considering how brutely and beastly the people now be governed. "O what a godly act should it be to your Excellent Highness to bring such a sort of people to a knowledge of God's laws, the country so necessary to your dominions by reason whereof so many souls should live also in quietness."

The older men saw the Marches less rhapsodically. Southampton noted that they were "barren, wild, cold and utterly ungarnished with wood." Norfolk sourly complimented Sir George Lawson as one of the best knights "who ever spurred a cow"; he had failed to provide beer. The soldiers had to drink water. They had to "lie on the wet ground." The invasion of Scotland was no pastime.

Neither was the invasion of England. A great army that was to escort Cardinal Beton, who would pronounce the papal interdict on English soil, was caught in November on the wrong side of the incoming tide. Word flashed through them that Norfolk was in their path. They turned back. Dashing homeward in panic at Solway Moss, they were overtaken, twenty killed, twelve hundred captured, including a score or so of the notables.

The thirty-year-old King, waiting to second the blow, learned there was no blow to second. He rode away in deadly chagrin.

He was not with his French Queen at Linlithgow when she gave birth to a girl on December 8th. He was already dying, his life a broken bridge from Flodden to Solway. On December 12th, this man who had never tamed his nobles expired "from grief, regret and rage."

It was a national calamity worse than Pavia, and there was no Scottish Louise of Savoy. He left one heir, Mary, the baby four days old—Mary Queen of Scots she was to be.

Henry's "fatherly affection to the Scottish King" was now shown in a proposal that his pallid Edward, who was six and knew his Latin verbs, should be wedded to the baby Mary. He proposed, meanwhile, to treat Scotland as a "native state," to control its governor and tutor its Queen. It was suzerainty, not partnership. The earls and barons who had been taken at Solway were brought to London, and, assigning them as guests to his councilors, he wove the net in which to catch Scotland. He was to hold one end of it, they were to go home holding the other, and Scotland was to flounder into it. The Scottish lords willingly assented, even promising to come back in the spring to see King Harry. And Cranmer had deep confabulation with his guest, Kennedy, on giving his people the Word of God.

VII

Henry was a creature of habit. Every year he made his progress in summer. Every Christmas he came to Greenwich. He had never been farther from England than Lille, and he had only been in the North of England once in his life. Windsor, Hampton Court, Nonesuch, Oatlands, Westminster, Whitehall—these knew him, and his armchair knew him. More and more he was becoming the King sitting down.

And he was bored. The evenings were long and cheerless in his widower's November. Of course he had wept when Katheryn ruined their marriage, and swore he would never marry again. But his gift was not tragic. He drummed his fingers. A

wide gulf, like a gigantic yawn, stretched between his last marriage and his present detachment. He had been a widower a full
year. For a man whose grimaces and impatient interruptions
broke into any discourse when he was displeased, life without a
customary companion was emptiness and fidget. He could spend
his days with his councilors. A treaty with the Scots, a treaty
with the Emperor, subsidies, loans, the debased currency, the
King's Book that rounded away every heresy for Gardiner and
every papacy for Cranmer—these were bread and meat. But
wine? Henry's heart, which had seemed like an old blotting
paper black with impressions, began to thirst again.

It was not for himself, naturally, that he would ever marry
again. He was in his old days. Marriage to him, with his leg,
could only be a sacrifice. But his family needed a mother. A
man must think of his family.

Mary was now with her father, and Mary did need a mother.
She was shut out from the man who had blasted her life. She
knew there was talk of her marriage but she scorned it. She told
one of her damsels that "she would be, while her father lived,
only Lady Mary, the most unhappy lady in Christendom."

The other two children, who were at Hatfield, had scarcely
more sweetness in their lives. Edward was being educated, if
England was not. He was covered with tutors like an invalid
with cupping-glasses; he looked none the better for it. Elizabeth was brighter. She was wide awake at ten, clever to her
finger tips, born to play on the world as certain prodigies are
born to play on the piano, but if Henry had been certain that
she was Henry Norris's child, not his own, he could not have behaved more indifferently. As she did not yield to tragic gloom
like Mary, however, her little heart had tightened up like rubber, always to be impressionable but impervious and resilient.

Such cheerlessness, each person incarcerated in his ego, is
characteristic of the solitary confinement of the power-sick; even
Henry's lute had been laid away, and if he feasted enough to

cheer his spirits he ran the risk, like his friend Francis, of getting the colic.

In this cheerless household, with so many terrible memories and so much to make Henry look baffled and hunted as he sat silent, there began to emerge a new and charming figure, a figure of benignity and life.

VIII

She was one of those quiet women who see the virile sex in a light of their own. The children, too, were not so much royal as human to her, children without the tilth of kindness, without any center or any home.

Katharine Parr was a lady of the court, but one of those who push up by themselves in any society, out of season or in season, affluent in their natures, well-molded, rich, gracious, like a crocus under autumn leaves. She possessed the odd gift that can turn any one not a monster into a human being—the solvency of good will.

She had been reared in the lap of Westmorland, not far from Windermere, and she was of an age with Jane Seymour, coming from a family, like the Seymours, that had its own notion of nobility, but the high wall of whose privacy revealed little of the manifold richness within.

She had left Kendal quite young to marry the veteran Lord Borough. A widow at sixteen, she had later been married to Lord Latimer. And while her uncle, Sir William Parr, was vigorous in suppressing the Pilgrimage of Grace, her husband was one of the leaders in it, though by some sagacity, her uncle's or her own, he had come through those perils and did not die till the beginning of 1543.

His widow was thus a considerable heiress at the age of thirty or thirty-one. Her brother was in Henry's closest circle, married into the powerful family that had borne the title of Essex and that many found an odious family. She was related to the

Throgmortons, equally well-entrenched, and Catholic, George Throgmorton's candor about Henry's love-affairs having landed him in the Tower. She was not herself as Catholic as her fore-bears: she was intimate with Henry's admired young Duchess of Suffolk, with his niece Lady Margaret Douglas, and with other of the elect who, like Marguerite of Navarre, had begun to cull the ripe fruits of Erasmus and the New Learning.

In the dignified indifference which is bred by satiety, Henry did not observe Lady Latimer, or, as she is better known, Kath-arine Parr. His eye had always been fetched by scarlet, by crim-son, by cloth-of-gold. The kind of old families who wear tawny and plum and who, dull by protective coloration, manage at the same time to have the best of everything, even when others are going to the scaffold, had never stirred Henry's pulse. It was his instinct to ignore them until their plumpness became too obvious, when he managed to bring them home for Christmas, like fine birds who have foraged after harvest or well-clad and succulent boar. Thus at home in the court but not at first ob-served by his Majesty, Katharine was receiving the approaches of her compeer in age and class, Thomas Seymour.

Thomas Seymour was not yet Lord Admiral, prince of the sea. He was, generally speaking, Edward's younger uncle. But for an ardent woman who had been married twice to elderly noblemen encrusted with country estates, this free, lithe, swag-gering young grandee, who, even on the banks of the Thames, flashed a piratical fire, must have had an attractiveness hardly to be owned. His least oath was, "By God's most precious soul." He saw life as a golden apple to which only the audacious climb, and he saw a windmill not as something to grind fat bags of corn, but as something over which to fling his bonnet, prefer-ably against the wind.

Katharine Parr was not herself a romantic figure; she was small and positively made, with thick eyebrows, and a frank, cheerful, florid countenance. But this very fact enwrapped her in Thomas's dangerous flame. She was sufficiently class-bound to prefer him to his brother Hertford, who companioned little Edward as an eagle might companion a wren, and who united with his ambition to protect Edward a seriousness that made him more dangerous than his reckless gallant of a brother, and potentially a traitor to his class.

But Katharine did not succumb to Thomas Seymour in the first days of courtship. She was living in an age when passionate natures wrecked themselves and she was old enough to observe the world she lived in as well as to listen to her heart.

Hugh Latimer would stand before young King Edward in a few years and say, "For God's love, beware where you marry; choose your wife in a faithful stock. Beware of this worldly policy: Marry in God; marry not for the great respect of alliance, for thereof cometh all these evils of breaking of wedlock, which is among princes and noblemen." That would be her own instinct.

But while she was still free, Henry laid on her the weight of his approval. Perhaps he had seen how devoted she was to Mary, how she mothered Edward and won Elizabeth. Perhaps the narrowed field of choice, and her staid widowhood in contrast to the flagrant freshness of Katheryn Howard, caught his mind. She had been married to an impeccable Catholic, with Essex and Throgmorton to assure Gardiner, while her own tendency, as a devotee of the New Learning, would make her attractive to Cranmer. Her graceful movements, her dignity, her beautiful hands designed her to preside at his side. And the goodwill that flowed from her to him was as kind as the mild current that encircles favorless lands and embalms them with the bounty of the sun.

When Henry smiled on her and opened his mind to her in the spring of 1543, she was said to have given a cry of horror.

"It were better to be your mistress than your wife!"

But even as he looked at her with those pointed eyes, and as

she dropped her own, the long corridor of those five previous
marriages of his, with four graves in it, must have stopped Katharine's heart.

Still it was not in her to think any one evil. He was not a
happy man. He had been much opposed by women, crossed,
balked, wronged, misled. It was his plaintive art to convey that
he was infantile—despotic like a baby but bewildered and helpless—and his empty life seemed pitiable. A woman with compassion, in whom pity linked with humility and kindness with
the incomplete man who has missed the secret of happiness.
She could not give it to him. But she could nurse him. She
could, by his very incapacity to go outside the limits of his
egoism, give him much without losing all that he could never
find. He could never need the core of her being, which was
Thomas Seymour's. And she could give him what he needed,
and what his tormented country needed, the climate of goodwill.

The firm self-sacrifice of this unromantic woman was made
easier by knowing Henry. He was a tired elderly man, and she
did not shut her eyes. Few insurance companies would have
taken Henry in 1543. He was visibly slowing down and coming
to anchor. And had Katharine escaped him, she would have
changed favor to a bright animosity that might have destroyed
her young man's career.

Katharine did not see Henry as Solomon or King David. She
referred to him as Moses. And marrying Moses (who had little
horns) was hardly personal. But she did it with a heart that enveloped him to the exclusion of any other yearning. He needed
her. Mary and Elizabeth and Edward needed her. Had they
been parched flowers and she a gardener, her heart could not
have been more moved.

"The time seemeth to me very long," she was to write to him
next year, "with a great desire to know how your Highness hath

done since your departing hence; whose prosperity and health I prefer and desire more than mine own.

"And whereas I know your Majesty's absence is never without great need, yet love and affection compel me to desire your presence. Again the same zeal and affection forceth me to be best content with that which is your will and pleasure.

"Thus, love maketh me in all things set apart mine own convenience and pleasure, and to embrace most joyfully his will and pleasure whom I love. God, the knower of secrets, can judge these words to be not only written with ink but most truly impressed upon the heart."

So she plucked her downy plumage to make Henry's nest. And he loved it. His eye possibly caught every fifth word of this solemn league and covenant of wifely devotion. But he also wrote her, rather in a hurry but amiably: "Would write again with his own hand but is so busy."—"Is too busy to write more, but sends blessings to all his children and recommendations to his cousin Margett and the rest of his ladies and gentlewomen and to his Council." "No more to you at this time, sweetheart, but for lack of time and great occupation of business."

He was natural with her, as she had wished. And when it was all over, and Henry was dead, and she could write to explain herself to Thomas Seymour whom she now admitted to love, she said to him:

"I would not have you think that this, mine honest goodwill toward you, proceeds from any sudden motion of passion; for, as truly as God is God, my mind was fully bent the other time I was at liberty to marry you before any man I know. Howbeit, God withstood my will therein most vehemently for a time, and through his grace and goodness made that seem possible which seemed to me most impossible: that was, made me renounce utterly mine own will, and follow His most willingly. It were long to write all the process of this matter. If I live I shall declare it to you myself. I can say nothing; but as my lady of Suffolk saith: 'God is a marvelous man.' Kateryn the Quene."

God is indeed a marvelous man, and never more so than as matrimonial agent. Strengthened by Him, Katharine Parr was able to agree to marry Henry in the summer of 1543.

IX

Henry's sixth marriage did not seem to portend any change in policy, religious or political. He was wedded on July 12, 1543, in an upper chamber in Hampton Court. It was a pleasant and simple ceremony, with both his daughters there to be glad for their new stepmother, and "none opposing but all applauding the marriage." Henry said "Yea" with beaming goodwill to the questions that Bishop Gardiner put to him in English, and Katharine, clasping hands with him on her promise, plighted herself "to be bonayr and buxome in bed and at board, till death us depart."

It was a blow, however, to Henry's good sister, Anne of Cleves. She had survived the first slight, Katheryn Howard being young and pretty. But Katharine Parr was not so young and not so pretty. Chapuys, who did not love the disloyal Cleves, reported that "the said lady would like to be in her shift with her mother, having especially taken great grief and despair at the King's espousal of this last wife, who is not nearly so beautiful as she." It ended, certainly, any prospect that Henry might double in his tracks, and Anne of Cleves permitted herself to say of her successor, "A fine burthen Madam Katharine hath taken on herself."

The burden was lightened by Henry's merry humor. So long as his own importance was in no way abraded, no man was more good-natured or more indulgent in the first months of a marriage. He had just signed a treaty with the Scots at Greenwich. He had announced his league with the Emperor against the

French. He had relaxed the severity of the Six Articles. Gardiner, who performed the wedding, was indispensable to him, and three heretics were burned on the green of Windsor Castle not long after the marriage, though Henry loved music too well to let John Marbeck, who had gone from his love of melody to the love of the English Bible, be burned alive because he had immersed himself in Scriptures. But this dark episode showed no fanaticism in Henry. He had not interfered with the young Earl of Surrey's going to prison in April for eating flesh in Lent and behaving like a "roister." But these things were not his doing and did not reveal a personal animus. The King's Book, even, which caused Gardiner and Cranmer to glower at one another, represented no passionate feeling in his nature. He objected to priests marrying because he feared they would become dynastic, but where the state was not impaired he had the leniency of the unprincipled.

Katharine Parr, however, had charity, not leniency. And she had her part in a subtle change in Henry's course. The post-Cromwellian tendency went on. Cranmer, petulant under pressure from his chapter at Canterbury, had shot out, "Ye will not leave your old mumpsimuses, but I will make you to repent it." The Chapter, encouraged by Gardiner, had retorted by charges of heresy, and for a time it looked as though the Archbishop might be tripped up. But Henry owed three divorces to Cranmer. No man, no matter how tempted, is likely to pull down his fire-escape. The charges against Cranmer, hot as they were, cooled as Henry pursued them.

"The King on an evening," wrote Cranmer's secretary, "rowing on the Thames in his barge, came to Lambeth bridge, and there received my lord, Cranmer, into his barge, saying unto him merrily, 'Ah, my chaplain, I have news for you—I know now who is the greatest heretic in Kent! And so pulled out of his sleeve a paper, wherein was contained his accusation, articled against him and his chaplains and other preachers in Kent, and subscribed with the hands of certain prebenderies and justices of the shire."

And Henry, out of a lifetime of political craft, coached Cranmer how to turn the tables on his accusers. In fact, he did it for him. He appointed a commission to investigate the charges, with Cranmer as its head.

x

Henry's craftiness with the Scots was the double of this. He had given Arran full instructions for the best way to suppress the monasteries. First, the Governor was to send commissioners "as it were" to take order for their living more honestly, but secretly to examine the religious: and "if it were well handled," the Governor shall learn their abominations. Then, armed with proof of monastic immorality, "he and the chief nobles agreeing together for the distribution of some of the abbey lands among them," he should treat with the most "tractable" bishops apart, assuring them of their own fortune and "devising" with them. It was Henry's approved method of reward and punishment, based on making moral capital out of "the intolerable idleness and filthiness" and "hypocrisy and superstition" of the monks.

Cardinal Beton was too virulent a force, however, for this program to thrive. Even the treaty of Greenwich had been signed in the spirit of that story later applied by Paget to the French. It concerned a poor man that Louis XI had condemned to death, and who, to save his life, undertook to make Louis's favorite ass speak within a year. "But it is impossible," said an open-mouthed comrade. The man responded, "Hold thy peace, for within a year the King may die or the ass may die or I may die or the ass may speak!"

The Scots had rewarded Henry for treating with them by allowing Cardinal Beton to reappear. The baby Mary was crowned Queen of Scots at Sterling in the autumn of 1543. By December Scottish patriotism hounded the "English lords" out of power, and the treaty of Greenwich was at an end.

The vileness of the Scots became too apparent. Henry "could find it in his gentle heart" to forget their unkindness if they would knowledge their bounden duties of allegiance, but these Scottish nobles "a sort of wolves" were barbarous, inconstant, disloyal. You bribed the Douglases and they did not stay bribed. Cardinal Beton was to be imprisoned, but he did not stay imprisoned. The common people reeked of patriotism. And though the plan for assassinating Beton was being fostered by Sadler, it was necessary to send Hertford in the spring to burn Edinburgh and butcher the rebellious so that the war with France, to which Henry was pledged, could be undertaken.

Hertford's harsh work was done in May, 1544. Litanies in mellow English celebrated the victory and chanted Henry's approaching departure to France.

He still could get into armor, but it had to be armor with a paunch on it. You can see it to-day on a wooden horse in the Tower of London. To get into it, for a young man, would be like getting into a roomy hansom-cab. Henry, encased in this hardware, was carefully hoisted on board his war-horse. He left for Calais with thirty or thirty-five thousand troops. His own sails, as heretofore, were cloth-of-gold.

But the war of 1544 was not the war of 1523. At that time the world was young and Henry and Charles and Francis had everything before them. Now they were veterans and they maneuvered like three crabs.

Francis was perhaps the most dilapitated of the three. He was described by the Imperialists as vile and wicked, wringing his hands and saying, "Shall I be taken prisoner again? Shall I lose my Kingdom? Shall I be killed? Shall I die?" This melodramatic picture did not correspond in the least with Monluc's

quick impression of him in this same year: sunk in his chair, old
before his time, his skin white, his body weary, his mind light
and quickly moved. "We are both great Kings and well stricken
in years," he had pleaded to Henry the previous year, when he
asked for a conference with James of Scotland and Henry, "for
the sake of peace." He had become prudent, and after his fruit-
less offensive of 1543 and his useless victory of Ceresole he
now relied on rear action and letting time and space fight the
invaders.

Charles was invading Champagne in person, the proud warrior that Titian has painted. He had just come from Barbara
Blomberg, the good woman of Ratisbon who next February
would hang Don Juan of Austria around his neck. It was one
of his few lapses, since he was a prim Emperor. He had been
enduring gout a great deal, his thin shanks wrapped in cloths,
and no solace but the wood of Inde. Then some one thought of
Barbara, the washerwoman with a voice. Barbara was a pungent and warming creature who only needed a little sun to ex-
pand alarmingly. Charles listened to her and consoled himself
with her. But what to him was a thing apart was Barbara's
whole existence. Her contact with royalty drove her husband,
one Pyramus Kegell, into the ignoble shade. She reverberated
from Ratisbon to the Alhambra. Nothing short of a general
council could handle her. And Charles, "cheese face" though
Heine called him, had for the rest of his life, "wondrous and
secret close man" that he was, to ponder on the miserable
truth that the wages of irregularity is publicity.

It was his plan in invading France to work west while Henry
worked south. He came along the Marne—Châlons, Epernây,
Château-Thierry. But Henry, blinking his obligations to the
south, sat down to consummate the capture of Boulogne of
which Wolsey had balked him twenty years before. And by
September 14th he had secured Boulogne while Charles, well

informed as to Francis's complaisance, hastened to sign an independent peace at Crépy. This was September 18th. Henry was not violently angry. He had a huge asset, he considered, in this new English foothold in France. And he hurried home to be ready for naval raids.

XI

Henry reposed at home. He was tired but happy. In many ways it was a pleasant autumn. Peace was being discussed on the basis of a captured Boulogne, with Gardiner shouting at the French, "both saying mass and responding." Cranmer was safe under Henry's wing in the meantime. The King was victorious. He could now savor the praises of London that the Spanish visitors of the summer had so spontaneously lavished. "O London," he could say as Dekker was to say, "thou art great in glory, and envied for thy greatness; thy towers, thy temples, thy pinnacles stand upon thy head like borders of gold; thy waters like frindges of silver hang at the hammes of thy garment. Thou art the goodliest of thy neighbors, but the prowdest; the welthiest but the most wanton."

Had he made peace, "we establish the valiantness of England forever, if we leave the game now." But the joy he felt had always in it the appetite for greater joy. "So fat that such a man had never been seen," he knew not how to "leave the game." He looked over the table, scanning every move of player and croupier, and it was thus Henry Howard was to see the immoderate yet hungry man "whose glutted cheeks sloth feeds so fat, as scant their eyes be seen."

The Narrow Seas he would make his own. He would control shipping. He would decree who should, and who should not, export to belligerents in wartime. And as his mind pushed him to encroachment, he ran once more into resistance. In January Chapuys came to him. "Neither of us seems so well as we did in the camp at Boulogne," Henry greeted him. "And indeed," says Chapuys, "he seems much broken." But he said "very loudly" that the French had been whipped both by land and by sea.

He made Chapuys comfortable, "graciously insisted on his being seated before himself." But he listened impatiently and broke in angrily, repeatedly declared that "he would a hundred times capture Boulogne than Paris," and insisted unpleasantly that the Emperor had failed in his obligations. It was his way of doing business. Chapuys was used to it. And the King with the "foul gout and the ambassador with the ordinary gout wrangled like two old curmudgeons thumping the oak settle.

Chapuys, "the old fox," began to be hated. "In words they overcome us." And the French had reason to be grateful to the Emperor for the peace of Crépy, as they planned to invade England in the summer.

XII

Small as they were beside the French, the English were ready for them on land and sea. "My lord," said the men of Norfolk to the Duke, "if they come, for God's sake bring us between the sea and them, that we may fight with them ere they get their ships again." Gallant and resolute, the nation braced itself to be invaded. The talk was all of "tall ships" and hulks, French barges and the folly of bringing galleys from "Marcelles." By means of beacons twenty-five to thirty thousand could be mustered in two hours. "They are confident in their strength," reported Van Der Delft to Charles, "and delighted to see the enemy near."

Francis was near Rouen with his Queen on June 14th, to see the setting forth of his army to sea. The Salamander, the Holy Ghost, the White Greyhound, the Crucifix, were among the ships ready with twelve thousand men to board them. Lisle had an equal force to sally forth to Havre.

In July Henry himself was at Portsmouth. And on Sunday

the 19th, as he was dining on the flagship the Great Harry, the French fleet appeared. Henry hurriedly left the flagship as it prepared to meet the French. The Mary Rose, named after Henry's sister, was unfortunately caught with gun portholes open, swamped, five hundred men trapped, and all but twenty drowned. The French had over three hundred sail but an ineffectual landing on the Isle of Wight and an indecisive action in the Channel, brought to its futile ending one of the biggest efforts to square the taking of Boulogne that had yet been made.

XIII

Henry had foreseen and even provoked this invasion. Thanks to his shrewdness, thanks to years of preparation at huge expense, the island had quilled like a porcupine at the mere smell of a Frenchman. "All men of sixty to sixteen" had been ready at an hour's warning to defend the seacoasts. The attack rose up black and formidable but it swung away across the Channel like a thundershower.

This escape, however, was far from clearing Henry's future. The Council of Trent was assembling, and ever since Charles had signed the easy peace of Crépy it had been apparent that greater wars were in the air. Charles had been circling the North like an imperial eagle, all claw and rounded eye, showing by the fearful singleness with which he had torn Gelderland from Henry's former brother-in-law Cleves what the other princelings might expect when his beak had been whetted at Trent.

It was perhaps the most anxious period, in fact, the crisis of Henry's career. He wanted to see Charles, but Charles politely evaded him, sending word that the Low Countries were unsafe to visit, "scourged by epidemics and crowded with soldiers." And this was true. The mercenaries, blood-thirsty brigands, had passed from Château-Thierry to Antwerp. No one could control them—Spanish, Italian, German, Balkan. They wrangled

over non-combatants like crows in the upturned field. They bargained with Kings as fiercely as they soldiered, and Henry had
been outrageously swindled by those he had been trying to hire
for Boulogne. It was the unrest preliminary to the general
council in which, for the first time since Luther, Catholic
genius was massing its forces to recover prestige and repulse
the Reformation.

There was no one more in the eye of this Counter-Reforma-
tion than the monarch whom the Pope wooed as "Henry, son of
Perdition and Satan." Henry had good cause to watch the
Council of Trent.

So far he had no reason for panic. He had just captured
Boulogne and repulsed the French fleet. There was no clear
unity in any Church, in any country, in any party, in any
camp. The political weather changed every instant. No one
trusted any one or was entitled to trust any one. Not until there
was a trial of strength could he or any other ruler in Europe
know whether the papacy was a hulk held together by mere
appearance or a ship that could ride the storm.

Charles, he was aware, did not put his full weight on the
Pope. Francis had not prevented the monstrous massacre of the
defenseless Vaudois, but he was treating with the Protestants
and still dallying with the Turk. The Danes and Swedes made
common cause with the German Protestants. As for himself, he
had just given Cardinal Beton a lesson. Hertford had destroyed
Melrose, and Dryburg, demolished seven monasteries, sixteen "piles," five market towns, 243 villages, thirteen mills and
three hospitals. "We are at war with France and Scotland," said
Bishop Gardiner mournfully in October; "we have enmity with
the Bishop of Rome; we have no assured friendship here with
the Emperor, and we have received from the Landgrave, chief
captain of the Protestants, such displeasure that he has cause to
think us angry with him."

In this gravest of emergencies, Henry did not share Gardiner's pessimism. But he gave up the bluster that used to characterize him and gathered himself into the eight-legged ingenuity that he had inherited from his spider of a father. He knew that this Church Council would come with the distaff of wisdom in one hand, the spear of war in the other. Reginald Pole, in spite of him, would be present at Trent to turn the whetstone for the papal spear. It portended many things, this great Council, but for Henry it portended nothing but the fate of Henry: his whole mind was set on combatting the reprisal that had been hanging over him for ten years.

XIV

Leaning against a window on a cold September afternoon, he talked to Van Der Delft, Charles's ambassador. "I have been King for forty years," he said, "and no man can say that I have ever acted otherwise than sincerely and openly."

Van Der Delft made no comment.

"I have never broken my word," Henry frowned, "I have always loved peace and now I am simply defending myself against the French. The French will not make peace without Boulogne, which I have honorably won and mean to keep."

So much for ritual. But he said all this coldly and without anger, his brain busy calculating. Until he knew what Charles himself was planning, he could not know whether to burst forth into righteous anger or hold himself ready to be wooed.

Still tempted by the multitude of possibilities and pricked by the necessity to choose, he confessed to Gardiner, "I stand amazed after which deer to run."

"Give up Boulogne," his timid councilors edged him. But Henry opposed them. He knew that as long as he held Boulogne he had a vital grip on French pride. They might promise to pay to get rid of him, but the French "when out of need forget their bonds." With Boulogne in his hands, he held the diplomatic tiller.

He closed his eyes to the ruinous cost. He called Boulogne his "daughter," but he spent no such fortune on any daughter of his flesh. "I am at my wits' end," Wriothesley confided to Paget, "how we shall possibly make shift for the next three months." To carry out his fight with Rome, Henry had been debasing the currency as he had debased marriage and debased parliament. And no one dared interfere with him. He had spent £1,300,000 to get Boulogne, where his special taxes had netted him £30,000. The cost of living was already insupportable in England. The economic consequences were hideous. And even if Catholic solidarity could not launch the sentence of deprivation, England staggered to its knees.

But Henry was in the grip of his own master-passion and he did not waver. He would spend eight million more to vindicate the course he had pursued since the divorce of Catherine of Aragon.

He began his autumn campaign by sending his wife's secretary, Buckler, to the German Protestants. They responded by dispatching negotiators. Applying everything he had ever learned from Wolsey and Cromwell, he started a three-ringed diplomacy with the whip in his own hand. He commissioned Gardiner, who had the Europeanism of the papacy in his bones, to negotiate with Charles at Brussels. Gardiner was to "suck out the secrecy and bottom of the matters treated between France and the Emperor," chosen to do this because the Bishop really said to himself, "God send us a good end of our Protestants," and "I never saw that the King's Highness of himself had any affection to them."

Affection or not, Henry dispatched Paget to work with the Protestants, deceiving Gardiner. Paget was to undercut the Emperor and point out the "crafty devices of the French." "If all used the same integrity as the Protestants and the English!" Paget murmured, and the eager Protestants brought from their

French sympathizers to Paget the inwardness of French intentions.

Anti-Protestant with the Emperor, anti-Catholic with the Germans, Henry's third effort was to pry Francis loose from Rome. To do this he kept hoodwinking his own man Gardiner. And meanwhile young Surrey angered every sane man by "animating" Henry to keep Boulogne.

A course so complicated, so devious, so oppressive, so madly expensive, could only proceed from the self-will of this indomitable egoist. Gardiner, sitting alone in Bruges, in the middle of November, reflected in a melancholy practical way, torn between his sympathy with Henry's contentions, which he had supported during the divorce, and the sober and rational ideals that had been framed by More and Colet thirty years before.

"Our war is noisome to our realm and to all our merchants that traffic through the Narrow Seas, who here cry out wonderfully . . .

"We are in a world where reason and learning prevail not, and covenants are little regarded . . .

"Bayard is a stout fellow and would fain have peace; and so would we, but how shall it be if the French King is thus stubbornly set? As he stirred the world for Milan, so he may be expected to move against us indirectly . . .

"I have written vehemently for peace, noting that the worst peace is better than the best war; but the peace the Frenchmen offer is so underfoote and so uncertain of observation that I cannot take comfort in it . . .

"Thus I muse in the night and write in the day when I am at leisure from talking and a little reading."

But Gardiner's sober thoughts could not touch the secret passions of the aging King.

These passions, however, which had driven him from sport to love, from love to war, were now sending him from war to reli-

gion. He had passed through all the stages of the power-sick
from the first docility to the last docility, from the willingness to
keep step with Ferdinand and Maximilian in the first place to
the final assertion that he was keeping step with God.

For the sake of war outside the realm, he was eager to preach
peace inside the realm, to that parliament which, meaning no
harm, he called his "spouse."

On Christmas Eve he came to parliament in person. Of the
two types of "moderation" which are preached in this world—
the hard moderation of consent, and the soft moderation of the
opiate—Henry could only plead for the old-fashioned, lulling,
authoritarian kind. He detested as much as any Council of
Trent the scrutiny of authority that had begun with the reading
of the Bible. He had no faith in the "inferior people." A plain
religious table d'hôte, such as the King's Book provided, seemed
to him indisputably more orderly and more productive of group-
power than the dubious anarchy of à la carte. Knowing the state
to depend for its power on the concentration of right opinion,
he saw no more reason for diversity of religious belief than for
self-will in human mobility, in prices, in food, in clothes.

So he rose to speak to his parliament, "so sententiously, so
kingly, or rather fatherly," that those who heard him could not
keep from weeping and "watering their plants." "I reckon this
day," sobbed a glistening young secretary, who listened to
Henry, "one of the happiest of my life."

As he might have had an inkling that it might be the last
time he would speak in this place, and as his message bore on
charity, Henry put into his argument the perfect accent of the
father who, acknowledging how "bare and barren" he is, still
declares himself appointed by God.

"Of such small qualities as God hath imbued me withal, I
render to His Goodness my most humble thanks, intending with
all my wit and diligence, to get and acquire to me such notable

virtues, and princely qualities, as you have alleged to be incorporated in my person."

He touched on the war he was waging with France, "not for our pleasure, but for your defence." He thanked them for the subsidy. He rejoiced at "the perfect trust and confidence" which they showed by committing to his order "all chantries, hospitals, colleges, and other places." He would regard it as a special "trust." Surely if he should suffer learning to be minished or poor and miserable people to go unrelieved, he "were no trusty friend to you, nor charitable to mine, even as a Christian, neither a lover to the publick-wealth, nor yet one that feared God, to whom account must be rendered of all our doings."

"Now sith I find such kindness in your part towards me, I cannot choose but love and favor you; affirming that no prince in the world more favoreth his subjects than I do you; nor no subjects or commons more love or obey their sovereign lord, than I perceive you do; for whose defence my treasure shall not be hidden, nor (if necessity require) my person shall not be unadventured."

Yorkshire was forgotten. The beastly realm of Lincolnshire was forgotten. The rebellion of 1541 was forgotten. Here or near here, the Happy Warrior began to cry. To speak on Christmas Eve of adventuring a person which so resembled a plum pudding, partook of tears and laughter, especially since his prudent behavior at Portsmouth. But Henry's imagination was busy with his ideal fatherliness and he turned to fatherly admonition.

He could not love them, he said, unless they would amend one thing: "Charity and concord is not amongst you, but discord and dissension beareth rule in every place. St. Paul saith charity is gentle, charity is not envious, charity is not proud, and so forth. Behold then, what love and charity is amongst you, when one calleth another heretic and anabaptist; and he calleth him again papist, hypocrite, and Pharisee! Be these tokens of charity amongst you? Are these signs of fraternal love betwixt you?"

The good political object that bulged under the plea that all was old mumpsimus wrangling with new sumpsimus related to the present importance of lying low. He wanted no religious eruption during the Council of Trent.

"Amend these crimes, or else I, whom God hath appointed," will correct these enormities. Although you be permitted to read holy Scriptures, and to have the Word of God in your mother tongue, you must not dispute and make Scripture a railing and taunting of the priests. "I am very sorry to know and hear how unreverently that most precious jewel, the Word of God, is disputed, rhymed, sung and jangled in every alehouse and tavern." "Love, dread, and serve God, to the which I, as your Supreme Head and sovereign Lord, exhort and require you."

So the encyclical ended. And as Henry, burdened with the flesh, labored from his high seat to go into the palace, those who had memory of the real meaning of this charity—stretching back from the sacramentaries of Windsor to old Lady Salisbury, Robert Aske, Nicholas Carew, Dr. Barnes, Dr. Abel, young Lambert, Father Forest, the monks of the Charterhouse, old John Fisher, Thomas More, the wife of his bed, the mother of Elizabeth, the royal seedlings like Buckingham and Montague, the minister like Cromwell, the traitors like Constable and Darcy,—charity that breathed from these gray lips, the charity that cloaks a multitude of sins, could have made angels mingle their tears with those of his loyal listeners.

xv

Henry was not well, in the new year. All sorts of people were dying: the young Orleans had been snuffed out in September, Suffolk had gone later, so had Richard Cromwell. Audley was dead. Luther died in February. And beside these nudges from the skeleton, which came when his leg was causing him fever, there were political difficulties that troubled him exceedingly. The currency was sick and growing sicker. The Protestants were anxious in Germany. In Scotland Cardinal Beton still gave backbone to Catholic policy; his murder as difficult as Reginald Pole's murder. And the Earl of Surrey had lost favor; he had made a daring excursion from Boulogne which ended in a repulse and hurt prestige.

"We ought to study to preserve the King's repose of mind," Gardiner had said to a fellow-councilor. But it was extraordinarily difficult to repose a man whose leg troubled him, whose war troubled him, whose bank troubled him and whose wife troubled him.

Katharine Parr had not changed. But while she was pursuing those elevated thoughts that she revealed in "The Lamentations of a Sinner," and was counseling the University of Cambridge not so much to hunger after profane learning as to set forth "Christ's sacred doctrine," Henry was reported to be growing restive. She had borne him neither boy nor wench. He was said to be thinking of a gentle lady, his friend Suffolk's widow. In Antwerp he was seeking a loan from the Fuggers and the English merchants there were wagering "that the King's Majesty would have another wife." But those who saw him in March, when he was hoisted from Greenwich to London, got an impression that he would never have a seventh. He greeted Van Der Delft gently and went out of his way to say how his robust constitution had helped him in his illness. "But verily," Van Der Delft told Charles, "his visage shows that it was worse than he pretends."

Charles had always figured for a good deal in Henry's life, but now more than ever. To carry on against the French Henry needed gold and grain and wagons. His country was tired of the war, and he could feel Boulogne slipping. When, to tighten the alliance, he proposed Edward for an imperial match, the Emperor suggested his brother's daughters; and when asked how many his brother had, facetiously counted up to fifteen. There were, in reality, only ten. But the tone of the discussion irritated Henry. The dowry was trivial. He complained, grew hot, showed great displeasure, until Van Der Delft and his colleagues concluded "it was high time to get away and avoid irritating him further, considering his malady."

But the malady went back to Spain. Cromwell's policy had been to Protestantize England to emancipate it from the Empire, and now the Protestants seemed to be in for it. The Council of Trent was showing Spanish edge. Reginald Pole was mute but the Jesuits were there to mail the fist, and the wildest rumors were coming to England: the Bishop of Rome had bound himself to help the Emperor with seven millions of gold, 22,000 infantry, 4,000 horsemen. The seven millions dwindled to 200,000 crowns in fact, but Charles, much as he resented the emphasis on dogma as against reform, and on the Pope as against the Emperor, could not reject any tangible help, ghostly or earthly, against German princes who were undermining the Church wealth, the Hapsburg electorate and his own supremacy.

"If we are beaten in the Pope's quarrel," a morose nobleman told John Mason, "your King's turn will follow."

Mason saw nothing to fear. "God and nature," he explained blandly, "have made so good a wall round the realm that the English never have war unless they go abroad to seek it."

The good Protestant German tried to enter into the feeling of splendid isolation. But it was no use. As Mason chatted on, he "suddenly would fall in a dump and, forgetting himself, bless him, and say 'Sic transit gloria mundi!'"

His feeling was not entirely unlike Henry's. Though far from a Protestant, Henry was worried. He agreed with Charles that the Emperor "must correct the disobedient." "Rebel vassals" must be quelled. But the Pope's soldiers, the Spanish, the German Catholic soldiers, were thronging to the Emperor. "If the armies meet," said Vaughan to Henry, "there will be a bloody fray, and these countries (the Low Countries) are wonderfully fearful of the result. Trade is at a standstill."

Henry could not help biting his lips. He knew the papal doctrine which assimilates baptism with an oath of allegiance and regarded himself as a rebel. He reluctantly allowed Hertford and Gardiner to talk peace with the French. "The King continues melancholy," the report went out, "and does not go into his garden as his habit is in summer."

XVI

In a crisis like this it had become Henry's habit to take out a little Catholic insurance.

Cranmer kept out of the way. But there were others who freely invited trouble. John Lassells, who informed on Katheryn Howard, had been on the Gardiner-Norfolk black-list. He was arrested for heresy. So was the preacher Crome. So was Latimer. So was Shaxton. And a woman of family, Anne Askew, who had been twice arrested in 1545, but proved to have many influential and solicitous friends at court, was once again landed into trouble.

This woman was "very obstinate and heady in matters of religion." But those who were good Imperialists were not breaking Anne Askew as a heretic. They were pursuing her as Elizabeth Barton had been pursued in 1533. The Holy Maid of Kent was a Catholic: Anne Askew was a Protestant. But the men who racked Elizabeth were no friends of Catherine of Aragon: the men who racked Anne Askew sought to reach Katharine Parr.

Anne Askew was found guilty, after a terrible quizzing conducted by Gardiner. But afterward, in the Tower, she had to deal with two men whom Henry intimately trusted: one was Wriothesley, the new Lord Chancellor, whom he had made wealthy and powerful; the other was Rich, who had been epitomized by Thomas More.

Anne Askew lived long enough to write her account of what happened in the Tower with these two men.

"Then Master Rich sent me to the Tower, where I remained till three o'clock, when Rich and one of the Council came, charging me upon my obedience to show them if I knew any man or any woman of my sect. Answered that I knew none. Then they asked me of my lady of Suffolk, my lady of Sussex, my lady of Hertford, my lady Denny and my lady Fitzwilliam. Answered that if I should pronounce anything against them I could not prove it.

"Then they said the King was informed that I could name, if I would, a great number of my sect.

"Answered 'that the King was as well deceived in that behalf as dissembled with in other matters.'"

But she had needed money to pay for food in the Tower; divers ladies had sent her money.

"I answered that there was a man in a blue coat who delivered me ten shillings and said that my lady of Hertford sent it to me; and another in a violet coat gave me eight shillings, and said my lady Denny sent it me: whether it were true or not, I cannot tell; for I am not sure who sent it me, but as the maid did say.

"Then they said, there were of the Council that did maintain me: and I said No.

"Then they did put me on the rack, because I confessed no ladies or gentlewomen to be of my opinion, and thereon they kept me a long time; and because I lay still, and did not cry, my lord Chancellor [Wriothesley] and Master Rich took pains to rack me with their own hands, till I was nigh dead.

"Then the lieutenant caused me to be loosed from the rack. Incontinently I swooned, and then they recovered me again.

"After that I sat two long hours reasoning with my lord Chancellor upon the bare floor; where he, with many flattering words, persuaded me to leave my opinion. But my lord God

(I thank his everlasting goodness) gave me grace to persevere, and will do, I hope, to the very end."

XVII

Anne Askew was burned to death at Smithfield, July 16th, mainly for denouncing the mass. Lassells was one of the other heretics who suffered.

Katharine Parr had been strong enough a year before to keep Cranmer's enemies from sending him to the Tower. The Primate was willing to bend to the Council but Henry, wrothy at this move of Gardiner's which Katharine exposed to him, sent for Cranmer under cover of night, told him he was a fool to put his head in the noose, and gave him his ring to produce when the Council renewed the attack.

Between 1545 and 1546, however, there was all the difference created by imperial mobilization. When the Queen tried to debate with Henry on the points in religion that were raised by all these trials, he became suddenly furious. To be challenged in his opinions, in his old age, by his wife, seemed to him insufferable. He quivered with a rage that gave an opening to Gardiner and Wriothesley. They drew up articles against her, and presented them to Henry. She was not with him. In a paroxysm of obscure passions, he set his name to the indictment.

Word was brought to Katharine by one of Henry's physicians. On hearing it she broke down. She had no illusion that this was a game to try her. She saw in it the wrath, the tempestuous fury, the malign cruelty, of which he was never incapable. The horror and terror of it dethroned her calm.

When the commotion of her weeping came to Henry, he forgot his own part in it. He sent his physicians. Budging along heavily, he came himself to her chamber, "where compassionating her estate," as Herbert puts it, "he used such kind words as did help recover her."

Attended by Lady Herbert, her sister, she later went to the

King's bedchamber. His attack was over, and the sun shone. "He courteously welcomed her and began to talk of religion."

But Katharine had learnt. She excused herself. A woman's place, she intimated, was on the footstool. She referred herself in this and all other causes to his Majesty's wisdom.

"Not so, by Saint Mary!" quoth the King. "You are become a doctor, Kate, to instruct us, as we take it, and not to be instructed or directed by us."

Katharine demurely replied that what she had said "was rather to pass away the time and pain of his infirmity than to hold argument." She hoped by hearing his Majesty's learned discourse to receive some profit thereby.

"And is it even so, sweetheart?" he beamed. "Then are we perfect friends again."

But the warrant he signed had gone out of his head. He and his Queen were talking merrily in the garden when Lord Wriothesley, with forty of the guard, came to enact the usual tragic scene.

Henry saw him and hobbled down the alley to him. "Fool, beast, knave, arrant knave, fool!"

Wriothesley's slow comprehension turned to dismay and horror. He disappeared.

As Henry puffed back, Katharine began to excuse the Chancellor.

He looked at her pityingly. "You, poor soul, do not know how evil he deserves his grace at your hands."

XVIII

Katharine Parr barely missed the Tower. The blow that Henry struck at her was deadly: but, curiously enough, it was also idiotic. In July Anne Askew was burned for saying, "Your mass is the most abominable idol in the world." In August Henry himself was trying to persuade Francis to join him in abolishing the mass.

And the counterpart of this insane frivolity was supplied by Francis when the French peace was arranged in June. He "laid his hand upon Knyvet's shoulder and said that nothing grieved him more than the war, but there never had been rancor nor malice, and the love of reconciled friends was without comparison." The Gascons and men of Kent, the Hodges and John Dulls, had not known that the war was so friendly. Some of them had gone to it, like defiant Alderman Reed of London, by the scruff of the neck, and many of them had not Reed's fortune to be taken prisoner.

Henry's government, like Henry's body, was beginning to be overripe, but, with the nonchalance which is nine-tenths of politics, he had contrived to turn to the world a new aspect which still had the appearance of being intact.

That aspect was the peace with France. Though Boulogne had cost five million crowns to capture, and though it was now being held and fortified at great expense, Henry had made terms about it that were drowned in joy-bells: it was to be ceded to the French in eight years for two million crowns. To hold it had stirred the French into hornets, and the whole grand policy, on which Henry had opposed his Council and lavished his talent, was big only with lost labor and debt.

But another triumph consoled Henry. Cardinal Beton had at last been assassinated. The men who killed him as he sat in his chair, Norman Leslie and Henry Balnavis, would be with him at Greenwich by the end of the year. They had stabbed Beton saying, "A vengeance upon thee! We from God are sent to avenge Wishart, thou obstinate enemy to Christ Jesus and his Holy Evangel!" And the priest died moaning and crying. His body was hung over the wall by arm and foot, for "the people to see their God," and the evangelists boasted they put salt on his body because the weather was hot.

These were the short steps toward civilization that Henry's friends and pensioners were taking. And he was doubly glad of

Beton's fate because his own political direction was changed again.

The signal for change came from Rome itself. A dove named Bertano flew from the ark with an olive-branch. He arrived by way of France. But Henry's attitude toward the olive-branch was like King David's attitude toward the Lord in regard to his dying boy. If the boy was dead, what was the good of praying any longer? If the flood was over, Henry folded his prayer-rug. He had only burned heretics to propitiate the gods. When the gods sent ambassadors, he knew he had burned heretics enough. Hence he regained his audacity and suggested abolishing the mass.

The furious war that had broken out in Germany between Charles and the Protestant princes increased his courage. The adjournment of the Council of Trent added to it. And as these signs of remitted danger sank into his consciousness, he became more open to the studied suggestions with which the New Men were plying him.

He had always fluctuated with the market. But while he denied he was unwell, he really had become a mountain of ailment. As he suffered, his customary baths doing him little good, he became quicker to see the aspect of things that his native obsessions prompted. This was understood by no men better than Hertford and Lisle, "the only nobles of age and ability," as Chapuys judged, "to undertake affairs."

They were New Men, "great stirrers of heresy." They had moved into the palace to be near Henry. As his own shadow lengthened, Norfolk saw that these were the coming men. Only the previous year he had blocked their sending Gardiner to the Tower. Only at Whitsun he paid his greatest tribute to the Seymours, tried to arrange two cross marriages with them, through the King. Norfolk's son, the most exasperated of the young generation, was less placatory. He dared to raise his voice.

"These newly erected men would by their wills leave no noble men on life."

The pane through which Henry himself was looking at the political scene was no longer clear. It was iridescent with his sick and writhing body. And as he dictated orders to Boulogne to respect the French forts, while sending verbal orders to tear them down, it was only an automatic act, the long habit of intrigue and connivance.

And at last, half-raising his eye to the visitor who half-opened the door, he sighed a great sigh and made his will.

He was to be buried as he had long intended, in the still unfinished chapel at Windsor. Jane Seymour, his true and loving wife, was to lie with him. She had borne him a son.

His will began with reassurance to the Catholics: "In the name of God and of the Glorious and Blessed Virgin our Lady St. Mary, and of all the Holy Company of Heaven."

He confessed his sincere faith that, mortal and born in sin, living here in this wretched and transitory world under God, dying in steadfast and perfect faith, he verily trusted to be saved by Christ's passion and to obtain eternal life.

He wished to be prayed for, and to have mass said for him, in case of purgatory.

Edward and his heirs, Mary and her heirs, Elizabeth and her heirs, and next the children of his sister Mary's two daughters, were bequeathed the crown.

Cranmer, Hertford, Lisle, Tonstall, Wriothesley, Browne, Paget, Russell, Denny, Herbert, and some others, were to direct the government during Edward's minority.

So he balanced the game with God and matched his councilors from both parties.

The shrewdness with which he faced both ways was not lost on the more observant citizen. "There will be a change of religion in England," wrote Hooper to Bullinger in December, "and the King will take up the Gospel of Christ if the Emperor be defeated in this most destructive war. Should the Gospel sustain a loss, he will then retain his impious mass, for which he has this last summer committed four respectable and godly persons to the flames."

This was the prospect. But at the eleventh hour, when the door gently opened and Henry's fate silently groped forward to claim him, Hertford and Lisle, with Cranmer behind them, raised before him the enraging threat of a new conspiracy.

Surrey was this new conspirator, this Buckingham. His father Norfolk was his abettor. And behind them was Gardiner, without whom "evangelical truth cannot be restored."

The effect on Henry was terrific. He had been so ill that his two legs had to be cauterized. Even Katharine and Mary could not see him. But with the mad vehemence of which he was capable, when the sick nerve was touched in him, he took the way that was shown to him. And Norfolk, who was not loved in London, followed Surrey through the streets to the Tower.

Empson and Dudley had been Henry's first offerings on the political altar. Then he had been young, gallant and untried; the newcomer, the Prince Charming. Now he was worn. His eyes were bloodshot. He could not lift a pen. His great body declared unhappy fatigue and misery in every crumpled line. Yet something inside him that distrusted every man and woman and that yet gripped for certainty and security drove him to sign away his oldest confederate and to lay hands on the one treasure of that hardened and sordid veteran, his only son.

The quickness of Norfolk, the sly wit of him, the nimble subservience, had served him often. But it availed nothing. He was devoured at last by this omnivorous suspicion.

The suspicion dressed itself in legal clothes. Henry was much better after Christmas. He sat up. He talked calmly. His boy Edward thanked him for a New Year's gift and "will strive to follow his father's example in virtue, wisdom and piety." The pith of Henry's nature still seemed rational and human. But that quick, terrified eye did betray the fissure in his nature, and the flood of sullen and lusterless feeling in the sunless depths of it rolled in its salt circle, forever turning on itself and never reaching the sea.

XIX

Surrey had no chance. The "foolish proud boy" was now thirty. He had always been insolent, since the days he went to France with Henry's boy Richmond. The braggart in him struggled with the noble poet. The daylight of high intelligence quarreled with a forest of antipathies. He lived in a green gloom. Knyvet could not bear his unkindness, his malice. "No, no, cousin Knyvet, I malice not so low, my malice is higher, my malice climbs higher." "The King loved him not," he said. And he had been rash; he had quartered the royal arms on his own; he had spoken unfeelingly of William the Conqueror; he had told his sister to become Henry's Madam "De Temps" at a period when Henry was in a condition to be moved by block and tackle. Those offenses he turned into quintessence in his final speech: he took his life in both hands and crashed it in the face of his accusers. There was a moment, perhaps, when something in this desperate act turned to his favor; but a single word from the man who directed the result quelled the impulse. Surrey was declared guilty. On Tower Hill, where he once had stood watching his cousin Katheryn Howard, he was brought to death, on January 19th.

Norfolk was stunned. He had never run counter to his own interests, and as he had always identified them with the King's, he could not understand the fortune that brought him to the same Tower as Darcy and Thomas Cromwell, Robert Aske and Robert Constable, Katheryn and Anne. It bewildered him, as if water were accused of running up hill.

He forgot that he had aspired; he chose only to remember that he had never conspired.

"I am a true poor gentleman," the old soldier protested. The Bishop of Rome he had renounced. "If I had twenty lives I would rather spend them all than that he should have any power in this realm, for no man knows better than I, by reading story, how his usurping power has increased."

So he defended himself. But it looked bad for him. His voice went up into the shriller registers of self-defense. "Who tried out the falsehood of Lord Darcy, Sir Robert Constable, Sir John Bulmer, Aske and many others but only I . . . I have always shown myself a true man to my Sovereign, and, since these things done, have received more profits of his Highness than before. Who can think that I should now be false?"

Norris might have said this, but Norris disdained it. Before Surrey was executed the father was also judged guilty. He was destined to be beheaded January 28th.

XX

While Norfolk signed a confession and begged for pity, Henry did not hear him. The usurer in his soul had forgotten that "charity is gentle." Every day, in spite of his own terrible sickness, Henry drove himself to come to council and to see ambassadors. Almost up to Surrey's execution, the 19th, he was busy with foreign affairs, while Hertford was near him, and Cranmer hovered by little Edward. But in spite of himself, in spite of his obstinate and tenacious nature, he could no longer sit up. His physicians ordered him to bed. He kept Katharine and his daughter Mary out of the sick-chamber, which had become repulsive. But he sent for them. Mary he saw alone. He regretted that he had never accomplished a marriage for her. He was prevented by fortune or misfortune.

"I pray thee, my daughter, try to be a mother to thy brother, for look, he is little yet."

Mary wept. As he spoke of the councilors he was naming, she cried, "I hope to God that your Majesty will live many days yet, and will not do me so much harm as to leave me an orphan so soon."

He did not answer. As he could not bear to see her weeping, he made signs with his hand that she should go away, for he could not say it in words.

He sent for Katharine. "It is God's will that we should part," he said with his masterful simplicity, "and I order all these gentlemen to honor you and treat you as if I were living still."

He had just named Thomas Seymour a member of the council. He had remembered a number of legacies in his will. He spoke to Katharine about her jewels and ornaments; he wished her to have them.

She could not answer for weeping, and he ordered her to leave him.

His condition grew worse hour by hour, while parliament, like a good dog, watched for a movement or token of the master. A quiet charged with hushed orders and rapid movements was tense in the galleries of Whitehall. Every breath was watched. The councilors who came out of the sick-chamber marked a grave change; he could not last. But he would not hear he was sinking. He talked, gave commands, taxed his strength. The crew without their captain were helpless. Who was to tell him? At last, on the evening of the 27th, with the physicians afraid to break the news, Sir Anthony Denny, the gentleman of the chamber, had the boldness to go in and tell him. His Majesty was in such case, he said, that to man's judgment he was not like to live. He therefore exhorted him to prepare himself to death.

Henry heard him. He knew he was sinking. He had much abused, he confided to Denny, but he gathered himself quietly for the end that was approaching. Although he had much abused "yet is the mercy of Christ able to pardon all my sins, though they were greater than they be."

Was there any learned man, Denny inquired timidly, to confer withal and open his mind unto?

"Cranmer," Henry answered, "but he not yet." He would take a little sleep, "and then," he said prudently, "as I feel myself, I will advise upon the matter."

And Denny bowed out.

XXI

As Henry fell into sleep that was stupor, propped in his great bed, those who looked at him could fear that life was extinct. The candles must have cast washing shadows on the livid face that fronted immobile to the approaching night. He could hardly speak to Denny. His tongue, which had tasted many delights, lay thick in his mouth. A cup of wine was ready to moisten his lips when he signaled for it, but unless it was clinked against his teeth without demand he went parched; he no longer had any power to signal. His arms fell torpid and inert. He had not been able to lift them to sign Norfolk's death warrant by hand; he could not lift them to avert his own.

Pain was no longer evident. His face had been black with it, but his legs that had dripped raging fires were now becoming two pillars of ice. There he lay, his eyes transfixed, his nightcap boyishly awry. The proud fortress was crumbling: already the outer walls were taken, the five senses were yielding their avenues, and nowhere if not in the hidden citadel was there a point where he still resisted his end.

Like a whisper from his past there softly entered the one man he had asked to see. It was Cranmer, come from Croydon, the cold breath of the January Thames still on his fresh face. He had come faithfully. He had obeyed his King in every desire since Catherine was put away: he had attended his master like the bird who ever attends the adventurer of the sea.

There was something fit and touching in this final conjunction of the pale-blooded priest and the hot-blooded man who had required his sanctions. Henry had been a piece of life, a lump of the energy that is conjured out of the sun. His naked force had eaten into the corrupt and into the sacredly healthy. He had attacked his life greedily. He had tried to rule it. He had multiplied with royal hand the legacy of human pain. Revolving on himself with precious apprehension, he had toward the end passed into an autumn serenity that dripped in its decay. Perhaps within his mind there had been an implacable witness to this decay: or maybe the weary witness had dried his tears and folded his hands. But the eight and thirty years in which he had dominated England had left their mark. He had channeled character, molded statecraft, and, by a marvelous maneuver, made himself the Supreme Head of a religion. Not for many years would this be scrutinized in its full meaning and some of its perversity of origin be cleansed in sun and wind.

Now the man was dying, bit by bit, the huge mass of him disputed in the grooves of instinct with the encroaching, high-headed worm. As Cranmer came to him the King's eyes, swiveling in their sockets, could give no recognition. The Primate knelt in the thick presence, others kneeling with him, and in his supple hand he took the King's cold and massy hand that hung relaxed on the coverlet.

Cranmer's voice had been persuasive in Henry's ears. "Do you die in the faith of Christ?" he asked earnestly.

Already in those ears there were other sounds. The ocean of oblivion was rolling its long wave toward him, the thunder of its surf engulfing him, while a blind mortality was crushing him toward obliteration with a steady hand.

Did he hear Cranmer? Did the word Christ gleam white on a far wing in the high heavens above this spent swimmer? Was there still a sting of consciousness in him? Was it intent on

Christ or was it enmeshed in the terror and turmoil of old battles repeating themselves, their phantom armies still grappling in the mist?

While life and death haggled over this powerless man, the heirs of authority were already disputing the heritage outside. Hertford, who had little Edward in his keeping, was bidding for the scepter. Paget stood with him. Gardiner, across the river, tightened his muscles. Wriothesley wavered. The soldiers champed. The lawyers sharpened dried quills. The clergy, much confused, prepared themselves for a Supreme Head aged nine years and three months. Katharine Parr, Kateryn the Quene K P, her eyes closed and her heart open, thought of Thomas Seymour. The council, the parliament, the law, the people, the whole hand of England, felt itself working free from the opposing thumb.

As Hertford, spare and feverish, walked the shadowed gallery with Paget, his long gestures betokening "liberty, liberty," and his lips declaring the plight of the people, there was something so keen in his words, so thirsty after the years in the desert, that Paget could only urge him to take his time and go slow. But could he go slow? The halberdiers at the end of the gallery, statues of attention against stone wall and tapestry, declared the crisis in the palace. With every word that Hertford uttered and every step he paced, the fate of Norfolk quivered. Should pale morning step into London before Henry had expired, then would it lay its cold hand on the papist's shoulder and steer him to his doom. Midnight had already sounded from Westminster. The King still lived. And Hertford's silver charity began to draw black judgment over it as each minute swerved the needle to the Tower.

One o'clock struck. Cranmer was on his knees. Henry convulsed. He resisted his enemy, his veins bursting. His hold on life, his hold on Norfolk's throat, he fought to keep, but death garroted him and Norfolk was saved.

Cranmer, weeping mildly, rose to his feet. Henry, he told the councilors, had pressed his hand. He had died in the faith of Christ, Christ's passion would save him, and thus he would enter into eternal life.

XXII

Soon, "in goodly time," he was taken from Whitehall. He was buried at Windsor, though not as he had planned. His council named a Protector, not as he had decided. The French took back Boulogne, not as he had treated. Out of the wreck of all his marriages, the female child, Elizabeth, at whose birth he had winced, whom he despised and rejected, took the scepter he meant for war-lords and raised it to heights of which the poets sing. The Cromwell whom he beheaded would have a fellow, a branch of the same tree. In 101 years, on this site of Whitehall, almost on the anniversary of his own death, Oliver Cromwell would behead the King of England. Strong passions breed strong passions.

But England had first to crown Henry's male heir. It is crying, "Vive le noble roy Edward!" And "the trumpets sound with great melody and courage."

BOOK EIGHT

The Background

> *"The great and glorious masterpiece of man is to know how to live to purpose: all other things, to reign, to lay up treasure, to build, are, at most, but little appendices and props."*
>
> MONTAIGNE

I

HENRY was a king. His trade, which is a hard one, will not distract us from his manhood, but one cannot pretend that he lived in that private condition which would save us from clustering historic detail: from very early he belonged to that important class of marked people who live in the thick of politics and in the pith of society, seeing much of men and of women and having their hand forced by their public position much as the hod-carrier gets a sunken shoulder, or the city man gets angina pectoris, because of his way of life. Henry cannot be seen apart from his occupation, its nature and its diseases. He was a man before everything, but his kingship colors his drama and sets his scene.

The class to which he belonged has been marvelously extended since the sixteenth century. The number of new dynasties since 1500, the lard dynasty, the tin dynasty, the steel, the railway, the newspaper, the cotton, the copper, the coal, the rubber, the oil, the motor, has so crowded upon, and depressed, the waning reputation of kingship that modern magnates are not unlikely to be unfair to their prototypes, and to see Henry and his kind in the light of nominal monarchy, instead of seeing them as men and brothers, the founders or managing directors of great corporations and trusts.

Henry was a magnate of a type so genuine that to approach him as a picture on a playing-card is to miss his significance. What he had at stake was not money. It was power that took a different form and had grander and wider implications. With the oil that anointed him there came more than fleets, foundations, researches, or even war; there came the direct handling of three million people, an effigy not only on the parliament and on the coins but in the people's corporate heart. The effulgence of a whole people with a longish history was shed upon him, and from him there came a vivid sense of the authority, if not of the duty, to which he had been consecrated. But if Henry was anointed with holier oil than Rockefeller-Morgan or Inchcape-Leverhulme, he pursued power in a manner no less typical and no less instinctive. He was a magnate to his fingertips. He was a magnate before he was a king. Hence, to make him intelligible, he has to be seen in the complicated throes of those rivalries that create his personal drama and give it such tremendous character. He has to be seen, particularly, in the Europe of 1500-1550, and in the company of Francis and Charles.

In the year 1500 itself, Henry and Francis and Charles were three small dukes. Within fifteen years, they would come to power, and this power would bring the three of them into the juxtaposition and interaction that would last to the middle of the century when the curtain rings down. Before looking at the thrones they would inherit, and the Europe that would surround them, a glimpse may be taken of the three children who, wholly unknown to themselves, would act in such a manner that we feel the effects of it even to this day.

II

In 1500 Henry is a boy of nine. He is a big dimpled child
with cream and rose complexion, self-willed yet ductile. He can
be managed, if his petulance is understood, and his tutor finds
him intelligent and full of application, considering that, like
most human beings, he cannot keep his mind on anything for
any length of time. He is the Duke of York, etc., etc., while his
older brother Arthur will be King of England. You see him at
his best when he comes from table where he has eaten well,
and orders his page to hand him his flute. With his flute to his
little mouth, his curled lip on the stop, his fingers flickering and
his eyes delightfully absorbed and intent, as he sits upright in
satin doublet, he changes to an artist, not a rapturous Italian
artist, but a jolly English one, with melody and sweetness and
zest in his nature, fluting for his solace like any shepherd boy
on any weald in England.

The boy Francis is most at home with his mother Louise. He
is now in 1500 one of those little brown French lads, long as
an haricot, already a perfect little gentleman and a perfect little
devil, with gay manners, a deftness that will combine with
lightning movements and hard daring, a shimmer of words
already allowing his mother and little sister to understand how
versatile his intelligence is, an intelligence that will be like his
own long, discriminating, inquisitive, sensuous nose. He is the
idol of his mother. Francis's sister was conceived at an age not to
be mentioned, and born when the mother was fourteen. The
boy will sleep in his mother's room until he is that same age.
He adores his mother, and counts on her to guide him, to indulge him, to save him, to be God for him, and to see in him the
Cæsar worthy of her dreams. He is not in line to be King of
France unless the present King die childless. He is Duc d'Angoulême, and his little sister who also worships him is Marguerite
d'Angoulême.

The youngest of the three dukes is Charles, a baby in his cradle, who is just opening those vast blue eyes on Ghent. His mother is a Spaniard, his father a blond German-Burgundian, but the language heard around his cradle is French Walloon. This must have been an amazingly placid baby, but already he was probably sleeping with his mouth open and moaning restlessly, not because he is going to be Emperor of the Holy Roman Empire—a trade name for Germany, more or less—but because he has adenoids. He will have the heavy adenoidal chin that Titian and Velasquez will make famous as the Hapsburg-Aragon contribution to human beauty. He is a blond infant, and no one cares for him more than his widowed young aunt, Margaret of Austria, who will be his regent in a few years.

These three dates are worth remembering: Henry born in 1491, Francis in 1495, Charles on that convenient date 1500. And the boys are worth identifying. Henry and Francis will die in the same year, 1547: Charles will outlive them, though not by many years. They are the central European figures of the first half of the sixteenth century, in that walk of life to which it had pleased God to call them, Henry's father having aided God by direct action.

III

The Europe which these three monarchs were so largely to inherit had not a purely political character. The stream of its politics was merely one influence, one current in the ocean, which was ebbing and flowing under vaster influences, some of them of this earth and others from beyond the earth, uncontrolled by sovereignties that were to call themselves imperial.

It was the world of 1500-1550: Europe opening its astonished gaze on the sea-routes to America, Africa and India; on the spread of travel, the marvel of ship and compass, the rich harvests of commerce and exchange springing mainly from the enterprise of the mounting middle class; the diversity and violence

of humanist criticism, the power of Biblical revelation passing
from the priests to the people, from Latin torpor into living
common speech; the weakness of the papacy and the strength of
kings; the confusion of values, the deep and at the same time
terrifying possibilities of mental and spiritual self-assertion, the
growing personality and increasing wealth of the "barbarian"
nations, and the keener sweetness of actual life.

This was a Europe in which strong impulse crowded on the
heels of new inventions and popularizations, pushing out the
boundaries of ambition and the frontiers of habit, and yet carrying into this enlargement of experience, as always happens, much
of the attitude and many of the impedimenta of the older art
of life. Names hurtle across the bold skies of the early sixteenth
century like wild squadrons of the air—Botticelli, Perugino,
Mantegna, da Vinci, Albrecht Dürer, Raphael, Michelangelo,
Titian, Breughel, Holbein, Cellini, Columbus, Cabot, Vasco da
Gama, Cortéz, Pizarro, Chevalier Bayard, Gaston de Foix,
Gonsalvo de Córdoba, Pescara, Linacre, Ambroise Paré,
Servetus, Bernard Palissy, Erasmus, Budé, Colet, Thomas More,
Melanchthon, Martin Luther, Rabelais, Ferdinand, Maximil-
ian, Louis XII, the Popes Julius, Leo X, Adrian VI, Clement
VII, Isabella, Louise of Savoy, Margaret of Austria, Margaret of
the Heptameron, James IV, James V, Charles V, Francis I,
Henry VIII, Wolsey, Cranmer, Thomas Cromwell, Machiavelli,
Ignatius Loyola, Copernicus, Calvin—a swarm, a whirl, of brilliant and extravagant vitality, that throbbed and danced in the
heavens and that, in the glowing distance, still coruscates and
blazes fire. It was not the revival of learning, since the reunion
of Italy and the classic had already accomplished itself, nor was
it a definite renaissance or resurrection, like an act in a play,
but it had, outside Spain, the common character of the breakdown of disciplines, an upheaval against the parenthood of the
past, a striding insurgence into new plenitudes of experience,
and, with this, a subjection to new empires of power.

Europe turned to Italy as Italy had turned to Greece. But it was the Italy of a new beauty and a new truth. The old universal control was gone and new fidelities proposed themselves through the fitful deliciousness, the immorality of emancipation, that crisped and thrilled men's hearts.

The garden had to have its serpent. A career like Michelangelo's, a single reflective gaze like Leonardo da Vinci's, broke through the Lorenzos and the Lorenzaccios to give back to human beings the mournful search of the infinite beyond the little ecstasy of young hope. But at least it was no longer that early fidelity, that simple obedience of the child. It was the piercing scrutiny of free intelligence, the sun that had been slain and was arisen.

And in the towns, in the little world of the workshops as in the dark recesses of the by-streets, this light, shattered into its prism by twisted window panes, fell in its wonder on the embruted and the enslaved. Plants reach for the light: in every nation of this turbulent and palpitating Europe there was that secret quiver in the breathlessness of a fresh experience which is like the glad hidden trembling of first love.

Yet with all this disposition to dethrone the theology that had dominated mature life, with all this zest for happiness that sought to create new hierarchies of value, the field of political authority was left gapingly open for the least inspired and least controlled of leaders. Save for Switzerland, Europe at this moment was politically imbecile. It was the direct ancestor of our present Europe, a concert without its director, a blare and clang of lusty sound with immense creative impulse and no exterior design. In 1500-1550 it was on the very threshold of that bloody nationalism which celebrated itself on so large a scale in 1914-1918. The main difference, from an historical point of view, is the more evident dynastic character of 1500-1550. The people of Europe dethroned the church by a sudden surge of instinct but, except for disputing power in a few peasant risings and a few restless communes, left political control to the hungry dynasts, a narrow and imperious master-class.

The Europe of emperor-pope had proved utterly unable to stretch itself to include the great plural vitalities that were now developing. This old notion and practice of a European society might have survived if the councils of the church had been extraordinarily flexible and emancipated, but as the Italians had no true interest in Europe, Europe could not group itself around the Italians. The ferment of new ideas, the yeast of the printed word, the self-assertion of army-and-treasury grasped by one dynast in each country, was too much for a papacy that had no religious tradition imposing enough to hold the people and thus enmesh the dynastic will.

The people were not entirely headless and feeble and ignorant. The day of the crusades was over, feudalism was gone, communities were no longer land-locked, the sea was not in the grip of the barons, and even on land the grip of the barons was loosened; in spite of priest and noble and judge and master, in spite of the old men of the tribe, the populations who had been immobilized as 'well as pacified under medievalism began to communicate. Out of the air itself a mental nitrogen was seized by even the most static of peoples, and growth accelerated, surging from the bottom, breaking bonds. But this burst of human vitality was superintended by nothing better than the existing habit. The church, having a feebler grip on the revenue and the army than the dynast, was indeed partially dislodged, out of honest revolt against its cynical selfishness. The people henceforward submitted to the dynasts, having mastered no opposite will.

The mind of Europe was not politically effective. It was the mind of poets, of saints, of speculators, of savants, of teachers and of artists. Unless the saint joined hands with the demagogue, the voice of a new faith was not heard in this turbulent, chaotic, liberated Europe, while the voice of skeptical and critical in-

telligence, the little metronome that goes on when people are
all talking or when they are all asleep, the word of just measure-
ment and melancholy account-keeping, was even less comprehended by the people than by their kings. And the kings only
listened out of caution: they were warrior-kings still encased in
their martial lobster-shells and still engaged in the old entranc-
ing occupation of building up their dynasties, exaggerating
their importance, magnifying their glory and their power.

IV

It was, one would have thought, a magnificent moment for men
of clear ambition and intrinsic power. This Europe, in which
Charles and Francis and Henry were to play leading parts, was a
Europe palpitating with humanist hope and opportunity. The
prestige of kings could not have been greater, conferred on
them by the power of their fathers or won by them in their own
right. But brute aggrandizement was the central appetite of
kingship. It dominated the lives of Francis, Charles and Henry.
They were dynasts with the military tradition of kingship. They
were warring princes. And they generally pursued their advancement by military methods while discussing, advocating
and pledging "universal peace."

In the game of power that occupied these royal lives, the
magnet was not a continent like Africa or a gold-mine of un-
developed resources like China. It was Italy. Italy was the
shining target of the high preoccupation. Every king in Europe
was intent on building up his personal control, and every king
in Europe had his eye on Italy. It had for centuries been the
strength and weakness of Italy that it had no central king. When
the dynastic states began to take form, and when every king began to see himself master in his own house as against his border
states and as against his insatiable nobles, the desire of conquering and dominating Italy became the essence of foreign policy.
Italy, a young goddess, nude and radiant, was to be held by any

one powerful enough under arms. So long as one power could cripple another by arousing a border state (and France and Spain were rimmed with toxic principalities), the main object beyond the border could not be pursued. But once let the dynastic state feel secure, the lust for Italy became paramount. It was the dream of Ferdinand and Isabella. It kept the French kings drunk for a hundred years. It inflamed Maximilian. It drew the Turks into Europe, since Italy was the jewel of the Mediterranean. And in Italy itself the papacy caught this passion and bartered its authority to become a third-rate military power.

But Italy, the exterior object of war and diplomacy, could not have come within reach until each European nation had faced the preliminary work of consolidating its own government under a dynasty and bringing the nobles, so greedy, so wasteful, so disruptive, under one control and one head. This work of consolidating the trusts was still unfinished at the opening of the sixteenth century, and has to be understood as the concrete political problem underlying the rivalry and ambition of the subsequent years.

The dynasts, in a sense, were unavoidable. The moment had come for each nation to assemble its features, to come into focus under a single head, to work as a unit. National war became more than ever a fateful though rude measure of the fires that were alive underneath, the forces and potentialities of national will. From looking over Europe at a glance, it would have been hard to tell which nations were nuclear as to language, religion, fellow-feeling, education, commerce, army, navy, statecraft, pugnacity. Elements of instinct, elements of national resources in the way of raw material, questions of an effective capital, a good leader, a seaboard, all came into play. Was it geographical that France should be a unit, where Spain could not incorporate Portugal with itself? Was persecution the only force that would induce the Netherlands to raise ramparts against international inundation? Why should Granada and Brittany, Navarre and Burgundy, Scotland and Milan succumb, while Switzerland and Sweden could integrate themselves, just as Venice and Naples were sinking into impotence? The larger units might seem to have had a predestined form, but national Italy was as conspicuous a failure as national England, national Spain and national France were to prove successes. The Blood Bath of Stockholm did not lead to a unification of Denmark and Sweden. It was a problem, in short, that presented itself to Peoples and Cultures but devolved in detail on unique men.

The work of consolidation that was engaging the unique men in 1500 has, therefore, to be viewed in simple outlines, to recall the life-heritage of Henry and his peers. The master-dynasts were Ferdinand and Isabella in Spain, the parents of Henry's first queen: Maximilian in Germany, Charles's grandfather: Louis in France, Francis's father-in-law: Henry VII, Henry's father: and Pope Julius a little later in Italy, the Holy Father of all. The Turk was about to appear in Europe, his head and shoulders hoisted above the horizon, his long arm reaching as far as Vienna. But the Turk remained a threat. We cannot complicate the story with the unspeakable Turk.

Spain, a country of eight million inhabitants, is of the first importance as a great power. Isabella had shown an unseeing world that a woman could be a manly sovereign even in a country where men were ordered to ride the horse exclusively and to leave the mule to unhorsed creatures like ecclesiastics and women. She had come to the rule of Castile after her brother. She had married Ferdinand of Aragon. Ferdinand sulked when he could not have the whip hand, but Isabella, working through him as the executive, drove him to the ideal of Spain as a unit. She was clear-willed, steady-minded and indomitable. She spared herself in nothing. To rally her soldiers against the invasion by Portugal, she raced into command when bearing a child; the unborn child was sacrificed but Portugal was re-

pulsed, and she set about breeding another child to make her
Queen of Portugal.

To Isabella and Ferdinand their children were not human
beings to be indulged—they were instruments of duty and
power. From the dream of Spain for the Spaniards, the parents
advanced to the dream of Spain as an empire, and in the grip of
this ambition, which was stupendous, neither Isabella nor Ferdinand
thought it was wrong to cement the edifice with their
living children. To make war for Spain, to bully for it, to lie
for it, to enslave for it, all in the name of Sant' Iago, was a
victory not only over the enemy but over the very nature of
the Spaniard himself. Isabella knew her place as a female, and
when she rode into a camp, settled into a silver saddle chair on a
crimson-clad mule, with her husband prancing on a charger,
she took the salutation of drum and trumpet as a meek woman.
She had earned these grand demonstrations and brilliant ceremonies,
she had wrested them from a people accustomed to eat
its head off out of pure unmanageability. But her own soul was
never diverted by bombastic ceremony from her program: she
was too intent on the commissariat, on the supply of gunpowder,
on the winter camps, on the hour of benediction.

It was an epoch of masterful national impulse, and this
heroic expansion was set by Ferdinand and Isabella into the
perspective of their dynastic will. It was only a few months
since King Manuel had written exultantly from Lisbon, in
1499: "We learn that our captains did reach and discover India
and other Kingdoms and lordship bordering upon it; that they
entered and navigated its seas, finding large cities, large edifices
and rivers, and great populations, among whom is carried on all
the trade in spices and precious stones which are forwarded in
ships to Mecca and then to Cairo, whence they are dispersed
throughout the world. We hope, with the help of God, that the
great trade shall be diverted, in consequences of our regulations,
to the natives and ships of our own kingdom, so that henceforth

all Christendom in this part of Europe shall be able in a large measure to provide itself with these spices and precious stones"— So, with the help of God, Ferdinand and Isabella also arranged and managed. And so, the doomed Christopher Columbus was now coming home across the ocean, bowed in chains, the prisoner of monarchs whose jealousy always leaped quicker and longer than their gratitude.

America for them was Power. Isabella and her husband wanted to put a weapon in the hands of every Spanish male, and to have a stream of gold pouring into Spain from America with which to buy weapons. The discovery of the new world was first of all gold, gold by the fleet-load, to pile into mountains and shovel into guns, so that a road could be blasted from Castile to Burgundy, to link Spain and Austria by land, and to ensure Spanish dominion from Antwerp to Sicily. To hold France in the nutcracker, an imprisoned France, was to be the grand culmination of a union between Spain and the Holy Roman Empire. And in this attempt to hinge half Europe into the destinies of Spain, the children and grandchildren of Ferdinand and Isabella were but the most natural of rivets, flesh and blood though they might be. These monarchs were no more conscious of exploiting their children than a beggar-woman who exploits a baby. Ferdinand and Isabella acted by hot instinct. They worked for their own glory, the glory of Spain and the still greater glory of God.

Portugal at this time, archaic in its chivalry, had the most resplendent court in Europe. It was important to Spain. Thanks to a dispensation of the Pope, the Portuguese monarch married two of Isabella's daughters in succession. The children of the Spanish court that were destined to link Spain with the Holy Roman Empire were equally useful to placate Portugal, which was Spain's Scotland.

Until Ferdinand and Isabella united three-quarters of Spain by their marriage, a jealous separatism had distinguished the peninsula. It was a string of states bound by circumstance, but jangling and jostling like bells on a mule. Its economy was agricultural, its inhabitants mainly rude and illiterate serfs of gorgeous individuality, with a strong church, great numbers of rich Moors and Jews, and vast estates that islanded families of astonishing pride, self-regard and self-assertion. The country had many mountains, which are conservative. It had a number of languages if not literatures, a tradition of tough municipal privilege that rivaled the bold tradition of the nobility. Such a nation, bristling with individualism, rife with lawlessness, hot with temperament, called for something like the parental hand.

Before Ferdinand died he had brought most of it under his thumb, leaving it to be consolidated under Charles's autocratic government. Ferdinand had won the gages of Roussillon and Cerdagne and ousted the local king from Navarre, as he had earlier made the conquest of Granada. This conquest occupied ten extremely bloody, costly and arduous years in which Ferdinand proved himself bold and slippery both as soldier and as schemer. "I will pick out the seeds of this pomegranate one by one," he had foretold, and with the aid of his new artillery he had dislodged the Moors. This was the great occasion of his and Isabella's intrenching their family and unifying Spain, and no sooner had he plowed the ground than the churchmen descended like rooks. There was no love lost between the man Ferdinand and the church, but he cheerfully associated it with his success, linked it with his perpetuation and tempted it with his spoils. He purchased survival for his family, however, at the price of national development. Civic suspicion was made institutional in the Inquisition, commerce was tied to monopolists, and the brain of the country ossified. The notion of liberty, so troublesome when the statesman has to brace the will for radical effort, is eventually as necessary as springs to the cart, but outside their specific work of founding a dynasty, Ferdinand and Isabella were dolts. They rounded out Spain to its maximum as a homogeneous state, but they reposed this state on bayonets. Only if one regard the dynasty as a goal, did Ferdinand prove to be a monarch of the first rank, nimble, astute, resourceful, insinuating and contemptuously unscrupulous He played his hand like a gambler, his love of power unqualified. He despised waste and pomp. He feared no exposure, physical or moral. He tricked the Vatican, the French, the English, the Moors, the Italians.

Of all his alliances, by far the most important was that already indicated with Maximilian. Maximilian (1459–1519) was almost the exact contemporary of Ferdinand (1452-1516). No less nimble and flexible, Maximilian was confronted with a different set of circumstances. He was at once an emperor and an adventurer, a magnate and a mendicant. The papacy was in theory the hub of his wheel, and he the rim, but the spokes that would give him an army, tangible resources, concrete territory, had been subtracted by all the big and little nobles and municipalities that composed his friable Germany. He still trundled the empty rim of power, but it was a prestige without a bank-balance. A kind of insubstantiality, therefore, attended Maximilian, who always had his hand out for contributions that melted as he touched them. He appeared and disappeared with almost comic facility. He had the quality of something disembodied— a rainbow immanent in Europe and yet visible in its tenuous splendor only when rain and shine were commingled. But this evanescence was highly misleading.

Maximilian was no beauty. High-nosed and dewy-eyed, his face a brick-red, his wet lower lip protruding as if to catch his crocodile tears, "as harmless as a babe unborn," he was one of the shrewdest manipulators in a changing world. He started off by marrying Mary of Burgundy, about which he wrote romantic poems, and which gave him a grip on Flanders and the Netherlands. He very nearly captured Charles of France as a son-in-law and he sought Anne of Brittany as his second wife.

His spotty military activity in the East of Europe gave him real control of the Hapsburg territory, and, while he seemed merely interstitial in the Empire, rummaging in the wainscots of Germany, his son Philip, Charles's father, had a definite address at Brussels. Having married into the Netherlands, which was attached to Burgundy, he did his best to saddle himself on the bucking burghers of Ghent and Bruges and Lille.

It was his ubiquity that attracted Ferdinand to an alliance, and out of this alliance came the powerful Hapsburg-Aragon connection.

Charles, the baby in his cradle, the baby of Maximilian's son and Ferdinand's daughter, is the creature for whom Ferdinand and Maximilian had worked so hard. He was soon to stand at the confluence of two great streams of inheritance—that which the spasmodic Maximilian bore to him and that which came to him from the ruses of Ferdinand in Italy and Spain. Charles would be Spanish-Gothic, Maximilian's German romanticism becoming gradually subordinate to Spanish sternness and stubbornness. By nineteen he would be emperor, the historic co-equal of the Pope, and his mission would be to constrict on every side his brilliant rival Francis I.

In the center of this whorl of Ferdinand and Maximilian, therefore, lay the pleasant land of France. Louis XI had striven to carry on the same work of dynastic consolidation as had Ferdinand in Spain, and, meeting the same unworkable combination of small selfishnesses and rude baronial insatiability, he had proved to be equally ready to match ruse with ruse, lie with lie, murder with murder. Out of a brutal welter of wills and forces he organized something like a centralized France. His successor, or rather his successors, kept marrying Anne of Brittany, to keep out Maximilian and to cement into the union this most important Celtic nation, so that, even with the Franche-Comté and Navarre and Picardy and Calais still loose claw and of wit, ruthless, lone. Such men cared nothing for effect and everything for result. Like the archetype millionaires of early Chicago, who themselves were modestly founding their beef dynasties and plow dynasties, dry-goods dynasties, clothespin and cathartic dynasties, these European monarchs who were creating a new organization of human power were at once petty in habit and avid in appetite, iron in self-rule and sinuous fishline in negotiation, men of such simplicity of personal life that they seemed less formidable than fifty of their high-living little competitors.

By 1500 Henry was one of the most seasoned monarchs in Europe. Branded by his melodramatic antagonist, Richard the Third, as "that great rebel, Henry ap Tuddor," the word "rebel," a flourish of Richard's hot imagination, was never worse applied. Security, not insubordination, was Henry's passion.

He had landed in England according to the set pattern of the Wars of the Roses, backed by two thousand of the ugliest customers he could collect in Brittany. He killed Richard the Third. The crown of England, rolled for so long in the field of battle, was lifted by Stanley and planted on this Tudor head. The wise men like Morton and Fox who had stood by Henry and backed him in adversity now thronged round the young victor and came into their own.

But this victory was no melodrama to Henry VII. It was a necessary coup d'état. It was plain and realistic business to a man who had in him the steady English desire to advance himself without friction, the French ability to see facts as they are, and the ruse and tenacity of a Celtic peasant.

Henry was not the sort of man to murder babies in the Tower and then trust himself to envious allies. He trusted nobody and he murdered legally. Early adversity had sharpened him. He saw the world with that bitter appreciation of its cruel enmity that grows on an ambitious man who has frequently been checkered in his youth and chased from hole to corner and

in the fabric, the France we now know was practically secured. Its wealth, its industry, its military fire, its imperial pretensions, provoked envy and fear in England, Spain and Germany. And this was especially so because the French were a land of fourteen millions, ready time after time to descend on that Italy which gleamed and beckoned to every greedy eye.

Louis XI's two successors, the first fantastically, the second soberly imperial, devoted their main strength to the conquest of Italy, to which, as Machiavelli pointed out at the time, they brought no true social intelligence. Each of them married Anne of Brittany, and to do it one of them had to break with his fiancée and the other, the Pope agreeing, with his wife. These two royal careers added less to the power of France than the corresponding dynastic careers of neighboring countries, but so well integrated was this kingdom, so handsomely dowered by nature, that even the most extravagant of military expeditions could not eat out its resources. It had recuperated after the Hundred Years' War. It repossessed its keen mind, its fine nervous organization, its dashing courage, its comedy of spirit. A range of human comprehensiveness that could run on the human keyboard from Rabelais to Calvin at the same moment of history was hardly to be rivaled. France was in great heart at the beginning of the sixteenth century, and when it was inherited by the galliard Francis I in 1515 it might have been reckoned the first nation in Europe, with a revenue ten times that of England.

England's population was three millions. The passage from Spain to England at this period was that from an empire in the full swing of its grand opening movement to a new monarchy tuning up. On land and sea the Spaniard was reaching out, strong in his proud will, his medieval convictions and his passionate certitude of soul, glorying in the faith and offering the oblation of blood. In this warfare he was pitiless. From this posi tive and limited nature, to which young Henry would ally himself by marriage, it was a long passage to the green and white of the Tudors.

The North, cool and damp, could but smolder and smoke in its dynastic impulse, bursting at times into fuming fire where the South could burn with flame. Yet interwoven with these instincts that nuzzled the Englishman, there pushed a weighing intelligence, a mind that held itself to actuality, that insisted on reasonableness, and was carried away by no gorgeous flights into the sun. Nature in England, slow and evident in its process, mild in its changes, warm in color and plump in outline, full of an equable, thick, pervading life, could inspire men less to violent decision than to ready effort and the ebullitions of a feeling hearty, jovial, caressing. A rich volume of slow spirit, a stream of imperturbable being, fed on beef and beer and bubbling like mud, buried Englishmen at times in sodden excesses yet buoyed them on a powerful flood of energy into stout assertion of will. This quality of the nation, stubborn in conceit, practical, afraid to discover in truth some awkward exaction that might not be useful, and at the same time finding inside itself odd humor and emotion and aëration, was at one with the Spaniard in the stubborn vigor of its life.

"The land is a little land," wrote William Morris, "too much shut up within the narrow seas, as it seems, to have much space for swelling into hugeness; there are no great wastes overwhelming in their dreariness, no great solitude of forests, no terrible untrodden mountain-walls: all is measured, mingled, varied, gliding easily one thing into another: little rivers, little plains, swelling, speedily changing uplands, all beset with handsome orderly trees; little hills, little mountains, netted over with the walls of sheepwalks: neither prison nor palace, but a decent home."

He recalled "the little towns, well bechurched, often walled; the villages just where they are now (except for those that have

nothing but the church left to tell of them) but better and more populous; their churches, some big and handsome, some small and curious, but all crowded with altars and furniture, and gay with pictures and ornament; the many religious houses, with their glorious architecture; the beautiful manor-houses, some of them castles once, and survivals from an earlier period; some new and elegant; some out of all proportion small for the importance of their lords."

And "a people rustic and narrow-minded indeed, but serious truthful, and of simple habits."

Since the days of Chaucer, however, this little England ha tasted bitterness. For forty years before 1500 it had known co trary winds and racking storm-battle, lawlessness, change kings, the stocks, the gibbet, sudden death.

In the red snow of Towton field the heralds had coun twenty-eight thousand corpses. This was only one of five or terrible battles, in a country of three millions. The comm had been seized. The landless men were restless and move town. Soldiers turned robber and cutthroat roamed the coun side, taxes had whipped the Cornishmen into wild revolt, defeat had sold the Cornishmen into slavery. It was an Eng of short views and ugly rumors, broken weather and alarm and off new claimants to the throne had landed in Eng arousing old loyalties and whetting ambitions, upsetting dations while the country still heaved with the after-sw Henry VII's own seizure of the crown. The law, the c the parliament, had lost their eminence, and only the beli Henry VII was cunning had kept the people from disorder.

Henry VII was cunning. He ranked with Ferdinan Maximilian, with Louis XI, with Cosimo de' Medici, as type of nation-builder; acquisitive in every fiber; not but the lesser feline, quick to strike and quick to retrea and wary; a schemer; fertile in plans, active in brain,

driven to the meaner dodges of the penniless exile. He did not need to make up his mind to the deep dynastic secret that money is power. This conviction had been bred in him by hunger and thirst, the hunger of unsatisfied fortune, the thirst of the mill-wheel for water. But he was, if you could imagine it, a man of prey with a pawky humor. His eye ran quizzically along the surface of every person and every situation he encountered, to catch the glint of gold that was in it, and he was one of the few kings anywhere who ever took in the special possibilities open to a monarch for extortion, monopoly, larceny and blackmail.

Stanley had crowned him, but he broke Stanley at a hint of treason and absorbed his wealth. He devoured the resources of the Warwicks. He sold justice and pouched the price of every pardon, sniffing even after odd marks and florins. He was circumspect as a pawnbroker, well-informed as a banker, alert as the founder of a trust, and patient as the originator of a chain of grocery stores. And as the managing director of this new style of business, a competitive national monarchy, he pursued his path without admitting any partner into his confidence. He shared his counsel but not his will. He practically dispensed with parliament. He put a ring through the nose of the law and led it into the Star Chamber. He made bishops his tools. From his accession in 1485 almost up to Catherine of Aragon's arrival in England, he had had to hold the throne against every species of aspirant. He had defeated pretenders in the field and beheaded rivals in the Tower. He used ridicule as much as terror, and seduction as much as intimidation. "Masters of Ireland," he had chuckled, "ye'll crown apes at the last."

Instability had not shaken Henry's nerve, but it had drained his energy: it had made him crave for a material security beyond everything on earth. He hoarded the wealth he reached on, which had pointed his look, curved his spine, and hooked his talons. He grouped round him the institutions of England with this acquisitive morbidity as the source of his policy, and he managed his relations to the rest of Europe from the same moral center.

His four marriageable children, Arthur, Henry, Margaret and Mary, he wished to employ in exactly the same spirit as did Maximilian and Ferdinand. No sooner was he on the English throne than his wife's brother went cap-a-pie to Spain, and out of his valiant services to Ferdinand and Isabella came much of their conviction that Catherine of Aragon ought to be wedded to the Prince of Wales. Since Scotland was so troublesome on one side, and France on the other, Henry VII proposed to placate Scotland with Margaret and buffer France with young Henry. Mary was the baby, but she was affianced to Maximilian's grandson Charles. That is to say, she was one of ten little princesses of Europe who, at one time or another, were bestowed by their throbbing parents on that heir of half Europe.

Thus the people of England, sharing the common fate, had become the citizens of a dynast, a hollow-chested, cool, sniffing, quizzical king.

Scotland at this moment was an independent kingdom. It had a tiny population, half a million, but its kings were monarchs in the romantic sense, highly cultivated and personally distinguished, with every intention of keeping Scotland a state complete in itself. The enemy, of course, was England. The English did not propose to have so expensive a neighbor as Scotland, always ready to stab England in the back when England wanted to stab some one else in the front. In such a situation as this, where the smaller nation creates friction, seeks for alliances, and is self-assertive, the enterprise of the stronger nation demands a judicious combination of force and fraud: and Henry VII offered a matrimonial alliance to the Scottish royal family while he tried to corrupt the nobles and create an English party inside Scotland. It was precisely the same as French policy in regard to Brittany, and it worked equally well. The Scottish nobles had never been welded into subordination, as had arrived with the French and the Spanish and the English nobles. The Douglases were venal. The Campbells were mercenary. Their detachment from their Scottish loyalty could be decided by time and place. Such defeats as Flodden were to reveal how great-hearted were the Scottish kings, who staked their own lives on victory, but also how shallow was their statecraft. The lowland rubble gave way under every pressure that England put on Scotland, and where fire and sword did not destroy national spirit in the people, bribery and assassination at length wore down the leaders and cost the nation its autonomy.

Ireland, with a million population, was even less integrated as a national unit. Where the English pale of Calais could not derange France, the English pale of Dublin could completely derange Ireland. Ireland was isolated. Cork is as far from Cherbourg as Esbjerg is from Harwich, and the isolation of Ireland from the Continent left it politically insignificant. It belonged naturally in the zone of Charles V, but he made far less use of it than the French made of Scotland. It was poor, backward, chaotic and distracted. The Fitzgeralds could have dominated it but for the Butlers. The Butlers could have dominated it but for the Fitzgeralds. It had no Ferdinand, no Maximilian, no centralizer and nation-builder. Thanks to invasion, it had not evolved.

Italy, strangely enough, had been equally inhibited by the same intrusion of selfish "barbarians," and its efforts to extrude the barbarians had been equally incompetent. It was this feeling of oppression, quite unintelligible to people who have never experienced it, that drove Pope Julius into his career as a soldier, and that gave such cutting edge to the keen mind of Machiavelli. Everything Pope Julius dreaded, everything Machiavelli dreaded, was later to be experienced by a divided Italy that was forced to drain impotence to the dregs. The arrest of its evolution as a national state cost it centuries of political normality. To the unhappiness of every other nation were added the shame, the frustration, the degraded "peacefulness" of subjection. And this degraded peace was thrust on Italy by Charles because the Italians weakened themselves by those princeling dissensions that were curbed elsewhere by the trust-builders.

The papacy, the oldest sovereignty in Italy, can then hardly be blamed for its mimicry of the rising dynasts. The papacy was accustomed to sovereignty. It had been father of the simple people so long, and had been the guardian of human infantility so much, that it could not resist fighting the dynasts for dominion on their own military terms.

Such a struggle, however, was doomed to failure. The kings who had stood behind papal prestige, which had inherited Roman prestige, had never done so out of religious conviction. They had done so because of poverty and mud. Peace in Europe had been preserved, if at all, because it cost so much money to wage war in winter and because credit was so hard to procure. But with the opening of new sea routes, the increase of production and commerce, the discovery of ore, the multiplication of ships and various other developments affecting transport and mobilization, the demands for national centralization had become imperative. The Future then began to fertilize the Present through those international bankers who now had a reason for being.

The papal tradition was bound to decline in the North as soon as these facilities of national credit mounted. The Reformation had been long overdue—Reformations are always overdue—but not until the Fuggers and the Welschers arose, and not until financial credit extended the possibilities of making war on land and sea, was it practicable for the Northern nations to increase their self-assertion. The beauty of credit is the power it gives to leaders to energize the natural rhythms. So long as the natural rhythms could not be quickened, so long must power have reposed with those whom Nature favored, the inhabitants of the Mediterranean. But invention and discovery gave the North the margin it needed. The blond monarchs thereupon reached out for that sovereignty to which the brunette papacy had grown accustomed. A new "ideology," the national ideology, was promptly developed to suit human infantility. This left the Catholic Church without either the bag or the pig in it. And not until Ignatius Loyola arrived, and the Counter-Reformation developed, did the church work effectually through the National State to compete for the control of human inertia, human docility and human immaturity.

Machiavelli called for his Prince to a deaf Italy.

Pope Julius was to advance from his own princeling attacks on the selfish oligarchy of Venice to a sudden and tardy discovery of the dreadful plight of the land in which the papacy is encysted. He became a fierce soldier, a fierce Italian, dauntless at seventy years of age. Italy for the Italians became his principle, and it carried him into something beyond his duties as pontiff. His successors, the descendants of a pawnbroker, were less scandalous. They found themselves threatened by more formidable barbarians than was Julius, and surrounded by nimbler negotiators. They did business less as soldiers than as bankers. They said, not Italy for the Italians, but Italy for the Medicis. They arranged dynastic marriages with Francis and with Charles. They tried to impose themselves by artifice. But fraud and force, as Machiavelli understood, can always conquer fraud. The Medicean popes founded an ignoble little dynasty that subserved the barbarians.

v

This elder generation of dynasts, the fathers and grandfathers of our heroes, had labored hard as fond and artful parents. They had founded their family fortunes. With religion no more pacific than the old warrior Pope Julius, with nationalism rising for the very reason that the peoples lent themselves to the nearest leader in their quest for salvation as a group, the new group-leaders could hardly be expected to do anything but continue the struggle, to make their own kingly managements absolute, to commit themselves to a war policy and to give themselves to the glorious instincts that their fathers had whetted.

Death prepared the drama. Henry's father died in 1509, Pope Julius in 1513, Louis XII in 1515, Ferdinand in 1516 and Maximilian in 1519. The old and cautious men, that is to say, followed one another to the grave in a procession. Within a mere decade the grand responsibility for Europe was thrown into dispute between three young and emulative men, the oldest of whom was twenty-four in 1515—and this at a moment when artillery was becoming the common language in place of Latin, when parliaments were nerveless, when morals were in chaos, when women had little or no control over their liege lords, when statesmen were virtually viziers and European diplomacy was at once miserably servile and miserably ineffectual.

VI

But the conflict that was brewing, which no faith could suspend, no temper avoid, no wisdom quell, was a double conflict in which the kings gave a political meaning to life, while the people sought to give it a religious meaning. Desperate efforts were made by the intellectuals to unite these two tendencies. Erasmus wrote a book, was said to write a book, of counsel for Charles. Budé was hired to give Francis the benefit of his wisdom. Henry was in the closest touch with those spiritual advisers who saw politics as the rôle of philosopher-kings. But these two tendencies, the political and the religious, were not easily marriageable. On the contrary, Henry and Francis and Charles came with glistening appetites to their banquet of life, which varied for them in their sense of responsibility but was perfectly similar in their desire and their intention to be absolute, to eat at a high table above their kind, to have one human being for a fool and another for a footstool.

Charles was to prove the most important man of the three, viewed politically. Had Juan lived, the eldest son of Ferdinand and Isabella, Charles would probably have made no more impression than his own younger brother. But though Maximilian sent his blooming daughter Margaret to marry Juan, that sickly youth died in a few months, physically weak like all the Aragons though probably not, as they supposed, killed by early marriage.

Margaret, whose Northern nature was little attracted by the somber religion, the inflexible ritual, the touchy pride, the fixed ideas that recalled the Orient in this Spanish dynasty, went home North again, self-possessed and colorful, as different from the Spaniards as a Rubens from an El Greco.

But her handsome brother Philip had married Juan's sister Juana, and Charles was their eldest child. Juana was an El Greco, a fiery, eccentric, crackling personality. She was of a disposition so jealous and of a nature so headstrong that even before her insanity she might well have been called Mad Juana.

Mad Juana completely lost her reason when her husband died "of a sudden." Charles was then only six years old, in 1506, and from that time to her death as a very old woman, Juana was "cumbered with sprites by witchcraft."

Though his aunt Margaret brought him up at Brussels, Charles had all the dismal traits of the orphan. His childhood was grave to the point of gloom. He was a long-faced, shut-in youth, with a jaw of great length but marvelously intent and burning eyes. He was rather a poor scholar, knew no Spanish, next to no Latin, no German, but got up at any hour of the night, from the time he was fourteen, to read whatever dispatches were arriving. He seemed to take life slowly and ponderously, the Burgundian predominating. He hunted a little, but only enough to make his lively grandfather Maximilian say, "We're certainly glad that our boy Charles takes so much pleasure in hunting, otherwise people might suspect he was a bastard." He had few outlets of animal spirits, even if he had possessed them, and he inherited the grim frugality of both grandfathers. But he was so dogged that when it came to a tournament, this youth in white frieze could prove as tough and formidable as the most athletic. He made a doughty soldier. His docility, on which his educators based their extreme confidence, covered thick and smoldering passions.

The heaviest hand that was laid on Charles was that of his tutor, Adrian of Utrecht, whom he afterward made Pope in between the two Medicis. This was Adrian VI, who would have liked to burn Luther to death and who tried to drape the renaissance in sackcloth. When he died the Romans erected a monument to his Physician, "The Liberator of His Country."

Reared in the cold shadow of his towering responsibilities, Charles himself gave the impression of coldness. When he was urged to be a Don Juan, he showed too great conscientiousness: at seventeen it had to be admitted, "his amours be succeeded very cold." His one sensuality, the dullest of deadly sins, was guzzling. He ate himself torpid and drank himself bilious. On the world, as a result, he turned a gaze of lead. But this lust he had for downing his quart of ale at a draught, for devouring eels and prawns and pasties and the rest, did not prevent his becoming the most studious, long-headed and deeply purposeful monarch of his period.

His rivalry with Francis might have been avoided if the young Francis had possessed a less lively imagination. But Francis not only disputed Italy when he came to the throne: he also disputed the election to the Empire that was to come when Maximilian died in 1519. It was this conflict over the Empire, impetuous and greedy but absolutely faithful to the impulses of a dynast, that decided the political temper from 1519 to 1550.

The French incursions into Italy, brilliant as military exploits, lacked social conviction. The French were predatory, but also skeptical. Had Francis killed off the native of the Milanese systematically and planted a colony of ironsides, the brute success of his intrusion would have been secured. But his was the imperial zest without the conviction of moral superiority, the brick without the mortar, the flood of impulse without the dam. Hence the same task of conquest had to be forever repeated, and French imperialism in Italy was a sparkling fizzle.

The conflict between Francis and Maximilian in Italy was so formidable, however, that when Maximilian died in January, 1519 and Francis thereupon dashingly sought the Empire for himself, he precipitated the most reckless and exhausting of all European duels.

VII

The Holy Roman Empire was, on the surface, a relic of the medieval world of the emperor-pope. No one had seemed more like the whale with his empty barrel than Maximilian with his hollow empire, and every caprice of his—the epic he wrote in Dutch, the university for poets, his dream-lore, his secretiveness, his penury, the Triumphal Chariot that Dürer was commissioned to make and not paid for making, the coffin he had with him at his latter end—all strengthened the general notion that this was a prince himself hollow and medieval, improvident and fantastical. But when the election for Emperor came to be held in Frankfort in the June of 1519, it was discovered that Maximilian had been canvassing for his grandson since 1517. Henry and Wolsey had been cheated. Charles was already fulfilling Maximilian's pledges to the electors when Francis was wildly snatching at the prize.

The election was an orgy of Catholic hypocrisy and dynastic hypocrisy, right in the heart of Luther's Germany. It was soon glaringly realized for what it was, a gamble surprisingly interesting, more kingly than throwing away six thousand ducats on tennis or mumchance. Not only to be Holy Roman Emperor, in all the orotundity of the title, but to be given this leverage in Europe—Wolsey and Henry were no less feverishly aroused to its possibilities than Francis, and were all the more stimulated by the eagerness with which Francis began soliciting their support.

The election was in the hands of the seven most imposing of German princes, three of them church magnates. In this small group the key Electors were a margrave and an archbishop, both Hohenzollerns. It was quite obvious to the archbishop, a bright man under thirty (particularly famous for his collection of forty-five saintly mummies, all of them guaranteed to work miracles) that the best chance for an auctioneer is to excite one keen and moneyed bidder against another. The archbishop himself wanted a cardinal's hat, as his brother wanted a royal bride, and both of them needed to build up their material fortunes. In this conviction they approached Francis soon after his capture of Milan, and let him know that they would support him as Emperor, and advise him where he could secure two other votes.

No sooner was the enterprise of the Hohenzollerns displayed in this direction than Maximilian began to canvass Charles's supporters and offer his bribes. The auction continued up to June, 1519. The two chief bidders being young and shot with desire, the object for sale being an Empire, and the Electors numbering only seven, an army of expert corruptionists hastened from every corner of Europe to Germany to open purses, to offer cash, to promise cardinalates, to guarantee territory, to assure pensions and promotions and churches and tapestries, until all the Electors except one honest man, Frederic of Saxony, had pledged themselves (in writing) to take a side and stay put.

Francis was handicapped because the Fuggers refused him the actual cash, yet he made his market. The Hohenzollerns sold themselves outright six times over, three times to Charles and three times to Francis, and at each solicitation they raised their figure and made a new deal on the basis of the other fellow's unexpected profusion.

One of Francis's counselors regretted the necessity of corrupting the Electors. Francis mournfully agreed with him, but added, "in times like these, whoever wants to have anything, whether the Papacy or the Empire, or anything else must get there by using force or fraud." The principle was so evident that both Wolsey and Henry had long made the most natural of inferences, namely, that if force and fraud could procure the Empire, Henry might as well have it as Charles or Francis. Henry's candidature could hardly be announced openly, since he had promised both Francis and Charles to support their claims with the Electors, but this had not prevented subsidies equal to thirty million dollars to Maximilian in 1516. It did not prevent secret canvassing and suborning, so that the English King let it be known quietly and to the right people that he was now in the field.

It was an odd enterprise. Henry had entered the same race as Charles and Francis for the balance of power in Europe, and especially Italy. It was an instance of the ravenous competitive instinct, but clumsy and pretentious. The one competitor whom the Electors could have honestly sworn to treat on his merits was Henry, since his direct bribes were not significant: Bonnivet, hidden by the obliging archbishop of Mainz behind a hanging, overheard the limping English argument. But only toward the end did Francis accept the intrinsic folly of his own candidature. He had asked for the crown himself instead of using all his strength to block Charles by setting up a German prince who would not amalgamate Germany and Spain. Charles alone had foreseen the immense economy of this amalgam: he had almost bitten Margaret's head off when she had meekly proposed that a surer candidate would be the younger brother. Charles had a dull presence and a sober persistence, but inside the leaden casket there burned a limitless ambition. At sixteen he had broken his sister's love match with ferocity. At nineteen he revealed to Margaret every step in his long-sighted European program. Charles, the tortoise, was a better runner than Francis, the hare.

The burgesses of Frankfort took the election on its surface appearance. They nodded approvingly when Law and Order, a chancery official and four trumpets and a guard, read out in a loud clear voice the lengthy edict, "exhorting the citizens to a becoming behavior, worthy of the circumstances." The Imperial Quartermaster, dispatched by the Hereditary Grand Marshal, had come, according to custom, to arrange and designate the ambassadorial suites, and Frankfort, sweating with obsequiousness, ran hither and thither saying, "The Imperial Quartermaster! The Hereditary Grand Marshal!!" It was something marvelous for this town of honest burgesses, with its marketplace, its wineshops, its Saalhof, its butcheries, its booths, its Ghetto, its churches, its moat, its battlements, its lime trees, its "gilt cross on the old cross near the middle of the bridge," to become suddenly a town that was to see the entrance of each of the Electors, to have the Jews locked up in their quarter, the gates closed, the ringing of bells, the thunder of cannon, the imperial bodyguard, the city keys on red velvet cushions, jewels, court dress, insignia, feathers and fur. The Hereditary Chamberlain, the Hereditary Carver, the Hereditary Cup-bearer, would all be in the offing, as well as the hereditary religious ritual and the hereditary plague.

The election hovered in uncertainty to the end. The night before the voting became a dizzying whirl of offers and commitments. Charles punted close on thirty million dollars of modern money (1,500,000 crowns). The election itself began with the solemnest oaths of impartiality in the hall of the Emperors, while thousands of soldiers hovered on the outskirts of Frankfort, to remind the Electors that "the German nation" should not be betrayed. And at last, with a Hohenzollern as bellwether, the seven votes went to a nineteen-year-old youth, henceforth Charles V, who would be crowned by his Holiness with an iron crown.

VIII

The debauchery of the Electors, so shameless though so secret, marks the collapse of a European epoch. It showed serious men that oaths were hollow, the papacy futile, the Empire a mere dynastic convenience, and nationalism a force not yet moralized. Nothing could have suggested more bitterly the need for a general upheaval of society and a revivification of moral values than this picture of the trough in which the little principalities grunted and snouted while the great principalities slung them their golden swill. The law of nature had openly reëmerged: man was pure appetite: and outside the hall of Frankfort multitudes of concerned human beings who had no political power echoed the words of one of the corruptionists who had to deal with the young Hohenzollern debauched by a Valois, a Hapsburg and a Tudor in turn, "J'ai honte à sa honte."

This was the dazzling archbishop of Mainz, with his good taste in tapestries, who had turned aside Martin Luther's glowering protest against the indulgences, and who, in effect, escorted Luther into "heresy."

IX

The imperial election is the dynastic entrance-gate to the Reformation. From Frankfort, rather than from Rome, one can best see the double problem that was to confront Charles; how to keep his empire together on the one hand and to keep it Catholic on the other. He had a magnificent heritage—Spain, the Low Countries, Germany, Austria, Naples, Sicily. But if he had to encounter the Turk on the outside, whether it was

Selim or Francis, he had to encounter a worse Turk on the inside. On him, as Emperor, fell the brunt of the German Reformation and the religious self-assertion of the German people.

An engineer cannot run on tracks that spread. Charles could temporize with, but he could not master, so vital and so radical an impulse. The red-tiled towns of Germany, those stout, well-nourished, garrulous, lusty, positive communities, where a popular religious impulse sent out ten verdant theological shoots in a month, were not made to fit into the light lath-work of Charles's empire. All the maneuvering of Maximilian had produced but a rickety organization, and when Charles had at the same time to face the truculent insurrectionaries in Spain, the question became one of survival.

But no emperor was to have better captains and better legionaries. He was to be served in Italy by soldiers like Toledo blades, cutthroats as fierce, quick and apt as had ever campaigned, led by such hard veterans as Pescara, Moncada, and de Leyva. So long as the enemy was Francis, Charles could girdle him and could hold Italy by the scruff of the neck, Pope and all included, but this was the mere arrest of evolution, the rolling of the stone before the tomb. Where Charles was powerless, either as statesman, as soldier or as emperor, was in the highly complex and subtle task of grouping the animated and bellicose multiplicity of Germany with the medieval unity of Spain. It was a task that a Constantine could not have mastered. It was too much for Charles's sunless temperament. He was not driven to violence, like his son. He mastered the spurts of furious temper that he had inherited from Juana. He accepted defensive strategy. He was brave, he was long-enduring, he was singularly simple and unostentatious. But the fatigue that was to lead to his resigning the throne was really the fatigue of an inadequate imagination. There are honest men whose very restraint defeats them, unwilling to force the lock and unable to change the key. Charles could block his enemies. He could conserve.

But he could not liberate the forces that surged under him. He was at his best in fighting the Turk and quenching Italy. But he tried to rivet a political "universality" on a collection of peoples in the utmost religious chaos. His dynastic assumptions and their religious assumptions being in the deepest conflict he could only reach an impasse and turn it over as gilded legacy to his unfortunate son.

X

Heresy is but the bridge between two orthodoxies. It is easy now to see the immobility that was bound to anchor the springing arch of the German Reformation. But the Reformation was, in itself the outcry of a genuine human dignity, a vivid sense of what Pope Adrian was within five years to describe as "great abominations."

Observe the contrast between the central ideas of the sixteenth and the twelfth centuries. In that medieval time the cathedral fringed out into the university, and every road ran through it. It stood in the center of man's city, open to every one always, catholically conceived, custodian of birth and death and marriage, as broad as its nave and as exalted as its spire. It did not oppose human nature. It marshaled human nature behind it, seeking the good of common humanity as perceived by reasoned common sense, and merely subordinating the tendencies and the variations that gleamed with strange desire. It answered need, extended charity, served and counseled and fathered, and consulted nothing so much as the will of the tribe. It clothed itself in beauty. The roof that shed the Northern snow, and the cool gulf of shade that gave escape from the Southern sun, were equally popular and equally religious. The miracle and the mystery were in every case the burning heart of the cathedral, and authority consoled and subdued the widow, the murderer, the burdened captain, the child. By sanctuary, if not by justice, the church declared its potence, and the lawless came to it in crime as the artist in creation, the king in majesty and the churl in sin. It was a focus of the will, docile yet presumably universal. Energy rushed from it in crusade, in sainthood, in scholasticism, in empire, like free radiants of a fixed and central star. This double movement, out into adventure and home to fidelity, seemed to complete the most perfect of disciplines with the widest of excursions. Outside this there was only exile and desolation, the defiance of the Word, the pride of Lucifer, the iniquity of Apollyon.

And yet esthetic man could not tolerate this bondage. He rebelled against reasoned authority. He declared that the medieval soul had prolonged and even perpetuated the spirit of infantility. That guided soul had remained happy with its toys and symbols, but credulous, dependent and full of fear. It saw a clump of trees as a bright greenwood in the daylight, and at night time as a dark forest of the werewolf where the pilgrim's heart could but scamper at every howl of the wind. This was not because the imagination had stronger wings, but because the forces of the universe were hidden in a willful father, towering and unknown. It was a world in which children knew scabrous facts, saw the scrofulous, the epileptics, the leprous, the insane, strewn on helpless cities and moaning or gibbering on the isolated countryside. There was nothing in nature so hideous that it was not obtruded on the very tenderest spirits, so that tenderness was in itself something to be jeered at by those who had throttled their fears. The virile man was not civilized, he was merely hardened. He took his sport grimly as his Father in the Old Testament did, in the midst of extruded guts and bleeding flesh torn from slaughtered animals. The slaughter of beasts, the way to nourishment, was companioned by the slaughter of men, the way to power. A battlefield was a shambles in which blood, viscera, and mounds of red amputations were as familiar as the ax and spear with which these butcheries were performed. Being half-civilized, these warriors were wholly religious, their religion compounded of a yearning for favor and an unwholesome fear. The princes and the barons inevitably supported this God of terror who whipped mankind with never-ceasing war and scourged him with poverty and plague. They too could count on resignation only by deepening fear. Fear was the tholepin of medieval religion; and the essential impulse of the renaissance was to turn away from this tension to a more human comedy that saw in misgovernment a mere failure of rational device and in warfare "a most bestial frenzy."

At Rome, the crucible, the medieval mind was released from fear in the fifteenth century before it had been prepared for charity, and savagely erupted in all the panoply of freedom. Yet this was not the strangest consequence of dislocated faith.

The effort to escape from authority was not new. In this body of the church there had always been the germs of heresy. It was not merely Wyclif and Huss who had to be stamped out; the list of heretics was only limited by the imaginable hypotheses of a metaphysical order. But not until the vitality of the church was lowered by its own infidelities, by its greed, its worldliness, and its desire for dynastic power, distracting it from the constant emendation of its own metaphysical order, did the heretics multiply their invading hosts and mature their rival existences.

So long as the state could be subjected to the church, so long could heresy be suffocated or shattered. Once the state became centralized, developing transport and taxation, coinage and a standing army, a national policy and a national language, the heavy hand of the church could no longer be laid on the meddlesome mind of man. His old discipline was thrown off, no matter how the supernatural was invoked or the infallible proclaimed. The national state awoke to find itself the jealous competitor of the Church Universal, and began to brew its own metaphysics. The state was no more jealous, in point of fact, than the church itself had been in the frightful particularism of the crusades, the name of which traduced the cross, as the name of the Jesuits was to traduce Jesus. The crusades were not universal. They were orgies of ecclesiastical imperialism. Noble in specific detail, they were the ugly and barbarous provincialism of a European religion pitting itself against Asiatic religions in the name of the Savior of *mankind*. The Turks, like the Jews, were declared and believed not to be "mankind." This was the seamy side of Christianity as a world truth. It required Official Christianity to belittle the other varieties of religion. Its very narrowness endangered it, once knowledge was extended. The authoritative egoism of Christianity as such invited and fostered the anarchical egoism of the national state.

XI

In his amiable opportunism and naturalism, what was Pope Julius's successor to do? At the very moment that Martin Luther was battling with the devil, striving with frantic German sincerity to give birth to German nationalism, no less than a new gesture of ease in Zion, the soul of Italy was exalted by the art of Botticelli, of Leonardo, of Raphael, of Perugino, of Michelangelo. In line, in color, in sonnet, in prose, man had been celebrating in Italy his achievement of an almost Greeklike individuality, while Germany was turning over in its snoring sleep. The burning naturalness of the German, the fierce morality, the fear of sensuousness that at the same time reverberated into rich and rhythmic song, all formed itself into a folk accent that called itself religious and was at one with the plangent, barbarous, ruthless, herd-vociferations of the Bible. There was something in these warm-hearted masses of Germany that wanted a maternal milk which Rome could no longer offer them. The black night of the plague, the dread shadows of the forest, the memories of wolf and bandit, of siege and starvation, of disease and death, poured and trooped through the German soul until every nerve and instinct cried out with heart-breaking voice for the solace of unity with God, the reassurance of faith. The common clay of Martin Luther was turned on the wheel of anguish and molded by the Word. He became the voice of a people, Germany heard in him that homely, irascible, whole-hearted protest which was the protest of a people hitherto mute and despised. The Anabaptists wished to go further than he did, to take over the full inheritance on the terms of the disinherited. But Luther contented himself to protest and reform. It was a moment in which Titan smote Olympus. The Catholic Church had not for a century preoccupied itself with the imitation of Christ, and in its aversion from the aridity of scholasticism it had become insensitive to the true religious experience. The wheel of Rome had fitted into the wheel of Florence, into that exquisite intensive quest as to the nature of man himself and the cultivation of his marvelous susceptibilities to beauty and enjoyment. To capture the glow of dawn on high peaks had become the breathless task of plastic genius. The son of a German miner saw this theater of beauty as a hideous infidelity to Christ crucified. Like a clang of iron in the midst of music, like the hammering of brutal metal on a gilded door, like the eruption of a guttural tribesman into the most liquid and the most modulated of discourses, Luther, turbulent, groping, obstinate, kindly yet scurrilous and scornful, demanded that this consecration of the spirit to the glory of man be suspended in the name of an appalling eternity.

Dürer's attitude, in 1520, was eloquent. He begged the Elector of Saxony, "in all humility to take the praiseworthy Dr. Martin Luther under his protection for the sake of the Christian Truth, which touches us more nearly than all the powers and riches of this world; because all things pass away with time, Truth alone endureth forever. If God ever helps me to see Dr. Martin Luther, I will draw him carefully and engrave him on copper, as a lasting remembrance of a Christian man who helped me out of great distress. And I beg your Worthiness to send me for my money anything new that Dr. Luther writes."

The spirit that breathes in this letter is the spirit that rushes through Dürer's portraits of the Germans round him, where the light in their faces is like that of a fresh fire ardent in a breeze. The Gothic artist in Dürer responded to the instinctive artist in Dr. Martin Luther, it yet being as true for Luther as Lombardi said it was true for Dürer: "he would have been much greater, if he had been acquainted with the antique." But the antique, the poised, the patient, was impossible in the deep waters where no light of any star could penetrate. Luther caught his impulse from the rejected and despised. Himself a muddled and often inconsistent man, he fought with a new weapon, which Rome was unprepared to answer. He carried the people with him. Not for a whole generation did the fresh impetus of the renaissance die out, or the Catholic Church fully collect itself to meet Lutheranism. Italy, indeed, was to lie parched and desolate, the victim at once of the papacy and the empire, its promise of union between Hellas and Judea cut off by the arrested renaissance, its nationalism sacrificed to Spain and the endless, merciless Counter-Reformation. The flower of the new synthesis hung broken from the tree, wrenched by the tornado from Germany.

XII

The dynastic state, directed by men of action, could not fulfill the duties it had usurped, and to which common people gave the name of "religion." Spain under the Inquisition, Italy paralyzed, France entering on the terrible wars of religion, Germany advancing to the Thirty Years' War, Holland to be sentenced to death by Philip, England to evade under Elizabeth and to reap under Cromwell, combined to testify to the blindness of this dynastic preoccupation of 1500 to 1550.

But the minds of men of action, centered on one order of facts, are totally blind to a different order. Just as Erasmus, bent on philology, could cross the Alps without remarking any "scenery," and could pass through Florence without noticing the Baptistery or the Duomo, so Wolsey and Henry, active in dynasty, took the religious question as essentially political.

Thereafter, from 1519 to 1550, the course was set. Once Francis grasped that he had missed the Empire and lost Leo, he knew that his Day had come. He girded for the gigantic duel; the stake would be Italy, the enemies Spaniard and German. Francis fully believed that he was stronger than the Emperor. Machiavelli, who knew Europe, said that "among the best ordered and governed kingdoms of our time is France," and this power and security Francis enthusiastically contrasted with Charles's poverty in Germany and his weakness in Spain.

Spain especially was difficult. The Flemish council spoke of "our Indians"; "the Flemings treated Spain as the Spaniards had treated America." And even when the great news of his election reached Charles at Barcelona, he was not particularly happy, since both nobles and commons had been responding like anything except Indians, kicking hard against his regent Ximenes and kicking harder against himself.

But if this youth of nineteen was of a slow consistency, there sank into this retentive consistency a hatred of his rival Francis. The great Ximenes died. Charles borrowed from Henry. He gave the regency to the faithful tutor from Utrecht whom he was soon to make Pope; and then he fulfilled exactly the same impulse as his rival Francis; he sought the good graces of Henry VIII.

The drama that succeeded, in which both sides besought Henry, was a drama charged with personal hatred. As events unroll themselves, the fate of the Empire and of France is perpetually swayed by the directing passions of Charles and Francis, and the opportunism of Henry. When Francis, radiant and reckless, toppled from the brave enterprise of Pavia into the degradation of his Madrid imprisonment, Charles hated him too deeply not to demand his pound of flesh, and never forgave him for dishonorable evasion. The amazing challenges, the demand for a duel that spurted like flame from Charles year after year, showed how personal was the keynote of European politics. And while the dynasts thus locked themselves in the drama of power, the drama of values passed from More and Erasmus through Luther and Zwingli to men of action like Loyola and Calvin.

Such were the main issues, the issues of empire and of reformation, into which Henry VIII was moving. But he had not yet arrived there. He is still a younger son, a mere Duke of York, while his older brother Arthur is expecting to marry a girl from Spain. So we leave Henry for the present, a buoyant youngster, sitting by the leaded window-pane and playing his flute.

INDEX

591